*Handbook of
Human Resource Management
in Government*

Handbook of
Human Resource Management
in Government

Stephen E. Condrey, Editor

Consulting Editor
Public Management and Administration
James L. Perry
Indiana University

Jossey-Bass Publishers
San Francisco

Copyright © 1998 by Jossey-Bass Inc., Publishers, 350 Sansome Street, San Francisco, California 94104.

Jossey-Bass books and products are available through most bookstores. To contact Jossey-Bass directly, call (888) 378–2537, fax to (800) 605–2665, or visit our website at www.josseybass.com.

Substantial discounts on bulk quantities of Jossey-Bass books are available to corporations, professional associations, and other organizations. For details and discount information, contact the special sales department at Jossey-Bass.

Manufactured in the United States of America

Credits are on p. 706

Library of Congress Cataloging-in-Publication Data

Handbook of human resource management in government / Stephen E. Condrey, editor.—1st ed.
p. cm.—(The Jossey-Bass nonprofit & public management series)
Includes bibliographical references and index.
ISBN 0-7879-4099-2
1. Civil service—United States—Personnel management—Handbooks, manuals, etc. 2. Civil service—United States—Salaries, etc.—Handbooks, manuals, etc. I. Condrey, Stephen E., date. II. Series: Jossey-Bass nonprofit and public management series.
JK765.H33 1998
352.6'0973—ddc21

98-9093

HC Printing 10 9 8 7 6 5 4 3 2

CONTENTS

FIGURES, TABLES, AND EXHIBITS

EXHIBITS

To my mother, Virginia Evans Condrey

PREFACE

Over the past several decades the once staid field of public personnel administration has emerged as the rapidly changing field of human resource management. Although some may consider this a mere difference in nomenclature, court decisions concerning test validation and employee rights, legislation such as the Americans with Disabilities Act of 1990, technological and demographic changes in the workplace, and political pressures for reinvention, decentralization, downsizing, and pay-for-performance compensation systems have thrust the human resource manager into a pivotal position in rapidly changing governmental organizations. These changes have transformed personnel administration from an insulated administrative function performed in relative isolation to a crucial managerial function performed at many organizational levels.

The *Handbook of Human Resource Management in Government* is designed to provide the reader—whether a student, scholar, or seasoned human resource manager—with a reference point from which to assess the needs and challenges of his or her organization within the current public human resource management environment.

AUDIENCE

Practitioners argue that much of what is printed in academic journals is obtuse and often does not inform effective human resource management practices. Conversely, many academic researchers may tend to discount the collective knowledge of practicing human resource managers. Of course, the truth lies somewhere between these two extremes. Much academic research supports effective human resource management practices, and there is much to be learned from managers who have spent years managing public personnel systems. Thus the aim of the *Handbook* is to bring together a collection of well-researched, timely, and informative materials dedicated both to providing practical guidance and advice for practicing managers and students in the field and to maintaining contextual relevancy for those who study and teach human resource management.

OVERVIEW OF THE CONTENTS

The *Handbook* is divided into five major parts. Each part clusters around a specific theme; however, many topics are reinforced throughout the book. The first part, "Human Resource Management in a Reinvented Government," provides the reader with an appreciation of the current prospects and challenges of the public human resource management profession. This part begins with a discussion of how the role of the human resource manager is changing in reaction to the new organizational milieu. It also includes overviews of state civil service systems, the organizational and political environment of public human resource management, and the increasing diversity within public organizations. The part concludes with an overview of organizational culture and climate that also describes how human resource managers can position themselves to positively affect both these factors.

The second part, "The Legal Environment of Human Resource Management," provides the reader with an appreciation for the legal context in which human resource management is practiced in public organizations. The part begins with an overview of the major statutes affecting the practice of public human resource management. The special constitutional rights and responsibilities of public employees and employers are addressed, as is the need to retain qualified legal counsel. Three separate chapters address and provide practical advice concerning equal employment opportunity and affirmative action, sexual harassment in the workplace, and the Americans with Disabilities Act. The part concludes with a discussion of alternative ways to resolve disputes and conflicts in the workplace.

The third part, "Managing Human Resources," provides practical advice on an array of functions performed by human resource managers. Individual chapters examine ways to create an environment conducive to a high-performance organization, to restructure and improve union-management relations, and to design and implement effective training and development programs.

The fourth part, "Tools for Integrating Human Resources into the Organization Mission," maps out the avenues human resource managers can take to break out of the often self-imposed box that has constricted the profession, and it describes instruments they can use to become more involved in the overall management of their organizations. Individual chapters furnish empirically based guidance on benchmarking and assessing organizational productivity; conducting strategic planning and analysis; designing and administering employee attitude surveys; implementing Total Quality Management systems; preparing for technological change in the workplace; using volunteers; evaluating, hiring, and managing human resource consultants; and performing essential budgeting functions. The part also provides an overview of employee recruitment and selection methodologies, along with specific guidance on how to conduct an effective job analysis, construct an assessment center, create a content-valid written examination, and design an employee performance appraisal system.

The final part, "Motivating and Compensating Employees," begins with an overview of the different theories and methodologies for rewarding and motivating public employees. Individual chapters lend specific guidance on constructing a position classification system, designing and creating an effective compensation system, implementing pay-for-performance compensation systems, and assessing an organization's array of employee benefits.

ACKNOWLEDGMENTS

I would like to thank the many people who helped me in bringing this volume together. James L. Perry, editor of the Jossey-Bass Public Administration Series, and Alan Shrader, senior editor at Jossey-Bass, provided guidance, insight, and encouragement at many crucial junctures in the *Handbook*'s conception, development, and revision. Two anonymous reviewers went well above the call of duty in their thoughtful, thorough, and instructive comments on each of the *Handbook* chapters. Additionally, Susan Williams, associate editor, Darren Hall, and Jennifer Morley, editorial assistants at Jossey-Bass, were always available to facilitate the editorial process. I appreciate the assistance of Xenia Lisanevich, senior production editor, and of Elspeth MacHattie and Bruce Emmer in the copyediting and production process.

Linda Pittman, research technician with the Vinson Institute, served a very significant role as my assistant during the entire process of creating the *Handbook*. Kelly Purvis, program coordinator with the Vinson Institute, served ably and with good humor in helping me craft the materials that brought the *Handbook* together as a whole. Michele Ross, doctoral candidate in public administration, and Rosalind Mays, Svitlana Chavarha, and Melanie Hardman, of the

Vinson Institute staff, also provided valuable assistance at various points in the process of preparing the *Handbook*.

Each of the chapter authors is to be commended for his or her efforts in writing an insightful, practically oriented chapter for the *Handbook*. Without exception, they were thoughtful and responsive throughout the process.

My sincere gratitude to each of you.

Athens, Georgia   Stephen E. Condrey
April 1998

THE EDITOR

Stephen E. Condrey is senior associate and program director, Human Resource Management Technical Assistance in the Carl Vinson Institute of Government and adjunct professor of Political Science at the University of Georgia. He has consulted with over two hundred organizations concerning organizational and personnel management issues. He presently serves on the editorial boards of *Public Administration Review* and *Public Personnel Management.* His research has appeared in the *Journal of Public Administration Research and Theory, Review of Public Personnel Administration, Public Productivity and Management Review, American Review of Public Administration, Journal of Urban Affairs, International Journal of Public Sector Management,* and *Publius: The Journal of Federalism.* His research interests include public management, human resource management reform efforts, and federal personnel policy. Before joining the Vinson Institute, he held administrative positions with the University of Georgia, the Personnel Board of Jefferson County (Birmingham, Alabama), and the Tennessee Comptroller of the Treasury. Condrey holds a D.P.A. degree from the University of Georgia (1990) and an M.P.A. degree in public administration from the University of Tennessee (1979), where he was also a fellow in the Southern Regional Training Program for Public Administration. He received a B.S. degree with highest honors from the University of Montevallo in 1978. He is the recipient of the University of Georgia's Walter B. Hill Award for Distinguished Public Service and Outreach.

THE CONTRIBUTORS

David N. Ammons is associate professor of public administration at the University of North Carolina's Institute of Government in Chapel Hill. His work focuses on issues of productivity improvement in local government and includes his recent book *Municipal Benchmarks: Assessing Local Performance and Establishing Community Standards* (1996). He received his Ph.D. degree (1983) from the University of Oklahoma.

Carolyn Ban is dean of the Graduate School of Public and International Affairs at the University of Pittsburgh. She previously taught public administration at the State University of New York at Albany and served as chief of a research division at the U.S. Office of Personnel Management. She has published extensively on civil service and public management issues and is the author of *How Do Public Managers Manage?* (1995) and coauthor of *Public Personnel Management: Current Concerns, Future Challenges* (with Norma M. Riccucci, 2nd ed., 1997). She obtained her M.A. degree (1966) from Harvard University in Russian Area Studies and a Ph.D. degree (1975) from Stanford University in political science.

Mary Maureen Brown is assistant professor of public administration at the University of North Carolina at Charlotte. Her current work focuses on information resource management in public organizations. Her interests concentrate on the use of information-based technology for reengineering operations to improve service delivery throughout the federal, state, and local levels of government.

Her research and service activities in strategic planning and information resource management span both the national and international arenas. Her most recent publications on information resource management have appeared in *International Journal of Public Administration, Social Sciences Computer Review,* and *State and Local Government Review.* She received a D.P.A. degree (1995) from the University of Georgia.

Roger G. Brown is professor and chairman of the Political Science Department at the University of North Carolina at Charlotte. He earned his Ph.D. degree from Johns Hopkins University in 1983. Brown taught previously at Towson State University and Iowa State University. His areas of research and publication include human resource management, organization theory, and conflict management.

Jeffrey L. Brudney is professor of political science and director of the Doctor of Public Administration (D.P.A.) Program at the University of Georgia. He received a B.A. degree at the University of California-Berkeley (1972) and M.A. and Ph.D. degrees at the University of Michigan-Ann Arbor (1974 and 1978). He is the author of *Fostering Volunteer Programs in the Public Sector: Planning, Initiating, and Managing Voluntary Activities* (1990), for which he won the 1991 John Grenzebach Award for Outstanding Research in Philanthropy for Education. Brudney has published a large number of journal articles and book chapters in the areas of public administration and the voluntary nonprofit sector, and he is the coauthor of *Applied Statistics for Public Administration* (with Kenneth J. Meier, 1997).

David G. Carnevale is Samuel R. Noble Presidential Professor at the University of Oklahoma. He is the author of *Trustworthy Government* (1995) and several articles and book chapters. His primary research interests concern the dynamics of dispute resolution and the development of human capital in organizations. He received his Ph.D. degree (1989) in public administration with an emphasis in human resources administration from Florida State University.

N. Joseph Cayer is professor of public affairs at Arizona State University. He is the author and coauthor of books on public personnel management, labor relations, general public administration, and public policy. He also is the author of numerous journal articles dealing with public affairs issues and emphasizing public personnel. He is received his B.A. and M.P.A. degrees from the University of Colorado at Boulder and his Ph.D. degree (1972) from the University of Massachusetts.

Keon S. Chi is professor of political science at Georgetown College and senior fellow for the Council of State Governments. His research and consulting interests include state policy innovations and management improvement. He is the author or coauthor of numerous book chapters, articles, and monographs on state program innovations, personnel administration, privatization, Total Quality Management, and restructuring state government. He is a section editor for *Public Administration Review,* a senior editor of *Spectrum: Journal of State Government,* and a columnist for *State Government News.* At the 1994 annual meeting of the American Society for Public Administration, he received the James E. Webb award for the outstanding paper. He received his M.A. degree (1968) and Ph.D. degree (1970) in government from Claremont University Center and Graduate School.

Charles K. Coe is professor of political science and public administration at North Carolina State University. Formerly the budget officer of Grand Rapids, Michigan, and a public service consultant at the Vinson Institute of Government, University of Georgia, he is the author of *Public Financial Management* (1989) and numerous articles on financial and urban management. He earned an M.P.A. degree (1969) at the University of Michigan and a D.P.A. degree (1982) at the University of Georgia.

Dennis M. Daley is associate professor of political science and public administration at North Carolina State University. He is the author of *Performance Appraisal in the Public Sector: Techniques and Applications* (1992). He teaches classes in human resource and personnel management and policy analysis. His research on human resource management has been widely published in the public administration journals. He received his Ph.D. degree (1980) from Washington State University.

James N. Danziger is professor of political science in the School of Social Sciences and also dean of undergraduate education at the University of California-Irvine. His B.A. degree (1966) in political science is from Occidental College, he has an M.A. degree (1968) in comparative politics from Sussex University, England, and M.A. (1969) and Ph.D. (1974) degrees in political science from Stanford University. He has received awards for his research from the American Political Science Association and the American Society for Public Administration, and he was recipient of UC-Irvine's first Distinguished Faculty Lectureship for Teaching. His research analyzes information technologies in organizations, and his most recent book is *Understanding the Political World* (1996).

Robert F. Durant is professor of public administration and policy in the George Bush School of Government and Public Service and the Department of Political Science at Texas A&M University. He earned his B.A. degree in political science from Maryville College (1970), and his M.P.A. (1979) and Ph.D. (1981) degrees in political science from the University of Tennessee-Knoxville. His research on public management, policy implementation, and bureaucratic politics has been published in several books and in such leading journals as *Public Administration Review, Administration and Society,* and the *American Journal of Political Science.* He was the recipient in 1993 of the American Political Science Association's Gladys M. Kammerer Award for the best book published the preceding year in U.S. national policy, *The Administrative Presidency Revisited.*

Mark R. Foster serves as a consultant at the Vinson Institute of Government, University of Georgia, working with municipal, county, and state government agencies. He previously held the position of industrial psychologist with Federal Express Corporation in Memphis, Tennessee. His primary areas of consulting are job analysis, test development and validation, assessment center design, administration and feedback, and biodata. Foster has conducted more than seventy-five job analysis studies using various techniques and developed and validated numerous selection and promotional instruments. He received his Ph.D. degree (1995) in industrial and organizational psychology from the University of Georgia.

Gerald T. Gabris is professor in the Division of Public Administration, Northern Illinois University. He has published numerous articles on the topics of performance appraisal and merit pay, with special attention on how these technologies can be made to fit within cooperative organizational cultures. His research has also recently focused on job burnout and organizational leadership, as factors effecting organizational performance and reform success. Gabris also currently serves as managing editor of *Public Administration Review.* He earned his M.A. and Ph.D. degrees (1973 and 1977) in political science at the University of Missouri-Columbia.

Christopher L. Gianos is a doctoral student in the Department of Politics and Society at the University of California-Irvine. His interests lie in public policy and the effects of emerging technologies on government and organizations. He received his B.A. degree (1992) in political science from the University of California-Irvine and his M.A. degree (1995) in political science with a specialization in public policy from San Diego State University.

Mary E. Guy is Jerry Collins Professor of Public Administration, Askew School of Public Administration and Policy, Florida State University, and president of the American Society for Public Administration. Her research interests include public management and workforce diversity. Her recent works in this research stream include *Women and Men of the States: Public Administrators at the State Level* (1992), along with numerous journal articles and book chapters on the subject. She holds an M.A. degree (1976) in psychology and a Ph.D. degree (1981) in political science, both from the University of South Carolina.

Arie Halachmi has served as consultant to various government agencies in the United States and abroad. He served on the national council of the American Society of Public Administration and chaired its publication committee, and he started and chairs the International Working Group on Public Sector Productivity for the International Institute of Administrative Sciences (IIAS). He is the associate editor of *Public Productivity and Management Review,* after serving as its managing editor from 1985 to 1995. He is the author or coauthor of more than 150 chapters and articles. Recent books that he authored or coedited include *Competent Government* (with Marc Holzer, 1995), *Public Productivity Through Quality and Strategic Management* (with Geert Bouckaert, 1995), *La productividad y la calidad en la gestion publica* (with Rafael Banon and Geert Bouckaert, 1995), *The Enduring Challenges in Public Management* (with Geert Bouckaert, 1995), *Reengineering and Performance Measurement in Criminal Justice and Social Programs* (with Geert Bouckaert, 1996), *Organizational Performance and Measurement in the Public Sector* (with Geert Bouckaert, 1996), and *Enterprise Government* (with Kenneth L. Nichols, 1996). He earned his Ph.D. degree in 1972 (with distinction) from the State University of New York at Buffalo.

Gerald S. Hartman, a member of the Washington, D.C., law firm of Swidler & Berlin, specializes in equal employment law, class action litigation, and labor law, representing management. His practice includes matters before the federal trial and appellate courts, National Labor Relations Board, Equal Employment Opportunity Commission, and Office of Federal Contract Compliance Programs. He previously served in the Department of Justice, Civil Rights Division, Employment Law Section, where as senior trial attorney he had lead responsibility for many pattern-and-practice cases. Previously, Hartman was professor of law at Wake Forest University Law School, teaching courses in employment discrimination and labor law and adjunct professor at George Washington University Law School, teaching employment discrimination litigation. He is a frequent lecturer for professional groups in equal employment law. He holds B.A. and M.B.A. degrees (1966 and 1968) from Columbia University and a J.D. degree (1972), with honors, from George Washington University Law School.

Steven W. Hays is professor in the Department of Government and International Studies at the University of South Carolina. A specialist in public personnel administration, organization theory, and judicial management, he has published widely in these fields. He currently serves as the managing editor of *The Review of Public Personnel Administration.* He earned his M.A. and Ph.D. degrees (1973 and 1975) in political science at the University of Florida.

Margaret S. Herrman is a senior public service associate with the Vinson Institute of Government, the University of Georgia. She is the author or coauthor of numerous articles and monographs on collaborative problem solving and is the editor of *Conflict Resolution: Strategies for Local Government.* She has also authored or coauthored over thirty-five technical reports and has contributed to over fifty professional meetings, often as keynote speaker, plenary speaker, session organizer, or conference organizer. She received her B.S. degree (1966), and her M.A. and Ph.D. degrees (both in 1977) in sociology from Emory University.

Gregory W. Homer is a member of the Washington, D.C., law firm of Swidler & Berlin. He has worked extensively with experts in statistics and labor economics in the preparation and execution of defense strategies and case analyses in complex class action litigation. In addition to defending numerous individual Title VII, age and disability discrimination, and employment tort actions, Homer has both defended and prosecuted breach of contract claims, particularly in the context of injunction proceedings. He is a member of the Section on Labor Law of the American Bar Association, Bar Association of the District of Columbia, and Pennsylvania Bar Association. Homer received his B.A. degree (1976), cum laude, from Yale University and his J.D. degree (1979) from the University of Virginia School of Law.

Michele M. Hoyman is associate professor of political science and public policy administration at the University of Missouri-St. Louis. She coedited *The Informal Economy* (1987), *Joint Training Programs: A Union Management Approach to Preparing Workers for the Future* (1991), and *New Developments in Worker Training: A Legacy for the 1990s* (1990). Her forthcoming book, *Power Steering* (1997), is a study of public administration impacts of large industrial sitings in rural communities. Hoyman also has authored articles on union democracy, the impact of *Alexander* v. *Gardner-Denver* on labor arbitration decisions in sex and race claims, on sexual harassment and on litigiousness of workers. She obtained her M.A. and Ph.D. degrees (1974 and 1978) in political science at the University of Michigan.

Donald E. Klingner is a professor of public administration at Florida International University in Miami, where he is also associate dean of the College of Urban and Public Affairs and book review editor of the *American Review of Public Administration.* His *Public Personnel Management* text, now in its fourth edition (1998), has become a standard in the field. He was a member of the National Academy of Public Administration's advisory panels on the federal classification reform project (1990–1991) and the judicial salary plan project (1991–1993). He received a B.A. degree in political science from the University of California-Berkeley (1968), an M.A. degree in government from the George Washington University (1971), and a Ph.D. degree in public administration from the University of Southern California (1974).

John E. Menditto is a member of the Swidler & Berlin Employment Law Department, where his work focuses on the defense of employment-related claims and litigation. He has provided advice and counsel to employers on all aspects of the employment relationship and has represented management in issues of employment law before administrative agencies and in federal and state courts. He received his B.A. degree (1986) from George Washington University, with distinction, and his J.D. degree (1989) from the University of Virginia School of Law.

Meredith A. Newman is assistant professor in the Department of Political Science, Washington State University, teaching public administration in the master of public affairs program. Her research interests include public management, gender and politics, organization theory and behavior, and comparative public policy. Her articles appear in a number of scholarly journals, including *Public Administration Review, American Review of Public Administration, Public Administration Quarterly,* and *Public Productivity and Management Review.* Newman is an executive board member of the Section for Women in Public Administration, vice chair of the National Campaign for Public Service, and Region IX representative on the National Council of the American Society for Public Administration. She received her M.P.A. degree (1990) from the University of Central Florida and her Ph.D. degree in policy studies (1993) from Deakin University, Australia.

J. Steven Ott is associate professor of political science at the University of Utah, where he is also director of public administration education in the Center for Public Policy and Administration. He has authored and edited books and articles in the areas of administrative theory, organization theory, organizational behavior, organizational culture, and organizational incompetence in the public and nonprofit sectors; interfaces between organizations in the public and nonprofit sectors; and rural development. He received his Ph.D. degree (1986) in public administration from the University of Colorado.

David Pfeiffer is resident scholar in the Hawaii University Affiliated Program on Disabilities and a visiting scholar in the Department of Political Science at the University of Hawaii at Manoa. He maintains an affiliation with the Sawyer School of Management of Suffolk University, Boston, where he was professor of public management. He has a number of publications in the field of disability studies and other policy areas, most recently in the *Policy Studies Journal* and *Disability and Society.* He received his B.A. degree (1956) in philosophy and M.A. degree (1963) in government form the University of Texas at Austin. His Ph.D. degree (1975) is in political science from the University of Rochester. He is a past president of the Society for Disability Studies and is presently the editor of the *Disability Studies Quarterly.*

Glenn W. Rainey Jr. is professor of public administration and political science and director of the Institute of Government at Eastern Kentucky University. For ten years, his responsibilities have included organizing and delivering training, certification programs, and technical services for human resource, training, and benefits administrators in local and state government. He has published a variety of articles, papers, and reports on public-sector organization and management as well as human resource management in the public sector. He received his Ph.D. degree from the University of Georgia in 1975 and served as a National Association of Schools of Public Affairs and Administration (NASPAA) Faculty Fellow with the U.S. Social Security Administration from 1977 to 1979. He currently serves as chair of the Certification Committee of the Kentucky Public Human Resources Association and as university representative on the Certification Committee of the State and Local Government Benefits Association. He has served regularly as an officer, board member, or committee member for a variety of national and state professional associations.

Catherine C. Reese is assistant professor of public administration at Arkansas State University. She received her B.A. degree (1984) in political science from Rhodes College (formerly Southwestern at Memphis), her M.P.A. degree (1989) from the University of Memphis (formerly Memphis State University), and her D.P.A. degree (1995) from the University of Georgia. Current research interests include the use of the line-item veto power in Southern state governments, state and local government financial management practices, and state and local government personnel management methods.

Norma M. Riccucci is professor of public administration and policy at the Rockefeller College of the State University of New York at Albany. She has published extensively in the areas of public personnel management, affirmative action, and public-sector labor relations. She is the author of *Unsung Heroes: Federal Execucrats Making a Difference* (1995) and *Promoting and Managing Diversity in Municipal Government Work Forces* (1992) and a coauthor of *Personnel Management in Government* (4th ed., 1992). She received her M.P.A. degree (1981) from the University of Southern California-Los Angeles and a Ph.D. degree (1984) in public administration from Syracuse University.

Gary E. Roberts is associate professor of public administration at Fairleigh Dickinson University. His research focus is on human resource management, with special emphasis on performance measurement and appraisal. He is currently conducting research in performance appraisal, the influence of fiscal stress on personnel policies, and performance measurement in health care settings. Roberts received his Ph.D. degree (1990) from the University of Pittsburgh.

Gilbert B. Siegel is C. C. Crawford Distinguished Professor of Public Productivity Improvement, Emeritus in the School of Public Administration of the University of Southern California. Most of his academic work has been in the fields of public management, with particular emphasis on human resource management. On the latter subject, his work has focused on compensation and performance improvement. Recent consulting assignments include participation in a study of Los Angeles County's municipal service delivery to unincorporated areas (for the Los Angeles County Citizen's Economy and Efficiency Commission) and development of a compensation system for the civil service of the Palestine National Authority. He is the author or editor of seven books, over sixty articles, and numerous consulting reports. His most recent book is *Mass Interviewing and the Marshaling of Ideas to Improve Performance: The Crawford Slip Method* (1996). He holds B.S. and M.S. degrees (1952 and 1957) in public administration from University of Southern California and a Ph.D. degree (1964) in political science from the University of Pittsburgh.

Lana Stein is associate professor of political science and public policy administration at the University of Missouri-St. Louis. She is the author of *Holding Bureaucrats Accountable: Politicians and Professionals in St. Louis* (1991) and of articles on urban politics and administration, published in the *Journal of Politics, Public Administration Review,* and other journals. She is currently working on a collaborative project on civic capacity to reform the public schools in large cities and a book on St. Louis's factional machine politics. She received her M.A. degree (1980) in political science from San Francisco State University and her Ph.D. degree (1984) in political science from Michigan State University.

Charles R. "Mike" Swanson is a senior public service associate in the Vinson Institute of Government, University of Georgia. He is the author or coauthor of five books on criminal justice and has consulted widely on public safety management and operations. He also serves as an expert in federal district courts on personnel issues, including testing practices and the Americans with Disabilities Act. He has designed some fifteen promotional systems for public agencies and conducted promotional testing for various state law enforcement agencies and for local departments. In addition to his experience in job analysis studies, he has developed and administered approximately two hundred assessment centers. His prior work experiences include service in the Marine Corps, as a uniformed officer and detective in Tampa, and as the deputy director of the Florida Governor's Council on Criminal Justice. He holds an M.S. degree (1971) in criminology from Florida State University and a D.P.A. degree (1979) from the University of Georgia.

Robert M. Tobias is in his fourteenth year as president of the National Treasury Employees Union. Prior to that, he served as NTEU's general counsel for twenty-three years. He also served on the adjunct faculty of the George Washington

University School of Law from 1970 to 1992. Tobias currently holds presidential appointments to the National Partnership Council, Advisory Committee on Federal Employee Pay, and National Commission on Restructuring the Internal Revenue Service. He received a B.A. degree from the University of Michigan in 1965, an M.B.A. degree from the University of Michigan in 1968, and an L.L.B. degree from George Washington University School of Law in 1969.

Theo van der Krogt is associate professor of organizational sociology at the Faculty of Public Administration and Public Policy of the University of Twente in Enschede, the Netherlands. He also is director of the Public Management Training Centre of that faculty. This center organizes contract education, and its main course is a two-year part-time postexperience executive program, Master of Public Management. Besides several publications on professionalization, Van der Krogt publishes mainly on subjects relating to the management of public organizations, especially local government. His research interests include management by contract, quality management in public organizations, and human resource management. He earned his M.A. and Ph.D. degrees (1972 and 1981) in sociology at the Catholic University of Brabant.

Montgomery Van Wart is associate professor of political science at Iowa State University, where he conducts state and local government programs. He received his B.A. degree from Franklin and Marshall (1973), his M.A.T. degree from Lewis and Clark College (1981), and his D.P.A. degree from Arizona State University in (1990). He is the education and training editor for *Public Productivity and Management Review.* He is the coauthor of *Handbook of Training and Development for the Public Sector* (with N. Joseph Cayer and Steve Cook, 1993) and has written many articles on human resource development in various journals.

Jonathan P. West is professor and chair of the Department of Political Science at the University of Miami. He is also director of the department's M.P.A. program. His interests are in the areas of human resource management, public policy and administration, and U.S. government. He is the author or coauthor of more than sixty articles and book chapters dealing with these topics. His most recent book is *Quality Management Today: What Local Government Managers Need to Know* (1995). He is a graduate of the University of Utah and received his M.A. and Ph.D. degrees (1966 and 1969) from Northwestern University. He taught previously at the University of Houston and the University of Arizona.

Toward Strategic
Human Resource Management

Stephen E. Condrey

Calls for reform permeate the field of public human resource management. No longer can personnel or human resource managers be content to practice their profession in relative isolation. Increased pressures for relevance and oversight are becoming the norm. It appears that all the language of downsizing, rightsizing, reinventing, reengineering, devolution, decentralization, and the like has become part of the public human resource management lexicon. The challenge for the human resource manager is to anticipate and be prepared for necessary and relevant changes to the profession. As James Perry and Debra Mesch (1997) observe: "Powerful economic, demographic, and technological forces have arisen that are radically reshaping longstanding assumptions about organizations and management. These forces represent the challenges that will be driving human resource management in the future" (p. 22).

The purpose of this introductory section is twofold. First, a brief historical sketch of the field is presented to bring context to the chapters that follow. Second, three organizing models for the delivery of human resource management services in public organizations are explicated. The strategic human resource management model that is discussed melds positive features of the traditional and reform models of human resource management.

1

REINVENTING HUMAN RESOURCE MANAGEMENT

John Kamensky (1996), deputy project director for the National Performance Review, posits that calls for "reinvention" and change in public and human resource management make up "only one piece of a larger reexamination of governance in democratic institutions in response to changing demographics, technologies, global competition and public expectations" (p. 249). Frank Cipolla (1996), director of the National Academy of Public Administration's Center for Human Resources, concurs with Kamensky, noting that "change of incredible proportions continues to dominate the world of human resource management. . . . The human resources function has been especially turbulent as institutions and organizations of all types discover that the old ways will not work in today's world of empowerment, accountable line managers, and performance-based organizations" (p. 17).

Although the new path is not yet clear, change and the potential for change in U.S. public-sector human resource management are evident, as they have often been throughout its history. As civil service systems slowly emerged in state and municipal governments after the Pendleton Act of 1883 established the federal civil service system, the personnel profession began to take on distinct functions in the recruitment, examination, and classification of public employees. Van Riper (1958) states the notion that public employees be selected and retained on the basis of *merit* was a novelty at that time: "Before the nineteenth century most civil servants were chosen upon what have been called, not always appropriately, political grounds. That is, most public appointments were made on the basis of partisanship, influence, wealth, family, personal loyalty, blackmail, or charity, rather than intelligence or competence to do their work" (p. 8).

Mosher (1982) posits that civil service systems, established in many instances to protect against the influence of partisan politics, were afforded an extraordinary amount of independence to develop and administer programs to protect our bureaucratic structures from the "evils" of those spoils politics. The nascence of many civil service systems, with their moral overtones of "good" versus "evil," coincided with the emergence of the field of scientific management. Given this *one best way* mentality, many classification and examination procedures became frozen in place, outside the purview of elected officials, other organizational departments, and managers. As time progressed, central civil service agencies designed to protect and professionalize public workforces became characterized as hindrances to effective management.

Fairly or not, to many the personnel profession today represents rule-bound bureaucrats more interested in achieving their own short-term goals than the goals of the larger organization. Consider Savas and Ginsburg's classic analysis of the New York City personnel system: "The system prohibits good management, frustrates able employees, inhibits productivity, lacks the confidence of the city's taxpayers, and fails to respond to the needs of the citizens" (1973, p. 72). Although many critics fail to consider that personnel rules, regulations, and procedures were devised to professionalize government employees and protect them from undue political pressures, in many cases, means and ends have indeed been reversed: line managers view human resource managers as an impediment rather than as full partners in achieving organizational mission and goals. Conversely, human resource managers view line managers as a hindrance to proper human resource management. If human resource management is to remain an intact profession, it must strive to achieve relevance to organizations as a whole.

HOW WE GOT WHERE WE ARE TODAY

Two relatively recent key events called the relevancy and viability of central human resource management agencies and functions into question. The first was the application of the Civil Rights Act of 1964 to state and local governments by the Equal Employment Opportunity Act of 1972. Following the passage of the latter legislation, there was a great deal of introspection by central personnel agencies, civil service systems, government managers, and citizens about the relevance of traditional hiring practices and their results as seen in the composition of U.S. workforces. In some cases this introspection was voluntary; in other cases it was not. Numerous charges of unfair recruitment, testing, and performance appraisal techniques were brought to light through lawsuits, consent decrees, and the like. Government agencies, now forced to defend their respective personnel systems, were obligated to prove their techniques' validity and viability in cases where adverse impact on protected groups was detected. Traditional practices such as the *rule of three* (hiring restricted to the top three candidates for a position as measured by a civil service examination) and written tests based on scanty or nonexistent job analyses came crashing down. When personnel managers were required to justify their methods, in many cases these methods were found to be sorely lacking. This increased scrutiny forced personnel agencies to rethink time-honored practices and to become acquainted with more readily defensible, sophisticated psychological methodologies: validated assessment centers often replaced written tests, broadbanding of test scores replaced strict rules of one or three, and performance appraisal systems moved from trait-based systems toward more job-related and interactive measures. In this way, implementation of the Equal Employment Opportunity Act of 1972 helped professionalize and energize a once dormant field. Conversely, it also laid the groundwork for a serious questioning of the role that central personnel agencies had in managing modern organizations.

The seeds of this questioning began to show evidence of fruition in the Civil Service Reform Act of 1978 (CSRA), the second major event that helped shape the current environment of public human resource management. Whereas the Equal Employment Opportunity Act of 1972 eventually disclosed tried-but-not-true personnel practices, response to the CSRA initiated a steady call to decentralize personnel functions and decisions.

Enacted during the Carter Administration, the Civil Service Reform Act sought to bring businesslike procedures to the federal government, most notably through a *merit pay* experiment for federal midlevel managers. Espoused as a proven private-sector technique, merit pay sought to link managerial performance to compensation, eliminating time-in-grade step increases (which, ironically, were first designed to be associated with individual performance). Although time has proven the federal government's merit pay experiment a failure, merit pay diffused and continues to diffuse to many state, city, and county government organizations.

Merit pay, like many of the provisions of the Civil Service Reform Act, was born of the idea that government bureaucracies and the public personnel administrators that had great influence in controlling them had become insulated from executive and political input and control. With the advent of the Reagan administration and a coinciding era of *cutback management,* government organizations at all levels began to question bureaucratic structures and processes. Organizations were instructed to *do more with less* and to become more efficient, effective, and accountable to executive and public oversight and control. Soon government organizations were called upon to *reinvent* themselves. In many instances, reinvention has focused on personnel practices; this, for example, was the case for the National Performance Review. Headed by Vice President Gore, the National Performance Review called for decentralizing many federal human resource management functions and encouraged the empowerment of managers to act with discretion rather than purely through applying rules and regulations (Gore, 1994).

PERSONNEL ADMINISTRATION AND THE CALL FOR REFORM

Personnel administration lies at the very core of administrative management. Its thrust should be positive and substantive, not negative and protective, not specialized and procedural as had been the emphasis of the predecessor civil service movements. . . . It should operate primarily as a service to managers up and down the line, not as a watchdog and controller over management. . . . Personnel operations . . . should be decentralized and delegated to bring them into more immediate relationship with the middle and lower managers whom they [serve].

This view of human resource management comes not from reports of the National Performance Review or the Winter Commission on State and Local Government but rather from Frederick Mosher's synthesis (1982, p. 86) of the 1937

Brownlow Committee report. In the six decades that have elapsed since the publication of the Brownlow report, many of its key tenets for reform remain viable and are discussed and debated in academic journals, classrooms, contemporary reform commissions, and city halls and county courthouses across the United States. These consistent and recurring criticisms focus on the traditional model of personnel administration as being more concerned with rules and procedures than with the effective functioning and management of public organizations. As Carolyn Ban states in Chapter One of this book: "For well over twenty years, personnel offices have been exhorted to change their roles. From the Civil Service Reform Act of 1978 and before to the reports of the National Performance Review in the 1990s, reformers have argued that personnel offices should move away from their traditional role, with its focus on routine processing of personnel transactions and on control and enforcement of arcane civil service laws, to new roles more aligned with management and more responsive to management's needs."

In a similar vein, Perry and Mesch (1997) explicate a new vision and role for public human resource management, stating that "advocates of strategic human resource management . . . contend that the human resource function can contribute more effectively to mission accomplishment and the achievement of organizational goals" (p. 21). Perry (1993) calls for a redefinition of the relationship between the Office of Personnel Management (OPM) and federal agencies and among the managers inhabiting both. He states that "one idea associated with strategic human resource management is that the style of human resource management is consistent with the strategy of the organization and that human resource practices are adjusted, accepted, and used by line managers and employees as part of their everyday work" (pp. 59–60). He explains that the strategic delivery of human resource services helps narrow the gap between the competing needs of line managers and human resource managers because its central focus is on the optimal functioning of the organization, not on two distinct sets of values or priorities. Perry proposes a system whereby operating departments contract for human resource management services with OPM. With OPM's role changed from regulatory body to service provider, Perry envisions more "knowledge-based" public-sector organizations, responsive to organizational needs but with a renewed "capacity for the federal civil service to pursue meritocratic values" (p. 68).

In an empirical test of the strategic approach to human resource management, Mesch, Perry, and Wise (1995) examined two personnel systems employed by the Veterans Administration and found no significant differences in employees' perceptions of the traditional or bureaucratic model and their perceptions of a model incorporating some features of a strategic human resource management delivery system. They note that their findings were not based on the "ideal" model of a strategic human resource management system but leave open the possibility that any personnel system is always open to bureaucratic gamesmanship: "Decentralization and line manager involvement may give greater control to professional elites who use the personnel system to pursue their norms. Thus it seems probable that decentralization and devolution are as likely to facilitate self-aggrandizing behaviors by lower-level participants as they are to produce goal-directed behavior" (p. 397).

DELIVERY OF HUMAN RESOURCE MANAGEMENT SERVICES: THREE MODELS

The purpose of this section is to explicate three distinct models for the delivery of personnel and human resource management services in public organizations. The intent is to provide an organizing focus for the *Handbook* and also to foster discussion of a service delivery model that combines the positive features of the traditional centralized personnel service delivery model with the features of a reform model predicated upon decentralization of personnel service delivery to the lowest possible operational level. Although no one model can address the particular needs and concerns of every public organization, this discussion is intended as a step toward generating introspection in the field, with the ultimate goal of creating and maintaining a viable and relevant home for the practice of personnel and human resource management within public organizations.

Traditional Model

The traditional model of public human resource management focuses on a central personnel organization dictating rules and procedures, ostensibly to achieve fairness and equity in public-sector organizations. Little thought is given to line functions of the organization, whether they be paving roads, providing recreation services to citizens, delivering social services to clients, or fostering diplomatic relations with a foreign country. Of course such a focus was not the original intent. As Van Riper points out in his study of the U.S. Civil Service, central personnel functions were aimed at professionalizing the workforce and providing equity and fairness in distributing a public good: government jobs. Beginning in the late 1800s, the federal government and major U.S. cities began to centralize personnel functions such as hiring, testing, recruitment, and classification. Influenced by the progressive reform movement and theories of scientific management, personnelists sought the one best way to hire, classify, appraise, reward, and promote public employees. Additionally, the Intergovernmental Personnel Act of 1970 encouraged local governments to create civil service systems with the promise of ensuing federal revenue-sharing dollars.

Reform Model

The reform model seeks to decentralize personnel authority and decision making to line managers. Almost a mirror image of the traditional model, the reform model values dispersal of real personnel authority to various organizational units, allowing them to make crucial decisions concerning employee recruitment, selection, classification, and remuneration. In many instances these decisions may be made by line managers having little formal knowledge of or training in modern human resource management practices and techniques. The result may be responsive to the immediate needs of the organization; however, with no central organizing focus, problems of equity and fairness within and among organizational units may appear. For example, effective and consistent management of equal employment opportunity goals may be hampered, pay disparities may become prevalent, and employee assessment inequities may arise.

Strategic Model

The strategic model suggests merging the two archetypal models just discussed. Borrowing from Perry's 1993 discussion of a strategically oriented federal civil service system, the strategic model seeks to balance the competing demands of the traditional and reform models, recognizing the benefits of some centralizing efforts but also realizing that human resource management takes place throughout an organization and should support, not hamper or subvert, the organization's overall goals. Under the strategic model the personnel function is shared between personnel authorities and the line departments that use human resource services. Examples of activities that can use such cooperative arrangements include devising and administering assessment centers, recruiting key personnel, and restructuring organizational classification systems. Here the human resource manager is an organizational consultant, a valued member of the managerial team, not a roadblock to be avoided. Mesch, Perry, and Wise (1995) note that "the strategic human resource management model emphasizes decentralization and devolution of authority. It seeks not uniformity but variety in personnel policies and practices. [Strategic human resource management] attempts to pare down excessive rules and regulations, enabling managers to function more efficiently and to focus on achieving their organizational mission within a competitive environment" (p. 398).

TRADITIONAL, REFORM, AND STRATEGIC MODELS COMPARED

The following sections compare and contrast the three models of public human resource management in terms of eight important factors: service delivery, goal orientation, communication patterns, feedback characteristics, value orientation, the role of the personnel/human resource manager, the internal and external perception of the personnel function, and the role of education for human resource managers. The comparison is summarized in Table I.1.

Table I.1. A Comparison of Three Models of Public Human Resource Management.

Function	Traditional Model	Reform Model	Strategic Model
Service delivery	Centralized	Decentralized	Collaborative
Goal orientation	Uniform enforcement of rules, policies, and procedures	Manager centered	Respectful of human resource management and organizational goals
Communication pattern	Top-down	Two-way	Multidirectional
Feedback characteristics	Formal and informal complaints	Muted	Continuous
Value orientation	"Merit"	Immediate responsiveness to organizational mission and goals	Effective organizational functioning coupled with a respect for effective human resource management practices
Role of human resource manager	Enforcer of "merit"	Diminished authority and control	Organizational consultant
Perception of human resource management profession	Hindrance to effective organizational functioning	Adjunct collection of skills	Full managerial partner
Role of education	Public personnel administration	Adjunct to managerial skills	Human resource management, general management, practical focus

Service Delivery

Under the traditional model, personnel service delivery is centralized through a unitary personnel authority, be it a civil service commission or personnel department. It is within this central unit that decisions affecting an organization's total personnel program are made, including decisions concerning recruitment, selection, classification, performance appraisal, and compensation. The archetypal reform model strips important functions from the central personnel authority and drives them downward to the operating units of the organization. Here, personnel decisions may be made by managers having little formal training in or appreciation of modern human resource management techniques.

The strategic model views service delivery as a collaborative effort between line managers and a human resource management delivery unit. Under the strategic model, important personnel decisions are made with the joint cognizance and cooperation of personnel professionals and operating unit managers. Examples of collaborative service delivery include the joint development of selection and appraisal devices, the use of the operating unit's expertise in designing effective recruitment and training strategies, and the development of classification and compensation systems that respect equity but allow managerial personnel discretion to reward employee development and performance through the use of career ladders and skill- or knowledge-based pay incentives and adjustments. Collaborative service delivery requires the personnel professional to break out of the central personnel agency box and to become intimately aware of the functional specifics of operating departments. Likewise, line managers are exposed to the opportunities and constraints that influence the delivery of public human resource management services.

Goal Orientation

A critical element in moving toward a strategic approach to human resource management is a shift in goal orientation. The traditional goal of central personnel agencies focuses on the uniform enforcement of rules, policies, and procedures, that is, the effective objectification of personnel decision making. Taken to an extreme, this concentration on rule enforcement becomes the agency's primary end. Unintended consequences include a dissociation of the central personnel agency from the organization's operational goals and objectives. In the words of Wallace Sayre (1948), personnel administration obsessed with a dependency upon rule orientation represents a "triumph of techniques over purpose." For example, strict enforcement of a rule of one or three for personnel selection, originally intended to reward merit and discourage patronage and favoritism, actually may impede managers in appointing staff responsive to organizational needs.

In an opposite but similar fashion the goal orientation of the reform model is manager centered. Here, the decentralization of the personnel function forces the goal orientation to cluster around the individual goals of agency managers. At the same time, such an orientation may hamper overall organizational goals, such as pay equity and affirmative action efforts.

The strategic model of public human resource management seeks a goal orientation that is respectful of effective human resource management practices yet responsive to the organization's overall goals. For example, the banding of examination scores into highly qualified and qualified groupings might meet the goal of allowing managerial discretion in employee selection yet also maintain respect for the principle of merit-based appointments.

Communication Patterns

Under the traditional model, communication is primarily top-down: directives from the central personnel authority are disseminated to line managers. The reform model seeks two-way communication between personnel administrators and line managers; however, under this model, standard notions of hierarchy and authority may be retained. Building upon the two-way communication of the reform model, the strategic model relies upon multidirectional communication, including communication with the ultimate consumers of human resource management services: employees. Multidirectional communication is the natural result of strategic human resource management's integration into organizational mission and function.

Feedback Characteristics

Related to communication patterns are feedback characteristics. Under the traditional model, feedback consists primarily of formal and informal complaints from line managers to the central personnel authority. Feedback to human resource managers under the reform model may be muted because many personnel functions are performed in relative isolation within line departments, without the benefit of a central organizing focus for the delivery of services. The strategic model envisions continuous feedback among central personnel agency staff, organizational managers, and employees.

Value Orientation

Frank Thompson (1990) notes that "multiple values, uncertainty, and the political culture present major challenges to those who seek to improve civil service systems and to those who manage within them" (p. 368). The traditional model values merit. The central personnel authority is viewed as the neutrally competent guardian of the merit principle. The reform model values immediate responsiveness to organizational mission and goals, which may or may not be in conflict with traditional notions of merit. The strategic model seeks to enhance effective and responsive organizational functioning while still respecting the traditional values of merit and equity. This is possible when personnel service delivery is collaborative and when there is a mutual understanding of both organizational and human resource system goals.

Role of the Human Resource Manager

The role of the public human resource manager varies widely under the three models. Although the traditional model reinforces the manager's role as guardian of the merit principle, the reform model, brought to its logical extreme, provides no substantive role for the manager. Under the strategic model the human resource manager's role is that of organizational consultant, knowledgeable of personnel techniques and practices in addition to having a substantive knowledge of the organization in which he or she works. This role is compatible with that envisioned by the National Academy of Public Administration (1995): "The role of HR professionals must shift dramatically from reactive paper processors to accountable consultants and advisors" (p. 5). Perry (1993) agrees, stating: "The role of the personnel specialist must become broader. These jobs must be enlarged and enriched as a means of integrating functional activities" (p. 66).

Perception of the Human Resource Management Profession

Similarly, the perception of the human resource management profession varies widely as seen through the lens of the three models. The profession is viewed as a stilted and isolated administrative function under the traditional model; as such, it is perceived as a hindrance to effective organizational functioning. The reform model leaves little room for human resource management as a distinct profession; rather, this model perceives human resource management as a collection of skills to be added to skills in standard managerial functions. The strategic model seeks to elevate the human resource management profession to the role of full managerial partner, with substantive knowledge of human resource management as well as general management.

Role of Education

Under the traditional model, education for human resource managers is limited to topics such as employee recruitment, staffing, selection, and position classification. Because the reform model envisions no substantive role for the human resource manager, the role of education is relegated to elective selections from the traditional topics. As evidenced by the discussion of the preceding seven factors, the strategic model places demands upon educational institutions to produce human resource management professionals knowledgeable of human resource management theory, general management, organization theory and behavior, and consulting theory and practice, and possessing a substantive and practical focus on sophisticated human resource management techniques and practices. Such an educational background will enhance the role of the human resource manager, the perception of the profession, and most important, the relevance of human re-source management to general management and administration.

CONCLUSION

The strategic model of personnel service delivery is presented as a viable alter-native to the traditional and reform service delivery models. Borrowing positive features from both models, the strategic model seeks to place the public per-sonnel administrator or human resource manager in a viable and critical role in managing modern public organizations. This role is key to the effective and eq-uitable functioning of public organizations and, likewise, critical to enhancing and maintaining a viable field of public human resource management.

The *Handbook of Human Resource Management in Government* appears at a critical juncture in the development of public administration and human re-source management. As change abounds, it is imperative that practicing human resource managers and scholars and students in the field push human resource management toward a role in public organizations that helps ensure the rele-vance and viability of the field. It is to this end that this *Handbook* is dedicated.

References

Cipolla, F. P. "Human Resources Management in the Federal Government: A Retrospec-tive." *The Public Manager*, 1996, 25(1), 17–19.

Civil Rights Act of 1964. U.S. Code, vol. 42, sec. 1981 et seq.

Civil Service Reform Act of 1978. U.S. Code, vol. 5, sec. 1101 et seq.

Equal Employment Opportunity Act of 1972. U.S. Code, vol. 42, sec. 2000e et seq.

Gore, A. "The New Job of the Federal Executive." *Public Administration Review*, 1994, 54(4), 317–321.

Intergovernmental Personnel Act of 1970. U.S. Code, vol. 42, sec. 4701 et seq.

Kamensky, J. M. "Role of 'Reinventing Government' Movement in Federal Manage-ment Reform." *Public Administration Review*, 1996, 56(3), 247–255.

Mesch, D. J., Perry, J. L., and Wise, L. R. "Bureaucratic and Strategic Human Resource Management: An Empirical Comparison in the Federal Government." *Journal of Public Administration Research and Theory*, 1995, 5(4), 385–402.

Mosher, F. J. *Democracy and the Public Service.* (2nd ed.) New York: Oxford University Press, 1982.

National Academy of Public Administration. *Strategies and Alternatives for Transform-ing Human Resources Management.* Washington, D.C.: National Academy of Pub-lic Administration, 1995.

Perry, J. L. "Strategic Human Resource Management." *Review of Public Personnel Administration,* 1993, *13*(4), 59–71.

Perry, J. L., and Mesch, D. J. "Strategic Human Resource Management." In C. Ban and N. M. Riccucci (eds.), *Public Personnel Management: Current Concerns, Future Challenges.* (2nd ed.) New York: Longman, 1997.

Savas, E. S., and Ginsburg, S. G. "The Civil Service: A Meritless System?" *The Public Interest,* 1973, *32*(2), 70–85.

Sayre, W. S. "The Triumph of Techniques over Purpose." *Public Administration Review,* 1948, *8*(2), 134–137.

Thompson, F. J. "Managing Within Civil Service Systems." In J. L. Perry (ed.), *Handbook of Public Administration.* San Francisco: Jossey-Bass, 1990.

Van Riper, P. P. *History of the United States Civil Service.* New York: HarperCollins, 1958.

PART ONE

HUMAN RESOURCE MANAGEMENT IN A REINVENTED GOVERNMENT

*Devising ways to make government work better
is not a task for the fainthearted or shortwinded.*
—Frank Thompson, *Revitalizing State
and Local Public Service*, 1993

As governments at all levels—federal, state, county, and municipal—search for ways to *reinvent* themselves, it is imperative that human resource managers be positioned to assist, survive, and thrive in this new public-sector milieu. The *Handbook of Human Resource Management in Government* begins with an introspective look at how public human resource management has changed and continues to change as it finds its place in our reinvented government environment. The six chapters in Part One examine reinvention and change in the public human resource management field as they pertain to the role of the personnel office, the reform of centralized civil service systems, the political environment in which human resource management operates, the increase in workforce diversification, and the internal organizational environment of public organizations.

In Chapter One, "The Changing Role of the Personnel Office," Carolyn Ban calls upon human resource managers to maintain the relevance of the profession. Ban traces the role of the personnel office from a regulatory and clearinghouse function toward a more strategic model in which human resource managers are actively involved in making key organizational decisions : "The new charge is to support the mission of the organization. This model also entails a new power relationship within the organization, with the HR senior staff functioning as part of the management team, sitting at the table with top management when major policy or program decisions are being made and considering the HR implications. In sum, in this view HR is no longer simply handling routine tasks or providing consulting services on a voluntary basis; it is a major player" in making important organizational decisions.

Originally created to professionalize public workforces and insulate public employees from the influences of spoils politics, civil service systems have of late been vilified as examples of much that is wrong with public human resource management in the United States. In Chapter Two, "State Civil Service Systems," Keon Chi supplies the reader with a thorough and objective overview and analysis of U.S. state civil service systems. Chi presents data from two recent national surveys that elucidate reform efforts in state government civil service systems. Selected reform proposals and recommendations from various studies, changes in state classification and compensation systems, and an overview of major human resource management issues are highlighted. Chi concludes with a discussion of plausible future reform and redefinition of state civil service systems.

Donald Klingner, in "Beyond Civil Service: The Politics of the Emergent Paradigm" (Chapter Three), describes the historical development of public human resource management in the United States and its relationship to the competing values of responsiveness, efficiency, employee rights, and social equity. He then traces the shift in values over the past two decades toward the *emergent values* of personal accountability, limited government, and community responsibility. These values are consistent with the reinvention movement in that they can support efforts to downsize and rightsize government, and they are apparent in recent reform efforts, such as the National Performance Review. Klingner argues that these emergent values signal a shift in the role that human resource professionals play in managing public organizations and that their role "is becoming more like the role of their private-sector counterparts, in that they are less responsible for resolving value conflicts than for increasing productivity."

Responding to affirmative action and equal employment opportunities, public organizations are becoming increasingly diverse. In Chapter Four, "Toward Diversity in the Workplace," Mary Guy and Meredith Newman trace the history and probable future of including women, minorities, persons with disabilities, and Generation X workers in the workplace. They discuss the legal and social impacts of this inclusion and conclude with specific examples of how the "human resource manager can help to create a work climate receptive to and respectful of diversity."

Jonathan West builds upon Guy and Newman's theme of inclusion in Chapter Five, "Managing an Aging Workforce: Trends, Issues, and Strategies." Using three case studies, West charts the effects of demographic changes in the population and the effects of economic restructuring. Debunking myths associated with older workers, he outlines managerial strategies for successfully incorporating these workers in the current public-sector work environment.

Steven Ott continues the theme of reinvention and organizational change in Chapter Six, "Understanding Organizational Climate and Culture." The chapter describes a theoretical basis and practical applications that provide the human resource manager with a greater understanding of organizational culture and climate. Ott explains that "organizational climate and culture hold keys that a human resource (HR) manager can use to unlock the status quo—to help the organization advance to a higher plane of performance, productivity, flexibility, innovation, effectiveness, or diversity. . . . They also hold keys that an HR manager can use to help maintain organizational excellence while the world around the organization changes and 'batters' against it." Human resource managers can position themselves to become crucial players in organizational change efforts, Ott suggests, and he provides two survey instruments that can be readily used to assess an organization's climate.

In these first six chapters, the authors delineate some of the many factors, both within and beyond the control of the public human resource manager, shaping the current environment of the public human resource management profession. Recognizing and reacting to these changes is vital as we seek to position our profession as integral to the reinvented public sector. The chapters that follow guide us toward this objective.

Reference

Thompson, F. *Revitalizing State and Local Public Service: Strengthening Performance, Accountability, and Citizen Confidence.* San Francisco: Jossey-Bass, 1993.

The Changing Role
of the Personnel Office

Carolyn Ban

For well over twenty years, personnel offices have been exhorted to change their roles. From the Civil Service Reform Act of 1978 and before to the reports of the National Performance Review in the 1990s, reformers have argued that personnel offices should move away from their traditional role, with its focus on routine processing of personnel transactions and on control and enforcement of arcane civil service laws, to new roles more aligned with management and more responsive to management's needs. This chapter explores the reasons for these calls for change and the specific critiques of the traditional personnel office roles. It then presents three related models for reform. Finally, it looks at specific attempts to implement change and at the sources of resistance to change.

Before we turn to the issue of new roles for the personnel office, it is useful to look briefly at the context for this discussion—the structure of the personnel process in the public sector. In the private sector each business or organization is free to establish its own personnel system, although it must work within the constraints imposed by a growing body of employment law governing such issues as affirmative action, labor relations, rights of the disabled, and family leave. In the public sector, in contrast, individual agencies typically have little freedom to design their own personnel systems; they must operate within civil service laws. Although there are variations between states and between municipal governments, most civil service systems are complex and highly formalized, and they stress uniformity rather than flexibility. Further, in many jurisdictions an external body—a civil service commission or, at the federal level, the Office of Personnel Management—sets the rules. That external organization may actually do much of the work, developing and administering civil service examinations for hiring or promotion, and it typically has the responsibility of oversight for agency personnel offices. However, this chapter focuses not on the role and functions of those central personnel organizations but on the operating personnel offices within government agencies or departments, offices that work on a daily basis with managers and employees.

WHAT IS THE PROBLEM?
NEGATIVE PERSONNEL OFFICE IMAGES

The traditional role of the personnel office in government, as it evolved since the creation of civil service systems in the late nineteenth century, emphasized two functions: routine processing of administrative tasks relating to payroll and retirement benefits and the like and enforcement of an increasingly convoluted set of laws, rules, and regulations governing the civil service system. Although agency managers recognize the need for both functions, they are increasingly dissatisfied with how personnelists handle them. They critique the inefficiency with which routine processing is managed. More important, they are strongly critical of the negative stance of personnelists, their heavy focus on compliance and their tendency to be naysayers, that is, to tell managers that they cannot do what they want rather than helping them to find a way to meet their goals within the system.

Managers interviewed by the U.S. Merit Systems Protection Board (MSPB) (1993) gave a variety of explanations for their dissatisfactions with personnelists. Many recognized that the problems they encountered were rooted in the civil service system itself—in the complexity and rigidity of personnel policies and procedures. But almost an equal number (69 percent in each case) perceived the problems as stemming from "personnel staff's excessive concern with strict compliance with the rules and procedures rather than results" and from "lack of sufficient staff resources in the personnel office." Finally, over half the managers interviewed blamed "lack of sufficient skill in the personnel staff" for the problems they encountered (p. 21).

Such critiques of the traditional personnel role are not new. They reach back well over twenty years. Alan Campbell (1978), who spearheaded the effort for the Civil Service Reform Act of 1978 and became the first head of the Office of Personnel Management, excoriated personnelists for "rigidity, inflexibility, and a turn of mind . . . that thinks in terms of protecting the system; can't do, rather than can do" (p. 61). The same message was echoed by scholars, who called for personnelists to abandon their traditional focus on the "compliance officer" role (Nalbandian, 1981).

At the root of the problem is a deep-seated role conflict between personnelists and line managers. As I have said elsewhere: "Personnel staff saw themselves as the 'keepers of the flame,' charged with preserving merit in the merit system—a probably accurate reflection of congressional intent. This view of their role was also instilled by their socialization, both inside most agencies and particularly in training given by the Office of Personnel Management (OPM) and its predecessor, the Civil Service Commission (CSC), which reinforced in budding personnelists an adversarial view of the system. They were conditioned to see managers as the people asking them to break the rules—to violate the merit system" (Ban, 1995, p. 91).

In addition to the conflict between personnelists and managers that is rooted in this traditional compliance function, conflict arises because personnel offices must serve multiple clients. They work for managers and also for employees; thus they risk being seen as either "management tool or employee advocate" (Straus, 1987).

THREE MODELS OF REFORM

Although reformers' descriptions of the problems with the traditional system have much in common, the new personnel office roles they have suggested over the years differ along three dimensions. First, reform proposals may focus on how the personnel office does its work. The model for this reform, which I term the *customer service model*, assumes that the personnel office will perform most or all of the same functions it currently handles, but exhorts it to do what it does better and faster, recognizing that the manager is its key customer.

Second, reform may focus on what the personnel office actually does. Thus the second model, the *organizational development or consulting model*, urges personnelists to take on new functions within the organization, serving as internal consultants to managers on a wide range of organizational issues. This proposal is sometimes combined with the suggestion that personnel offices give up some of their traditional functions.

Finally, reform may focus on where the personnel office sits within the organization—on its power and role in organizational policy. The third model, the *strategic human resource management model*, focuses on this issue, urging personnel staff to act as full members of the management team, linking personnel and human resource (HR) policy to agency mission, goals, and policy.

Although it makes sense to separate out these strands of reform for analytic purposes, in practical terms they are often intertwined, with organizations pursuing reform along two or three of these dimensions simultaneously. Thus as we examine each model, it is important to look at the ways that strategies for change reinforce or conflict with each other.

Model 1: Customer Service

The customer service model for reform has existed in the literature for over twenty years (Balk, 1969; Campbell, 1978; Nalbandian, 1981). Quite simply, it urges personnelists to do what they do better and faster and to be more responsive to the needs of their primary clients, managers. More specifically, this means improving accuracy and speed in processing routine administrative actions. It also means taking a more positive attitude toward managers' requests, helping them to find creative ways to do things within the constraints of the system instead of simply saying no to them.

Model 1 Change Strategies

As we have seen, both managers and scholars have recognized that much of the problem they see in personnel offices is inherent in the rules and regulations within which personnelists are forced to work. Thus a key thrust of reform proposals is to deregulate civil service systems. At the federal level a National Performance Review (NPR) report critiqued the excessive complexity and rigidity of civil service regulation and argued that "we must enable all managers to pursue their missions, freed from the cumbersome red tape of current personnel rules" (1993a, p. 22). Indeed, one of the first actions taken under the NPR was to abolish the federal government's ten-thousand-page *Federal Personnel Manual.* Similarly, the National Commission on State and Local Public Service (1993) (chaired by former Mississippi governor William Winter and also known as the Winter Commission) decried "rule-bound and complicated systems" and argued that "we must not be so hidebound in order to protect against failure that we quash the spirit of innovation" (p. 25).

In addition to deregulation, proposals to implement the customer service model call for increased reliance on new technology to improve efficiency and responsiveness. This includes use of computers for rapid scoring of civil service tests and for drawing up lists of eligibles and use of telephone hot lines or the Internet for distributing information about vacancies. The federal government has even implemented a system for applying for some jobs directly by push-button telephone.

But simplifying the formal rules and providing new technology will not of themselves change the traditional culture of personnel offices. A number of reform efforts have focused on the structure and style of work, linking reform to culture change. Foremost among these has been the introduction of Total Quality Management (TQM) in personnel offices both in the federal government (Ban, 1992) and in state and local governments (Berman, 1997). TQM encourages personnel staff to examine their relationships with their customers and to set measurable goals for their work. It is often linked to a restructuring of work, with a movement away from narrow specialization, with one group handling hiring and another classification, toward a more generalist approach, with cross-training so that one staff person or a team can follow through on all the related steps of a complex personnel action. In fact, some personnel offices that have implemented TQM have moved to the use of self-managed teams. Barzelay's description of reform in the state of Minnesota encompasses this combination of approaches: "The new organizational structure—involving agency services teams—signaled the change in emphasis from performing a set of separate technical functions to providing a unified service to a segment of the customer base. As part of the same strategy, operating-level staffing professionals were given the intellectual tools to respond proficiently to whatever problem customers brought to their attention. Through cross-training, for example, employees who had known only about position classification learned how to deal competently with recruiting and examining. Conversely, specialists in the hiring process learned how the system of position classification worked" (1992, pp. 58–59).

As Barzelay makes clear, improving the quality of customer service may also require upgrading the skills of personnel staff. The recent MSPB study of the personnel function found that "more than half (56 percent) of managers and almost half (48 percent) of personnelists thought that either 'to a large extent' or 'to some extent' carrying out their personnel management responsibilities was more difficult than it ought to be because of a lack of sufficient skill among personnelists" (U.S. Merit Systems Protection Board, 1993, p. 28). What is particularly striking here is that the personnel staff agreed; in fact, when asked, "To what extent do you feel that you know enough and are skilled enough to provide excellent service?" over half (57 percent) responded, "To a small extent; there's a lot I don't know," and nine percent responded, "To no extent; I'm overwhelmed and need a lot more development" (p. 28).

These skill deficits are exacerbated by the fact that many personnel offices are short staffed. But increasing personnel staff is not a viable option in most jurisdictions. Indeed, in the federal government, personnel staff (along with other "overhead" staff) have been targeted for significant cuts. Although the rationale for such cuts is that in a deregulated environment fewer control staff are needed, the cuts have far outstripped the process of deregulation, putting even greater pressure on the staff who remain.

A final issue in implementing the customer service model is more controversial. Many proposals for change have stressed the need to decentralize personnel functions in large organizations down to the operating level in order to give managers the service they need. Both the NPR and the Winter Commission expressly called for decentralization. In the area of hiring, the NPR called for giving "all departments and agencies authority to conduct their own recruiting and examining for all positions" and for "abolish[ing] all central registers and standard application forms" (National Performance Review, 1993a, p. 23). Yet some research has found that centralized personnel offices may actually give superior service (Ban, 1995), and a recent report by the National Academy of Public Administration (1996a) showcases reinvention efforts that included extreme centralization with a single central personnel office, often combined with smaller offices that could provide some face-to-face service.

Model 2: Organizational Development and Consulting

The second model goes beyond improving customer service to advocate that the personnel office take on broader functions, serving as an internal organizational consultant to management, not just on narrow personnel issues but in such areas as organizational design, organizational development (OD), employee motivation, and productivity. Advocates of this role see personnel staff acting as change agents, helping to introduce new management approaches. For example, in many organizations it is the personnel office that is charged with implementing Total Quality Management in the organization (Berman, 1997). Terminology becomes important here; advocates of a broader role also often support use of the term *human resource management* (HRM) rather than *personnel management*. As a Government Accounting Office (GAO) report explained it:

> The term "human resource management" was introduced in the 1950s to expand the focus of personnel management from its emphasis on traditional functions such as recruiting, selection, and pay and benefits. HRM introduced additional strategies to address the needs of increasingly complex organizations, the changing work force, advanced technology, and the external environment. According to the literature, an organization employing an HRM strategy:
>
> - emphasizes the integration of its mission and future direction with the planning and management of its work force,
>
> - fosters a collaborative relationship between management and employees and encourages employee involvement, and
>
> - addresses not only the development and motivation of individual employees but also the development of work units and the organization as a whole [U.S. General Accounting Office, 1987, p. 60].

Indeed, in 1987, the GAO found that over half the agency HR offices surveyed offered organizational assessment and diagnosis or OD services to management.

Model 2 Change Strategies

Moving to model 2 poses even greater challenges than we saw with model 1. First, personnel staff must offer their new services on a voluntary basis, relying on requests from their customers, that is, from managers. This requires a very different relationship with management than does the old oversight function and thus a far greater culture change for personnel staff. Additionally, model 2 requires staff with a whole new range of skills and knowledge. Staffing and classification specialists do not automatically know how to do employee surveys or how to counsel managers on strategies for improving productivity.

The potential for conflict with traditional roles is, of course, also greater with model 2. A recent report on civil service reform points up the difficulty of reconciling personnel's roles of "auditor and consultant," and quotes a personnel director who explains the dilemma vividly: "I assure you that when folks have a difficult question about a financial decision, they don't call the state auditor. They call somebody who will help them decide what the state auditor might say. Balancing performance review with being consultative is difficult because it will mean that it will be in the agencies' best interest to hide all difficult or questionable decisions instead of seeking advice" (Carnevale, Housel, and Riley, 1995, p. 25).

One argument, then, is that the two functions should be separated in some way. One approach is that of the U.S. Environmental Protection Agency, which has two connected units: a personnel unit performing the traditional functions and a human resource unit providing consulting services to managers (Ban, 1995). Another approach is the franchising or outsourcing of the routine personnel functions. The argument is that this outsourcing will save money via economies of scale and will free internal resources to provide consulting services.

Another strategy linked both to improved customer service and to changing personnel office roles is to delegate greater authority over personnel decisions to line managers themselves. The intention is to empower managers by giving them authority over such personnel decisions as classifying positions. At the same time, in theory, such delegation of authority should lead to a changed role for personnelists, who are no longer controllers but consultants who help managers exercise this new authority. As Nigro (1990) has put it, this approach "imposes extraordinary demands on administrators while saying very little about how they should go about meeting this challenge" (p. 195). Particularly at a time when federal managerial ranks are being thinned and spans of control broadened, asking managers not only to supervise more people but also to take on responsibility for personnel functions may make them feel overburdened and resentful. Indeed, there is already some evidence that managers given authority over classification will sometimes reject it (Ban, 1995).

Model 3: Strategic Human Resource Management

The third model focuses on a strategic human resource management approach. This model envisions not only a changed role for the personnel or HR office but a changed way of thinking about that office's primary responsibility; no longer should the focus be on carrying out the rules and regulations. The new charge is to support the mission of the organization. This model also entails a new power relationship within the organization, with the HR senior staff functioning as part of the management team, sitting at the table with top management when major policy or program decisions are being made and considering the HR implications. In sum, in this view HR is no longer simply handling routine tasks or providing consulting services on a voluntary basis; it is a major player—an integral part of the strategic planning process.

Model 3 Change Strategies

Model 3 differs from model 2 in both level of involvement and scope of issues covered. The consulting provided under model 2 is targeted to operating levels, with personnel specialists working with individual line managers to solve organizational problems. Under model 3, HR staff are working at the very top of the organization, hand in hand with senior managers. The scope of the issues covered also varies; model 2 personnelists are typically working on short-term operational planning and consulting. Under model 3, the focus is longer-term and proactive, with HR specialists charged with avoiding problems via strategic planning, including projecting future staffing needs.

The concept of strategic human resource planning originated in the private sector. As Schuler (1992) describes it: "Strategic human resource management is largely about integration and adaptation. Its concern is to ensure that: (1) human resource (HR) management is fully integrated with the strategy and the strategic needs of the firm; (2) HR policies cohere both across policy areas and across hierarchies; and (3) HR practices are adjusted, accepted, and used by line managers and employees as part of their everyday work" (p. 18).

In a business environment, becoming a *strategic partner* means, in the words of one business leader, that "HR must become bottom-line valid. . . . The HR function must perform in a measurable and accountable way for the business to reach its objectives" (Caudron, 1994, p. 54).

That bottom-line focus is difficult to transfer to the public sector, but some agencies are succeeding in linking HR to the strategic concerns of the organization. A recent interview with Barbara Sundquist of the Minnesota Department of Transportation, winner of an Agency Award for Excellence from the International Personnel Management Association, gives a good sense of the dynamics of this approach:

> The Human Resource Planning Board (HRPB) is the strategic human resource planning body . . . responsible for identifying, prioritizing, and strategically planning for emerging human resource issues, trends, and opportunities which will impact the agency. The focus of the HRPB is on longer term, strategic, human resource planning rather than tactical or operational human resource planning. The HRPB is composed of managers from each division within the

agency and supported by a working team of human resource professionals from within the Office of Human Resources. . . . I consider our major accomplishment to be obtaining the involvement of management in addressing human resource issues on a long-term strategic basis. . . . With the HRPB we have a partnership with managers as human resource staff are directly involved along with the managers. This will prevent the "dumping" of ideas on the human resource office without any input from us. It also will give managers a better understanding of the many varied human resource issues and the difficulty in solving some of the resultant problems ["Minnesota Department of Transportation," 1993, p. 1].

There is little hard information about the diffusion of the strategic HR approach in government. The 1987 GAO study of agency productivity improvement practices found that thirty-nine of the seventy-one agencies studied were doing some strategic HR planning, but only 36 percent of that group thought it contributed significantly to operations. In their analysis of strategic human resource management, Perry and Mesch (1997) provide case studies of organizations successfully implementing strategic HR management. For example, the state of Washington, which is in the early stages of transition to a strategic human resource management approach, has introduced a number of changes in personnel policy, including "simplified classification, broad banding, a performance management system that emphasizes program results and management skills, and strengthened management training and career development" (p. 30). Further, the director of the Department of Personnel serves as a member of the governor's cabinet. "The close working relationship between the governor and director of personnel facilitates the consideration of human resource issues in strategy making" (p. 31).

Federal agencies are currently implementing a major management reform, the Government Performance and Results Act of 1993 (GPRA), which requires agencies to develop five-year strategic plans with measurable goals. Its intention is to hold agencies and managers accountable for results. As a report of the National Academy of Public Administration (NAPA) (1995) points out, GPRA holds great potential for encouraging strategic HR—potential that is not yet being tapped: "GPRA allows agencies to propose waivers to administrative requirements. In return for the waivers, agencies are to be held accountable for achieving the promised performance improvements. This allows agencies to propose flexibilities to improve HR programs and processes to more closely align HRM with organizational goals and strategic plans. A review of a sample of agency plans submitted under GPRA pilot tests does not demonstrate that agencies have fully recognized the human component of improving organizational performance. Nor do [the plans] . . . reflect clear emphasis on the linkage between effective human resource management and achievement of mission objectives" (p. 6).

CHALLENGES TO REFORM

Each of the three models presented here is controversial, and each will encounter some resistance if personnel leadership chooses to implement it, either singly or in combination. To some extent the sources of resistance will be common to any of the three approaches, although each raises some specific issues. This section discusses challenges in four areas: cultural and legal issues, management attitudes, personnel staff competencies, and resources.

Cultural and Legal Issues

Each of the three models requires a major change in the culture of the personnel office, away from the traditional compliance and control orientation. A customer service approach means that personnelists need to let go of the assumption that their main function is to uphold the integrity of the merit system. Although many personnel staff welcome this change, they point to some enduring problems. Even within a somewhat deregulated environment, the civil service law remains the basis on which they must act, and they have no desire to expose themselves to charges that they have been so flexible that they have violated the law. Further, some complain that no matter how helpful they are, managers will push them to do even more, making demands that are patently unreasonable. As a personnelist in an agency that was implementing TQM explained to me, "The TQM focus on the client doesn't deal with clients who have unreasonable demands. You can't go to Burger King and ask for a Big Mac" (Ban, 1995, p. 101). As we saw earlier, the conflicts over role and culture are even greater in agencies implementing the organizational development model of reform, because the continuing compliance role makes it difficult for managers to accept personnel staff as helpful consultants.

Finally, the strategic human resource management approach poses some potentially serious values conflicts. There has been considerable debate in the public administration literature about the applicability of private-sector administrative reforms to the public sector. Making top human resource staff part of the management team raises quite different problems in government agencies than in private companies. Personnel staff are typically career civil servants. Further, as Nalbandian (1981) points out, "Historically . . . the development of merit personnel systems went hand in hand with government reform, and consequently took on an anti-political, moralistic spirit, which by and large endures" (p. 40). Personnelists imbued with that spirit have long struggled against pressure from political appointees. Those pressures will be even greater under strategic human resource management, but advocates have failed to recognize this values conflict. For example, the report *Reinventing Human Resource Management*, issued by the National Performance Review (1993b), states that "in the future . . . HRM staff advisers should be viewed as part of the management team, not servants of management or the system's police." But it then argues that "the ideal system is free of political influences and embodies merit system principles" (pp. 3–4). Meeting both of these goals simultaneously may be difficult, given the likelihood of pressure from political appointees to put loyalty to the team above maintaining merit system principles.

Management Attitudes

Attitudes of managers toward a changed role for personnelists are also problematic. This source of resistance is compounded by the reformers' calls for related changes in managers' HR role. Models 2 and 3 assume that managers actively desire or will at least accept a new conception of the role of the personnel office. But it is not clear that senior political appointees will, in fact, accept and trust personnel staff as full members of the management team. The level of acceptance may depend to a great extent on the philosophical posture of the administration and its stance toward political-career relations. Under the Reagan administration, for example, senior officials argued for "jig-saw puzzle management" as a way of dealing with career staff, in which staff members were given only the information they needed for their narrow areas of responsibility and never allowed to see the big picture (Sanera, 1984).

At the operational level it is evident that line managers are very supportive of the customer service model. But it is not clear that line managers want to turn to the personnel office for broad consulting assistance in areas outside of personnel. Public and private line managers surveyed for a study of HR roles (King and Bishop, 1994) thought the top three purposes of HR from their perspective were to advise the line, maximize use of HR, and ensure legal compliance (in short, rather traditional role definitions). An interesting private-sector study examining how multiple constituencies assessed the effectiveness of their human resource departments found a difference by level of management: "The constituencies in the operating levels have a strong preference for their HR departments to perform administrative and employee support activities, while the constituencies at the corporate level tend to emphasize planning and development activities or activities that have organization-wide implications" (Tsui, 1987, p. 64). Tsui concludes from her findings that "the HR department should first satisfy existing needs before creating new needs" (p. 67). In sum, although some agencies' HR staffs have been successful in developing a clientele for their consulting services, organizations considering such an approach need to recognize that acceptance by managers is far from automatic; managers may be more interested in an improved customer service focus.

Perhaps a more serious problem is an issue raised earlier in relation to model 2: that changing the role of the personnel office may also entail expanding line managers' roles vis-à-vis the personnel process. It is far from clear that the majority of line managers would buy into that change.

Personnel Staff Competencies

Certainly, one of the challenges for personnel offices taking on new roles is that new approaches require different competencies of staff. As we saw in the discussion of managers' dissatisfaction with their personnel staff, not only do many managers feel that staff do not have the skills needed to do their current jobs but many personnelists have admitted that they feel they lack competence and need additional training.

New roles, particularly those required by models 2 and 3, require not just upgrading current skills but acquiring some quite different competencies. There is a considerable body of private-sector literature concerning HR competencies. For example, after considerable empirical research, Ulrich and his colleagues (Ulrich, Brockbank, Yeung, and Lake, 1995) conceptualized HR competencies within a "three-domain framework: . . . knowledge of business, delivery of HR practices, and management of change processes" (p. 474). The National Academy of Public Administration report *A Competency Model for Human Resources Professionals* (1996a) focuses on five key roles and competencies: business partner, HR expert, change agent, advocate, and leader. Figure 1.1 illustrates these roles in more detail and shows how they are interrelated.

Personnel offices, then, face a dilemma. The NAPA report argues that "a wide gap appears to exist between the potential and actual performance of the federal HR community in delivering services needed to accomplish the agency mission" (p. 4). The same can be said of personnel and HR staffs at the state and local levels. To acquire the new competencies they need, they can either upgrade the skills of current staff or hire new staff. Neither will be easy.

Resources

The dilemma underlying any reconceptualization of personnel roles is that resources are tight and are likely to become even tighter. This is particularly true at the federal level, where personnel and other "overhead" functions are taking a disproportionate share of the cuts as a result of the National Performance Review. From 1992 to 1996, the number of people employed in personnel occupations declined by 18 percent. In comparison, procurement staff declined by 12 percent and budget staff by 6 percent (U.S. Merit Systems Protection Board, 1997).

Yet even before those reductions in staff size, both managers and personnelists agreed that their personnel offices were understaffed (U.S. Merit Systems Protection Board, 1993). One personnelist quoted in the 1993 MSPB study pointed to the relationship between understaffing and lack of competence: "We're so understaffed that we can't get away to take training. There just isn't anybody to handle the work while you're gone, so we aren't developing at all" (p. 31). The NPR has argued that deregulation will lessen the burden on per-

Figure 1.1. Competency Model for Human Resource Professionals.

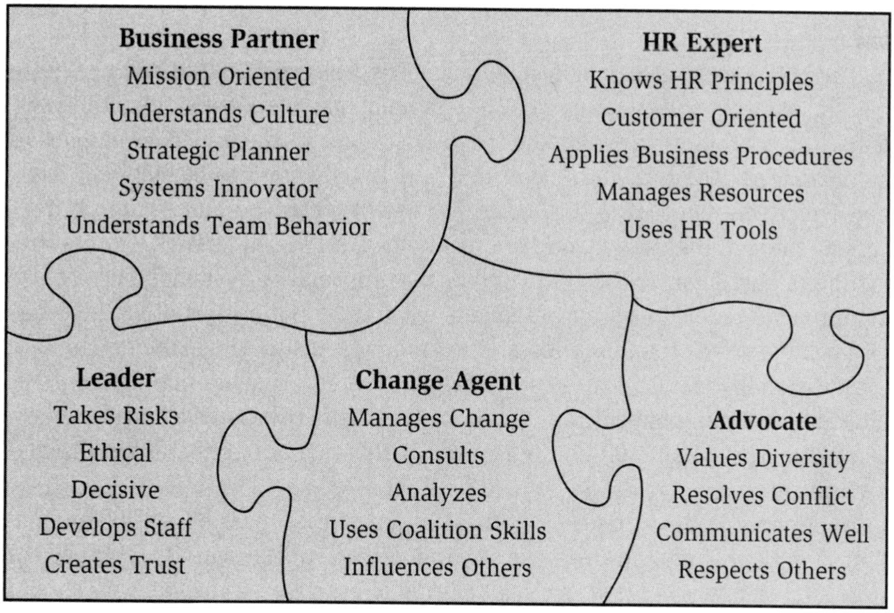

Business Partner
Mission Oriented
Understands Culture
Strategic Planner
Systems Innovator
Understands Team Behavior

HR Expert
Knows HR Principles
Customer Oriented
Applies Business Procedures
Manages Resources
Uses HR Tools

Leader
Takes Risks
Ethical
Decisive
Develops Staff
Creates Trust

Change Agent
Manages Change
Consults
Analyzes
Uses Coalition Skills
Influences Others

Advocate
Values Diversity
Resolves Conflict
Communicates Well
Respects Others

Source: National Academy of Public Administration, 1996a, p. 9. Reprinted with permission.

sonnel staff, but realistically, even if staff choose not to take on new roles, they will continue to find resources very tight for the foreseeable future.

Personnel offices, like other organizations, have been looking for ways to cope creatively with scarce resources. The National Academy of Public Administration (1996b) has compiled many of the creative approaches taken by both public and private organizations to cut costs and improve productivity, focusing on three areas: reengineering, information technology, and alternative service delivery. The reengineering cases presented provide concise descriptions of both the process and results of restructuring HR in both public and private organizations. As noted previously, several organizations profiled moved to extremely centralized HR structures, with dramatic cuts in HR staffing. For example, Sears reduced the number of employees working in HR and payroll "from over 700 to approximately 200 working in a single service center" (p. 7). Similarly, the Small Business Administration (SBA) consolidated its five regional personnel offices into two locations, Washington and Denver, and moved from a specialist to a generalist concept, cutting overall staffing levels from ninety-one full-time equivalent positions to sixty-one. One of the lessons that SBA learned was that "procedures should be streamlined and standardized prior to consolidation so the organization is not trying to do the same amount of work with fewer staff" (p. 16).

The NAPA study also explores the links between reengineering and new technology, with consolidated service centers using service kiosks, telephone systems, and computer-accessed systems to offer greater self-service for employees and managers. The study also notes that "the general effort to increase efficiency and effectiveness of HRM has led to the use of increased automation of processing through the use of workflow technology, increased attention to the integration of payroll and HRIS [human resource information systems], and the use of automation tools to support functions which may not be part of a shared service center such as training, succession planning and strategic planning" (p. 23).

Additionally, NAPA explores the range of alternative service delivery approaches, including franchising (that is, hiring another federal agency to manage some or all HR functions) and outsourcing (that is, contracting out to private-sector firms).

Although it is clear that each of these approaches, separately or in combination, can be a useful strategy for dealing with resource scarcity, such broad structural changes as reengineering or using alternative service delivery should be driven by decisions about the appropriate roles for the personnel office, not just by a desire to cut costs.

CONCLUSION

In some ways it is depressing to review the literature and to be reminded that we have been calling for similar reforms in the role of the personnel office for over twenty years. It appears that private-sector organizations are far ahead of government agencies in accepting new roles for their personnel and HR staffs. Certainly, the failure to change may be due to inertia or to resistance on the part of personnel staff who are set in their ways. But it is also apparent that fundamental change in the role of government personnel offices faces a number of challenges that private organizations do not encounter, foremost among them the structure of the civil service system itself. Agencies that wish to streamline hiring, for example, do not have the discretion to throw out the existing system and design their own. Even though increased delegation of hiring authority may have given agencies greater flexibility, they are still forced to work within the confines of the system. At the federal level this means enforcing the rule of three and veterans' preference, for example.

Further, the fact that public-sector top management comprises political appointees, who are often short-timers and sometimes ideologues, limits the potential for personnel directors to be full partners of management. And as we have seen, line managers also may be resistant to accepting personnel staff as either partners or consultants.

Thus although some change is clearly both necessary and overdue, the critical question is whether fundamental change is possible within the confines of current civil service systems.

References

Balk, W. "A Harsh Light on 'the' Personnel Function." *Public Personnel Review,* 1969, *30*(3), 136–141.

Ban, C. "Can Total Quality Management Work in the Federal Government? The Politics of Implementation." Paper presented at the annual meeting of the American Political Science Association, Chicago, Sept. 1992.

Ban, C. *How Do Public Managers Manage? Bureaucratic Constraints, Organizational Culture, and the Potential for Reform.* San Francisco: Jossey-Bass, 1995.

Barzelay, M. *Breaking Through Bureaucracy.* Berkeley: University of California Press, 1992.

Berman, E. M. "The Challenge of Total Quality Management." In C. Ban and N. M. Riccucci (eds.), *Public Personnel Management: Current Concerns, Future Challenges.* (2nd ed.) New York: Longman, 1997.

Campbell, A. K. "Revitalizing the Federal Personnel System." *Public Personnel Management,* 1978, *7*(6), 58–63.

Carnevale, D. G., Housel, S. W., and Riley, N. *Merit System Reform in the States: Partnerships for Change,* Norman: Programs in Public Administration, University of Oklahoma, 1995.

Caudron, S. "HR Leaders Brainstorm the Profession's Future." *Personnel Journal,* 1994, *73*(8), 54–61.

Civil Service Reform Act of 1978. U.S. Code, vol. 5, sec. 1101 et seq.

Government Performance and Results Act of 1993. U.S. Statutes at Large 107 (1993) 285.

King, A. S., and Bishop, T. "Human Resource Experience: Survey and Analysis." *Public Personnel Management,* 1994, *23*(1), 165–180.

"Minnesota Department of Transportation: Recipient of IPMA's Agency Award for Excellence: Medium Agency." *Public Personnel Management,* 1993, *22*(1), 1–6.

Nalbandian, J. "From Compliance to Consultation: The Changing Role of the Public Personnel Administrator." *Review of Public Personnel Administration,* 1981, *1*(2), 37–51.

National Academy of Public Administration. *Strategies and Alternatives for Transforming Human Resources Management.* Washington, D.C.: National Academy of Public Administration, 1995.

National Academy of Public Administration. *A Competency Model for Human Resources Professionals.* Washington, D.C.: National Academy of Public Administration, 1996a.

National Academy of Public Administration. *Improving the Efficiency and Effectiveness of Human Resources Management.* Washington, D.C.: National Academy of Public Administration, 1996b.

National Commission on State and Local Public Service (Winter Commission). *Hard Truths/Tough Choices: An Agenda for State and Local Reform.* Albany, N.Y.: Rockefeller Institute of Government, 1993.

National Performance Review. *From Red Tape to Results: Creating a Government That Works Better and Costs Less.* Washington, D.C.: U.S. Government Printing Office, 1993a.

National Performance Review. *Reinventing Human Resource Management: Accompanying Report of the National Performance Review.* Washington, D.C.: U.S. Government Printing Office, 1993b.

Nigro, L. G. "Personnel for and Personnel by Public Administrators: Bridging the Gap." In N. B. Lynn and A. Wildavsky (eds.), *Public Administration: The State of the Discipline.* Chatham, N.J.: Chatham House, 1990.

Perry, J. L., and Mesch, D. J. "Strategic Human Resource Management." In C. Ban and N. M. Riccucci (eds.), *Public Personnel Management: Current Concerns, Future Challenges.* (2nd ed.) New York: Longman, 1997.

Sanera, M. "Implementing the Mandate." In S. M. Butler, M. Sanera, and W. B. Weinrod (eds.), *Mandate for Leadership II.* Washington, D.C.: Heritage Foundation, 1984.

Schuler, R. S. "Strategic Human Resource Management: Linking the People with the Strategic Needs of the Business." *Organizational Dynamics,* Summer 1992, pp. 18–32.

Straus, S. K. "Municipal Personnel Department: Management Tool or Employee Advocate?" *Popular Government,* Fall 1987, pp. 21–26.

Tsui, A. S. "Defining the Activities and Effectiveness of the Human Resource Department: A Multiple Approach." *Human Resource Management,* 1987, *26*(1), 35–69.

Ulrich, D., Brockbank, W., Yeung, A., and Lake, D. "Human Resources Competencies: An Empirical Assessment." *Human Resources Management Journal,* 1995, *34*(4), 473–496.

U.S. General Accounting Office. *Human Resource Management: Status of Agency Practices for Improving Federal Productivity.* GAO/GGD-87-61FS. Washington, D.C.: U.S. General Accounting Office, 1987.

U.S. Merit Systems Protection Board. *Federal Personnel Officers: Time for Change?* Washington, D.C.: U.S. Merit Systems Protection Board, 1993.

U.S. Merit Systems Protection Board. Calculations of Office of Personnel Management's central personnel data file, 1997.

CHAPTER TWO

State Civil Service Systems

Keon S. Chi

The past two to three decades have witnessed an era of administrative growth in state governments, as evidenced by a steady increase in employment and proliferation of agencies. The number of state employees grew from 2.7 million in 1970 to nearly 5 million in 1996. Each of the fifty states today has hundreds of administrative agencies—cabinet departments, divisions, bureaus, branches, sections, and units—performing more than 150 different functions, including education, welfare, transportation, corrections, and natural resources. In the meantime, state civil service systems, created a half century or so ago to standardize human resource management, ensure stability, and protect merit employees, have become much more complicated or have been dismantled in many states.

"We need more flexibility and less control." "It takes too long to get employees hired." "The system is too bureaucratic and complicated." "There isn't a strong commitment to employee development" (Commission on Reform and Efficiency, 1993, pp. 3–5). These and similar comments represent the feelings of many state officials involved in personnel systems across the states. The common complaints about state civil service systems address the time-consuming examination and hiring processes, the great number of narrow classifications, the dependence on excessive paperwork, the deficient and outdated information systems, the lengthy dismissal processes, the rigid reduction-in-force policies, the entitlement mentality among state workers, the lack of linkages between performance and rewards, and the lack of flexibility for agency managers.

This chapter presents an overview of state personnel agencies; highlights trends in state civil service reform activities, focusing on hiring, classification and compensation, and performance management; and discusses challenges to traditional civil services systems, such as downsizing, privatization, and Total Quality Management.

STATE PERSONNEL AGENCIES

State personnel agencies vary greatly in their legal basis, methods of appointing agency directors, reporting procedures, and staffing patterns. However, all but one state (Texas) has a central personnel agency, and these central personnel agencies perform similar functions across the states. This section summarizes recent trends in the structural and functional characteristics of state personnel agencies.[1]

The following list (National Association of State Personnel Executives, 1996b) shows the many names currently given to central personnel agencies, and these differences appear to reflect organizational variations. No two state structures are alike. Although a majority of states have kept the same personnel agency names over the years, several states have recently altered their agency names to include the term *human resources.* Until 1990, for example, only three states used that term. By 1995, six states had adopted it. Twenty-three states have separate personnel agencies; the remaining agencies are part of larger administrative organizations, such as departments of administration, administrative services, or management services.

State	*Name of State Personnel Agency*
Alabama	State Personnel Department
Alaska	Personnel Management
Arizona	Personnel Division
Arkansas	Office of Personnel Management
California	Department of Personnel Administration
Colorado	Department of Personnel
Connecticut	Bureau of Personnel
Delaware	State Personnel Office
Florida	Division of Personnel Management Services
Georgia	State Merit System
Hawaii	Department of Human Resources Development
Idaho	Personnel Commission
Illinois	Bureau of Personnel
Indiana	State Personnel Department

Iowa	Department of Personnel
Kansas	Division of Personnel Services
Kentucky	Personnel Cabinet
Louisiana	Department of Civil Service
Maine	Bureau of Human Resources
Maryland	Department of Personnel
Massachusetts	Department of Personnel Administration
Michigan	Department of Civil Service
Minnesota	Department of Employee Relations
Mississippi	State Personnel Board
Missouri	Division of Personnel
Montana	State Personnel Division
Nebraska	State Personnel Division
Nevada	Department of Personnel
New Hampshire	Division of Personnel
New Jersey	Department of Personnel
New Mexico	State Personnel Office
New York	Department of Civil Service
North Carolina	Office of State Personnel
North Dakota	Central Personnel Division
Ohio	Division of Human Resources
Oklahoma	Office of Personnel Management
Oregon	Human Resource Services Division
Pennsylvania	Civil Service Commission
Rhode Island	Office of Personnel Administration
South Carolina	Office of Human Resources
South Dakota	Bureau of Personnel
Tennessee	Department of Personnel
Texas	(No central agency)
Utah	Department of Human Resource Management
Vermont	Department of Personnel
Virginia	Department of Personnel and Training
Washington	Department of Personnel
West Virginia	Division of Personnel
Wisconsin	Department of Employment Relations
Wyoming	Personnel Division

Today fewer state personnel executives are appointed by or report to their governors than in the past. Directors of state personnel agencies in twenty-six states are currently governor appointed, compared to thirty-three in 1986. Thirty-nine directors reported directly to their governors ten years ago, and that number decreased to twenty-five in 1996. Meanwhile, the number of personnel executives appointed by umbrella agency heads or personnel boards has increased. The implication here is that governors tend to have less direct control over state personnel administration than in the past, and therefore it has become more complicated for personnel agency directors to remedy weaknesses in civil service systems, unless they have support from the upper-level department heads to whom they report. Changing the way state personnel administrative agencies work is also complicated. In a majority of states, personnel administration cannot be changed by executive actions alone. Because statutes are the legal basis of personnel agencies in most states, legislative commitment and support are necessary for agency reform.

Personnel staffing patterns vary from state to state. The number of employees performing personnel duties in central agencies ranges from 9.5 in North Dakota to 570 in New Jersey. A majority of states (twenty-six) have reduced the number of these employees in recent years. The number of full-time employees in line agencies performing personnel duties varies from 30 in Vermont to more than 1,000 in Florida. And the number of full-time state employees served by the central personnel department ranges from 6,600 in North Dakota to nearly 179,000 in New York.

Despite various agency names the major functions of state personnel administration are very much the same across the states; they deal with merit testing, employee qualifications, human resource management information systems, classification, position allocation, compensation, recruitment, selection, performance evaluation, position audits, employee promotion, employee assistance and counseling, human resource development and training, employee health and welfare programs, affirmative action, labor and employee relations, collective bargaining, grievances and appeals, alternative dispute resolution, retirement, incentive and productivity systems, attitude surveys, child care, workers' compensation, group health insurance, drug testing, and budget recommendations to the legislature.

Finally, the debate over centralization and decentralization in state personnel administration continues. Nearly every state is trying to decentralize at least some of its centralized personnel functions. But the real debate is not around the question of whether decentralization in general is desirable or not or whether a specific state should have a more decentralized personnel system. Rather, the debate appears to be around such questions as: How extensive should decentralization be? What elements of the civil service system should be consistent across state agencies? What issues should be up to individual line agencies to determine? and, What should the role of the central personnel agency be in a decentralized system? In Florida's decentralized system, for example, the central personnel agency plays a facilitator's role, consulting with agencies, assisting them in developing agency policies and programs, providing training and technical assistance, and performing a systemwide oversight function (Wechsler, 1993).

STATE CIVIL SERVICE REFORM

Beginning in the late 1980s, many states initiated a variety of civil service reform activities. According to a survey conducted by the National Association of State Personnel Executives (NASPE) (1993), for example, thirty-five states were undergoing some form of civil service reform in 1992. As the rationale behind their reform efforts, these states cited the need to change rules, regulations, and policies to meet executive leadership needs and to implement quality management initiatives. The NASPE survey identified governors and personnel agency executives as the main forces behind the reform initiatives in most states, but several states indicated that other agencies and personnel agency customers were driving the reform efforts. "Wholesale" civil service reform was being undertaken by six states and one territory (Florida, Massachusetts, Minnesota, New Jersey, Ohio, Oklahoma, and the Virgin Islands); the other states were carrying out incremental reform activities, typically over a period of several years. Classification, compensation, and performance evaluation were the main targets for reform in most states, followed by merit testing, employee benefits, selection procedures, incentive and productivity programs, retirement methods, and training. By 1994, South Carolina had joined the group of states with wholesale civil service reform. A 1996 National Association of State Personnel Executives survey (1996b) showed that state personnel agencies were currently involved in reform activities in the same functional areas as in 1992: classification (in forty-five states), compensation (forty-three), performance evaluation (thirty-five), selection (thirty), recruitment (twenty-seven), merit testing (twenty-six), training (twenty-five), employee relations (twenty-one), and benefits (nine). The following sections highlight state trends in three major reform areas: selection and hiring, classification and compensation, and performance evaluation.

Selection and Hiring

A majority of state personnel agencies continue to use traditional methods of selection and placement. Written tests are used for entry and promotional evaluation in thirty-five states, and some type of credential evaluation is used in thirty-nine states. Although several states are exploring new methods of assessment, such as skills assessment, job simulations, and video testing, a majority of states (thirty-one) use traditional methods to rank candidates. For example, when a number of top candidates are eligible for appointment through credential evaluation, the majority of states certify five to twenty candidates. When written test scores are used, candidates with the top five or ten scores are determined to be eligible. Nearly all states give systematic preference to veterans in employment. Most add to the final examination score five points for veterans and ten points for disabled veterans applying for entry positions. Systematic preference for minorities and women seems far less common than in the past. Montana reported that it gives preference in hiring only to Native Americans.

A common complaint is that existing hiring systems are too slow or inflexible. Many states are recommending reformed systems that will enhance and facilitate the flexible deployment of state employees, quickly and efficiently satisfying needs identified through workforce planning; that will develop a centralized recruiting effort that has more access to protected groups of applicants and that helps hiring managers and supervisors recruit for unique high-level or hard-to-fill positions; that will hire for specific jobs, not general job classifications; that will revise the current system to encourage position-specific hiring processes; and that will implement a database of hiring-related information accessible to all agencies (Commission on Reform and Efficiency, 1993, p. 1). In 1996, Kansas, for example, initiated a new method to recruit state employees without going through traditional hiring practices. For fifty years, applicants for classified positions in the Kansas state government were supposed to be selected for interviews based on their performance on a written exam. But when state officials determined that only one-third of all classified vacancies were actually being filled through the examination process, they replaced it with a computerized system that selects interviewees based on their skill levels. Currently, applicants complete registration forms that indicate their education and experience in terms of proficiency levels, and these forms are scanned into the state's computerized personnel database. When a state government position needs to be filled, the requirements and proficiency level preferences are entered into the same database, and the computer electronically matches applicants to the position, ranking them by the fit of the proficiency levels. From this ranked listing, agency recruiters select interviewees. The computerized selection system resulted from business process reengineering in the Kansas state government.

Wisconsin's much publicized Recruiting the Best and the Brightest program was developed in response to criticism that a slow, inflexible civil service hiring process was stifling the state's ability to attract a talented and diverse workforce. Beginning in 1991, the state Department of Employment Relations instituted four innovative programs to enable state agencies to compete successfully with private and other public employers for the best candidates to fill more than three thousand jobs each year. By minimizing the use of a rigid multiple-choice testing procedure and increasing the number of candidates eligible to be interviewed, the Entry Professional Program has helped the state compete for the most talented among entry-level professionals. The new Critical Recruitment Program, which introduced a focused and flexible applicant-screening process, has enabled state agencies to hire qualified candidates in more than six hundred traditionally hard-to-fill positions in such technical fields as engineering, health care, and the sciences. Under the new walk-in civil service testing program initiated in 1992, job applicants are not required to submit applications in advance. Instead, they can now simply show up at the test site, fill out an application, and take their exam. According to state officials, the program provides agencies with employment registers from written exams 40 percent faster than before. The Department of Employment Relations no longer has to process applications for no-shows, who applied but never tested, and no longer has to send out notices to applicants confirming their exam dates. Finally, the department began making job vacancy bulletins available to state agencies via computer. JOBS—Job Online Bulletin Service—provides users with a computerized listing of all vacancies in both of the department's job vacancy bulletins (Wisconsin Department of Employment Relations, 1995).

Washington state has developed Executive Search Services (ESS). This program, housed in the Washington state Department of Personnel, carries out an effective method of identifying, screening, interviewing, and ultimately hiring top-level executives for state government. The program designs and leads nationwide searches for positions at the director, deputy director, and assistant director levels. Its main purpose is to provide quality public-sector executive recruitment expertise at a very reasonable price. ESS is available to any state agency, board, commission, or institution of higher education, and it provides its services for a flat fee of 10 percent of the position's first-year salary, plus any expenses for advertising or travel. This fee is less than the national average for private search firms of 33 percent of the salary plus another 15 percent for expenses. In addition to providing quality services at a significant cost savings, ESS also has an excellent reputation for providing client agencies with a highly diverse pool of qualified candidates (National Association of State Personnel Executives, 1995).

Classification and Compensation

Classification and compensation are the most talked about topics in state civil service reform. California appears to reflect the typical problems with state government classification systems. The California civil service system currently consists of about 4,500 job classifications. But more than 1,600 of them contain five or fewer employees. "This excessively detailed partition of state service greatly conflicts the ability of individuals and all state government to serve California. It punishes those employees who quickly master skills by locking their pay to 'time in grade.' It frustrates managers who need to deploy and redeploy the knowledge, skills and abilities of their employees to maximize performance" (California Governor's Office, 1996, p. 62). Despite an outcry for a reduction in the number of classifications, however, states have been very slow in implementing reform measures. Some have added more job classes in recent years. The report of the National Commission on the State and Local Public Service (1993) recommended a drastic reduction of the number of classifications—from several hundreds or thousand to no more than a few dozen. The report also advocated a simple pay structure to allow agency managers to use greater discretion in rewarding productive employees. Currently, more than twenty states are in the process of reforming their classification and compensation systems.[2]

There are several basic purposes for these classification systems. In some states the classification system is regarded as a rational means for sorting and naming positions, and in other states it is an important administrative tool. In still other states it is merely a tool in developing position specifications. Job classifications currently range in number from 551 in South Dakota to more than 6,000 in New Jersey. The following list shows the number in each state (National Association of State Personnel Executives, 1996b; Council of State Governments, 1996).

Number of Classifications, 1986–1996

State	1986	1996
Alabama	1,340	1,481
Alaska	1,000	1,000
Arizona	1,450	1,575
Arkansas	2,100	1,854
California	4,400	4,500
Colorado	1,600	951
Connecticut	2,500	4,060
Delaware	1,100	1,300
Florida	1,839	3,100
Georgia	1,500	1,500
Hawaii	1,583	1,719
Idaho	1,100	1,633
Illinois	1,600	1,039
Indiana	1,525	1,501
Iowa	1,200	851
Kansas	1,200	762
Kentucky	1,442	1,700

Louisiana	2,440	2,875
Maine	1,497	1,300
Maryland	3,000	2,389
Massachusetts	850	1,150
Michigan	1,766	1,691
Minnesota	1,794	2,269
Mississippi	1,700	2,500
Missouri	1,080	1,307
Montana	1,500	1,350
Nebraska	1,300	1,460
Nevada	1,200	1,300
New Hampshire	1,470	1,251
New Jersey	6,500	6,169
New Mexico	800	1,200
New York	7,300	5,950
North Carolina	3,012	3,500
North Dakota	960	980
Ohio	1,737	2,000
Oklahoma	1,136	1,407
Oregon	1,185	815
Pennsylvania	2,700	2,782
Rhode Island	1,500	1,500
South Carolina	2,400	2,298
South Dakota	510	551
Tennessee	1,409	1,680
Texas	1,324	1,148
Utah	2,100	2,200
Vermont	1,063	1,300
Virginia	2,100	1,800
Washington	2,400	1,750
West Virginia	950	750
Wisconsin	2,011	2,800
Wyoming	1,350	774

Between 1986 and 1996, approximately half of the states reduced the number of job classifications, and the other half increased them. Many of the states that reduced the number began doing so in the late 1980s and early 1990s, in response to increasing use of technology and new management techniques that changed the education and experience needed to perform state jobs. In general the number of classifications appears to be associated with the number of state employees. The more state employees, the more job classifications. California, New Jersey, and New York are examples. But there are exceptions. Texas, for example, employs almost as many people as New York but has only one-fifth the classifications. And Georgia, which has a level of state employment similar to New Jersey's or North Carolina's, has thousands fewer job classifications. The number of job classes may be related to such factors as how often the classification system is updated, how involved the personnel department is in the state budgeting process, how often the legislature requests more titles to support a new or expanded program, how difficult it is to get rid of job classifications once they get in the system, and how much opposition there is from employee unions. Two other factors affecting the number of job classes are organizational structure (hierarchical or horizontal) and the need for new occupations, especially in information technology.

One recent development in the classification field is the use of *broadbanding,* introduced to state governments from the private sector. Under broadbanding, a state typically pares away many salary grades and ranges, collapsing them into fewer or broader and more inclusive classes of positions. The most common reason for adopting this practice, usually applied to both classification and compensation, is to complement the move to a flatter organization. Other reasons are to encourage a broadly skilled workforce, support a new culture or climate, support career development opportunities, reduce salary administration efforts and costs, and minimize job analysis and evaluation costs. Currently, nineteen states are using broadbanding, and many are planning to implement it. California and Texas are among the states already trying to reduce the number of job classes through broadbanding or similar methods that allow managers the flexibility to manage. The largest state in the nation is trying to reduce by 75 percent its largest group of job classes (the 400 classifications that together make up 83 percent of state jobs). In addition the governor recently directed the State Personnel Board to reduce the 1,617 classes with five or fewer employees (California Governor's Office, 1996). Texas is trying to delete 422 job classes, create 47 new classes, change the titles of 215 classes, and reallocate 41 classes. The total number of classes in Texas could decrease from 1,148 to 773. In addition the state is planning to consolidate most agency-specific classes or to rewrite job descriptions so that each class can be used by all agencies as appropriate (Texas Office of the State Auditor, 1996).

The Washington Management Service emphasizes flexibility, decentralization, and individual accountability instead of standardization and procedure. This state program, implemented in 1994, covers more than 2,800 midlevel management positions. They retain the protections of the civil service system but function under a separate set of rules adopted by the director of the Department of Personnel. These streamlined rules fill only eight pages of text, compared to more than one hundred pages for the traditional civil service rules. There are no centralized structure of minimum qualifications, employment registers, job specifications, classifications, and salary ranges. Instead, personnel decisions are made on a position-by-position basis at the agency level. The compensation system departs radically from the tight structure of conventional civil service systems. Approximately 750 job classifications—and the administrative processes associated with them—have been consolidated into four broad management bands. Agencies are responsible for making salary decisions within the context of their agency budgets and the minimum and maximum salaries assigned to each band. By reducing red tape, the Washington Management Services program saves agencies, applicants, and employees considerable time, effort, expense, and frustration. Georgia is implementing a totally new system. A recently enacted law requires that all state positions filled on or after July 1, 1996, be placed in an unclassified service. Workers hired after that date are employed at-will and are not covered by the merit system. This radical reform law spelling out the new roles and responsibilities of the state's agencies and merit system in administering the personnel system also decentralizes authority for personnel management to individual agencies and moves the Georgia state merit system to a consultative role (Lopez and Tanner, 1996). The new system will be phased in gradually over the next several years. Under it, agencies will define agency-unique job classes in the unclassified services, assign these job classes to appropriate pay ranges on the statewide compensation plan, administer applicant screening devices to ensure the integrity of the selection process, and develop policies that will ensure compliance with applicable employment-related federal and state laws (National Association of State Personnel Executives, 1996a).

When identifying the primary purpose of their compensation systems, some states see them as key elements in attracting and retaining a high-quality workforce. A compensation system can ensure that employees are paid equitably based upon a consistent, objective methodology or help reinforce organizational values or help meet organizational goals. However, one problem with traditional classification systems is that job titles are connected to salary ranges. An employee who reaches the ceiling of a position's salary range cannot get a pay increase unless he or she gets a new title.

Compensation systems in a majority of states are authorized by statute, in fourteen by regulations, and in fourteen through collective bargaining. Systems in nineteen states are authorized on two or even all three of these bases. Twenty-six states have reported a regular program for awarding merit increases. One recent survey by the Council of State Governments (CSG) found that most states still rely on traditional systems of compensation, including across-the-board increases (forty-five states), merit increases (thirty-three states), and seniority-based pay (twenty-seven states). But states have also at least begun to try new and creative ways of paying employees. A number of states reward employees based on performance, through noncash incentives (seventeen states), bonuses (thirteen states), and incentive-based pay (eleven states). Survey respondents have said the use of these types of performance-based pay will increase during the next five years ("Downsizing," 1995).

Performance Evaluation

Performance evaluations now are mandatory, and all but five states require annual evaluations of all employees. The remaining five require evaluations only for a select group. One-third of the states have separate evaluations for managers and other employees, and about two-thirds allow agency heads some degree of customization.[3]

Two new approaches to performance evaluation deserve special mention here: Georgia's GeorgiaGain and Michigan's pay-for-performance for division directors. The transition to the GeorgiaGain Performance Management Process (PMP) officially got under way in October 1995, as managers and employees began to develop new performance plans, and some Georgia state employees have been evaluated on these plans since 1996. Each performance plan specifies four levels of performance: "did not meet expectations," "met expectations," "exceeded expectations," and "far exceeded expectations." Managers are now required to prepare for transition of all classified employees to the new PMP. Each transition requires a one-on-one meeting between manager and employee to develop a new performance plan (National Association of State Personnel Executives, 1996a).

In March 1996, the Michigan Civil Service Commission approved a proposal to expand the state's pay-for-performance plan to cover six hundred division directors and deputy division directors. At that time about three hundred higher-level employees (such as bureau and office directors) were already under merit pay plans. Under the approved proposal, managers who meet expectations are eligible for merit increases or lump-sum bonuses of up to 8 percent. Raises are subject to available funds, however. Managers with poor evaluations can have their pay cut by up to 8 percent. Moreover, managers cannot bump other managers from similar positions or be bumped from their own jobs by more senior managers in periods of downsizing. The plan also provides a pay-protection clause for employees affected by a reduction in force. Agencies have been instructed to train employees, develop individual performance standards and objectives, and submit any necessary documents for civil service review.

CHALLENGES TO STATE CIVIL SERVICE SYSTEMS

In a 1995 NASPE survey, state personnel directors identified downsizing, Total Quality Management (TQM), federal mandates, budget cuts, and civil service reform as the five most important issues for them in the past five years. They also selected downsizing, compensation reform, privatization, TQM, pay-for-performance, and technology as the most important issues facing state personnel executives in the next five years ("Downsizing," 1995). This section focuses on three of these important issues: downsizing, privatization, and TQM.

Downsizing

Workforce reduction was one of the biggest issues in the early 1990s. And half of the personnel executives surveyed predicted that shrinking the workforce will continue to be a primary concern in the second half of the decade. But is real reduction of state employment possible in light of continued population growth and increasing responsibilities for state governments? Some states have been successful in reducing the number of state employees, but state personnel executives tend to say that downsizing can have a downside—because state government is so labor intensive, reducing staff limits the ability to provide services.

Reductions in force, mandatory hiring freezes, and job sharing are the most popular ways of downsizing for states. Out of forty-six states responding to a survey, thirty-six used reduction in force, thirty-six used mandatory hiring freezes, and thirty-four used job sharing. Other methods used were deferred payment for time worked, mandatory pay increase freezes, telecommuting, early retirement, voluntary unpaid leave, and retraining. Comparing recent trends, it appears that telecommuting has become more popular in the past few years and that fewer states are making use of mandatory unpaid leave and mandated pay increase freezes now than five years ago. Twenty of the forty-six states reported using mandatory unpaid leave in 1991, but only fourteen were using it in 1996. In the same group, thirty-five states were using mandated pay increase freezes in 1991, and twenty-six were using them in 1996 (National Association of State Personnel Executives, 1996b, p. 157).

New York is among the states with the largest reduction in workforce. Between 1991 and 1995, for example, more than ten thousand permanent employees from sixty-four agencies were laid off. In 1996, another six thousand workers were let go. Several hundred, however, have been reemployed at the same or a lower grade level. Agencies with the largest number of layoffs are those dealing with mental health and mental retardation, correctional services, and general services. Although the full impact of this downsizing is not yet clear, several trends appear evident. One trend is that the average age of state employees is rising. In 1991, for example, the average age was 41.8; by 1994, it had risen to 43; and by 1995, it had increased to 43.3. Another trend appears to be a longer average length of service. The average length of service increased from 10.9 years in 1991 to 13 years in 1994. According to a report by the New York State Department of Civil Service (1995), one of the consequences of downsizing is a lack of new opportunities for growth and development for the remaining workers. The report pointed to a significant reduction in promotion opportunities and the difficulty of moving to another assignment.

Connecticut is an example of a state that like many others has invested extensive time and effort to assist state employees displaced by downsizing. The state personnel division conducted numerous outplacement workshops and job fairs. Employees were assisted in qualifying for jobs through many skill-developing sessions and special test administrations (Connecticut Department of Administrative Services, 1993).

Privatization

Privatization is increasing in state government. As reflected in the NASPE and CSG surveys of state personnel executives, it has become a major challenge to state policymakers and civil service systems in recent years. According to a 1993 national survey of privatization in the fifty state governments, conducted by the Council of State Governments, despite persistent resistance and skepticism, the extent of privatization activities has steadily increased in recent years. More than 85 percent of state auditors, budget directors, and comptrollers who responded to the survey predicted increased privatization activities in the foreseeable future. Privatization was most common in the areas of administration and general services, mental health and mental retardation, social services, corrections, and transportation. The major reasons for privatization cited by survey respondents were cost savings (24 percent), flexibility and less red tape (23), lack of agency personnel or expertise (19), speedy implementation (17), and high-quality service (17) (Chi, 1993). But privatization initiatives have met opposition. The strongest and most persistent opposition in many states has come from state employee associations or unions, often led by the public employee department of the AFL-CIO or the American Federation of State, County and Municipal Employees (AFSCME). In fact the AFL-CIO has led antiprivatization campaigns across the states. In short, privatization is often viewed by government employee union leaders as *union busting.* Thus unions believe that before states attempt to contract out certain functions or services to the public, it should be essential for state managers to seek union or employee association approval.

Oregon was one of the first states to devise privatization guidelines, and they do provide that an agency must notify the state employee union within one week of its decision to do a formal privatization feasibility study and must indicate job classifications and work areas affected; the union must be given a thirty-day notice before the agency issues bids if contracting the work will displace bargaining unit workers; the agency must also tell the union the results of the feasibility study, including the assumptions used, cost details, projected cost savings, and expected quality changes if any; the union must submit an alternative proposal, such as a productivity improvement program, during the thirty-day notice period; and the agency and the union are required to discuss the effect contracting the work will have on bargaining unit workers if any full-time worker will lose his or her job. The guidelines also say: "Don't think employees won't know what's going on. They will and what they imagine is happening may be worse than what is happening. Unions are concerned about employment of their members. As it affects their members, unions are as interested in the success of contracting state work as they are about union-developed alternative proposals" (Chi, 1988, p. 8).

In addition to union opposition, state policymakers and managers face legal barriers in implementing privatization. The examples of New York and California can help us comprehend the legal obstacles state managers must overcome when initiating privatization projects. New York's state constitution has been generally interpreted as limiting privatization activities for state and local government. Article 5, section 6 reads in part: "appointments and promotions in the civil service of the state and all of the civil divisions thereof . . . shall be made according to merit and fitness to be ascertained as far as practicable by examination which, as far as practicable shall be competitive." Moreover, a 1989 study by the New York Legislative Commission on State and Local Relations reported: "In addition to collective bargaining, other legal impediments inhibit privatization more than in other states. Although the power of New York governments to contract with private firms is broad, it is not unlimited." Furthermore, the existing state labor law (sec. 220) requires private contractors to pay the prevailing union wage rates to their employees who are working on public projects (Chi, 1992). Similarly, California's ability to privatize public services is often hampered by constitutional and legal barriers. Article 2 of the state constitution, which established the civil service system in 1934 to end the corrupt spoils system of political patronage, has been interpreted by the courts as severely limiting, if not preventing, privatization. There also are laws, such as California Civil Code section 19130, that according to California officials insulate state employees from the rigors of competition (California Governor's Office, 1996, pp. 30–31).

State policymakers and managers are likely to confront several major issues when deciding whether to privatize. First, they should develop cost comparison formats for state agencies to use in the privatization decision-making process and in assessing outcomes of privatization projects. Without such formats and other carefully devised preprivatization analyses, it is difficult to determine if privatization is likely to be cost efficient. Second, they should note that cost savings may be realized when several qualified private providers compete for a privatization project or when carefully structured competitive bidding takes place between state agencies and private firms. Without true competition, a government monopoly could simply be replaced by a private monopoly. Third, state managers should realize they will have to work as planners, managers, and monitors of privatization activities, because privatization does not delegate state authority or responsibility to private providers. That is, privatization changes the nature of state government, forcing managers to increase oversight. Fourth, managers should not initiate privatization projects without first considering the future status of affected state employees. State managers need to address the employee displacement issue before privatizing state services or programs. In certain areas, however, privatization may be used as a tool for not hiring additional state workers. Fifth, in planning, implementing, and monitoring privatization activities, state managers should pay attention to the dangers that agency service may be interrupted and that there may be corruption, mismanagement, or unfair labor practices on the part of private firms.

Total Quality Management

Total Quality Management, a management philosophy recently introduced in state government, is another challenge to state civil service systems. TQM, among other programs, is designed for a climate of employee empowerment, teamwork, and decentralized decision making, approaches not always compatible with traditional, hierarchical management. Moreover, many state managers are asking if TQM is just another fad, like management by objectives. According to a national survey of TQM activities by the Council of State Governments in 1993, TQM, either in pure or hybrid form, has been initiated in selected executive branch agencies in more than forty states. These states have initiated their TQM efforts under gubernatorial executive orders (in thirteen states), agency heads' directives without gubernatorial executive orders (eleven states), special legislation (two states), or other means (thirteen states, including those where TQM was initiated in agencies not under the governors' direct jurisdiction). The trend is toward more widespread use of TQM (Chi, 1994).

Why is TQM needed? Traditional management approaches, such as management by objectives and zero-based budgeting, certainly have their place. Under appropriate circumstances they may have quite useful consequences. In fact some state agencies have reported encouraging outcomes from such approaches, although others have yet to realize measurable management improvement. But the principal difficulty with traditional management and productivity improvement approaches is that they are either detached from daily management or result in piecemeal changes. In addition, none has a comprehensive philosophy of management linked to a method of process improvement and of changing organizational culture. TQM emphasizes horizontal decision making with employee empowerment and teamwork, customer-defined quality, and continuous improvement. Although TQM has been variously defined as a philosophy, approach, tool, process, system, method, set of guiding principles or procedures, or array of organizational behaviors, and although state TQM efforts contain several components, TQM proponents tend to share at least one underlying assumption: namely, management problems are primarily system based, not employee based. According to quality management proponents, most problems that an organization confronts are self-inflicted and usually created by management. They maintain that more than 85 percent of organizational problems are systems problems. Management created the systems (policies, rules, procedures, legislation) to deal with such things as training, rewards, service delivery, information, and finances, and therefore it is management's job to improve the systems so that people can work more effectively in them.

Why is TQM important in state government now? Management reformers contend taxpayers and customers of government services are forcing state policymakers to rethink how they operate. In the wake of recent budget shortfalls, many state governments have been implementing strategic planning, restructuring their executive branch agencies, advocating civil service reform, and conducting cost control and efficiency studies to improve management and service delivery. The ultimate goal of TQM is to close the gap between what customers expect to receive and what they actually get from state government. These customers are both internal (workers in state agencies) and external (agency clients and constituents). If state governments do not adopt what is becoming the standard for service (customer friendly, fast, flexible, individualized, and so forth) and simply stay constant, they will for all practical purposes fall behind.

A number of practical issues arise when implementing TQM in state agencies. Managers and employees must be convinced that TQM is not a fad. Over the years they have been subjected to many new management fads; many of them tend to regard TQM as just another craze and think it, too, will eventually go away. To carry out effective and successful TQM initiatives, TQM initiators and supporters must overcome resistance from state agency executives, especially midlevel managers and often employee organizations and unions, who tend to favor traditional management approaches or the status quo. Because improvement efforts have a major impact on employees' work, organized labor has an important role to play in shaping the directions TQM takes in state government. Also, governors and agency heads must address structural barriers to TQM implementation, such as existing civil service systems and multiple layers of hierarchy, to create a new environment for change. TQM training is the first step for management improvement. It takes resources and time, but it represents an investment in the people who will actually carry out change within any organization. It promotes an understanding of the vision, mission, and goals of the initiative as it promotes buy-in to process change. As many as thirty-seven states have reported using business executives and outside management consultants to train state managers and employees; twenty-nine of these states also have used state TQM coordinators and facilitators. In general terms, six TQM training models can be considered by state agencies: no formal training is provided, and self-education is up to each person; formal training is provided, decentralized to each department; formal training is voluntary, but central leadership is provided; a training model is provided for all departments, along with central leadership; a unified, integrated approach is provided on a multiagency level; and a unified, integrated approach is provided on multistate and multigovernment levels.

Finally, once TQM is in place, it is important to sustain it. In order to maintain TQM activities in state government, some TQM experts propose that state officials consider these four needs: an ongoing external advisory board (to provide strategic vision, key result areas, financial and in-kind support, accountability, media visibility); career civil servant buy-in; TQM-compatible infrastructures (recognition and reward structures, human resource management, recruitment and selection practices, sufficient internal training capacity); and strategic experiments to test and refine TQM process (volunteers in different areas can report results and recommend process improvement and select key results for rollout). Additional strategies may include gaining support of constituents (client groups and unions); institutionalizing the quality process through statutes, rules, and regulations; depoliticizing the quality process; selling the quality process, not the label; courting legislatures and oversight organizations; conducting continual training programs reflecting the new culture and long-term changes in the labor force; protecting and nurturing institutional memory; grooming candidates for succession in elective state offices; and emphasizing the quality process in transition documents. However, the attitudes and decisions of senior agency managers may be the most crucial factor in sustaining TQM. After pro-TQM governors leave office, for instance, top-ranked civil servants as well as midlevel managers will determine the fate of TQM. Two crucial questions thus arise: How can we make top civil servants more aware of these quality management practices? And, How might we get these folks to decide to support continuous quality improvement and to sustain the quality effort over time?

CONCLUSION

The foregoing analysis raises two significant implications for state civil service systems. First, states need clearly defined long-term visions for their civil service systems. Second, state civil service systems cannot be changed without strong gubernatorial leadership and continual legislative commitment.

States need to define their strategic visions for human resource management for the twenty-first century. Minnesota and California are among the states with clearly defined visions that appear to be leading the way. In 1993, the Minnesota Commission on Reform and Efficiency set the state's visions for the state human resource system, defining a system that is outcome based, customer oriented, simple, and user friendly and also strategic, proactive, and change based. The vision describes an ideal human resource system that reflects community values and that "encourages quality employers with creative optional work force development and increased effectiveness of statewide management teams" (Commission on Reform and Efficiency, 1993, p. 6). According to California's vision, "The ideal system would allow managers to hire the best and brightest—quickly; train, retain and motivate the workforce; compensate fairly by rewarding merit; empower workers to apply their skills in ways that support the mission of their department; empower managers to reward high performance, and to discipline or remove under-performers; and train employees for the challenges of competitive government" (California Governor's Office, 1996, p. 60). In 1995, New York state also completed a five-year (1995 to 1999) workforce management plan with similar goals and objectives (New York State Department of Civil Service, 1995).

To implement successful civil service reform, it is imperative that governors and legislative leaders walk their talk. They must overcome political pressure to rout the status quo from all quarters, including employee unions. They must tackle the obstacles to change encountered by state personnel executives, including budget problems and fiscal constraints, reluctance to change on the part of agency managers, and union concerns and opposition. In removing these obstacles, union cooperation is what is needed the most. This brief discussion of privatization and TQM leaves no doubt that state managers, with union support, can achieve a great deal more with less or do better with the same amount of resources, especially in times of fiscal austerity and the *devolution revolution.* State employee unions have remained strong in more than half of the state governments. In 1996, there were twenty-seven states that guaranteed collective bargaining rights to state employees. Unions will continue to exert their influence on civil service reform efforts, downsizing, privatization, and quality management in the states. Lastly, legislative leadership counts in comprehensive civil service reform. The issue of civil service reform is more important today than ever before. But without total leadership commitment, neither ongoing civil service reform efforts nor alternatives to traditional state management approaches can be successfully implemented. Without the necessary financial resources, state managers cannot give the needed higher priority to human resource management.

Notes

1. For more information on state personnel administration, see National Association of State Personnel Executives (1996b).

2. As of 1995, twenty-one states were undergoing reform of their classification and compensation systems and another eleven states were planning to reform these systems, according to the 1995 National Association of State Personnel Executives survey. The twenty one states (with the years their reforms began) are Kansas (1985), Michigan (1986), Rhode Island (1987), Pennsylvania (1988), New Hampshire (1988), Arkansas (1989), Wisconsin (1989), West Virginia (1990), Ohio (1990), Maryland (1990), Florida (1991), Connecticut (1992), Minnesota (1993), Georgia (1992), Montana (1992), North Carolina (1993), Virginia (1993), Idaho (1993), Washington (1993), New Jersey (1994), and Texas (1994).

3. According to a survey conducted by the Minnesota Commission on Reform and Efficiency in 1993, states use four basic types of job evaluation methods: classification (thirteen states), the Hay method (eight states), point factor system (sixteen states), and the whole job method (South Carolina and Texas). A common strength of the three major methods is their ability to evaluate all jobs. More than half of the respondents using classification listed this as a strength.

References

California Governor's Office. *Competitive Government: A Plan for Less Bureaucracy, More Results.* Sacramento, Apr. 1996.

Chi, K. S. *Privatization and Contracting for State Services: A Guide.* Lexington, Ky.: Council of State Governments, Apr. 1988.

Chi, K. S. "What Other States Are Doing." In E. S. Savas (ed.), *Privatization for New York: Competing for a Better Future.* Albany: New York State Senate Advisory Commission on Privatization, Jan. 1992.

Chi, K. S. "Privatization in State Government: Options for the Future." *State Trends and Forecasts,* Nov. 1993 (entire issue).

Chi, K. S. "TQM in State Government: Options for the Future." *State Trends and Forecasts,* Oct. 1994 (entire issue).

Commission on Reform and Efficiency. "Human Resources Management in Minnesota State Government." In *Summary Report.* St. Paul, Minn., 1993.

Connecticut Department of Administrative Services. *Personnel Division Annual Report, 1992–93.* Hartford, 1993.

Council of State Governments. *Book of the States, 1996–97.* Lexington, Ky.: Council of State Governments, 1996.

"Downsizing: The Mantra for State Personnel Directors in the '90s." *State Trends Bulletin,* Spring 1995, *1*(2), 1.

Lopez, J. F., and Tanner, J. D. "How Can We Fix the Merit System?" *State Government News,* June-July 1996, pp. 26–27.

National Association of State Personnel Executives. *Civil Service Reform Survey.* Lexington, Ky.: National Association of State Personnel Executives, 1993.

National Association of State Personnel Executives. *State Personnel View,* Winter 1995, pp. 1–4.

National Association of State Personnel Executives. *State Personnel View,* Winter 1996a, pp. 1–4.

National Association of State Personnel Executives. *State Personnel Office: Roles and Functions.* (3rd ed.) Lexington, Ky.: National Association of State Personnel Executives, 1996b.

National Commission on the State and Local Public Service (Winter Commission). *Hard Truths/Tough Choices: An Agenda for State and Local Reform.* Albany, N.Y.: Rockefeller Institute of Government, 1993.

New York State Department of Civil Service. *1995 New York State Work Force Management Plan.* Albany, Nov. 1995.

Texas Office of the State Auditor. *A Biennial Report of Recommended Changes to the Classification Plan.* Austin, Sept. 1996.

Wechsler, B. "Florida's Civil Service Reform." *Spectrum,* Winter 1993, pp. 45–51.

Wisconsin Department of Employment Relations. *Recruiting the Best and the Brightest: Reinventing Wisconsin's Civil Service Hiring System.* Madison, Sept. 1995.

CHAPTER THREE

Beyond Civil Service

The Politics of the Emergent Paradigm

Donald E. Klingner

In September 1993, Vice President Gore unveiled the main report of the National Performance Review (NPR), stating that "we stand at the crossroads of the future of our federal government, of public service, of public confidence in government" (National Performance Review, 1993a, p. 3). This reform fervor was generated by nationwide interest in *reinventing government,* to use Osborne and Gaebler's phrase (1992). The reforms recommended by the NPR were widely and hotly debated within the federal government community. Could the federal government adopt customer service, lower costs, and employee empowerment as values (Walters, 1992)? Were the reforms consistent with agency efficiency, political responsiveness, and employee rights? Could they win Congressional approval?

Yet fundamental as these issues were, the debate changed in fourteen months: the Republican party gained control of Congress in the November 1994 election, claiming a mandate to make much more radical changes. In this new context, Republicans claimed that the marginal increases in program effectiveness, service, and flexibility promised by NPR were simply not enough to solve the problem.

From a historical perspective the events of the past several years signify a shift in the politics underlying public human resource management. The purpose of this chapter is to present a historical perspective on traditional public personnel management functions, processes, systems, and values; examine the politics and values of the emergent antigovernment paradigm (personal accountability, limited and decentralized government, and community responsibility for social service delivery); evaluate the emergent paradigm's impact on traditional values; and explore how the emergent paradigm affects the role of the public personnel manager.

A HISTORICAL PERSPECTIVE

Public human resource management in the United States can be viewed from at least four perspectives (Klingner and Nalbandian, 1998). First, it is the *functions* (planning, acquisition, development, and discipline) needed to manage human resources in public agencies. Second, it is the *processes* by which public jobs, as scarce resources, are allocated.

Third, it is the interaction among fundamental societal *values* that often conflict. These values are responsiveness, efficiency, employee rights, and social equity. *Responsiveness* means a budget process that allocates positions and therefore sets priorities and an appointment process that considers political or personal loyalty along with education and experience as indicators of merit. *Efficiency* means staffing decisions based on ability and performance rather than political loyalty. *Employee rights* mean selection and promotion based on merit, as defined by objective measures of ability and performance, and employees who are free to apply their knowledge, skills, and abilities without partisan political interference. And *social equity* means public jobs allocated proportionately, based on gender, race, and other designated criteria.

And fourth, public human resource management is the embodiment of human resource *systems*—the laws, rules, organizations, and procedures used to fulfill personnel functions in ways that express the abstract values. Historically, U.S. public human resource management systems developed in at least four evolutionary stages (summarized in Table 3.1). First came *patronage* systems (1789 to 1883), which, in their first phase, awarded public jobs on the basis of social and family status and, in their second, awarded them according to political loyalty or party affiliation. Second, the increased size and complexity of public activities led to the emergence of a *civil service* model (1883 to 1933), which emphasized efficiency (modernization) by defining personnel management as a neutral administrative function and which emphasized individual rights (democratization) by allocating public jobs, at least at the federal level, on merit (Heclo, 1977). Third, a hybrid *effectiveness* model emerged (1933 to 1964), which combined the political leadership of patronage systems and the merit principles of civil service systems, because even pure merit systems must be responsive to political leadership if government is to be effective (Fischer, 1945; Sayre, 1948). Fourth, the values of the effectiveness model remained in force, and two more systems emerged (1964 to 1992), as advocates of two additional values. *Collective bargaining* emerged to represent collective employee

Table 3.1. Evolution of Public Human Resource Management.

Stage of Evolution	Dominant Values	Dominant Systems	Pressures for Change
One (1789–1883)	Responsiveness	Patronage	Modernization Democratization
Two (1883–1933)	Efficiency Employee rights	Civil service	Responsive and effective government
Three (1933–1964)	Responsiveness Efficiency Employee rights	Patronage Civil service	Employee rights Social equity
Four (1964–1992)	Responsiveness Efficiency Employee rights Social equity	Patronage Civil service Collective bargaining Affirmative action	Dynamic equilibrium (self-correcting) among four competing values and systems

rights (the equitable treatment of members by management through negotiated work rules for wages, benefits, and working conditions), and *affirmative action* emerged to represent social equity (through voluntary or court-mandated recruitment and selection practices to help ameliorate the underrepresentation of minorities and women in the workforce). In this fourth stage, U.S. public human resource management could be described as a dynamic equilibrium among the four competing values, each championed by a particular system, for allocating scarce public jobs in a complex and changing environment. As one might expect, this conflict has exhibited a commingling of technical decisions (*how* to do a personnel function) with political ones (*what* value to favor or *what* system to use) (Nalbandian, 1981; Ban and Riccucci, 1991; Freedman, 1994).

THE POLITICS AND VALUES OF THE EMERGENT PARADIGM

In the traditional view of public personnel management it was possible to evaluate techniques based on their contribution to the maximization of one or more of the four competing values. Thus, for example, affirmative action programs could be evaluated favorably based on their contribution to social equity but unfavorably based on their denial of individual rights for nonminorities. The state of the field at any one time could be evaluated in terms of the balance among the four competing values, with public personnel managers and others functioning to resolve conflict arising from the simultaneous implementation of these competing values and systems. Thus the traditional model of public human resource management reinforced all four values and the role of personnel managers and others in mediating the resulting value conflicts.

Because evolutionary change is by nature slow, it is difficult to pinpoint the precise point at which this consensus began to alter. But if pressed, one could do worse than pick the 1976 presidential campaign, won by Jimmy Carter, who ran against the national government as a Washington "outsider." Following the election, he proposed the 1978 Civil Service Reform Act on grounds that included poor performance in the public service and difficulty in controlling and directing bureaucrats. Beginning in 1981, the Reagan administration, though starting from fundamentally different values and policy objectives, continued to cast government as part of the problem and to campaign against the infrastructure of public agencies and public administrators.

The antigovernment assumptions behind this shift were paralleled by a related transition from political to economic perspectives on public policy (Lan and Rosenbloom, 1992). This shift in perspectives emphasized market forces, rather than program implementation by government agencies and employees, as the most efficacious tools of public policy related to both individuals and the economy. Although public administration retained its role as the *great compromiser* among competing values, the emphasis on economic perspectives and the value of administrative efficiency clearly reflected the intense pressures on the public sector to "do more with less," a mandate that has come with the territory of public management since 1981. The first pressure—do more—caused governments to become more accountable, through such techniques as program budgeting, management by objectives, program evaluation, and management information systems. The second pressure—to do more with less—caused governments to lower expenditures, through such methods as tax ceilings, expenditure ceilings, deficit reduction, deferred expenditures, accelerated tax collection, service fees, and user charges and through a range of legislative and judicial efforts to shift program responsibilities and costs away from each affected government.

Because from 50 percent to 75 percent of public expenditures goes toward employee salaries and benefits, efforts to increase accountability and reduce expenditures have focused on those managerial functions, the ones subsumed by public personnel management. The shift focused on philosophies and techniques used to enhance accountability in previous eras (such as the 1930s and the 1960s), emphasizing program outputs and rationally tying program inputs to outputs. Examples of these techniques were program budgeting, human resource forecasting, job evaluation, management by objectives, objective performance appraisal, training needs assessment, cost-benefit analysis, and gainsharing (productivity bargaining). Moreover, the information systems revolution has expanded access to information formerly used by management for coordination and control, and this change has been reflected in organizational restructuring and the downsizing of middle managerial positions.

The presidential election of 1992 was fascinating from the perspective of civil service reformers, for it pitted proponents of sweeping major change against proponents of even greater change. Less than a year after taking office, Vice President Gore issued the National Performance Review report that aimed at creating a government that "works better and costs less." The changes initiated by this report have been intensely debated in the public management literature since then, with an emergent consensus on these broad conclusions: increased government effectiveness requires (1) fundamental changes in organizational structure and accountability, epitomized by the term reinventing government; (2) a decentralization of most public personnel functions to operating agencies and a corresponding reduction in the functions and authority of the Office of Personnel Management; and (3) a 10 percent reduction in federal civilian employment, largely in staff positions (personnel, budget, auditing, procurement, and middle management).

The Republican Party swept into control of Congress in 1994 for the first time in over forty years, pledging to carry out the reforms in its Contract with America. The emphasis of this contract was that government, especially the federal government, should be doing less—and with less resources. The Republican electoral victory was a result of a contemporary shift toward three emergent *antigovernment* values: personal accountability, limited and decentralized government, and community responsibility for social services.

First, proponents of *personal accountability* expect that people will make individual choices consistent with their own goals and accept responsibility for the consequences of these choices, rather than passing responsibility for their actions on to the rest of society. Collectively, we are responsible for providing each other with equal opportunity to develop our individual knowledge, skills, and abilities, but the responsibility for that development (or lack of it) falls on the individual.

Second, proponents of *limited and decentralized government* believe, fundamentally, that government is to be feared for its power to arbitrarily or capriciously deprive individuals of their rights. It is this libertarian belief that gave rise to the Constitution's Bill of Rights, which basically seeks to limit the national government's power to infringe on individuals' freedoms of speech, press, association, and privacy. Proponents of this value also believe that public policy, service delivery, and revenue generation can be controlled efficiently in a smaller unit of government in a way not possible in a larger one. And for some limited government proponents, a reduction in government size and scope is justified by perceived government ineffectiveness; by a high value accorded to individual freedom, responsibility, and accountability; and finally, by a reluctance to devote a greater share of personal income to taxes.

More specifically, it is argued that smaller units of government are more effective because, at the local level, decision makers are known, revenues are predictable and the amounts understandable (millions versus trillions of dollars), and services are directly visible. Decentralization of government to the local level raises issues of equity in service delivery and regulation, but proponents argue that these issues are generally best addressed not by uniform national policies or standards but by increasingly representative legislative bodies and increasingly powerful ethnic group representation. The fact that they see this diversity and representativeness as likely to result in political gridlock at a national level is a primary reason for limiting and decentralizing government and for avoiding attempts to level the playing field through income redistributive policies and programs.

Third, the values of limited and decentralized government and personal accountability are supplemented with the value of *community responsibility for social services.* Even civil libertarians and free enterprise capitalists recognize that some individuals are unable to compete economically and politically because they lack the necessary knowledge, skills, ability, or emotional makeup to do so, regardless of the incentives they are offered. The answer to this distributional problem is not government "handouts," but a safety net maintained through the combined efforts of government social service agencies and nongovernment social institutions. A key development here is the emergence of not-for-profit nongovernment organizations responsible for social services, recreation, and community development activities. These may be churches, community centers, neighborhood associations, or other community-based organizations; the kinds of groups that President Bush praised in his "thousand points of light" speech in 1992. The most significant consequence of the emergence of this value, at least as far as public human resource management is concerned, has been the creation of this alternative to the traditional notion that government has to fund *and* deliver social services. The trend toward downsizing and decentralizing government would be incomplete without the thousands of nonprofit organizations that routinely provide local government social services funded by taxes, user fees, and charitable contributions.

The model of public human resource management presented in Table 3.1 is the traditional paradigm, one that is both descriptive and normative. That is, it is intended both to describe the historical and contemporary reality of the field and to defend the role public human resource managers play as they compromise among competing values. The emergent paradigm emphasizes two general descriptive characteristics of contemporary public human resource management: (1) using alternative organizations and mechanisms to deliver public services, and (2) increasing the flexibility of employment relationships for those public employees that remain. The primary alternative mechanisms are service purchase agreements with other public or nongovernment organizations, privatization, franchise agreements, subsidies, vouchers, volunteers, self-help, and regulatory and tax incentives (International City Management Association, 1989). The primary ways of increasing the flexibility of the public employment that remains are increased use of contingent employees and of exempt positions outside the civil service filled through employment contracts. The existence of these alternative instrumentalities is not new. But a review of recent examples indicates how commonplace they have become, and how much they have supplanted traditional service delivery by civil service employees hired through appropriated funding of public agencies.

Alternative Mechanisms

Service *purchase agreements* with other government agencies and nongovernment organizations (NGOs) have come into increasing use. For example, metropolitan Dade County now provides fire and rescue services to almost every small- and medium-size municipality in Dade County. These arrangements were negotiated because they offer persuasive advantages for the county and its municipalities. For Dade County, there is the opportunity to expand services within a given geographic area and gain economies of scale. For municipalities, there is the opportunity to reduce capital costs, personnel costs, and legal liability risks. In addition, because firefighters are heavily unionized, there is the opportunity to avoid the immediate political and economic costs associated with collective bargaining.

As another example, many local governments contract with individual consultants or private businesses to conduct such personnel services as employee development and training. The use of outside consultants and businesses (hired under fee-for-service arrangements on an as-needed basis) not only increases available expertise but also increases managerial flexibility by reducing the range of qualified technical and professional employees the agency would otherwise hire. The costs of service purchase agreements might be lower for the service provider than for the agency, and the agency reduces its own legal liability risks.

Privatization is the performance of a formerly public function by a private contractor. It differs from service purchase agreements primarily in philosophy and scope. Service purchase agreements contract for delivery of a particular service to a public agency, but privatization effectively means that the government stops providing a service and replaces its agency infrastructure with an outside contractor that then provides all services formerly provided by the public agency. Privatization has become commonplace over the past fifteen years because it offers all the advantages of service purchase agreements on a larger scale. It has become prevalent in areas, such as solid waste disposal, where there is an easily identifiable *benchmark* (standard cost and service) for comparison with the private sector and where public agency costs tend to be higher because of higher pay and benefits (Mahtesian, 1994). Privatization is also spreading rapidly in certain areas that have previously been almost entirely the prerogative of the public sector: schools and prisons.

In 1994, for example, the school board of a faded working-class Pittsburgh suburb was facing desperate problems. It had the highest tax rate in the county, only one of 40 students who took the Scholastic Assessment Test in the year from June 1993 to June 1994 scored above the national average on math and verbal test results, and the number of high school graduates had plummeted from 225 in 1978 to 60 in 1994. It sent layoff notices to teachers at one of four schools, and hired a Tennessee company to run the school, picking its own teachers. Not surprisingly, it made this decision over strong opposition from unionized teachers and school administrators, who intimated that the purpose was union-busting rather than educational reform. A state court issued an injunction forbidding the contract; the district is considering an appeal (Applebome, 1995).

In 1990, a record number of over one million people were incarcerated in federal and state prisons. Despite heavy increases in prison construction, most states have been at capacity for the past five years. Privatization is one option for increasing government performance while attempting to hold down costs. Thus, during the past five years, a number of private corporations have gotten into the business of managing prisons, halfway houses, boot camps, and detention facilities. These organizations offer elected officials an alternative to public construction and management of prison facilities, which is a soaring cost for most state governments.

Franchise agreements allow a private business to offer a previously public function within a geographic area, charge competitive rates for it, and then pay the appropriate government a fee for the privilege. Examples are the private shuttle bus companies that are developing in many major cities, using vans instead of buses. The vans frequently duplicate public transportation services and skim riders from popular bus routes, but municipalities often encourage the procedure because it reduces their own costs, provides some revenue in return, and results in a continuation of a desirable public service. Private van companies may also have a big financial advantage in their ability to pay wages and benefits substantially lower than those paid by publicly owned transit companies.

Subsidies enable private businesses to perform public services funded either by user fees from clients or cost reimbursement from public agencies. Examples are airport security operations (provided by private contractors and paid for by both passengers and airlines), some types of hospital care (such as emergency medical services provided by private hospitals and reimbursed by public health systems), and some higher education programs (a state may pay a private university to operate a specialized program, rather than assign program responsibility and resources to a public institution; similarly, local housing authorities may subsidize rent in housing projects, based on tenant income, to encourage occupancy by low-income residents).

Vouchers enable individual recipients of public goods or services to purchase them from competing providers on the open market. Recent public opinion has focused on educational vouchers as a possible alternative to public school monopolies. Under this system, parents would receive a voucher that could be applied to the cost of education for their child at a number of competing educational institutions—both public and private. Another variant uses housing vouchers as a substitute for publicly constructed and managed housing. These vouchers allow public housing recipients to purchase the best possible housing for their money on a competitive basis from private landlords.

Volunteers are widely used by a range of public agencies to provide services that might otherwise be performed by paid employees. Examples include the volunteers involved in community crime watch programs, which work in cooperation with local police departments, and the volunteer teacher's aides who provide tutoring and individual assistance in many public schools.

Self-help is common in community development programs and correctional facilities. Community development programs frequently use resident volunteers to provide recreation, counseling, and other community support services. Frequently, such volunteer contributions are required to leverage a federal or state grant of appropriated funds. Contrary to the popular image of minimum-security prisons as vacation resorts, prison inmates are usually responsible for laundry, food service, and facilities maintenance.

Regulatory and tax incentives are typically used to encourage the private sector to perform functions that might otherwise be performed by public agencies with appropriated funds. The Job Training Partnership Act of 1982, for example, set up a tax incentive–based national system for workforce training that replaced the system set up by the Comprehensive Employment and Training Act of 1973 (CETA). CETA passed federal money through to state and local governments for assessment, training, and job placement activities. Its successor offers income tax deductions for corporations that hire, train, and retain disadvantaged employees. The intended effect—human resource development and employment—is the same as with CETA, only the mechanism is different.

Flexible Employment Relationships

All the mechanisms just described provide public services without using public employees and in many cases do so through funding sources besides appropriated funds. Yet even in those cases where public services continue to be provided by public employees working in public agencies funded by appropriations, massive changes have occurred in employment practices. Chief among these are increased use of temporary, part-time, and seasonal employment and increased hiring of exempt employees (those outside the classified civil service) through employment contracts. These two devices, along with the increased use of outside contractors, have markedly changed the face of the public workforce (U.S. Merit Systems Protection Board, 1994).

Increasingly, employers reduce costs and enhance flexibility by meeting minimal staffing requirements with *permanent* or *regular* employees and by meeting peak workload demands with *contingent* (temporary, part-time, or seasonal) workers. These contingent employees usually receive lower salaries and benefits than career employees. Additionally, they do not enjoy the enhanced job protections of the civil service or of collective bargaining agreements. The skill requirements of their jobs are often reduced by job redesign or work simplification. Where commitment *and* high skills are required on a temporary basis, agencies may seek to save money or maintain flexibility by using contract or leased employees for positions exempt from civil service protections.

THE IMPACT OF THE EMERGENT PARADIGM ON TRADITIONAL VALUES

These two emergent public human resource management systems—using alternative mechanisms for delivering public services, and increasing the flexibility of employment relationships for the public employees who remain—have implications for each of the four values that underlie the traditional model of public personnel management.

Employee Rights

The value of employee rights is diminished by the new paradigm. Employees are more likely to be hired without civil service protections, more likely to be hired into temporary and part-time positions, more likely to receive lower pay and benefits, and more likely to be unprotected by civil service regulations or collective bargaining agreements (Kilborn, 1995).

Social Equity

It is most probable that social equity is also diminished by the new paradigm. For example, comparisons between the public and private sectors over the past twenty years have concluded rather uniformly that minorities and women in public agencies are closer to equal pay for equal work than are their private-sector counterparts. Managerial consultants are overwhelmingly white and male. Part-time and temporary positions are less likely to be covered by the Americans with Disabilities Act of 1990 and the Family and Medical Leave Act of 1993. And retrenchment in federal agencies responsible for enforcing affirmative action compliance means that agency activities will be less visible and effective. In addition, many positions are being removed from these agencies' purview.

Efficiency

The impact of the emergent paradigm on public agency efficiency has been both positive and negative. On the positive side the emergent paradigm has characteristics that clearly increase public agency productivity and lower costs, particularly for civil service employees in appropriated positions. In many cases the threat of privatization or layoffs has forced unions to agree to pay cuts, reduced employer-funded benefits, and changed work rules (Cohen and Eimicke, 1994). A common example of the latter result is that municipal trash collectors now are more likely to work a full shift by the clock, rather than being allowed to leave work when their route is completed.

On the negative side, the personnel management techniques that have become more common under the new paradigm may actually *increase* some personnel costs, particularly costs for independent contractors, reemployed annuitants, and temporary employees. Downsizing may eventually lead to higher recruitment, orientation, and training costs. Maintaining minimum staffing levels also results in increased payment of overtime and higher rates of employee accidents and injuries. As the civil service workforce shrinks, it is also aging. This means eventual increases in several critical areas: pension payouts, disability retirements, workers' compensation claims, and health care costs. These are costs that agencies should but may not yet foresee.

The impact of the new paradigm on public program effectiveness is also debatable. Although the intention may be to create a government that works better and costs less, the paradigm may have several less-desirable unintended consequences (Peters and Savoie, 1994). First, downsizing causes a flow of human capital from an agency. Although this may have no short-term costs, in the long run it reduces organizational memory, hampers the development of clear and efficient procedures, and increases the orientation and training burden on the employees and supervisors who remain.

Second, the new paradigm tends to increase workforce tension and fear. For the past two decades, public employees have been told that they are part of the problem rather than part of the solution. Most managerial analysts would conclude that this does not enhance employees' professionalism, self-respect, or performance. In addition, career employees may be afraid of losing their jobs, afraid of training temporary workers who may become their replacements, and afraid of taking risks. Temporary workers, too, are unhappy about working side by side with career employees who have higher pay, benefits, and job security.

Third, increased outsourcing makes contract compliance rather than traditional supervisory practices the primary control mechanism for the quality of service. This sets up a real possibility of fraud and abuse (Moe, 1987). Services supplied under poorly drafted or inadequately enforced contracts can cost much more than the same services provided by public agencies and employees. For example, a state audit in Florida recently revealed that taxicab companies hired by Palm Beach County to provide transportation services to indigent public health patients had submitted exorbitant bills for reimbursement. In one flagrant case, auditors calculated that a driver would need to drive a cab twenty-four hours a day at forty miles per hour to have accumulated the miles for which the county was being billed. In another, U.S. Immigration and Naturalization Service officials canceled a contract with a private prison management company after releasing a scathing report detailing an atmosphere of abuse and penny-pinching in a jail for illegal immigrants and asylum seekers (Sullivan and Purdy, 1995).

Fourth, downsizing squeezes all programs, effective and ineffective alike. Continual budget cuts result in agencies that are budget driven rather than mission driven. That is, they tend to focus on achievement of short-term performance indicators that will maintain their appropriated funding levels. At the same time, long-range planning, or indeed any planning beyond the current budget cycle, becomes less important. This means they will not be able to do effective capital budgeting, maintain adequate capital assets (human or infrastructure), or request incremental resources for long-range projects. And budget-driven agencies that address public problems with short-term solutions designed to meet short-term legislative objectives are not likely to be effective.

Political Responsiveness

Political responsiveness is the ultimate value. This is so because stakeholders (voters and special interests) support elected officials when the actions the officials support are perceived by the stakeholders as being beneficial to themselves or to their conception of the public interest. Political responsiveness for elected and appointed officials means favoring the value that has the most, or the most vocal, public support.

It is in its different approach to political responsiveness that the emergent paradigm has had the greatest impact on public administration in general and public personnel management in particular. The traditional paradigm assumed that government, particularly a powerful central national government, was the major societal institution concerned with setting national objectives and reallocating the resources to pay for program implementation. The emergent paradigm places much less importance on the role of national government (particularly with respect to domestic issues, those not connected with defense or international affairs), because the new paradigm's first value of personal accountability generally reduces the role of government in society. If a person's problems are viewed as the results of his or her choices, then the responsibility for consequences is personal rather than societal. By emphasizing decentralization the new paradigm's second value replaces the primary focus of national government activity with a focus on state and local activity. And by calling for a safety net made up of some state and local government agencies and other not-for-profit NGOs, the new paradigm's third value deemphasizes the role of the national government in making social welfare policies and redistributing income, a role central to the concept of national government since 1933.

Although it may be unfair to expect the values behind an embryonic paradigm to be explicit or immediately validated by reality, critics view the emergent paradigm as an abdication of political responsibility rather than as a shift toward personal responsibility, decentralization, and community-based social services. These critics charge that the current paradigm shift represents less a redefinition of political responsiveness than the exercise of political and economic opportunism. Rhetoric aside, reducing the power of the national government limits income redistribution from the wealthy and limits public scrutiny over the actions of public officials.

So the transition from one paradigm to another leaves fundamental issues unresolved, at least for now. What *is* the appropriate role of government? To what extent are persons responsible for their choices and the consequences of these choices? Who owns the vast public infrastructure now up for privatization—current taxpayers or future ones? To what extent are elected and appointed officials who preside over the dismantling of social and public infrastructure for the sake of short-term political gain abdicating their responsibility to the public welfare? Are states, local governments, not-for-profits, and community-based organizations capable of maintaining a social safety net once the national government abandons its hegemonic role in social welfare policy? Or are we essentially abandoning the political and social ideal of government as a provider of public goods and services in favor of the economic ideal of government as protector of private wealth and privilege? Does the emergent paradigm indeed reflect alternative values, or does it reflect simply the rationalization of covert self-interest by political and economic elites? Are personal accountability, limited and decentralized government, and community responsibility for social services the beliefs of an emergent paradigm, or are they fundamentally rhetorical sound bites and political slogans designed for emotional and symbolic appeal rather than rational clarification and compromise among competing values.

These troubling issues can be examined further in the cuts in local and state government services now occurring in California. That state's Proposition 13, passed in 1976, was the initial grassroots effort to limit government growth by capping property taxes for current residents. With Washington cutting back, the state facing perpetual deficits, and its county governments in danger of bankruptcy, facing the impact of the resulting twenty years of budget cuts may now be unavoidable. Perhaps the greatest question to answer in evaluating the impact of budget cuts on political responsiveness is this: How much decline in quality of public life will people accept as the price of lower taxes? And there can be no doubt that the quality of public life in California has declined. Thirty years ago, for example, California had the fifth highest rate of spending per pupil in the country and an envied educational system. Today it ranks forty-second in spending, it has one of the highest dropout rates in the country (only two states are worse), and in 1994 its fourth graders tied for last place in an educational assessment test given in thirty-nine states (Sterngold, 1995).

Perhaps the contrast between the two paradigms is best illuminated by the different responses of their adherents to such events. Adherents of the traditional paradigm see the declining quality of public life as equivalent to a declining quality of individual life; adherents of the emergent paradigm view it as enhanced opportunity for persons to make choices about their own spending priorities, including community responsibilities. Adherents of the emergent paradigm see their values as liberating, in the sense that the values emphasize individual choice and community responsibility. Adherents of the traditional paradigm see the emergent values as a hypocritical overlay atop greed and self-interest.

The paradigm shift may also be difficult to define and discuss because it reflects a fundamental shift in the nature of political discourse as well as its substance (Clymer, 1995). So deep is the current mistrust of government that any discussion of its role remains mired in the short-term jockeying for position that routinely takes place among candidates seeking to position themselves favorably in electoral campaigns.

THE CHANGING ROLE
OF PUBLIC HUMAN RESOURCE MANAGEMENT

Over the past two centuries, human resource management has evolved from compliance to consultation to contract compliance. This evolution has been driven by the gradual and sequential emergence of alternative competing values. As each value has gained political strength, its increased importance has been reflected in the emergence of a corresponding public personnel system and its related techniques. (Table 3.2 illustrates this evolution.) Most significant, this evolutionary process gave implicit recognition to the importance of public administration (and of public personnel management as a subset of this discipline), because it assigned to public administration and public administrators the authority to (1) incorporate diverse values and perspectives and (2) resolve conflicts over the implementation of these values in particular administrative situations (Meier, 1994).

The evolution of public human resource management has meant corresponding changes in the role of the public human resource manager. During the development of public personnel management, as part of the transition from patronage to merit systems (stage two), it functioned as the champion of merit

Table 3.2. Role of the Public Human Resource Manager.

Stage	Dominant Values	Dominant Systems	Public Personnel Manager's Roles
One (1789–1883)	Responsiveness	Patronage	
Two (1883–1933)	Efficiency Employee rights	Civil service	Compliance: • Watchdog against the spoils system
Three (1933–1964)	Responsiveness Efficiency Employee rights	Patronage Civil service	Compliance: • Watchdog against the spoils system • Watchdog for legislative mandates
Four (1964–1992)	Responsiveness Efficiency Employee rights Social equity	Patronage Civil service Collective bargaining Affirmative action	Consultation Balance among four competing values and systems
Five (1992–present)	Personal accountability Limited government Community responsibility	Alternative organizations and mechanisms Flexible employment relationships	Compliance with legislative limits Compliance with contracts

Note: The dominant values and systems represented by stages one through four repeat the information given in Table 3.1; the left-hand column summarizes the analysis of the public human resource manager's role in each stage. Stage five is the emergent paradigm.

system principles. It operated within civil service systems whose development was characterized by a bipolar dynamic of competition between political patronage and civil service systems. In this context the public personnel manager was viewed as a watchdog, whose responsibility it was to protect employees, applicants, and the public from the evils of the spoils system. This required knowledge of civil service policies and procedures and a willingness to apply them in the face of political pressure.

During stage three (1933 to 1964), public personnel managers sought to maintain bureaucratic compliance, efficiency, and accountability through budgetary controls and *position management*. It became the role of public personnel management, through such devices as personnel ceilings and average grade-level restrictions, to control the behavior of public managers and to help ensure compliance with legislative authority.

During stage four (1964 to 1992), due to a variety of political and economic pressures, the focus of public personnel management shifted to *work management,* as managers and public personnel specialists continued to demand flexibility and equitable reward allocation through such alterations to classification and pay systems as rank-in-person personnel systems, compensation broadbanding, and group performance evaluation and reward systems. This trend coincided with *employee* needs for appropriate utilization, development, and recognition (National Performance Review, 1993b). In addition, because this period was characterized by a dynamic and self-correcting equilibrium among four competing values, the role of the public personnel manager involved political (mediating and conflict resolution) skills in addition to technical knowledge.

The current period (stage five, 1992 to present) calls for two types of behavior by public human resource managers. The first is responsiveness to legislative mandates for cost control. The second is contract management. The first is compliance oriented; the second, contract compliance oriented. It has become the responsibility of the public human resource manager (along with the budget officer, attorney, and risk management specialist) to develop and manage the alternative techniques by which human resources are managed. Experience with civil service rules and collective bargaining continues to be important, for many public employees (particularly schoolteachers and administrators, police, and firefighters) are still covered by union contracts and collective bargaining agreements. But also critical is experience related to management of other types of employment contracts, such as individual performance contracts for exempt employees, temporary employees, independent contractors, and so forth. (It is noteworthy that a recent search-and-screen process for the personnel director of a midsize Florida city resulted in the highest ranking being given to a person with no previous civil service personnel experience. Instead, this candidate, a labor attorney, had extensive private-sector experience negotiating and administering employment contracts with outside vendors and contractors.)

The most troubling impact of this paradigm shift on the role of the public human resource manager emerges when the shift is viewed as the public policy rationalization (through emotive and symbolic value statements) of private privilege. If this view is true, then the emergent public management role of ensuring contract compliance and compliance with legislative limits is merely a facade covering a reality of cuts in public programs and taxes to maintain the income of those who would rather not support policies or programs that redistribute income. And the public human resource manager's traditional function (like that of other public administrators) of mediating value conflicts has become something not only different but diminished professionally and ethically. If justice is nothing more than the interest of the stronger, then concepts such as the rule of law and substantive and procedural equity no longer have meaning. And if this is true, then public human resource managers (like other public administrators) will find it hard to maintain professionalism. Nor will ethical decision making be an issue, unless public human resource managers work on two levels: one overtly accepting the status quo and performing the expected role of contract compliance and cost reduction; the other covertly rejecting the status quo and performing the subversive role of seeking to preserve and articulate the now-archaic values of social equity, individual rights, efficiency, and political responsiveness to a public service ideal that characterized their role in the preceding paradigm.

CONCLUSION

The last twenty years have marked a turning point in the evolution of public personnel management. Until recently, the field was a dynamic equilibrium among four competing progovernment values. But beginning in 1992, strong political pressures to do more with less supplanted this evolutionary process with a new emergent paradigm characterized by three antigovernment values: individual accountability, limited and decentralized government, and community responsibility for delivery of social services. The emergent paradigm has changed the role of the public human resource manager: from resolving conflict among competing values to implementing contract compliance and compliance with legislative limits. The role of public human resource managers is becoming more like the role of their private-sector counterparts, in that they are less responsible for resolving value conflicts than for increasing productivity (as defined legislatively). And their role is diminished to the extent that the values idealized following the paradigm shift assume less importance for public agencies and employees in the accomplishment of public policy objectives.

Finally, their emergent role may present professional public human resource managers with ethical dilemmas if the values underlying the emergent paradigm are in fact nothing more than the rationalization of the protection of private privilege.

References

Americans with Disabilities Act of 1990. U.S. Code, vol. 42, sec. 12101 et seq.

Applebome, P. "Private Enterprise Enters the Public Schools." *New York Times,* Apr. 9, 1995, p. Y10.

Ban, C., and Riccucci, N. M. (eds.). *Public Personnel Management: Current Concerns, Future Challenges.* New York: Longman, 1991.

Clymer, A. "No Deal: Politics and the Dead Art of Compromise." *New York Times,* Oct. 22, 1995, sec. 4, pp. 1, 3.

Cohen, S., and Eimicke, W. "The Overregulated Civil Service." *Review of Public Personnel Administration,* 1994, *15*(2), 11–27.

Comprehensive Employment and Training Act of 1973. U.S. Code, vol. 29, sec. 801 et seq.

Family and Medical Leave Act of 1993. U.S. Code, vol. 29, sec. 2601 et seq.

Fischer, J. "Let's Go Back to the Spoils System." *Harper's,* Oct. 1945, pp. 362–368.

Freedman, A. "Commentary on Patronage." *Public Administration Review,* 1994, *54*(3), 313.

Heclo, H. *A Government of Strangers.* Washington, D.C.: Brookings Institution, 1977.

International City Management Association. *Service Delivery in the '90s: Alternative Approaches for Local Governments.* Washington, D.C.: International City Management Association, 1989.

Job Training Partnership Act of 1982. U.S. Code, vol. 29, sec. 1501 et seq.

Kilborn, P. T. "Take This Job: Up from Welfare: It's Harder and Harder." *New York Times,* Apr. 15, 1995, sec. 4, pp. 1, 4.

Klingner, D. E., and Nalbandian, J. *Public Personnel Management: Contexts and Strategies.* (4th ed.) Upper Saddle River, N.J.: Prentice Hall, 1998.

Lan, Z., and Rosenbloom, D. H. "Public Administration in Transition?" *Public Administration Review,* 1992, *52*(6), 535–538.

Mahtesian, C. "Taking Chicago Private." *Governing,* Apr. 1994, pp. 26–31.

Meier, K. J. "Public Administrative Theory, or Breathes There a Man with Soul So Dead Who Never to Himself Hath Said, This Is My Own, My Paradigm." *SPAR* (Newsletter of the Section on Public Administration Research, American Society for Public Administration), Oct. 1994, pp. 1–5.

Moe, R. C. "Exploring the Limits of Privatization." *Public Administration Review,* 1987, *47*(6), 453–460.

Nalbandian, J. "From Compliance to Consultation: The Changing Role of the Public Personnel Administrator." *Review of Public Personnel Administration,* 1981, *1*(2), 37–51.

National Performance Review. *From Red Tape to Results: Creating a Government That Works Better and Costs Less.* Executive Summary. Washington, D.C.: U.S. Government Printing Office, 1993a.

National Performance Review. *Reinventing Human Resource Management: Accompanying Report of the National Performance Review.* Washington, D.C.: U.S. Government Printing Office, 1993b.

Osborne, D., and Gaebler, T. *Reinventing Government: How the Entrepreneurial Spirit Is Transforming the Public Sector.* Reading, Mass.: Addison Wesley Longman, 1992.

Peters, B. G., and Savoie, D. J. "Civil Service Reform: Misdiagnosing the Patient." *Public Administration Review,* 1994, *54*(6), 418–425.

Sayre, W. S. "The Triumph of Technique over Purpose." *Public Administration Review,* 1948, *8*(2), 134–137.

Sterngold, J. "The Budget Knife Boomerangs Home." *New York Times,* July 30, 1995, p. E3.

Sullivan, J., and Purdy, M. "In Corrections Business, Shrewdness Pays." *New York Times,* July 23, 1995, pp. A1, 13.

U.S. Merit Systems Protection Board. *Temporary Federal Employment: In Search of Flexibility and Fairness.* Washington, D.C.: U.S. Merit Systems Protection Board, 1994.

Walters, J. "Reinventing Government: Managing the Politics of Change." *Governing,* Dec. 1992, pp. 28–40.

CHAPTER FOUR

Toward Diversity in the Workplace

Mary E. Guy
Meredith A. Newman

Despite an increase in the entry of "others" into the workforce, diversity is more than a function of demographics and numbers. Capitalizing on the multiple strengths and perspectives that others bring to the workplace results in fresh perspectives to old problems. Much as an alloy is stronger than a single metal, a diverse workforce is more capable of adjusting to complexity and new demands than was the homogeneous workforce of the past. Not to be overlooked, diversity promotes equity in the workplace just as democracy promotes equity in society.

Human resource managers who skillfully choreograph changes in the workforce with every new hire, promotion, and training opportunity take advantage of the best that the American labor force has to offer. The focus of the presentation that follows is on *valuing* diversity. To this end, we address the following questions: What is diversity? How diverse is the workplace? What are the challenges of workplace diversity? We conclude with a discussion on the role of human resource managers in creating, maintaining, and advocating a diverse workforce. Strategies that represent diversity in action and that serve to sharpen efforts to diversify the workforce are offered.

Note: The authors gratefully acknowledge the research assistance of Donna Loper, Sherri Maljkovic, and H. Perry Stevens Jr.

WHAT IS DIVERSITY?

There are currently 127 million people in the American labor force. By the year 2005, there will be 150 million. As the numbers grow, so do the dimensions to diversity, with gender, race, age, and workers with disabilities being most prominent.

Men currently outnumber women by 11.4 million, but by the year 2005, as women continue to enter the labor force in increasing numbers, men will outnumber women by only 7 million. With more African Americans, Hispanics, and Asians, along with the aging of the baby boomers, the face of the workforce will change even more. The power to capitalize on these shifts hinges on understanding the opportunity that diversification offers.

In productivity terms, diversity is a competitive necessity. The unique contributions made by different groups of workers are instrumental to success. To take advantage of this opportunity, however, requires moving beyond fears, prejudices, and stereotypes. It requires finding common ground and capitalizing on fresh insights and the contributions these findings make to organizational health. The opportunity that diversity provides is premised on the principles of trust and respect for differences. It is an action-oriented perspective that moves beyond the letter of the law to embrace respect for others and the spirit of affirmative action.

Clearly, the way an employer defines diversity shapes, if not predicts, an organization's response to the changing workforce. Judging from a recent survey by the Society for Human Resource Management and Commerce Clearing House, many human resource managers see managing diversity as a legal issue rather than a productivity opportunity (Losey, 1993). Those who see diversity through a legal lens are likely to rely solely on diversity training and meeting the letter of the law and thus are unlikely to gain the benefits that accrue to those who make diversity work for the betterment of the organization. How can human resource managers capture, express, and advance the best spirit of diversity within their organizations, especially in the current context of downsizing? It is to this question that we now turn.

HOW DIVERSE IS THE WORKPLACE?

This section presents issues that surround the workplace integration of women, minorities, workers of widely varying ages, and persons with disabilities. The U.S. labor force is composed of the supply of workers who are sixteen years of age or older and who are either working or looking for work. This represents about 66 percent of all Americans. (Members of the armed forces are excluded from this count.) By the year 2005, the U.S. Department of Labor projects that

69 percent of the population will be included in the labor force, due to population growth and immigration patterns (*Occupational Outlook Quarterly*, 1993, p. 6). The following tables and discussion explore labor force demographics in terms of gender, race, age, and disability status.

Table 4.1 shows the increasing proportion of women workers from 1966 through the year 2005, as projected by the Department of Labor. The percentage of women in the labor force has increased steadily over the last three decades—from 36 percent in 1966 to a projected 48 percent in 2005. And the number of women in the labor force has shown a dramatic increase over the same period—from 27.3 million in 1966 to a projected 71.8 million in 2005.

As the number of women in the workforce has achieved a critical mass, it has set a series of changes in motion. Cafeteria benefit plans now provide worker choices among an array of insurance and dependent-care plans. Closer scrutiny is given to classification and compensation schemes, and family and medical leave is in place. Women are less frequently excluded from top ranks simply for the fact of being women, and the notion that a leader is a "he" is diminishing. Expectations of and demands for comparable pay for comparable work are on the rise, sexual harassment is less often tolerated, and numerous other changes are taking place.

Table 4.2 shows the current racial diversity of the labor force, along with the Department of Labor's projection for labor force characteristics in the year 2005.

Table 4.1. Gender of the Labor Force.

	Percentage of Labor Force		Size of Labor Force (in millions)	
Year	Women	Men	Women	Men
1966	36	64	27.3	48.5
1979	42	58	44.2	60.7
1992	46	54	57.8	69.2
2005	48	52	71.8	78.7

Source: Occupational Outlook Quarterly, 1993, p. 10.

Table 4.2. Racial Diversity in the Labor Force.

Year	White (non-Hispanic)	Black (non-Hispanic)	Hispanic (all races)	Asian, Pacific Islander, American Indian, Alaska Native
1992	78 percent	11 percent	8 percent	3 percent
2005	73	11	11	5

Source: Occupational Outlook Quarterly, 1993, pp. 12–13.

According to the U.S. Bureau of Labor Statistics, white non-Hispanics will continue to comprise the vast majority of workers and will account for about two-thirds of all labor force entrants over the 1992 to 2005 period (*Occupational Outlook Quarterly*, 1993, p. 4).

Notwithstanding this projection, however, Hispanics, Asians, Pacific Islanders, American Indians, and Alaska Natives, collectively, will continue to increase their representation in the labor force, and blacks are projected to maintain their 1992 level well into the future. With the face of the workforce changing from white to a collage of colors come adjustments in workplace habits. Tolerance for those of different races and cultural backgrounds is essential, in words as well as deeds. For teams to function well, members must be able to see beyond skin color and stereotypes. Cultural differences and traditions must be incorporated into the workplace milieu.

Table 4.3 displays the age distribution of the labor force from 1966 through projections for the year 2005. Unlike the period from 1979 to 1992, in which there was a sharp decline in the size of the labor force sixteen to twenty-four years of age, the period from 1992 and 2005 is predicted to experience an increase in new entrants to the labor force (*Occupational Outlook Quarterly*, 1993, p. 4). These new entrants, called Generation X, are the children of the baby boomers. They enter the workforce with experiences quite different from those of their parents, and their work habits differ significantly from those of their elders (Tulgan, 1995). Having come of age playing computer games, they have grown accustomed to rapid feedback and computers that perform tasks for them. With both parents in the workforce, they learned to entertain themselves during after-school hours by watching television or by relying on friends to while away the afternoons. More comfortable in teams than hierarchies, they resist the top-down bureaucracies that pepper the organizational landscape. These generational differences require managers to move to more consultative supervisory styles.

Table 4.3. Distribution of the Labor Force by Age.

Age	1966	1979	1992	2005 (estimated)
16–24	20 percent	24 percent	16 percent	16 percent
25–34	19	27	28	21
35–44	22	19	26	25
45–54	21	16	18	24
55 and older	18	14	12	14
Size of labor force	75.8 million	104.9 million	127 million	150.4 million

Source: Occupational Outlook Quarterly, 1993, pp. 8–9.

The distribution of employees with disabilities is more difficult to quantify precisely. Overlapping statistics give estimates of 36 million to 50 million Americans with disabilities (Henderson, 1994). The passage of the Americans with Disabilities Act of 1990 has been the impetus for an increasing number of people with disabilities to enter the workforce and to seek opportunities equal to those of their nondisabled peers. Employers are required to make reasonable accommodation for handicapped workers. With the dawning tolerance for those with disabilities come additional responsibilities on the part of employers to make sure the workplace is as worker-friendly as possible.

WHAT ARE THE CHALLENGES OF WORKPLACE DIVERSITY?

As the face of the workforce changes, so does the shape of the workplace. Hierarchies are giving way to flattened structures; individual effort is giving way to teamwork; the universal "he" is giving way to "she"; racial intolerance is giving way to sensitivity; work habits are changing as the computer generation moves in; and stereotypes about people with disabilities are being tested and found wanting. Women's private lives and public (and workplace) lives are mixing as dependent care moves from family concern to employer concern. Interactions between men and women at work are becoming bracketed into acceptable behavior and unacceptable behavior now that sexual harassment is legally actionable and better understood. Thus a diverse workforce requires an expanded appreciation for human capacity and individual differences.

Team-building becomes the norm rather than an innovation. Old-timers on the job have significant adjustments to make as newcomers look less and less like them. As agencies downsize and jobs become fewer, resentments build when those who have been traditionally advantaged find themselves having to compete for jobs that in prior days would have come to them almost as entitlements. As women are promoted over men, as African Americans are promoted over whites, jealousies increase and tensions rise. As workers with disabilities claim the right to reasonable accommodations, employers find themselves spending more time on personnel issues than they had anticipated. These are but a few of the workplace challenges that are accompanying increased diversity. The following sections examine these challenges and their implications more closely.

Gender and the Law

Here we briefly review the legislation intended to integrate women into the workforce and to move them closer to economic parity with men. Each of the laws in the following list was passed after there were significant numbers of women in the workplace who insisted that Congress play a role in leveling the playing field.

Equal Pay Act of 1963

Civil Rights Act of 1964

Executive Order 11375

Equal Employment Opportunity Act of 1972

Civil Service Reform Act of 1978

Pregnancy Discrimination Act of 1978

Civil Rights Act of 1991

Family and Medical Leave Act of 1993

The laws show a pattern of continued effort to change the workplace from a man's world to a worker's world. They progress from insistence on equal pay or on an equal chance in hiring and promotion, to acknowledgment of women's right to be treated with the same respect accorded men, to an understanding that women's capacity to bear children must be incorporated into workplace practices.

The Equal Pay Act of 1963, an amendment to the Fair Labor Standards Act of 1938, requires that employers pay equal wages for work that is substantially equal unless the employer can show that a wage difference is attributable to some factor other than sex. The right to equal pay for equal work is also addressed in the provisions of the Civil Rights Act of 1964. According to Title VII, employers may neither refuse to hire nor discharge any person on the basis of color, race, sex, national origin, or religion. Nor may employers discriminate with respect to compensation and to terms, conditions, or privileges of employment. Nor may employers limit, segregate, or classify employees or applicants in any way that deprives them of employment opportunities or otherwise adversely affects their employment status.

Despite the inclusion of sex discrimination in the discrimination forbidden by the 1964 Civil Rights Act, the primary attention of the 1960s-era civil rights legislation was on race, not gender. Executive Order 11375 (President, 1971) was issued by President Lyndon Johnson in 1967 to extend to women the protections that had been afforded to minorities in Executive Order 11246 (President, 1967), which he had issued two years earlier. Executive Order 11375 requires federal contractors to practice nondiscrimination and to take positive action (including recruitment, employment, and training) on behalf of women.

The women's movement gained momentum in the late 1960s and crystallized around support for the Equal Rights Amendment in the early 1970s. A growing pressure for action brought the Equal Employment Opportunity Act of

1972 to amend the earlier Civil Rights Act and strengthen the Equal Employment Opportunity Commission (EEOC). Among other things, it gave the EEOC the ability to go to court when necessary for direct enforcement action.

Discrimination against pregnant women is prohibited by Title VII of the 1964 Civil Rights Act, as amended by the Pregnancy Discrimination Act of 1978. It had became clear in the 1970s that the Supreme Court was unlikely to treat gender inequality as a violation of the Constitution. The Court had refused to find classifications based on gender to be inherently suspect. Even though the Court offered a heightened degree of scrutiny when government treats people differently on the basis of gender, it was willing to invoke equal protection as a barrier only in extreme cases. The Court had indicated that it would take constitutional action if, and only if, the government took discriminatory steps not merely in spite of the knowledge that women would be disadvantaged but because of a specific intent to injure them. And the Court had rejected the assertion that differential treatment on the basis of pregnancy was gender discrimination, suggesting that pregnancy was a self-inflicted wound. To remedy the Court's unwillingness to frame gender inequality as a constitutional violation, the 1978 act prohibits discrimination on account of pregnancy by stating that "women affected by pregnancy, childbirth, or related medical conditions shall be treated the same for all employment-related purposes, including receipt of benefits under fringe benefits programs, as other persons not so affected but similar in their ability or inability to work" (*U.S. Code,* vol. 42, sec. 2000e[k]).

The Civil Rights Act of 1964 has also been interpreted as prohibiting sexual harassment. The Equal Employment Opportunity Commission, which was created by the act to administer the employment provisions of the law, issued guidelines in 1969 on sex discrimination. These guidelines barred hiring based on stereotyped characterization of the sexes, classifying jobs as men's or women's, and advertising under male and female listings (Equal Employment Opportunity Commission, 1997b). As amended in 1972, the law covers federal government, state and local governments, and most companies of at least fifteen employees. Despite the pent-up demand for legal remedy, the courts allowed class actions and class relief in only 13 percent of all sex discrimination cases brought under Title VII between the years 1965 and 1976 (Blum, 1991).

Although not directly related to gender, the Civil Service Reform Act of 1978 called for a federal workforce that reflects the nation's diversity. To that end it effectively codified the push to diversify the federal workforce and make the bureaucracy representative of the population, both horizontally and vertically. With women severely underrepresented, this act served to heighten employers' sensitivity to the absence of women in civil service posts, especially at the middle and upper ranks.

The Civil Rights Act of 1991 set standards for employers when they attempt to justify discriminatory actions or policies based on business necessity, shifted the burden of proof to the employer after the plaintiff has established a *prima facie* case, and provided the right to a jury trial. It also put more teeth in remedies. Under Title VII of the 1964 Civil Rights Act, prevailing parties could recover only back pay and attorney's fees. The Civil Rights Act of 1991 added a provision to permit victims of intentional discrimination to recover compensatory and punitive damages in addition to back pay and attorney's fees. Punitive damages are allowed when the defendant is found to have engaged in discriminatory practices with malice or reckless indifference to the federally protected rights of the plaintiff. Compensatory damages are allowed for future pecuniary losses, emotional pain, suffering, inconvenience, mental anguish, loss of enjoyment of life, and other nonpecuniary losses. Damages are capped at $100,000 for employers with fewer than 200 employees and $300,000 for larger employers. These caps do not extend to back pay or other relief originally authorized under Title VII.

The Family and Medical Leave Act of 1993 covered all employers with fifty or more employees who are employed for at least twenty weeks during a calendar year. Under this law an employee is entitled to up to twelve weeks of unpaid leave during any twelve-month period in order to care for a recently born or adopted child; for a seriously ill child, spouse, or parent; or for the employee's own serious health condition that precludes employment.

In combination with one another, these laws serve as levers available to women to pry open the doors of economic opportunity and to maintain reasonable working conditions once inside. Demands for these laws resulted from discrimination in a variety of forms: unfair salary disparities; denial of promotion opportunities; penalties for pregnancy, childbearing, and child rearing; and sexual harassment. It is incumbent on human resource managers to be aware of these protections for women workers.

Race and the Law

The workforce is increasingly racially diverse. Table 4.2 reflects the demographic shift in favor of minorities over whites. During the decade 1980 to 1990, the white population grew 6 percent, the African American population grew 13.2 percent, the American Indian population grew 37.9 percent, the Hispanic population grew 53 percent, and the Asian population grew 107.8 percent (Henderson, 1994).

African Americans currently make up 12.1 percent of the U.S. population, almost 30 million people. They are the largest minority group in the workforce, constituting 11 percent. Despite more than thirty years of equal opportunity legislation, gains for African Americans in the workplace have been slow. For example, in 1983, there were 482,000 (4.5 percent) African Americans in executive, administrative, and managerial positions; in 1991, there were 858,000

(5.7 percent)—a modest gain of only 1.2 percent (Henderson, 1994). These national laws provide protections on the basis of race.

Civil Rights Act of 1964

Civil Service Reform Act of 1978

Civil Rights Act of 1991

Title VII of the Civil Rights Act of 1964, as amended by the Equal Employment Opportunity Act of 1972, prohibits discrimination in employment based upon race, national origin, and color, as well as sex and religion, by employers of fifteen or more employees. Such discrimination is unlawful in employee hiring, firing, wages, fringe benefits, classification and promotion, and training. In addition, the EEOC issued guidelines in 1980 defining discrimination based on national origin. Such discrimination includes the denial of equal employment opportunity "because an individual has the physical, cultural or linguistic characteristics of a national original group" (Equal Employment Opportunity Commission, 1997a, sec. 1606).

The Civil Rights Act of 1991 strengthened the scope and effectiveness of federal civil rights protections and provided additional protections against unlawful discrimination in the workplace. Title I of the act defines federal civil rights remedies; Title II, referred to as the Glass Ceiling Act of 1991, established the Glass Ceiling Commission; Title III, the Government Employee Rights Act of 1991, provides procedures to protect the rights of government employees (Henderson, 1994).

Age and the Law

As Table 4.3 demonstrates, gender and race are not the only changes in workforce demographics. The median age of the workforce, which was 34.6 years in 1980, will increase by the year 2000 to 38.9 years, a change of more than 12 percent (Losey, 1993). This is projected to occur despite the entry of Generation Xers. In fact, some researchers predict that within twenty-five years, one out of four workers will be age fifty-five or older (Blank and Slipp, 1994).

Generations have different work attitudes, experiences, and expectations at work (MacManus, 1996). Cohorts also change priorities as they progress through their careers. During child-rearing years, child care and family leave benefits are especially important; for empty-nesters, retirement planning and salary predictability are priorities. Likewise, challenges on the job may be motivating to some workers but demotivating to others (Guy, 1984). Understanding and valuing such differences is the essence of diversity. These national laws address age issues:

Age Discrimination in Employment Act of 1967

Employee Retirement Income Security Act of 1974

Age Discrimination in Employment Act Amendments of 1978

Age Discrimination in Employment Act Amendment of 1986

Older Workers Benefit Protection Act of 1990

The Age Discrimination in Employment Act (ADEA) serves to promote employment of older people between the ages of forty and sixty-five based on their ability rather than their age. The ADEA prohibits arbitrary age discrimination in employment, including hiring, referral, classification, and compensation on the part of employers with twenty-five or more employees (Henderson, 1994). Amendments to ADEA in 1978 rendered legally unenforceable most mandatory retirement policies for people up to age seventy. Mandatory retirement after age seventy was abolished in a 1986 amendment. Research into the impact of job protection up to age seventy indicates, however, that little change has occurred in the labor force participation of aged men. Lawlor (1987) concludes that age protection has more of a symbolic impact than a real one. However, as baby boomers age and the cost of health care escalates, it is possible that more of the aging workforce will choose to delay retirement longer than in the past.

The 1974 Employee Retirement Income Security Act (ERISA) gives employees greater protection for their pension programs. Prior to ERISA, employees who enrolled in private pension plans frequently lost their pensions, sometimes after decades of participation, due to job transfers, companies' going out of business, and employers' mismanagement of pension funds (Henderson, 1994). The 1990 Older Workers Benefit Protection Act (OWBPA) provides additional safeguards against employers' pressuring workers to accept early retirement. The act prohibits "capricious and discriminatory acts to get employees to waive their employment and retirement rights" (Henderson, 1994, p. 81).

Notwithstanding these laws, ageism continues to define the work experience of many older workers. They remain underutilized and undervalued (Nelton, 1993), and the number of age discrimination cases filed with the Equal Employment Opportunity Commission continues to grow. In 1990, the EEOC had a backlog of age discrimination cases exceeding 45,000, and it received 17,000 more complaints the following year. By September 1992, a record 60,000 discharge-because-of-age cases were filed. In addition, private lawsuits alleging age discrimination increased 2,200 percent from 1969 to 1989 (Henderson, 1994).

Three decades after enactment of the ADEA, discrimination based on age continues unabated. Henderson (1994) refers to the subtle discrimination against older workers as the *Detroit syndrome:* devalue them, demote them, discount them, and dump them (p. 86). Ageism is manifest at work when older middle- and lower-level employees are relegated to positions with little responsibility. The perception that older workers are less productive than their younger colleagues then becomes a self-fulfilling prophecy as the less productive assignments result in their being less productive, reinforcing the stereotype.

An examination of the difference that age makes at work is not complete without once again mentioning Generation Xers. Children of the baby boomers, they were born between 1965 and 1981 (Tulgan, 1995). Xers reflect the social ferment of the times. They came of age with greater protections of equality in terms of race and gender than any generation in the past. But after working for a few years, they learned that the laws on the books are not necessarily reflected in workplace practices. This knowledge couples with the cynicism that marks their generation to produce a potent combination of thwarted expectations and a drive to breathe life into the protections they were taught to expect.

Many Xers grew up as latchkey kids and learned to entertain themselves with television and fast-paced computer games. Having grown accustomed to self-reliance, they seek autonomy. They inherited a political system that grew weaker throughout their formative years. First, there was Watergate in the early 1970s, and then came Presidents Gerald Ford's and Jimmy Carter's limited effectiveness. President Reagan's powerful rhetoric about the "evil empire" made the U.S. system seem necessarily strong as a counterforce, but the evil empire crumbled before their eyes, much as the Wizard of Oz turned out to be an illusion, leaving Dorothy and her friends to find their strength from within. With this backdrop to their lives, Xers are not loyal to institutions or employers because they do not expect institutions and employers to be loyal to them.

Unlike their fathers and grandfathers, this is a generation that has come of age in the era of a volunteer army. Thus most of the corps of young men now entering the workforce have not served in the military, and they lack the common socialization to hierarchy and deference to authority that military training brought to earlier generations of young men turned veterans. For this reason, Xers as a whole, and men especially, can be expected to be more comfortable than their predecessors in flattened organizational structures that rely more on teamwork than on downward chains of military-like command and control.

Although Xers want recognition for their individual effort, they enjoy working in teams. They are a nonidealistic generation, expecting rewards now from their work, rather than trusting institutions to reward them in the future. They are skeptics. The women expect to receive equal rights and when they do not, they are more intolerant of inequities than their mothers. The increasing number of sexual harassment claims, for example, gives evidence of this. Although their mothers were taught to tolerate harassment and discriminatory work conditions, women of this generation have learned to just say no. At the same time, what older generations found shocking, Xers have become inured to after years of television talk shows that hype eccentric lifestyles as if they were the norm.

Bruce Tulgan (1995) encourages supervisors to delegate and to anticipate that Xers will solve problems differently than boomers. They are not disloyal, disinterested, cynical slackers; in fact their work and careers are fundamental to their definition of self. To maximize productivity of Xers, Tulgan recommends that employers differentiate between arrogance and independence and that they provide Xers with opportunities to excel; focus on results, not process; provide as much information as possible; outline and clearly define goals; build feedback loops; and make feedback accurate, specific, and timely. Some of these recommendations are unique to Xers, and some are equally applicable to workers of all ages.

Disability and the Law

Along with gender, race, and age, disability is a dimension to diversity. Despite an estimated 930,000 workers with disabilities (Alexander, 1994), there are more than 7.7 million disabled Americans who are either out of the labor force or unemployed (Henderson, 1994). Although the existence of a disability often has no direct relationship to a prospective employee's ability to do the job, it has nonetheless been used to exclude individuals from being hired (Mello, 1995). Among the barriers individuals with disabilities face when seeking employment are lower wages, employers' negative attitudes, and coworkers' discomfort (Henderson, 1994). Elderly people with disabilities may be more discriminated against than others. As noted earlier, in terms of productivity very little is expected of the elderly in general, and almost nothing is expected of those with disabilities. But failure to invest in their potential is shortsighted. These national laws provide protections to the disabled:

Smith-Fess Act of 1920

Barden-LaFollette Act of 1943

Vocational Rehabilitation Act Amendments of 1965

Rehabilitation Act of 1973

Americans with Disabilities Act of 1990

Americans with Disabilities Act Amendments of 1994

The Smith-Fess Act of 1920 established federal and state rehabilitation programs. Rehabilitation services for persons with physical disabilities were to be vocational; physical restoration and sociopsychological services were excluded. The Barden-LaFollette Act of 1943, also known as the Vocational Rehabilitation Act of 1943, strengthened vocational rehabilitation programs by providing physical restoration services to people with disabilities. It also extended vocational rehabilitation services to the mentally challenged. The Vocational Rehabilitation Act Amendments of 1965 further strengthened the earlier acts. These amendments were superseded by the Rehabilitation Act of 1973. Significant provisions of Title V of this act included establishment of the Interagency Committee on Handicapped Employees (sec. 501); establishment of the Architectural and Transportation Barriers Compliance Board (sec. 502); introduction of *affirmative action* into the language of rehabilitation (sec. 503); and calls for nondiscrimination in employment (sec. 504).

The Americans with Disabilities Act of 1990 (ADA), as amended in July 1994, provides a clear and comprehensive national mandate for the elimination of discrimination against individuals with disabilities. More extensive in scope than its predecessors, the act covers the majority of state and local government agencies as well as federal agencies. Moreover, it adds an enforcement mandate and charges the federal government to play a central role in such enforcement.

Congress passed the ADA after concluding that individuals with disabilities are a discrete and insular minority who face restrictions and limitations that result from stereotypical assumptions not truly indicative of their ability to contribute to society. According to the law, a "qualified individual with a disability" is an individual who, with or without reasonable accommodation, can perform the essential functions of the job in question (Kohl and Greenlaw, 1992; Susser, 1990). When the act was passed, there were an estimated 43 million Americans with one or more physical or mental disabilities. That number is expected to increase as the baby boom generation ages (Susser, 1990). Congress held that the nation's proper goals regarding individuals with disabilities are to ensure equality of opportunity, full participation, independent living, and economic self-sufficiency for such individuals.

An individual who brings a claim under the ADA is entitled to a jury trial and has the potential to collect punitive and compensatory damages in an amount commensurate with the size of the employer's workforce. Legal advisers recommend that employers review existing policies and practices and redouble their efforts to train supervisory personnel so that hiring, daily management, and termination decisions do not result in expensive litigation (Naidoff, 1992).

The EEOC found that 80 percent of "reasonable accommodations" for the disabled cost less than $500, with most (51 percent) of the accommodations having no cost at all. Simply rearranging work flows or office furniture often suffices (Kohl and Greenlaw, 1992). Human resource managers should undertake job analyses to determine the essential functions of each job. This information helps supervisors place disabled workers in settings where they can be most productive and avoids claims that an otherwise qualified applicant is not capable of performing a job. Despite legal protections, people with disabilities continue to experience marginalization. By placing physical and economic barriers in the paths of individuals with disabilities, organizations send these individuals messages that translate into "you are inferior" (Henderson, 1994). Valuing diversity ensures that the workplace is inclusive of all groups, including individuals with disabilities.

Of course it is one thing to hammer away at discriminatory practices at work—it is another thing to nail down equity of opportunity therein. The law can go only so far in dismantling gender and racial barriers to career advancement. Mere adherence to the letter of the law may protect employers from litigation, but it fails to achieve the intended goal of a representative workforce. Women, minorities, and the disabled continue to experience work "outside" the prevailing (able-bodied white male) model. The tension inherent in the process of assimilation exacerbates this dynamic; valuing diversity begins to address it.

STRATEGIES FOR CAPITALIZING ON DIVERSITY

Diversity matters. An increasingly heterogeneous workplace and an organizational culture that values diversity and tolerance combine to improve decision making, increase productivity, and enhance morale. Studies show that diversity leads to better organizational decisions—the greater the diversity of employees, the greater the diversity of ideas. For example, a 1993 study conducted at the University of North Texas pitted, without the teams' knowledge, heterogeneous teams of business students against all-white teams. By the end of the seventeen-week experiment, the diverse groups were viewing situations from a broader range of perspectives and offering more innovative solutions to problems (Rice, 1994). Thus a diverse workplace can sharpen an organization's competitive edge.

The human resource manager can help to create a work climate receptive to and respectful of diversity. Strategies that advance diversity at work include relying on teams rather than hierarchy, supplying cross-functional training that capitalizes on individual differences rather than specializations, broadening position classifications to accommodate cross-functional performance, and concomitantly, moving away from viewing each worker with similar training as an interchangeable part on an assembly line.

Specific examples of constructive diversity efforts occur more frequently than one might think from the lack of publicity about them. At the federal government level, U.S. Forest Service workforce diversification efforts go beyond legal mandates and have broad implications for organizational change and adaptation. The basic tenets of the program have become an integral part of the Forest Service's management philosophy: "individual skills and cultural diversity are valued and sought out as important assets of the organization and key resources for solving problems" (Brown and Harris, 1993, p. 87).

At the local government level, San Diego's Diversity Commitment has resulted in a paradigm shift in organizational culture. According to Ossolinski (1992), the upper-level city administrators "shifted from an emphasis on a high performance team to an emphasis on valuing diversity first and promoting the value of a diverse high performance team" (p. 18). At the department level, the

Human Services Department of Arlington County, Virginia, is committed to a diverse workforce reflective of the citizens it serves. The challenge of responding to dramatic demographic changes with effective service delivery was met head on by the department. It developed a long-range strategy to empower its culturally diverse workforce and ensure responsive service delivery (Ossolinski, 1992). At the forefront of its efforts are its *cultural consultants,* approximately thirty-six volunteers from all racial and ethnic groups in the department, who work to facilitate communication between diverse groups.

As the workforce changes, classification schemes must be updated to accommodate workers and the needs of the workplace. In attempts in a number of different settings to broaden the scope of workers' tasks, jobs once narrowly defined are being combined into cross-functional assignments. In Birmingham, Alabama, for example, Cooper Green Hospital, a county-owned and -operated indigent-care facility, has started employing patient care technicians. In the past, different workers were hired for the positions of nursing assistant, phlebotomist, and EKG technician. Now an assembly line version of patient care has given way to teamwork and group accountability, as patient care technicians (PCTs) are cross-trained to perform all three functions. Patient care technicians are paid more than individuals who held one of the previous job classifications and get to use a broader base of skills and interests. These new workers are also asked to use more individual discretion than workers in the past, and they become part of a team that is held accountable for the performance of an entire unit in the hospital.

Job redesign results in unit supervisors who must think more globally about unit operations. Capacity building, as in this example, accommodates workers who do not fit easily into the pigeonholes of the narrow classification and compensation systems of the past. As the wave of the future, broadening the scope of work calls attention to the importance of teamwork, flexibility, and reframing jobs.

CONCLUSION

Diversity is not a zero-sum game where one side wins and one side loses. Rather, it is a gradual loosening of the old way of doing things and a move toward greater involvement of all segments of the population. To achieve diversity, organizations must hire and promote the most capable candidates for jobs, being always mindful of the necessity to build a workforce that is representative of the citizens being served.

Recruitment strategies need to be inclusive because new recruits are important catalysts for organizational change. Human resource managers can broaden candidate pools by, for example, advertising in publications read by African

Americans and Hispanics, recruiting at schools with high minority enrollments, and actively seeking minority job candidates. Managers who scrutinize their selection processes, especially job requirements and testing, can ensure that protected groups are not inadvertently or disproportionately screened out during those processes (Nobile, 1991).

Once workers are on board, their skills and perspectives must be brought to bear to devise solutions and to achieve the organization's goals. To hire a representative workforce but then insist that all organizational processes be conducted in the future exactly as they were in the past is to leave an armament of resources untapped.

In the long run, diversity brings cultural change. For human resource managers, this means there will be tension as practices shift and workers make room at the table for those who are "different." The expedient course of providing training to supervisors on how to avoid litigation stops short of teaching them how to develop the advantages and opportunities a diverse workforce presents. Training in tolerance and in sensitivity to differences are the substrata upon which any formal workshops on compliance with laws should be built. Formal laws, regulations, and policies to eliminate discrimination and voluntary strategies for encouraging diversity are necessary but not sufficient to address the problems and opportunities of a pluralistic workforce (Bernotavicz, Barringer, and Clasby, 1993). Proactive human resource managers should be change agents, helping the workplace embrace diversity as a central value. A managerial philosophy of fostering a multicultural approach helps diminish the tension that arises naturally from change.

Promotion from within is an effective way to signal the importance of diversity. Promotion policies should be reviewed and promotion statistics monitored to ensure that all protected groups are advancing throughout the organization (Nobile, 1991). Performance appraisal and reward systems should reinforce the importance of effective diversity management. For example, Amtrak ties compensation to manager performance on diversity management efforts (Cox, 1991). It is also important to realize that traditional assessment tools may have limited utility for evaluating people who are different from the evaluator (Galagan, 1993).

Changes in human resource policies and benefit plans that make it easier for employees to balance work and family role demands are essential. So too is ongoing training. For example, training to confront issues concerning the employment of workers with disabilities begins with the preparation of detailed job descriptions for each position. Mentoring programs that target women and minorities serve to connect these "outsiders" with their organizations' informal networks, and they facilitate career advancement in the process. The state of South Carolina's Budget and Control Board has implemented an effective mentoring program to overcome the shortage of women in the upper ranks of state agency administration. By establishing recognized mentoring relationships, the program ensures that up-and-comers who in the past might have been overlooked for leadership positions are groomed for promotion.

Following these collective recommendations can help to create an environment that develops the full potential of all members of a diverse workforce and achieves strategic advantage in the process. Once enacted, these recommendations can ensure that diversity is managed not at the edges but in the mainstream of an organization's operations—that the philosophy of diversity is woven into the basic fabric of organizational life.

References

Age Discrimination in Employment Act of 1967. U.S. Code, vol. 29, sec. 621 et seq.

Alexander, S. "Preemployment Inquiries and Examination: What Employers Need to Know About the New EEOC Guidelines." *Labor Law Journal,* Nov. 1994, pp. 667–678.

Americans with Disabilities Act of 1990. U.S. Code, vol. 42, sec. 12101 et seq.

Bernotavicz, F., Barringer, R. E., and Clasby, M. *Addressing Issues of Diversity: A Sourcebook.* Portland: Edmund S. Muskie Institute of Public Affairs, University of Southern Maine, 1993.

Blank, R., and Slipp, S. *Voices of Diversity: Real People Talk About Problems and Solutions in a Workplace Where Everyone Is Not Alike.* New York: American Management Association, 1994.

Blum, L. M. *Between Feminism and Labor.* Berkeley: University of California Press, 1991.

Brown, G., and Harris, C. C. "The Implications of Work Force Diversification in the U.S. Forest Service." *Administration and Society,* 1993, *25*(1), 85–113.

Civil Rights Act of 1964. U.S. Code, vol. 42, sec. 1981 et seq. (Title VII at 2000e.)

Civil Rights Act of 1991. U.S. Statutes at Large 105 (1991) 1071.

Civil Service Reform Act of 1978. U.S. Code, vol. 5, sec. 1101 et seq.

Cox, T., Jr. "The Multicultural Organization." *Academy of Management Executive,* 1991, *5*(2), 34–47.

Employee Retirement Income Security Act of 1974. U.S. Code, vol. 29, sec. 1001 et seq.

Equal Employment Opportunity Act of 1972. U.S. Code, vol. 42, sec. 2000e et seq.

Equal Employment Opportunity Commission. *Guidelines on Discrimination Because of National Origin. Code of Federal Regulations,* 1997a, vol. 29, sec. 1606. (Originally issued 1990.)

Equal Employment Opportunity Commission. *Guidelines on Discrimination Because of Sex. Code of Federal Regulations,* 1997b, vol. 29, sec. 1604. (Originally issued 1969.)

Equal Pay Act of 1963. U.S. Code, vol. 29, sec. 206 et seq.

Fair Labor Standards Act of 1938. U.S. Code, vol. 29, sec. 201 et seq.

Family and Medical Leave Act of 1993. U.S. Code, vol. 29, sec. 2601 et seq.

Galagan, P. "Leading Diversity: An Interview with Ann Morrison." *Training and Development,* Apr. 1993, pp. 38–43.

Guy, M. E. "Passages Through the Organization: Old Dogs and New Tricks." *Group and Organization Management,* 1984, *9*(4), 467–479.

Henderson, G. *Cultural Diversity in the Workplace: Issues and Strategies.* Westport, Conn.: Quorum/Greenwood, 1994.

Kohl, J. P., and Greenlaw, P. S. "The Americans with Disabilities Act of 1990: Implications for Managers." *Sloan Management Review,* 1992, *33*(3), 87–90.

Lawlor, E. F. "The Impact of Age Discrimination Legislation on the Labor Force Participation of Aged Men: A Time Series Analysis." *Evaluation Review,* 1987, *10*(6), 794–805.

Losey, M. R. "Making Changing Workplace Demographics Work for You." *Managing Office Technology,* 1993, *38*(8), 38.

MacManus, S. A. *Young vs. Old: Generational Combat in the 21st Century.* Boulder, Colo.: Westview Press, 1996.

Mello, J. A. "Employment Law and Workers with Disabilities: Implications for Public Sector Managers and Human Resource Practices." *Public Personnel Management,* 1995, *24*(1), 75–87.

Naidoff, C.E.I. "Understanding the Civil Rights Act of 1991." *Management Review,* Apr. 1992, pp. 58–59.

Nelton, S. "Golden Employees: In Their Golden Years." *Nation's Business,* 1993, *81*(8), 34–35.

Nobile, R. J. "Can There Be Too Much Diversity?" *Personnel,* 1991, *68*(8), 11.

Occupational Outlook Quarterly, Fall 1993, *37* (special issue titled *The American Work Force: 1992–2005*).

Older Workers Benefit Protection Act of 1990. U.S. Code, vol. 29, sec. 621n. et seq.

Ossolinski, R. S. "Celebrating Workplace Diversity." *Public Management,* Apr. 1992, pp. 18–21.

Pregnancy Discrimination Act of 1978. U.S. Code, vol. 42, sec. 2000e(k).

President. "Equal Employment Opportunity," Executive Order 11246. *Code of Federal Regulations,* 1967, vol. 3 *(The President: 1964–1965 Compilation).*

President. "Amending Executive Order No. 11246, Relating to Equal Employment Opportunity," Executive Order 11375. *Code of Federal Regulations,* 1971, vol. 3 *(The President: 1966–1970 Compilation).*

Rehabilitation Act of 1973. U.S. Code. Vol. 29, sec. 701 et seq.

Rice, F. "How to Make Diversity Pay." *Fortune,* Mar. 1994, pp. 78–83.

Susser, P. A. "The ADA: Dramatically Expanded Federal Rights for Disabled Americans." *Employee Relations Law Journal,* 1990, *16*(2), 157–176.

Tulgan, B. *Managing Generation X.* Santa Monica, Calif.: Merritt, 1995.

CHAPTER FIVE

Managing an Aging Workforce

Trends, Issues, and Strategies

Jonathan P. West

A spate of articles has been published recently speculating about the impacts of the oldest wave of baby boomers (those individuals born between 1946 and 1964), who turned fifty in 1996 (see, for example, Solomon, 1995). Such impacts will not be limited to the health care and leisure-time industries (Posner, 1995). As 76 million boomers enter the ranks of *older workers* (defined by the U.S. Bureau of Labor Statistics [BLS] as workers fifty-five years old and older), the workplace will be influenced in many ways, and these influences will be felt in government settings at all levels (Elliott, 1995; Moody, 1995; West and Berman, 1996b). There are numerous myths and stereotypes surrounding the effects of the aging process and the capabilities of older workers, and government jurisdictions have traditionally done little to combat these erroneous perceptions, to identify the particular needs of older workers, and to tailor programs that meet their array of concerns. This is likely to change, albeit gradually, in the future; indeed it has already changed in the few innovative jurisdictions that are out front in responding to this emerging human resource issue (Roberts, 1995; West and Berman, 1996b).

This chapter describes the demographic trends and economic restructuring initiatives that compel interest in the issue of older workers, arguing that

---

Note: The author wishes to thank Erika Fueyo and Kevin Taylor for their assistance in gathering materials for this chapter.

this back-burner issue will move to the front burner in coming years. It explores the myths and realities and the legal concerns surrounding this segment of the workforce and examines management strategies for creatively coping with aging workers' special needs. It also discusses the results achieved and barriers encountered when managers respond to older workers' concerns, and it presents selected case studies of targeted efforts that offer practical guidelines for those concerned with innovative human resource management.

TRENDS

Demographic Developments

The graying of America is highlighted by key demographic facts. In 1994, there were 33.2 million people who were sixty-five years or older, about one in every eight Americans (12.7 percent of the population). The number of Americans in this age group has increased by 7 percent (2.1 million) since 1990; the comparable increase for the under-sixty-five age group is 4 percent. The percentage of Americans over sixty-five has more than tripled since 1900, and the number has ballooned from 3.1 million to 33.2 million (Fowles, 1995). These trends are expected to continue in the future, with the biggest spurt anticipated when the baby-boom generation turns sixty-five, between 2010 and 2030. By 2030, those sixty-five and older will number 70 million; those eighty-five and older will number 8 million (Administration on Aging, 1997; Fowles, 1995).

These general population trends are mirrored in the aging of the U.S. workforce. The first wave of baby boomers will turn fifty-five by the year 2001, qualifying as older workers according to the BLS definition. The fifty-five-plus segment of the workforce is projected to grow from 12.3 percent currently to more than 20 percent by 2020 (Barth, McNaught, and Rizzi, 1993) and to increase at double the rate of the rest of the population during the next ten years (Strouse, 1995). In 1990, the median age of workers was 36.6 years; the projection for the year 2005 is 40.6 years. By the year 2000, roughly half of the labor force will be middle-aged (between ages 35 to 54) (Kelly, 1992). The future portends major manpower shortages, with only 56 million baby busters (born between 1965 and 1976) available to replace the 76 million baby boomers (Solomon, 1995). In short the next two decades will see the number of older workers increase substantially, as the number of younger workers decreases significantly. These trends present challenges and opportunities for managers who must harness and effectively channel the talent, experience, and knowledge represented by older workers.

Public administrators confront an aging government workforce that poses the same challenges and opportunities. Table 5.1 reports the percentage of each state's population and the percentage of its public-sector workforce that is fifty-five or older (U.S. Bureau of the Census, 1995). The proportion of the total population that is fifty-five or older is 21.84 percent. Local governments have the highest

Table 5.1. Percentage of Population and Public-Sector Workforce over Age Fifty-Five.

	Percentage over Age 55		
	Nation/State Population[a]	Local Government Workforce	State Government Workforce	Federal Government Workforce
United States	21.81	19.39	16.78	15.28
Alabama	22.95	22.15	19.79	19.24
Alaska	8.97	8.85	9.88	4.05
Arizona	21.36	19.11	16.62	15.07
Arkansas	25.19	25.35	19.69	18.75
California	18.87	20.98	18.07	13.88
Colorado	18.29	18.75	13.16	17.62
Connecticut	23.05	24.61	21.29	13.69
Delaware	24.14	20.41	24.16	14.42
Florida	21.68	23.91	21.15	18.08
Georgia	18.91	18.82	16.15	14.86
Hawaii	20.00	16.50	20.48	11.16
Idaho	20.83	25.38	21.19	16.67
Illinois	22.37	23.08	19.26	17.17
Indiana	22.06	21.60	16.67	19.28
Iowa	26.20	24.86	19.52	29.78
Kansas	24.73	29.14	21.49	17.97
Kentucky	22.08	20.95	19.52	17.51
Louisiana	20.11	20.76	17.58	14.20
Maine	22.28	24.56	23.55	14.43
Maryland	19.71	18.63	17.31	13.60
Massachusetts	22.69	24.82	20.69	20.05
Michigan	21.15	22.32	15.52	19.10
Minnesota	21.69	23.38	19.36	22.88
Mississippi	21.81	24.55	29.26	17.85
Missouri	24.33	23.44	19.41	19.83
Montana	23.07	19.22	16.98	18.81
Nebraska	25.26	27.76	20.52	20.52
Nevada	19.92	19.47	17.57	15.21
Hew Hampshire	19.30	16.43	21.01	22.29
New Jersey	23.04	24.87	19.35	18.19
New Mexico	19.44	16.97	18.46	16.11
New York	23.09	23.16	19.56	18.04
North Carolina	22.38	20.44	19.88	11.24
North Dakota	26.22	24.01	22.41	16.10
Ohio	22.45	20.71	19.13	21.20
Oklahoma	23.74	23.64	21.63	18.58

Table 5.1. Percentage of Population and Public-Sector Workforce over Age Fifty-Five, cont'd.

	Percentage over Age 55		
	Nation/State Population[a]	Local Government Workforce	State Government Workforce	Federal Government Workforce
Oregon	22.88	20.21	19.24	21.18
Pennsylvania	25.31	25.38	21.97	20.79
Rhode Island	24.61	17.98	23.77	14.41
South Carolina	20.98	19.75	17.94	11.91
South Dakota	25.39	25.00	19.25	17.39
Tennessee	22.79	22.53	16.70	18.76
Texas	19.04	18.69	16.42	14.79
Utah	15.25	19.53	17.86	20.46
Vermont	19.14	25.50	15.29	18.87
Virginia	19.90	16.82	18.17	11.16
Washington	20.23	20.81	15.59	11.68
West Virginia	25.42	22.51	22.72	19.27
Wisconsin	22.18	24.49	19.33	21.71
Wyoming	18.68	19.31	13.40	14.07

[a]U.S. percentage over age fifty-five is a weighted average based on state populations.

Source: U.S. Bureau of the Census, 1995.

proportion of older workers, followed by state government and then by the federal government. The overall percentage of local government workers fifty-five and up is 22.09 percent. Comparable figures for state and federal government employees are 19.15 percent and 17.42 percent, respectively. Data for the general population range from a low of 8.97 percent in Alaska to a high of 26.22 percent in North Dakota. The highest percentages of older workers in local government are found in the Plains states, especially Kansas (29.14 percent) and Nebraska (27.76 percent); in state government, older workers are disproportionately located in Mississippi (29.26 percent) and Delaware (24.16 percent); and in the federal government, higher concentrations of workers fifty-five and over are found in the Plains states of Iowa (29.78 percent) and Minnesota (22.86 percent). Because it is not unusual for one out of five public-sector workers to be in the fifty-five and older age group, it is incumbent upon management to give careful consideration to developing strategies that address the needs of this critical workforce segment.

Economic Restructuring

Economic and social trends add to the challenge and strategic complexity of responding to an aging workforce. For example, over 4.3 million jobs have vanished in the United States since 1979, and three-fourths of all U.S. households "have had a close encounter with layoffs since 1980" (*The Downsizing of America,* 1996, pp. 4–5). Older workers have been especially hard hit. Five private-sector trends affecting all jobs but resulting in disproportionate displacement of older workers have been identified in a 1995 report by the American Association of Retired Persons (AARP): (1) a combination of rising global competition, slow economic growth, and demands by consumers for better value for dollars spent and by Wall Street for better short-term performance has exerted downward pressure on corporate profits; (2) strategic responses to lower profits have focused on cost cutting, primarily reductions in force (RIFs), downsizing, and reduced benefit packages; (3) most newly created jobs in the era of downsizing have been low-wage service-sector positions or knowledge jobs requiring advanced training; (4) an emphasis on the bottom line and pragmatic approaches has accentuated workplace upheavals associated with downsizing, rightsizing, reengineering, and restructuring; and (5) long-standing notions of paternalism (which offered job security, seniority, and income and benefits growth) have been supplanted by a corporate culture of expendability.

In the "new organizational reality" that has emerged, "organizations that once saw people as assets to be nurtured and developed have begun to view those same people as costs to be cut. Employees who took job security for granted and expected to be taken care of in return for their work and loyalty have had to face a new reality in which organizations can no longer provide long-term employment or career paths" (Noer, 1993, p. 1). A recent *New York Times* series on corporate downsizing and some Kettering Foundation studies have increased public awareness of these issues and their effects on older workers (*The Downsizing of America,* 1996; Yankelovich, 1995). One quick fix to increase corporate profitability is to reduce labor costs by replacing older, higher-paid workers with younger, cheaper workers. But such actions are not without painful consequences. Research has documented that compared to younger workers, older workers who are displaced or considered expendable remain out of work for longer periods, have greater difficulty finding replacement jobs, and encounter more problems when changing fields. They also experience a greater loss of earnings when subsequently employed (Love and Torrence, 1989; Morris and Caro, 1995). Surveys of human resource decision makers indicate that the plight of older workers as a result of downsizing has been devastating, marked by feelings of fear, resentment, and worry about stagnant wages and diminished benefits (American Association of Retired Persons, 1995).

Restructuring and downsizing have also become part of the new reality in the public sector, albeit less drastically. From 1979 to 1993, 454,000 public service jobs disappeared (*The Downsizing of America,* 1996).[1] Terms and phrases like cutback management, RIF, reengineering, productivity improvement, privatization, and doing more with less have become commonplace in the public sector at all levels. President Clinton has declared that "the era of big government is over," and actions at all levels have scaled back the size of government.

A persistent culture of protectionism, reinforced by civil service provisions and union contracts, has slowed the pace but not diminished the ardor of those advocating cost-cutting personnel reductions. Although firing workers with tenure, seniority, and bumping rights over other workers is difficult, use of early retirement incentives, buyouts, privatization, part-time or lower-paid workers, and other strategies can reduce the size of the payroll. Given these environmental pressures to downsize and institutional safeguards that make such downsizing difficult, government managers must decide whether to support workforce reductions and, if so, whether older workers should be among the expendables. In this context the myths and stereotypes regarding aging and its link to performance take on new importance.

ISSUES

Myths and Stereotypes Versus Results

Some of the myths concerning aging and the competence of older workers have been debunked in the professional and academic literature; others persist. Myths and stereotypes are important because they can guide actions. When managers hold stereotypical views of older workers, their responses can be inappropriate and counterproductive. Similarly, policies based on erroneous ideas can debilitate worker performance and morale. Some of the most commonly expressed myths and stereotypes regarding older workers assert that compared to younger workers, they are less flexible and more resistive to change, unable to get along well with others, unwilling or unable to learn new skills, anxious to retire as soon as possible, less productive, more prone to frequent absences from work, more susceptible to work-related stress and accidents, more expensive, averse to new technology, less viable for development, less likely to be available over time (because they have the option to retire), and not as "with it" as their younger coworkers (American Association of Retired Persons, 1993; Blocklyn, 1987; Buonocore, 1992; Galen, 1993; Nelton, 1993; Rosen and Jerdee, 1976; Wooldridge and Maddox, 1995).

These myths have been challenged and in several instances refuted by empirical research, survey findings, and organization-specific experiences of informed observers. The literature supports a number of counterassertions about older workers, stressing that compared to younger employers, they have lower rates of absenteeism, fewer accidents, and less alcoholism and drug addiction; show few or no differences in adaptability and productivity; experience less stress at work; often cost their employers less; and have lower turnover rates. They also tend to arrive at work on time or early; receive high ratings on job skills, loyalty, reliability, maturity, interpersonal relations, and a strong work ethic; and benefit from training and education. Further, older workers sometimes take longer to learn certain skills, but their learning capabilities are similar to those of younger workers when training methods are calibrated to their unique learning styles (American Association of Retired Persons, 1993; Gilsdorf, 1992; Hagen, 1983; Kaeter, 1995; Palmore, 1990; Rosen and Jerdee, 1989; Shea, 1991; Strouse, 1995; Wooldridge, 1995).

Although it is difficult to sort out the validity of claims and counterclaims, it is important to recognize the negative consequences of stereotypical thinking. Both managers (especially those in the human resource field) and first-line supervisors, need to be alerted to the misconceptions that exist regarding aging in general and the effects of aging on older workers in particular. Research in the mid-seventies on managerial stereotypes by Rosen and Jerdee (1976) found that managers viewed older workers as change resistant, uncreative, slow and cautious at making judgments, lower in physical capacity, disinterested in technological developments, and untrainable. Research in the mid-eighties found age stereotypes to be so ubiquitous that even personnel managers had them (Beutell, 1983). Clearly, managers and supervisors need to be educated "to view older workers as a valuable asset rather than a liability" (Snyder and Brandon, 1983, p. 47). Many of today's human resource managers already hold more enlightened views—valuing older workers "for their experience, knowledge, work habits and attitudes" (Bove, 1987, p. 78). Indeed, research in the mid-nineties found that overwhelming majorities of human resource people felt older workers possess good attendance and punctuality, commitment to quality, solid performance records, loyalty and dedication, practical as well as theoretical knowledge, ability to get along with coworkers, solid experience in their job or industry, and emotional stability (Solomon, 1995). Myths and stereotypes are diminishing, but they have lingered longer than is justified by the facts.

Workshops for supervisors are one effective way to confront stereotypes about aging. Kaminski-da Roza (1984) describes an example from a large research and development laboratory that sponsored a workshop on optimizing older workers' productivity. One component of the twelve-hour workshop addressed age stereotypes by (1) having supervisors examine their assumptions, communication patterns, tools, reports, assignments, and overall treatment of employees with regard to age-related stereotypes; (2) having both younger and older workers evaluate supervisors in terms of their use of stereotypes about aging; and (3) having supervisors subject stereotypes to reality testing (asking, for example, Are employees who are fifty-plus really retired on the job?). Workshops of this type can lead to appropriately customized action steps for supervisors to follow in enhancing the older workers' contributions.

Legal Concerns

The passage of the Age Discrimination in Employment Act (ADEA) in 1967 and its amendments in 1986 gave managers another reason to examine their attitudes, policies, and practices regarding older workers. The ADEA's purpose is to get employers to make decisions based on employee or applicant qualifications and to discourage the use of ageist assumptions. The ADEA protects workers aged forty-plus from workplace discrimination in hiring, promotion, training, and retirement and from actions against employees with regard to pay, working conditions, or terms of employment. The ADEA encompasses private-sector firms of twenty or more employees and labor unions of twenty-five or more members as well as federal, state, and local government employers. In 1990, further protection was provided with the passage of the Older Workers Benefit Protection Act, which amended the ADEA and prohibited employers from denying benefits to older workers. Most states also have their own laws protecting older workers from age discrimination

Enforcement of the ADEA was initially handled by the Wage and Hour Division of the Department of Labor but subsequently shifted to the Equal Employment Opportunity Commission (EEOC). Excellent guides are available to assist older workers who wish to take informal or formal action against age discrimination (for example, American Association of Retired Persons, 1994). The number of formal charges of age discrimination filed annually with the EEOC increased from 11,397 in 1980 to 24,190 in 1987 (American Association of Retired Persons, 1993). More than one-fourth of EEOC cases concern age discrimination (Stark, 1996). Of the $71.1 million EEOC recovered for victims of workplace discrimination in 1992, over $56 million came from suits filed under the ADEA (Cozzetto, Pedeliski, and Tipple, 1996). (Despite such data, not all evaluations of ADEA impact have been positive; see, for example, Posner, 1995.)

In assessing the potential impact of the ADEA, demographics once again become important. Table 5.2 reports the average age of each state's population and the average ages of its local, state, and federal government workforces (U.S. Bureau of the Census, 1995). The average age for the U.S. population as a whole is 35.52. The age profile pattern of the public-sector workforce in Table 5.2 is similar to that reported in Table 5.1: the average age of local government workers (43.16) is slightly higher than that of state (41.35) or federal workers (39.48). The mean age of state populations ranges from a low of 28.42 in Alaska to a high of 38.86 in Florida. It is not surprising that in all but two instances (North Carolina and Florida) the average ages of the local, state, and federal government workforces exceed the average age of the state's population in each of the fifty jurisdictions. The average age of the local government workforce exceeds forty years in forty-nine of the fifty states (the exception being Alaska), and the average age of the state government workforce exceeds forty years in forty-seven states (the exceptions are Alaska, Colorado, and Wyoming), but the average age of the federal workforce is *below* forty years in a majority of states. With significant numbers of local and state government employees (and to a lesser extent federal employees) over the age of forty, the antidiscrimination provisions of the ADEA that stress the continued employment of qualified workers age forty and above become especially relevant to human resource and other public managers.

Table 5.2. Average Age of Population and Public-Sector Workforce.

	Average Age			
	Nation/State Population[a]	Local Government Workforce	State Government Workforce	Federal Government Workforce
United States	35.52	43.16	41.35	39.48
Alabama	35.42	42.65	41.79	41.27
Alaska	28.42	38.28	39.49	34.21
Arizona	34.40	41.63	40.12	38.46
Arkansas	36.45	43.32	42.06	40.55
California	33.55	42.62	41.11	36.92
Colorado	33.79	41.96	39.79	39.15
Connecticut	36.39	44.85	41.70	36.92
Delaware	35.91	41.04	44.83	36.50
Florida	38.86	43.44	41.89	38.64
Georgia	33.65	41.19	40.61	38.29
Hawaii	33.86	40.34	42.06	34.97
Idaho	33.48	44.56	41.70	39.88
Illinois	35.33	43.50	40.78	39.67
Indiana	35.10	42.89	40.34	41.19
Iowa	37.10	44.05	41.06	44.67
Kansas	36.15	44.84	41.14	39.38
Kentucky	35.13	42.47	41.43	39.17
Louisiana	33.40	42.33	40.66	38.11
Maine	35.47	43.80	43.25	37.80
Maryland	34.63	42.73	40.56	39.64
Massachusetts	36.08	44.42	41.21	40.34
Michigan	34.51	43.35	40.30	40.03
Minnesota	34.71	43.31	41.02	42.52
Mississippi	33.97	42.78	41.52	38.10
Missouri	36.17	43.00	40.96	41.20
Montana	35.36	42.96	40.35	40.66
Nebraska	36.43	45.36	41.07	40.86
Nevada	34.30	43.04	40.56	38.64
New Hampshire	34.07	41.47	41.31	41.50
New Jersey	36.33	44.34	41.28	40.00
New Mexico	33.16	40.35	41.25	39.63
New York	35.95	43.38	41.86	40.07
North Carolina	35.59	41.67	42.22	34.64
North Dakota	36.48	43.33	41.84	38.66
Ohio	35.33	42.74	40.58	41.76

Table 5.2. Average Age of Population and Public-Sector Workforce, cont'd.

| | Average Age | | | |
	Nation/State Population[a]	Local Government Workforce	State Government Workforce	Federal Government Workforce
Oklahoma	35.80	42.98	42.17	40.02
Oregon	35.86	43.59	41.17	42.40
Pennsylvania	36.91	44.09	42.72	41.75
Rhode Island	36.70	42.01	42.40	37.10
South Carolina	34.38	40.57	40.74	34.94
South Dakota	35.69	43.35	40.37	39.62
Tennessee	35.88	43.06	40.53	41.21
Texas	33.19	41.56	40.06	38.00
Utah	29.37	42.21	40.77	42.17
Vermont	34.08	45.15	41.36	40.21
Virginia	34.68	41.85	40.35	37.52
Washington	34.58	43.36	41.49	37.43
West Virginia	36.93	42.96	42.57	41.58
Wisconsin	35.05	44.43	40.53	41.52
Wyoming	33.02	42.22	38.77	39.81

[a]U.S. average age of population is a weighted average based on state populations.

Source: U.S. Bureau of the Census, 1995.

Managers need to be vigilant to avoid potential liability under the ADEA and to conform to both the letter and spirit of this legislation. Age-related discrimination has been detected in the areas of hiring (for example, rejecting applicants for age-related reasons), promotion (advancing younger candidates over older or more qualified ones), training (excluding older workers from training or retraining), reductions in force (terminating or forcing retirement of older workers exclusively or disproportionately), termination (linking firing decisions to declining performance or medical problems tied to age), and other aspects of personnel management.[2] Managers must take care not only in what they do but also in what they say. Snyder and Brandon's sage advice is "to sensitize all managers to the fact that any type of age reference, even in informal conversation, may have a negative impact on the organization's position [in an age discrimination suit]" (1983, p. 41). The bulk of age discrimination charges filed against state and local governments in fiscal year 1994, according to the EEOC, were in the areas of hiring and discharge, followed by terms of employment, harassment, wages, layoffs, and retirement and pensions, in that order.[3] A 1995 survey of cities over fifty thousand (West and Berman, 1996a) found a similar pattern of age-discrimination complaints reported by city managers. Thus in addition to myriad demographic, social, and economic challenges, managers of older workers must be aware of the legal requirements and tread cautiously to avoid lawsuits arising from age-related missteps.

MANAGERIAL STRATEGIES

What are some managerial strategies that will sidestep legal and fiscal pitfalls and still respond to the legitimate needs of older workers? This section singles out four strategic categories for examination: supportive workplace relations, training, career development, and performance appraisal.

Supportive Workplace Relations

Three types of strategies fall under the rubric of supportive workplace relations: those dealing with stress and health, alternative work arrangements, and retirement (Dennis, 1987). Older workers face certain unique stressors (for example, caregiving responsibilities) that can adversely affect performance at work. Organizations that offer in-house stress management or referrals via employee assistance programs help employees manage stress before it erodes productivity. Older workers also benefit from employer-sponsored health or wellness programs that foster proper nutrition, sensible exercise, appropriate drug use, and relaxation instruction (Tager, 1987). Such employer-sponsored initiatives help young and old employees alike, but may be especially helpful to aging workers if they address special needs (for example, health screening and blood pressure monitoring). Alternative work arrangements, a second form of supportive workplace relations, provide work flexibility and balance organizational and individual needs. A menu of arrangements helpful to older workers might include leave policies (parenting, elder care), job modifications (transfer, rotation, and redesign), part-time work schedules (job sharing, phased retirement, rehiring retirees part-time), workstation and workplace modifications (equipment redesign, adaptation to functional losses), flextime, and volunteer opportunities for retirees. Many items on this menu benefit old and young workers; others target specific needs of mature employees. The final set of supportive workplace relations pertains exclusively to older workers and deals with pension planning and early retirement incentive programs. By providing assistance in pension planning, employers help employees consider their long-range financial needs while they still have time to take appropriate steps to ensure security. Early retirement incentives sometimes go hand in hand with downsizing, but they do provide both an inducement and a buffer against more painful forms of job loss.

Training

Organizations may be reluctant to train older workers (Rosen and Jerdee, 1985; Sonnenfeld, 1978), and mature employees may be hesitant to avail themselves of training opportunities (Sterns and Doverspike, 1987). Fear of failure or anxiety about competing with younger coworkers might explain this reluctance of seasoned employees to become trainees. Employers can make training more palatable to such employees by adapting it to adult learning styles. Such adaptations might require organizing information in a more logical sequence, allowing trainees more time to digest information, encouraging trainee participation, and emphasizing the familiar when presenting material (Van Wart, Cayer, and Cook, 1993). Knowles and Associates (1984) suggest additional modifications that will add to adult training efficacy: altering the physical design and ergonomics of the training setting to achieve a comfort level promotive of learning; incorporating experiential teaching techniques rather than traditional lecture methods; acknowledging the valuable contributions adult learners can make to the learning process; and understanding how mature trainees' career stage may influence their willingness to learn. Making training widely available and adapting it to adult learning styles will signal management's recognition that mature workers are among the valuable assets the organization wishes to nurture and encourage.

Career Development

Creating an effective workplace involves cultivating a *learning environment;* indeed, continual learning opportunities are critical to the cutting-edge management tools of Total Quality Management and process reengineering. Organizations can facilitate such opportunities by helping employees assess their skills, knowledge, and abilities (SKAs); analyzing the task-SKA mix; and providing opportunities to develop new SKAs. Employers can encourage employees to design annual development objectives and can provide stimulating work assignments, institute mentor programs matching experienced with less-experienced workers, and enrich job content (West and Berman, 1993, 1995; Wolf, Neves, Greenough, and Benton, 1987). Such initiatives are valuable to younger and older workers alike. Career planning, revitalization, and counseling support for older workers is vitally important if they are to avoid career plateaus and SKA obsolescence. Yet organizational decision makers may erroneously conclude that investments in mature workers will bring insufficient performance benefits to the employers. Such judgments may be based on two questionable assumptions: that most of these workers will retire soon and that short-term benefits won't repay the expenditure. Enlightened managers and policymakers will avoid such shortsighted thinking.

Performance Appraisal

To be fair to older workers, managers should use objective performance appraisal methodologies that are valid, reliable, and free of age bias. Careful job analysis and clear, valid performance standards can help ensure that performance appraisals are reasonable and job relevant (Lovrich, 1995). Proficiency testing is a useful tool to assess current SKAs and supplement on-the-job performance ratings (Davis and Dotson, 1987). In contrast, chronological age is a poor predictor of job-related performance and, under the ADEA, an illegal basis for personnel decision making (American Association of Retired Persons, 1994). Nonetheless, age-related stereotypes persist among supervisors, who may require training to sensitize them to problems of rater bias and encourage them to use objective, age-neutral appraisal criteria.

Some age discrimination litigation has rested in part on smoking-gun phrases that managers have used in assessing employee performance: "you can't teach an old dog new tricks"; "you are too damn old for the line of work you are in"; "it would be cheaper to replace you with a younger worker"; "we need to get some 'young blood' in this organization." Managers have referred to older workers as "deadwood" and have suggested the need for "old-coot hatcheting." Such statements have been offered as proof of prejudice against older workers. Two types of prejudicial ageism have been identified by Posner (1995): (1) *animus discrimination*—which is a "systematic undervaluation" of the vocational capabilities of older workers, motivated by "ignorance, viciousness, or irrationality" (p. 320); and (2) *statistical discrimination*—which occurs when managers rely on stereotypes, attributing "to all people of a particular age the characteristics of the average person of that age" (p. 322). The first type is less common than the second. An example of the second type is found in the case of *Liebovitch* v. *Administrator, Veterans Administration* (33 FEP 777 [D.D.C. 1982]) where "the court reasoned that the supervisor's opinion of the employee's performance appeared to be derived more from a preexisting expectation of the capabilities of a 60-year old person than from a fair evaluation of the plaintiff's actual skills" (Miller and Schuster, 1990, p. 560). Plaintiffs who have evidence that managers acted on such misperceptions in evaluating performance can use this information in pressing their age discrimination cases. Managers must avoid actions based on stereotypes and smoking-gun language reflecting ageism.[4]

ACCOMPLISHMENTS AND BARRIERS

Research on the accomplishments of private and public organizations in addressing older workers' needs and concerns shows mixed results. National survey data from the private sector show a gap between policies toward older workers that personnel managers thought should be in place and those actually in place in surveyed companies. Theorists speculate that because companies have not yet experienced the full impact of the related demographic trends (the most dramatic of which may be a decade and a half from fulfillment), they are not proactively seeking to prevent problems (Commerce Clearing House, 1988). Waiting for the problems to become more severe is characteristic not only of the private sector but is also reflected in national and state survey results from the public sector (West and Berman, 1996b; Roberts, 1995). Similarly, an aspiration gap[5] has been noted in public organization initiatives where the need for future improvements beyond past accomplishments is greatest: adapting performance appraisals to the older workers' needs, adopting older worker policies, providing outplacement assistance, and using third parties (mediators or arbitrators) in age discrimination suits.

Notwithstanding such aspiration gaps and a general reluctance to act aggressively with a multifaceted strategy, there is evidence of progress and accomplishments. West and Berman (1996b) asked city managers an open-ended question about their cities' greatest accomplishments to date with older worker programs. Among the most frequently mentioned achievements were treating all employees equally and fairly regardless of their demographic groups, retention of older workers, reemploying retirees in full- or part-time work, well-funded retirement and benefit plans, early-retirement incentive programs, and active volunteer efforts. This survey and other published surveys report the frequency with which public and private organizations use particular human resource management strategies to address older worker needs, and usage patterns show considerable variation. Several reasons are offered to explain the mixed record of accomplishments. Barriers that are difficult for city governments to circumvent include lack of resources (funds, staff) and lack of will (awareness, interest, priority), reflecting the fiscal squeeze and the tendency to delay action until serious negative consequences occur. (Exhibit 5.1 presents some samples of the achievements and obstacles described by city managers during West and Berman's survey.) Despite such barriers, some jurisdictions have been more successful than others in effectively managing aging employees. Case studies provide concrete examples of success in meeting the needs of older workers. The three specific cases offered in the following sections illustrate creative efforts at training adults by the Wackenhut Training Institute, pre-retirement planning in the city of Tacoma, Washington, and mobilization of retirees in Fort Myers, Florida. They show creative ways to effectively use current older workers, soon-to-retire workers, and already-retired potential workers.

CASE STUDIES

Wackenhut Training Institute

The Wackenhut Corporation frequently negotiates contracts with the public sector to provide security officer services. The Wackenhut Training Institute (WTI)

Exhibit 5.1. City Managers' Descriptions of Achievements and Obstacles.

Management Accomplishments

"Early Retirement Programs—Needed to downsize. 2/3rds went out under ERP. Remainder laid off. One of 156 filed suit. Program was successful."

"Placing displaced workers in funded, vacant positions."

"Following the letter of the law on ADEA and offering pre-retirement and financial planning (mostly attended by older workers). We have a very thorough and aggressive wellness program integrated into our benefits package that has a very positive impact on older workers."

"Job redesign and job transfer programs for older workers. Older workers can remain on the job longer and continue to be productive."

"Our willingness to adapt work environments to older or disabled employees."

"Working with the local AARP for part-time workers as needed."

"Providing a workplace relatively free of age bias."

"Liberal retirement benefits and continuation of medical insurance benefits on retirement reducing financial need for employees to work until they are almost dead; we promote good health through our wellness program. Offer access at no cost to a well-equipped fitness facility, require annual job task in fitness testing for policy and fire personnel to keep employees and mentally sharp."

"We are very proud of our retirees who return to volunteer in our "senior core" program—they assist us in police, library, and recreational and park services!"

"The tuition assistance program is of great benefits to [older workers]; it allows them opportunities to acquire education/skills necessary for job security, competitiveness, and promotion opportunities."

"Reasonable job restructuring to accommodate older workers' situations. Hiring retirees as part-time, flex hours. Special skills training for older worker target groups."

Obstacles

"(1) money in the budget; (2) eliminating bias of managers toward older workers; (3) time to train for skills enhancement; (4) priority given to training."

"Support by management of humane/social interest programs."

"(1) developing interest in elder care; (2) giving recognition to/appreciating contributions of senior employees."

"Budgetary shortfalls are the greatest obstacle to implementing more programs."

"Downsizing of Government limits opportunity for job redesign and job transfer."

Exhibit 5.1. City Managers' Descriptions of Achievements and Obstacles, cont'd.

"Some workers begin to develop a 'short-timer's attitude' before retirement."

"The average person is not knowledgeable of the laws on the needs/concerns of older workers, particularly concerning work, so it's battle to (1) educate everyone (2) integrate (successfully) older workers into the workplace (3) create a positive environment conducive to high productivity and morale. We deal with the issues day by day: (4) training and more training, hiring and retaining more older workers."

"Budgetary constraints and competency pressures for new programs of all types, along with demands for downsizing and productivity improvements. We need to add these issues to our list of priorities and educate managers on the needs of older workers."

"Lack of funds devoted to training has impacted the entire workforce; lack of funds directed toward human resource programs in general has been detrimental; however, the city has provided substantial computer training which has benefited 'older' workers who otherwise may have remained computer illiterate."

"Senior management attitudes that young workers are less resistant to change."

Source: West and Berman, 1996b, p. 54.

bases its officer training on the adult learning model of *andragogy,* which encompasses four tenets: adults prefer self-directed learning, they bring unique life experiences to the learning process; their readiness to learn is linked to what they consider relevant; and they seek immediate application of newly acquired knowledge. This adult learning model is used by WTI to develop security officer training programs that include the following elements:

1. Preassessment of the learning styles of security employees, using tests to assess preferred methods of information processing. Results have indicated a preference for instruction that emphasizes the "why" of learning, real-world applications of newly acquired knowledge, logical sequencing of subject matter, and active participation in the learning process.

2. Instructional materials such as guides, self-study workbooks, and handouts that present information in a structured, logical format and make clear the students' responsibility in the learning process. Interactive exercises, role-plays, and self-quizzes involve the learner and provide quick feedback.

3. Instruction for trainers in how to facilitate learning by moving away from exclusive reliance on traditional "I'll talk, you listen" lecture methods.

4. Development of student-teacher *learning contracts,* in which trainees agree on the action plans they will use to apply learned concepts in workplace settings.

5. A cost-benefit approach to training evaluation, using student critique sheets that ask trainees whether they feel like participants in the learning program, whether the material is validated by their experiences, whether the material is relevant to their needs, and whether they feel the concepts taught were applicable to their security role (Goodboe, 1995).

The WTI experience is instructive for public personnel managers. It shows how an adult training methodology is applicable even in a private industry experiencing high turnover and a transient workforce. And WTI methods are especially relevant in training the relatively more stable public-sector workforce, where the fruits of such human capital investments promise to be more plentiful and enduring. The better trained the workforce, including older workers, the higher the quality of the service it is likely to deliver.

Tacoma Pre-Retirement Program

The award-winning Tacoma Employees' Retirement System Pre-Retirement Program has been recognized by the Government Finance Officers Association as containing "exceptional elements of creativity, transferability and sound management" (Pabst, 1987, p. 24). The program is designed to help aging employees prepare—emotionally, physically, and financially—for retirement. Benefits from this pre-retirement planning accrue not only to the workers but also to the employer because of increased productivity, retention, and improved morale.

The Tacoma system began with an employer-subsidized pilot program in 1983. The pilot program enrolled forty employees and was offered one day a week, three hours a day, for eight weeks. The successful pilot resulted in a twenty-four-hour course divided into two twelve-hour segments. This format gives participants time to complete reading and homework assignments and to receive feedback on their efforts. The course is now offered three or four times a year. It covers retirement options, fears about the future, tax information, Social Security eligibility and benefits, health issues, time and money management, living arrangements and lifestyle considerations, and goals and continuing work options. Pabst (1987) identifies these key lessons in Tacoma's experience: use a single instructor for each course rather than multiple instructors, use an instructor with a strong financial background (to supplement other information sources), use an instructor knowledgeable about employee benefits, and use a required text and course materials. Further, hold courses in the evenings and make them available to spouses, carefully screen potential speakers and their messages, have employees evaluate the program, provide refresher courses, and limit classes to twenty to thirty participants. Finally, speakers should include financial planners, gerontologists, mental health professionals, legal counselors, Social Security representatives, tax consultants, and stock brokers.

Programs like Tacoma's can help older workers resolve important financial and emotional issues prior to retirement and make informed decisions about their future. Such programs signal management's concern about older employees and may result in improved worker loyalty and on-the-job performance.

Fort Myers G.R.A.M.P.A.-Cop Program

Fort Myers, Florida, is located 125 miles south of Tampa on Florida's Gulf Coast. A large part of the city's population is retired or semi-retired, and there are more than one thousand senior citizens with some law enforcement experience. The city responded to the era of tight financial resources and citizen demands for continued services with an innovative G.R.A.M.P.A.-Cop school resource officer program, which hires retired police officers, certifies them through the regional academy as auxiliary officers, trains them in school resource functions, and assigns them to area schools. The acronym G.R.A.M.P.A. stands for Getting Retirees Actively Motivated to Policing Again.

To be eligible, program applicants must have at least five years of sworn law enforcement experience, be at least forty years old, pass a department physical examination at their own expense, meet basic requirements for state-sponsored training as reserve and auxiliary officers, and meet other traditional requirements of job applicants (valid driver's license, letters of recommendation, complete background investigation). Appointments are made by the chief of police, and officers serve at the chief's pleasure; they are not protected by civil service rules. G.R.A.M.P.A. cops are used principally to promote drug abuse prevention and intervention in city schools through education and counseling. They may also be called upon to help regular school resource officers in developing and delivering more conventional services, such as bicycle safety and child molestation prevention. Their training includes information about school resource officer functions and school board policies and programs, and specific instruction on various types of drugs, profiles of abusers, and both referral treatment and prevention programs.

The bottom-line benefits of such a program are obvious: the city capitalizes on years of valuable law enforcement experience at less than half the cost of regular police officers, and G.R.A.M.P.A. cops exert a positive influence on the youths of the community. The program is particularly budget-friendly in that Florida, like many other states, has a law providing that police departments having an aggressive policy with regard to "seizing and selling contraband articles, vessels, motor vehicles, aircraft or other personal property [are permitted] to finance their G.R.A.M.P.A.-Cop programs either partially or wholly from their forfeiture funds" (City of Fort Myers, 1989, p. 10).

Public personnel officers in other jurisdictions can learn a valuable lesson from such a program. Many government programs can benefit by tapping the

resources of skilled retirees who may need additional sources of financial support to offset expenses not covered by their pension plans or who may want a
job to break the monotony or boredom of retirement. In the latter instance they
might not need supplemental income and might be enthusiastic volunteers who
seek employment as a source of stimulation, satisfaction, and camaraderie. This
low-cost strategy of resource expansion is especially attractive in the current period of fiscal austerity.

CONCLUSION

Demographic, economic, and legal trends converge to raise the salience of older
worker issues. Although management has been slow to respond to this combination of forces, such neglect will become more costly in the future as the problems become more severe. Impending labor shortages and skill deficiencies,
citizen demands for better services, and the desire to avoid litigation will prompt
managers to place a higher value on the talent and life experience of older employees and to recognize the importance of treating them fairly. Public managers and human resource professionals must be especially observant of current
trends and take whatever actions are required in their organizational settings to
ensure that attitudes, policies, and practices are sensitive to the needs of *all*
workers. Attention may need to be devoted to combating myths and stereotypes
about aging and older employees' capabilities. Strategic leverage points for addressing older worker issues are training, career development, performance appraisal, and the creation of supportive workplace relations. Innovative programs
such as those designed and implemented by Wackenhut and the cities of
Tacoma and Fort Myers are transferable to other settings and show some ways
to get the most from mature employees. Despite the new organizational realities that undervalue aging workers, these workers continue to be valuable assets to employers. Cultivating the potential of today's mature workers and
tomorrow's older workforce is a creative challenge for public administrators and
human resource leaders now and in the future.

Notes

1. Although these jobs are no longer found in the public sector, many of them continue to exist in the private sector due to outsourcing.

2. Proving age discrimination is difficult in each of these areas. For example, employers may contend that firing decisions are based solely on "declining performance" and not on age, but evidence of deteriorating performance would need
   to be offered to show that rational nondiscriminatory reasons caused the termination. Plaintiffs might argue in rebuttal, as noted by Cozzetto, Pedeliski, and Tipple
   (1996), that "statements of employers and supervisors that aim at 'getting rid of

the good ole joes' or the 'old buzzards' or the 'Alzheimer brigade' may be probative that age was the controlling factor in the adverse action against the employee" (p. 249).

3. Data provided by Ester Cosby, public affairs specialist, EEOC, Office of Communications and Legislative Affairs, Mar. 1995. Data are compiled by the Office of Program Operations for the EEOC's Charge Data System (CDS) national database. The CDS is continually updated as data are submitted to EEOC headquarters by EEOC field offices and state and local Fair Employment Practices Agencies around the country; statistics may therefore change slightly over time.

4. Miller and Schuster (1990) discuss the following four specific cases under the rubric of "age bias in performance appraisal systems": *Buchholz* v. *Symons Mfg. Co.* (445 F. Supp. 796 [E.D. Wis. 1978]); *Guthrie* v. *J. C. Penney Co., Inc.* (803 F. 2d 202 [5th Cir. 1986]); *Liebovitch* v. *Administrator, Veterans Administration* (33 FEP 777 [D.D.C. 1982]); *Krodel* v. *Dept. of Health and Human Services* (33 FEP 689 [D.D.C. 1982]).

5. West and Berman (1996b) define the aspiration gap as "the difference between policies and practices currently in use (reality) and the percent of organizations reporting that important improvements are required (aspiration) in a particular area in the next five years" (p. 50).

References

Administration on Aging. *The Administration on Aging and the Older Americans Act.* Unpublished manuscript, Administration on Aging, U.S. Department of Health and Human Services, Washington, D.C., 1997.

Age Discrimination in Employment Act of 1967. U.S. Code, vol. 29, sec. 621 et seq.

American Association of Retired Persons. *America's Changing Workforce: Statistics in Brief.* Washington, D.C.: American Association of Retired Persons, 1993.

American Association of Retired Persons. *Age Discrimination on the Job.* Washington, D.C.: American Association of Retired Persons, 1994.

American Association of Retired Persons. *American Business and Older Workers: A Roadmap to the 21st Century.* Washington, D.C.: American Association of Retired Persons, 1995.

Barth, M. C., McNaught, W., and Rizzi, P. "Corporations and the Aging Workforce." In P. H. Mirvis (ed.), *Building the Competitive Workforce.* New York: Wiley, 1993.

Beutell, N. "Managing the Older Worker." *Personnel Administrator,* 1983, *28*(8), 31–38.

Blocklyn, P. L. "The Aging Workforce." *Personnel,* 1987, *64*(8), 16–19.

Bove, R. "Retraining the Older Worker." *Training and Development,* 1987, *41*(1), 77–78.

Buonocore, A. J. "Older and Wiser: Senior Employees Offer Untapped Capabilities." *Management Review,* 1992, *81*(7), 49–53.

City of Fort Myers. *Fort Myers Police Department G.R.A.M.P.A.-Cop School Resource Officer Program.* Unpublished paper, Fort Myers, Fla., 1989.

Commerce Clearing House. *ASPA-CCH Survey.* Chicago: Commerce Clearing House, 1988.

Cozzetto, D. A., Pedeliski, T. B., and Tipple, T. J. *Public Personnel Administration.* Upper Saddle River, N.J.: Prentice Hall, 1996.

Davis, P. O., and Dotson, C. O. "Job Performance Testing: An Alternative to Age Discrimination." *Medicine and Science in Sports and Medicine,* 1987, *19*(2), 178–185.

Dennis, H. (ed.). *Fourteen Steps in Managing an Aging Workforce.* Lexington, Mass.: Heath, 1987.

The Downsizing of America. New York: Times Books, 1996.

Elliott, R. H. "Human Resource Management's Role in the Future Aging of the Workforce." *Review of Public Personnel Administration,* 1995, *15*(2), 5–17.

Fowles, D. G. *A Profile of Older Americans.* Unpublished paper, prepared for the Program Resources Department, American Association of Retired Persons, and the Administration on Aging, U.S. Department of Health and Human Services, 1995.

Galen, M. "Myths About Older Workers Cost Business Plenty." *Business Week,* Dec. 20, 1993, p. 23.

Gilsdorf, J. W. "The New Generation: Older Workers." *Training and Development,* 1992, *46*(3) 77–79.

Goodboe, M. E. "Should Security Practice Andragogy? Adult Learning Model." *Security Management,* 1995, *39*(4), 65–74.

Hagen, R. P. "Older Workers." *Supervisory Management,* 1983, *28*(11), 2–9.

Kaeter, M. "Age-Old Myths." *Training,* Jan. 1995, *23,* 61–66.

Kaminski-da Roza, V. "A Workshop That Optimizes the Older Worker's Productivity." *Personnel,* 1984, *61*(2), 47–56.

Kelly, J. "The Rising Tide of Older Workers." *Nation's Business,* 1992, *80*(19), 22.

Knowles, M. S., and Associates. *Andragogy in Action: Applying Modern Principles of Adult Learning.* San Francisco: Jossey-Bass, 1984.

Love, D. O., and Torrence, M. D. "The Impact of Worker Age on Unemployment and Earnings After Plant Closing." *Journal of Gerontology,* 1989, *44*(5), 140–145.

Lovrich, N. P."Performance Appraisal: Seeking Accountability and Efficiency Through Individual Effort, Commitment and Accomplishment." In S. W. Hays and R. C. Kearney (eds.), *Public Personnel Administration: Problems and Prospects.* (3rd ed.) Upper Saddle River, N.J.: Prentice Hall, 1995.

Miller, C. S., and Schuster, M. H. "The Impact of Performance Appraisal Methods on Age Discrimination in Employment Act Cases." *Personnel Psychology,* 1990, *43,* 555–578.

Moody, B. "The Political Landscape of Aging Policy: Important Actors and Trends." *Review of Public Personnel Administration,* 1995, *15*(2), 18–35.

Morris, R., and Caro, F. "The 'Young-Old,' Productive Aging, and Public Policy." *Generations,* 1995, *19*(3), 32–38.

Nelton, S. "Golden Employees: In Their Golden Years." *Nation's Business,* 1993, *81*(8), 34–35.

Noer, D. M. "Leadership in an Age of Layoffs." *Issues and Observations,* 1993, *13*(3), 1–5.

Older Workers Benefit Protection Act of 1990. U.S. Statutes at Large 104 (1990) 978.

Pabst, P. F. "Tacoma Employees' Retirement System Pre-Retirement Program." *Government Finance Review,* Apr. 1987, pp. 21–24.

Palmore, E. B. *Ageism: Negative and Positive.* New York: Springer, 1990.

Posner, R. A. *Aging and Old Age.* Chicago: University of Chicago Press, 1995.

Roberts, G. "Age-Related Employment Issues in Florida Municipal Governments: Are Municipal Governments Preparing for Change?" *Review of Public Personnel Administration,* 1995, *15*(2), 62–83.

Rosen, B., and Jerdee, T. "The Influence of Age Stereotypes on Managerial Decisions." *Journal of Applied Psychology,* 1976, *61*(4), 428–432.

Rosen, B., and Jerdee, T. *Older Employees: New Roles for Valued Resources.* Homewood, Ill.: Business One Irwin, 1985.

Rosen, B., and Jerdee, T. "Investing in the Older Worker." *Personnel Administrator,* 1989, *34*(1), 70–74.

Shea, G. F. *Managing Older Employees.* San Francisco: Jossey-Bass, 1991.

Snyder, R. A., and Brandon, B. "Riding the Third Wave: Staying on Top of ADEA Complaints." *Personnel Administrator,* 1983, *28*(2), 41–47.

Solomon, C. M. "Unlock the Potential of Older Workers." *Personnel Journal,* 1995, *74*(11), 56–65.

Sonnenfeld, J. "Dealing with the Aging Work Force." *Harvard Business Review,* Nov.-Dec. 1978, pp. 80–90.

Stark, D. E. "Age Discrimination in the Workplace." *High Technology Careers Magazine.* [http://www.vjf.com/pub/docs/age.html]. 1996.

Sterns, H. L., and Doverspike, D. "Training and Developing the Older Worker: Implications for Human Resource Managers." In H. Dennis (ed.), *Fourteen Steps in Managing an Aging Workforce.* Lexington, Mass.: Heath, 1987.

Strouse, C. "Older Workers Fight for Acceptance." *Miami Herald,* Mar. 12, 1995, p. A16.

Tager, R. M. "Stress and the Older Worker." In H. Dennis (ed.), *Fourteen Steps in Managing an Aging Workforce.* Lexington, Mass.: Heath, 1987.

U.S. Bureau of the Census. *1990 Census of Population and Housing: Public Use Microdata 1 percent Sample.* Washington, D.C.: U.S. Department of Commerce, 1995.

Van Wart, M., Cayer, N. J., and Cook, S. *Handbook of Training and Development for the Public Sector: A Comprehensive Resource.* San Francisco: Jossey-Bass, 1993.

West, J. P., and Berman, E. M. "Human Resource Strategies in Local Government: A Survey of Progress and Future Directions." *American Review of Public Administration,* 1993, *23*(3), 279–297.

West, J. P., and Berman, E. M. "Strategic Human Resource and Career Development Planning." In S. W. Hays and R. C. Kearney (eds.), *Public Personnel Administration: Problems and Prospects.* (3rd ed.) Upper Saddle River, N.J.: Prentice Hall, 1995.

West, J. P., and Berman, E. M. "Agism in Local Government." Unpublished poster-board presentation delivered at the annual meeting of the American Society for Public Administration, Atlanta, July 1996a.

West, J. P., and Berman, E. M. "Managerial Responses to an Aging Municipal Workforce: A National Survey." *Review of Public Personnel Administration,* 1996b, *16*(3), 38–58.

Wolf, J. F., Neves, C. M., Greenough, R. T., and Benton, B. B. "Greying at the Temples: Demographics of a Public Service Occupation." *Public Administration Review,* 1987, *47*(2), 190–198.

Wooldridge, B. "Meeting the Challenge: Being a Successful Leader of an Increasingly Diverse Workforce." *Journal of Public Management and Social Policy,* 1995, *1*(1), 26–41.

Wooldridge, B., and Maddox, B. "Demographic Changes and Diversity in Personnel: Implications for Public Administrators." In J. Rabin, T. Vocino, W. B. Hildreth, and G. J. Miller (eds.), *Handbook of Public Personnel Administration,* New York: Dekker, 1995.

Yankelovich, D. "Three Destructive Trends." *Kettering Review,* Fall 1995, pp. 6–15.

CHAPTER SIX

Understanding Organizational Climate and Culture

J. Steven Ott

Do more. Do it with less. Focus on customers. Streamline. Downsize.
Walk the talk. Coach. Do it better. Work smarter. Be number one. Reinvent.
Reengineer. Benchmark. Practice quality management. Find a mentor.
National Performance Review. Executive orders. Government Performance
and Results Act. Transform. Faster. Faster. Faster.
—Michele Hunt, "Freeing the Spirit of Public Service in All of Us," 1995

Many factors and forces shape an organization's receptivity or resistance to change including its legislative mandates, the design of its structure, the clientele it serves, and the types of functions it performs. Changing the culture and climate of the organization, however, is the first emphasis of almost every current book and article on Total Quality Management (TQM), reinventing government, quality of work life (QWL), self-empowered work teams, sexual harassment, or diversity (Atkinson, 1990; Ott, 1995; Wilson, 1992).

Organizational climate is like the space that surrounds the core of an "organizational donut" (Handy, 1994, chap. 4); *organizational culture* is the fabric of the core *and* the surrounding space. Together climate and culture make up the area wherein an organization's identity, personality, and distinctiveness develop and reside. They collectively determine the areas in which an organization can place claims on employees' energies, enthusiasms, and loyalties. As we all know, a manager can use legitimate authority to issue formal policies prohibiting or requiring specific acts, types of behavior, and compliance. However, we also know that few managers can use authority to mandate positive attitudes, creativity, or respect or to mandate risk taking on behalf of an agency or its clients.

Not many failures of organizational improvement initiatives are caused by inadequate policies or management incompetence (Ott and Shafritz, 1994, 1995). More often, the culprit is the culture of the organization and the operating climate that emerges from it (McNabb and Sepic, 1995; Moran and Volkwein, 1992). It is not easy to convince employees who have worked for decades in an organizational culture of, for example, "no mistakes" to start taking personal risks, such as communicating openly with their supervisors when they exceed their official authority or ignoring counterproductive policies (Lipsky, 1980) in order to respond effectively to agency or client problems.

Organizational climate and culture hold keys that a human resource (HR) manager can use to unlock the status quo—to help the organization advance to a higher plane of performance, productivity, flexibility, innovation, effectiveness, or diversity (Atkinson, 1990; Downey, Hellriegel, and Slocum, 1975; Ganesan, 1983; Hunt, 1995; Kopelman, Brief, and Guzzo, 1990; Lawler, Hall, and Oldham, 1974; Litwin and Stringer, 1968; McNabb and Sepic, 1995; Pritchard and Karasick, 1973; Putti and Kheun, 1986; Siehl and Martin, 1990; Whipp, Rosenfeld, and Pettigrew, 1989). They also hold keys that an HR manager can use to help maintain organizational excellence while the world around the organization changes and "batters" against it (Hunt, 1995).

The culture and climate of an organization thus can hold the keys to influencing people to change—or to maintain—their beliefs, values, attitudes, and patterns of behavior: for example, their willingness to truly listen to clients' opinions, their approach to work, or their willingness to network and collaborate with people in other units of government or in the private sector (particularly when the environment is turbulent). Organizational culture and climate may encourage government employees to participate (or prohibit them from participating) in organizational improvements such as Michele Hunt lists in the quote at the start of the chapter. As the profession of public human resource management (HRM) continues to grow away from its insulated *personnelism* history into a central agency role that often includes leading change initiatives, an HR manager's tool bag needs to include methods for identifying, interpreting, changing, and maintaining organizational culture and climate. The good news is that HR managers in many units of municipal, state, and national governments are emerging as pivotal actors who are central to their organization's effectiveness and—not uncommonly in the 1990s—its continued survival as an independent or intact agency. HR managers are leading initiatives that affect organizational productivity, flexibility, funding, and grievance filings and outcomes that control the frequency of unwanted newspaper headlines. The power, influence, and ability of HRM departments to attract increasingly scarce organizational resources have risen along with the increasing importance of department roles (Salancik and Pfeffer, 1977).

There is also not-so-good news, however. Altering or maintaining organizational culture and climate can be a complex, time-consuming, expensive, unpopular, fuzzy, lengthy, and risky endeavor. And knowing when such actions have been successfully accomplished is almost as difficult and controversial (Dutcher, Hayashida, Sheposh, and Dickason, 1992). HRM departments that take on roles as leaders of change need an array of skills, attitudes, and abilities that may not be readily available in those departments or from reliable consultants. Thus when an organization's climate or culture must be altered, higher public officials must be convinced of the need for patience and resources to accomplish all the fuzzy tasks involved—at a time and in an environment when both are in short supply.

Departments within organizations typically have their own subcultures, and the subcultures of some public HRM departments are ill-suited for leading important initiatives. Too often, HRM subcultures and subclimates stifle, suppress, and eventually repel people who have abilities and attitudes that are suited to organizational change. Traditional personnel systems (the interrelated policies and procedures for classifying positions; screening and selecting potential employees; establishing compensation grades, steps, and ranges; evaluating employee performance; and awarding increases) are both products of and sustainers of change-resisting organizational cultures (Shafritz, Riccucci, Rosenbloom, and Hyde, 1992). To the extent that traditional personnelists and the systems they administer dominate the HRM subculture, it will be difficult for the department to be a pivotal and effective leader of change.

Thus far I have discussed ideas and characteristics common to both organizational climate and organizational culture. However, although they share many attributes, they are substantively different phenomena, and their differences are important for practicing HR managers to understand. Organizational climate is the easier of the two to change and to measure; but it can be transitory, like a mood. Organizational climate is close to the surface and relatively easy to sense. Changes in events or leadership can cause it to swing, and the changes can be noticed. Organizational culture is different. It is embedded in the fabric of an organization. When executives or consultants claim that an organization's culture has been changed, they usually do not understand that only the climate has changed. When the culture is altered, it doesn't snap back; it remains.

The purposes of this chapter are practical, not theoretical. It is an attempt to help HR managers understand the reasons for, implications of, and challenges involved in identifying, changing, and maintaining a climate or a culture. There are sound reasons, methods, and techniques for working with both, but because climate and culture are not the same phenomenon, they differ. Each phenomenon needs to be understood for what can and cannot be done with it.

ORGANIZATIONAL CLIMATE

Organizational climate has been an established topic in the literature of organization theory, organizational behavior, survey research, and HRM for more than twenty-five years. It has been defined variously as "psychological environments in which the behavior of individuals occurred" (Trice and Beyer, 1993,

p. 19); "a summary perception of the organization's work environment that is descriptive rather than evaluative" (Joyce and Slocum, 1984, p. 721); and "the internal environment of an organization that (a) is experienced by its members, (b) influences their behavior, and (c) can be described in terms of the values of a particular set of characteristics (or attributes) of the organization" (Tagiuri, 1968, p. 27). Because climate is a *social construct* (Berger and Luckmann, 1966), *the* definitive definition does not exist. Constructs are *social facts* (Durkheim, 1963), and "once created . . . they acquire their own power and serve as forceful constraints on the individual's social behavior" (Fink and Chen, 1995, p. 494).

As a perception and a *feeling tone*, organizational climate is not, for example, the incentive pay program or the work environment. Rather, it is how people feel about and react emotionally to the incentive pay program or the work environment—how they let it affect them collectively. Changing an organizational climate, therefore, is not a monumental ground-breaking feat, at least under ordinary circumstances and in the short-term. Difficult, yes; extraordinarily difficult, no. Too often, though, proponents of TQM, reinvention, reengineering, and other organizational improvement initiatives confuse organizational climate change with organizational culture change.

"'First (or second), the culture of the organization must be changed.' (Often, the first step is equally sweeping: 'create a shared vision and mission'. . . . Having made the pronouncements—warning would-be TQM implementers that they cannot succeed without first changing the organizational culture—too many TQM articles and books simply proceed to the next implementation step with a clear conscience" (Ott, 1995, p. 365).

Changes in events or leadership can cause an organizational climate to swing noticeably, and when an organizational climate has been altered, it can and will change again. Often changes occur as quickly as pressures are removed. When organizational climate has been altered by a newly elected strong mayor or governor, for example, it often drifts or snaps back to the old climate as soon as the executive's attention moves on to the next new initiative—or elected position. When an organizational culture has been altered, beliefs, attitudes, values, behaviors do not snap back or revert easily. Changing the culture of an organization is changing its character or identity.

ORGANIZATIONAL CULTURE

Whereas climate is a somewhat temporary feeling tone in an organization, culture is integral to an organization and cannot be manipulated easily (U.S. General Accounting Office, 1992). "Organizational culture is not just another piece of the puzzle, it is the puzzle. . . . A culture is not something an organization has; a culture is something an organization is" (Pacanowsky and O'Donnell-Trujillo,

1983, p. 126). A culture is an interactive blend of change-resisting (or enhancing) beliefs, socially constructed realities, values, professional traditions, norms, ways of thinking about and doing things, and language or jargon that is shared by members of an organization. This blend may vary somewhat across an organization, resulting in subcultures (Martin and Siehl, 1983; Trice, 1993). The organizational culture performs the important task of helping employees create meaning in the face of organizational ambiguity and uncertainty (Feldman, 1991). It provides clues and guides that help employees understand what to expect and what is expected of them.

Organizational culture—like climate—is a social construct, and thus its meaning has been subject to ongoing disagreement (Ott, 1989; Trice and Beyer, 1993). Rather widespread agreement has emerged, however, that organizational culture is

- The culture that exists within an organization, similar to a societal culture but on an organizational scale
- A phenomenon made up of such things as values, beliefs, assumptions, perceptions, behavioral norms, artifacts, and patterns of behavior
- A socially constructed, unseen, and unobservable force behind organizational activities
- A social energy that moves organizational members to act
- A unifying theme that provides meaning, direction, and mobilization for organizational members
- An organizational control mechanism, informally approving or prohibiting behaviors [Ott, 1989, p. 50].

Schein (1993) identifies three levels of organizational culture (which this chapter applies later to the task of identifying organizational culture): *artifacts, patterns of behavior,* and the deepest and most difficult level to get at, *underlying basic assumptions,* ideas likely to have moved from people's conscious minds to their preconscious minds. Basic assumptions are "like applying brakes while driving a car. After years of pushing the brake pedal and the car slowing, we quit thinking about brakes and braking: we just hit the brakes instinctively, *assuming* the car will slow down. If hitting the brakes works repeatedly, we cease thinking about braking. Our belief in the relationship between braking and slowing turns into a basic assumption" (Ott, 1989, p. 42).

Organizational culture is not easily discernible, measurable, or alterable. Frequently, executives and consultants who claim that organization's culture has changed are in fact seeing only a climate change. A manager cannot simply go out and change the organizational culture—as some consultants and writers about TQM, reinvention, and reengineering would have us believe (Ott, 1995). Organizational climate is considerably easier to work with.

IDENTIFYING ORGANIZATIONAL CLIMATE

Identifying organizational climate is not a particularly difficult endeavor. Organizational surveys (Desatnick, 1986; Dunnington, 1993; Dutka and Frankel, 1993; Edwards and Thomas, 1993a, 1993b; Glick, 1985; Landis, Dansby, and Faley, 1993; Marsden, Cook, and Knoke, 1994; Rosenfeld, Booth-Kewley, and Edwards, 1993) and longitudinal studies that identify climate (Jackofsky and Slocum, 1988) require careful planning and execution, but they are not *that* difficult to administer. Many organizational climate surveys already exist (Cullen, Victor, and Bronson, 1993; Hellriegel and Slocum, 1974; Litwin and Stringer, 1968; Nave, 1986; Siegel and Turney, 1980; Tagiuri, 1968). (Two examples appear in Exhibits 6.1 and 6.2, at the end of the chapter.)

Two measurement issues are (1) aggregating climate from individual perceptions (Dansereau and Alutto, 1990; Joyce and Slocum, 1984) and (2) resolving the inevitable problems encountered when using quantitative techniques to describe phenomena from the arm's-length perspective of an objective observer (Edwards and Thomas, 1993a, 1993b; Glick, 1985; Hellriegel and Slocum, 1974).

The stickiest part of measuring organizational climate, however, is a third issue—reaching agreement about the *operational definition* of the organizational climate. That is, precisely how will climate be defined for the purposes of the measurement? This task may sound straightforward, but it is not, because it is usually not truly a measurement issue but a political issue.

First, organizations do not set out to identify or measure organizational climate purely for the interest value. They have practical reasons: for example, to identify the need for change, to gauge readiness for a new program, to identify attitudinal or feeling-tone barriers that may cause problems for a planned initiative, to focus a planned change, or to establish a baseline against which they will be able to determine the effects of organizational change (Burns, 1996).

Second, the process of identifying organizational climate surfaces implicit values or beliefs about organizational goodness. What makes an organization "good," "healthy," or "effective"? What level of which climate indicator(s) signals the need for change? (Culbertson and Rosenfeld, 1993; Kerce and Booth-Kewley, 1993; Landis, Dansby, and Faley, 1993; Toulson and Smith, 1994). Would improving (what aspects of?) organizational climate increase (what indicators of?) organizational effectiveness? These are hard questions to which there are only social fact answers, and the answers often will influence which—or whose—program is implemented.

Third, identifying organizational climate usually is caused by a desire or a plan to improve an organization in a predetermined manner. Such improvement might involve employee motivation, job satisfaction, or personnel management practices (Downey, Hellriegel, and Slocum, 1975; Ganesan, 1983;

Lawler, Hall, and Oldham, 1974; Pritchard and Karasick, 1973; Putti and Kheun, 1986; Toulson and Smith, 1994). All dimensions of organizational climate reflect implicit normative views about what should be done to improve an organization. When a survey is designed to identify social constructions, only the needs and variables it addresses are capable of being found. If a dimension is not included, it does not exist! Thus on the one hand, if TQM advocates thought it likely that TQM would improve the organizational climate (defined in terms of employee perceptions of empowerment), they would fight to include questions about empowerment in the instrument. On the other hand, if the HRM director or the agency chief believed organizational improvements could be accomplished best by improving supervisors' communication skills or by clarifying currently ambiguous rules, the instrument would be designed to gather information about these different dimensions. Thus deciding which operational definition of organizational climate to measure can develop into a political donnybrook.

The changeability of organizational climate also poses interesting problems of interpretation. All of us react differently to tension-producing situations. Likewise, not all employees react or respond in the same ways to the same stimuli. If HR managers were to survey the climate after introducing an incentive pay program or work environment change, they would probably get some patterned responses but also different perceptions (readings) of the organizational climate across workgroups and at different points in time (Glick, 1985; Turnipseed and Turnipseed, 1992). These differences might be interpreted either as reflecting the existence of subclimates or as revealing the absence of a pervasive organizational climate. Unless managers are methodologically careful, they might pick the incorrect interpretation for their organization.

The important point, however, is not to get caught up in the complexities. Be clear about why a reading of organizational climate is wanted, and design or select an instrument or other measurement process that suits the purpose.

IDENTIFYING ORGANIZATIONAL CULTURE

The task of identifying an organizational culture is considerably more complex than measuring a climate. The obstacles are plentiful and difficult to circumvent—without trivializing what organizational culture is. The most serious problem in identifying an organizational culture is that culture is not *something*: it is woven into the fabric or character of the organization. Analogously, it is more difficult to measure peoples' personalities than it is to measure their beliefs or behaviors. Here are some additional substantial barriers to identifying organizational culture:

- Most organizational culture studies use qualitative or near-qualitative rather than quantitative research methods. Qualitative methods are excellent for describing and explaining but not for predicting and generalizing.

- Organizational culture research has relied on qualitative research methods because it is almost impossible to use quantitative methods to study such things as preconscious basic assumptions. Qualitative methods, however, do not meet quantitative research design standards for ensuring validity and reliability. Thus qualitative studies of organizational culture are not valid by quantitative research standards and will often be subjected to severe criticism.

- Most qualitative research efforts take many months or even years to complete. When information about organizational culture is needed quickly—for input to strategy decisions, for example—qualitative methods cannot deliver.

- Qualitative studies are expensive to conduct.

However, when human resource management decisions must be made, information is needed, and an HR manager may be called upon to undertake the complex and sometimes risky task of studying the organizational culture. Anyone who initiates this task faces many decisions about what to investigate, the methods and strategies to use, and the claims that can be made about the findings.

Practical concerns should prevail: the level of culture to be studied and the methods to be used to collect information should be appropriate to the reasons for conducting the study. For example, the methodological approach used by an HRM department to study the limits an agency's basic assumptions impose on agency ability to implement a pilot team-based incentive pay plan should not be the same as the methods used by a General Accounting Office team to prepare a report for Congress on the factors that determine the effectiveness of team-based incentive pay plans across the Department of Defense (U.S. General Accounting Office, 1992). Different organizational purposes require designs and methods that can identify different levels and dimensions of culture—and also produce results at different costs, within different time frames, and with different levels of confidence in the findings.

The first step is to decide which level of culture to investigate:

- Material artifacts (level 1A)
- Patterns of behavior (level 1B)
- Beliefs, values, and ideologies (level 2)
- Basic underlying assumptions (level 3)

Once again, the choice of level should be driven by purposes—the reasons why the organization wants the culture identified. Methods can and should be chosen to fit the study's purposes. Methodological trade-offs can be made, particularly between the costs and time it takes to identify a culture and the confidence an organization can place in the findings. Thus if an HRM department needs information now to decide on the feasibility of a new program and if confidence-level requirements are not high—if the department can tolerate a margin of error—study approaches can be designed to hold down costs and produce information relatively quickly. Conversely, if the department can take a few months for the study, methods can be used that yield results in which management can have higher confidence. Awareness of such trade-offs is crucial: the choice of methods for identifying organizational culture should be based on how quickly results are needed and how findings will be used. The remainder of this chapter explains how to identify organizational culture and which indicators to study at each level of organizational culture.

Artifacts: Level 1A of Organizational Culture

Clues about organizational culture can be collected quickly and inexpensively by looking at material artifacts, such as physical settings and archives. However, artifacts should be used only as clues or as confirmations of other findings about the culture. They cannot be trusted to provide accurate information by themselves, and it is difficult to piece cultural patterns together accurately from them. Techniques that can be used to observe them include

- Wandering around and looking at physical settings (Gagliardi, 1990; Steele, 1973)

- Rummaging through archives and other organizational records (Clark, 1970; Pettigrew, 1979)

- Reading between the lines on organization charts (Greenfield, 1984; Meyer, 1984; Weick, 1976)

- Listening to the everyday language, jargon, humor, and metaphors used in halls, rest rooms, and lunch areas (Boland and Hoffman, 1983; Evered, 1983; Louis, 1981; Pondy, 1978)

- Absorbing the myths, stories, sagas, and legends told at new employee orientations and other celebrations and rituals (Clark, 1970; Feldman, 1991; Martin, 1982; Martin and Powers, 1983; Martin and Siehl, 1983; Pettigrew, 1979; Pondy, 1983; Wilkins, 1983).

Patterns of Behavior: Level 1B of Organizational Culture

Innumerable instruments, questionnaires, and surveys already exist for identifying norms and patterns of behaviors in organizations (Alexander, 1978; Allen and Kraft, 1982), but designing and developing effective instruments can be expensive and time consuming (see Chapter Twenty-One). When such surveys are done carefully, they can provide a plethora of useful information, and findings can be compared among organizational units and within units over time.

Surveys of norms also have limitations and dangers. First, norms that are not addressed by an instrument cannot be identified by it. Second, people tend to believe survey results because they *look* scientific, which can lead to dangerous practical consequences. Third and most important, it is tempting to use questionnaires to identify norms and then hope the norms are accurate reflections of the deeper levels of organizational culture—the basic underlying assumptions (Cooke and Rousseau, 1988). Sometimes they are, but it is not easy to know when they are or are not. Norms by themselves are not organizational culture. Thus norm surveys provide only *one measure* of *one indicator* of *one level* of organizational culture.

Beliefs, Values, and Ideologies: Level 2 of Organizational Culture

Artifacts and behavioral patterns can be seen, touched, or heard directly. Norms can be inferred from patterns of behavior or surveyed. Beliefs, values, and ideologies are one step further removed from observable behavior. Relationships between what is observed and assumptions buried deep inside peoples' heads can be blurred by intervening factors. Inferring beliefs and values from observable behavior thus can be a risky endeavor (Beyer, Dunbar, and Meyer, 1988; Conway, 1985; Dougherty and Kunda, 1990). Roger Harrison has developed an interesting paper-and-pencil instrument for diagnosing organizational culture, or as he calls it, *organizational ideology* (Harrison, 1993; Harrison and Stokes, 1992). Ideology establishes a rationale for norms and explains the behavior of an organization's members. Thus, for example, Al-Khalaf and I (Al-Khalaf and Ott, 1994) chose Harrison's instrument to identify cities whose ideologies, or cultures, indicated a readiness for TQM implementation.

Basic Underlying Assumptions: Level 3 of Organizational Culture

Attempting to decipher an organization's basic assumptions richly and accurately is a substantial undertaking. It requires a lengthy involvement (usually more than one year), a combination of outsider and insider perspectives, almost unrestricted access to people and records, the use of multiple data collection strategies, and an understanding that when all is completed, the results will not necessarily be widely accepted by the organization as valid or useful (Burns, 1996; Ott, 1989, chap. 5; Pettigrew, 1979; Rousseau, 1990; Schein, 1993; Trice and Beyer, 1993, chap. 1; Van Maanen, 1983; Van Maanen, Dabbs, and Faulkner, 1982). Thus except in the most unusual circumstances, HR managers are advised to settle for a strategy that avoids trying to identify basic underlying assumptions and instead uses the *proxy measures* (substitute indicators) at a more observable level of organizational culture.

Identifying Organizational Culture: Summary of Advice

For most purposes, HR managers should not try to decipher basic assumptions. Instead, they should be practical and

1. Use proxy indicators of organizational culture. Proxy measures at level 2 of organizational culture (beliefs, values, and ideologies) usually are preferable. The potential for making grievously wrong inferences about culture is higher when using artifacts than when using beliefs, values, and ideologies.

2. Use more than one type of measure of more than one indicator of organizational culture (Hofstede, Neuijeu, Ohayv, and Sanders, 1990; Rousseau, 1990).

3. Select strategies and tools to fit the purposes. For example, focus groups are the wrong methodological choice when the purpose is to make comparisons between organizations.

4. Keep in mind that qualitative research methods in general are most useful for *describing* aspects of organizational culture. They are not of much use for generalizing and are virtually useless for testing hypotheses about relations between variables, for example, between organizational culture and organizational productivity or adaptability.

5. Be prepared to be criticized. Any strategy or tool used to identify organizational culture will be criticized by someone. It comes with the territory! So be clear in your purpose, as this chapter has emphasized, and be prepared to justify your selection.

CONCLUSION

Human resource managers should realize the important functions that culture and climate perform in their organizations, particularly in enabling or inhibiting change. Also, HR practitioners need to be alert to the distinctive natures of these two phenomena—and thus to the different purposes, methodologies, and strategies for identifying them.

Exhibit 6.1. Organizational Climate Index.

The following survey will be used to determine the state of our organizational climate. Rate each item on the basis of the following:

90–100 Excellent

80–89 Good

70–79 Fair

60–69 Poor

0–59 Very Poor

Your thoughtful, accurate responses will help make our organization stronger and a better place to work. If you have questions about the survey, please ask your supervisor. If you do not have sufficient information to answer a question or have no opinion on a topic, do not answer that question. Place your complete unsigned survey in the box located at _____

(location)

by _____ _____ .

(date)   (time)

Section I: Job

1. Our organization provides adequate training for new employees.   _____

2. Our organization provides adequate training for new employees to develop new skills.   _____

3. Job expectations are realistic and clearly stated.   _____

4. Our facilities are clean, safe, and functional.   _____

5. Information, materials, and equipment necessary to do my job are provided.   _____

6. My job is challenging and contains enough variety to be interesting. _____

7. The quantity of work associated with my job is not too much or too little.   _____

Subtotal   _____

Section II: Communication

1. Our organization has clear, well-written policies, procedures, and guidelines.   _____

2. There is an adequate amount of communication within our organization.   _____

3. Methods of communication within our organization are varied (individual contact, group meetings, memos/letters, newsletters, etc.).   _____

Exhibit 6.1. Organizational Climate Index, cont'd.

4. Communication within our organization is timely, accurate, and complete. _____

5. Two-way communication is encouraged and present in our organization. _____

6. There is regular direct person-to-person contact and opportunity for communication between supervisors and staff. _____

    Subtotal _____

Section III: Management

1. Effective planning is a characteristic of our organization. _____

2. Decision making is timely and effective. _____

3. People are given an opportunity to participate in decisions that affect them all. _____

4. Evaluations are handled in a fair and professional manner. _____

5. Disciplinary action is taken only when justified and actions taken are appropriate. _____

6. Grievance situations are handled in a fair and unbiased manner. _____

    Subtotal _____

Section IV: Motivation and Morale

1. Salaries are fair in relation to job requirements, experience, and quality of work. _____

2. Benefits are adequate. _____

3. Working relationships with coworkers are positive and enjoyable. _____

4. Working relationships with supervisors are positive and enjoyable. _____

5. There is tolerance for individual differences and dissent within our organization. _____

6. Good work brings appreciation and recognition. _____

7. A spirit of cooperation and respect for others exists in our organization. _____

8. Employees take pride in their work and our organization. _____

    Subtotal _____

    Organizational Climate Index _____

Source: J. L. Nave, "Gauging Organizational Climate," *Management Solutions*, 1986, *31*(6), 14–18. Reprinted with permission of American Management Association Periodicals.

Exhibit 6.2. **Survey of Organizational Climate.**

GENERAL SURVEY INSTRUCTIONS

Most of the questions in this survey will ask you:

- **How much you agree with things**
- **How important things are**
- **How often things happen**

Each of the questions is answered by circling a number.

For example:

How much do you agree or disagree with the following statements about your work group?

	Strongly Disagree				Strongly Agree
My group works well together.	1	2	3	4	(5)
In my group, everyone's opinion gets listened to.	1	2	3	(4)	5

In this example, Jane Doe was asked how much she agreed or disagreed with certain statements about her workgroup. She feels very strongly that her group works well together. However, she does not feel quite as strongly that everyone's opinion gets listened to although she does agree that this occurs.

Some of the questions may look like this:

	Not Important at All				Very Important
How important is the respect you receive from the people you work with?	1	2	3	(4)	5

In this example, there are written descriptions above only some of the numbers. However, any of the 5 numbers can be used. Jane Doe feels that the respect she receives is more than "somewhat important" but not quite "very important." So she answered by circling 4.

Before each set of questions, special directions will be given on how to answer. Please be sure to read the directions and the choices for the answers. You may believe that you do not have enough information to answer some of the questions. We ask that you answer every item that you can based on the information that you have. If none of the choices seems strictly appropriate, please choose the one that comes closest to your feeling or opinion.

Exhibit 6.2. Survey of Organizational Climate, cont'd.

The following statements are about your organization and the experiences you have had working there. How much do you agree or disagree with each statement?

	Strongly Disagree				Strongly Agree
1. In general, I am satisfied with my job.	1	2	3	4	5
2. Management is flexible enough to make changes when necessary.	1	2	3	4	5
3. People in this organization will do things behind your back.	1	2	3	4	5
4. The information that I get through formal channels helps me perform my job effectively.	1	2	3	4	5
5. In this organization it is unclear who has the formal authority to make a decision.	1	2	3	4	5
6. During this next year I will probably look for a new job outside of this organization.	1	2	3	4	5
7. Employees do not have much opportunity to influence what goes on in this organization.	1	2	3	4	5
8. Overall, this organization is effective in accomplishing its objective.	1	2	3	4	5
9. It takes too long to get decisions made.	1	2	3	4	5
10. I am told promptly when there is a change in policy, rules, or regulations that affects me.	1	2	3	4	5
11. This organization is responsive to the public interest.	1	2	3	4	5
12. When changes are made in this organization, the employees usually lose out in the end.	1	2	3	4	5
13. Employees here feel you can't trust this organization.	1	2	3	4	5
14. When a commitment or promise is made by management, it will be carried out.	1	2	3	4	5
15. I often think about quitting.	1	2	3	4	5
16. In this organization authority is clearly delegated.	1	2	3	4	5
17. All in all, I am satisfied with the work on my present job.	1	2	3	4	5

Exhibit 6.2. Survey of Organizational Climate, cont'd.

The next two questions ask about the frequency of conflict in your work setting.

	Never				Very Often
18. How often does conflict interfere with getting your work done?	1	2	3	4	5
19. How often have you personally had work conflicts?	1	2	3	4	5

The next few questions ask about your immediate supervisor—the individual that you report to directly. How much do you agree or disagree with each statement?

	Strongly Disagree				Strongly Agree
20. My job duties are clearly defined by my supervisor.	1	2	3	4	5
21. My supervisor encourages subordinates to participate in important decisions.	1	2	3	4	5
22. My supervisor knows the technical parts of his or her job well.	1	2	3	4	5
23. My supervisor gives me adequate feedback on how well I am performing.	1	2	3	4	5
24. My supervisor and I discuss things that I need to do for my career development.	1	2	3	4	5
25. My supervisor helps me solve work-related problems.	1	2	3	4	5
26. My supervisor demands that subordinates do high quality work.	1	2	3	4	5
27. My supervisor encourages me to help in developing work methods and job procedures.	1	2	3	4	5
28. When a conflict occurs between two people in my work group, my supervisor listens to both sides of the story.	1	2	3	4	5
29. My supervisor handles the administrative parts of his or her job well.	1	2	3	4	5
30. My job performance is carefully evaluated by my supervisor.	1	2	3	4	5

Exhibit 6.2. Survey of Organizational Climate, cont'd.

31. My performance rating presents a fair and accurate picture of my actual job performance.	1	2	3	4	5
32. My supervisor attempts to resolve conflicts in private with the persons involved.	1	2	3	4	5
33. My supervisor insists that subordinates work hard.	1	2	3	4	5
34. My supervisor sets clear goals for me in my present job.	1	2	3	4	5
35. My supervisor asks my opinion when a problem related to my work arises.	1	2	3	4	5
36. My supervisor deals with subordinates well.	1	2	3	4	5
37. My performance appraisal takes into account the most important parts of my job.	1	2	3	4	5
38. My supervisor keeps adequately informed about how I think and feel about things.	1	2	3	4	5
39. My supervisor helps to resolve conflicts that occur in my work group.	1	2	3	4	5
40. My supervisor maintains high standards of performance for his/her employees.	1	2	3	4	5

The following questions ask about the frequency of performance feedback. Please indicate the most appropriate response for each item.

	Never				Very Often
41. How often do you receive feedback from your supervisor for good performance?	1	2	3	4	5
42. How often would you like to receive feedback from your supervisor for good performance?	1	2	3	4	5
43. If you are a supervisor, how often do you give your subordinates feedback for good performance? (Leave item blank if you are not a supervisor.)	1	2	3	4	5
44. If you are a supervisor, how often do you give your subordinates feedback that helps them improve their performance? (Leave blank if you are not a supervisor.)	1	2	3	4	5

Exhibit 6.2. Survey of Organizational Climate, cont'd.

45. How often do you receive feedback from your supervisor that helps you improve your performance? 　1　2　3　4　5

46. How often would you like to receive feedback from your supervisor that helps you improve performance? 　1　2　3　4　5

Here are some statements that may or may not describe your workgroup, that is the people with whom you work most closely on a day-to-day basis. How much do you agree or disagree with each statement?

	Strongly Disagree				Strongly Agree
47. In my group, everyone's opinion gets listened to.	1	2	3	4	5
48. There are feelings among members of my workgroup that tend to pull the group apart.	1	2	3	4	5
49. The people I work with generally do a good job.	1	2	3	4	5
50. Coordination among workgroups is good in this organization.	1	2	3	4	5
51. If we have a decision to make everyone is involved in making it.	1	2	3	4	5
52. My coworkers encourage each other to give their best effort.	1	2	3	4	5
53. I have confidence and trust in my coworkers.	1	2	3	4	5
54. In this organization, competition between workgroups creates problems in getting work done.	1	2	3	4	5
55. I feel I am really part of my workgroup.	1	2	3	4	5
56. In this organization, conflict that exists between groups gets in the way of getting the job done.	1	2	3	4	5
57. Because of the problems that exist between groups, I feel a lot of pressure on the job.	1	2	3	4	5
58. My group works well together.	1	2	3	4	5

Exhibit 6.2. Survey of Organizational Climate, cont'd.

The next questions are about your job and the kind of work you do. How much do you agree or disagree with each statement as a description of your job?

	Strongly Disagree				Strongly Agree
59. I have a great deal of say over decisions concerning my job.	1	2	3	4	5
60. The things I do on my job are important to me.	1	2	3	4	5
61. I do not have enough training to do my job well.	1	2	3	4	5
62. The work I do on my job is meaningful to me.	1	2	3	4	5
63. I feel personally responsible for the work I do on my job.	1	2	3	4	5
64. I have too much work to do everything well.	1	2	3	4	5
65. I have all the skills I need in order to do my job.	1	2	3	4	5
66. My job is challenging.	1	2	3	4	5
67. I work hard on my job.	1	2	3	4	5
68. It's important to me that I do my job well.	1	2	3	4	5
69. I have a great deal of say over what has to be done on my job.	1	2	3	4	5
70. My job gives me the opportunity to use my own judgment and initiative.	1	2	3	4	5
71. My job makes good use of my abilities.	1	2	3	4	5
72. I feel that I am making a contribution to the overall objectives of my organization.	1	2	3	4	5
73. It always seems as if I have too much to do.	1	2	3	4	5
74. In general, I like working here.	1	2	3	4	5

Here are some things that could happen to people when they do their jobs especially well. How likely is it that each of these things would happen to you if you perform your job especially well?

	Not at All Likely				Very Likely
75. How likely is it that you will be promoted or given a better job if you perform especially well?	1	2	3	4	5

Exhibit 6.2. Survey of Organizational Climate, cont'd.

76. How likely is it that your own hard work will
lead to recognition as a good performer?   1   2   3   4   5

77. How likely is it that you will get a cash award
or unscheduled pay increase if you perform
your job especially well?   1   2   3   4   5

78. How likely is it that you will have better job
security if you perform especially well?   1   2   3   4   5

79. In general, the current level of conflict that exists in my work setting is

1	2	3	4	5
Very Low	Low	Moderate	High	Very High

80. Please rate the amount of effort you put into work activities during an
average workday.

1	2	3	4	5
No Effort		Some Effort		Extreme Effort

**This completes the survey. We appreciate your cooperation in taking the time
to answer these items thoughtfully.**

Source: Siegel and Turney, 1980.

References

Alexander, M. "Organizational Norms Opinionnaire." In J. W. Pfeiffer and J. E. Jones
(eds.), *The Annual Handbook for Group Facilitators.* San Francisco: Pfeiffer/
Jossey-Bass, 1978.

Al-Khalaf, A. M., and Ott, J. S. "TQM Implementation in Small U.S. Cities: Factors
That Affect Successful Implementation." Paper presented at the National Conference of the American Society for Public Administration, Kansas City, Mo., July
1994.

Allen, R. F., and Kraft, C. *The Organizational Unconscious.* Upper Saddle River, N.J.:
Prentice Hall, 1982.

Atkinson, P. E. *Creating Culture Change: The Key to Successful Total Quality Management.* San Francisco: Pfeiffer/Jossey-Bass, 1990.

Berger, P. L., and Luckmann, T. *The Social Construction of Reality.* New York: Doubleday, 1966.

Beyer, J. M., Dunbar, R. L., and Meyer, A. D. "Comment: The Concept of Ideology in
Organizational Analysis." *Academy of Management Review,* 1988, *13*(3), 104–127.

Boland, R. J., and Hoffman, R. "Humor in a Machine Shop: An Interpretation of Symbolic Action." In L. R. Pondy, P. J. Frost, G. Morgan, and T. C. Dandridge (eds.), *Organizational Symbolism.* Greenwich, Conn.: JAI Press, 1983.

Burns, G. "Measuring Climate to Create a Roadmap, Not a Report Card." *Journal for Quality and Participation,* 1996, *19*(1), 46–50.

Clark, B. R. *The Distinctive College: Antioch, Reed, and Swarthmore.* Hawthorne, N.Y.: Aldine de Gruyter, 1970.

Conway, J. A. "A Perspective on Organizational Cultures and Organizational Belief Structure." *Educational Administrative Quarterly,* 1985, *21*(4), 7–25.

Cooke, R. A., and Rousseau, D. M. "Behavioral Norms and Expectations: A Quantitative Approach to the Assessment of Organizational Culture." *Group and Organization Studies,* 1988, *13*(3), 245–273.

Culbertson, A. L., and Rosenfeld, P. "Understanding Sexual Harassment Through Organizational Surveys." In P. Rosenfeld, J. E. Edwards, and M. D. Thomas (eds.), *Improving Organizational Surveys.* Thousand Oaks, Calif.: Sage, 1993.

Cullen, J. B., Victor, B., and Bronson, J. W. "The Ethical Climate Questionnaire: An Assessment of Its Development and Validity." *Psychological Reports,* 1993, *73*(2), 667–674.

Dansereau, F., and Alutto, J. A. "Level-of-Analysis Issues in Climate and Culture Research." In B. Schneider (ed.), *Organizational Climate and Culture.* San Francisco: Jossey-Bass, 1990.

Desatnick, R. L. "Management Climate Surveys: A Way to Uncover an Organization's Culture." *Personnel,* 1986, *63*(5), 49–54.

Dougherty, D., and Kunda, G. "Photograph Analysis: A Method to Capture Organizational Belief Systems." In P. Gagliardi (ed.), *Symbols and Artifacts: Views of the Corporate Landscape.* Hawthorne, N.Y.: Walter de Gruyter, 1990.

Downey, H. K., Hellriegel, D., and Slocum, J. W., Jr. "Congruence Between Individual Needs, Organizational Climate, Job Satisfaction and Performance." *Academy of Management Journal,* 1975, *18*(1), 149–155.

Dunnington, R. A. "New Methods and Technologies in the Organizational Survey Process." In P. Rosenfeld, J. E. Edwards, and M. D. Thomas (eds.), *Improving Organizational Surveys.* Thousand Oaks, Calif.: Sage, 1993.

Durkheim, E. "Sociology and Philosophy." In G. Simpson (ed.), *Emile Durkheim.* New York: Crowell, 1963.

Dutcher, S. D., Hayashida, C. A., Sheposh, J. P., and Dickason, D. K. *Pacer Share: Fourth-Year Project Evaluation Report.* San Diego, Calif.: Organizational Systems Department, U.S. Navy Personnel Research and Development Center, 1992.

Dutka, S., and Frankel, L. R. "Measurement Errors in Organizational Surveys." *American Behavioral Scientist,* 1993, *36*(4), 472–484.

Edwards, J. E., and Thomas, M. D. "The Organizational Survey Process." *American Behavioral Scientist,* 1993a, *36*(4), 419–442.

Edwards, J. E., and Thomas, M. D. "The Organizational Survey Process: General Steps and Practical Considerations." In P. Rosenfeld, J. E. Edwards, and M. D. Thomas (eds.), *Improving Organizational Surveys.* Thousand Oaks, Calif.: Sage, 1993b.

Evered, R. "The Language of Organizations: The Case of the Navy." In L. R. Pondy, P. J. Frost, G. Morgan, and T. C. Dandridge (eds.), *Organizational Symbolism.* Greenwich, Conn.: JAI Press, 1983.

Feldman, M. S. "The Meanings of Ambiguity: Learning from Stories and Metaphors." In P. J. Frost and others (eds.), *Reframing Organizational Culture.* Thousand Oaks, Calif.: Sage, 1991.

Fink, E. L., and Chen, S.-S. "A Galileo Analysis of Organizational Climate." *Human Communication Research,* 1995, *21*(4), 494–521.

Gagliardi, P. (ed.). *Symbols and Artifacts: Views of the Corporate Landscape.* Hawthorne, N.Y.: Walter de Gruyter, 1990.

Ganesan, V. "Knowledge Workers: Organizational Climate and Motivation." *Psychological Reports,* 1983, *52*(3), 884–886.

Glick, W. H. "Conceptualizing and Measuring Organizational and Psychological Climate: Pitfalls in Multilevel Research." *Academy of Management Review,* 1985, *10*(3), 601–616.

Greenfield, T. B. "Leaders and Schools: Willfulness and Nonnatural Order in Organizations." In T. J. Sergiovanni and J. E. Corbally (eds.), *Leadership and Organizational Culture.* Urbana: University of Illinois Press, 1984.

Handy, C. *The Age of Paradox.* Boston: Harvard Business School Press, 1994.

Harrison, R. *Diagnosing Organizational Culture: Trainer's Manual.* San Francisco: Pfeiffer/Jossey-Bass, 1993.

Harrison, R., and Stokes, H. *Diagnosing Organizational Culture.* San Francisco: Pfeiffer/Jossey-Bass, 1992.

Hellriegel, D., and Slocum, J. W., Jr. "Organizational Climate: Measures, Research and Contingencies." *Academy of Management Journal,* 1974, *17*(2), 255–280.

Hofstede, G., Neuijeu, B., Ohayv, D. D., and Sanders, G. "Measuring Organizational Cultures: A Qualitative and Quantitative Study Across Twenty Cases." *Administrative Science Quarterly,* 1990, *35*(2), 286–316.

Hunt, M. "Freeing the Spirit of Public Service in All of Us." *Public Productivity and Management Review,* 1995, *18*(4), 397–406.

Jackofsky, E. F., and Slocum, J. W., Jr. "A Longitudinal Study of Climates." *Journal of Organizational Behavior,* 1988, *9*(4), 319–334.

Joyce, W. F., and Slocum, J. W., Jr. "Collective Climate: Agreement as a Basis for Defining Aggregate Climates in Organizations." *Academy of Management Journal,* 1984, *27*(4), 721–742.

Kerce, E. W., and Booth-Kewley, S. "Quality of Work Life Surveys in Organizations: Methods and Benefits." In P. Rosenfeld, J. E. Edwards, and M. D. Thomas (eds.), *Improving Organizational Surveys.* Thousand Oaks, Calif.: Sage, 1993.

Kopelman, R. E., Brief, A. P., and Guzzo, R. A. "The Role of Climate and Culture in Productivity." In B. Schneider (ed.), *Organizational Climate and Culture.* San Francisco: Jossey-Bass, 1990.

Landis, D., Dansby, M. R., and Faley, R. H. "The Military Equal Opportunity Climate Survey: An Example of Surveying in Organizations." In P. Rosenfeld, J. E. Edwards, and M. D. Thomas (eds.), *Improving Organizational Surveys.* Thousand Oaks, Calif.: Sage, 1993.

Lawler, E. E., III, Hall, D. T., and Oldham, G. R. "Organizational Climate: Relationship to Organizational Structure, Process and Performance." *Organizational Behavior and Human Performance,* 1974, *11*(1), 139–155.

Lipsky, M. *Street Level Bureaucracy: Dilemmas of the Individual in Public Services.* New York: Russell Sage Foundation, 1980.

Litwin, G. H., and Stringer, R. A. *Motivation and Organizational Climate.* Boston: Division of Research, Graduate School of Business Administration, Harvard University, 1968.

Louis, M. R. "Culture in Organizations: The Need for and Consequences of Viewing Organizations as Culture-Bearing Milieux." *Human Systems Management,* 1981, *2,* 246–258.

Marsden, P. V., Cook, C. R., and Knoke, D. "Measuring Organizational Structures and Environments." *American Behavioral Scientist,* 1994, *37*(7), 891–910.

Martin, J. "Stories and Scripts in Organizational Settings." In A. H. Hastorf and A. M. Isen (eds.), *Cognitive Social Psychology.* New York: Elsevier, 1982.

Martin, J., and Powers, M. E. "Truth or Corporate Propaganda: The Value of a Good War Story." In L. R. Pondy, P. J. Frost, G. Morgan, and T. C. Dandridge (eds.), *Organizational Symbolism.* Greenwich, Conn.: JAI Press, 1983.

Martin, J., and Siehl, C. "Organizational Culture and Counterculture." *Organizational Dynamics,* 1983, *12*(2), 52–64.

McNabb, D. E., and Sepic, F. T. "Culture, Climate, and Total Quality Management: Measuring Readiness for Change." *Public Productivity and Management Review,* 1995, *18*(4), 369–385.

Meyer, J. W. "Organizations as Ideological Systems." In T. J. Sergiovanni and J. E. Corbally (eds.), *Leadership and Organizational Culture.* Urbana: University of Illinois Press, 1984.

Moran, E. T., and Volkwein, J. F. "The Cultural Approach to the Formation of Organizational Climate." *Human Relations,* 1992, *45*(1), 19–47.

Nave, J. L. "Gauging Organizational Climate." *Management Solutions,* 1986, *31*(6), 14–18.

Ott, J. S. *The Organizational Culture Perspective.* Belmont, Calif.: Wadsworth, 1989.

Ott, J. S. "TQM, Organizational Culture, and Readiness for Change." *Public Productivity and Management Review,* 1995, *18*(4), 365–368.

Ott, J. S., and Shafritz, J. M. "Toward a Definition of Organizational Incompetence: A Neglected Variable in Organization Theory." *Public Administration Review,* 1994, *54*(4), 370–377.

Ott, J. S., and Shafritz, J. M. "The Perception of Organizational Incompetence." In A. Halachmi and G. Bouckaert (eds.), *The Enduring Challenges in Public Management: Surviving and Excelling in Public Management.* San Francisco: Jossey-Bass, 1995.

Pacanowsky, M. E., and O'Donnell-Trujillo, N. "Organizational Communication as Cultural Performance." *Communication Monographs,* 1983, *50*(2), 126–147.

Pettigrew, A. M. "On Studying Organizational Cultures." *Administrative Science Quarterly,* 1979, *24*(4), 570–581.

Pondy, L. R. "Leadership Is a Language Game." In M. W. McCall Jr. and M. M. Lombardo (eds.), *Leadership: Where Else Can We Go?* Durham, N.C.: Duke University Press, 1978.

Pondy, L. R. "The Role of Metaphors and Myths in Organization and in the Facilitation of Change." In L. R. Pondy, P. J. Frost, G. Morgan, and T. C. Dandridge (eds.), *Organizational Symbolism.* Greenwich, Conn.: JAI Press, 1983.

Pritchard, R. D., and Karasick, B. W. "The Effect of Organizational Climate on Managerial Job Performance and Job Satisfaction." *Organizational Behavior and Human Performance,* 1973, *9*(1), 126–146.

Putti, J. M., and Kheun, L. S. "Organizational Climate: Job Satisfaction Relationship in a Public Sector Organization." *International Journal of Public Administration,* 1986, *8*(3), 337–344.

Rosenfeld, P., Booth-Kewley, S., and Edwards, J. E. "Computer-Administered Surveys in Organizational Settings: Alternatives, Advantages, and Applications." *American Behavioral Scientist,* 1993, *36*(4), 485–511.

Rousseau, D. M. "Assessing Organizational Culture: The Case for Multiple Methods." In B. Schneider (ed.), *Organizational Climate and Culture.* San Francisco: Jossey-Bass, 1990.

Salancik, G. R., and Pfeffer, J. "Who Gets Power—and How They Hold On to It: A Strategic-Contingency Model of Power." *Organizational Dynamics,* 1977, *5,* 2–21.

Schein, E. H. *Organizational Culture and Leadership.* (2nd ed.) San Francisco: Jossey-Bass, 1993.

Shafritz, J. M., Riccucci, N. M., Rosenbloom, D. H., and Hyde, A. C. *Personnel Management in Government.* (4th ed.) New York: Dekker, 1992.

Siegel, A. L., and Turney, J. R. *Manager's Guide to Using the Survey of Organizational Climate.* Washington, D.C.: Workforce Effectiveness and Development Group, U.S. Office of Personnel Management, 1980.

Siehl, C., and Martin, J. "Organizational Culture: A Key to Financial Performance." In B. Schneider (ed.), *Organizational Climate and Culture.* San Francisco: Jossey-Bass, 1990.

Steele, F. I. *Physical Settings and Organization Development.* Reading, Mass.: Addison Wesley Longman, 1973.

Tagiuri, R. "The Concept of Organizational Climate." In R. Tagiuri and G. H. Litwin (eds.), *Organizational Climate: Exploration of a Concept.* Cambridge, Mass.: Harvard University Press, 1968.

Toulson, P., and Smith, M. "The Relationship Between Organizational Climate and Employee Perceptions of Personnel Management Practices." *Public Personnel Management*, 1994, *23*(3), 453–468.

Trice, H. M. *Occupational Subcultures in the Workplace.* Ithaca, N.Y.: ILR Press, 1993.

Trice, H. M., and Beyer, J. M. *The Cultures of Work Organizations.* Upper Saddle River, N.J.: Prentice Hall, 1993.

Turnipseed, D. L., and Turnipseed, P. H. "Assessing Organizational Climate: Exploratory Results with a New Diagnostic Model." *Leadership and Organization Development Journal*, 1992, *13*(5), 7–14.

U.S. General Accounting Office. *Organizational Culture: Techniques Companies Use to Perpetuate or Change Beliefs and Values.* GAO/NSIAD-92–105. Washington, D.C.: U.S. General Accounting Office, 1992.

Van Maanen, J. "The Fact of Fiction in Organizational Ethnography." In J. Van Maanen (ed.), *Qualitative Methodology.* Thousand Oaks, Calif.: Sage, 1983.

Van Maanen, J., Dabbs, J. M., Jr., and Faulkner, R. R. (eds.). *Varieties of Qualitative Research.* Thousand Oaks, Calif.: Sage, 1982.

Weick, K. E. "Educational Organizations as Loosely Coupled Systems." *Administrative Science Quarterly*, 1976, *21*(1), 1–19.

Whipp, R., Rosenfeld, R., and Pettigrew, A. "Culture and Competitiveness: Evidence from Two Mature U.K. Industries." *Journal of Management Studies*, 1989, *26*(6), 561–585.

Wilkins, A. L. "Organizational Stories as Symbols Which Control the Organization." In L. R. Pondy, P. J. Frost, G. Morgan, and T. C. Dandridge (eds.), *Organizational Symbolism.* Greenwich, Conn.: JAI Press, 1983.

Wilson, D. C. *A Strategy of Change: Concepts and Controversies in the Management of Change.* London: Routledge, 1992.

PART TWO

THE LEGAL ENVIRONMENT OF HUMAN RESOURCE MANAGEMENT

What Congress has commanded is that any tests used must measure the person for the job and not the person in the abstract.
—Chief Justice William Burger, *Griggs* v. *Duke Power Company*

The case of *Griggs* v. *Duke Power Company* clearly heralded the increasing legal concerns faced by human resource management. With the advent of the Equal Employment Opportunity Act of 1972, public human resource managers were greeted with a successive array of court cases challenging their recruitment, selection, and appraisal methodologies. Heretofore excluded or underrepresented groups demanded workforce representation, and these demands led to two decades of federal legislation and court decisions that transformed the public human resource management landscape. Gender stereotypes were challenged, workers with disabilities began to take their place in public organizations, and public employees began to more aggressively assert their constitutional rights in the workplace.

As public employees continue to turn to the law for workplace remedies, the increasing number of legal issues that public human resource management must comply with and help others comply with places new demands upon the human resource manager. Part Two of this *Handbook* provides the reader with a healthy appreciation for the complex legal environment in which human resource management is practiced in today's public organizations.

Chapter Seven, "Human Resource Management Legal Issues: An Overview," written by Gerald Hartman, Gregory Homer, and John Menditto, all practicing labor attorneys with the Washington, D.C., law firm of Swidler & Berlin, opens this section by reviewing major employment law issues and suggesting why the human resource manager should retain a knowledgeable labor attorney suitable for his or her organization. The authors explain major federal antidiscrimination laws such as the Equal Employment Opportunity Act of 1972, the Rehabilitation Act of 1973, and the Americans with Disabilities Act of 1990. Turning to a discussion of the constitutional rights and responsibilities of public employees and employers, they stress that public human resource management legal terrain is indeed rocky and that successful human resource managers must keep abreast of and actively respond to the constant changes in the field.

In Chapter Eight, "A Practical Guide to Affirmative Action," Norma Riccucci focuses on steps that human resource managers can take to increase workforce diversity. She states that "there is perhaps no function of human resource management that has generated more controversy and debate as affirmative action. . . . Within this tumultuous environment, human resource managers and personnelists are particularly challenged to manage affirmative action programs and policies for their organizations." Riccucci reviews relevant federal legislation and case law, discussing the political and managerial environment surrounding equal employment opportunity and affirmative action, and she presents specific guidance for practicing managers in the development of an affirmative action plan for a municipal government.

In Chapter Nine, "Sexual Harassment in the Workplace," Michele Hoyman and Lana Stein define sexual harassment, outline associated federal guidelines, and review relevant case law. They explain that "sexual harassment in the workplace is pervasive" and that fully one-half of all working women have experienced "some form of sexual harassment at some time on their jobs." Hoyman and Stein furnish clear guidance to practicing managers through the explication of a model action plan to ameliorate sexual harassment in public workplaces.

While U.S. workforces have expanded over the past several decades to include women and minorities, workers with disabilities have just recently won increased statutory claim to employment opportunities through passage of the Americans with Disabilities Act of 1990 (ADA). David Pfeiffer provides insight into this important piece of federal legislation in Chapter Ten, "Understanding the Americans with Disabilities Act." After reviewing the history of the disability movement and the related laws that preceded the passage of the ADA, he turns to specific ADA provisions, discussing their implementation and giving readers guidance and examples regarding the "reasonable accommodation" provisions in particular. Pfeiffer also outlines resources available to assist government organizations in proactively implementing the Americans with Disabilities Act.

Margaret Herrman's "Managing Conflict in the Workplace" (Chapter Eleven) concludes Part Two. A nationally recognized leader of the conflict resolution movement, Herrman explains how potential legal conflicts can be ameliorated with a cognizant and conscientious effort to resolve disputes in the workplace before legal action becomes necessary.

The chapters in Part Two emphasize that public human resource managers must not only understand but also be prepared to, as Hartman, Homer, and Menditto state, become "minor constitutional scholars" in order to successfully negotiate the constantly evolving legal environment of public human resource management. As statutory and case law evolves, it is imperative that these managers position themselves to ensure that their organizations are proactive rather than reactive in dealing with public human resource management legal issues.

CHAPTER SEVEN

Human Resource Management Legal Issues

An Overview

Gerald S. Hartman
Gregory W. Homer
John E. Menditto

Pick up a copy of any newspaper, and you are almost certain to see an article detailing another significant lawsuit involving employment discrimination. Most of the press headlines have involved claims against private-sector employers, such as the race discrimination lawsuits against Denny's Restaurants and Texaco, Inc. But public-sector employers have not been immune, as evidenced by the highly publicized sexual harassment lawsuit brought against President Clinton.

Perhaps overshadowed by the publicity given the few high-profile cases is the unprecedented rise in the overall number of employment claims being asserted. During the three-year period between 1991 and 1994, the number of charges of discrimination filed with the Equal Employment Opportunity Commission increased over 50 percent. Even more significantly, the number of employment discrimination lawsuits filed in federal court has more than doubled in the last four years.

Although not as well documented, constitutional claims against public-sector employers also have increased dramatically in recent years. These employment-related claims—raising such important issues as privacy and equal protection rights—have forced human resource management generalists to become minor constitutional scholars as they struggle to ensure that personnel policies and decisions follow the dictates of the U.S. Constitution.

This chapter introduces the public-sector human resource manager to the legal landscape where the personnel function now must operate. The first section provides a broad overview of the significant statutory laws governing the human resource management function, focusing on the federal discrimination laws that regulate public-sector employment. The second section analyzes the important constitutional issues that bear upon the public-sector personnel function.

FEDERAL DISCRIMINATION LAWS

Title VII

Title VII of the Civil Rights Act of 1964 is perhaps the best known of all the federal laws prohibiting employment discrimination. As amended, it prohibits discrimination on the basis of race, color, religion, sex, or national origin. Title VII applies to all personnel functions: hiring, discharging, compensation, promotion, classification, training, apprenticeship, employment referrals, union membership, and terms, conditions, or privileges of employment. In addition, under Title VII it is illegal to harass an employee based upon his or her sex, race, color, religion, or national origin.[1]

Statutory exceptions exist permitting discrimination where a person's sex, national origin, or religion is a bona fide occupational qualification (commonly referred to as a BFOQ) reasonably necessary to a business operation or where an institution of higher learning closely affiliated with a particular religion hires employees of that religion. Both of these exceptions, however, have been narrowly construed.

An employer is defined by Title VII as "a person engaged in an industry affecting commerce who has fifteen or more employees for each working day in each of twenty or more calendar weeks in the current or preceding calendar year, and any agent of such a person"[2] (*U.S. Code*, vol. 42, sec. 2000e). The Equal Employment Opportunity Act of 1972 extended the coverage of Title VII to state and local governments, as well as to federal employees, and Title VII's principles apply to government and private employers in a similar manner (*Dothard* v. *Rawlinson*, 433 U.S. 321 [1977]). The 1972 amendments to Title VII did not apply to employees of the House of Representatives and the Senate who were not in competitive service. Congress, however, extended the protections of Title VII to its own employees as part of the Civil Rights Act of 1991.

The Equal Employment Opportunity Commission is responsible for receiving and processing charges of discrimination filed by state and local government employees. The EEOC (and, in certain cases, the Merit Systems Protection Board) also has jurisdiction over Title VII claims by federal employees (other than Congressional employees).

Enforcement. A public-sector employee who believes that he or she has been the victim of employment discrimination covered by Title VII may bring suit in his or her own name as an "aggrieved party." However, this individual must first file a charge of discrimination with the Equal Employment Opportunity Commission and must provide that agency with an opportunity to resolve the grievance. Where there is no approved state or local agency with authority to investigate claims of discrimination (that is, a section 706 deferral agency), a complainant must file his or her charge with the EEOC within 180 days of the occurrence of the alleged unlawful employment practice in order for the charge to be timely. Where a qualified deferral agency exists, the charge must be filed with the EEOC within 300 days of the occurrence.

Charges must be in writing and made under oath or affirmation. Upon receipt of a charge the EEOC must serve notice on the party being charged (typically an employer, labor organization, or employment agency) within ten days. The EEOC must then investigate the charge and determine whether "reasonable cause" exists to believe that the charge is true.

A complainant must bring suit within ninety days after being notified by the EEOC of his or her right to sue. A right to sue notice will be issued when a no cause determination has been made by the EEOC, or this notice may be requested by the charging party at any time during the administrative process.

After a right to sue notice has been issued, a public-sector employee may commence a legal action on his or her own behalf. In addition, the U.S. Department of Justice may bring suit on behalf of the employee or, if the alleged discrimination affects a class of individuals, may bring a "pattern or practice" action against the public employer.

Remedies. Prior to the Civil Rights Act of 1991, remedies under Title VII were limited to back pay and, where appropriate, reinstatement. The Civil Rights Act of 1991 overhauled the remedial scheme of Title VII and thereby precipitated a wave of litigation under that statute.

Most notably, the Civil Rights Act of 1991 authorized the award of compensatory damages (for example, for emotional distress) where an employer has "engaged in unlawful intentional discrimination (not an employment practice that is unlawful because of its disparate impact)" (*U.S. Code*, vol. 42, sec. 1981). Although the Civil Rights Act of 1991 also authorized the award of punitive damages against private-sector employers, such damages may not be awarded against a state or local government employer. The act sets caps on the total award of compensatory and punitive damages, based upon the size of the employer. The current maximum award of compensatory damages against a public-sector employer is set at $300,000. Where a plaintiff seeks compensatory damages, a jury trial may be demanded.

Another significant aspect of Title VII's remedial scheme concerns court-awarded attorneys' fees. Title VII empowers a court to award the prevailing party its attorney fees and fees paid to experts. Notwithstanding Title VII's caveat that such awards are discretionary, the Supreme Court has ruled that a plaintiff "who succeeds in obtaining an injunction under that Title should ordinarily recover an attorney fee unless special circumstances would render such an award unjust" (*Newman* v. *Piggie Park Enterprises,* 390 U.S. 400 [1968]). A prevailing employer, however, may receive attorney fees only when the plaintiff's action was frivolous, unreasonable, or without foundation (*Christianburg Garment Co.* v. *E.E.O.C.,* 434 U.S. 412 [1979]).

Civil Rights Act of 1871

The Civil Rights Act of 1871, also known as the Ku Klux Klan Act, was passed pursuant to the Fourteenth Amendment, which provides that "no State shall make or enforce any law which shall abridge the privileges or immunities of citizens of the United States; nor shall any State deprive any person of life, liberty, or property without due process of law; nor deny any person within its jurisdiction the equal protection of the laws."

Section 1 of the Civil Rights Act of 1871 was codified at section 1983 of the *U.S. Code,* volume 42. Section 1983 provides that "every person who, under color of any statute, ordinance, regulation, custom or usage, of any State or Territory, or the District of Columbia, subjects, or causes to be subjected, any citizen of the United States or any person within the jurisdiction thereof to the deprivation of any rights, privileges or immunities secured by the Constitution and laws, shall be liable to the party injured in an action at law, suit in equity, or other proper procedure for redress." The purpose of section 1983 is to deter state actors from using the badge of their authority to deprive individuals of their federally guaranteed rights and to provide relief to victims if such deterrence fails (*Wyatt* v. *Cole,* 504 U.S. 158 [1992]).

Thus section 1983 applies only to persons who act under color of state law. The statute does not reach solely private conduct nor does it extend to conduct of federal agencies and officials in most instances.[3] Its precondition to suit that a defendant must act under color of state law is known as the state-action requirement. The state-action requirement clearly is met where government agencies and officials have engaged in discriminatory practices. Accordingly, section 1983 has been relied upon to remedy employment discrimination involving public schools, colleges, and universities; fire and police departments; public and semipublic hospitals; and other state agencies. A more difficult question of applicability occurs where a private institution is so heavily involved with the state that state action arguably is present. This sort of state involvement may come through receipt of public funds, through state licensing or regulation, through the private entity's engagement in functions normally exercised by the state, or through some combination of these factors (see *Rendell-Baker* v. *Kohn,* 457 U.S. 2764 [1982]).[4]

Another difficult question of applicability is what constitutes a "person" under section 1983? Although Congress could have created a right of action directly against state and local governments, as it did with the 1972 amendments to Title VII noted above, it did not do so explicitly under section 1983. Thus initially, section 1983 was construed not to authorize suits against state or local governments. In *Monroe* v. *Pape* (365 U.S. 167 [1961]), the Supreme Court—construing the statute literally—held that section 1983 covered government officials, not government entities. Seventeen years later, the Supreme Court overturned *Monroe* as it applied to local governments, in *Monell* v. *Department of Social Services* (436 U.S. 658 [1978]). The Court reasoned that "our analysis of the legislative history of the Civil Rights Act of 1871 compels the conclusion that Congress *did* intend municipalities and other local government units to be included among those persons to whom Section 1983 applies." However, the Supreme Court ruled in *Alabama* v. *Pugh* (438 U.S. 781 [1978]) that a state remains insulated from a section 1983 suit in federal court based upon the immunity granted states by the Eleventh Amendment. Thereafter, in *Will* v. *Michigan Department of State Police* (491 U.S. 58 [1989]), the Supreme Court—again relying upon a strict interpretation of section 1983—ruled that a state also is insulated from liability in state court.

However, these two Supreme Court rulings do not mean that a person who is the victim of illegal discrimination committed by a state has no recourse under section 1983. Government officials who implement such discrimination can be sued under section 1983 in their official and individual capacities. However, because damage awards may require payment from the state treasury and are therefore barred by the Eleventh Amendment, only prospective injunctive relief may be awarded against state officials sued in their official capacities.

Scope of Coverage. Where section 1983 does apply, it covers discrimination based on any of the five protected classifications set out in Title VII—race, color, religion, sex, or national origin—and a number of other protected classes. Thus the Supreme Court has held that a public employer may not discriminate against a noncitizen (*Sugarman* v. *Dougall*, 413 U.S. 634 [1973]). In addition, other distinctions—such as classifications based on age, disability, or sexual preference—have been found to violate section 1983 when such classifications are not rationally related to some legitimate state interest.

Enforcement. Unlike Title VII, section 1983 does not specify any procedural perquisites to filing suit. Thus a suit under section 1983 may be filed directly in either the federal district court or the appropriate state court of general jurisdiction.

Age Discrimination in Employment Act

The Age Discrimination in Employment Act (ADEA) was enacted in 1967 to prohibit discrimination in any aspect of employment against employees aged forty and over. The law originally protected only individuals between forty and sixty-five. However, in 1978, the maximum age was raised to seventy, and since January 1, 1987, the maximum age for the protected group has been eliminated.

Scope of Coverage. The ADEA defines an employer as "a person engaged in an industry affecting commerce who has twenty or more employees for each working day in each of twenty or more calendar weeks in the current or preceding calendar year" (*U.S. Code*, vol. 29, sec. 630). Coverage under the ADEA was extended to federal, state, and local government employers by the 1974 amendments to the Fair Labor Standards Act. State and local employment services are also covered. Under the EEOC's interpretive guidelines, so long as an agency regularly procures employees for at least one employer covered by the ADEA, that agency falls within the act's coverage with respect to all its activities, whether or not it performs those activities for covered employers.

Enforcement. Administrative enforcement of the ADEA is vested in the EEOC. Both private actions and actions brought by the EEOC may be filed under the ADEA. Like Title VII actions, ADEA suits may be brought in state or federal court and may be tried by a jury. Unlike Title VII remedies, however, ADEA remedies are limited to reinstatement, back pay (which may be doubled for "willful" violations), and attorney fees.

Rehabilitation Act of 1973

Scope of Coverage. The Rehabilitation Act of 1973 prohibits discrimination by federal government contractors or by recipients of federal financial assistance against individuals with disabilities. An individual with a disability is defined as any person who: "(i) has a physical or mental impairment which substantially limits one or more of such person's major life activities, (ii) has a record of such an impairment, or (iii) is regarded as having such an impairment." However, the Rehabilitation Act excludes from its definition "an individual who is currently engaging in the illegal use of drugs, when a covered entity acts on the basis of such use," and "any individual who is an alcoholic whose current use of alcohol prevents such individual from performing the duties of the job in question or whose employment, by reason of such current alcohol abuse, would constitute a direct threat to property or the safety of others" (*U.S. Code*, vol. 29, sec. 706).

Sections 793 and 794 of the Rehabilitation Act are the heart of the statute. Section 793 provides that all federal contracts in excess of $10,000 must contain a provision requiring affirmative action to employ and advance the employment of individuals with disabilities. Section 793 also prohibits employers holding federal government contracts in excess of $10,000 from discriminating against disabled individuals. Section 794 prohibits discrimination against qualified individuals with disabilities by programs that receive federal financial assistance. This includes all aspects of state and local government programs, including employment.

Enforcement. Under section 793(b), any individual with a disability may file a claim with the Department of Labor against a covered contractor. The Department of Labor is responsible for investigating such claims and taking action as warranted by the investigation.

Americans with Disabilities Act of 1990

Scope of Coverage. The Americans with Disabilities Act of 1990 (ADA) is the most comprehensive piece of civil rights legislation to be passed since Title VII. The ADA proscribes discrimination on the basis of an individual's disability. This proscription extends to hiring, promoting, prejob testing, training, and other "terms, conditions, and privileges of employment." In addition, the ADA mandates that individuals with disabilities have equal access to all types of goods, services, public facilities, accommodations, interstate communications, and transportation, whether state or privately operated.

The ADA defines discrimination to include both intentional and unintentional discrimination. It also requires employers to reasonably accommodate employees' disabilities unless to do so would result in undue hardship to the employer. "Reasonable accommodation" is defined to include restructuring jobs, modifying work schedules, hiring readers or interpreters, reassigning job incumbents to vacant positions, making facilities readily accessible, acquiring equipment, and modifying testing materials and current policies. The ADA adopts the term "qualified individual with a disability" found in the Rehabilitation Act and defines this term to include all persons with a disability who with or without reasonable accommodation are capable of performing a particular job. Under the act, individuals who use illegal drugs are not considered disabled.

The ADA covers state and local government employers who employ fifteen or more individuals for twenty or more calendar weeks annually. It also covers state and local entities and their agents when these entities provide public services. The employers the ADA exempts from its coverage are the United States and any bona fide 501(c) tax-exempt private membership club.

Defenses. An employer is not required to "reasonably accommodate" an individual with a disability if such accommodation would constitute an "undue hardship." Undue hardship includes any action that requires significant difficulty or expense, in light of

1. The nature and cost of the accommodation
2. The overall financial resources of the facility, or facilities, including number of persons employed and impact upon the facility

3. The overall financial resources of the covered entity, including the size of the business

4. The type of employer operation, including the composition, structure, and functions of the workforce and the geographical separateness and administrative or fiscal relationship of the facility in question to the covered entity

In addition, an employer may defend the application of a qualification standard or test that tends to screen out individuals with disabilities, on the ground that the test is "job-related and consistent with business necessity." Also, the ADA allows employers to refuse to hire individuals with infectious and communicable diseases as defined by the secretary of Health and Human Services if such prospective employees would handle food.

Enforcement. Enforcement of Title I of the ADA is through the provisions of Title VII of the Civil Rights Act of 1964, as amended by the Civil Rights Act of 1991, and includes the requirement that a charge of discrimination be filed timely with the EEOC. Prevailing public-sector employees may be awarded back pay, compensatory damages (subject to the statutory caps), injunctive relief, and attorney's fees.

FEDERAL WAGE, HOUR, AND BENEFIT LAWS

Fair Labor Standards Act

The Fair Labor Standards Act (FLSA) was enacted in 1938 to regulate minimum wages and overtime pay and to restrict "oppressive child labor" practices in the work place. The act has been amended several times since its initial passage, and covers all individuals engaged "in commerce or in the production of goods for commerce or in any enterprise engaged in commerce or in the production of goods for commerce." FLSA applies to almost all categories of federal, state, and local government employees. However, police officers and firefighters are subject to different overtime measuring provisions, due to their unique hours of employment. For all other categories, overtime at the rate of one and one-half times the normal hourly rate must be paid for all hours in excess of forty in any work week. However, overtime need not be paid to "exempt" employees.

The administrative body authorized to enforce FLSA is the Wage and Hour Division of the Department of Labor. Remedies available are injunctions, payment of unpaid wages, liquidated damages, and criminal penalties. Typically, the Department of Labor solicitor's office pursues wage claims before an administrative law judge. In addition, actions by state employees for FLSA violations may be brought directly in state court by aggrieved individuals.[5]

Family and Medical Leave Act

The Family and Medical Leave Act of 1993 (FMLA) is the first broad-based federal law providing employees with rights to take leave from work in order to care for themselves or family members. It is intended to allow employees to balance their work and family life by taking reasonable amounts of medically or family-necessitated leave.

Employees of federal, state, and local government generally have the same leave rights as employees of private companies under the FMLA. Thus eligible public employees, in general, may take up to twelve weeks of leave every twelve months to care for a newborn or newly placed adopted or foster child, for a seriously ill family member, or for the employee's own health. The employee can choose, or be required by the employer, to substitute accrued paid leave for unpaid leave. With limited exceptions, the employee is entitled to return to the same or an equivalent position following the leave period. The FMLA applies to all public employers who employ fifty or more employees at a single worksite or employ fifty or more employees at worksites within a seventy-five-mile radius of each other.[6]

State and local employees seeking enforcement of the FMLA may file an administrative complaint with the Department of Labor or may commence a lawsuit in federal court. Federal employees may seek enforcement through grievance procedures established by a collective bargaining agreement or agency management. Remedies are limited generally to lost wages (doubled where the employer fails to demonstrate that it acted in good faith) and attorney's fees.

Special FMLA rules apply to elementary and secondary teachers who take leaves near the end of the academic term or whose intermittent leave or leave on a reduced work schedule amounts to more than 20 percent of the total number of working days during the leave period. Thus instructional employees who start a leave near the end of a term can sometimes be required to continue it through the end of the term. When this happens, the employee continues to enjoy the same employment and benefit protections. In addition, instructional employees who request intermittent leave for a planned medical treatment may have to choose either (1) a temporary transfer to an available alternative position or (2) leave for a continuous period not to exceed the duration of the planned medical treatment, if the requested intermittent leave is for more than 20 percent of the total number of workdays in a leave period.

State and Local Laws

State and local governments remain free to regulate personnel matters over and above the federal requirements. In many cases, state and local law may provide greater or different protections to certain groups, allow different remedies for unlawful acts, and provide different enforcement mechanisms. The trend in this direction has accelerated as many jurisdictions perceive federal government unwillingness or inability to adequately protect employees in such areas as sexual preference and drug testing. Thus public employers and human resource managers need to be familiar with the laws peculiar to their jurisdiction.

CONSTITUTIONAL CONSTRAINTS ON THE PUBLIC EMPLOYER

Statutory law only is one-half of the legal landscape facing the human resource manager. In addition, he or she must be knowledgeable about the constitutional considerations that affect the public human resource management function. This section first describes the theoretical background of constitutional law as it relates to the government as employer. Then it discusses current protections afforded government employees with respect to the constitutional issues of freedom of speech, procedural due process, freedom of association, right of privacy, and equal protection.

Constitutional Background

The U.S. Supreme Court's analysis of constitutional law as it relates to the government as employer has passed through three theoretical stages over the past century (see "Developments in the Law—Public Employment," 1984, p. 1738). During the first stage the Court maintained that because a public employee has no "right" to public employment, an employer can condition employment on any reasonable terms, including the employee's relinquishment of certain constitutional rights. During this stage, courts held that the "privilege" of public employment could be withdrawn or extended at the whim of the public employer, in much the same way as private employers could act under the employment at will doctrine (see *Adler* v. *Board of Education*, 342 U.S. 485 [1952]).[7]

The notion that constitutional protections turn upon whether a government benefit is characterized as a right or a privilege was undermined, and eventually rejected, in a series of freedom of association cases decided by the Supreme Court during the 1950s and early 1960s. In *Wieman* v. *Updegraff* (344 U.S. 183 [1952]), the Court invalidated a state statute requiring public employees to take an oath denying past affiliation with Communists; in *Shelton* v. *Tucker* (364 U.S. 479 [1960]), the Court invalidated a state statute requiring teachers to disclose all associational ties; and in *Keyishian* v. *Board of Regents* (385 U.S. 589 [1967]), the Court invalidated a state statute that barred members of certain "subversive" groups from teaching. These freedom of association cases led to the Court's landmark freedom of speech decision, *Pickering* v. *Board of Education* (391 U.S. 563 [1967]), where the Court, employing a balancing test, held that a public school teacher could not be discharged for speaking out on a matter of public interest. The Court's reasoning left no doubt that the right-privilege test no longer applied:

"The theory that public employment which may be denied altogether may be subjected to any conditions, regardless of how unreasonable, has been uniformly rejected." *Keyishian* v. *Board of Regents* (385 U.S. at 605). At the same time it cannot be gainsaid that the State has interests as an employer in regulating the speech of its employees that differ significantly from those it possesses in connection with regulation of the speech of the citizenry in general. The problem in any case is to arrive at a balance between the interests of the teacher, as a citizen, in commenting upon matters of public concern and the interest of the State, as an employer, in promoting the efficiency of the public services it performs through its employees.

This second stage has been termed the *individual rights* approach because of the Supreme Court's recognition that public employees retain certain individual rights when they enter government employment.

The Court today continues to apply the *Pickering* balancing test in the arena of free speech, procedural due process, and a host of other constitutional areas involving public employment, although its continued application has been characterized by greater deference to the government's need to manage its workforce effectively so that it may provide public services efficiently. Thus this third stage of analysis has been termed the *public service* model.

Freedom of Speech

As noted above, the *Pickering* balancing test continues to be applied by the Supreme Court in its analysis of what constitutes constitutionally protected free speech. The Supreme Court more recently applied this test in the public employment context in *Rankin* v. *McPherson* (483 U.S. 378 [1987]). This case concerned the firing of Ardith McPherson, a deputized clerical employee in the law enforcement office of Harris County, Texas. On March 30, 1981, McPherson heard a radio report of an attempt to assassinate then-president Ronald Reagan. Upon hearing the report, McPherson engaged a coworker in a conversation in which McPherson expressed the opinion, "I hope if they go for him again, they get him." McPherson's remark was overheard by another employee, who reported it to the chief law enforcement officer, Walter Rankin. In response to the remark, Rankin discharged McPherson.

The *Rankin* Court began its analysis by noting that the threshold question was whether McPherson's remark might be characterized as speech on a matter of "public concern." Rarely will purely private or personal speech enjoy constitutional protection. Here, the majority concluded that statement dealt with a matter of public concern because it was made in the course of a conversation addressing the policies of the president's administration and it came on the heels of a news bulletin regarding an attempted assassination of the president.

Next, the Court employed the *Pickering* balancing test to conclude that Rankin's interest in discharging McPherson was outweighed by her rights under the First Amendment. In applying the test, the Court focused its analysis on the nature of the position held by McPherson:

> Where, as here, an employee serves no confidential, policymaking, or public contact role, the danger to the agency's successful functioning from that employee's private speech is minimal. We cannot believe that every employee in Constable Rankin's office, whether computer operator, electrician, or file clerk, is equally required, on pain of discharge, to avoid any statement susceptible of being interpreted by the Constable as an indication that the employee may be unworthy of employment in his law enforcement agency. At some point, such concerns are so removed from the effective functioning of the public employer that they cannot prevail over the free speech rights of the public employee.

Thus *Rankin* cautions public human resource managers to closely review personnel decisions based upon employee speech. Such a review should consider (1) whether the speech involved a matter of public concern; (2) whether the context in which the statements were made (including the manner, time, and place of the statements and the position held by the employee) was significant; (3) whether the statement impairs discipline by superiors or harmony among coworkers; and (4) whether the statement impedes the performance of the speaker's duties or interferes with the enterprise's regular operation.

Procedural Due Process

The requirements of procedural due process apply only to the deprivation of interests encompassed by the Fifth and Fourteenth Amendments' protection of life, liberty, and property. Thus in the realm of public employment, to merit the protection of due process the employee must possess a "property" or "liberty" interest that has been threatened by some government action (*Board of Regents v. Roth,* 408 U.S. 564 [1972]). If the employee enjoys such an interest, he or she is entitled to a predeprivation hearing whose requisites the courts are to determine on a case-by-case basis through a balancing test that pits the employee's interests against those of the government.

Property. The *Roth* Court established that a public employee may have property interest in continued employment, but such an interest must be based upon existing rules of law, such as state law, that secure certain rights and support claims of entitlement to those rights. In *Roth,* the Court found that a nontenured state university professor had no property interest in continued employment: "the terms of the respondent's appointment secured absolutely no interest in reemployment for the next year. . . . Nor, significantly, was there any state statute or University rule or policy that secured his interest in reemployment or that created any legitimate claim to it." The Court concluded that "in these circumstances, the [employee] surely had an abstract concern in being rehired, but he did not have a property interest sufficient to require the University authorities to give him a hearing when they declined to renew his contract of employment."

Subsequent to *Roth* the Court's decisions initially placed further limitations on a public employee's property interest in continued employment and the process due when such a right exists. In *Arnett* v. *Kennedy* (416 U.S. 134 [1974]), for example, a former federal employee challenged the procedures by which he was dismissed. The Court, in a plurality opinion, held that where the legislation conferring the property right also sets out the procedural mechanism for enforcing that right, the two cannot be separated:

> The employee's statutorily defined right is not a guarantee against removal without cause in the abstract, but such a guarantee as enforced by the procedures which Congress has designated for the determination of cause. . . .
>
> Where the grant of a substantive right is inextricably intertwined with the limitations on the procedures which are to be employed in determining that right, a litigant in the position of appellee must take the bitter with the sweet.

The "bitter with the sweet" approach was rejected eleven years later in *Cleveland Board of Education* v. *Loudermill* (470 U.S. 532 [1985]). In *Loudermill,* the Supreme Court firmly established that procedural due process will usually apply where a public employee is dismissed, even if the process due is limited by federal statute. The Court went on to hold that such a process will usually require "a pretermination opportunity to respond" coupled with sufficient posttermination administrative procedures to ensure constitutional fairness.

Liberty. In *Roth,* the Court expansively defined liberty to encompass the freedom to contract, marry, worship, and enjoy other "privileges long recognized . . . as essential to the orderly pursuit of happiness by free men." Applying this definition, however, the Court found that only two liberty concerns can trigger administrative hearing rights following the discharge of a public employee: the employee's interest in his or her good standing in the community and interest in being able to pursue a career elsewhere.

Since *Roth,* the Supreme Court has further limited its definition of liberty interests. To establish such an interest, a public employee must now (1) demonstrate that he or she was stigmatized in connection with an alteration of employment status; (2) allege that the stigma arose from substantially false characterizations of the employee or his or her conduct; and (3) show that the damaging characterizations were made public through channels other than employee-initiated litigation ("Developments in the Law—Public Employment," 1984, p. 1789).

Freedom of Association

The First Amendment guarantees that the government will not infringe on the right of citizens to freely associate. Thus it is now well settled that public employees enjoy the right to join organizations, as well as the right to refrain from such associations. But to what extent may a public employer condition employment on affiliation with a particular political party?

Prior to 1976, it was generally understood that political patronage dismissals did not violate a public employee's constitutional rights. However, in *Elrod* v. *Burns* (427 U.S. 347 [1976]), the plurality opinion of a divided Supreme Court applied the doctrine of unconstitutional conditions in determining that patronage dismissals constitute impermissible violations of the First Amendment rights to freedom of association and freedom of political belief, unless an employee's political beliefs would interfere with the discharge of his or her public duties. In *Elrod*, the Court held that the newly elected Democratic sheriff of Cook County, Illinois, had violated the constitutional rights of certain non–civil service employees by discharging them "because they did not support and were not members of the Democratic Party and had failed to obtain the sponsorship of one of its leaders." In his concurrence, Justice Stewart noted that the duties of the public employees were "nonpolicymaking" and "nonconfidential."

Four years later, a majority of the Court relied upon *Elrod* in concluding that two county assistant public defenders could not be discharged based upon their party affiliation (*Branti* v. *Finkel*, 445 U.S. 507 [1980]). The Court reasoned that "the ultimate inquiry is not whether the label 'policymaker' or 'confidential' fits a particular position; rather, the question is whether the hiring authority can demonstrate that party affiliation is an appropriate requirement for the effective performance of the public office involved."

Elrod and *Branti* establish that a public employer will rarely be able to justify an employee's dismissal based upon party affiliation. But does the rule of *Elrod* and *Branti* extend to other personnel actions? In *Rutan* v. *Republican Party of Illinois* (110 S. Ct. 2729 [1990]), the Court answered this query in the affirmative. There, the Court held that "the rule of *Elrod* and *Branti* extends to promotion, transfer, recall, and hiring decisions based on party affiliation and support."

Right of Privacy

The Fourth Amendment to the U.S. Constitution prohibits the U.S. government from engaging in unreasonable searches and seizures and establishes, derivatively, a right to privacy. These protections and positive rights apply to the states and their agents by virtue of the Fourteenth Amendment.

In the public employment setting the issue of an employee's right to privacy has been most recently and vociferously raised with respect to constitutional challenges to employee drug- or alcohol-testing programs. These challenges have been asserted against federal employers; state employers, such as hospitals and universities; and local governments. In such instances the courts typically have concluded that the state action requirements of the Fourth and Fourteenth Amendments have been met when a government entity (1) seeks to test its own employees or applicants for employment or (2) seeks to regulate private actors by requiring that they test their own employees.

In Fourth Amendment search and seizure cases in general, the government's interest in the challenged activity is balanced against the individual's privacy expectations to determine whether the particular intrusion is *reasonable*. Generally, a substance-abuse testing program imposed by a government entity will survive a constitutional challenge if the program is substantially related to legitimate government interests and is no more intrusive than is reasonably necessary to serve those interests.

In *Skinner* v. *Railway Labor Executives' Association* (489 U.S. 602 [1989]), the Supreme Court specifically considered the search and seizure implications of substance abuse testing required in the private sector as a result of federal regulation. The Court recognized that government-mandated urinalysis testing invades legitimate privacy expectations and therefore amounts to a search when given to detect illicit drug or alcohol use. Nevertheless, the Court upheld Federal Railroad Administration rules requiring railroad employee blood and urine testing in the event of an accident and permitting similar tests when there is a reasonable suspicion that an employee is impaired by alcohol or drugs. According to the Court, the expectation of privacy is diminished by employment in a pervasively regulated industry and when the compelling government interest in public safety in that industry warrants the use of drug testing, even when there is no suspicion of drug use by specific individuals.

In the companion case of *National Treasury Employees Union* v. *Von Raab* (489 U.S. 656 [1989]), the Supreme Court applied a similar analysis in upholding U.S. Customs Service rules that make testing for the illegal use of drugs a job condition for positions involving drug interdiction, carrying a firearm, or handling classified material. (See also *Vernonia School District 47* v. *Acton,* 115 S. Ct. 2386 [1995], which upheld random, suspicionless testing of high school athletes against a Fourteenth Amendment challenge.)

Although both the *Skinner* and *Von Raab* opinions found the probable cause and search warrant requirements inapplicable to public-sector testing programs and allowed random testing absent reasonable suspicion in those industries that unquestionably affect public safety, the Supreme Court also indicated that such determinations must be made case by case. Thus a drug-testing program's ability to pass constitutional muster will depend upon the scope of the particular intrusion, the manner in which it is conducted, the justification for initiating it (apart from the normal need for law enforcement), and the place in which it is conducted.

Applying this type of analysis, courts both before and after the *Skinner* and *Von Raab* decisions have reached varying conclusions about the constitutionality of government-imposed testing programs. For example, in *Transport Workers Local 234* v. *Southeastern Pa. Transp. Auth.* (863 F. 2d 1110 [3d Cir. 1988]), the court upheld the state transportation authority's use of random drug and alcohol testing of employees in safety-sensitive positions but rejected return-to-work testing; in *McDonnell v. Hunter* (809 F. 2d 1302 [8th Cir. 1987]), the court upheld testing for state prison employees in medium- and maximum-security facilities who have regular contact with prisoners; in *Fowler v. New York City Dep't of Sanitation* (704 F. Supp. 1264 [S.D.N.Y. 1989]), the court upheld pre-employment and follow-up testing during city sanitation workers' probationary periods because of the potential harm if they operated sanitation trucks while under the influence of drugs; in *Burka v. New York City Transit Auth.* (739 F. Supp. 814 [S.D.N.Y. 1990]), the court upheld the city transit authority's periodic testing of employees in safety-sensitive positions and testing of employees in non-safety-sensitive positions following an on-duty "incident" or accident, but rejected testing of employees in non-safety-sensitive positions upon their return to work after a long absence, their application for promotion, or during periodic physical exams; and in *Penny v. Kennedy* (915 F. 2d 1065 [6th Cir. 1990]), the court upheld the plan of Chattanooga, Tennessee, to have mandatory drug testing of city police and firefighters.

In *National Treasury Employees Union v. Yeutter* (918 F. 2d 968 [D.C.C. 1990]) and *Hartness v. Bush* (919 F. 2d 170 [D.C.C. 1990]), the U.S. Court of Appeals for the District of Columbia Circuit held that a portion of a federal drug-testing program exposing all Department of Agriculture employees to urinalysis was unconstitutional. In *National Treasury,* the court stated that only testing done on reasonable suspicion of on-duty drug use or drug-impaired work performance would be allowed unless the worker held a safety- or security-sensitive job. The court allowed the random drug testing of certain motor vehicle operators, however. Because the drug testing was part of the Drug-Free Workplace Program and the government was disclaiming any law enforcement purpose in its testing, the government's interest in employee drug testing extended only as far as work performance and work responsibilities. Therefore, the court held that absent a safety- or security-sensitive job, random testing would not be within the government's legitimate interest, and testing would be allowed only on a reasonable suspicion of drug use. Government employees who have access to secret information or who have secret clearances may, however, be subject to random drug testing regardless of their frequency of exposure to secret documents. In *Hartness,* the court held that national security interests are involved in ensuring that persons who have access to secret documents do not become the victims of blackmail or coercion due to drug use and that these security interests outweigh individual Fourth Amendment and privacy interests.

Equal Protection

The Fourteenth Amendment proscribes the states from enforcing any law denying persons "the equal protection of the laws," and the due process clause of the Fifth Amendment contains an equal protection component prohibiting the

U.S. government from doing the same. Public employees have used the equal protection clause as grounds for myriad claims opposing adverse personnel policies and actions. This section discusses equal protection law as it relates to one area currently of particular concern to public personnel managers: reverse discrimination.

Reverse Discrimination: An Introduction. One of the most highly publicized and emotionally charged issues in human resource management is reverse discrimination. It has been raised in many contexts, from admission to professional schools, to the granting of government contracts, to employment. In the public employment context, white male employees and job applicants have brought suits under Title VII, section 1983, and the equal protection clause, challenging preferences for minorities and females designed to remedy past discrimination. As a result the Supreme Court and lower federal courts have grappled with the conflict between prohibitions of preferences on the basis of race and sex on the one hand and the need to redress past discrimination against minorities and females on the other. Federal court treatment of this issue has developed along two lines of analysis: whether the affirmative action plan challenged was voluntarily imposed or whether it was imposed pursuant to a court order.

Voluntary Programs. Affirmative action programs voluntarily instituted by public employers face a more rigorous test of their constitutionality than those implemented pursuant to court order, although—as demonstrated by the leading case in the area—such voluntarily implemented programs can be upheld. In *Johnson* v. *Transportation Agency, Santa Clara County* (480 U.S. 616 [1987]), the Court rejected the reverse discrimination claim of a male who scored slightly higher on an interview than the female who was selected for promotion. The Court held that the female's selection was justified by the manifest imbalance between the number of women in the job classification (none) compared to the number of women in the labor market. Because women were concentrated in traditionally female jobs and significantly underrepresented in traditionally male categories, the employer could properly consider, among other factors, the gender of the qualified candidates. In order to be justifiable, however, an employer's affirmative action plan must not authorize blind "hiring by the numbers" in order to meet a numerical goal and must not unnecessarily trammel the rights of male employees or create an absolute bar to their advancement. *Johnson* did not specifically address whether the affirmative action plan voluntarily adopted by Santa Clara County was constitutional. However, drawing on the Court's analysis in *Johnson* and other nonemployment Supreme Court cases involving equal protection analysis, it is possible to form a general understanding of the characteristics necessary for a voluntary affirmative action plan to pass constitutional muster: (1) voluntary affirmative action at the state and local level must not be based upon quotas or quota-like approaches, must serve a compelling state interest, and must be narrowly tailored so as to not unnecessarily trammel the rights of others; and (2) voluntary affirmative action at the federal level must serve important government objectives and must be substantially related to the attainment of those objectives.

The U.S. Supreme Court recently indicated that it will continue to subject voluntary affirmative action efforts to close scrutiny. In *Adarand Contractors, Inc. v. Peña, Secretary of Transportation* (115 S. Ct. 2097 [1995]), the Court held that explicit race-based preferences in government contracts were unconstitutional unless there is a compelling government interest to institute such a program and unless the program is narrowly tailored to serve that interest.

Court-Ordered Programs. Remedial affirmative action is designed to redress proven past discrimination by an employer against members of a particular group. Such remedial schemes typically are implemented pursuant to court order and usually allow employers broad latitude to rely upon race or gender in making personnel decisions.

The leading case, *United States v. Paradise* (480 U.S. 149 [1987]), decided the same term as *Johnson*, upheld the remedial affirmative action program at issue. Under that program, African American state troopers in Alabama were promoted one-for-one for each white state trooper promoted. The Court found that such a broad race-conscious order was justified by the state's compelling interest in eradicating the pervasive, systematic, and obstinate discriminatory exclusion of blacks by the Alabama Department of Public Safety.

The Supreme Court plurality opinion did note significant constitutional constraints on the design of remedial affirmative action. Thus in a concurring opinion, Justice Powell explained that such constraints required attention to five factors:

> (i) the efficacy of alternative remedies; (ii) the planned duration of the remedy; (iii) the relationship between the percentage of minority workers to be employed and the percentage of minority group members in the relevant population or workforce; (iv) the availability of waiver provisions if the hiring plan could not be met; and (v) the effect of the remedy on innocent third parties.

CONCLUSION

This chapter presented an overview of the major statutory laws and constitutional issues currently influencing public-sector employment. But case precedent in the field of employment law is continually redefining the personnel rules that public employers must follow. As a result, public-sector employers must reevaluate the way in which they staff and manage their human resource function. Gone are the days when public organizations could afford to transfer clerical employees untrained in personnel issues into human resource management positions. Gone too are the days when human resource professionals could rely upon less than up-to-date training to guide their decision-making processes.

One product of this revolution is the need for the human resource manager to establish a professional relationship with experienced employment counsel. Just as individuals in the field of human resources have been forced to specialize as a result of the explosion in employment litigation, so too have members of the legal profession. Attorneys who practice employment law now faithfully follow emerging trends in employment litigation. This allows them, as employment counsel, to alert human resource managers of developments that otherwise might go unnoticed. Simply put, human resource managers who forego the services of experienced labor counsel may find they are applying obsolete personnel rules and exposing themselves and their organizations to unnecessary risk.

Notes

1. Sexual harassment is the most prevalent form of prohibited harassment, although federal law prohibits harassment based upon all protected classifications. The Equal Employment Opportunity Commission has issued extensive guidelines, defining in detail what constitutes sexual harassment and the circumstances under which the EEOC would hold the employer responsible for such conduct. Briefly, unwelcome sexual advances, requests for sexual favors, and other verbal or physical conduct of a sexual nature constitute sexual harassment when "(1) submission to such conduct is made either explicitly or implicitly a term or condition of an individual's employment; (2) submission to or rejection of such conduct by an individual is used as the basis for employment decisions affecting such individual; or (3) such conduct has the purpose or effect of unreasonably interfering with an individual's work performance or creating an intimidating, hostile, or offensive working environment" (Equal Employment Opportunity Commission, 1997).

2. Whether the phrase "any agent of such person" establishes individual liability for supervisors engaging in discriminatory conduct is an issue that has divided the courts. Some courts have interpreted this provision to allow individuals to be sued personally under Title VII, along with the employer (see, for example, *Hamilton v. Rodgers*, 791 F. 2d 439 [5th Cir. 1986]; *Paroline v. Unisys Corp.*, 50 Fair Empl. Prac. Cas. 306 [4th Cir. 1989]). Other courts have disagreed, finding that the provision is intended only to incorporate the doctrine of *respondeat superior* liability into the statute (see *Smith v. St. Bernard's Regional Medical Ctr.*, 19 F. 3d 1254 [8th Cir. 1994] and *Busby v. Orlando*, 931 F. 2d 764 [11th Cir. 1991]).

3. Federal officials, however, may be held liable for acts of employment discrimination where such actions amount to a violation of the Constitution (see *Davis v. Passman*, 442 U.S. 228 [1979], which allowed a secretary to maintain a Fifth Amendment due process claim where she alleged that a U.S. Congressman terminated her employment due to her gender).

4. In *Rendell-Baker*, employees of a privately owned school who were terminated for protesting school policies alleged a violation of section 1983. They alleged this section was applicable because the school received over 90 percent of its funds from state and federal agencies through tuition funding plans. The Supreme Court, however, held to the contrary, finding insufficient state funding and state regulation.

5. Applying the holding of *Seminole tribe* v. *Florida*, 116 S.Ct. 1114 (1996), a number of courts have recently held that state employees could not bring suit in federal court to enforce FLSA. For example, in *Mills* v. *State of Maine*, 118 F.3d 37 (1st Cir. 1997), the court held that the amendments to FLSA which abrogated states' sovereign immunity by extending FLSA to states and state employees were not rationally related to the elimination of any unreasonable and arbitrary state action, or effects of such action, and thus were not a valid exercise of Congress' power to enforce the Fourteenth Amendment. Other federal courts have continued to hold that state employees may maintain FLSA suits in federal court.

6. The act's fifty-employee coverage threshold does not apply to elementary or secondary schools, whether private or public.

7. In *Adler*, the Court upheld New York civil service laws that barred members of subversive groups from teaching. In its ruling, the Court provided a clear elucidation of government employment as a privilege approach: "It is clear that such persons have the right under our law to assemble, speak, think and believe as they will. . . . It is equally clear that they have no right to work for the State in the school system on their own terms. . . . They may work for the school system upon the reasonable terms laid down by the proper authorities of New York. If they do not choose to work on such terms, they are at liberty to retain their beliefs and associations and go elsewhere."

References

Age Discrimination in Employment Act of 1967. U.S. Code, vol. 29, sec. 621 et seq.

Americans with Disabilities Act of 1990. U.S. Code, vol. 42, sec. 12101 et seq.

Civil Rights Act of 1871, U.S. Code, vol. 42, sec. 1983 et seq.

Civil Rights Act of 1964. U.S. Code, vol. 42, sec. 1981 et seq. (Title VII at 2000e.)

Civil Rights Act of 1991. U.S. Statutes at Large 105 (1991) 1071. (Compensatory damages at *U.S. Code*, vol. 42, sec. 1981.)

"Developments in the Law—Public Employment." *Harvard Law Review*, 1984, *97*, 1738–1800.

Equal Employment Opportunity Act of 1972. U.S. Code, vol. 42, sec. 2000e et seq.

Equal Employment Opportunity Commission. *Guidelines on Discrimination Because of Sex. Code of Federal Regulations*, 1997, vol. 29, sec. 1604. (Sexual harassment at 1604.11.) (Originally issued 1969.)

Fair Labor Standards Act of 1938. U.S. Code, vol. 29, sec. 201 et seq.

Family and Medical Leave Act of 1993. U.S. Code, vol. 29, sec. 2601 et seq.

Rehabilitation Act of 1973. U.S. Code, vol. 29, sec. 701 et seq.

CHAPTER EIGHT

A Practical Guide to Affirmative Action

Norma M. Riccucci

There is perhaps no function of human resource management that has generated more controversy and debate as affirmative action. Since its inception, it has been the target of damaging attacks and misrepresentations that have often left human resource managers and personnelists confused about its purpose and meaning. Perhaps most insidious have been the misguided claims equating affirmative action with *quotas* or *reverse discrimination*. Within this tumultuous environment, human resource managers and personnelists are particularly challenged to manage affirmative action programs and policies for their organizations.

This chapter provides practical information about the operation of affirmative action and equal employment opportunity (EEO) in government settings. Rosenbloom's three approaches (1983) to public administration—managerial, political, and legal—form an appropriate framework for this information. This chapter focuses in particular on the managerial approach and the steps human resource managers take in developing affirmative action plans. However, because affirmative action planning does not occur in a vacuum, this chapter also examines the environmental forces that influence the scope and boundaries of affirmative action. Thus the statutory, regulatory, and common law that human resource managers must be knowledgeable of is briefly reviewed. And because political milieux also influence the operation of affirmative action and especially the realization of its goals, this chapter also addresses the politics surrounding affirmative action. To begin, the following section briefly defines the terms and concepts of EEO and affirmative action.

DEFINING THE CONCEPTS

Equal employment opportunity is largely viewed as a means to prevent discrimination in the workplace on the basis of race, color, religion, gender, national origin, age, and physical and mental abilities. Because of its emphasis on nondiscrimination, a major facet of EEO is legislative mandates, such as civil rights laws. Although efforts to promote EEO initially spurred a good deal of resistance in this country, a policy of nondiscrimination is widely accepted today by policymakers and, for the most part, the general citizenry.

Affirmative action, in contrast, which emerged in response to pervasive employment discrimination, refers to proactive efforts to diversify the workplace in terms of race, ethnicity, gender, and even physical abilities. The proaction emphasis has led to a great deal of controversy and public debate over affirmative action as an employment tool or social policy (Rosenbloom, 1977; Riccucci, 1997; Cornwell and Kellough, 1994; Nalbandian and Klingner, 1987). In particular the legal and political disputes around affirmative action have greatly influenced its operation in public- and private-sector workforces. The next section takes a closer look at how law and politics have affected human resource managers' use of affirmative action in the public sector.

THE LEGAL ENVIRONMENT OF AFFIRMATIVE ACTION

A wide body of law governs the operation of affirmative action in the public sector. Statutory law and the U.S. Constitution provide an important framework for affirmative action, as do regulatory and common, or case, law.

Statutory and Constitutional Law

Title VII of the Civil Rights Act of 1964 (amended by the Equal Employment Opportunity Act of 1972 to include public-sector employers) provides the most comprehensive protection against employment discrimination on the basis of race, color, religion, gender, and national origin.[1] Although Title VII *does not* mandate affirmative action, it is serving as a framework for judicial interpretations of the legality of affirmative action plans and programs.[2] In fact, with the exception of the Rehabilitation Act of 1973 and federal set-aside programs, both of which are discussed later in this chapter, there are no federal statutes mandating affirmative action on a broad scale.

Likewise, although the Fifth and Fourteenth Amendments to the U.S. Constitution do not require affirmative action on the part of public employers, they are serving as the basis for judicial determinations of the constitutionality of affirmative action programs. As will be seen shortly, a wide body of case law governs affirmative action in the public sector.

It is worth noting that the Rehabilitation Act of 1973, which prohibits discrimination on the basis of disability, also has an affirmative action component for federal employers and federal contractors. (The Americans with Disabilities Act of 1990 [ADA], which is much broader than the Rehabilitation Act, applies to all public- and private-sector employees with the exception of those the executive branch of the federal government, which continues to be covered by Title V of the Rehabilitation Act. Federal contractors are covered by both the ADA and the Rehabilitation Act.) Sections 501 and 503 of Title V, respectively, require that the federal government and federal contractors (with contracts in excess of $2,500) take affirmative action to provide employment opportunities to persons with disabilities. Thus, although the ADA does not mandate affirmative action for the employers it covers, the Rehabilitation Act does mandate it for the federal government and for federal contractors. In any event, however, affirmative action for disabled persons may currently be more a promise than a reality.

There are also federal, state, and local statutes or ordinances that mandate affirmative action in the awarding of government contracts. Known as *set-asides,* such programs are a more narrow form of affirmative action where the government requires or encourages a certain portion of federal, state, or local contracting dollars to be earmarked, or set aside, for minority- or women-owned businesses. However, the future of set-asides, at least at the federal level, is precarious at best, given the Supreme Court decision in *Adarand Contractors, Inc. v. Peña, Secretary of Transportation* (115 Sup. Ct. 2097 [1995]), which creates stringent standards for set-asides (discussed in more detail later), and given the Clinton Administration's 1996 decision to suspend, for at least three years, all federal set-aside programs (Holmes, 1996).

Regulatory Law

In addition to statutory and constitutional law, affirmative action is also greatly affected by various federal, state, and local regulations. For example, numerous executive orders have been issued on the subject by chief executive officers at every level of government. The most prominent of these regulations is President Johnson's 1965 Executive Order 11246 (as amended by the 1967 Executive Order 11375) (President, 1967, 1971), which prohibits federal contractors with contracts exceeding $10,000 from discriminating on the basis of race, color, gender, religion, and national origin. It also requires those contractors with contracts in excess of $50,000 and fifty or more employees to take affirmative action to recruit, hire, and promote women and people of color whenever these groups are underused by the employer. State and local governments are regulated by 11246 if they have contracts or subcontracts with the federal government to furnish supplies or services or to provide the use or lease of property (Schlei and Grossman, 1983, p. 874). However, under some circumstances a contractor or subcontractor working for a unit of a state or a local government and not participating in the actual work may be exempt from 11246 provisions (Levin-Epstein, 1987, pp. 18–19).

Executive order 11246 is administered and enforced by the U.S. Department of Labor and its Office of Federal Contract Compliance Programs (OFCCP). In the event of noncompliance with the executive order the secretary of labor can take several actions, including canceling, terminating, or suspending the contract. In practice, federal contractors rarely lose their contracts, providing they can demonstrate good faith efforts toward achieving their affirmative action goals. Indeed, of the hundreds of thousands of contractors—employing millions of workers—only thirteen lost their contracts under the Carter Administration and two under the Reagan Administration (Press, 1985).

Affirmative action executive orders may also be issued at the state and local levels of government. For example, in 1983, then-governor Mario Cuomo of New York state issued Executive Order 6, which requires affirmative action in the state government workforce for women, people of color, persons with disabilities, and Vietnam-era veterans. It remains in force even today.

Other regulations in addition to executive orders govern and guide the use of affirmative action. For example, the Equal Employment Opportunity Commission (EEOC), which oversees and enforces various antidiscrimination laws including Title VII of the Civil Rights Act, has issued numerous regulations, most notably the 1978 Uniform Guidelines on Employee Selection Procedures and the guidelines in Affirmative Action Appropriate Under Title VII of the Civil Rights Act of 1964, as Amended. The Uniform Guidelines (Equal Employment Opportunity Commission, 1997c), issued jointly by the EEOC, the Department of Labor, the Department of Justice, and the Civil Service Commission (now the Office of Personnel Management), are a set of rules around employment decisions, intended to assist human resource managers and affirmative action officers to comply with requirements of federal law prohibiting discrimination on the basis of race, color, religion, gender, and national origin. The guidelines in Affirmative Action Appropriate Under Title VII, addressed in more detail later in this chapter, provide further assistance by interpreting the "legal principles which govern voluntary affirmative action under Title VII and other employment discrimination laws." Both sets of guidelines are ultimately intended to assist human resource managers in the development of affirmative action plans.

Case Law

The courts have interpreted statutory and constitutional law in deciding and defining the legal contours and boundaries of affirmative action, and it is perhaps the resulting case law that has had the greatest impact on the operation of affirmative action in the public sector. Court decisions ultimately influence the way in which human resource managers and affirmative action officers develop and implement affirmative action plans. Even the EEOC has amended some of its guidelines in accordance with Supreme Court decisions (Equal Employment Opportunity Commission, 1989).

Since the Court issued its *Regents* v. *Bakke* (438 U.S. 265) decision in 1978, which upheld the principle of affirmative action, the U.S. Supreme Court has upheld affirmative action in various forms, at least through 1989.[3] Table 8.1 presents a snapshot of Supreme Court affirmative action rulings from 1979 to 1987. As the table illustrates, it is only in the area of layoffs that the Court has not permitted the use of affirmative action.

By 1989, however, when the next series of decisions was issued, the high Court abruptly shifted its position on affirmative action programs. For example, in 1989, it issued a severe blow to set-aside programs in *Richmond* v. *Croson* (88 U.S. 469 [1989]). In *Croson,* the Court opined that state and local governments must justify their affirmative action programs under a *strict scrutiny* analysis. Strict scrutiny is a two-pronged test that asks (1) whether there is a compelling government interest for the program (for example, to redress past discrimination) and (2) whether the program is sufficiently narrowly tailored to meet its specified goals (for example, whether alternative programs could be employed that do not classify people by, for instance, race).[4] Subsequent to the *Croson* ruling, state and local governments wishing to maintain their set-aside programs had to modify them to comport with the strict scrutiny criteria, and a number of governments across the country carried out such revisions.

At the federal level of government, set-aside programs are moribund, but not because of the *Croson* decision, which, as noted, governs the operation of only state and local government set-asides. Rather, the Supreme Court's 1995 decision in *Adarand Contractors, Inc.* v. *Peña, Secretary of Transportation* (115 Sup. Ct. 2097) struck the first blow. In *Adarand,* the Court majority ruled that *all* federal affirmative action programs had to be subjected to the strict scrutiny inquiry. *Adarand,* in effect, overturned two earlier Court decisions that upheld federal set-asides: *Fullilove* v. *Klutznick* (448 U.S. 448 [1980]), and *Metro Broadcasting* v. *Federal Communications Commission* (497 U.S. 547 [1990]). In *Fullilove,* the Court had ruled that the federal government has broad authority to develop set-aside programs; thus the Court did not subject the federal program to a vigorous strict scrutiny analysis (Riccucci, 1997). In *Metro Broadcasting,* the Court had upheld a federal set-aside program seeking to increase the number of broadcast licenses awarded to people of color, also without applying a vigorous strict scrutiny test.

Human resource managers at the federal level received final word on the operation of set-asides in 1996, when President Clinton ordered the suspension of all federal set-aside programs for at least three years. (It must be kept in mind, however, that Clinton's directive does not affect the requirements under Executive Order 11246, which, as discussed, governs a contractor's workforce but does not require set-asides.)

Table 8.1. Supreme Court Decisions on Affirmative Action: 1979–1987.

Case	Legality or Constitutionality of Affirmative Action In			
	Hiring	Promotions	Layoffs	Federal Set-Asides
United Steelworkers of America v. *Weber,* 443 U.S. 193 (Title VII)	Yes[a]			
Fullilove v. *Klutznick,* 448 U.S. 448 (1980) (Fifth and Fourteenth Amendments)[b]				Yes
Memphis v. *Stotts,* 467 U.S. 561 (1984) (Title VII)			No	
Wygant v. *Jackson Board of Education,* 476 U.S. 267 (1986) (Fourteenth Amendment)			No	
Sheet Metal Workers' International Association v. *EEOC* 478 U.S. 421 (1986) (Title VII and Fifth Amendment)	Yes[c]			
International Association of Firefighters v. *City of Cleveland,* 478 U.S. 501 (1986) (Title VII)	Yes	Yes		
Johnson v. *Transportation Agency, Santa Clara County,* 480 U.S. 616 (1987) (Title VII)		Yes		
United States v. *Paradise,* 480 U.S. 149 (1987) (Fourteenth Amendment)		Yes		

[a]Involved selection of trainees for in-plant program.

[b]And various antidiscrimination statutes.

[c]Involved recruitment, selection, training, and admission to union.

Another Supreme Court ruling that dealt a blow to affirmative action was *Martin* v. *Wilks* (490 U.S. 755 [1989]).[5] Here, the Court threatened the continued existence of affirmative action programs in general, holding that white firefighters faced no time limitations in challenging affirmative action consent decrees approved by lower courts. In effect this left open the possibility of an endless series of lawsuits challenging long-standing court-approved affirmative action programs.

In response to the Supreme Court's regressive 1989 rulings, Congress enacted the Civil Rights Act of 1991, which, among other things, overturned the *Wilks* decision (Cayer, 1996; Bureau of National Affairs, 1991). It should be noted, however, that the 1991 act did not overturn the Court's *Croson* ruling. So human resource managers overseeing set-aside programs at the state and local levels of government must continue to adhere to the strict scrutiny requirements established in *Croson*.

THE POLITICAL ENVIRONMENT OF AFFIRMATIVE ACTION

The political culture of a jurisdiction can also impinge upon the management of affirmative action in that it sets a tone for the overall support that will be provided for affirmative action efforts. Support from a mayor or city council can affect the resources devoted to affirmative action and, ultimately, implementation effectiveness. For example, Norman Rice, the African American mayor of Seattle, Washington, has made affirmative action and cultural diversity programs priorities of his administration, and the city's diversity coordinator, Joanne Anton, has pointed out that the success of Seattle's efforts is largely due to the mayor's strong commitment and to his insistence that department heads actively support affirmative action and diversity initiatives (Chambers and Riccucci, 1997).

Conversely, when there is little or no support from political institutions, affirmative action efforts can be hampered. Perhaps the best and most publicized example can be found in the state of California. In May of 1995, Governor Pete Wilson ordered an end to all state affirmative action programs not required by law or court order. He also pushed the University of California Board of Regents to end the use of affirmative action in college admissions, hiring, and contracting, which it did in July of 1995.

In short, political and legal environments can greatly influence the operation of affirmative action. Against this backdrop, let's now turn to a primary managerial task of affirmative action—the development of affirmative action plans.

THE MANAGERIAL ASPECTS OF AFFIRMATIVE ACTION

Human resource managers and affirmative action officers are responsible for two key affirmative action functions: reporting and planning. First, Title VII of the Civil Rights Act as amended requires public-sector employers with one hundred or more employees to compile and submit annual reports on workforce gender and racial composition to the EEOC (Equal Employment Opportunity Commission, 1995). The purpose of the reporting requirements is to aid in EEOC's administration and enforcement of Title VII (Equal Employment Opportunity Commission, 1997b). In addition, once processed and summarized, the reports allow employers to compare the racial and gender makeup of their workforces with that of other jurisdictions across the country and with their local labor market.

The second critical affirmative action function performed by human resource managers or affirmative action officers is affirmative action planning. The following section discusses what is involved in developing an affirmative action plan.

Developing a Plan

There is no definitive affirmative action plan, nor is there a cookbook approach to developing viable, effective plans. Although affirmative action plans come in a wide variety, there are nonetheless some common ingredients in well-developed plans:

1. Financial and human resources for administering the plan
2. Evaluation of current EEO and affirmative action efforts and overall personnel policies and practices
3. Utilization analyses
4. Goals and timetables for achieving a representative workforce
5. Recruitment strategies for reaching and attracting job candidates from all sources
6. Training programs for employees and supervisors
7. Procedures for evaluating an organization's progress toward achieving its affirmative action goals (see, for example, Shafritz, Riccucci, Rosenbloom, and Hyde, 1992; Klingner and Nalbandian, 1985; Dresang, 1984).

Perhaps one of the first steps in effective affirmative action planning is to ensure that the organization or government entity will invest an appropriate amount of resources in the overall effort. If serious about diversifying its workforce, a government employer must appropriate resources so that its *entire* plan can be implemented effectively.

In addition, organizations will often review and evaluate their current EEO and affirmative action efforts. This entails a host of activities, including examining current recruitment, hiring, promotion, retention, and transfer policies and practices and analyzing their effects on all employees. Such a review may reveal inequities in the treatment or representation of protected classes throughout the organization.

Utilization analyses are also important to affirmative action planning. A utilization analysis compares the numbers and percentages of protected-class persons in the organization or government workplace with their percentages in the local or relevant labor market (Klingner and Nalbandian, 1985). The analysis also reviews the skills requirements for job vacancies, the skills usage of protected classes (including disabled and older workers) within the organization, and the general availability of protected-class persons with the requisite skills in the local labor market. Organizations may also consider the availability of protected-class persons in the local geographic area who are promotable, and the training opportunities it will make available so that these persons are competitive for job advancement.

Development of goals and timetables has also been encouraged. They may be calculated in any number of ways, but they should establish benchmarks and target dates for diversifying the workforce. Goals, contrary to popular belief, *are not* quotas; *quotas* are generally set by courts after a finding of employment discrimination; and in theory, courts can impose sanctions (fines) if organizations do not meet quotas. In practice, sanctions are rarely imposed because the courts tend to look favorably on an organization's good faith efforts toward fulfilling the established quota.

Goals, in contrast, are flexible benchmarks or indicators of an organization's desired level of protected-class employment. If an organization does not fulfill its goals within a given time period, it will reexamine its efforts and set more realistic goals. Needless to say, the organization does not impose sanctions on itself if the goals are not met.

Active recruitment efforts should also be outlined in the affirmative action plan. Outreach is critical for an organization's overall affirmative action efforts and requires the development and maintenance of contacts with appropriate groups and communities (for example, women's groups, African American communities, Latino communities, groups representing citizens with disabilities, and so forth). Contacts should also be maintained with schools, colleges, and universities that have large populations of women or students of color. It is also common to make job announcements through specific radio stations and other media outlets (for example, specific newspapers) that appeal to people of color, women, and other protected-class groups.

Training and education programs for managers, supervisors, and rank-and-file employees should also be addressed in the affirmative action plan. Managers and supervisors should receive training on their organization's overall EEO and affirmative action policies and programs, and employees should be offered training programs for skills acquisition, promotion opportunities, and career growth and development.

Finally, periodic reviews and evaluations of the affirmative action plan and its implementation will enable the organization to determine whether it is meeting its goals. Problems can thus be identified and rectified.

In developing and implementing a plan, employers may find it beneficial to rely on EEOC's technical assistance, compliance manuals (for example, Equal Employment Opportunity Commission, 1991), and guidelines on affirmative action (Equal Employment Opportunity Commission, 1997a).[6] These guidelines govern how the EEOC will handle charges that complain about actions taken in accordance with an affirmative action plan. The EEOC issued these guidelines expressly in conjunction with section 713(b)(1) of Title VII, which protects from challenge an employer's omission or action taken "in good faith, in conformity with, and in reliance on written opinions or interpretations of the [EEOC]." Thus, adhering to the EEOC's guidelines on affirmative action protects employers who take "reasonable actions" under legitimate affirmative action plans (Equal Employment Opportunity Commission, 1993).

There are many other components that may be included in affirmative action plans. Some are presented in the sample affirmative action plan in Exhibit 8.1 at the end of the chapter. It should be stressed that Exhibit 8.1 illustrates a single example of a plan, not a model plan. As noted earlier, each affirmative action plan will be unique to the employer producing it and to the problems and opportunities it faces.

Monitoring the Plan

Affirmative action and EEO planning are ongoing processes that do not end once a plan has been completed and implementation begun. In particular, monitoring the plan involves constant attention to how the plan is being implemented and whether its goals are being met. In some circumstances, administrative bodies may arrange formal audits. For example, the Department of Labor's OFCCP conducts periodic compliance audits of current federal government contractors as well as pre-award audits of prospective contractors. The initiation of an audit does not depend upon receipt of a complaint from an aggrieved individual. Rather, the OFCCP routinely selects employers for review (Schlei and Grossman, 1983).

To begin the audit, the OFCCP requests a copy of the employer's affirmative action plan, reviews it, and makes a determination as to its soundness. If the plan is sound, the audit is immediately terminated (B. Ellis, Associate Director for Affirmative Action, State University of New York-Albany, interviewed by the author, Apr. 26, 1996). If the plan is unsound, a *desk audit* is arranged. Here, an OFCCP compliance officer or team is assigned to the case and spends several days, sometimes weeks, randomly reviewing affirmative action files on hiring, promotions, and terminations within the *entire* organization, not just the program or unit receiving federal funding. The team will, for instance, (1) investigate the numbers of women and persons of color hired, promoted, and terminated within a designated time period; (2) ascertain whether any of the employer's personnel procedures have adverse impact; (3) conduct a compensation analysis to determine if there are pay inequities between women and men or between people of color and whites; and (4) randomly select employees to be interviewed on the employer's EEO and affirmative action practices.

The purpose of the desk audit is to determine which areas, if any, warrant further investigation. For example, if a compensation analysis reveals pay inequities, a more comprehensive investigation into the pay policies and practices of the employer is launched. The employer is then given the opportunity to explain or justify the pay disparities. If the employer can provide a satisfactory explanation, the investigation is terminated. If it cannot, the OFCCP compliance team will offer recommendations and remedies that can bring the employer into compliance with federal law.

Afterward, the employer is required to provide periodic progress reports to the OFCCP indicating what steps it is taking to remedy the problem. For example, if the OFCCP found that the employer's recruitment efforts failed to yield female job candidates, the employer would need to illustrate that it is now making a good faith effort to recruit women. If the employer fails to demonstrate a good faith effort, it may be sanctioned (Ellis, interviewed by the author, Apr. 26, 1996). As noted earlier, although the employer's federal funding can be suspended or terminated, this rarely happens, even when employers are not in compliance with OFCCP requirements.

Although there is no definitive preparation for OFCCP audits, it appears clear that employers can eschew sanctions—and indeed full-fledged audits—if they have well-developed affirmative action plans in place.

Affirmative action plans are also monitored by the courts when employment discrimination claims have arisen from the plans. In addition, plans may be monitored by administrative bodies such as the Merit Systems Protection Board (for plans for federal employees) and, more broadly, the EEOC.

As noted earlier the EEOC reviews and monitors equal employment opportunity and affirmative action progress through the EEO reports submitted to it by public employers. Any EEOC commissioner may initiate an investigation under Title VII to address a perceived widespread pattern of employment discrimination (Equal Employment Opportunity Commission, 1995, p. A4).[7] If the investigation leads to a finding of systematic discrimination, the EEOC may seek to conciliate a settlement between the employer and the aggrieved person(s). If this fails, the U.S. attorney general, on behalf of the EEOC and the aggrieved public employee(s), may bring a civil action in federal court. The court may enjoin the employer from engaging in the unlawful employment practices and may order reinstatement, hiring, or promotion of employees, with or without back pay.

In sum, an important managerial function of affirmative action planning is monitoring the plan once it has been implemented. Not only is this sound management practice but it can also prove cost effective because the costs of challenges to affirmative action plans are staggering.

CONCLUSION

Human resource managers at every level of government have equal employment opportunity and affirmative action responsibilities and tasks that are legal, political, and managerial. As this chapter shows, affirmative action planning is a critical function of human resource management, but human resource managers must also have practical knowledge and be vigilant about the relevant law and politics if their affirmative action plans are not only to be effective but to survive judicial scrutiny as well. The EEOC and many other administrative bodies provide technical assistance on affirmative action to human resource managers. Such assistance is imperative and can help an organization ultimately reach its affirmative action goals while also avoiding costly administrative hearings or lawsuits emanating from challenges to its affirmative action programs and policies.

Notes

1. State and local statutes, constitutions, or ordinances may also prohibit discrimination, but this discussion is primarily limited to federal mandates. It should further be noted that this chapter does not review the wide body of employment discrimination (that is, EEO) law made under the various federal mandates, but limits the discussion to law pertaining solely to affirmative action.

2. So, too, do section 1983 of the Civil Rights Act of 1871 and, on a more limited basis, section 1981 of the Civil Rights Act of 1866 (for example, since the U.S. Supreme Court, in *Brown* v. *General Service Administration*, 425 U.S. 820 [1976], found Title VII of the Civil Rights Act of 1964 as amended to be the exclusive remedy for federal employees, section 1981 cannot be used against federal defendants).

3. An exception is the Court decision in *Grove City College* v. *Terrel H. Bell* (465 U.S. 555 [1984]), where the Court ruled that the gender discrimination provisions of Title IX of the Education Amendments of 1972 applied *only* to programs receiving federal financial assistance and not to the entire educational institution. The Civil Rights Restoration Act of 1987 then restored the broad coverage of civil rights laws, making it clear that discrimination is prohibited throughout an entire organization or agency and not just in the program receiving federal assistance.

**Exhibit 8.1. Sample Table of Contents and Selected Language
for an Affirmative Action Plan for Midtown, USA.**

I. Introduction.
  A. Organizational structure of city of midtown and organizational chart
  B. Statement of workforce applicant pool
II. Policy Statement on Equal Opportunity and Affirmative Action
  A. Institutional commitment
    The City of Midtown is committed to a policy of nondiscrimination and equal employment opportunity in conjunction with an affirmative action program that ensures that regular position vacancies are disseminated in a fashion calculated to reach a race/gender representative cross section of qualified potential applicants in each profession, discipline, or trade within the geographic recruiting area.
  B. Mayor's commitment
    The Mayor of Midtown issues annual statements delineating the City's policy of equal employment opportunity and nondiscrimination and reaffirming her own personal commitment to affirmative action. The Mayor is committed to communicating the importance of the City's affirmative action program to all City employees, making certain that individual responsibilities for efforts toward its affirmative action goals are clearly understood and actively pursued.
III. Dissemination of Affirmative Action Policy
  A. Internal dissemination of policy statement
  B. External dissemination of policy statement
  C. Dissemination of affirmative action plan: availability and location of affirmative action plans
    1. The Office of Affirmative Action
    2. The Mayor's Office
    3. The Personnel Department
    4. The Office of Public Information
    5. The Public Library
IV. Responsibility for Implementation
  A. The Office of Affirmative Action
    It is the responsibility of this Office to work with Midtown's supervisors, equal employment opportunity officers, and any requesting employee to ensure compliance with Midtown's affirmative action plan and policy and applicable laws (for example, Title VII of the Civil Rights Act of 1964, the Equal Pay Act of 1963, the Age Discrimination in Employment Act of 1967, the Americans with Disabilities Act of 1990, Executive Order 11246, and other applicable laws).
  B. Equal employment opportunity officers
  C. Department of Personnel

Exhibit 8.1. Sample Table of Contents and Selected Language for an Affirmative Action Plan for Midtown, USA, cont'd.

D. Supervisors

Responsibility for implementation of affirmative action efforts is extended to Midtown's supervisors. They should be made to understand that their work performance is being evaluated on the basis of their equal employment and affirmative action efforts and results, as well as other criteria.

V. Workforce Analysis

The City of Midtown's analysis is an organizational profile by unit by position in ascending salary order. The institutional workforce analysis is maintained for audit purposes. Each major unit will periodically be provided copies of workforce analyses for its subordinate units. The institutional workforce analysis appears in Appendix A of this affirmative action plan.

VI. Job Groups

Each job group is described herein and includes a list of job titles within each group. Also included is desired training and experience with likely patterns of advancement. The job group analysis reflects the composition of each job group by race and gender. Institutional job groupings appear in Appendix B of this plan.

VII. Availability Determination

The most specific estimates of availability are used, though in some cases figures for persons with specific skills were not available and more general categories were used that tend to overestimate availability. In some cases a general persons of color figure is used because more specific race/ethnicity data are not available. The availability analysis is furnished in Appendix C of this plan.

VIII. Utilization Analysis

The utilization analysis is a comparison of actual representation in the workforce with the estimated availability in each job group. Underutilization is the number of additional white women or people of color needed to match availability estimates for the current size of the group. Table A shows the City of Midtown's current utilization analysis.

IX. Goals and Timetables

A. Review of prior year's goals

B. City of Midtown's goals

C. Agency goals

D. Department goals

Table B shows the City of Midtown's current goals

X. Identification of Problem Area: Application Flow and Selection Rate

XI. Action-Oriented Programs

A. Statement on training policy and programs for managers, supervisors, and administrators

Exhibit 8.1. Sample Table of Contents and Selected Language for an Affirmative Action Plan for Midtown, USA, cont'd.

- B. Steps toward the improvement of employment opportunities for women and people of color: recruitment, hiring, and promotion procedures

XII. Internal Audit and Reporting Systems: Monitoring EEO and Affirmative Action Efforts
- A. Responsibilities of the City of Midtown's Office of Affirmative Action
- B. Statement of support at institutional level for auditing and reporting

XIII. Sexual Harassment Policy
- A. Statement of policy
- B. Processing of complaints
- C. Sanctions

XIV. Workers with Disabilities
- A. Statement of policy
- B. Rehabilitation Act of 1973
- C. Americans with Disabilities Act of 1990
- D. Review of physical and mental job qualifications
- E. Reasonable accommodation of disabilities
- F. Recruitment of and outreach to persons with disabilities
- G. Processing of complaints
- H. Sanctions

XV. Veterans
- A. Statement of policy on veterans' preferences
- B. Vietnam-Era Veterans Readjustment Assistance Act of 1974
- C. Review of physical and mental job qualifications
- D. Reasonable accommodation of disabled veterans
- E. Recruitment of and outreach to veterans with disabilities
- F. Processing of complaints
- G. Sanctions

XVI. Gays and Lesbians
- A. City of Midtown's ordinance prohibiting discrimination against gays and lesbians in employment
- B. Processing of complaints
- C. Sanctions

XVII. AIDS Policy
- A. Statement of AIDS policy
- B. Americans with Disabilities Act of 1990
- C. Processing of complaints
- D. Sanctions

XVIII. Family Leave
- A. Family and Medical Leave Act of 1993

Exhibit 8.1. Sample Table of Contents and Selected Language
for an Affirmative Action Plan for Midtown, USA, cont'd.

Table A. Example of Utilization Analysis.

Job Group	Total in Job Group	People of Color				Women			
		Available (percent)	Expected Number of	Actual Number of	Under-utilization	Available (percent)	Expected Number of	Actual Number of	Under-utilization
1A1	21	5.10	1.00	1		10.41	2.00	2	
1A2	174	5.92	10.30	6	4.30	10.32	17.95	15	2.95
1B1	135	10.14	13.68	7	12.68	26.04	31.15	29	6.15
1B2	102	9.94	10.13	9	1.13	37.48	38.22	32	6.22
1B3	69	7.33	5.05	6		34.16	23.57	41	

Table B. City of Midtown's Goals.

Job Group	People of Color			Women		
	Desired Goal (percent)	Target Date Goal (percent)	Years to Desired Goal	Desired Goal (percent)	Target Date Goal (percent)	Years to Desired Goal
1A1	0	—	—	7	4	3
1A2	9	2	6	6	2	5
1B1	5	2	5	2	1	2
1B2	18	1	9	22	3	4
1B3	2	1	4	0	—	—

4. For further discussion of strict scrutiny and the statistical evidence sufficient to justify a conclusion of discrimination, see, for example, *Employment Discrimination Law*, 1989.

5. Other 1989 Supreme Court rulings that changed EEO practices or employment discrimination law include *Lorance* v. *AT&T* (490 U.S. 900 [1989]); *Wards Cove Packing Co.* v. *Atonio* (490 U.S. 642 [1989]); *Price Waterhouse* v. *Hopkins* (490 U.S. 228 [1989]); and *Patterson* v. *McLean Credit Union* (491 U.S. 164 [1989]).

6. Some government jurisdictions have special offices (for example, offices or departments of minority and women's business development) that could also provide technical assistance.

7. The Merit Systems Protection Board is also empowered to take remedial action, depending upon the circumstances, in EEO cases involving federal employees.

References

Age Discrimination in Employment Act of 1967. U.S. Code, vol. 29, sec. 621 et seq.

Americans with Disabilities Act of 1990. U.S. Code, vol. 42, sec. 12101 et seq.

Bureau of National Affairs. "Civil Rights Act of 1991: Text and Analysis." *Employment Guide,* Nov. 11, 1991 (special supplement).

Cayer, N. J. *Public Personnel Administration in the United States.* (3rd ed.) New York: St. Martin's Press, 1996.

Chambers, T., and Riccucci, N. M. "Models of Excellence in Workplace Diversity." In C. Ban and N. M. Riccucci (eds.), *Public Personnel Management: Current Concerns, Future Challenges.* (2nd ed.) New York: Longman, 1997.

Civil Rights Act of 1866. U.S. Code, vol. 42, sec. 1981 et seq.

Civil Rights Act of 1871. U.S. Code, vol. 42, sec. 1983 et seq.

Civil Rights Act of 1964. U.S. Code, vol. 42, sec. 1981 et seq. (Title VII at 2000e.)

Civil Rights Act of 1991. U.S. Statutes at Large 105 (1991) 1071.

Civil Rights Restoration Act of 1987. U.S. Code, vol. 20, 1687 et seq.

Cornwell, C., and Kellough, J. E. "Women and Minorities in Federal Government Agencies: Examining New Evidence from Panel Data." *Public Administration Review,* 1994, *54*(3), 265–270.

Dresang, D. J. *Public Personnel Management and Public Policy.* New York: Little, Brown, 1984.

Employment Discrimination Law. Five-Year Cumulative Supplement. Washington, D.C.: Bureau of National Affairs, 1989.

Equal Employment Opportunity Act of 1972. U.S. Code, vol. 42, sec. 2000e et seq.

Equal Employment Opportunity Commission. "Interpretive Memorandum: *Martin* v. *Wilks.*" Washington, D.C.: Equal Employment Opportunity Commission, Oct. 17, 1989.

Equal Employment Opportunity Commission. *EEOC Compliance Manual.* Vol. 2, sec. 607.3–607.4. Washington, D.C.: Equal Employment Opportunity Commission, 1991.

Equal Employment Opportunity Commission. *Technical Assistance Program: Resource Manual.* Washington, D.C.: Equal Employment Opportunity Commission, 1993.

Equal Employment Opportunity Commission. *Employer EEO Responsibilities.* Washington, D.C.: Equal Employment Opportunity Commission, 1995.

Equal Employment Opportunity Commission. *Affirmative Action Appropriate Under Title VII of the Civil Rights Act of 1964, as Amended. Code of Federal Regulations,* 1997a, vol. 29, sec. 1608.

Equal Employment Opportunity Commission. *Recordkeeping and Reporting Requirements Under Title VII and the ADA. Code of Federal Regulations,* 1997b, vol. 29, sec. 1602.

Equal Employment Opportunity Commission. *Uniform Guidelines on Employee Selection Procedures. Code of Federal Regulations,* 1997c, vol. 29, sec. 1607. (Originally issued 1978.)

Equal Pay Act of 1963. U.S. Code, vol. 29, sec. 206 et seq.

Family and Medical Leave Act of 1993. U.S. Code, vol. 29, sec. 2601 et seq.

Holmes, S. A. "Clinton Administration Suspends Set-Asides." *Albany Times Union,* Mar. 8, 1996, p. B12.

Klingner, D. E., and Nalbandian, J. *Public Personnel Management: Contexts and Strategies.* (2nd ed.) Upper Saddle River, N.J.: Prentice Hall, 1985.

Levin-Epstein, M. D. *Primer of Equal Employment Opportunity.* (4th ed.) Washington, D.C.: Bureau of National Affairs, 1987.

Nalbandian, J., and Klingner, D. E. "Conflict and Values in Public Personnel Administration." *Public Administration Quarterly,* 1987, *11*(1), 17–33.

President. "Equal Employment Opportunity," Executive Order 11246. *Code of Federal Regulations,* 1967, vol. 3 *(The President: 1964–1965 Compilation).*

President. "Amending Executive Order No. 11246, Relating to Equal Employment Opportunity," Executive Order 11375. *Code of Federal Regulations,* 1971, vol. 3 *(The President: 1966–1970 Compilation).*

Press, A. "The New Rights War." *Newsweek,* Dec. 30, 1985, pp. 66–68.

Rehabilitation Act of 1973. U.S. Code, vol. 29, sec. 701 et seq.

Riccucci, N. M. "Will Affirmative Action Survive into the 21st Century?" In C. Ban and N. M. Riccucci (eds.), *Public Personnel Management: Current Concerns, Future Challenges.* (2nd ed.) Reading, Mass.: Addison Wesley Longman, 1997.

Rosenbloom, D. H. *Federal Equal Employment Opportunity.* New York: Praeger, 1977.

Rosenbloom, D. H. "Public Administrative Theory and the Separation of Powers." *Public Administration Review,* 1983, *43*(3), 219–227.

Schlei, B. L., and Grossman, P. *Employment Discrimination Law.* (2nd ed.) Washington, D.C.: Bureau of National Affairs, 1983.

Shafritz, J. M., Riccucci, N. M., Rosenbloom, D. H., and Hyde, A. C. *Personnel Management in Government.* (4th ed.) New York: Dekker, 1992.

Vietnam Era Veterans' Readjustment Assistance Act of 1974. U.S. Statutes at Large 88 (1974) 1578.

CHAPTER NINE

Sexual Harassment in the Workplace

Michele M. Hoyman
Lana Stein

On an autumn weekend in 1991, millions of Americans sat transfixed in front of their television sets. It was not an important football contest that captured their attention but rather the Senate deliberation on the confirmation of Clarence Thomas, President Bush's nominee to the Supreme Court. In very rare weekend proceedings the all-male Senate Judiciary Committee heard the testimony of law professor and former Thomas colleague at the Equal Employment Opportunity Commission (EEOC) Anita Hill, who charged that Thomas had used sexually explicit language and innuendo during private meetings with her. Ironically, Thomas had headed the compliance agency that handles sex discrimination complaints, including sexual harassment. Thomas denied Hill's charges. Other witnesses attested to the character of either Hill or Thomas. No one else had been present during these alleged incidents, and Hill had not reported them at the time. Although Thomas in the end was confirmed by a narrow margin, many questions had been raised about his character and about what constitutes sexual harassment. The issue was brought home to many Americans. A large number of women strongly identified with Hill based on their own workplace experiences.

The public sector again became a well-publicized arena for charges of sexual harassment in 1991 following the U.S. Navy's annual Tailhook Association convention of naval aviators. The event was marred when females were forced to run a gauntlet of their groping male colleagues. Unwelcome horseplay resembled assault in a few instances. According to a Pentagon report, "The assaults varied from victims being grabbed on the buttocks to victims being groped, pinched and fondled on their breasts, buttocks and genitals. Some victims were bitten by their assailants, others were knocked to the ground and some had their clothing ripped or removed" (Gordon, 1993, p. A1). The report stressed that this was not an isolated event. In 1994, the Senate permitted Admiral Frank B. Kelso II, chief of naval operations, to retire with all of his four stars. Republican and Democratic women of the House of Representatives and the Senate had lobbied to strip Kelso of two of the stars because of the handling of the Tailhook incident. Republican Senator Kay Bailey Hutchison, of Texas, said that "it's no secret to anyone that few officers believed that the Navy was serious about getting to the bottom of Tailhook '91. Officer after officer stymied the investigation" (Dowd, 1994, p. 1). The Senate vote was fifty-four to forty-three; the actions of the Congressional women had narrowed the margin considerably. The Navy actually has now taken some steps to prevent such incidents and has met with a little success. In a recent survey of women in the Navy, 53 percent reported experiencing incidents of sexual harassment, down from 66 percent in 1988 ("Navy Makes Progress," 1996).

In 1996, television viewers and newspaper readers learned of a class action suit by a number of female workers at a Mitsubishi factory in Illinois. These women charged that they had been continually sexually harassed with unpleasant verbal comments and suggestions as well as sexually explicit photographs left at their lockers or workstations. They are pursuing the matter in court. The company in turn has denied knowledge of any wrongdoing and is strenuously fighting the suit. It even organized a counterdemonstration by some women plant workers, who carried signs saying, "I love Mitsubishi."

Most recently, the U.S. Army has had to handle charges of sexual harassment made by female recruits against their male drill instructors. Perhaps learning a lesson from Tailhook, the Army has acted relatively expeditiously. In May 1997, it brought charges of sexual misconduct and indecent assault against its highest-ranking enlisted soldier (Schmitt, 1997, p. A1).

These well-publicized cases document problems that certainly are not absent from public and private worksites in the United States. Women or men may be subjected to unwelcome verbal or physical advances by coworkers. These advances may make the person approached very uncomfortable and may affect work performance or advancement. If unwelcome and affecting work status or deleterious to work performance, they are illegal: they are sexual harassment.

The Clarence Thomas hearing illustrates some of the difficulty an employer or a court can have in examining charges of sexual harassment. Sometimes there are no witnesses, and cases become a matter of (most frequently) "he said, she said." Often cases hinge on a one-on-one credibility finding by an arbitrator, judge, or convenor of an internal investigation. Yet, if a court of law finds harassment occurred, an employer can be liable even when unaware of the behavior at the time it occurred. In addition, the line between office romance and objectionable behavior may be a fine one. Many people have met their future mates at work. How does an employer draw the line and train and monitor workers to ensure that incidents of sexual harassment do not occur?

The problem of sexual harassment is an old one. Historically, many female employees fending for themselves and "minority women were especially subject to abuse. . . . Refusal of an unwelcome overture could result in retaliation, dismissal, and an unfavorable reference. In the long term, acquiescence presented comparable risks and carried additional social and psychological costs" (Rhode, 1989, p. 231). Various forms of harassment were also tools to maintain *occupation subordination.* As Rhode notes, offensive behavior could be used to rid worksites of females and this may be one reason incidents have continued to occur as women enter nontraditional fields and are employed at all types of work locations. Although men have been and continue to be victims of harassment as well, women are predominantly on the receiving end.

The issue of sexual harassment is of importance to public and private employers alike. Since the 1960s, women have entered the workforce in increasing numbers and certainly have increased their presence in nontraditional occupations. Employer liability is clear.

In the pages that follow, we provide a legal definition of sexual harassment, outline the federal guidelines that deal with it, and offer a précis of relevant court cases. Finally, we offer advice to administrators about how they might address the issue at their job sites to protect both their employees and themselves.

LEGAL STATUS OF SEXUAL HARASSMENT

Judge Howard Smith, a venerable congressman from Virginia, added the word "sex" to the list of affected classes in the 1964 Civil Rights Act. Some feel Smith acted with sincerity; others take the position that this amendment was meant to kill the legislation. In any case, discrimination in employment based on gender came to be prohibited except in jobs in which gender was a bona fide occupational qualification: for example, employment as an actor playing certain a role or as a sperm donor or wet nurse. Title VII of the 1964 act addressed employment and covers any business employing at least fifteen individuals. Subsequent to the passage of this act, the courts began to treat sexual harassment as a form of sex discrimination under Title VII and suits began to be filed on a tort basis at the state level. On September 23, 1980, the Equal Employment Opportunity Commission issued a set of guidelines that continue unchanged to this day. These guidelines state that "unwelcome sexual advances, requests for sexual favors, and other verbal or physical conduct of a sexual nature" will be considered harassment when

- Submission to such conduct is made either explicitly or implicitly a term or condition of an individual's employment;

- Submission to or rejection of such conduct by an individual is used as the basis for employment decisions affecting such individual, or

- Such conduct has the purpose or effect of unreasonably interfering with an individual's work performance or creating an intimidating, hostile, or offensive working environment [U.S. Bureau of National Affairs, 1980, p. E-2].

The EEOC guidelines place considerable responsibility on the employer in the event that instances of sexual harassment are established. The EEOC interprets its charge to mean that "employers will be held liable for the acts of supervisors and agents 'regardless of whether the specific acts alleged were authorized or even forbidden by the employer and regardless of whether the employer knew or should have known of their occurrence'" (U.S. Bureau of National Affairs, 1980, p. A-5).

In 1986, in *Meritor Savings Bank, F.S.B.* v. *Vinson* (477 U.S. 57), the U.S. Supreme Court held as unlawful two different types of sexual harassment claims. First is *quid pro quo harassment* in which "sexual demands are made specifically in exchange for employment benefits, such as being hired, being promoted or to avoid being fired" (Sherman, 1992, p. 45). The second category for which the Court established employer liability is *hostile work-environment harassment.* This occurs "when there is a work atmosphere which is so pervasively hostile, offensive, or abusive that it alters or interferes with an employee's ability to do a job" (Sherman, 1992, p. 45). The employer in this case attempted to avoid broad liability, but the Court held that it was completely liable under the hostile environment standard.

The atmosphere, or environment, standard is the most far-reaching and radical in its implications. It provides the greatest protection to employees and has been applauded by many feminist groups. On the other hand it presents numerous difficulties to employers. They are asked to create a particular work atmosphere not governed solely by their desire for profit or, in the public and nonprofit sectors, their particular service mission. The EEOC guidelines require that employers maintain an atmosphere that does not allow any harassment to interfere with productive labor.

The EEOC guidelines require subjective judgment; they do not set forth clearly recognizable objective behaviors that are forbidden. Therefore one baseline requirement for determining that a behavior is harassment is whether it results in an employment consequence, that is, promotion or denial of promotion, firing or hiring, positive or negative performance appraisal. However, because the guidelines do not list lawful and unlawful behaviors, often it is a person's perception of behavior that makes it harassment or not.

Nonetheless any employer covered by Title VII is liable for behavior considered to be harassment by its supervisors, employees, or even nonemployees unless it takes prompt remedial action. A nonemployee might be a customer or a repair person with whom an employee has to interact. The strictest standards of liability are reserved for supervisors, once again, "regardless of whether the specific acts complained of were authorized or even forbidden by the employer and regardless of whether the employer knew or should have known of their occurrence" (Equal Employment Opportunity Commission, 1980). An employer is responsible for acts of sexual harassment toward an employee by fellow employees when the employer "knew or should have known of the conduct" unless it can be shown that "immediate and appropriate corrective action" had been taken (Equal Employment Opportunity Commission, 1980). In the case of objectionable conduct by nonemployees, liability is more limited and will be assessed case by case. Prompt remedial action to protect employees is viewed favorably by the EEOC. In establishing its guidelines in 1980, the EEOC rejected earlier employer defenses such as "boys will be boys" and "we didn't know our supervisor was doing that" (Hoyman and Robinson, 1981).

The EEOC has received an inordinate amount of complaints. More persons have filed in recent years, perhaps spurred on by the changes in the law made by the Civil Rights Act of 1991. This act allows a jury trial and compensatory and punitive damages in sexual harassment cases. In 1995, the EEOC counted a record number of sexual harassment complaints (15,549), more than double the number filed in 1990. California in 1995 had three times its 1990 number (Alger and Flanagan, 1996a, p. 107). Because of this sheer volume, there often are considerable delays in investigation and prosecution (Yang, 1996, p. 98).

FREQUENCY OF SEXUAL HARASSMENT

Sexual harassment in the workplace is pervasive. A number of surveys have found that at least half of women responding have experienced some form of sexual harassment at some time on their jobs. For example, findings from a survey by the Center for Policy Studies and Program Evaluation at Sangamon State University (now University of Illinois-Springfield) of a random sample of Illinois public employees[1] showed that 59 percent of women respondents had experienced "one or more incidents of sexual harassment in their current place of employment" (Hoyman and Robinson, 1981, p. 2). Table 9.1 elaborates the types of harassment these women encountered. Because the women were asked only about their present jobs, instances of harassment over their entire work lives could have been considerably higher.

Crull's 1979 survey of women workers found that in 79 percent of the cases of harassment reported, the harasser had the authority to fire the victim (Crull, 1980,

Table 9.1. Sexual Harassment Reported by Women on Present Job.

Event	Percentage Experiencing It
Sexual remarks or teasing	52
Suggestive looks or leers	41
Subtle sexual hints and pressures	26
Physical touching or grabbing	25
Sexual propositions	20
Repeated pressures for personal relationships	14
Miscellaneous forms of unwanted sexual attentions	9
Coercive sex	2

Source: Data from Hoyman and Robinson, 1981, p. 2; Robinson, 1981, p. 31.

pp. 67–71). In 16 percent of the cases, explicit threats were made when women refused unwanted attention. Although in 76 percent of the cases women complained to the harasser or another party that they wished this conduct to stop, 42 percent of those who complained eventually resigned. Crull found that almost every case was accompanied by psychological stress.

Most harassment consists of a male directing undesired attention toward a female. A survey of a large random sample of federal workers found that those most likely to be harassed were under thirty-four years of age and female, single or divorced, very dependent on their jobs, at the low end of the wage spectrum, working as trainees or in nontraditional jobs, working in a group largely of the opposite sex. Among men, minorities were more likely to be harassed (*Sexual Harassment in the Federal Government,* 1980, p. 16). Forty percent of women respondents reported having experienced some form of harassment. In a 1988 follow-up study, 42 percent of the women surveyed reported experiences with sexual harassment in some form (Strickland, 1995, p. 493). In addition, the immediate victim may not be the only person negatively affected by the harassment. In one recent case a judge allowed a male worker to sue his employer after he claimed that his career was stymied because his wife had filed a sexual harassment claim against the company where both worked and the company had then retaliated against him (Brady, 1996, p. 20).

These data clearly indicate that many workers have encountered a form of sexual harassment on their jobs. Given the magnitude of this problem, it is also evident that many instances are never reported, whether out of fear, modesty, or lack of knowledge. Again, there sometimes is a fine line between casual flirting and harassment. The definition is a personal one. One individual may perceive certain words or action as harassment while another individual may be flattered by them. What constitutes harassment may also be culturally bound. As the number of African Americans, Asians, and Latinos in the U.S. workforce increases, subjective views of harassment may present greater variation because different subcultures may not agree on definitions of unacceptable behavior. All these issues of definition necessitate increased supervisory awareness, promulgation of a clear policy, and training for employees.

IMPACTS OF SEXUAL HARASSMENT

The impacts of sexual harassment are myriad. First, the victim is affected, psychologically or professionally. Second, the accused harasser is affected, and there may sometimes be false accusations. If due process is not guaranteed, then a person falsely accused of harassment may incur damages for which the employer could be held responsible, such as loss of job, blacklisting, or loss of income. Third, the claim of harassment is destructive of the work environment. Three other impacts also are noteworthy: (1) the high monetary cost to the agency; (2) the tarnish and possible disgrace that falls on the agency's top officials; (3) the damage to the image of the agency (or to a product in the private sector).

Lars Bildman, chief executive of the drug company Astra, resigned the day before *Business Week* released the results of a six-month investigation of complaints against him by dozens of women working for the company (Maremont and Sasseen, 1986). Because the person at the top was involved, there was considerable adverse publicity for both him and the company. In such a case, the entire hierarchy might be perceived to be part of a cover-up. One of the first public cases of sexual harassment involved a secretary who worked for the U.S. Department of Justice. She successfully brought suit against her supervisor. Ironically, the Department of Justice had sole responsibility for compliance on this issue before the EEOC became empowered to appear in court on these compliance cases.

Another interesting impact is the dual attitude toward sexual harassment that has emerged in the business community. The private sector is not of one mind about the size of the problem. Some employers, for either ideological or ethical reasons, are making serious efforts to comply, as are those who wish to avoid the potentially high costs of litigation. Some, however, are outraged that the behavior in question has even become an issue. *Forbes* recently declared, "Of all the crusades Washington ever embarked upon, the current commitment to stamp out sex in the workplace surely ranks among the daffiest" (Alger and Flanagan, 1996b, p. 106). The magazine noted that an employee dismissed for telling dirty jokes could hit the company with a wrongful discharge suit. *Forbes* was reacting to an EEOC spokesperson's estimate that seven hundred employees might be involved in the Mitsubishi suit and that each might be liable under federal law for as much as $300,000 in damages.

PERTINENT COURT RULINGS ON SEXUAL HARASSMENT

The unanimous Supreme Court ruling in *Meritor Savings Bank* v. *Vinson* established the two-pronged definition of harassment, quid pro quo or hostile environment, and it set parameters for subsequent court rulings, although Hoff (1991) has questioned whether *Meritor* could be applied to other instances of on-the-job harassment because the circumstances of *Meritor* were so blatant. She cautions that the *Meritor* Court allowed evidence of "possible seductive or provocative behavior" on the part of victims, and she notes that "cultural perceptions about women, especially with respect to 'harms' accruing to them because of their sexuality, still do not strike most men as being real, let alone detrimental or offensive" (pp. 358–359).

The notion that boys will be boys was a popular and successful defense in litigation before the issuance of the 1980 EEOC guidelines. However, in the *Meritor* case the Court did set a standard for how intrusive the conduct must be for an employer to suffer liability. To constitute a violation of Title VII, the harassment must be sufficiently severe and pervasive to alter the conditions of the victim's employment and create an abusive work environment. But the Court declined to adopt a categorical rule that would, on the one hand, automatically impose liability on an employer for harassment by a supervisor or, on the other hand, protect an employer who had no knowledge of such conduct. In the latter case, if an employer's nondiscrimination policy is silent on sexual harassment, an employer may still be liable for an employee's behavior.

In subsequent cases, courts have made a distinction between quid pro quo and hostile environment cases. They have found the strict liability of employers more readily in quid pro quo cases (those in which the supervisor has authority over employment decisions), even when the employer has no knowledge of the supervisor's conduct (see, for example, *Volk* v. *Coler*, 845 F. 2d 1422 [1988], and *Henson* v. *City of Dundee*, 682 F. 2d 897 [1982]). In cases involving hostile environment, the courts have tended to require actual employer knowledge of a supervisor's misconduct to find employer liability (*Equal Employment Opportunity Commission* v. *Hacienda Hotel*, 881 F. 2d 1504 [1989]; *Steele* v. *Offshore Shipbuilding*, 867 F. 2d 1311 [1989]; see Sedmak and Levin-Epstein, 1991). However, a literal reading of the guidelines and the *Meritor* ruling supports broad employer liability, meaning that employers are responsible for the actions of their supervisors under the assumption that the employers should have known (agency theory).

Various court decisions have found sexual harassment to exist in a wide variety of circumstances. The classic case is that of a male supervisor offering a woman a promotion in exchange for sexual favors. However, a third party denied a promotion because of sexual favors exchanged between a supervisor and another employee is also construed to be a victim of harassment (*King* v. *Palmer*, 778 F. 2d 878 [1986]; *Priest* v. *Rotary d/b/a Fireside Motel and Coffee Shoppe*, 634 F. Supp. 571 [1986]; *Toscano* v. *Nimmo*, 570 F. Supp. 1197 [1983]; *Broderick* v. *Ruder*, 685 F. Supp. 1269 [1988]; *Spencer* v. *G.E. Co.*, 894 F. 2d. 651 [1990]).

The definition of sexual harassment includes homosexual as well as heterosexual activity. In *Wright* v. *Methodist Youth Services* (311 F. Supp. 307 [1981]), the parties involved were homosexual, and harassment was established. Further, it has become clear from various decisions that sexual harassment does not have to include physical contact; it can be verbal or nonverbal (for example, the display of lewd photographs) if such behavior is linked to an employment consequence.

The decisions of the various federal courts continue to exhibit a certain ambiguity or foot dragging on enforcement. This 1995 case from the Seventh Circuit is illustrative. In *Baskerville* v. *Culligan International Co.* (1995 W.L. 11597), the Seventh Circuit Court overturned a $25,000 damage awarded by a jury at the lower level to a plaintiff who had been hired as a secretary in 1991. The supervisor of the secretary was a regional manager who made a series of comments carrying sexual overtones. Chief Judge Posner ruled that these incidents, spread out over seven months, did not constitute sexual harassment because the supervisor never touched the employee or invited her to go out on a date or have sex with him. In addition, the judge noted that the employer took prompt remedial action to protect the employee from the supervisor. In its decision the court reasoned that the concept of sexual harassment is designed to protect working women from an atmosphere that is "hellish," not to rid the workplace of vulgarity.

This decision might be seen as narrowing both the bounds of employer liability and definitions of harassment. Yet it is not a Supreme Court ruling and rather reflects the vagaries of the U.S. judicial system in which any type of precedent can be located if one scours the findings of all the appellate and state courts. Nonetheless, it demonstrates that there is no certitude in cases of this kind. Another relatively recent court decision (*Paroline* v. *Unisys Corp.*, 879 F. 2d 100, 1990]) maintained that to avoid liability, an employer who knew or should have known of the sexual harassment "must take prompt, effective remedial action. A reasonable response does not include transferring the victim to her disadvantage. [In dealing with the offender,] [r]eprimands, reassignments, and denials of scheduled pay increases, coupled with counseling, may be adequate. Discharge of the offender is not always required" (Player, 1992, pp. 211–212). The various courts have not agreed on severity or on damages, although they continue to maintain that harassment in some form represents misconduct that carries a liability. Since 1991, victims of sexual harassment can recover damages, raising the stakes even higher for employers who are not vigilant. Prior to the enactment of the 1991 Civil Rights Act, the only remedies were *make whole remedies.*[2]

In 1993 (with Clarence Thomas as one of its members), the nation's highest court rendered a unanimous decision that demonstrated that it had taken firm ground in cases of sexual harassment. In *Harris v. Forklift Systems Inc.* (510 U.S. 17), the Court ruled on the case of Teresa Harris, who had been subjected to a lengthy series of sexually demeaning comments by the president of the firm she worked for. In addressing the issue of hostile environment, Justice Sandra Day O'Connor, author of the decision, wrote that "a discriminatorily abusive work environment, even one that does not seriously affect employees' psychological well-being, can and often will detract from employees' job performance, discourage employees from remaining on the job or keep them from advancing in their careers." Concurring, Judge Ruth Bader Ginsburg said that what is important is "whether members of one sex are exposed to disadvantageous terms or conditions of employment to which members of the other sex are not exposed." This case established that severe psychological injury did not have to be proven in order to establish that a hostile environment existed (Strickland, 1995, p. 501). However, the plaintiff was not awarded victory. Instead, the Supreme Court sent the case back to the Court of Appeals (Greenhouse, 1993, pp. A1, 22).

Managing all the issues related to sexual harassment constitutes a personnel challenge. The law has been designed to protect the victims, and that is its main concern. However, the alleged harasser also has a set of rights to due process. He or she has the right to refute the charges and to have a full and fair hearing. An employer should hold an investigation when charges are raised and then hold a hearing. The process must also be reasonably quick.

The question of sexual harassment is clearly a matter of concern to personnel managers in both the public and private sectors. The courts have established that employers must have a policy in place and that channels for remedial action must exist. Courtroom challenges to personnel policies or activities are costly in terms of both monetary expense and unfavorable publicity. Given the EEOC guidelines and litigation to date, certain procedures are recommended for public personnel managers, and it is to these that we now turn.

WHAT CAN PUBLIC PERSONNEL MANAGERS DO?

Public personnel managers need to create an atmosphere that makes sexual harassment unlikely. They must make it clear to all that this behavior is undesirable and carries serious consequences. They also need to move quickly and decisively when charges of sexual harassment do occur at one of their worksites (Hoyman and Robinson, 1980). In order to achieve these ends, personnel managers need to establish the following elements:

1. A policy statement prohibiting sexual harassment
2. The public promulgation of the statement
3. A civil service provision prohibiting harassment, if appropriate
4. Routine inclusion of information about the sexual harassment policy in new employee orientation and in training for existing employees
5. Uniform enforcement of the policy
6. A progressive set of disciplinary measures for infractions of the policy
7. Training of supervisors
8. Training of all employees
9. A plan to take prompt remedial action when an allegation occurs, pending an investigation
10. An in-house investigation capability
11. The availability of alternative dispute resolution devices, in order to avoid more costly litigation

Developing a clear policy statement on sexual harassment is the most important first step for public personnel administrators. This policy statement must explicitly mention sexual harassment. A statement forbidding discrimination by race or sex is not sufficient. Defining sexual harassment for the policy statement is not an easy task. However, it is the authors' view that the definition should be as broad and all-inclusive as the legal definition. As mentioned earlier, that definition states that sexual harassment is unwanted sexual advances that have one of three employment consequences: submission to such conduct is made either explicitly or implicitly a term or condition of an individual's employment, submission to or rejection of such conduct by an individual is used as the basis for employment decisions affecting such individual, or such conduct has the purpose or effect of unreasonably interfering with an individual's work performance or creating an intimidating, hostile, or offensive work environment.

The most important factor here is that the conduct be *unwanted*. This definition encompasses all possible forms of harassment and ensures that the employer mentions all behavior that could violate government guidelines. If an employer's policy statement falls short of the federal guidelines enumerated here, considerable liability could be incurred if litigation took place.

Second, this policy should be posted publicly in the various worksites. Many workers may be reluctant to bring forth charges of harassment, out of either fear for their jobs or reticence to pursue action in this charged area. Through comprehensive training of both supervisors and employees, it should be made clear that the employer does not desire to have any form of harassment in the workplace and wants to be made aware of any unpleasant situation as soon as it occurs. In this training, that fine line between office romance and harassment must be made clear: sexual harassment is unwelcome behavior that interferes with job responsibilities. No should mean no. In addition, the policy should extend prohibitions against harassment to either gender and to homosexual and heterosexual alike. The policy has to make clear that harassment is a serious problem; it is not boys will be boys but carries consequences for work performance and potential liability for the employer. This type of training must be continuous. Further, the sexual harassment policy statement should be contained in all employee handbooks and be made part of civil service rules in those jurisdictions with a formal civil service. It can be posted on bulletin boards, in employee lounges or restrooms, and on the work floor. The policy can also be distributed periodically in employees' paycheck envelopes.

Employees who encounter sexual harassment need to know the route to remedial action. If the agency has an ombudsman, an interview with that person might be a suitable course; an employee might wish to discuss the matter in confidence before pursuing a formal complaint. Once an appropriate supervisor is made aware of allegations of improper behavior, management needs to act quickly. The employee making the complaint must be removed from the situation that is causing distress and interfering with job performance, with no loss in benefits.

Agencies must practice uniform enforcement of their sexual harassment policy. Rules become worthless when they are not enforced or when they are enforced differentially. A discharge or disciplinary activity can be overturned when the employer has not enforced the rules uniformly and in all cases. An employer increases its liability when differential treatment can be established.

What is the role of a union in sexual harassment cases? Obviously, if the contract requires that the union be allowed a role in bargaining rules, the union will have input into the sexual harassment policy or the work rules governing it. However, by far a union's biggest role is that of defending those who have been disciplined. Normally, then, the union is relegated to the role of defending the person accused of harassment.

Progressive discipline is a sound method for dealing with infractions of the sexual harassment policy. An employee charged with harassment should face a series of successively more severe penalties; thus the first infraction of a rule may not be grounds for discharge, unless it is an egregious infraction or has been previously established as a dischargeable offense. Usually, the employee first receives a warning, and our advice is that it be a written warning. In some locations the first warning is verbal and the second is written. In any case, clear records must be kept of the infractions and the penalties proffered. Due to the ongoing liability of the employer and the vulnerability of the victim, the employee may also be transferred. A second violation might invoke a two-week suspension without pay; the third might bring about a four-week suspension. Warnings would be contained in the written responses to these latter violations.

Progressive discipline emphasizes a course of action in response to repetition of the same offense, and the employee is given a chance to change his or her ways.

Some behaviors may be so extreme as to warrant immediate dismissal. Rape falls into that category. For liability considerations if for nothing else, the employer will want to act immediately to terminate the offender or suspend the accused without pay.

If accusations of harassment are permitted to continue and are then found to be true, the agency has placed itself in grave jeopardy. If complaints accumulate, the employer may want to suspend the accused without pay pending an internal investigation and perhaps a criminal or EEOC investigation as well.

In order to prevent sexual harassment in the workplace, it is important to provide training to all supervisory personnel. Both lower-level supervisors and those on the higher rungs need to have the same information to ensure consistency in their treatment of any incidents and to prevent the reversal of any disciplinary measures. The first-line supervisor, of course, is most critical in the enforcement of the agency's policy. It is the first-line supervisor who can condemn or condone an atmosphere that tolerates harassment.

The Supreme Court's adoption of the hostile environment standard has increased the importance of educating employees as to what constitutes unlawful or offensive behavior. Naturally, the training should address basic do's and don'ts. But, as mentioned in relation to establishing a policy, it also has to explain where the line between flirtation or romance and unwanted behavior lies. In addition to familiarizing all employees with the main facets of agency policy, it should give them a clear idea of what discipline to expect for a first minor infraction, for repeated infractions, and for a severe infraction. Role-playing or sensitivity sessions may be useful in raising employees' awareness of others' perceptions or feelings. Because fear or shame has probably led to a significant underreporting of various forms of sexual harassment, training sessions and other reminders should encourage victims to come forward when genuine problems exist.

Employers will have to develop an internal mechanism to investigate complaints of harassment. This mechanism should embody speed, thoroughness, objectivity, and due process. Speed is important because liability may be ongoing. Any investigation should be as thorough as possible in order to accurately reveal the parties at fault and identify any broader problem behind the precipitating event. Objectivity, of course, is important but often difficult to achieve. All the witnesses will be acquainted and generally partisan to one side or the other. Defenses of illegal behavior may be offered by friends, fellow workers, or supervisors. They may close ranks, claiming that the behavior is just "par for the course."

Because findings often come down to the judgment of one person's credibility over another and because internal neutrality is sometimes difficult to obtain, an outside party may be employed to investigate and do fact finding on the recommendation of counsel. This person will not be familiar with the parties in the case and may be an arbitrator or equal employment opportunity specialist. The employer will still select the punishment or remedy. Information regarding the course of an investigation for harassment can become part of an agency's normal grievance procedure.

Obviously, a completely detached investigation is the most credible and will be viewed as such by the EEOC or state agency if it reexamines the charge. Therefore, a public agency may want to keep a roster of EEO-qualified arbitrators to resolve such disputes. The advantages of arbitration are that it produces a final and binding result and it is less costly and faster than litigation.

Several recent studies have looked at the role of arbitration in sexual harassment grievances. Elkiss (1987) studied eighty-three sexual harassment cases. She found that the arbitrator sustained the discipline in over 50 percent of the cases. This is similar to findings regarding arbitration in other areas, measured in a random sample, where the grievant prevailed 57 percent of the time (Hoyman and Crews, 1996; see also Hauck, 1995).

CONCLUSION

Sexual harassment is a major workforce problem. If harassment creates a quid pro quo situation or if an environment hostile to work performance is created, employers may be held liable. Although there is variation among court decisions in this area, it has been made clear by the Supreme Court that sexual harassment constitutes sex discrimination and is not lawful. Employers need to understand the gravity of the problem and, to protect themselves and their employees, must create policies that define and try to prevent sexual harassment, take action to create a work atmosphere that does not condone offensive behavior, follow up promptly any allegations, and put in place disciplinary measures to deal with perpetrators. These actions must be accompanied by training, investigative capability, and possibly use of outside resources. The gravity of the problem has to be appreciated by all employers and especially those that hire women in nontraditional jobs.

Notes

1. The Sangamon survey and the 1981 survey of federal employees used random samples. Subsequent surveys in both private and public settings often used convenience samples and therefore are less scientific. In addition, the Sangamon study remains an excellent data source because all strata of occupations are represented.

2. A make whole remedy merely restores the plaintiff to his or her status prior to the unlawful action, without any compensatory or punitive damages. A make whole remedy in the case of wrongful discharge is reinstatement and back pay.

References

Alger, A., and Flanagan, W. "A Field Day for Lawyers." *Forbes,* May 6, 1996a, p. 107.

Alger, A., and Flanagan, W. "Sexual Politics." *Forbes,* May 6, 1996b, pp. 106–110.

Brady, R. L. *HR Focus,* May 1996, p. 20.

Civil Rights Act of 1964. U.S. Code, vol. 42, sec. 1981 et seq. (Title VII at 2000e.)

Civil Rights Act of 1991. U.S. Statutes at Large 105 (1991) 1071. (Compensatory damages at *U.S. Code,* vol. 42, sec. 1981.)

Crull, P. "The Impact of Sexual Harassment on the Job." In D. Neugarten and J. Shafritz (eds.), *Sexuality in Organizations: Romantic and Coercive Behaviors at Work.* Oak Park, Ill.: Moore, 1980.

Dowd, M. "Senate Approves a 4-Star Rank for Admiral in Tailhook Affair." *New York Times,* Apr. 20, 1994, p. 1.

Elkiss, H. "Why Do Arbitrators Uphold Discipline? Examples from Sexual Harassment Grievances." *Journal of Individual Employment Rights,* 1987, 5(2), 101–123.

Equal Employment Opportunity Commission. *Final Guidelines on Sexual Harassment in the Workplace.* Washington, D.C.: U.S. Government Printing Office, 1980. (*Federal Register,* 1980, vol. 45, sec. 74676.)

Gordon, M. R. "Pentagon Report Tells of Aviators' Debauchery." *New York Times,* Apr. 24, 1993, pp. A1, 22.

Greenhouse, L. "Court, 9–0, Makes Sex Harassment Easier to Prove." *New York Times,* Nov. 10, 1993, pp. 1A, 22.

Hauck, V. *Arbitrating Sexual Harassment Claims.* Washington, D.C.: Bureau of National Affairs, 1995.

Hoff, J. *Law, Gender, and Injustice: A Legal History of U.S. Women.* New York: New York University Press, 1991.

Hoyman, M. M., and Crews, S. "Impact of Gender on Arbitral Outcomes." Paper presented at the annual meeting of the Industrial Relations Research Association, San Diego, Calif. Jan. 2–5, 1996.

Hoyman, M. M., and Robinson, R. "Interpreting the New Sexual Harassment Guidelines." *Personnel Journal,* Dec. 1980, 59(12), 996–1000.

Hoyman, M. M., and Robinson, R. "The EEOC Guidelines on Sexual Harassment: The Solution or Just the Beginning?" Paper presented at the forty-first annual meeting of the Academy of Management, San Diego, Calif. Aug. 2–5, 1981.

Maremont, M., and Sasseen, J. "Abuse of Power." *Business Week,* May 13, 1986, pp. 86–98.

"Navy Makes Progress Against Sex Harassment." *St. Louis Post-Dispatch,* July 4, 1996, p. 3A.

Neugarten, D. A. "Sexual Harassment in Public Employment." In S. W. Hays and R. C. Kearney (eds.), *Public Personnel Administration: Problems and Prospects.* Upper Saddle River, N.J.: Prentice Hall, 1990.

Player, M. A. *Federal Law of Employment Discrimination in a Nutshell.* (3rd ed.) St. Paul, Minn.: West, 1992.

Rhode, D. L. *Justice and Gender: Sex Discrimination and the Law.* Cambridge, Mass.: Harvard University Press, 1989.

Robinson, R. "Sexual Harassment in the Workplace." Unpublished tutorial, Institute of Labor and Industrial Relations, University of Illinois, 1981.

Schmitt, E. "Top Army Soldier Named in Sex Case." *New York Times,* May 8, 1997, p. A1.

Sedmak, N., and Levin-Epstein, M. D. *Primer on Equal Employment Opportunity.* (5th ed.) Washington, D.C.: U.S. Bureau of National Affairs, 1991.

Sherman, A. J. "Sexual Harassment Policies a Must." *D&B Reports,* Jan.-Feb. 1992, p. 45.

Strickland, R. A. "Sexual Harassment: A Legal Perspective for Public Administrators." *Public Personnel Management,* 1995, *24*(4), 493–513.

U.S. Bureau of National Affairs. "Strict Standards of Employer Liability Stay in EEOC Sexual Harassment Guidelines." *Daily Labor Report No. 186,* Sept. 23, 1980, pp. A-5, E-2–E-3.

U.S. Merit Systems Protection Board. *Sexual Harassment in the Federal Government.* Washington, D.C.: U.S. Government Printing Office, 1988.

Yang, C. "Getting Justice Is No Easy Task." *Business Week,* May 13, 1996, p. 98.

CHAPTER TEN

Understanding the
Americans with Disabilities Act

David Pfeiffer

On July 26, 1990, President George Bush signed into law the Americans with Disabilities Act (ADA). This act fulfilled a campaign promise made in 1988. Some observers said, based upon public polling results before and after the 1988 election, that this promise caused a sufficient number of persons with disabilities to switch from Michael Dukakis to George Bush to provide Bush's winning margin or at least a major part of it. In the 1992 and 1996 presidential campaigns both parties paid attention to the issues relevant to the community of people with disabilities. Some observers say that people with disabilities are today a major player in presidential politics; whether that is true or not, meeting the provisions of the ADA is now a significant part of human resource management.

The passage of the ADA represents the maturing of the disability movement in the United Stated. Up through the end of World War II, disparate groups of people with disabilities and their family members sought new policies and programs. But after a number of war veterans returned disabled, the disability movement took on a new image. Rather than simply seeking services, it began to challenge society about the way in which persons with disabilities were viewed and treated.

Disabled veterans, because they were veterans, provided more clout to the movement. Still, however, most policies were crafted and programs implemented by persons without disabilities. Not until the 1970s was there a critical mass of advocates who were themselves disabled. The White House Conference on Handicapped Individuals in 1977 gave recognition to that fact. The regulations implementing the Rehabilitation Act of 1973 (containing, in section 504, the first civil rights provision for persons with disabilities) were also promulgated in 1977, four years after the passage of the statute. Political demonstrations and protestors' occupation of the Western regional and national offices of the then-named U.S. Department of Health, Education and Welfare gave evidence that the disability movement knew how to apply pressure to the system.

During the 1980s, a number of federal and state laws were passed in order to protect the rights of people with disabilities. In November of 1980, Massachusetts incorporated almost the exact wording of section 504 in the state constitution as amendment 114. Using this constitutional amendment as a base, the disability movement in Massachusetts obtained passage of the state's Public Accommodations Law, Employment Discrimination Law, and other related laws, and strengthened the Architectural Accessibility Law. All of this legislation had been recommended by the White House conference.

On the federal level, a number of laws recommended by the White House conference were passed. The Voting Accessibility for the Elderly and Handicapped Act of 1984, revisions of the special education laws, now incorporated into the Individuals with Disabilities Education Act of 1970, the Air Carrier Access Act of 1986, and the 1988 amendments to the Fair Housing Act of 1968 all embody recommendations from the White House conference.

One of the strongest recommendations of the White House conference was to amend the 1964 Civil Rights Act to include persons with disabilities. In the mid-1980s, the National Council on Disability (also created as a result of the White House conference) started a series of investigations that led to the publication of reports stressing the need to protect the civil liberties of people with disabilities. Out of this activity came the Americans with Disabilities Act, which was finally passed in 1990.

OVERVIEW OF THE ADA

Title I of the ADA

Title I of the Americans with Disabilities Act of 1990 extends the nondiscrimination provisions found in section 504 of the earlier Rehabilitation Act of 1973 to the private sector. Under section 504 (*U.S. Code,* vol. 29, sec. 794) any program or activity receiving federal financial assistance is prohibited from discriminating against an otherwise qualified person on the basis of disability. Generally, however, only public entities (states, territories, local governments, and instrumentalities created by them) came under this prohibition. Title I extended this protection for people with disabilities to the private sector.

Reasons for the ADA

As just outlined, ADA is deeply rooted in the history of the disability movement (Mayerson, 1993; Pfeiffer, 1993; Watson, 1993; West, 1993). Before the 1980s, federal and state policies consigned people with disabilities to second-class (or worse) citizenship through exclusion, segregation, and denial of equal protection. The ADA is an attempt to change this situation.

Although statistics depend upon definitions, it is generally agreed—no matter which source is used—that the unemployment rate for people with disabilities is at least 40 percent and may be as high as 80 percent. In terms of income some 80 percent of persons with disabilities are below the country's median income, and some 60 percent are below the poverty level no matter which definition is used. In terms of housing and education, persons with disabilities are worse off than the nondisabled (Barnartt and Christiansen, 1985; Pfeiffer, 1990, 1991; U.S. Bureau of the Census, 1993). Persons with disabilities are viewed as one of the disadvantaged groups in this country (Young, 1990).

In passing the ADA, Congress found discrimination on the basis of a disability to be a serious problem in most areas of society, including employment. This discrimination, Congress found, violates the equal protection of persons with disabilities and is unnecessarily costly in terms of tax dollars spent and lost tax revenues. Congress, therefore, provided a clear mandate in the ADA to eliminate this discrimination.

Definition of Disability

Disability is often defined by whether or not a person can carry out the so-called normal activities of daily living. This functional definition underlies only part of the ADA definition, because by itself it carries many problems of interpretation. For example, what is the normal way of moving about: by car, by public transportation, by bicycle, by wheelchair, or by foot? What is the normal way of working? With all the people who do not work 9 A.M. to 5 P.M. or who have unusual occupations, how can one arrive at a statement of a normal way of working? To define disability on the basis of normal activities only is to perpetuate discrimination.

For this and other reasons, disability is defined in the ADA as "(A) a physical or mental impairment that substantially limits one or more of the major life activities of such individual; (B) a record of such an impairment; or (C) being regarded as having such an impairment" (42 USC, sec. 12102). Major life activities include, but are not limited to, the ability to walk, talk, see, hear, breathe, care for oneself, learn, work, perform manual tasks, socialize, and be active in the community. Having "a record of such an impairment" covers individuals who have recovered from some condition or illness or who were misclassified as disabled. Being "regarded as having such an impairment" covers individuals who are perceived as disabled when they are not. There is no mention of normal in this definition.

What Title I Says

Title I says that no employer (of fifteen or more persons in the private sector) "shall discriminate against a qualified individual with a disability because of the disability of such individual in regard to job application procedures, the hiring, advancement, or discharge of employees, employee compensation, job training, and other terms, conditions, and privileges of employment" (42 USC, sec. 12112). Employment agencies, labor organizations, and joint labor-management committees are also covered by this prohibition. Exceptions are corporations owned by an Indian tribe and nonprofit private membership clubs. Although the services and programs of state, territorial, and local governments are primarily covered by Title II, as employers these governments are also covered under Title I.

A "qualified individual with a disability" is one who can perform the essential functions of the job. It does not matter whether or not the person requires or has a "reasonable accommodation" (defined later in this chapter). If the person can perform the essential functions (perhaps with a reasonable accommodation), he or she is qualified.

Title I also prohibits discrimination against anyone on the basis of association with a person with a disability. Therefore a person must not experience discrimination because a spouse, child, family member, or friend is disabled.

Role of the Title I Regulations

Almost all federal statutes have accompanying regulations. These regulations are drawn up by the agency in charge of implementing the law and usually promulgated by the cabinet secretary or independent agency administrator in charge. They are the way in which the law will be enforced, and human resource managers should be aware of the regulations relating to relevant acts and understand their purpose and how they might change.

The regulations are of most use to the agency, but they are also a valuable source of information to the persons subject to the law. For example, the ADA regulations contain examples of disabilities and examples and discussions of reasonable accommodations and other topics. They and other documents with examples serve to interpret and, it is hoped, clarify any ambiguity in the law. However, they must conform to the law. Sometimes courts find that regulations are written in ways that contradict the law, and these regulations are struck down.

The Equal Employment Opportunity Commission, which implements and enforces Title I, published its related regulations in the *Code of Federal Regulations* (Equal Employment Opportunity Commission, 1997b) with an appendix entitled

"Interpretive Guidance on Title I of the Americans with Disabilities Act." The statute uses the term "essential functions" to help define who is otherwise qualified for a position but does not define it. In the regulations (29 CFR, sec. 1630.2[n]) this term is defined and discussed, and it is discussed further in the appendix.

The appendix can be changed quite easily. However, any change in the regulations must be publicly announced, with sufficient time before it takes effect for persons to make written comments. These comments must be answered or somehow dealt with. Only then can the change become part of the regulation, sometimes after a further period for comments.

One agency can incorporate another agency's regulations into its own. For example, the Department of Justice—which implements and enforces Title II in public entities—says (U.S. Department of Justice, 1997) that the Equal Employment Opportunity Commission regulations just discussed are to be used by public entities in regard to employment. And agencies can issue joint regulations. The Equal Employment Opportunity Commission and the Department of Labor's Office of Federal Contract Compliance, for example, have published joint regulations for filing charges of discrimination against a government contractor (Equal Employment Opportunity Commission, 1997a).

Impact of the Other Titles of the ADA

There are five parts, or titles, in the ADA. Title I, as mentioned, covers employment discrimination in the private sector. Title II covers discrimination by state, territorial, and local governments and anything created by them such as regional compacts and local school boards. Title II gives special attention to public transportation authorities and transit systems run by private entities to serve the public on behalf of a public entity.

Title III covers public accommodations. A public accommodation is anything that is open to the public, such as restaurants, stores, recreation facilities, and town halls. Probably Title III will have no distinct impact on employment. Anything it requires in regard to employment will already be required under the other two titles.

Title IV requires that every state establish a relay system so that persons who use text telephones (TTs) can call a central number and be connected with an operator who answers with a TT. That operator can then place a call to a hearing person and convey the messages back and forth. (Many persons use the term TDD [telecommunication device for the deaf] for this device. The community of persons using these devices prefers TTY [teletypewriter], the original name of the device.) Title IV's requirement may have a positive impact upon employment in the sense that an employee can use the system to place work-related phone calls. However, a person who has a job that requires extensive, direct telephone conversations—telemarketing, for example—may not benefit at all from a relay system.

Title V has a number of miscellaneous provisions. One prohibits retaliation against, interference with, or coercion or intimidation of anyone exercising a right or assisting (testifying, for example) in any proceeding under the ADA. Another provision states that a person with a disability who is a current illegal user of drugs is not protected in the case of an action based upon that illegal drug use.

Title V also states that homosexuality and bisexuality are not impairments and that the following conditions are not disabilities: "(1) transvestism, transsexualism, pedophilia, exhibitionism, voyeurism, gender identity disorders not resulting from physical impairments, or other sexual behavior disorders; (2) compulsive gambling, kleptomania, or pyromania; or (3) psychoactive substance use disorders resulting from current illegal use of drugs" (42 USC, sec. 12211).

The Value of Legal Counsel

Although the basic principle of nondiscrimination is quite clear, its application in various circumstances can be complicated. In addition, as with any nondiscrimination law, a number of provisions require judicial interpretation when new circumstances or complex situations are encountered. Therefore it is essential that the human resource manager establish open communication and trust with an organization's legal counsel.

Anytime a charge of discrimination is made, and especially before any formal action is taken, legal counsel should be informed. It may be that sufficient procedures have been established in the human resource function and that under these procedures legal counsel is consulted only at a certain level of seriousness, but communication with that counsel must be easily and clearly available. The circumstances will then dictate the actions.

Questions of court procedure and rules of evidence can be very arcane. Lawyers are trained to know and to use these procedures and rules. It is probably wise to err on the side of communicating with legal counsel too early than to wait and risk being too late.

ADA IMPLEMENTATION

State, territorial, and local governments in the United States have implemented the ADA. Although for various reasons some governments had already accomplished many of the ADA goals prior to the act's implementation, a remarkable amount has been achieved in governments because of the ADA.

State and Territorial Governments

Pfeiffer and Finn (1995, 1997), with a sample of forty-four states and three territories, show the extent of ADA implementation. They found that 63 percent had an ADA coordinator and that 58 percent had completed the self-evaluation of policies and physical plant regarding discrimination, with another 20 percent saying it was in process. Although not every entity was required to do so, 76 percent said that they had completed a transition plan of how required changes would be done, and another 9 percent had it in process.

Most states and territories had completed an access survey of major state offices, with the number varying from 76 percent to 96 percent depending on the facility. A TTY had been installed in major facilities, again depending on the facility, by 56 percent to 84 percent of the states and territories. Sign language interpreters were provided on request by 98 percent of states and territories, and 91 percent provided material in alternative formats. A reasonable accommodation had been provided by 87 percent of the states and territories. ADA and disability awareness training was provided by 75 percent.

Local Governments

Pfeiffer and Finn (1995, 1997) found that an ADA coordinator existed in 65 percent of the local governments. The self-evaluation had been completed by 70 percent and the transition plan by 66 percent. Again, not every local government had to complete a transition plan. Eighty-eight percent to 95 percent of major facilities had completed access surveys, the percentage depending on the type of facility. TTYs were installed in these major facilities by as few as 15 percent of schools but as many as 73 percent of police stations.

Sign language interpreters were provided by 65 percent of the local governments, and 36 percent provided materials in alternative formats. A reasonable accommodation was provided by 39 percent.

Implications

What these statistics show (along with others presented by Pfeiffer and Finn, 1995, 1997) is that many states and a lesser but significant percentage of local governments are taking steps to remove discriminatory barriers and policies. Although it will take time to identify and remove all barriers, the ADA is having an impact upon U.S. society.

Some commentators say that because the unemployment rate of persons with disabilities remains at a high level, the ADA must not be working. However, a decade after the enactment of the Civil Rights Act of 1964, the unemployment rate of African Americans remained high. This fact was taken to mean that discriminatory attitudes remained. Today the high unemployment rate of people with disabilities must be viewed in the same way. Attitudinal barriers are just as common as architectural and sensory barriers.

REASONABLE ACCOMMODATIONS

One of the ways in which an employer can avoid the legal penalties of discrimination under the ADA is to work out an accommodation with the employee with a disability. There are generally three considerations: the accommodation must be reasonable, it must not present an undue hardship to the employer, and both sides must agree on it.

What Is a Reasonable Accommodation

The term "reasonable accommodation" originated in EEOC regulations concerning religious holidays, but—for reasons not relevant here—those parts of the regulations were struck down by the courts (Burgdorf, 1995). Regulations for implementing the Rehabilitation Act of 1973 used the term, but gave only examples and not a definition. Over the last two decades, case law and administrative decisions have developed an interpretation of what the term means.

Based on this interpretation the EEOC regulations (Equal Employment Opportunity Commission, 1997b, sec. 1630.2[o]) define a reasonable accommodation as (1) any modification to the process of applying for a job which allows the person with a disability to be considered for the job; (2) any change in the work environment including the manner in which a job is usually done that allows a person with a disability to carry out the essential functions of the job; or (3) any adjustment of benefits provided which allows a person with a disability to utilize them as any other employee would. The accommodation could be a work schedule change, a job restructuring, such as having other persons carry out the nonessential functions, a reassignment to another position, the provision of an auxiliary aid or service, or physical modification to the workplace.

Cost of Accommodations

One employer concern is whether the accommodation will cost more than the employee is worth in terms of productivity. If available studies are correct, most employees with disabilities require no accommodation at all. When an accommodation is requested, a high percentage result in no cost or little cost. The expenditure will usually be part of the normal cost of doing business.

For example, in an in-depth study of Sears, Roebuck and Co., Blanck (1996) found that between January 1, 1978, and December 31, 1992, an end date shortly after Sears became subject to the ADA, 69 percent of the accommodations for employees with disabilities entailed no cost and another 28 percent cost less than $1,000. The average cost was $121. If the 3 percent that cost over $1,000 are removed, the average cost drops to $36. After Sears became subject to the ADA, Blanck (1996) found that from January 1, 1993, to December 31, 1995, 72 percent of the accommodations entailed no cost, and another 17 percent cost less that $100. The average cost was $45. In addition, employers have tax credits available for barrier removal.

The ADA provides that an accommodation is not reasonable when it presents an "undue hardship" to the employer, that is, when it entails a significant cost or difficulty, taking into account the financial resources of the facility where the job is carried out and the financial resources and size of the employer. Other factors to be considered are the type of business and the impact on the company.

Although not an employment case, *Roberts* v. *KinderCare Learning Centers* (8 NDLR 147 [8th Cir. 1996]), illustrates an undue burden. A day-care center was asked to provide a full-time personal care attendant for a child. It refused to do so, and the parents sued in federal district court. The court found that the high cost of providing this full-time attendant was an undue burden given the resources of the day-care center. It accepted the day-care center's figures that a full-time attendant would cost over $200 a week plus benefits but that tuition received would be only $105 a week. The decision was then upheld by the Eighth Circuit Court of Appeals.

In any event the employer must know that the employee has a disability before a reasonable accommodation is possible. In many cases the accommodation might be granted without such an identification, but to charge that an employer refused to provide a reasonable accommodation, the employee with a disability must self-identify and do so at a reasonable time before an accommodation is requested.

Neither the employer nor the employee has a veto over what is reasonable. Neither one has to accept the suggested accommodation. In cases of disagreement, negotiation about the accommodation should occur. However, if the accommodation is rejected by either side and the case goes to court, both sides run the risk of even higher costs than anticipated. Title V of the ADA suggests alternative means of dispute resolution where appropriate and authorized by law, and a dispute over a suggested accommodation is a candidate for such alternative resolution.

Examples of Reasonable Accommodation

Reasonable accommodations vary from employer to employer and from employee to employee, and instances of successful reasonable accommodations can be found in many places. Spechler (1996) provides the first three illustrations that follow.

For example, a man who is quadriplegic applied for a position in the chief financial officer's department at AT&T. Two virtually cost-free accommodations were provided during the interview process. A table was raised so the man's motorized chair could fit underneath and he could take the standard employment tests. He was also given additional time to complete the tests because he was a slow writer. Before he began work a local job accommodation specialist was brought in for a one-hour session with his new coworkers. It turned into a four-hour question-and-answer session, which made everyone more comfortable and made his coworkers more willing to help when asked to do little things like taking medication out of his shirt pocket. Hand splints enabled the man to use a computer, but they were cumbersome in other situations. After he was hired, a second set of hand splints was purchased by AT&T so he would not have to carry the splints back and forth between his home and the office. He also relied (when necessary) on personnel in the medical facility at his work location for personal care needs. After the medical facility was closed for budget reasons, an alternative was worked out.

BankAmerica Corporation not only provided reasonable accommodations for employees with disabilities, it also developed guides and a training curriculum on the ADA. Because banks are places of public accommodation, the company quickly produced a training video for all employees who directly served customers, and it provided training seminars for its human resource specialists. Spechler (1996) presents numerous details about these training and awareness activities.

The Florida Power & Light Company provided a number of reasonable accommodations over a broad spectrum of disabilities. For an engineer who began to lose peripheral vision, the company purchased software and hardware that magnified the computer screen. For a person who began to use a wheelchair due to a spinal cord injury, the company had only to raise the height of a desk to enable the person to return to work. For hearing-impaired employees in the customer service department, the company provided amplified phones.

The Job Accommodation Network (n.d.) also provides a number of illustrations of reasonable accommodation. The Network assisted in developing the solutions. For example, an employee with a eye disorder became fatigued from glare on the computer screen. For $39, an antiglare screen was purchased that greatly reduced the employee's fatigue. Another employee developed a condition that limited use of her hands. She could not reach across her desk to a set of files. For $85, a lazy Susan file holder was purchased that made it possible for her to keep her job. A police officer with dyslexia spent a great amount of time at the end of his shift filling out forms. For $69, a tape recorder was purchased. A secretary typed the other police officers' forms from handwritten copy and this officer's forms from the tape.

Two more accommodations mentioned by the Job Accommodation Network were a $35 one-handed can-opener for a cook who had only one hand and a costless schedule change for a person who developed a condition that necessitated a two-hour rest period during the day. She came in earlier and left later than before, still working the same number of hours but taking her needed break in the middle.

Both Spechler and publications available from the Job Accommodation Network present overviews of AIDS in the workplace. Both say that in the public and in the private sectors this disability raises unique and emotionally charged questions resulting in reasonable accommodation. Spechler also discusses how technology can facilitate reasonable accommodations. Access technology is both a useful and a little-known subject.

ACTIONS REQUIRED BY TITLE II

Except for actions required of public transportation authorities that are not relevant here, the statutory language of Title II does not require anything other than nondiscrimination. The statutory language of Title I requires nondiscrimination and the posting of a notice in an accessible format describing the provisions of the Americans with Disabilities Act. Because public entities are employers, they must post such a notice. However, the regulations issued by the U.S. Department of Justice for Title II (28 CFR, sec. 35) do require that public entities undertake a number of actions in order to comply with the ADA.

Any public entity with fifty or more employees must designate an employee to coordinate the responsibility of complying with the ADA, and it must establish a grievance procedure to resolve complaints under Titles I and II. The coordinator investigates any complaints about noncompliance. Public entities with less than fifty employees still must comply with the ADA, so the appointment of a coordinator and establishment of a grievance procedure would be useful to them even if not required.

All public entities must make available in accessible formats information about the rights and protections found in Title II. This information must be made available to job applicants, program participants, beneficiaries, and "other interested persons" (28 CFR, sec. 35.106). The last phrase is generally taken to mean the general public, but its definition has not been not specified.

Every public entity must undertake a self-evaluation of its services, policies, and practices to determine whether they violate Title II. All services, policies, and practices must be in compliance. Interested persons, including people with disabilities and organizations representing people with disabilities, must be provided an opportunity to participate. If a self-evaluation was carried out in compliance with section 504 of the Rehabilitation Act of 1973, then only policies and practices not included in that earlier evaluation are reviewed.

All public entities must comply with Title II; in addition, any public entity with fifty or more employees that determines that structural changes in facilities are necessary must prepare a transition plan. This plan must identify the physical barriers, how they will be modified to make the facility accessible, and a schedule for their modifications.

Adaptive Environments Center (1996) offers four principles for successful compliance with these requirements: (1) top leadership must demonstrate commitment to the ADA during the entire process; (2) compliance activities must be coordinated; (3) people with disabilities who are also knowledgeable about the process and about accommodations must be involved in the process (but note that being disabled does not guarantee this knowledge); (4) compliance must become institutionalized.

Spechler (1996) presents a ten-step process for implementing the ADA within organizations. The steps revolve around the four principles set forth by the Adaptive Environments Center. If these four principles and ten steps are followed, success is very probable.

CAUTIONS ABOUT THE ADA

The ADA is in its beginning stages and case law is still developing. Many questions remain to be answered although the main requirements are clear. Discrimination on the basis of a disability is prohibited. Whether certain acts are discriminatory and whether an individual is a qualified person with a disability and whether an accommodation is reasonable are all questions that have to be answered in the context in which they happen. Future developments may make the ADA and concerns over discrimination more complex or more simple. Many answers to current questions remain for the future to reveal, along with important questions we have not yet asked.

In any event the context in which the ADA is relevant is a volatile one. Being hired or fired, being promoted or paid more, and perceiving any type of discrimination are issues of great importance to the person with a disability. Cost considerations are of great importance to employers and to public entities. Accusations of discrimination are always unsettling. Human resource managers must approach ADA compliance and complaints carefully, but they must deal with them.

Finally, employers, public entities, and people with disabilities should emulate the announced strategy of the Department of Justice and the Equal Employment Opportunity Commission. This strategy is to educate and negotiate first. If there is no success, only then litigate. It is contended by many disability rights advocates that a large number of ADA complaints are resolved by education and negotiation. There is no need to litigate if a successful resolution can be achieved.

CONCLUSION: THE BENEFITS OF THE ADA TO EVERYONE

The Americans with Disabilities Act provides benefits to everyone. As Pfeiffer (1996) shows, people with disabilities are empowered by the ADA. They feel good about having rights, and they now have greater expectations about themselves and their place in society. In addition, the implementation of the ADA opened up employment to many persons with disabilities. The education of private-sector employers, public officials, and the public in general benefited all of society.

There is support for the ADA among private-sector employers. In part it has opened a new source for workers that they can tap. There is similar support among public officials because it is important that citizens be able to obtain services to which they are entitled. And there is general support in U.S. society for the ADA.

There are tax savings when people with disabilities who previously received tax monies in order to live become self-supporting. There is revenue enhancement when previously unemployed people with disabilities pay income and other taxes. There is a general feeling of enhanced self-worth from being self-supporting.

Understanding the ADA means knowing what is required by it. It also means knowing the role the ADA is playing in the lives of people with disabilities and in the larger society.

RESOURCES

Besides the publications cited in this chapter, there are a number of other resources. Both the Equal Employment Opportunity Commission (EEOC) and the Disability Rights Section of the Department of Justice (DOJ) have manuals and other publications on the ADA. They are available by phone from the EEOC (202–663–4900) and the Disability Rights Section (800–514–0301); however, the lines are often busy. Each federal region in the country has a Disability and Business Technical Assistance Center (DBTAC) that can provide the EEOC and DOJ publications and other ones. The telephone number is the same for all regions (800–949–4232 [800–9494-ADA] for both voice and TTY), and you will reach the DBTAC in your federal region.

The President's Committee on Employment of People with Disabilities (202–376–6200) funds the Job Accommodation Network (JAN), an important source for information about accommodations (800–232–9675 [800-ADA-WORK], both voice and TTY).

The workbook published in 1996 by the Adaptive Environments Center (617–695–1225) is specifically targeted to public entities. It provides step-by-step advice on compliance matters for human resource managers (and others) in the public sector. It is also useful for private-sector employers.

Burgdorf's 1995 legal treatise on disability-based discrimination in employment covers the Rehabilitation Act of 1973 (sections 501, 503, and 504), the ADA, and other related law. It is a very readable work and very complete.

A biweekly publication entitled *Disability Compliance Bulletin* carries news articles on court cases and agency actions pertaining to the ADA and related laws. It is published by LRP Publications (215–784–0860), which also publishes the *National Disability Law Reporter,* which contains the court decisions on which the *Bulletin* articles are based.

Finally, the following publications can be usefully consulted: Fersh and Thomas (1993), Gutman (1993), Morrissey (1991), Robinson (1993), and West (1996).

References

Adaptive Environments Center. *ADA Title II Action Guide for State and Local Governments and Supplement on Employment.* Boston: Adaptive Environments Center, 1996.

Air Carrier Access Act of 1986. U.S. Code, vol. 49, sec. 41705 et seq.

Americans with Disabilities Act of 1990. U.S. Code, vol. 42, sec. 12101 et seq.

Barnartt, S. N., and Christiansen, J. B. "The Socioeconomic Status of Deaf Workers: A Minority Group Perspective." *Social Science Journal,* 1985, *22,* 19–32.

Blanck, P. D. "Transcending Title I of the Americans with Disabilities Act: A Case Report on Sears, Roebuck and Co." *Mental and Physical Disability Law Reporter,* 1996, *20*(2), 279–286.

Burgdorf, R. L. *Disability Discrimination in Employment Law.* Washington, D.C.: Bureau of National Affairs, 1995.

Civil Rights Act of 1964. U.S. Code, vol. 42, sec. 1981 et seq. (Title VII at 2000e.)

Equal Employment Opportunity Commission. *Procedures for Complaints/Discharges of Employment Discrimination Based on Disability Filed Against Employers Holding Government Contracts or Subcontracts. Code of Federal Regulations,* 1997a, vol. 29, sec. 1641.

Equal Employment Opportunity Commission. *Regulations to Implement the Equal Employment Provisions of the Americans with Disabilities Act. Code of Federal Regulations,* 1997b, vol. 29, sec. 1630.

Fair Housing Act of 1968. U.S. Code, vol. 42, sec. 3601 et seq.

Fersh, D., and Thomas, P. W. *Complying with the Americans with Disabilities Act: A Guidebook for Management and People with Disabilities.* Westport, Conn.: Quorum/Greenwood, 1993.

Gutman, A. *EEO Law and Personnel Practices.* Thousand Oaks, Calif.: Sage, 1993.

Individuals with Disabilities Education Act of 1970. U.S. Code, vol. 20, sec. 1400 et seq.

Job Accommodation Network. *Job Accommodation Ideas: Job Accommodation Problems with Proposed Low-Cost Solutions.* Washington, D.C.: President's Committee on Employment of People with Disabilities, n.d.

Mayerson, A. "The History of the ADA: A Movement Perspective." In L. O. Gostin and H .A. Beyer (eds.), *Implementing the Americans with Disabilities Act: Rights and Responsibilities of All Americans.* Baltimore: Brookes, 1993.

Morrissey, P. A. *A Primer for Corporate America on Civil Rights for the Disabled.* Horsham, Pa.: LRP, 1991.

Pfeiffer, D. "Disabled People, Local Government, and Affirmative Action." In S. C. Hey, G. Kiger, B. Altman, and J. Scheer (eds.), *The Social Exploration of Disability.* Salem, Oreg.: Society for Disability Studies and Willamette University, 1990.

Pfeiffer, D. "The Influence of the Socio-Economic Characteristics of Disabled People on Their Employment Status and Income." *Disability, Handicap and Society,* 1991, *6*(2), 103–114.

Pfeiffer, D. "Overview of the Disability Movement: History, Legislative Record and Policy Implications." *Policy Studies Journal,* 1993, *21*(4), 724–734.

Pfeiffer, D. "'We Won't Go Back': The ADA on the Grass Roots Level." *Disability and Society,* 1996, *11*(2), 271–284.

Pfeiffer, D., and Finn, J. "Survey Shows State, Territorial, Local Public Officials Implementing the ADA." *Mental and Physical Disability Law Reporter,* 1995, *19*(4), 537–540.

Pfeiffer, D., and Finn, J. "The Americans with Disabilities Act: An Examination of Compliance by State, Territorial, and Local Governments in the USA." *Disability and Society,* 1997, *12*(5), 753–773.

Rehabilitation Act of 1973. U.S. Code, vol. 29, sec. 701 et seq.

Robinson, K. *Model Plan for Implementation of Title I of the Americans with Disabilities Act: The Human Resource Perspective.* Horsham, Pa.: LRP, 1993.

Spechler, J. W. *Reasonable Accommodation: Profitable Compliance with the Americans with Disabilities Act.* Delray Beach, Fla.: St. Lucie Press, 1996.

U.S. Bureau of the Census. *Americans with Disabilities: 1991–92.* Current Population Reports No. P70-33. Washington, D.C.: U.S. Government Printing Office, 1993.

U.S. Department of Justice. *Nondiscrimination on the Basis of Disability in State and Local Government Services. Code of Federal Regulations,* 1997, vol. 28, sec. 35.140.

Voting Accessibility for the Elderly and Handicapped Act of 1984. U.S. Code, vol. 42, sec. 1973ee.

Watson, S. D. "A Study in Legislative Strategy." In L. O. Gostin and H. A. Beyer (eds.), *Implementing the Americans with Disabilities Act: Rights and Responsibilities of All Americans.* Baltimore: Brookes, 1993.

West, J. "The Evolution of Disability Rights." In L. O. Gostin and H. A. Beyer (eds.), *Implementing the Americans with Disabilities Act: Rights and Responsibilities of All Americans.* Baltimore: Brookes, 1993.

West, J. (ed.). *Implementing the Americans with Disabilities Act.* Cambridge, Mass.: Blackwell, 1996.

Young, I. M. *Justice and the Politics of Difference.* Princeton, N.J.: Princeton University Press, 1990.

CHAPTER ELEVEN

Managing Conflict in the Workplace

Margaret S. Herrman

Why would human resource professionals, program managers, and staff of government agencies consider expending scarce resources of time, money, or personnel to create work settings that welcome conflict? The short answer is that they might consider the option because *conflict positive* workplaces tend to be creative and more responsive to internal and external pressures, often resulting in both effective and efficient service organizations. "To be alive is to be in conflict. To be effective is to be in conflict. Organizations cannot function without conflict and members of an organization cannot interact without conflict. If organizations are to be effective, and if members of an organization are to be competent, they must be able to manage and resolve conflicts constructively" (Tjosvold and Johnson, 1983, p. 1).

Today, nonadversarial or cooperative approaches to conflict are becoming more commonplace. Federal, state, and local agencies across the United States are incorporating positive dispute resolution processes into routine decision making. Over the past two and a half decades, dispute resolution (DR) strate-

---

Note: Many of the ideas in this chapter were suggested by chapters in *Resolving Conflict: Strategies for Local Government* (Herrman, 1994b), a publication of the International City/County Management Association Practical Management Series. In particular I relied on my own introductory chapter to that book and the chapters "Resolving Conflict in a Multicultural Environment," by Andrea Williams; "Cooperationist Institutions in Public Policymaking," by Steven Kelman; "A Proactive Approach to Organizational Conflict," by Ozzie Bermant; and "Developing a Comprehensive Internal Dispute Resolution System," by Douglas H. Yarn.

gies, especially those offering alternative dispute resolution (ADR) ways of (1) negotiating complex regulations and (2) resolving highly technical, multijurisdictional disputes (for example, disagreements over the siting of regional toxic waste dumps, regional water access, and housing development affecting a standard metropolitan region), have been permeating government settings.[1] Regulatory negotiations and multijurisdictional mediation still tend to be crisis driven, sporadic, and focused above commonplace office conflict. Yet the vast majority of conflict, especially chronic disputing, occurs well below regulatory or multijurisdictional levels; it is primarily between coworkers and/or between agency functionaries and the public.

Workplace morale, creativity, and responsiveness and the public's image of government can benefit from the institutionalization of systemic DR and ADR procedures. This chapter examines three possible applications: (1) increasing employee skills for responding to internal office conflicts, (2) extending cooperative problem-solving skills to confrontations that involve individual or small groups of constituents who challenge policies or agency rulings, and (3) developing a comprehensive DR/ADR system that a government agency can access easily for a variety of reasons.

UNDERLYING SOURCES OF CONFLICT

The workplace is in transition, and opportunities for conflict are increasing. Pressure on government programs to perform is mounting, and certain "givens" are slipping away. Common wisdom in the later half of the 1990s (see, for example, "Political Battlegrounds of the Future," 1997) is that our culture will quickly cease to be predominantly Caucasian and dominated by youth. The proportion of the population over sixty-five years of age is increasing. Many of these older citizens benefited from good educations and stable jobs, and they anticipate a comfortable retirement in communities that offer a range of support services designed to take them through the death experience. Many understand power brokering, and they are not reluctant to voice their expectations individually and collectively. At state and local levels, older constituencies are likely to challenge tax assessments, user impact fees, changes in zoning restrictions and planning maps, and on and on. In addition, graying baby boomers are not going to disappear anytime soon. Their demands for service represent a second wave that will continue well beyond the year 2000. Are employees of state and local governments equipped to serve an aging population while also addressing the tenacious needs of an ever growing lower (even under) class?

Furthermore, the workforce in government, as elsewhere, is more culturally diverse than was it was ten to fifteen years ago, and that trend will continue. In work settings once predominantly staffed by people of one culture (in this case,

Caucasian people of European descent), the probability for misunderstanding even in simple work routines increases with each new worker of a different culture (compare Williams, 1994). Plus, the potential for tension escalates as agencies add different categories of employees. In the past, tensions between career and appointed employees were expected, but now the traditional full-time workforce has been downsized and that smaller workforce is augmented by contractual, often marginalized part-time workers, creating further tensions.

Finally, it is almost impossible to visualize daily interactions both between workers in government offices and between government functionaries and the public that do not involve conflict. Misunderstandings from clashing agendas, unarticulated needs, and culturally based expectations are inevitable. At the same time, external pressures for both accountability and demonstrable performance are increasing. Government can no longer plead that social, economic, or environmental problems are too complex and that solutions are around the corner. Local constituencies as well as federal monitors expect answers and results.

THINKING ABOUT CONFLICT

As I wrote in 1994:

> Conflict is an expression of incompatibility: It exists when the actions of one person or group block the actions of another person or group. If the conflict surfaces—in other words, if both sides decide to take the conflict on—one of four outcomes is possible: (1) you win, and your rival loses; (2) your rival wins, and you lose; (3) the two of you compromise, and both of you lose to some degree; or (4) you put your combined energies into an integrative solution, and both of you win to some degree. . . . Historically, the American public including public officials has favored the first outcome, feared the second, and chosen the third only as a last resort. Until the 1980s, outcome four was rarely considered an option [Herrman, 1994a, p. xi].

Conflict is as complex as it is ubiquitous. Numerous things cause specific conflicts, and knowing a root cause sometimes allows us to predict how easy it might be to achieve cooperative solutions (that is, outcome four) (compare Coser, 1956, pp. 48–55).

Data-based disputes. Work settings seem to engender misunderstandings over data. For example, someone has access to important information others do not have, people do not have the same data on the same problem, or people interpret the same information in different ways. Personnel disputes are often about data, and gaps or misinterpretations of data may also lie at the heart of many client-agency disputes. Cues that a dispute is about data can include missed deadlines that have negative reverberations, overlapping or repetitious work assignments, miscalculations, proposals or policies that fail to reach the appropriate desk, or negative performance appraisals based on vague or inconsistent job specifications.

A program specialist (person A) and an administrative assistant (person B) in an agency were jointly responsible for conducting staff development workshops. Person A compiled registration lists and projected participant fees. Person B handled the mailings for conferences including notifying people of conference arrangements and fee structures. Person B also paid conference-related bills and invoiced participants who failed to pay during the registration process. In a mediation, it became clear that both were frustrated because there was no database accessible to both. Person B was expected to send out invoices in a timely way, but there was no easy way to obtain the information needed to fulfill the task. Person A assumed person B was apathetic and not very systematic in the work routine, and therefore avoided providing other information pertinent to person B's job performance.

Purely data-based conflicts are perhaps the easiest type of conflict to resolve. The first step requires facilitating sufficient conversation so that the protagonists can identify what data are missing, misplaced, or misunderstood. The second step involves creating clear and shared strategies for filling the gaps and/or clarifying differences in interpretation. This is exactly what happened in the dispute just described. Once person A and person B identified the gap, they were able to create a clear, easy system for sharing conference participant information.

Structural disputes. These disagreements affirm that change is ongoing in workplaces. Ever-shifting program mandates, new technologies, innovations in worksite setups, and changes in personnel can precipitate structural inequities and ambiguities. For example, a worker hired ten years ago and assigned to a specific job often finds that the job description that fit the work assignment perfectly ten years ago no longer applies because, over the years, new technologies and new mandates have changed the nature of the job. Specifically, computers and new software require knowledge and skills that newer workers possess and some older workers fear. One dynamic might be that newer workers receive rewards for their performance while some older workers begin to feel obsolete.

Like data-based disputes, structural disputes are relatively easy to resolve. Given the right atmosphere, the people experiencing a conflict can readily identify the source of tension, and they are often willing to change. Even so, a resolution requires not only party buy-in but sometimes policy changes, changes in the physical layout of a workplace, new rewards, and different incentives. Institutional response, possibly adaptation, and redefinition are important for lasting solutions of structural disputes.

Here is a simple example. Each of two secretaries was engaging in behaviors designed to irritate the other (forgetting to reload the paper tray in a copying machine, not giving the other telephone messages, opening each others' mail, and the like). In mediation they talked about how their work spaces were joined by a door that remained open. It appeared that this physical connection opened up communication that worked for one but not both of them. One liked to chat about family and current events as a way of reinforcing a pleasant work atmosphere. The other needed more private space and had a hard time concentrating on work when interrupted. Their solution was to close the door permanently as they opened other passages for other people in the office. This change involved a potential fire code violation and an issue of easy access for other workers. Toward the end of the mediation a management representative, who had the authority to make decisions, was brought into the problem-solving session to listen to proposed solutions and then, it was hoped, approve an option that would work for the two parties and the organization.

Structural conflict is more problematic in office settings than in interactions between agency personnel and clients. Still, structural issues may play out in tax assessment appeals, zoning disputes, and disputes over denied benefits. Here, too, resolution is possible when the agency involved has or can create flexibility in how policies are implemented and when the challenge allows the agency to reexamine how policies have evolved.

Relational disputes. It is no surprise that relational disputes occur frequently in office settings. Office settings engender proximity for extended periods of time, and people begin to care about each other just as they might outside an office. But just as in other settings, coworkers may struggle for dominance or control. People may experience the loss of relationships. For example, coworkers and supervisors form a close bond when one person is a new hire; the bond may be that of teacher or mentor, but the bond deteriorates over time as the new hire becomes a savvy veteran. Jealousy may also be an issue. For example, a person might think, "You and I worked together so well for so long; now you are teaming up with someone else. Why have you turned against me?" Finally, people expect and tolerate differing levels of familiarity and relational flexibility in an office. It is not unusual for relational tensions that technically fall beyond protected areas covered by equal employment opportunity (EEO) to be the root problem for EEO complaints. Filing an EEO complaint constitutes a red flag signaling that a problem exists. The act of filing is a cry for help.

Relational disputes can be more difficult to resolve than data or structural disputes. At the same time, relational tensions are usually ripe for a positive conflict-handling process. In the end, people recognize that they will be happier when relational boundaries are clarified and when personal exchanges like apologies begin the process of healing. Relational disputes, not addressed early, can span years, and time does not mellow a dispute. Over time these conflicts typically develop beyond toxicity almost to a pathology, what Coser (1956) refers to as unrealistic disputes. And in the later stages they are not easily amenable to cooperative conflict resolution processes. It is fortunate that they represent a very small proportion of the pool of conflicts found in a workplace.

They are also less problematic for stranger-to-stranger conflicts affecting client and agency representatives.

Interest disputes. These conflicts pertain to frustrations that arise when interactions irritate (compare Herrman, 1997, pp. 34–35). They stem from competition over perceived or actual incompatible needs. Interest conflicts occur over *substantive issues* (for example, money, including salaries, promotions, and raises; access to physical resources such as computers, agency vehicles, office space, and office location; and time, including attention from management, leave time, overtime, staff development time, and so forth), *procedural issues* (the way people clock in and out, the way leave time is defined, how memos are distributed in the office, how conflict is handled in the office and so forth), or *psychological issues* (primarily perceptions of trust, trustworthiness, fairness, desire for participation, respect, and so forth).

Generally, interests can be satisfied in a variety of ways (Fisher and Ury, 1983), and they are not the hardest type of conflict to resolve. Still, most disputes attributed to staff and management in government offices seem to fall into this category. Achieving clarity consistently in substantive and procedural policies helps to clear the air. Often, along with the need for institutional consistency in the operationalization of procedural policies, there is a need to ensure equity in the way substantive rewards are allocated. Lack of clarity and consistency twist over time into perceived violations of psychological interests. A very difficult office dispute began at the substantive and procedural levels, but the frustrations were not confronted early on. After a ten-year incubation period the dispute had deteriorated to a psychological level and could no longer be resolved in mediation.

By comparison many conflicts between an agency and a client begin at a psychological level (that is, agencies and the personnel who represent agencies are not trusted by skeptical clients or constituents) only to shift to interest- and substantive-based issues as trust is addressed and fears put to rest. If fears are not put to rest, the conflict will continue and expand.

Value conflicts. These problems are caused by perceived or actual incompatible belief systems. Values operate as personal beliefs that give meaning to social interactions. They help people define good versus bad, right versus wrong, just versus unjust. Differing values do not necessarily cause conflict. People can live together in harmony for years with quite different value systems. A dispute surfaces only when some people attempt to force their set of values on other individuals or when people lay claim to rigid value systems that disallow divergent beliefs (leading, for example, to the stance, "you can't work with me unless you believe as I do").

As the workforce becomes more diverse, substantially more interest- and value-based conflicts should emerge in office settings. As Williams (1994) notes, even the smallest exchanges can cause friction when an exchange crosses ethnic and cultural divides. Moreover, cultural divides may not be as obvious as one might think. In some regions of the United States and some rural communities, informal norms dictate how and when you greet someone when you see him or her in the morning. For example, in traditional communities in the South members of the younger generation are expected to initiate the ritual, and in some communities the use of a title *(Mr., Mrs., or Ms.)* is expected. Consider the friction when a young, brusque, preoccupied person from another region takes a job in a rural, southern setting. When behavioral expectations are violated, suspicions of anger or aloofness build up. Although expectations about greetings do not constitute formal procedures, they are part of subconscious and strongly held beliefs about how the world "should" operate. Values attached to personal space, dress codes, eye contact, permissible speech, and communication styles all fall into the realm of potential value conflicts. EEO disputes are becoming more common, and certainly there are very real EEO violations. But many accusations of EEO violations are rooted in unexplored value differences as well as in relational tensions.

Value disputes, whether internal to an office or involving a client of an agency are perhaps the most difficult type of dispute to resolve. First, they surface later than other disputes. Because these disputes are rooted in actions that are taken for granted and because they involve stereotyping, people often fail to recognize the nature of the problem until it takes on the obviousness of an elephant in the living room. Second, it is difficult to discuss value conflicts unassisted. They strike at the heart of a person's sense of self-identity, and risks associated with potentially exposing that identity to attack in the heat of anger are significant. Value conflicts assume that cherished beliefs about who you are will be called into question.

CONFLICT READINESS

Regardless of the type of complaint or the particular people implicated in a fight (for example, a supervisor and an employee, two employees, or a client or constituent and the agency), an individual's general feelings about conflict constitute the best predictor of how that person will respond. Is conflict seen as pleasant, a diversion, an opportunity to grow, a chance to achieve clarity, or a pain on the horizon? We North Americans, at this point in history, react to conflict in fairly predictable and negative ways. When one of us experiences some form of violation, his or her initial response is to avoid a confrontation. We bury our feelings, say nothing, and try to go about our normal routine.

If avoidance fails to improve the situation, our next step might be to talk to a trusted friend or colleague, a process known as triangulation.[2] The conversation might serve several important purposes—gathering needed information, rehearsing statements of the complaint, exploring likely outcomes, or requesting that the ally serve as an emissary. In a few instances avoidance and triangulation provide sufficient relief, but neither facilitate a face-to-face confrontation between the people directly associated with the dispute. Without that confrontation the person responsible for perpetrating the offense continues to operate in the dark and is never fully aware that something is wrong or needs to change. Under these circumstances, the situation is likely not to change and may deteriorate.

When avoidance and/or triangulation fails to eliminate the problem, confrontation finally begins to surface as an option, but not a preferred option. Our cultural scripts condition us to believe that we must win outright or we will fail, making confrontation a high-stakes game with a risky outcome. Aversion to that risk can be seen in workplaces as poor morale or apathy, lack of creative discussions about work-related problems, or simmering relationships between coworkers that eventually erupt into threats of violence, the "blue flu," or a dismissal after a straw-that-broke-the-camel's-back incident. Some workplace mediations involve people who have seethed together for seven, ten, or fifteen years. It is amazing that the protagonists have endured the situation for so long in their reluctance to confront one another.

In the domain of client-agency interactions, most aggrieved clients approach government officials as anything other than meek lambs. Hints that a client or constituent fears failure can be found in the way he or she complains about a tax assessment, an improperly calculated water bill, a proposed zoning variance, a letter from the IRS, or a ranking on an eligibility exam. Constituents come armed with an attitude and a stack of documents to justify their correct "position." These are not silly or temperamental people. Conflict is uncomfortable, and just like people who work for government, constituents have not been conditioned from childhood to work through or expect a process of constructive dialogue.

TRADITIONAL AND NONTRADITIONAL CONFLICT RESOLUTION STRATEGIES

Traditional strategies for working through personnel disputes in government settings, as elsewhere, require confrontation. That's fine. But typical human resource policies covering internal grievance mechanisms and union policies promote superficial communication and sparring at arm's length rather than reasoned, respectful, face-to-face problem solving. For example, under a standard grievance procedure the aggrieved person is instructed to discuss the problem with an appropriate supervisor or union representative, yet neither of these resource persons is institutionally predisposed to listen completely and without prejudice. One leans toward protecting the status quo, and the other wants to project a union image of advocate for the disenfranchised.

In addition, most managers grew up learning the same lessons about conflict as the staff, and few managers or union representatives have received explicit training in listening and problem exploration. Cultural messages, job pressures, and lack of both training and positive reinforcement combine forces to predispose managers and union representatives alike to listen quickly and often superficially ("just give me the facts") and to make even quicker judgments that a particular person is to blame or that the complaint is frivolous.

If no satisfactory solution emerges from an initial presentation of the problem, the person voicing the complaint is asked to prepare a written statement of the grievance. This could be an effective strategy, but most staff see the assignment as futile. They feel they lack sufficient knowledge of relevant institutional rules and the appropriate terminology to provoke a thorough and thoughtful review. Many people simply withdraw at this point, leaving the problem to fester a while longer. A smaller number go forward with a written grievance. Some of the latter may seek legal council before writing anything down. Although seeking advice from a lawyer may actually reflect a sense of insecurity and futility, the mere mention of this external resource by an employee immediately raises the stakes for the agency.

From the perspective of effective and efficient problem resolution, the pitfalls inherent in traditional organizational conflict-handling mechanisms are numerous. A primary concern is (1) the absence of safe structures that (2) encourage complete information gathering and nonincendiary information exchange between the primary parties and that (3) also ensure sufficient time for effective problem resolution at the earliest possible moment. Simply put, the parties in a conflict do not talk to each other, do not listen to each other, and do not feel comfortable correctly interpreting relevant policies. At the same time, they do feel organizational pressure to get on with their work.

Like these traditional strategies for handling employment problems, *constituent appeals* also suffer from communication gaps and an environment that undercuts reasoned problem solving. Envision a constituent trying to approach an agency with a request that a decision be reviewed or reversed. It is not unusual for the first contact to be by phone and to be accompanied by a number of frustrations—the phone is always busy, or the caller must navigate a sophisticated but complex computerized telephone answering system, or the agency representative ends up playing telephone tag with the constituent. This is not a good beginning if the goal is productive problem solving and a positive agency image.

The next step may be for the constituent to come into the agency. Here the potential for frustration remains substantial—either a lot of paperwork is required, or the first agency person available is abrupt, or a decision maker is nowhere to be found, or no decision can be made until the "case" has been presented to an appeals panel. The prospect of going before a panel is even less appealing and conducive to good problem solving than these typical initial face-to-face interactions. The sheer numeric imbalance (for example, one constituent to five panel members) fosters anxiety. To compensate, the constituent either shows up with half of the neighborhood as character witnesses, or with a book of documentation he or she is determined to read, or with an attorney in tow. None of these are attractive scenarios for either the constituent or the representatives of a governing body.

Nontraditional options for dispute resolution exist in business and can be easily imported into a government setting (compare Tjosvold, 1991; Ury, Brett, and Goldberg, 1988; see also Bermant, 1994; Yarn, 1994). These options seem to respond to the imperfections in traditional systems by supporting skilled problem solving in safe environments. The characteristics that support skill and safety as minimal requirements and that cut across each of the three applications to be described shortly typically include the following:

Common Characteristics

- Strategies are introduced from the top and bottom of the organization simultaneously.

- People are prepared to respond to the conflict as early as possible. Preparation involves

   Introducing and then reinforcing the idea that conflict is both normal and beneficial (and a lack of expressed conflict is stultifying to an agency and irritating to constituents) and that some people even find the experience of working through a conflict fun and creative.

   Teaching the skills associated with good communication and good problem solving at all levels of the organization (through both periodic training and ongoing mentoring or support groups).

- Policies reward good problem solving.

- No form of retaliation is authorized.

- Settings exist within the organization for effective confrontation; both privacy and uninterrupted time are also provided.

- People have access to multiple conflict resolution resources, such as the following DR, ADR, and traditional mechanisms (compare Yarn, 1994, p. 187):

   Dispute Resolution (DR) Mechanisms

   Active listening. People in the agency are trained to listen, giving associates in distress easy access to people who offer an opportunity to talk about the problem. Interaction is minimal: the person hearing the complaint (perhaps an agency representative, a coworker, or a supervisor or manager) takes no action except to *really* listen. This very quiet but extremely important activity often involves asking appropriate questions that stimulate the distressed person's thinking. What emotions are at play (what hot buttons are going off)? What are the sources of the tensions? Questions might also review factual events. The goal is for the distressed person to achieve (1) greater clarity and (2) a reduced state of anxiety that naturally follows clearer thinking and the sensation of being heard (compare Deutsch, 1973). The listener is not expected to validate the grievance (by saying, for example, "You are right to be angry about . . ."), to investigate, or even to problem solve. Quite the opposite, it is not necessary for the listener to be an expert in the area in dispute or to have any power in the organization. The key here is quiet listening and asking just the right questions. It is hard to convey in writing how critical this step is in building an effective DR process. It seems so simple, and yet few of us have been taught to listen without offering advice or moralizing or taking sides. (Active listening is also an example of how and when triangulation can be extremely helpful to, rather than undercutting, good problem solving.)

Appropriate self-help. Clarity often contributes to a greater sense of efficacy, propelling the distressed person into action, rather than apathy or passive aggressive responses, when action is necessary for the problem to be removed.

Two- (or more) person negotiation. Two-person dialogue for the purpose of problem solving lies at the heart of any DR process and extrapolates to ADR processes as well. Effective two-person negotiation (which can in reality easily involve many more people) assumes that every participant has a clear stake in an outcome. There are no neutrals here.[3] Listening, assertion, problem analysis, options generation, and option selection are all encompassed in effective person-to-person negotiation.

Alternative Dispute Resolution (ADR) Mechanisms

Facilitated group dialogue. This technique is a natural extension of two-person negotiation, the difference being that the group of problem solvers can be even larger and a neutral person assists by structuring and facilitating dialogue.

Conciliation. This technique is somewhat similar to traditional grievance procedures in that the people involved are not brought together face to face. A conciliator, who could be someone formally tapped by the organization—for example, a manager or coworker—speaks off the record to everyone involved in the dispute to see where commonalities exist and where trade-offs might facilitate a needed change. If common ground is identified, the conciliator may make offers and finalize an agreement. The conciliator is a little bit like an old-fashioned matchmaker.

Fact-finding or investigation. Essentially an ombudsperson (ombuds) function, this mechanism goes much further than the comparable traditional grievance process. An ombuds is usually accorded considerable institutional power, over and above that of a typical supervisor, to investigate a complaint. The ombuds receives a complaint, talks separately to all the people involved (as a conciliator would), gathers pertinent information about past practices and current policies, and then presents findings and perhaps recommendations to both the complainant and to people within the organization who can make things happen.

In-house mediation. Involving one or several agency personnel who have been trained to provide mediation services to people of the agency, in-house mediation provides a third party (that is, someone with no vested interest in the dispute or a particular outcome) who does not render decisions. In comparison to an ombudsperson or a conciliator, a mediator assists the people directly involved in the dispute to talk about the problem, explore individual and common agendas, develop options, and create a plan for implementing the preferred options. If in-house mediation is to be successful, everyone in the organization must recognize the types of fights suitable for mediation[4] and receive institutional encouragement to seek a mediator's services. (The section on comprehensive DR and ADR systems that follows offers more detail.)

External mediation. This mechanism is similar to in-house mediation in that employees are encouraged to bring their internal disputes to a mediator. However the mediators themselves are external, imported from other government agencies or from the nonprofit or private sector.

Shuttle diplomacy. This technique is a slightly more structured version of conciliation, extending into formal mediation. Here, generally, a decision is made by one or all of the protagonists or by the mediator that those involved have too much anger to sit in the same room. Negotiations are facilitated by a mediator who shuttles between the parties in their separate locations. President Carter's intervention in the Middle East peace talks, with the participants brought to Camp David, is a classic example of a process that is often seen in international mediation but is also relevant to local settings.

Traditional Mechanisms

An authoritative decision process might include several options: the decisions might be made by a supervisor, a grievance panel, a fact finder operating within a personnel or human resource department, or formal litigation.

- People know they have access to several strategies. If a good outcome is elusive using one strategy, no stigma is associated with seeking out other conflict-handling options.

- *Interface bodies* are a part of the DR/ADR system. For example, if citizen appeals boards or panel review boards exist under the aegis of an agency, board members will have been trained and mentored in cooperative problem-solving techniques. They likewise will understand the full scope of the system and the relevance of their work to that system.

- Solid information is collected on patterns of conflict. (For example: Do specific issues surface repeatedly? Are some units are more adept than others at working through conflict?) (See Exhibit 11.1 for a sample survey.) Someone tracks and analyzes patterns of conflict and resolution within the agency and between the agency and constituents.

- Resources are committed to conflict resolution training and ongoing support. This may be the best long-term investment an agency or program can make.

THREE APPLICATIONS

Increasing People's Skills for Working Through Conflict

Increasing people's skills and capacity to work through conflict is a dispute resolution option, based on two-person negotiation, that assumes employees of a government organization appreciate the positive potential of interoffice conflict, have been trained to work through a conflict together, and have a capacity to judge whether they are comfortable tackling a conflict alone or whether the conflict might benefit from the involvement of a neutral. This option works only where top and middle management support and encourage it and where structural incentives guide individuals in distress to use positive conflict-handling skills informally. For example, when a misunderstanding exists, people at all levels of the organization are encouraged to talk to each other before they triangulate a manager into an exploration of the problem. If a person approaches his or her manager before attempting a face-to-face conversation with the other person directly involved in the conflict, the manager will suggest that the primary people discuss the conflict before management gets involved.

Private space is set aside for these conversations, and inducements encourage people to take the time to work through a conflict. People do not fear losing pay or respect, and they do not experience any form of retaliation. Just the opposite, good problem-solving work is viewed by management as valid, productive, job-related work.

Support and encouragement must coincide with training and mentoring. Good initial training[5] will provide at least twenty hours of highly participatory classroom time that examines key topics like the concept of conflict, skills and strategies for communication and problem solving, the roles power and diversity play in office conflicts, and the ways training will be implemented in people's work setting. (See Exhibit 11.2 for a sample topic outline.)

To follow up the training, the agency can form focus groups or problem-solving groups in which experts in systems design, staff, and management develop a structure and then write policies that support putting the skills into practice.

The necessary *elements of a structure* are both simple and complex, simple from the perspective that very few new institutional substructures need to be created (for example, no new staff or offices) and complex in that effective implementation assumes ongoing, visible support for managers and employees working out their problems. Training, mentoring, even the development of written policies must be seen as a transition into a new way of interacting. With the DR option in place, people are encouraged to stop avoiding conflict and to engage in positive confrontive activities as soon as a problem surfaces. The confrontation might be as simple as someone's walking into a colleague's office, saying that there is a problem, and making an appointment for a problem-solving conversation (simple suggestions for this move can be a part of the dealing with difficult people exercise in the training outlined in Exhibit 11.2). It might also involve calling a meeting of the people affected by the conflict so that they can participate in a dialogue to solve the problem.

If the person raising the red flag feels that the problem involves significant emotions or complex issues or issues with significant policy implications, the training and ongoing support groups provide a framework for deciding which type of ADR mechanism to access next. If the new structure allows people to choose their third party (and realistically that may be very difficult), the training and support groups also help people decide what characteristics in a third party would be ideal.

Extending Cooperative Problem Solving to Client-Agency Confrontations

Once employees of an agency know that positive conflict-handling strategies are expected and rewarded when internal conflicts surface, a natural next step is to extend the practices to agency clients and constituents. An extension of good problem resolution skills to constituent complaints does not necessarily imply changing existing policy or invoking new formal procedures, unless existing policies require decision making according to arbitrary deadlines that work against reasoned problem solving. Nevertheless, even though major policies may not change, intentional use of good conflict-handling skills and strategies is critical. A few examples of options are instructive.

If a client-initiated confrontation occurs in an office rather than a hearing setting, quickly move any discussion to a physical environment conducive to respectful listening and dialogue. The change can demonstrate concern for the complainant (for example, an employee might tell the client that working on the problem in a constructive way is important), diffuse anger, and allow a free flow of crucial information.

Certainly all of the skills associated with dealing with difficult people apply (for example, listening respectfully, attending to open body language, using a calm voice, and so forth). One skill people sometimes forget to apply is slowing the confrontation cycle down. The goal is to reduce the stress associated with client fears that there is a limited amount of time to work toward a resolution. Therefore, an effective strategy is to convey to the client that there is time for reasoned dialogue, today and in the future if need be.

Next, as a confrontation naturally evolves into a face-to-face dialogue, it is important for the employee to adopt a listening posture and also avoid defensive or assertive communication. Here, listening produces needed information about the root of the complaint. It may also enhance clarity.

Commonly, client-agency confrontations are data or procedural disputes, although as noted earlier value disputes will likely increase as population diversification continues in the United States. Listening permits the employee to identify whether relevant data are missing, how procedures have been violated or confused, and/or how values are clashing. Appropriate decisions about what steps to take and how to assign responsibility for those steps depend on a clear analysis of the origin of the problem. When the dispute is data based, the complainant and the agency representative may need to gather then share relevant missing data (a self-help strategy). An agency representative may also need to research facts and report to the complainant, and to offer recommendations up line (activity similar to an ombuds function). Mediation is a common alternative when benefits have been denied (for Medicaid and special education, for example) and when disputes occur over local zoning and siting. A facilitated dialogue might be a good option for land use planning and environmental crises.

Planning, tax assessor, personnel, and panel hearing boards will always provide an authoritative backstop whenever DR/ADR procedures fail to produce mutually satisfactory outcomes. But even these boards might consider how they appear to an angry constituent and what might be done procedurally to address complainant anger and fear.

From a cooperative problem-solving perspective, traditional public hearings that restrict the amount of time a constituent has to present a case are disasters. Although public officials are sometimes spared long monologues, the trade-offs are constituents further convinced that officials are heartless and the loss of potentially valuable information. The use of a dais or other structural barriers between officials and the public reinforces perceptions of alienation. Where there is concern for the safety of officials, extend the concern to the public by screening everyone for weapons before convening a problem-solving session.

Boards might consider, at least for preliminary hearings, removing both time limits and structural barriers that inhibit dialogue and increase anxiety. In a better model, the primary complainants sit with officials at a large table. They are allowed to speak without strict limits and interruptions (see Herrman, 1994b, especially part 4, for a wealth of other options). If the thought of a filibuster is a deterrent to using an alternative model, officials can ease the pressure toward extending talk by describing the structure of the entire session at the beginning of the meeting, including a proposed time for ending the meeting and the possibility of additional sessions.

Finally, use a facilitator. The presence of a facilitator simplifies the role of the public officials. With a facilitator, officials can speak as participants who want to solve the problem and avoid the role of process police. Where a facilitator controls the process, the facilitator absorbs a lot of the heat if the process goes badly.

When the less formal means of resolving a dispute fail and a board must turn to an arbitrative hearing format, many of the same listening skills appropriate for two-person dialogue can reduce citizen frustration and expedite the flow of information needed to make sound decisions. Panels that must decide from anecdotal feedback whether to return a child in foster care to his or her home of origin can gather more complete information quicker when they rely on cooperative communication techniques.

Developing a Comprehensive DR/ADR System

A comprehensive DR/ADR system requires more organizational resources than either of the two options previously described. A system encompasses both of these options and opens the entire organization up to more effective problem solving. By creating a DR/ADR system the organization sends signals to everyone from top management to the lowest staff position that positive responses are the coin of the realm. An important subtext to the message is that everyone is supported, through training, mentoring, and rewards, in his or her individual efforts to work through conflicts early (rather than avoiding a confrontation until a campaign or an organized dispute has jelled) and that positive options are available should an early two-person negotiation fail.

Many of the benefits of a system emerge once the two preceding options are in place, but the system contributes the structure that ensures longevity (the change is not seen as a fad or a bandage), legitimacy, and the flexibility to change as the needs of the organization change.

Structural Elements. A system encompasses all the basic elements listed earlier. It can even rely on both in-house and imported mediators should a need arise. But it also requires elements that go beyond the earlier list.

- The DR/ADR system needs a home within the organization. Placement within the overall organizational culture is situationally determined, but the ideal location is associated with neutrality. In one likely scenario the system functions from the chief administrator's office (CAO). A human resource or personnel office will also work, but these offices might restrict the scope of services, as might the office of a legal counsel (in comparison to the CAO, for example, these offices operate under more restricted definitions of legitimate functions).

- The home needs identifiable space. Although an ideal model calls on each employee to negotiate his or her own disputes as close to the source as possible, there should be no shame in asking for the assistance of a facilitator, mediator, ombuds, or even an administrative panel. Fears of bias and scrutiny can be reduced considerably when such hearing officers conduct business in neutral space that is removed from the normal flow of business. Also, dedicated office space ensures privacy for the conversations necessary when setting interventions up, answering questions that are bound to arise, making phone calls associated with fact finding, writing reports, conducting and compiling periodic conflict assessments, and conducting either training or mentoring.

- A system requires personnel dedicated to the system and not sharing their time across distinctly different job assignments. Setting up cases (that is, explaining the process to the uninformed); talking about a disputant's natural concerns (for example, whether he or she should bring an attorney to the session); locating an appropriate neutral party; and scheduling or rescheduling the session takes time. Record keeping takes time. Conducting conflict assessments and compiling the data take time. Planning and conducting training, staff development, and mentoring take time. Finally, it is important that everyone staffing a DR/ADR office be trained in a range of intervention skills. The training takes time, as do the actual interventions. One rule of thumb is that minimal staffing includes a receptionist and a senior intervenor or system administrator. Both can do intake. Both can provide services, although a judicious division of labor is appropriate. The number of calls or referrals in a month helps determine staffing above the minimum. Two people can work through ten cases a month, but it is questionable whether two people could handle a ten-case load and still complete training, staff development, and system monitoring tasks.

- Records produced by the system (primarily assessment data and minimal case data) must be protected and maintained. If a case is conciliated, facilitated, or mediated, the residual case file contains the final written agreement (if one exists) and basic intake information. Any information pertaining to what people say during an intervention is traditionally destroyed as the parties complete their work together. Because a system is costly, accountability is an issue. It is important to be able to describe clearly the nature of the workload, how conflict affects the organization, the costs and cost savings of providing services (this is especially relevant where in-house mediators provide service gratis in a community that could encompass intervenors who would charge fees), and the amount of time invested in the various intervention strategies.

- Policies must protect the system and the people using it. Policies serve to legitimate the system as they protect the integrity of the services provided. Although the organization need not develop additional layers of complex procedures, it does need to spell out minimal policies addressing issues of governance, training and qualifications for neutrals, referral procedures, assignment of cases to neutrals, role restrictions for neutrals (for example, it needs an operating definition of confidentiality and of exceptions to confidentiality), disposal of paper trails associated with any intervention, and repeated conflict assessments.

Costs and Benefits of Investing in a Nontraditional Model. It may be difficult for human resource managers or personnel directors to implement a really accurate cost-benefit analysis of a nontraditional DR/ADR system. How do you cost out improved morale except in reduced turnover rates and improved job performance? What is the true cost of a human resource professional's time when an employee comes back time and again with a complaint that just does not go away? What are the true costs of formal grievances, not just in personnel time but also in increased ill will on a worksite? How do you balance the cost of one case that goes through full litigation to a negative judgment against ten cases that look less serious but are resolved in mediation? Many intangibles make up the long-term benefits of a DR/ADR system.

When the field of dispute resolution was much younger than it is today, leaders projected that DR/ADR innovations would reduce both the fiscal cost of processing complaints and the time people had to wait to have their day in court. After living with the innovations for twenty-plus years, we have found that the original arguments missed the mark.

Initial responses of an organization to a newly implemented system seem to be a natural reluctance to send cases through the system, then a visible movement of cases some might define as frivolous, and then a leveling period. Even with training and with mentoring and support groups, people are reluctant to change and especially to trust that organizational disincentives are not lurking around the corner ("Will my pay be docked?" "Will I have to work overtime?" "Will I be perceived as a poor employee?"). Human resource officers can be instrumental in the success of the new services by not only referring cases but also assuring people that retaliation will not be tolerated. The payoff for human resource offices is that they will be able to safely release at least a third of their cases, many of which are not currently covered by agency policies, and at least 80 percent will not come back. People will continue to bring their troubles to human resources or personnel because those are the traditional resting grounds for complaints, but a sizable number of the complaints do not need to stay in human resources. They can be exported.

If the system gains a reputation as an effective and humane service, people will begin to ask for assistance much earlier in the cycle of a conflict. The implications are twofold. There may be an initial appearance that the agency or organization has become more conflicted. Do not buy into the myth or the fear. People are simply beginning to openly express problems before they become crises. In short, this is a slow process of change toward a healthier organization. In the end, human resource professionals may see fewer misplaced complaints and may be freed up to handle serious EEO and other deep-seated situations more effectively.

Legal Concerns. The American Bar Association and various state bar associations are concerned about the use of ADR mechanisms in statutory discrimination cases, in particular the use of employer or union waiver of the right to a judicial resolution or a jury trial. The concern appears well founded in settings where employees are neither (1) trained to determine for themselves in an informed way which DR options they would like to access nor (2) allowed to move freely between options; the concern does not seem pertinent to the type of system or set of informal options described in this chapter. The system described here is predicated on informed choice and no waiver. Even when human resource personnel refer cases to a DR/ADR system, the choice to actually use the system clearly remains with the employee, who can opt to access one or several steps in the system. In recent years the federal government has offered mediation services nationwide for various forms of discrimination complaints filed with the Department of Justice and the Equal Opportunity Employment Commission. Because of the seeming clout of any federal bureaucracy, a referral to mediation for a sexual harassment, racial bias, or Americans with Disabilities Act dispute may not seem at first blush to be voluntary. Even so, complainants and respondents have the option of removing themselves from mediation, and they certainly have the option of pursuing litigation in the event mediation fails. Waivers of one's litigation rights do not seem to be an issue.

CONCLUSION

Probably the key factor in the success of the options described in this chapter is that people are trained to use good conflict-handling skills. They are supported in their efforts both with colleagues and with the public; thus when an employee experiences difficulty on the job, a DR/ADR option looks like a scenic superhighway, not a blind alley.

Over time, people will be able to work through problems much more effectively and closer to the origin of the dispute. The upshot is that employees from the bottom to the top of the organization will develop a greater sense of personal efficacy that translates into better morale, better employee relations, a more creative work atmosphere, and perhaps a more effective agency.

Benefits spill over into improved public perceptions if the public also experiences the expertise of good conflict-handling skills. Although public complaints may not always end as the public desires, the simple acts of being heard with respect, of receiving a reasoned response, and of receiving assistance when self-help is insufficient could reduce public cynicism and increase public confidence that public needs are being served (compare Smith, 1983).

Notes

1. The Program for Community Problem Solving (PCPS), 1301 Pennsylvania Avenue, NW, Suite 600, Washington, DC 20004, (202) 626–3183, is an excellent resource for general information about DR and ADR in government and for a listing of ADR consultants across the nation.

2. Smith (1989) provides an interesting case study of the impact of triangulation on the workings of government decision making.

3. A neutral is simply a person who is disinterested in the outcome of the dispute but wants to ensure a sound process of problem solving.

4. In an August 26, 1997, e-mail to the author, John Keltner (an expert in the field of dispute resolution) nicely describes a conflict continuum consisting of (from less to more intense) unpolarized discussion (a conversation a person might have with a colleague before approaching the person associated with the problem or an exploratory discussion with the associated person), mild argument, organized argument (debate), unorganized argument (dispute), a campaign (people choose sides and try to overpower, outwit, or outmaneuver the other side), and finally more aggressive forms of conflict. Keltner believes that mediation is appropriate for the forms of conflict below a campaign, although campaigns do happen in government work settings, and my experience is that mediation can effectively uncover assumptions, false information, and positions driving the campaign. With time, mediation can also move the dispute toward a cooperative solution.

5. Note 1 lists one resource (PCPS) that might be helpful in locating training. Other resources include the Vinson Institute of Government at the University of Georgia; National Institute for Dispute Resolution (NIDR), 1726 M Street, NW, Suite 500, Washington, DC 20036–4512, (202) 466–4764; and Society of Professionals in Dispute Resolution (SPIDR), 815 15th Street NW, Washington, DC 20005–2201, (202) 783–7277. PCPS, NIDR, and SPIDR each maintain either a consultant or a membership list.

Exhibit 11.1. Sample Conflict Assessment for a Government Agency.

This survey is *completely confidential.* No one will see your answers except the researcher/resource person compiling the results. Once results have been compiled, the surveys will be destroyed. All answers will be compiled into a single report. Reported information will be in the nature of general trends in comments. Although no one's name will appear in the report, to maintain confidentiality, please don't sign the survey.

The first set of questions is about your experience in your work setting. Feel free to use the backs of pages if you need more space. Please, just number your answers.

1. How would you generally describe your work environment? Please check all the words that apply.

    ___Creative   ___Effective   ___Stressful   ___Unpleasant

    ___Fulfilling   ___Stifling   ___Tense   ___Threatening

    ___Rewarding   ___Exciting   ___Pleasant   ___Peaceful

    ___Dull   ___Boring   ___Overwhelming

2. Conflict often occurs in work settings, and as we think about ways the agency can help people work with conflict effectively, it would help us to know more about the types of conflicts you see or experience. How would you describe conflict in your work setting?

    • Conflict involving coworkers: _____

    _____

    _____

    How frequent is it?   *How much does it disrupt your work?*

    ___A lot   ___A lot

    ___Sometimes   ___Not much

    ___Not very often

    • Conflict involving coworkers and management: _____

    _____

    _____

    How frequent is it?   *How much does it disrupt your work?*

    ___A lot   ___A lot

    ___Sometimes   ___Not much

    ___Not very often

Exhibit 11.1. Sample Conflict Assessment for a Government Agency, cont'd.

- Conflict involving workers (either staff or management) and the public: _____

_____

_____

How frequent is it?   *How much does it disrupt your work?*

___A lot   ___A lot

___Sometimes   ___Not much

___Not very often

3. Are there particular types of conflicts or situations that are harder to deal with than others? Please describe: _____

_____

_____

4. When a conflict comes up, how do you or the people you work with usually deal with the conflict? _____

_____

_____

5. Have coworkers used any formal or informal procedures to resolve conflicts? (Please include your own experiences in your answer.)

___Yes, formal ones. Please describe: _____

_____

_____

___Yes, informal ones. Please describe: _____

_____

_____

___No, not formal ones.

___No, not informal ones

6. Do existing ways of working through conflict meet your needs or the needs of others you work with? _____

_____

_____

_____

_____

Exhibit 11.1. Sample Conflict Assessment for a Government Agency, cont'd.

The following information is optional, but it will allow resource people to look at patterns of conflict within the agency/organization.

7. My current position in the agency/organization is

   ___Staff   ___Full-time   ___Contract

   ___Management   ___Part-time   ___Consultant

8. I work in _____Division.

9. I have worked for this agency/organization for _____ years.

THANK YOU FOR YOUR ASSISTANCE. If there are any further thoughts or comments you would like to share, feel free to use this space.

Exhibit 11.2. Sample Dispute Resolution Training Agenda.

Module 1

- The struggle of change: experiencing how we react to requests to do things a different way and our vulnerabilities
- Conflict in workplaces:

  Types of conflict and sources of conflict
  How you and others typically react to conflict
  How organizational structures impact conflict
  What problem solving is

Module 2

- How communication hurts or helps when people try to resolve conflicts:

  Identifying and reducing normal static in listening and hearing
  Dealing with difficult people
  Understanding body language and unspoken messages
  Recognizing frame of reference: how your values and background affect what you hear and say
  Listening:

    How you take information in
    Affirmation: letting people know they have been heard
    Techniques for using listening to help others achieve greater clarity
    Barriers to effective listening
    Assertion: expressing your needs and frustrations in ways that facilitate understanding and recognition

Exhibit 11.2. Sample Dispute Resolution Training Agenda, cont'd.

Module 3

- Power dynamics in conflict and resolution processes:

  Types of power
  Responses to power
  Problem-solving steps

Module 4

- Experiencing one-on-one and group problem solving (a look at several models)

- Removing barriers to effective problem solving:

  Using physical space as an extension of body language
  Respecting confidentiality and the need for privacy
  Being aware of the number of people involved in the conflict
  Being aware of the relative status of people involved in the conflict
  Respecting how everyone deals with his or her feelings or works through his or her hot buttons
  Recognizing "tolerated" behaviors that are problematic

- Triangulation at work

Module 5

- How diversity influences your work and potential conflicts

Module 6

- The pros and cons of working through your problem one-on-one, with a problem-solving group, or with the help of a third party (becoming an informed consumer):

  Exploring various third-party roles: what third parties can and cannot do.
  What to look for in a third party
  How to ask for help

- Assessing your work environment:

  Identifying existing support for good problem solving
  Identifying things that might undercut the development of a conflict positive work setting
  Defining what you would like to create

Module 7

- Strategies for taking this training back into your work environment:

  Planning for periodic feedback, adjustments, and new skills (mentoring, small groups, ongoing support meetings)
  Keeping a diary of successes and failures (to look for your own hot buttons, things you want to learn more about, institutional issues to be addressed: confidentiality, time, space, privacy, and so on)

References

Bermant, O. "A Proactive Approach to Organizational Conflict." In M. S. Herrman (ed.), *Resolving Conflict: Strategies for Local Government.* Washington, D.C.: International City/County Management Association, 1994.

Coser, L. A. *The Functions of Social Conflict.* New York: Free Press, 1956.

Deutsch, M. *The Resolution of Conflict.* New Haven: Yale University Press, 1973.

Fisher, R., and Ury, W. L. *Getting to Yes.* Boston: Houghton Mifflin, 1983.

Herrman, M. S. "Introduction." In M. S. Herrman (ed.), *Resolving Conflict: Strategies for Local Government.* Washington, D.C.: International City/County Management Association, 1994a.

Herrman, M. S. *Resolving Conflict: Strategies for Local Government.* Washington, D.C.: International City/County Management Association, 1994b.

Herrman, M. S. *Mediation Training Manual: Basic Techniques for Magistrate and Juvenile Court Mediators.* Athens, Ga.: Vinson Institute of Government, University of Georgia, 1997.

Kelman, S. "Cooperationist Institutions in Public Policymaking." In M. S. Herrman (ed.), *Resolving Conflict: Strategies for Local Government.* Washington, D.C.: International City/County Management Association, 1994.

"Political Battlegrounds of the Future." *USA Today,* Aug. 8, 1997, p. A6.

Smith, B. E. *Non-Stranger Violence: The Criminal Court's Response.* Washington, D.C.: U.S. Department of Justice, 1983.

Smith, K. K. "The Movement of Conflict in Organizations: The Joint Dynamics of Splitting and Triangulation." *Administrative Science Quarterly,* 1989, *34*(1), 1–20.

Tjosvold, D. *The Conflict-Positive Organization: Stimulating Diversity and Creating Unity.* Reading, Mass.: Addison Wesley Longman, 1991.

Tjosvold, D., and Johnson, D. W. "Introduction." In D. Tjosvold and D. W. Johnson (eds.), *Productive Conflict Management: Perspectives for Organizations.* New York: Irvington, 1983.

Ury, W. L., Brett, J. M., and Goldberg, S. B. *Getting Disputes Resolved: Designing Systems to Cut the Costs of Conflict.* San Francisco: Jossey-Bass, 1988.

Williams, A. "Resolving Conflict in a Multicultural Environment." In M. S. Herrman (ed.), *Resolving Conflict: Strategies for Local Government.* Washington, D.C.: International City/County Management Association, 1994.

Yarn, D. H. "Developing a Comprehensive Internal Dispute Resolution System." In M. S. Herrman (ed.), *Resolving Conflict: Strategies for Local Government.* Washington, D.C.: International City/County Management Association, 1994.

PART THREE

MANAGING HUMAN RESOURCES

management . . . *judicious use of means to accomplish an end* . . .
—Merriam-Webster's Collegiate® Dictionary, Tenth Edition*

A s public organizations continue to change, the judicious and effective management of human resources is critical. This third part of the *Handbook of Human Resource Management in Government* provides new insights and practical applications for what have been considered many of the traditional functions of human resource management: managing relations with unions, conducting organizational training and development activities, and recruiting, selecting, and appraising employees.

David Carnevale sets the tone for the section with Chapter Twelve, "The High-Performance Organization in Government: Strategic Thinking and HR Administration." Carnevale's principal argument is that "the fundamental strategic human resource challenge is to devise an HR system and implement it in a fashion that supports, rather than inhibits, the achievement of an organization's overall strategic plan. The ultimate goal of all strategy is to realize high performance." He demonstrates how goal congruence in an atmosphere of organizational trust can strengthen the human resource management function and help propel organizations toward high performance.

In many regions of the country, no single factor can influence the practice of public human resource management more than an organization's relationship

---

*By permission. From *Merriam-Webster's Collegiate® Dictionary,* Tenth Edition ©1996 by Merriam-Webster, Incorporated.

with employee unions. Robert Tobias, president of the National Treasury Employees Union, provides insight into this often tenuous relationship in Chapter Thirteen, "Federal Employee Unions and the Human Resource Management Function." Tobias traces the historical relationship between unions and human resource management in the federal government, noting that human resources was traditionally called upon to help "protect" government organizations from union influence. This protection often manifested itself in the form of rules and regulations, and Tobias argues that this rule-bound protectionism fostered adversarial and hostile relations between union representatives and human resource managers and ultimately relegated the latter to the role of "technicians, performing not as managers but as representational advocates of the existing structure and protectors of the status quo." However, he sees potential for a redefined partnership between labor representatives and human resource managers, predicated upon the human resource function's being "fully integrated into the process for defining and achieving agency mission," with union leadership providing proactive rather than reactive stewardship. Although Tobias is not certain that such a partnership will evolve, he insists that the parties "have a chance to be partners if they truly seize the opportunity."

In Chapter Fourteen, "Organizational Investment in Employee Development," Montgomery Van Wart demonstrates how public organizations can increase their capacity by enhancing the "investment in employees as assets" and nurturing "an appreciation of the fact that employees form the core of a successful enterprise." Given the changing environment in which public organizations find themselves, Van Wart presents an investment model aimed at rethinking the employment relationship and human resource management. He argues that viewing employees as assets, as opposed to costs, is key toward improving organizational performance, and he furnishes examples of how human resource managers can enrich organizational capacity building by using organizational assessment surveys and training needs assessments. Van Wart also explains differing strategies for individual and organizational interventions aimed at increasing the performance of individual employees and organizations.

In Chapter Fifteen, "Staffing the Bureaucracy: Employee Recruitment and Selection," Steven Hays recognizes the importance of a proactive recruitment and selection strategy for government organizations. "Because any organization's performance is largely dependent upon the quality of its workers, those organizations that do an effective job of managing . . . entry functions are clearly the better for it. . . . Managers can save large amounts of time and aggravation by placing the right person in the right position." Hays notes that government organizations have often neglected recruitment and selection activities, with detrimental effects. He conveys methods for increasing the effectiveness of these activities, borrowing selectively from successful private-sector approaches.

One avenue toward improvement of recruitment, selection, and appraisal activities is delineated by Mark Foster in Chapter Sixteen, "Effective Job Analysis Methods." Foster explains that job analysis is the linchpin for an effective system of personnel administration, especially in validating examinations and performance appraisal devices. He discusses different job analysis methodologies, stressing the uses and sources of job analysis information. He then gives a step-by-step example of how to conduct a job analysis for a typical local government job.

Charles (Mike) Swanson builds on Foster's work in Chapter Seventeen, "A Practical Guide to Conducting Assessment Centers." Swanson draws on his considerable experience as a consultant to provide specific guidance to the practicing human resource manager on how to construct and administer an assessment center. He also defines and discusses the advantages of using the assessment center as a crucial feature of the employee selection process and presents specific examples of differing types of assessment center exercises.

Dennis Daley concludes Part Three with Chapter Eighteen, "Designing Effective Performance Appraisal Systems." As governments are increasingly called upon to become more efficient and accountable, the need for effective employee performance appraisal systems has become evident. Daley states that although there is no one "best" way to appraise employee performance, there are certainly wrong ways, and the challenge to the human resource manager is to "design an appraisal system around [the organization's] needs and capabilities." In a very succinct treatment, Daley discusses salient issues surrounding the appraisal process. He favors the application of behaviorally anchored rating scales (BARS) and management by objectives (MBO) approaches over more subjective measures, and he observes that "feedback is an integral and essential part of the performance appraisal process."

Human resource managers must constantly keep abreast of the critical and core human resource functions elucidated in the following chapters. The strategic management of human resources through employee recruitment, selection, appraisal, training, and development is basic to the overall functioning of public organizations. Mastery of these areas is crucial if organizations are to provide themselves with "the best and the brightest" and to accomplish organization goals and objectives in this era of doing more with less.

CHAPTER TWELVE

The High-Performance Organization in Government

Strategic Thinking and HR Administration

David G. Carnevale

Organizational strategy is the pattern of decisions, actions, and behaviors that enable an organization to realize its mission. Strategy is a conceptualization of what an organization intends to be and how it will realize that future. Typically, strategic planning involves defining the mission of an organization, identifying the needs of key constituencies, distinguishing opportunities and threats and also strengths and weaknesses (SWOT analysis), developing plans of action to achieve strategic objectives, allocating resources, implementing tactics, and evaluating the results of strategic action (Nutt and Backoff, 1992; Bryson, 1995). An important aspect of any organizational strategy is the design and management of the human resource (HR) component (Klingner, 1995). The fundamental strategic human resource challenge is to devise an HR system and implement it in a fashion that supports, rather than inhibits, the achievement of an organization's overall strategic plan. The ultimate goal of all strategy is to realize high performance.

High-performance work organizations

- Push authority and responsibility for work processes down the line

- Strengthen the skills of employees through a strong commitment to human capital development and organizational learning programs

- Create less bureaucratic, more decentralized organizational arrangements to enable faster response times to client and customer demands

- Invest in technology to enhance information flow and to monitor organizational achievement

- Commit to quality as a premier measure of individual, group, and organizational performance (compare Carnevale and Haupton, 1996).

This chapter examines the extent to which public human resource managers should rely on private-sector HR strategies to guide the development of HR designs in government. Similarly, it discusses the extent to which *managerialism,* the fundamental HR strategy in business, should be the principal basis of public HR strategy. It also reports on a recent study of civil service reform at the state government level. Managerialism is defined here as a functionalist orientation in which techniques that support the management of public enterprises are considered ideal.

Public HR officials are cautioned to be wary of HR innovations based upon a strictly managerialist orientation. Adopting managerialist HR programs from the business sector is a decidedly inadequate, perhaps even self-defeating, strategic response to the human resource requirements of public institutions. Such schemes cannot lead to high performance where the operating domain is more political than economic.

The realms of public organizations are buffeted by distinctive, often competing values (Rainey, 1991). As a result, the historical considerations that have informed the design and operation of public human resource management programs differ from those that have traditionally driven HR programs in business. The value orientation of human resource management in government suggests a unique, sector-specific HR strategy for creating high-performing public work systems. The meaning of high performance itself takes on a different cast in government. People interested in HR policy are warned that what works best in business may not work nearly as well in government.

THE CORE VALUES OF PUBLIC HR MANAGEMENT

The development of the U.S. public service at all levels has generally reflected an ever-shifting emphasis among a rich set of often competing goals and their underlying values. For instance, during the evolution of human resource management (HRM), it has moved from elitist origins at its founding to a determined attempt at ensuring a greater measure of egalitarianism. Insulating civil service systems from politics is an abiding goal, although that goal has simultaneously competed with the goal of finding a way to make human resource systems reasonably responsive to executive leadership. The idea of merit is a classic value, or operating ideology, of public HRM, but there is a tension between that principle and representativeness in government employment. Economy, efficiency, and effectiveness are important historical objectives of public HRM, just as they are in the business sector, but they are counterbalanced by the strong notion that government should be a model employer with a special responsibility to promote social equity. Finally, the goal of fostering a powerful measure of employee protectionism coexists with the goal of increasing managerial flexibility and control of day-to-day business (Van Riper, 1958; Mosher, 1968; Shafritz, 1975; Elliott, 1985). Different values have been ascendent at different times, but always the ideas of what constitutes an effective HR strategy and how high performance is evaluated have necessarily included consideration of all, not just some, of these competing goals and their supporting competing values.

The ongoing contest between these diverse values means that designing, operating, and reforming public HRM is as much a political difficulty as it is a technical problem, because the mission of human resource management systems in government traditionally embraces more than just realizing high levels of operational performance in instrumental terms alone.

HIGH PERFORMANCE IN GOVERNMENT ORGANIZATIONS

Internally, the high-performing work organization "competes on the basis of quality and faster time cycles. Its production is based on multiskilled work teams; its organizational design reduces hierarchy and enhances open communications throughout. Authority and responsibility are pushed down the line to personnel who have greater autonomy to make decisions about work arrangements. There is more employee participation, and continuous learning rather than intermittent training is emphasized. 'Reciprocal commitment,' based on mutual trust between the organization and the employee, is a major objective. The development of a more functionally democratic workplace featuring 'robust collaboration' is the principal goal" (Carnevale, 1995, p. 157).

The major external objectives of the high-performing organization are to satisfy client or customer requirements for quality, variety, customization, convenience, and timeliness—the operating standards in the *new economy* (Carnevale, 1991). Human resource management methods in government have been roundly criticized for not commissioning public organizations to adequately satisfy both internal and external stakeholder requirements.

The criticisms of public HRM systems are well known. Many contemporary HRM methods are generally viewed as out-of-date, better suited perhaps for an earlier time in the U.S. past when mainly bureaucratic mass-production plans were seen as the optimal way to create and run organizations. In the public case, the worst aspects of the traditional mass-production hierarchy were compounded by operational values that made public organizations especially rule bound, rigid, insensitive to executive leadership, blind to the needs of a diverse society, and insulated from the demands of a postindustrial economy. The classic summary observation about public HRM methods, strategic fit, and high performance is credited to Sayre (1948), who characterized public human resource strategies as having achieved "the triumph of technique over purpose." This criticism has proven timeless, as evidenced by a host of contemporary reviews (see, for example, State Academy for Public Administration, 1995; Milton Marks Commission, 1995; National Academy of Public Administration, 1993; National Performance Review, 1993; National Commission on the State and Local Public Service, 1993).

The litany of complaints about public HRM is familiar to all in public administration. One of the most consistent criticisms is the perception that public HRM misses connections with executive leaders and line managers in terms of supporting the daily operational requirements of public enterprises. For example, a constant complaint is that public service employment systems interfere with managers' ability to reward good performance and to apply sanctions for poor behavior. Moreover, public HRM methods are reproached for being too bureaucratic and negative, for being intentionally designed to ensure bad things don't happen as opposed to enabling good things to happen. Public HRM systems are said to staff public agencies inadequately, to be ineffective in recruiting and selecting outstanding persons into the public service. Additional condemnations address a lack of focus on human capital development and on the development of adequate compensation strategies. Finally, public HRM methods suffer from critics' perception (accurate or not) that business methods are comparatively better. This perception leads to the belief that business methods are appropriate for wholesale transfer into government. In summary, public HRM is an object of ridicule in many locales, scapegoated at every turn for what is wrong with government. Public HRM is seen as out-of-date and out of touch with the commonly understood mission requirements of high-performing organizations (Carnevale, 1992, 1995).

At bottom, the thrust of the contemporary criticism of public HRM systems implies that additional managerial discretion is required to produce effective government. This is the let-the-managers-manage model of human resource management, and it has widespread support among personnel reformers these days. There is, in this prescription, a great deal of concern for the internal strategic requirements of the high-performing work organization. But it is questionable whether this prescription adequately serves the external requirements of high-performing public organizations, where political, rather than strictly managerial, concerns are paramount. The question is whether this supposedly ideal HR strategy, posited to lead to high performance, these days represents but a partial response to the HR strategy–high-performance problem.

In government, managerial norms inevitably beg important political questions. HR strategies created to support high-performing work systems in government require a high-wire act of the first order, trying to balance the conflicting forces that naturally arise from competing values, such as merit versus representativeness and employee protectionism versus responsiveness to executive leadership. These are political matters as much as they are managerial or technical matters. The problem is whether equilibrium between simultaneously managerial and political aims is obtainable.

STUDY OF THE STATES:
IMPLICATIONS FOR HIGH PERFORMANCE

To understand current trends in using HRM to create high-performance work institutions in government, it is helpful to examine typical tendencies in present civil service reform ventures. Values emphasized in reform initiatives are significant clues to how high-performance work strategies are conceived in the public sector. What follows is a discussion, based on a study I conducted,[1] of civil service reform in all fifty state governments and its implications for understanding strategic HRM thinking in the public sector. Although the level of analysis is limited to state-level bureaucracies, it is clear that the findings reflect larger patterns found at the national level (compare, for instance, National Performance Review, 1993).

Study results show that contemporary personnel reform in the states strives to achieve two main strategic objectives that arise directly out of public HRM's history. First, there is a determination to make government work better by strengthening management control of human resource activities. This managerialist trend involves incrementally increasing the number and type of delegated authorities, authorizing model demonstration projects, and increasing the use of technology in human resource management. Broadly speaking, the principal tactic is to move away from centralized control of human resource functions, such as recruitment and selection, and to grant managers in line agencies more authority in various HR areas. Delegation rather than decentralization is the rule. This means that the devolution of control from centralized personnel agencies to line departments is usually achieved by written agreements that list the performance requirements expected of the departments. Failure to meet agreed-upon standards can lead to recovery of the function by the central personnel body.

Second, there is a companion commitment to sustain merit principles or to ensure that all employment decisions are made in accord with personnel laws and rules. This means, for instance, that applicants for open competitive positions will not be discriminated against because of various ascriptive criteria such as race or gender. Despite the host of criticisms leveled against public HRM systems, the truth is that their so-called bureaucratic excesses—their uses of rules rather than trust—were necessitated by real incidents of various forms of discrimination engaged in by assorted elected and appointed government officials at all levels of the U.S. public service. State reform efforts have sustained interest in protecting merit principles. However, study results suggest that this protection may be honored more in theory than in practice. For example, there is little indication that states are evaluating the effects of delegated authorities. This fact carries a significant implication about what people might consider effective HRM policies in government. At this juncture, it is sufficient to note that the forces for greater managerialism dominate current strategic thinking in public HRM (Carnevale, Housel, and Riley, 1995).

Overall, study results show that current reforms go a long way in satisfying the internal demands of high-performance work systems. However, the reforms do not evidence as much capacity for fulfilling the unique external operating requirements of high-performing public organizations.

FINDING THE RIGHT STRATEGIC FIT

A strategic plan aligns an organization's (1) mission, purpose, and goals, or what it intends to do; (2) external forces such as opportunities and threats, or what is feasible in its operating domain; and (3) internal forces such as strengths and weaknesses, or what it is really capable of doing (Barry, 1986). When this plan is realized, conditions for high performance are established.

In government, there are differences from business both in kind and degree among the three sets of strategic issues just listed. Although all organizations exist on some continuum of *publicness* (Bozeman, 1987), there are still enough significant differences between public and private institutions to warrant distinctly disparate strategic approaches in creating high-performing work systems. According to Nutt and Backoff (1992): "The strategic managers of [public] organizations should be wary of using private sector approaches that assume clear goals, profit or economic purposes, unlimited authority to act, secret development, limited responsibility for actions, and oversight through market mechanisms that signal financial results. In public organizations or, more accurately, in organizations with significant amounts of publicness, many of these assumptions are not valid. To cope with the demands posed by publicness, managers need approaches that go beyond strategic management ideas developed for the private sector" (pp. 22–23).

Government has traditionally imported management practices wholesale from the business sector. Certain managerial techniques will transfer well between sectors. However, there is significant evidence that some adjustments in thinking are in order when private ideas are brought into the public sector (Hyde, 1992), and this is the case when it comes to human resource administration and the triad of strategic issues evident in public organizations. The following sections discuss the strategic fit between public HRM and these issues.

Mission

High performance begins with strategic questions that clarify mission. In government the HR mission is often determined by forces outside the HR administrator's control. For instance, the views of elected leaders and the preferences of organized interests of all kinds combine to establish legal mandates and operating constraints that dramatically influence organizational mission. Because they arise from such complex political recipes, HR goals of public organizations are typically broad and conflicting. High-performance work institutions feature clear goals, a reasonable measure of control over issue identification and prioritization, established performance expectations, and good command over implementation. These factors are not easily realized in the public sector, with its political operating context.

In HRM terms the politicization of mission means that legislative bodies often impose such mission requirements as pay-for-performance, senior executive systems, appraisal methods, and broadbanding of job classifications, along with a host of ideas about wages and fringe benefits. Groups representing women, minorities, unions, and others play a major political role as they ensure that their concerns are incorporated into the mission requirements of government organizations.

It is not unusual, or inappropriate, for various interest groups to attempt to influence the human resource function in government through legislative action and other public pressures. Public unions, for instance, have the right to bargain wages, hours, and other terms and conditions of employment as they simultaneously carry the same battles directly to the legislative body. Political actors are numerous in the public HR operating domain, to an extent unknown and unimagined in most business organizations. External political forces contend with internal managerial considerations at every turn when it comes to the formulation of HR policy, and the result is multiple interpretations of what HR policies actually lead to high performance in government and multiple definitions of what high performance itself actually means. These are fundamentally political issues, not strictly managerial ones.

Opportunities and Threats

The external operating environment of organizations, public and private, presents both opportunities and threats. The strategic rule of thumb is to exploit opportunities and block threats. This assumes, however, that strategists can agree what these terms mean. Most public organizations have special problems in distinguishing threats and opportunities because the measures are ultimately political. In private organizations, economic markets provide clear feedback about the difference between threats and opportunities. Profits and losses categorize the various external contingencies. Public organizations exist in political markets that do not share common measures of return on investment, market share, profit margins, and the other elements that businesses can appraise to evaluate their progress in realizing strategic objectives. Because of this value disconsensus on most important public policy issues, the questions of what is a quality product or service, who is really a customer or client, and what constitutes the right organizational strategy are often contentious political matters. Likewise, the increasingly narrow common political ground across public policy issues makes it is difficult to agree on yardsticks of the public organization's success or on what is really a threat and what is really an opportunity. One person's threat is usually someone else's opportunity. The issues of opening up grazing lands, harvesting timber, building more prisons, reducing welfare payments, implementing school vouchers, funding abortions, or saving a certain species do not fall into neat threat versus opportunity categories when the body politic is badly divided on how to react to them. Every government strategy tramples upon someone's political interest.

Affirmative action policy is a good example of the kind of public HRM strategy that represents either opportunity or threat, depending upon where one sits in relation to the redistribution resulting from such programs. Enacting a comprehensive collective bargaining law with an interest-based arbitration dispute mechanism arguably either fosters greater stability in employee-employer relationship or compromises constitutional sovereignty rights of the citizenry, depending upon one's point of view. A comparable worth study addresses gender-related wage injustices or destroys supply and demand as the best determinant of a job's worth. The feedback from political markets is always tougher to read than signals from economic markets about strategic choice and organizational performance.

Strengths and Weaknesses

The third leg of the strategic triad involves evaluating an organization's internal strengths and weaknesses. The operating principle is to build on strengths and overcome weaknesses. Here, too, a number of differences between government and business must be taken into account in developing HRM programs that enable high performance.

Public managers have less direct control over subordinates at lower levels because of institutional constraints created by often very strong degrees of employee protectionism embedded in civil service rules. The managerial problems inherent in limited control of nonsupervisory personnel are exacerbated by the fact that public employees are organized into unions at far greater rates than comparable workers in business. The extent of this unionization is a considerable restraint on managerial authority in terms of pay, promotions, benefits, leave policies, discipline, and other important aspects of the public organization's reward and incentive structure. Public HRM strategies in support of the high-performing work system cannot be determined by management as unilaterally as they can be in the business sector, where unionization is in a present state of serious decline.

Compared to their private peers, public managers and employees see less connection between performance and extrinsic rewards like pay, promotions, and job security. This raises serious questions about, for example, the efficacy of pay-for-performance strategies based on expectancy theories of motivation. It also raises issues about employee performance appraisal and disciplinary systems. Unless employees see some cause-effect relationship between what they do (or what they do not do) and the kinds of rewards of sanctions they might expect, almost no motivational strategy can be effective in the long term.

Public employees may have, finally, different motivational sets from those typically found among business employees. Public employees differ in their public service motive and in the value given to related intrinsic factors, with important implications for HRM planning and organizational performance. Thus, for instance, public employees can be motivated strongly by public service ideals, not just pecuniary concerns (Rainey, 1979, 1983, 1991; Rainey, Traut, and Blunt, 1986; Rainey, Backoff, and Levine, 1976).

In summary, organizational mission requirements are more ambiguous for government agencies, external operating environments are more political, and internal strengths and weaknesses more difficult to measure. Business HRM strategists can pay more attention to the internal effects of their policies. They have less to fear about external considerations. Business strategy can be developed in greater isolation, insulated from the eyes of potentially interested publics. Business HRM plans do not need to run the same public oversight gauntlet that a public HRM administrator is bound to pass through. A business employee does not have the same claim over his or her employment status as does, for example, the typical "permanent" civil service worker, whose security is ensured in ways and for reasons unheard of in most business organizations. As the operational contexts are very different in the public and private sectors, so are the process expectations of the people who work in and are served by the two sectors.

WHY THE PROBLEMS ARE POLITICAL

The problems facing public administration in general, and human resource administration in particular, are essentially political, not managerial. Improving management methods will no doubt improve the performance of public organizations, but strengthening management techniques alone is an inadequate strategic response to the central issues that confront public institutions. This point was brought home recently to me while I attended a meeting of the National Academy of Public Administration in Washington, D.C., to discuss the future of public administration. We found ourselves debating this topic during the week the government was intentionally shut down by the Congress because of a political fight over the national budget. It became clear that the field's real future lay, not in coming up with yet another new management technique, but in developing a better grasp of government's role in the way public HRM addresses important questions, a better understanding of the larger political and economic environments within which public HRM is embedded. Ultimately, all roads are political in public administration.

THE QUESTION OF TRUST

Both internal traditions and external forces conspire to prevent meaningful reform of HR programs, such that they can effectively support conditions needed for high-performance and high-trust work systems.

Traditional designs of public HRM systems are low trust. This reflects both internal and external factors. Job design is specialized, in the best tradition of bureaucratic idealism. There is precious little attention given to work design and performance appraisal methods that foster teamwork. Employee involvement and participation in the creation and maintenance of work processes remains low despite the recent fanfare about quality improvement, reinvention, and reengineering. Pay systems remain focused on individuals and not groups. Agencies have little experience or interest in knowledge-based pay programs. Even pay-for-performance techniques, which have a high level of political appeal, seem designed to control not release the full productive potential of the public workforce. Commitment to human capital development continues to exist more in theory than practice. Where education and training are valued, they focus on behavior modification. The idea that development means inviting real change in how people think and work on the job is not adequately grasped. People are still taught to behave according to a predetermined set of standards rather than to think critically. Labor relations programs remain adversarial rather than cooperative for the most part, despite the introduction of partnership plans in some locales. Knowledge elites still control much of what goes on in the typically bureaucratic public organization, and real power remains up, not down, the line. The internal rules, roles, and relations in most modern public institutions remain low trust despite a continuing interest in bureaucratic reform (Carnevale, 1995).

High-performance work systems cannot be realized on the cheap. They require an investment mentality—investment in staff training and development, new technology, competitive compensation systems, and the like. No HR strategy, from whatever source, can overcome public leaders' lack of will to make the investments that facilitate high-performance conditions. High-performance and high-trust work systems necessitate the sharing of power and authority. Government managers, like their private equals, seem loathe to shift their work authority paradigm and elected officials seem nervous about empowering nonelected bureaucrats. The missions of government agencies typically offend powerful political interests. That is the nature of things in a pluralist society, where factions compete to dominate every aspect of the policy process. As a result, much strategic thinking about government these days appears designed to constrain rather than enable high levels of organizational performance. Bureaucracy has sticking power because, despite their claims to the contrary, public officials and too many top-level administrators have a vested interest in maintaining it. They trust what they can control and choose not to invest in alternative arrangements (Carnevale, 1995).

These problems cannot be resolved through greater focus on managerial technique alone. Management styles and methods are consequential but not determinant in creating high-trust, high-performing work systems. Surely the failure of an entire parade of management reforms during the past fifty years should underscore the limits of what managerialist methods alone can realize in creating high-performing public organizations. Improving management style and techniques is a necessary but not sufficient condition for improving the performance of public institutions.

CONCLUSION

If we rely too much on managerialist HR strategies in government as our premier tactic for improving organizational performance, we will encounter serious problems. Effective HRM strategy in government must address all the paradoxical challenges that arise from the galaxy of competing values in the public HRM operating domain. Managerialism addresses many but not all of these necessities. A goal of responding to executive leadership, for example, begs the question of employee protectionism, a contrary goal and one grounded in the historical experience that public officials have time and again engaged in corrupt activities in the name of the public good. Objectifying merit, as if it had no ideological dimension, will not satisfy those who expect government institutions to be representative and nondiscriminatory. The value of being like business does not fit with the value that government has a special responsibility to serve as a model employer, as it clearly has in the past, heeding social equity issues involving race and gender for example. Becoming more businesslike begs this strategic HRM question, Who will mind the merit principle store if managerial license is increased dramatically in government?

The results of the fifty-state study show a sharp turn toward managerialism. The impetus has been the real problems the modern civil service has encountered in dealing with a number of external and internal mission requirements. This shift acknowledges managerialism as legitimate and strategic, yet there is almost no evidence in the study that special attention is being paid to evaluating the results of managerialist reforms. Precious few data show that central HRM bodies are really monitoring managers' compliance with all the basic ideas reflected in the typical set of public merit principles. The eagerness with which public HRM strategists have embraced Total Quality Management, excellence programs, reinvention schemes, and reengineering programs should give merit principle enthusiasts considerable pause when these maneuvers draw attention from other, equally worthwhile concerns.

Management strategies that work in business cannot be transferred wholesale into government. Managerialism cannot serve as an effective *political strategy* in government, and it is in the politics of reform that the real opportunities for creating high-trust and high-performing public organizations reside. HRM reform programs that have never been implemented or have failed when implemented were abandoned not because they did not make technical sense but because they did not have adequate political support.

Some argue that mistrust of managerialist strategy is old-fashioned, out-of-date, reminiscent of a past that no longer exists, that can no longer be. There is a Madisonian kind of argument at bottom in such thinking, and it does have appeal. For example, why should such alarm be sounded against management innovation when merit principles will survive, perhaps even prosper, not because of personnel rules or central HRM oversight, but because the environment of public agencies in modern times is much more organized and attentive to issues of corruption and merit abuse than it was at the beginning of the twentieth century. These days there are good-government groups, unions, and organizations reflecting the interests of various protected classes, and the extent of bureaucratic professionalism in government, itself a check against mischief, has been strengthened. The political parties themselves, it is said, arrest one another from illegal patronage. The press is vigilant, and the public is wary of corruption. There is, in fact, a system of natural political checks and balances that will take care of merit principles. Merit principle protection is ensured goes the argument.

This reasoning suggests that HRM strategists can rely upon the natural politics of the HRM operating domain to guard against corruption, ensure a reasonable measure of employee protectionism, guarantee representative bureaucracy, prevent discrimination, and promote social equity. It insinuates that HRM strategists should appropriately concentrate on improving management methods.

Nevertheless, although this reasoning is true in many respects and although there is a compelling need for more trust in government and especially in the management of public human resource systems (Carnevale, 1992, 1995), there is also a need for *rational distrust* (Barber, 1983). That is, there should always be some measure of hearty skepticism present in individuals, groups, and organizations. Without rational distrust, for instance, even in a democracy people get duped and lose liberty. Without a fair amount of critical thinking and healthy cynicism, public HRM systems can fail strategically and be unable to honor their obligations to the entire array of worthwhile values that demand their attention.

The right HRM strategy in government is at once managerial but always more. It must address enduring issues of representativeness, equity, and employee protection and have a broad definition of the public good. If it does not, it will flounder in protecting the public trust, and once it fails politically, its managerialist techniques will soon be called into question, no matter how rational they may have once appeared.

The prescription for making public HRM work in political terms is to welcome, not resist, the involvement of attentive publics. This means for example that public personnelists need to stop hiding behind the supposed rationalism and scientism of their managerial procedures and begin to negotiate with various interests that do not feel well served by current practice. Specifically, developing and using conflict resolution skills like negotiation and mediation to resolve disputes between different legitimate interests is essential. Facilitating dialogue between competing interests through team building, strategic planning, and other group consensus methods is also essential. In mediating between competing forces the public personnelist must be prepared to realize workable solutions that are not just technically feasible but that also create constructive working relationships between all the stakeholders in the public personnel enterprise. Ultimately, this prescription means that although polishing one's technical expertise is important, it is no substitute for increasing one's knowledge of how to deal with differences.

The correct HR strategy in government is not entirely rational, nor is it meant to be. There are limits to what technique can accomplish or should be asked to reach. The strategy that is ideal and normative is inherently political; it is what will work in terms of the interests of outside stakeholders of all kinds. It is the product of a number of complex political transactions. It is negotiated (and the meaning of high performance is negotiated as well; standards of high performance cannot exist independently of people's political needs). It fosters people's confidence and trust in government internally and externally. Public HR strategy that conforms to this definition is developed through a political process: one that involves the public, is publicly accessible, and represents all interests. When the requirements of the definition and the development process are satisfied, high-trust and high-performance work systems will be achieved.

Note

1. The study (Carnevale, Housel, and Riley, 1995) was conducted on behalf of the Human Resources Management Advisory Committee of the state of Oklahoma. In-depth telephone interviews were conducted with eighty-five senior executive personnelists throughout the United States. Respondents were identified from recommendations solicited through the office of each state's human resource director. Questionnaires were provided to respondents in advance of the interviews. All interviews were recorded and transcribed.

References

Barber, B. *The Logic and Limits of Trust.* New Brunswick, N.J.: Rutgers University Press, 1983.

Barry, B. W. *Strategic Planning Workbook for Nonprofit Organizations.* St. Paul, Minn.: Amherst H. Wilder Foundation, 1986.

Bozeman, B. *All Organizations Are Public: Bridging Public and Private Organizational Theories.* San Francisco: Jossey-Bass, 1987.

Bryson, J. M. *Strategic Planning for Public and Nonprofit Organizations: A Guide for Strengthening and Sustaining Organizational Achievement.* (Rev. ed.) San Francisco: Jossey-Bass, 1995.

Carnevale, A. P. *America and the New Economy: How New Competitive Standards Are Radically Changing American Workplaces.* San Francisco: Jossey-Bass, 1991.

Carnevale, A. P., and Haupton, A. M. "The Economic, Financial, and Demographic Context of American Higher Education." Paper prepared for the Seminar on Change and the Public Comprehensive University, Aspen Institute Program on Education in a Changing Society, Aug. 1996.

Carnevale, D. G. "The Learning Support Model: Personnel Policy Beyond the Traditional Model." *American Review of Public Administration,* 1992, *22,* 423–435.

Carnevale, D. G. *Trustworthy Government: Leadership and Management Strategies for Building Trust and High Performance.* San Francisco: Jossey-Bass, 1995.

Carnevale, D. G., Housel, S. W., and Riley, N. *Merit System Reform in the States: Partnerships for Change.* Norman: Programs in Public Administration, University of Oklahoma, 1995.

Elliott, R. H. *Public Personnel Administration: A Values Perspective.* Reston, Va.: Reston, 1985.

Hyde, A. C. "The Proverbs of Total Quality Management: Recharting the Path to Quality Improvement in the Public Sector." *Public Productivity and Management Review,* 1992, *16,* 25–37.

Klingner, D. E. "Strategic Human Resource Management." In J. Rabin, T. Vocino, W. B. Hildreth, and G. J. Miller (eds.), *Handbook of Public Personnel Administration.* New York: Dekker, 1995.

Milton Marks Commission. *Too Many Agencies, Too Many Rules: Reforming California's Civil Service.* Sacramento: Milton Marks Commission on California State Government, Organization, and Economy, 1995.

Mosher, F. C. *Democracy and the Public Service.* New York: Oxford University Press, 1968.

National Academy of Public Administration. *Leading People in Change: Empowerment, Commitment, Accountability.* Washington, D.C.: U.S. Department of Health and Human Services, 1993.

National Commission on the State and Local Public Service. *Hard Truths/Tough Choices: An Agenda for State and Local Reform.* Albany, N.Y.: Nelson A. Rockefeller Institute of Government, 1993.

National Performance Review. *From Red Tape to Results: Creating a Government That Works Better and Costs Less.* Washington, D.C.: U.S. Government Printing Office, 1993.

Nutt, P. C., and Backoff, R. W. *Strategic Management of Public and Third Sector Organizations.* San Francisco: Jossey-Bass, 1992.

Rainey, H. G. "Perceptions of Incentives in Business and Government: Implications for Civil Service Reform." *Public Administration Review,* 1979, *39,* 440–448.

Rainey, H. G. "Public Agencies and Private Firms: Incentive Structures, Goals, and Individual Roles." *Administration and Society,* 1983, *15,* 207–242.

Rainey, H. G. *Understanding and Managing Public Organizations.* San Francisco: Jossey-Bass, 1991.

Rainey, H. G., Backoff, R. W., and Levine, C. L. "Comparing Public and Private Organizations." *Public Administration Review,* 1976, *36,* 233–246.

Rainey, H. G., Traut, C., and Blunt, B. "Reward Expectancies and Other Work-Related Attitudes in Public and Private Organizations: A Review and Extension." *Review of Public Personnel Administration,* 1986, *6*(2), 50–72.

Sayre, W. S. "The Triumph of Technique over Purpose." *Public Administration Review,* 1948, *8,* 134–137.

Shafritz, J. M. *Public Personnel Management: The Heritage of Civil Service Reform.* New York: Praeger, 1975.

State Academy for Public Administration. *A Time to Just Do It—Change: Recommendations for Changes in the New York State Human Resources Management System.* Albany, N.Y.: State Academy for Public Administration, 1995.

Van Riper, P. P. *History of the United States Civil Service.* New York: HarperCollins, 1958.

CHAPTER THIRTEEN

Federal Employee Unions and the Human Resource Management Function

Robert M. Tobias

Human resource managers and federal employee unions are often seen by others, and perceived by each other, as enemies. However, they are actually participants in a mutually reenforcing symbiotic relationship.

Historically, it was the function of human resources (HR) to keep the unions out of policymaking, planning, budgeting, program design, and program implementation and within the narrowly described federal scope of bargaining. Human resource managers became a perfect foil for unions. They represented all that was oppressive and demeaning about federal labor relations—a perfect rallying point for federal employee unions. And the actions of each, the manager and the union, had the effect of marginalizing the other.

That historical paradigm has been challenged by Congress, the administration, the public, and the members of federal unions. There is a growing awareness that unions and managers must create a more cooperative, less adversarial relationship in order to maximize productivity, efficiency, and employee satisfaction. There is a growing acceptance that program designs, budgets, and staffing are grist for labor-management discussion and resolution. There is a growing understanding by human resource managers and unions that each must create a new role and both must create a new relationship. And there is a growing acknowledgment that defining a new role is difficult, time consuming, frustrating, and complicated by the many downsizings facing human resource managers and unions.

It is unclear at this time whether unions and human resource managers will continue their march in from the cold or will once again be returned to the margin of agency decision making and a relationship that is hostile and adversarial.

HISTORICAL PERSPECTIVE

Management Structure

The federal government, contrary to public perception, adopts and incorporates the prevailing private-sector management philosophies. Congressional oversight committees, managers who are trying to do good work, and private-sector consultants selling the latest silver bullet that promises to "fix all/solve all" combine to keep private-sector managerial philosophies a constant source for public-sector debate, experimentation, and implementation.

In the 1930s, when the federal government was rapidly expanding in response to public needs during the Depression, the prevailing private-sector management philosophy reflected Frederick Taylor's scientific management and Theory X. The hierarchical command-and-control structure was created in the private sector to manage an unskilled workforce performing repetitive tasks. The philosophy also assumed that employees did not want to work and would not work unless constantly watched. Multilayered managerial structures were created to gather information from each lower level; in short, each level was created to watch the next lower level. Those at the top made decisions to be implemented by those at the bottom, with everybody in between reporting and watching.

Notwithstanding the differences in education between, say, Henry Ford's assembly-line worker and an employee in the National Labor Relations Board or the Department of Labor, or the difference between a routinized task in making steel and a more complex task of determining whether a particular labor law violation has occurred, the presumptive validity of private-sector management methods led to much initial acceptance and incorporation of this philosophy into the federal management structure.

It took deep root due to an additional circumstance. The small cadre of political appointees in public agencies, more concerned with public policy development than public policy management, wanted simply to issue managerial directives to the career civil servants and then get on with the seemingly more important business of enacting laws. That attitude went unchanged from administration to administration. Political appointees serving an average of eighteen months in office are not interested in managing. They want to make their historical mark in terms of legislation enacted. The hierarchal management structure was well accepted because it implied orders could be given and followed (even if the utility of this system has turned out to be illusory). This implication made it unnecessary for political appointees to spend time or effort managing; directives became an "efficient" substitute.

HR Functions Separated from Mission Accomplishment

Starting in 1883, Congress enacted a number of statutes seeking to separate the hiring, evaluation, promotion, and discharge of civil servants from the political process. Congress sought to eliminate patronage and to create a civil service based on merit. And Congress created the Civil Service Commission, now the Office of Personnel Management, to administer the laws enacted.

The Civil Service Commission implemented the laws by issuing the *Federal Personnel Manual,* ten thousand pages of regulations that were binding on every federal agency. This centralized personnel authority administered a centralized personnel system for 2.1 million federal civilian nonpostal employees. Agency managers had no authority to change the personnel rules. As a result, political appointees and agency managers with agency mission responsibility had no personnel authority or responsibility, and the human resource function was dissociated from mission accomplishment.

It was the responsibility of the human resource function to interpret and implement the unchangeable civil service rules in each agency. These rules were not directly related to accomplishing specific agency functions; they were developed to implement laws that may have had relevance when enacted but that often lost relevance over time. Coming from a centralized personnel authority, they could not respond to the needs of individual agency cultures and often became barriers to efficient accomplishment of the agency mission. Human resource managers were responsible for giving the bad news to agency line managers that the centralized personnel authority prohibited them from doing what everyone knew was more efficient.

The human resource role of high priest interpreter of the civil service laws and regulations did not endear the HR function to political appointees or ordinary line managers. HR managers were seen as gatekeepers to get around, not colleagues to engage in problem solving. They were often scapegoats, taking the blame for the inflexible rules outside of managerial control. They were an easy target because the real target was remote and amorphous. As a result they were often excluded from decision making by political appointees and agency managers at the top of the hierarchical management structure.

Restricted Bargaining Made HR Managers Technicians

The formal history of federal-sector labor relations began in 1962, when President Kennedy issued Executive Order 10988 (President, 1964). Labor unions instrumental in his campaign put a great deal of pressure on this Democratic president to support a statute allowing union recognition and requiring employee bargaining in the federal sector. Labor unions correctly saw the federal workforce as ripe for organizing. Only nineteen thousand employees in a total federal workforce of 2.8 million employees, including postal workers, were organized (*Labor-Management Relations in the Federal Service*, 1969, p. 31). The executive order was ultimately issued to defuse the pressure for a statute.

President Kennedy created a task force that made recommendations for a labor-management system; many of them mirrored the private-sector system under the National Labor Relations Act of 1935 (NLRA). The recommendation on scope of bargaining varied dramatically, however. When Congress enacted the NLRA, it believed that collective bargaining was an effective tool to resolve differences. Wages, hours, and other terms and conditions of employment were made mandatorily negotiable. In contrast, the president and high-level political appointees were afraid that the career civil service, given the same tool, might bargain away the discretion and power so coveted in a hierarchical management system. Therefore, the task force recommended, and the president adopted, a very narrow scope of bargaining that excluded a broad range of issues and problems labor unions would otherwise expect to be able to address and resolve. The order stated that "such obligation [to bargain] shall not be construed to extend to such areas of discretion and policy as the missions of an agency, its budget, its organization and the assignment of its personnel, or the technology of performing its work" (President, 1964, sec. 6[b]). The executive order also excluded from bargaining civil service rules and regulations, and broad areas of managerial discretion:

All agreements with such employee organizations shall also be subject to the following requirements. . . .

(1) In the administration of all matters covered by the agreement officials and employees are governed by the provisions of any existing or future laws and regulations, including policies set forth in the Federal Personnel Manual and agency regulations, which may be applicable, and the agreement shall at all times be applied subject to such laws, regulations and policies;

(2) Management officials of the agency retain the right, in accordance with applicable laws and regulations, (a) to direct employees of the agency, (b) to hire, promote, transfer, assign, and retain employees in positions within the agency, and to suspend, demote, discharge, or take other disciplinary action against employees, (c) to relieve employees from duties because of lack of work or for other legitimate reasons, (d) to maintain the efficiency of the Government operations entrusted to them, (e) to determine the methods, means and personnel by which such operations are to be conducted; and (f) to take whatever actions may be necessary to carry out the mission of the agency in situations of emergency [President, 1964, sec. 7].

In spite of the narrow scope of federal bargaining, unions began organizing aggressively. Within seven years, 52 percent of the workforce was organized in 2,305 exclusive units in thirty-five agencies (*Labor-Management Relations*, 1969, p. 31).

With the change from the Johnson to the Nixon administration in 1968, a new task force was convened. Unions, frustrated over their inability to fulfill campaign promises of creating a less arbitrary workplace through collective bargaining, urged that the scope of bargaining be expanded. The new task force rejected the general appeal but did recommend that a new executive order make clear that "agencies and labor organizations shall not be precluded from negotiating agreements providing for appropriate arrangements for employees adversely affected by the impact of realignment of workforces or technological change" (*Labor-Management Relations*, 1969, p. 39). President Nixon accepted this recommendation when he issued Executive Order 11491, and this language came to mean that unions could negotiate over the impact and implementation of a protected management right so long as the exercise of the management right was not negated. The task force also recommended, and the president accepted, the creation of a centralized structure to make negotiability determinations, consider whether agencies or unions committed unfair labor practices, and assist the parties in reaching agreement through mediation and final binding interest arbitration (President, 1971, secs. 4–6, 16, 17).

With the pent-up demand to bargain and a centralized authority to make negotiability decisions, human resource managers were presented with a unique opportunity to expand their sphere of influence. The skills and institutional knowledge developed by interpreting laws and the *Federal Personnel Manual* could be used to interpret the legality of union bargaining proposals. In addition, the political appointees and high-level career civil servants, the decision makers in the hierarchical management structure, needed someone to protect the scope of their decision-making discretion from the threat the growing unions now presented. Ironically, they viewed the expertise of human resource managers to provide a narrow construction of the law, *Federal Personnel Manual*, and applicable agency regulations as extremely useful when applied to an external force like unions.

As would be expected, individuals with specialized, technical expertise delegated new authority and responsibility wanted to perform well. And they did. Administrative and court litigation mushroomed. All potential incursions into the protected management rights arena were vigorously resisted by the HR function.

Human resource managers were delegated the responsibility to communicate the views and protect the interests of higher-level managers. In doing so, however, they became technicians, performing not as managers but as representational advocates of the existing structure and protectors of the status quo.

Unions Became Fierce Adversaries

The inherently narrow scope of bargaining defined in the executive order and subsequent legislation, coupled with the new human resource manager role, made it impossible for unions to address constant employee complaints about evaluation systems, preselection for promotions, shift starts and stops, switches from one shift to another, equipment provided, work processes and procedures, award amounts and methods of award allocation, health and safety provisions, training quality and availability, and work quality.

Unions felt the pressure of unsatisfied members and competition from other unions. With two large independent unions in the federal sector, raiding was a common phenomenon, and decertifications were not uncommon. Unions wanted finalized, comprehensive collective bargaining agreements.

Human resource managers' declarations of nonnegotiability at the bargaining table were vigorously resisted by unions. Any proposal accepted by unions that constricted the scope of bargaining was feared as setting a precedent that could be used by managers in a subsequent or parallel negotiation. Conversely, unions were typically interested in using a negotiation and litigation process to set a precedent that might minimally expand the scope of bargaining. Unions crafted bargaining proposals that may or may not have addressed the real problem in the workplace; the primary goal was to make the problem negotiable, to conclude a bargained agreement with the problem area generally covered and then arbitrate the ambiguity. Real issues were rarely directly addressed and never finally resolved.

The inherent ambiguity of the exclusions from bargaining, the felt responsibility of the human resource managers to interpret the exclusions as narrowly as possible, and the need for public action, if not results, from unions created fierce disagreement and hostile litigation over the scope of bargaining. For unions, fighting became the substitute for success, and for human resource managers, the measure of success.

Labor-Management Process Marginalized HR Managers

The task of keeping the unions at bay, although important to the decision makers, is analogous to the task of guarding a gate. The guard performing the task is the first line of defense, the first to fall in battle, and often described as a hero. But the guard is not a colleague of the general; the guard does not make recommendations on how guard training should occur or whether it should occur at all. The guard, like the human resource manager, is rewarded for successfully performing an important ministerial function.

This role further marginalized the HR managers. The primary focus on negotiability determinations made it difficult for these managers to accomplish their historical task of designing systems to support the development of human resources in the workplace. For example, it was already a challenge to design an employee evaluation system that would be consistent with laws and the *Federal Personnel Manual* and that would distinguish poor, good, and outstanding performance. Throw a union into the mix and stir with fears of whether a proposal or counterproposal is negotiable, and you cannot create an evaluation system that achieves its goals.

The human resource manager may achieve the goal of protecting management decision making, but the systems ultimately created will be criticized by those same managers who applauded the HR manager's guard role. The human resource manager is highly unlikely to receive accolades for substantive achievement in this system and is likely to become even more marginalized.

Labor-Management Process Marginalized Unions

Unions felt marginalized because the only way they could create an aura of union power and empowerment was by challenging the powerful outside the union. Unions excluded from operational and policy decisions could get their voices heard only through the adversarial process.

Unions filed lawsuits using First Amendment and due process arguments to create rights unattainable in bargaining. Freedom of Information Act lawsuits were filed to obtain information that would have been readily exchanged in constructive labor-management relationships. Lawsuits claiming violations of the Administrative Procedure Act of 1946 were filed to challenge substantive decisions unreachable in bargaining.

Unions sought to expand impact and implementation bargaining. In an attempt to change substantive decisions, proposals were drafted in the form of process. So long as a proposal was considered process, it could not be implemented until bargaining was completed. Aggressive impact and implementation bargaining could then delay the implementation of a substantive decision, ameliorate its adverse impact, or provide a rich source of litigation potential. Unions also aggressively protected the rights secured in collective bargaining agreements or Executive Order 11491. Grievances and unfair labor practice charges were used as weapons to enforce rights and punish transgressors. These union efforts generated publicity, gave unions a reputation as real fighters on behalf of federal employees, encouraged additional organizing, provided a measure of credibility, and led to a union management structure comprising a small number of federal employee union members waiting to react to management actions.

The union response gave human resource managers ample justification for expansion of their activities. The more grievances, unfair labor practices, and negotiation impasses generated, the more human resource managers were needed. And, of course, the more egregious the posture and position of human resource managers, the more justification for the union.

However, despite all the activity, issues were not resolved. Hostility and acrimony increased. Polarization thrived in the climate of distrust. Human resource managers were not elevated into the room where program management decisions occurred. And unions were ultimately unsuccessful at ameliorating employees' pain because of the inability to negotiate or even to discuss with agency program managers the root causes of the pain in the workplace.

HISTORICAL LABOR-MANAGEMENT PARADIGM

Political Appointees Received More Scrutiny

The congressional authorizing, oversight, and appropriation committees (each federal agency has one of each) have, of course, an abiding interest in how federal agencies implement enacted legislation. Even though congressional review of the executive branch is fractured because of the numerous congressional committees, a common theme began to emerge in the late 1980s and early 1990s: agencies needed to plan better on both a short- and long-range basis, and agencies needed to provide financial information to Congress, similar to that provided by corporations to stockholders.

In 1993, Congress passed the Government Performance and Results Act (GPRA), which requires agencies to prepare five-year strategic plans and annual operating plans, both plans to be submitted annually as part of the appropriations process. In addition, agencies must identify outcome measures of performance and report on whether the measures have been achieved (*U.S. Code*, 1994, vol. 5, sec. 306). Although GPRA was enacted in 1993, it did not become fully effective until 1997. Congress recognized that agencies needed time to change from the limited planning previously associated with annual appropriation cycles and to learn how to do strategic planning and define outcome measures.

Agencies are now in the midst of devising strategic plans. One of the important realizations this exercise brings to political appointees is that they must focus more time and energy on managing the agency. It is the political appointees who most often testify before congressional committees, historically in support of or in opposition to substantive legislation and a larger budget. It is becoming clear to them that they will now testify on the strategic management plan and on whether the outcome measures were reached and, if not, why not. Political appointees now have a stake in the management of agencies unlike at anytime in the past.

The Chief Financial Officers (CFO) Act, passed in 1990, has a corollary impact on political appointees. Historically, agency heads annually sought budgets while proclaiming excellent results from their prior year expenditures. It was very hard for members of Congress to keep in mind the financial history of each agency, particularly when an agency is engaged in a long-term financial investment. The CFO Act now requires agencies to prepare an auditable financial statement that includes a balance sheet (annual income and expenses) and a statement of assets and liabilities. Agencies have not maintained financial records in this manner and are having a great deal of difficulty meeting the test.

The responsibility and effort to comply with the CFO Act has focused agencies' political appointees on rocks long unturned, management practices that should be challenged. For example, if labor costs, including training, rent, and travel, can be accurately counted, should they be a "corporate" asset controlled by the agency, or should monies and control be transferred regionally or locally? An accurate cost-accounting system will allow agency managers to understand better which employees are value added to the work process and which are overhead. These management issues are now within the purview of the political appointees because Congress requires the information and because Congress, the press, and the public will evaluate it.

In addition, in 1993, Congress enacted legislation to reduce the government workforce by 12 percent, 272,000 positions, by 1997. In 1996, one year ahead of schedule, the number of nondefense federal employees fell below 2 million, the smallest number since 1963. Finally, Congress appropriated fewer dollars in 1995 than 1996 and fewer dollars in 1996 than 1997 for civilian discretionary spending. This was not a reduction in the rate of increase; it was fewer actual dollars appropriated.

Agency political appointees and agency managers are now subject to more scrutiny than before and to objective evaluation of results and are provided with fewer resources both in personnel and dollars.

Public Confidence in Government Reached a New Low

Wise politicians and political appointees recognize the nexus between public support for an agency and public support for "government." They know that taxpayer or customer satisfaction is much more a part of government decision making than ever before. The federal government and its supporting organizational structure exist because the public desires a service and is willing to pay the costs. To the extent that the public loses confidence in the ability of the federal government to deliver a service, the greater the demand to eliminate the service or shrink its financial support.

Polling and anecdotal evidence reflects the frustration felt today by the U.S. public: "Public confidence in the federal government has never been lower. The average American believes we waste 48 cents of every tax dollar. Five of every six want 'fundamental' change in Washington. Only 20 percent of Americans trust the federal government to do the right thing most of the time—down from 76 percent 30 years ago" (National Performance Review, 1993a, p. 1).

It is clear; the public will not support inefficient or ineffective federal programs.

Administration Focused Attention on Better Management

The National Performance Review (NPR) initiated by President Clinton in March 1993 and led by Vice President Gore accelerated the changing labor-management paradigm by announcing that the president and his cabinet secretaries were responsible for managing the executive branch of government. Policy development was no longer to be the sole criterion of agency success. Each agency was directed to appoint a deputy or undersecretary as a chief operating officer (COO). These COOs have the responsibility for "transforming the agencies' day-to-day management culture, for improving performance to achieve agencies' goals, [and] for reengineering administrative processes" (National Performance Review, 1993a, p. 89). Political appointees now must pay attention to resource, and particularly human resource, use.

The NPR recognized that the hierarchal multilayered management structure must be eliminated: agencies achieve this objective "by turning their entire management system upside down—shedding the power to make decisions from the sedimentary layers of management and giving it to the people on the ground doing the work" (National Performance Review, 1993a, p. 6). The NPR also recognized that empowering workers makes good business sense: "Removing a layer of oversight that adds no value to customers does more than save money: It demonstrates trust in our workers. It offers employees in dead-end or deadly dull jobs a chance to use all their abilities. It makes the federal government a better place to work—which will in turn make federal workers more productive" (National Performance Review, 1993a, p. 71).

Recognition was followed up with a directive to the Office of Personnel Management to deregulate personnel policy by eliminating the ten thousand–page *Federal Personnel Manual* and all agencies' implementing directives: "The directive should require that most personnel management authority be delegated to the agencies' line managers at the lowest level practical in each agency" (National Performance Review, 1993a, p. 22).

The president recognized that neither delegation of new authority nor increased productivity can be achieved in the context of adversarial labor-management relations. He issued Executive Order 12871, which set a direction: "The involvement of Federal Government employees and their union representatives is essential to achieving the National Performance Review's government reform objectives. Only by changing the nature of federal labor-management relations so that managers, employees, and employees' elected union representatives serve as partners will it be possible to design and implement comprehensive changes necessary to reform government" (President, 1994).

Executive Order 12871 also significantly expanded the scope of bargaining in the federal sector by making the "numbers, types, and grades of employees or positions assigned to any organizational subdivision, work project, or tour of duty, or the technology, methods, and means of performing work" substantively negotiable (sec. 2[d]).

Unions and human resource managers were confronting a new day with new expectations and significantly changed relationships.

Union Members Want More Participation in Work

Union members are increasingly insistent on participating in the development of new work processes and procedures. They recognize the increased emphasis by Congress on efficiency and effectiveness. They know that they have information and knowledge that can contribute to a more productive workplace. And they correctly equate future job security with agency success.

Union members who are provided an opportunity to participate have heightened job satisfaction. In a recent 165-item questionnaire administered to 88,000 IRS employees, the question that most closely correlated to overall job satisfaction was whether the employee believed his or her skills and abilities were being effectively used. Employees who scored highest on skill utilization, scored highest on job satisfaction. The correlation was twice as high as for any other question and did not change whether the respondents were managers or bargaining unit employees, men or women, whites or African Americans. The data show clearly that using employee skills creates a more satisfied workforce. It is only a short leap to conclude that using employee skills will create more productivity and a better agency bottom line.

Union members want a participatory role heretofore denied to them by the hierarchical management structure and hostile labor-management relationships. They want to be players, not automatons in a command-and-control structure.

PROSPECTS FOR THE FUTURE

Agency Recognition of Need for Union Involvement

Agency decision makers are beginning to recognize that substantial reorganizations and work process reengineering efforts are needed in order to respond to the external pressures to do more with less. Moreover, 80 percent of eligible federal employees are now organized (National Performance Review, 1993b, p. 79), in contrast to 37.1 percent of the state and local eligible employees and 10.4 percent of the private-sector eligible employees (U.S. Secretary of Labor's Task Force, 1996, p. 52). Therefore these same decision makers are being advised by human resource managers that the organized employees can significantly delay implementation of needed changes by asserting the right to negotiate on the substance or, if the substance is nonnegotiable, bargaining over the impact and implementation of the proposed changes. It is not unusual for bargaining to take one to two years, and during bargaining, implementation may not occur. Agency decision makers, newly responsible for agency management, cannot wait two years for change to occur.

The Frederick Taylor myth that efficiency and productivity can be increased only by increasing pressure on employees to produce more, because they do not really want to work, was explored by W. Edwards Deming, who proved that 85 percent of an employee's productivity is linked to work processes and procedures (Deming, 1986). Therefore working harder does not automatically improve productivity; usually the system must change first. This fact, coupled with the further fact that those working in the system have the knowledge, skills, and ability to understand the current work process and what must be done to improve it, enhances management decision makers' need for employee involvement and a less adversarial, more cooperative relationship with unions.

Union Recognition of Adversarialism's Shortcomings

Adversarial unionism creates a sense of action and drama. There are winners and losers. Right and wrong are publicly determined, and public punishment often provides sweet satisfaction. However, adversarial unionism is also based on rights enforcement and has serious limitations in the federal sector. First, because the scope of bargaining is so limited, the rights created in collective bargaining agreements are similarly limited, as is the scope of rights enforcement in the grievance procedure.

Second, lawsuits or grievances, even of the class action variety, touch only a few employees. The euphoria of anticipated action and of vindication felt by the aggrieved quickly dissipates because resolution comes often years after the injury. And a successful lawsuit or grievance may make a manager more careful to follow the applicable rules, but the adversarial system cannot force a fundamental change in the basic managerial policy and cannot change an environment that excludes employees to a collaborative environment where employee views are valued.

For example, the IRS employs approximately thirty thousand employees from February to June to process tax returns in ten IRS service centers. This pipeline operation is no different in organization from Henry Ford's assembly line. Major tasks are broken down into series of smaller tasks sequentially performed by separate employees. The work is boring, low skilled, and low paid and offers little likelihood of promotion. Federal unions have no right in statute or regulation to force a change in the work process created by the pipeline. Yet union members who work in the pipeline are not concerned with whether their union has a right to address a problem, they want a solution. And they want to participate in devising the solution.

Recognition That Partnerships Create Mutual Benefits

President Clinton clearly understood that labor-management partnerships can be advantageous to the public, and directed each agency head to create labor-management partnerships throughout the government: "The head of each agency shall . . . (a) create labor-management committees or councils at appropriate levels, or adapting existing councils or committees if such groups exist, to help reform government; (b) involve employees and their union representatives as full partners with management representatives to identify problems and craft solutions to better serve the agency's customers and mission . . . ; (c) provide systematic training of appropriate agency employees (including line managers, first line supervisors, and union representatives who are Federal employees) in consensual methods of dispute resolution, such as alternative dispute resolution techniques and interest-based bargaining approaches" (President, 1994, sec. 2).

President Clinton changed the labor-management dynamic. All issues involving "the agency's customers and mission" are discussable when the goal is to help "reform government." Strategic, tactical, program, budget, and operating decisions are matters for the parties to discuss and attempt to decide. In short, the scope of what may be discussed in the context of the labor-management partnership is virtually unlimited. The president recognized that the decision-making process of power bargaining and adversarialism must change to a consensus-making process of interest-based bargaining and alternative dispute resolution techniques. He also understood that training was an essential ingredient of success.

What distinguishes this effort to transform the process from past efforts was that it recognized that labor and management each have interests that can be satisfied only with the cooperation of the other. Management decision makers want fast decisions without the traditional delays of adversarial bargaining. Unions and union members want a broader, guaranteed scope of bargaining but, even more, want a role in shaping the inevitable reorganizations and the changes in work process and procedures. Management decision makers want more productivity and unions more job satisfaction through an empowered, involved workforce. Management decision makers want better decisions, and unions want employee knowledge to be used and recognized.

The symmetry of these interests creates an opportunity for transformation. Neither party can advance at the expense of the other, but each party can advance in conjunction with the other. Translating intellectual and conceptual agreement, or the beauty of the ideas, into changed behavior in the workplace requires a significant change in the role historically played by managers, human resource officials, union officials, and bargaining unit employees.

Recognition That Changed Roles Mean New Responsibilities

The command-and-control management style based on the hierarchical management structure must give way to leadership based on ideas, data, and decisions that reflect interests rather than power and position. Opening the door, sharing data, engaging in predecision discussion, and struggling to reach consensus decisions—not only between labor and management but also between managers—are necessary efforts in successful partnerships.

Management decision makers have a new role: the responsibility of creating and implementing changed work processes and procedures that increase productivity, work product quality, and taxpayer satisfaction.

As concluded in a recent General Accounting Office sponsored symposium to identify successful private-sector HR management "lessons learned," HR managers must be fully integrated into the process for defining and achieving agency mission: "Instead of isolating the 'personnel function' organizationally, integrate human resource managers into the mission of the organization. Tie the organization's human resource manager position into its mission, vision, and culture" (U.S. General Accounting Office, 1995, p. 6). Human resource managers must not be marginalized; rather they are integral to providing ideas, educating staff, supporting change, setting management strategies, and facilitating decision making, among other things. The previously organizationally isolated human resource manager has an important role to play that is critical to agency success.

Union officials are also required to adopt new leadership directions. Identifying what one's group does not have—reactive leadership—is totally different from identifying what employees want and effectively participating in setting and helping to implement agency policy. Identifying goals, setting priorities, creating action plans, responding to management policy initiatives, and effectively involving union members in the union decision-making structure are all elements of proactive union leadership.

It is extremely unlikely that either agency managers or union officials will change their leadership orientation and organizational structure in isolation. Although it is true each person must change individually, managers and officials can also develop a momentum in the context of change in relation to each other. A union leader develops the courage to change individually when viewing a management leader who is inclusive and shares information. A management leader becomes willing to change individually when a union leader is willing to risk being proactive rather than complaining about what has not been done.

Recognition That Partnerships Create Measurable Results

The early payoff from partnership activity has been primarily cost avoidance: fewer grievances and unfair labor practice charges filed, more filed grievances and unfair labor practice charges settled, fewer requests to negotiate the impact and implementation of management-initiated changes (because the union is now involved in the original decision to change), and faster negotiation of term and midterm agreements (because the parties are using alternative dispute resolution and interest-based bargaining).

Agencies have also reported significant cost savings. A report to the president by the National Partnership Council (NPC) (1995) identified several cost-saving projects created as a result of the partnership process (p. 15). Although no current method exists for gathering governmentwide calculations of cost savings, there is no question they are occurring and at an ever-increasing rate.

Similarly, the anecdotal evidence of increased employee job satisfaction is impressive. Those employees who have participated on reengineering work teams, work system design teams, or other forms of involvement report a newfound surge of purpose and feel a stake in what happens at their agency.

Recognition That Role Behavior Is Very Difficult

Creating partnerships envisions significant changes in behavior, significant changes in the institutional culture of agency management, in union officials, and in bargaining unit employees. Changes in culture require education, persistent pressure to change from committed leaders, and a growing cadre of cheerleaders among union officials, managers, and human resource managers. In addition, changes in culture require that people have time to learn what is expected, a willingness to take risks, opportunities to incorporate and exhibit changed behavior, time to develop trust associated with the new behavior, and a belief that the new behavior is predictable.

Taking time to change runs contrary to the enthusiasm and expectations associated with creating a new partnership. Union leaders expect to participate immediately at all levels of management and in all management decisions previously made unilaterally. And they expect their advice and counsel to be accepted. Managers expect the new sharing of information to result in no grievances at all, no impact and implementation bargaining, and automatic ratification of the agency agenda.

Then, when institutional resistance to change proves formidable, career managers wonder whether partnership is just another management fad that will disappear with a new political appointee or a new administration. Many managers like the command-and-control decision-making process. They have grown up in the system, feel comfortable with it, and do not want it to change. They have little shared understanding or acceptance for the need to change. They have little understanding and even less skill for reaching decisions using consensus among managers let alone among managers and union officials seated at the same table.

Union officials find that forming partnerships is politically risky. The adversarial labor-management relationship fosters a service or benefit rationale for joining a union. The union job in this case is to "protect" the union member from management, and for that service many employees have been willing to join and pay dues. Unions are becoming less adversarial, but broad-scale employee and union participation and empowerment has not yet occurred. As a result, employees feel less inclined to join the union for protection; they do not feel inclined to participate in change that has not reached them.

There is also a strong contingent of union officials who are philosophically opposed to "getting in bed with management." Arm's-length dealing is appropriate, they feel, because managers and management can never be trusted. And like managers, they often lack understanding of the need to change.

For all these reasons, it is critically important that the parties understand and accept that a partnership is not a legal contract, it is a long-term relationship. It is not linear. It does not get better every day. Some days it gets worse, some days it stays the same, and some days there are real breakthroughs. What is hoped for and is worked for is a positive trend line. But that happens only when the parties continue to talk and work at solving the problems associated with the needed cultural change.

Recognition That Progress Can Be Dissipated by One Catastrophe

The largest potential catastrophic event faced by union leaders and management officials is a threat to job security, such as downsizing. The sine qua non for a union is to protect jobs, and management officials often believe that survival of the agency depends on aggressive downsizing. In addition, President Clinton promised job cuts of 272,000 by 1997, and Congress is cutting, and is proposing to further cut, agency budgets, which will eliminate even more jobs. Will these events constitute a return to war or a strengthened, more mature partnership relationship?

The traditional model for managing downsizing is for management to announce a need, determine the number of employees to be eliminated, negotiate the limited bargainable issues, and implement the downsizing.

The traditional union response is to lobby Congress and the affected community, pointing out why management wisdom is lacking in the proposed reduction and why lost service will be detrimental to constituents. Rallies and other public events are staged to generate public education and interest. The several critical management decisions concerning who will be eliminated and in what order are aggressively challenged as violations of the complex statute governing federal downsizing. A union win in one or more administrative or judicial challenges is very expensive to agencies because it involves employee reinstatement, back pay, and attorney fees.

Changing this traditional model requires a truly contrarian approach. When parties to a disagreement are anxious, fear attack, and see a high risk of failure, the likelihood of their engaging in experimental behavior is low. Instead they do what has proven successful in the past: demonize each other, attempt to change or sustain, as the case may be, the fundamental decision, and trust to win before a third party. And blame the third party if they lose.

Use of the partnership process, in contrast, requires that managers include union leaders in exploring alternatives to downsizing before a final decision is made and power is used to implement the decision. If agreement is reached that downsizing is necessary, the same approach of inclusion, data-driven discussion, and consideration of the parties' respective interests must be used to determine which employees will lose their jobs.

This approach, although extremely difficult, will strengthen the partnership process and partnership relationship because it requires the parties to solve problems with high-stakes consequences to each. If agreement is reached, they share accountability and responsibility. This approach requires acts of leadership, courage, and results. Without those acts, the partnership process is in serious jeopardy, because so many agencies are planning downsizing, and it is so easy to revert to comfortable behavior.

CONCLUSION

Will the difficult decisions associated with downsizing, the impact of the election of a new union leader or the replacement of a political appointee, or the impact of the election of a new administration lead to the demise of the partnership effort between unions and human resource managers and a return to the adversarial wasteland? Will these parties conclude the decisions are too hard, the stakes too high, and the consequences too grave to trust the partnership process with the most contentious issues? Or will they trust the fledgling process being created, recognize the value of struggle, risk failure, and seek to further institutionalize an effort known to be better for unions, managers, and the taxpaying public? Will they spend time, use energy, and maintain focus on joint goals and individual interests, or will the tsunami of job security wash their efforts out to sea?

Only time will provide the answers. Agency managers, human resource managers, and union leaders have a chance to be partners if they truly seize the opportunity.

References

Administrative Procedure Act. 1946. *U.S. Code,* vol. 5, sec. 551 et seq.

Chief Financial Officers Act. 1990. *U.S. Statutes at Large* 104 (1990) 2838.

Deming, W. E. *Out of the Crisis.* Cambridge, Mass.: MIT Center for Advanced Engineering Study, 1986.

Government Performance and Results Act. 1993. *U.S. Statutes at Large* 107 (1993) 285.

Labor-Management Relations in the Federal Service: Report and Recommendations. Washington, D.C.: U.S. Government Printing Office, 1969.

National Labor Relations Act. 1935. *U.S. Code,* vol. 29, sec. 151 et seq.

National Partnership Council. *A New Vision for Labor-Management Relations: A Report to the President on Progress in Labor-Management Partnerships.* Washington, D.C.: National Partnership Council, 1995.

National Performance Review. *From Red Tape to Results: Creating a Government That Works Better and Costs Less.* Washington, D.C.: U.S. Government Printing Office, 1993a.

National Performance Review. *Reinventing Human Resource Management: Accompanying Report of the National Performance Review.* Washington, D.C.: U.S. Government Printing Office, 1993b.

President. "Employment-Management Cooperation and the Federal Service," Executive Order 10988. *Code of Federal Regulations,* 1964, vol. 3 *(The President: 1959–1963 Compilation).*

President. "Labor-Management Relations in the Federal Service," Executive Order 11491. *Code of Federal Regulations,* 1971, vol. 3 *(The President: 1966–1970 Compilation).*

President. "Labor-Management Partnerships," Executive Order 12871. *Code of Federal Regulations,* 1994, vol. 3 *(The President: 1993 Compilation).*

U.S. General Accounting Office. *Transforming the Civil Service: Building the Workforce of the Future.* Results of a GAO-Sponsored Symposium, GAO/GGD-96–35. Washington, D.C.: U.S. General Accounting Office, 1995.

U.S. Secretary of Labor's Task Force on Excellence in State and Local Government Through Labor-Management Cooperation. *Working Together for Public Service.* Washington, D.C.: U.S. Department of Labor, 1996.

CHAPTER FOURTEEN

Organizational Investment in Employee Development

Montgomery Van Wart

All the great management analysts agree that employees are any organization's key asset in this age of leaner, more flexible, and more dynamic organizations. In studying excellence over the years, Tom Peters (1987, 1992; Peters and Waterman, 1982) has become increasingly convinced of this; Rosabeth Moss Kanter (1983, 1989; Kanter, Stein, and Jick, 1992) has long attributed innovation to an employee orientation in management; Peter Drucker (1985, 1992), Warren Bennis (Bennis and Nanus, 1985), and Edgar Schein (1985) assert that genuinely valuing employees is the very essence of leadership; and W. Edwards Deming (1986) makes sure that people are the center of most of his famous fourteen points. Even the recently popular reengineering gurus Michael Hammer and James Champy (1993), originally keen on cutting processes without much real thought given to the people in those processes, later adjusted their messages substantially when they realized that without concern for the exceedingly important organizational asset of human capital, radical change cannot be successfully engineered, even by the most strong willed and brilliant organizational leaders equipped with good change maps (Champy, 1995; Hammer, 1995).

Further, the great management experts generally agree that the new types of organizations emerging—no matter whether in the private or public sectors, in the United States or abroad—require a whole new perspective on investment in employees as assets and an appreciation of the fact that employees form the core of a successful enterprise. Although learning and continued training of employees was important in the heyday of the classical hierarchical bureaucracy, typically organizations encouraged only learning that was well defined, technical, and repetitive, with creativity and innovation carefully limited to select groups. The underlying assembly-line principle operating in classical hierarchical bureaucracies (and in their learning strategies) meant that employees could be changed with relative ease because (1) the organization itself was relatively stable and (2) the jobs were easily broken down into discrete functional areas with high degrees of specialization. Organizations in the past could rapidly and relatively easily replace large numbers of employees by putting new employees through narrow-gauged training programs. Employees generally accepted this narrowness in jobs and training, despite its frequent overreliance on specialization and repetition, because of the job security it offered and the sense of expertise arising from easy job mastery.

Given today's rapidly changing organizational environment—an environment likely to continue undergoing rapid change for the foreseeable future—it is little wonder that we see a new emphasis on the *learning* organization (Senge, 1990; Garvin, 1993; Kettl, 1994). How else can organizations keep up with the enormity of current technological revolutions (the greatest since Edison, Ford, and Bell were at their creative height), the new global pressures for cost compression, and the new customer demand for much higher levels of quality?

Organizations in the postmodern era will be affected by a number of forces (Peters, 1994). In general, the new conditions will be typified by an unstable environment with growing competition, undependable funding, little notice of frequent mission changes, rapidly evolving technology, and a variable and part-time workforce (Howard, 1995; Benveniste, 1994). Unlike the past, when incrementalism was the bedrock experience of the public sector (Wildavsky, 1974), today downsizing, privatizing, and restructuring are being considered at every level of government and are constant topics of public discussion in newspapers, on talk shows, and among politicians from both major parties (see, for example, National Performance Review, 1993, 1994; National Commission on the State and Local Public Service, 1993).

Not only must employees go through an initial period of learning how to conduct their work, as they did in the past, but they must perform that work under constantly varying conditions requiring continual additional training and re-skilling. Further, they are also responsible for changing the structures they work in, due to the enormous streamlining of management and technical staff. These forces make the ability to learn a skill needed as never before. As the new information workers that we are all becoming, we are required to absorb facts, master new concepts, and refine old skills and pick up new ones everyday. Sporadically—rather than once a lifetime—we must master whole new technologies, missions, and worldviews with agility.

To summarize, the traditional notion of human resource development was based on organizational stability because organizations were in fact rather static. Training was relatively straightforward and heavily skewed toward the beginning of employees' careers. The current notion guiding human resource development is to deploy personnel strategically, through not only initial training but also retraining and refocusing, and to change management style and systems (see Figure 14.1). Training and education are more evenly spread through the entire career of the individual. They blend with organizational development initiatives that were generally apart from employee development in the past. But rather than losing their importance because of this conceptual merger, human resource (HR) or human resource development (HRD) managers find that organizational development is often among their most important responsibilities (Van Wart, Cayer, and Cook, 1993).

This chapter addresses both traditional learning functions and the contemporary expansion of learning. It describes surveying training and development needs from three levels, it provides an understanding of learning theory basics by examining seven fundamental learning principles, and it also offers an understanding of six different instructional families and discusses the recent emphasis on advanced forms of learning.

SURVEYING TRAINING AND DEVELOPMENT NEEDS

Training and development assessments can occur at the organizational, department, or individual levels. In the past most training personnel focused on only the department and individual levels. Today organizational needs analysis has become very common, often using personnel managers and training managers as the technical leaders of major organizational assessment strategies.

Figure 14.1. Changing Notions of Human Resource Development.

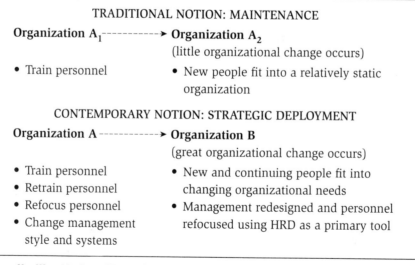

TRADITIONAL NOTION: MAINTENANCE

Organization A₁ ----------► Organization A₂
(little organizational change occurs)

- Train personnel
- New people fit into a relatively static organization

CONTEMPORARY NOTION: STRATEGIC DEPLOYMENT

Organization A ----------► Organization B
(great organizational change occurs)

- Train personnel
- Retrain personnel
- Refocus personnel
- Change management style and systems
- New and continuing people fit into changing organizational needs
- Management redesigned and personnel refocused using HRD as a primary tool

Source: Van Wart, M., Cayer, N. J., and Cook, S. *Handbook of Training and Development in the Public Sector.* San Francisco: Jossey-Bass, 1993, p. 14. Reprinted with permission.

Organizational Needs Analysis

Organizational needs analysis can be conducted in numerous ways, and therefore it is up to organizational leaders and those guiding them technically to be sure that the most effective strategies are selected for the organization. I analyzed seven major strategies in depth elsewhere (Van Wart, 1995) and thus only mention them here:

1. Ethics assessments
2. Mission, values, vision, and planning statement reviews
3. Customer and citizen assessments
4. Employee assessments
5. Performance assessments
6. Benchmarking
7. Quality assessments

Each strategy has its strengths and weaknesses, which only organizational managers and leaders can judge in light of their own circumstances. Briefly, *ethics assessments,* also called ethics audits, may either determine what the stated legal norms are or probe the gap between the stated legal values and the organization's actual performance. *Mission, values, vision, and planning statement reviews* examine the formal declarations of what organizations do, what they value, and how they plan to achieve their goals. The use of *customer and citizen assessments* has expanded immensely in the public sector because of the interest in values related to customer and citizen preferences. *Employee assessments* of employee opinions and values have also become much more common and important in helping organizations make significant adjustments. *Performance assessments* are used in all organizations to some degree; however, in the public sector, performance standards traditionally have suffered from at least six problems: weak comparability with standards in similar units, lack of knowledge about unit costs, lack of rewards for efficiency, inability to measure true effectiveness, inability to measure team and system performance, and deficiency in identifying and correcting systemic errors. *Benchmarking,* according to Bogan and English (1994), is systematically searching for superior performance and then using these best practices. *Quality assessments,* which are increasingly common and diverse, generally share a number of features: all are relatively comprehensive and emphasize customer satisfaction, employee involvement and development, continual learning and improvement, prevention over inspection, and supplier partnerships far more than assessments used to.

Because organizational assessment is both time consuming and expensive, generally only one or at most two organizational assessment strategies are implemented at one time. The checklist of questions in Exhibit 14.1 can steer organizational leaders and training personnel toward the most appropriate strategic assessment to use first.

Exhibit 14.1. Checklist to Determine the Best Organizational Assessment Strategy.

What areas might your organization consider improving through an organizational assessment (check the Yes responses)? If you check more than one Yes response, go back and prioritize them. Generally, one assessment strategy at a time is optimal. (The questions are keyed to the list of assessments in the text.)

Assessment #	Questions to Ask	No	Yes	Ranking
1.	Is there a perception of substantial noncompliance with legal regulations? Do regulations and significant organizational rules seem to be poorly understood?	____	____	____
2.	Is your organization's mission blurred, are the values unclear or conflicting, or is the planning poor? Does the organization seem to lack a dynamic and realistic vision for the future?	____	____	____
3.	Is your organization unaware of *precisely* what clients, recipients, or customers are thinking? Is there an absence of a stream of data about their perceptions that could powerfully affect your organization's decisions?	____	____	____
4.	Is your organization unaware of precisely what *all* its employees are thinking about the organization? Is there an absence of a stream of data about their perceptions that could powerfully affect your organization's decisions?	____	____	____
5.	Do your various departments, divisions, units lack data that could significantly affect their weekly and monthly performance? Do line employees lack performance data to correct their own errors and to institute self-improvements? Do annual performance data fail to *really* make a difference?	____	____	____

Exhibit 14.1. Checklist to Determine the Best Organizational Assessment Strategy, cont'd.

Assessment #	Questions to Ask	No	Yes	Ranking
6.	Does your organization fail to compare itself to other similar organizations on a regular basis? Do comparisons fail to be rigorous or to create a sense of healthy competition? Does your organization fail to occasionally seek out high-performing organizations to study with site inspection teams and in-depth analysis and comparison?	___	___	___
7.	Is your organization already routinely performing a number of organizational assessments, especially customer and employee assessments? Does your organiza-tion feel that it is ready to undertake the most rigorous level of assessment?	___	___	___

Department Needs Analysis

A second level of surveying is *department needs analysis.* The departments and the organization (especially as represented by the training department) must jointly decide what training needs exist and how to address those needs. The end result of this joint effort varies greatly, depending on the size of the orga-nization or training department and the emphasis given to training. In a small agency, on the one hand, with one employee responsible for training part-time, the training menu may be informal and limited to a few orientation programs, with all other training being either on the job or the responsibility of the em-ployees to obtain outside the organization. A large organization, on the other hand, may have a large catalogue of classes, a bulletin listing specific course dates and special offerings, and a sophisticated tracking system. Given the wide range of organizational capabilities and the wide range of department needs, the approaches to department needs analysis vary greatly. Only two are outlined here, as sample perspectives from a range of possibilities. (See Exhibit 14.2 for examples using the two alternate approaches.)

Performance Gap Approach. The simpler of the two strategies is called the *per-formance gap approach.* It focuses immediately on the perceived problem and

Exhibit 14.2. Examples of Two Approaches to Management Training Programs:
Performance Gap and Comprehensive.

Performance Gap Approach

A large city in Arizona realized that it had reached a size at which it needed to consciously inculcate similar values across departments and reinforce basic supervisory and management skills. Many supervisory skills had been taught on an ad hoc basis, but the city trainers, city manager, and the department heads informally agreed that it was time to formalize a management training program. A training advisory committee was informally constituted to determine what course of action would best suit the organization (perceived problem).

The training advisory committee entered a period of discussion and informal analysis. What departments were most interested in the program, what were some of the perceived management deficiencies, and finally, what program parameters might be suitable, given the moderate amount of resources available the first year (preanalysis)? After roughly sketching a program, the training advisory group sent the tentative plan in a memorandum to all department chairs for suggestions for change and for tentative commitments of program participants (data collection).

The memorandum received mixed responses that needed to be considered and acted upon. Some department heads had many substantial suggestions, and some large departments were unwilling to make any commitment whatsoever. The committee then conducted interviews with department heads to further understand and incorporate their ideas, as well as gather much needed support for the program (analysis). The interviews were successful in gathering the necessary support, and the first phase of the program was planned to begin in six months (results and implementation).

Comprehensive Approach

In 1991, the State of Arizona decided to review the management knowledge, skills, and abilities of its managers to enhance its comprehensive management training program (a part of the Certified Public Manager Consortium). The state used the already constituted statewide training advisory committee, with members from all major state agencies, to act as the oversight body for the study (planning). A subcommittee drafted an inventory of approximately fifty management skills that were thought to typify traditional and newer management characteristics (exploratory).

After this instrument was refined and approved by the committee, it was circulated to 6,500 supervisors, managers, and executives (skill inventory). Each of the questionnaires requested that respondents rate skills by importance and by deficiency in the general management population. The committee reviewed the results and decided what to include in the training and what to deemphasize, given the results (skill analysis).

The existing program was then reviewed against these data. Some new topics were added, some topics were deleted, and some of the material was simply adjusted (program design). Finally, the revised program was piloted and evaluated, with final adjustments based on the feedback of the participants.

works well when the perceived problem is fairly obvious, the training alternatives are relatively easy to identify, and piecemeal (rather than systemic) solutions are appropriate. It has five phases.

The performance gap approach is activated (its first phase) by the recognition of a perceived or potential problem—a gap between the desired performance and the actual performance. For example, the introduction of a new, divisionwide software program would ordinarily be a target for a new training program.

The following preanalysis phase can either be an informal scan of the problem or an extensive exploratory analysis to ensure that the training being designed is the right answer. During this phase a training advisory group can be formed, and exploratory information can be gathered through interviews, surveys, site visits, document examination, making a plan for systematic data gathering, or field testing possible data collection methods or tools. The idea during this phase is not to gather systematic information about the problem but to probe the problem sufficiently to make sure that the data-gathering phase is well focused and uses the most productive techniques.

The data-collection phase can use a variety of different methods to collect data, such as focus groups, structured observations (efficiency analyses), document surveys (including productivity reports, complaints, performance appraisals, grievance files, exit interviews, and policy and procedure manuals), interviews, questionnaires, and surveys with menu listings of options.

The analysis of needs (the fourth phase) looks for performance gaps in essentially two ways: first, by assessing the needs of the job (including the knowledge, skills, and abilities required to do the job) and, second, by assessing the current skills, knowledge, and abilities of the employee. Because performance deficiencies are caused by many things, not just employee inability, it is important to examine employees' strengths in these areas rather than make assumptions. Performance gaps also stem from sloppiness, poor management direction, inadequate equipment, poor job design, excessive job demands, morale problems, program obsolescence, and so on.

Finally, the results of the analysis, both training-related and non-training-related, are implemented (the fifth phase). Generally, a good analysis of needs will reveal some opportunities for job improvement. These should be implemented before or simultaneously with a new or revised training program.

Comprehensive Approach. The *comprehensive approach* to analyzing department needs takes a systems approach to the task of training. It generates a tremendous amount of data to be used in various aspects of the human resources function, of which the training and development aspect is only one. The comprehensive approach requires a systematic survey of the organization before a decision is made that action of any sort—whether changing job descriptions, reorganizing jobs, changing pay scales, or expanding current training—is necessary. (Because this approach relies heavily on job analysis skills, the reader is also referred to Chapter Sixteen of this book.)

The first of six phases in this approach is the planning phase. Because job analysis is time consuming and requires a systematic methodology, careful planning at the beginning is essential to the success of the approach. Establishing the scope, an advisory group, and training outcomes are recommended.

The second phase is the exploratory phase, in which the job analyst investigates the general parameters of the job and gathers information sources about it. The third phase is the task or skill inventory phase. One possibility here is to produce an exhaustive, detailed task inventory in which each of the tasks is broken down into microanalytic elements. This approach works well when the job has many tasks that are relatively straightforward and involve little judgment. A second possibility is to dissect the job into just a few task elements but generate a skills inventory that delineates those elements. This is often the preferred method for jobs requiring a great deal of professional judgment, perhaps dealing with complex human interactions (such as managing) or making complex decisions (such as policy recommendations). Most often organizations use a single approach for consistency, rather than suiting the method to the job.

The task or skill analysis phase goes beyond the description used in the previous phase to the analysis of functions. Analysis of tasks and skills reveals their importance, frequency, level of proficiency required, criticality, and degree of responsibility required. For example, a job inventory may find that a task of the assistant fire chief is to talk to the press, and the analysis finds that this happens somewhat infrequently, that it is very important when it does occur because of the public relations involved, and that it requires a high level of proficiency because this employee's work is responding to emergencies, activities that often elicit an aggressive or hostile press.

The program design phase takes the information gleaned and uses it for training purposes. A strength of the comprehensive approach is that it not only uncovers performance deficiencies but also provides a kind of broad training blueprint for new employee training (both for instruction and self-directed job manuals). Providing a process manual for new and continuing workers leads to greater uniformity, higher quality, and also increases in productivity.

In the last phase the new or revised program is actually implemented. Such a program may install thorough new employee training where none had existed, a narrow-gauged program to address a particular performance deficiency, or simply high-quality self-instructional materials such as job aids (simple one-page checklists and instructions that are easily accessible to the task) or manuals.

One of the important variations for analyzing department needs today uses a modified comprehensive approach for radical process improvement and job change (see Exhibit 14.2).

The strengths and weaknesses of the two approaches are fairly obvious. The performance gap approach is more direct, less expensive, faster, and more incisive. It is also more prone to be applied as a Band-Aid approach, with personal solutions and poor research leading to superficial training. The comprehensive approach is more rigorous and complete, leads to an excellent database, and tends to be less open to the influence of personalities. It is also prone to be substantial and often prohibitively expensive; to take very long lead times, sometimes years; and to produce data overkill. Good judgment must be used in deciding which approach to use or how to blend aspects of approaches to meet particular circumstances.

Individual Needs Analysis

Needs analysis occurs not only at the organizational and department levels but also at the *individual level.* Methods for deciding who needs and receives training vary across public-sector organizations and even within organizations. Some organizations have highly formalized systems, and others have very informal systems. In some organizations, much of the training is mandated by federal or state statutes, and in others, there are no mandated training requirements. In some organizations, training units establish training curricula and eligibility, and in others, operational units make these decisions. Some organizations define training needs narrowly, and others broadly.

Training units and departments are most often the key actors for performance testing and training once organizational standards have been set, for assessment centers for management improvement, and for mandated training inventories leading to specific skill level requirements. Supervisors are generally the key actors for the training stemming from performance appraisals, employee cross-training programs, and individual development plans (generally shared with employees). Employees are themselves the key actors in determining their need for compliance and mandated training in their profession (for example, required continuing education for finance officers), self-improvement, improved credentialing, and individual development plans.

In today's organization it is critical that all three primary players are constantly attuned to needs analysis of individuals because of the increasing obsolescence factor in both knowledge and skills. At the turn of the century, an individual might have had to learn only a single area of knowledge or set of skills and abilities. By 1940, it was more likely to be several areas or sets. Today, most workers must learn many areas and sets during their working career, even when they remain within the same field and subfield, a trait that is becoming less common. Therefore it is critical to have numerous concerned actors involved in assessing the needs of individuals, finding resources to support those needs, and providing the emotional and intellectual support to keep individuals developing and learning rapidly. (See Exhibit 14.3 for a checklist.)

Exhibit 14.3. Checklist of Possible Needs of Individuals.

Training departments	___Performance testing or training for organizational standards
	___Assessment centers
	___Mandated training inventories and suggested training
Supervisors	___Performance appraisals
	___Cross-training programs
	___Individual development plans
Employees	___Individual compliance with mandated training
	___Self-improvement strategies
	___Improving credentials
	___Individual development plans

UNDERSTANDING THE BASICS OF LEARNING THEORY

Although different learning theories emphasize different aspects of learning, they do not fundamentally disagree. For example, *behaviorism* stresses the idea that learning is behavioral change produced by the effect of external stimuli. Therefore learning is most effective when it is systematically arranged to reinforce the desired response. *Social learning* theory stresses the importance of observation and social context. According to this theory, people learn most often from models provided in context and from mimicry. *Cognitive learning* theory emphasizes learner activity in putting together patterns in unique and meaningful ways. It pays special attention to the individual's insight, learning patterns, and integration of meaning into already established cognitive structures, and therefore is particularly powerful at explaining problem solving. Finally, *adult learning* theory reminds educators of the adult learner's active curiosity, motivation for self-improvement, preference for practical (as opposed to academic) problem solving, and capacity for self-imposed learning management. It is possible to extrapolate seven fundamental training principles from these theories:

- Foster participant goal setting
- Increase the similarity of training to the work environment
- Use underlying principles
- Increase the organization of the material
- Actively involve the learner
- Give feedback
- Use a variety of techniques and stimuli

The first training principle is to *foster participant goal setting.* Setting goals at two levels is an important way to focus and enhance motivation. First are the goals that bring the employees into training. Second are the goals employed in the training itself (often called desired learning objectives). Without agreement between employee goals and instructional goals, the learning is likely to be superficial at best. Goal setting can often be substantially enhanced by supervisory attention prior to the training to ensure that the relevance of a particular program is explicit. Goal setting can also be enhanced by instructors who take the time to investigate individual learners' experiences and motivations, and then build some of the learning and assignments around those experiences and particular needs. Learners who are active in their own goal setting inevitably do better in the long run because their goals define an easy self-discipline for personal accomplishment. For example, at the beginning of a computer program training seminar, an instructor might quickly survey the class for the intended uses of the program. She can not only encourage all those goals that are appropriate (one hopes the vast majority) but can guide expectations and meld group goals from individual desires.

One of the oldest principles emphasized in training is to *increase the similarity of training to the work environment.* This similarity has particular relevance when specific tasks, skills, or behavior are being taught, including such relatively simple skills as machine operation, such intermediate skills as the application of procedural discipline, and such complex skills as negotiation. Three (progressive) devices for incorporating this similarity into training are examples, models, and simulation. Examples help students understand select aspects of what is taught and can include everything from visual artifacts to verbal stories. Case studies are another well-known type of example. Using a model is a visual or graphic technique to show the learners the entire process or at least major chunks of it. The modeling may be done on some actual machinery or through a training film, but the learner sees much of the process in context. In simulations, the trainees do more than observe the correct behavior; they themselves perform it. Simulations include role-plays, guided practice, and automated fabrications, such as computer simulations for pilots. Generally these ways of increasing similarity are used in sequence, with examples being first, models being second, and simulations being last.

Using underlying principles is one of the oldest educational principles; it emphasizes the learner's need to understand the broader applicability. Although teaching a specific application for a specific job is immediately useful, it does not equip the learner with the fundamental understanding to cope well with solving problems that arise or to adapt to new, related methodologies in the future. Principle-based learning lasts longer but has less specific utility; technical-based learning is more direct but may not be of much use if the technique changes. Blending some underlying principles with other training principles is the most effective; excessive concentration on underlying principles often leaves learners dazed and learning unanchored. For example, narrowly defined training about a computer program might show an employee how to use a specific protocol in entering data; however, without broader underlying principles about the computer application, the employee will be helpless in the face of any nonroutine occurrence such as a malfunction, a piece of unusual information, or a program change.

Increasing the organization of the material is a simple concept but is not easily translated into instruction. What is apparent to the instructor or writer is rarely as clear to the participant or reader. Because a clear organizational structure enhances not only understanding but recall many times over, it is important to make sure that material is (1) outlined for learners, (2) occasionally referenced during learning, and (3) rehearsed by participants if possible. There are innumerable ways to increase the organization of material being taught. When auxiliary readings are given to learners, questions focusing their reading beforehand are extremely useful. Clear definitions and labels are critical; they should often be listed separately for reinforcement. Figures and graphs can often help learners visualize the conceptual path being taught. Reviewing what has been taught not only clarifies the organization of the material but sets the material in the learner's mind as well. Learners themselves have a responsibility in organizing the material. Their first responsibility is to seek out the instructor's or writer's organization and try to understand it as fully as possible. Yet for deep learning to occur, each learner must modify the structure for his or her own usage, language, and experience. Learners who take the time and have the discipline to do this remember and use far more than those who do not. Some examples of organizing the material, then, include instructors' previews and reviews, participants' recapitulations and written summaries, and clear outlines and visual materials that condense the overall ideas.

Actively involving the learner is a principle critical to most quality learning. Learning either must be anchored to old experiences or must create new experiences to which it can be anchored. Actively involving the learner creates these rich experiences and avoids the shallower learning that occurs in more passive learning situations. Active learning can occur many ways. Asking questions, doing in-training practice, and doing nontraining practice are three common means. The ancient Socratic method of constantly asking questions is powerful because it requires the learner to stay engaged and to relate the topic to his or her own experience. Ultimately all discussion methodologies, such as small groups, debates, case studies, and individual conferences, enhance this mode of learning. Creating opportunities for practice during training, so that participants can be supervised and receive immediate assistance, is another powerful tool for active involvement. Such practice can range from simple note taking to full-scale simulations. Not all practice can be conducted during the training session itself so creating opportunities for outside practice is often necessary when high mastery levels are desired. Such opportunities may be as simple as homework or complex as apprenticeships in which the learner constantly reports back to a master instructor as tasks are completed. Ideally, process practice occurs first, in which the learner conceptualizes the learning. Guided practice occurs next under the instructor's watchful eye. Finally, outside exercises occur when the instructor is not present but can later monitor the outcomes.

Giving feedback is a principle that describes supplying learners with knowledge about the results of practice. Practice in this case includes exercises, tests, discussions, papers, simulations, and apprenticeships. The feedback on the practice can take many forms. It can be verbal praise or suggestions for improvement. It can be test scores, productivity reports, or performance measurements. It can be a subtle physical behavior by the instructor: a nod or shake of the head, a smile or frown, or a pat on the back. Good trainers tend to look for ways to increase the amount and immediacy of feedback. Although performance of tasks has an implicit feedback function, apart from the instructor, the trainee who receives instructor feedback is likely to outstrip those who do not. For example, mentoring is a particularly powerful technique because of the customized feedback on performance that participants constantly receive. Feedback allows for rapid extinction of errors, increases motivation and interest, and should lead to high standards and goal setting.

Using a variety of techniques and stimuli engages more fully a wide range of the participant's senses. This principle recognizes that when different sensory and cognitive channels are used in the learning process, learners have a greater opportunity to encode knowledge. Because everyone has a slightly different learning style in terms of favoring aural, visual, or tactile inputs, using different sensory channels ensures that all learning styles are being covered. It also seems to increase both interest and motivation; variety reduces boredom. It enhances motivation by providing a challenge to integrate the differently displayed materials. Thus, rather than hear a single long lecture, in the same amount of class time learners may be asked to do a preliminary reading, then asked a few preliminary questions about the reading, then listen to a short lecture enhanced by visual overheads and a brief demonstration, and then engage in a discussion integrating the lecture and the readings.

Although a very short training session might employ only a few basic training principles, longer programs should consciously try to use as many of the principles as possible. Few training programs suffer from employing too many principles; many programs suffer from overrelying on one or only a few principles.

Training principles are operationalized by instructional methods, the topic to which we now turn.

UNDERSTANDING THE SIX DIFFERENT FAMILIES OF INSTRUCTIONAL METHODS

Not only can instructional methods be grouped into families but also each of those families tends to emphasize just a few training principles. Therefore it is useful to mix families when trying to design a program with greater effect. Six families of methods are briefly examined in this section. (See Exhibit 14.4 for a complete checklist of the six families and the methods within each.)

Lecture methods are an excellent choice for presenting a great deal of information efficiently, stressing underlying principles, and highlighting the internal organization of the material presented. However, unalloyed, they tend to lack participant involvement, feedback, and direct connection to the work environment. All lecture methods shown in the checklist can be leavened by the use of examples, humor, quotations, statistics, comparisons, and personalizing touches.

Discussion methods, particularly case studies, occasionally are used as the dominant training method, but more often they are auxiliary to lecture and other methods. Most training programs, especially those that depend primarily on lectures, use some form of discussion method. Discussion enhances the participants' active role in the learning process, either voluntarily or structurally. Although often inefficient in terms of time consumed, discussion methods more than make up for this weakness in terms of increasing dynamic human interaction.

The importance of *printed materials* in training varies tremendously. Some programs do not use printed materials at all, most use them as an auxiliary source, and some rely on them as the primary mode of instruction. Printed materials have strengths similar to lecture methods' advantages; they are good at teaching underlying principles and providing clear organizational techniques. However, reading materials do not provide the same level of variety when combined with lecture methods that other instructional families do. Other than the types of printed materials that are used as supplementary tools in class (handouts, written exercises, overheads, and so forth), there are three main types of printed materials in training. The auxiliary reading materials are those not specially designed for the class and are used either before or after the training session. The training manuals are those materials specially designed for a job or an instructional class. Finally, a system of printed materials is a type of programmed instruction when it is used primarily for self-instruction, moving the trainee, step-by-step, in the direction of established goals and objectives and allowing the trainee to monitor his or her own progress through the answers he or she provides to questions.

The training principles most affected in *practice and feedback techniques* are actively involving learners, giving feedback, and providing work similarity. Although the more cognitive techniques, such as standard lectures, are efficient in relaying general principles, there is no certainty that trainees will retain and

Exhibit 14.4. Checklist of Instructional Methods by Instructional Family.

WHICH METHODS MIGHT OR DO YOU USE?

Lecture methods
___Standard lectures
___Team teaching
___Guest speakers
___Panels
___Student presentations

Discussion methods
___Question-and-answer techniques
___Large-group session
___Small-group session
___Case studies
___Debates
___Individual conferences

Printed materials
___Auxiliary reading materials
___Training manuals
___Programmed instruction

Practice and feedback techniques
___Note taking
___Adjunct questions
___Individual exercises
___Demonstrations
___Role-plays
___Simulations
___Survey and self-assessment techniques
___Tests
___Site visits

Behavior-shaping methods
___Coaching
___Apprenticeships
___Job rotation
___Self-training and embedded training
___Counseling

Technology-based techniques
___Audiotapes
___Slides
___Videotapes and films
___Computer-based training
___Teleconferencing
___Optical disk technology

store the information accurately and lastingly. It is rare for practice and feed-back techniques to be used alone, but they are extremely effective with other methods. Nine techniques have been placed in this category, although others mentioned elsewhere (such as discussion methods) have practice and feedback characteristics.

Behavior-shaping methods feature learning by doing. Effectively used, behavior-shaping methods are among the most powerful because they tend to emphasize participant goal setting, ideal similarity to the work environment, full learner involvement, and extensive feedback. Poorly used, behavior-shaping methods are little more than undirected learning situations, in which the process is haphazard and the learning outcomes uncertain. Behavior-shaping methods can largely be thought of as on-the-job training.

Technology-based techniques can either support other methods or be the pri-mary delivery method. Typically, they are good at teaching underlying princi-ples, increasing the organization of the material, and increasing the similarity to the work environment. The sophisticated technology-based methods, such as computer-based training (including the new Internet technologies), two-way videoconferencing (and fiber optic systems), and optical disk training, can also be good at involving learners and giving feedback.

MOVING INTO ADVANCED FORMS OF LEARNING

Most of the discussion so far has implicitly concentrated on learning for basic and intermediate knowledge, skills, and abilities. This type of learning has always been important and will become even more important as the pace of change re-quires ever more frequent replacement of knowledge and skill sets. However, or-ganizations increasingly must foster advanced forms of learning, those using more sophisticated methods of transmitting, expanding, and creating knowledge (Carnevale, Gainer, and Meltzer, 1990). Advanced forms of learning are espe-cially useful for solving totally new or complex problems, restructuring whole processes or systems, reanalyzing a job from a completely new perspective, or reengineering an organization to adapt to major environmental changes (see the pioneering work of Argyris, 1985, and Argyris and Schön, 1974, 1978; or the more recent work of Senge, 1990). Advanced forms of learning include

- Learning by sharing
- Learning by comparing
- Learning by systems thinking
- Learning by competing
- Learning by suspending disbelief

Learning by sharing is particularly powerful in the affective, or emotional, domain, which is often the gateway to the other domains of learning (the cognitive and the psychomotor). One form of learning by sharing is learning by teaching (seemingly contradictory to what we normally assume, which is that we learn by being taught). Teaching forces us into advanced modes of learning because it requires us to be clear, logical, and organized; to practice and manipulate the information; and to receive feedback about how well the information is being understood. Learning by discussing, another form of learning by sharing, although a frequent mainstay of basic learning, is important for advanced learning as well because it encourages inquiry and collaboration. Discussion leads to the discovery of nonroutine problems, anomalies, contradictory perspectives, hidden assumptions, and complementary ideas. In genuine discussion we abandon our advocacy roles and work on collaborative learning (Senge, 1990). And yet another kind of learning by sharing, learning by teaming, "may represent a whole new management paradigm" (Manz and Sims, 1993, p. 14). High-performing teams develop high levels of trust, establish a shared sense of purpose, have a belief in mutual learning and teaching, and group-enforce self-discipline (Katzenbach and Smith, 1993).

Given that the scientific method is based on *learning by comparing* and on the tremendous success of the scientific method in modern world history, there can be little doubt of its power. One form of learning by comparing is learning from systematic examination of past experience. People who take time to reflect and compare events in their lives, with the discipline to act on what they discover, generally accomplish more. Groups that systematically observe their past performance note high and low points, discover why these fluctuations occur, and increase performance. Even organizations that rigorously survey past experiences tend to encourage good practices and discourage poor practices. A second form is learning by systematic observation of others' experience, now commonly called benchmarking (Keehley, Medlin, MacBride, and Longmire, 1997). Although benchmarking can have a number of meanings, it most commonly refers to comparison with industry leaders whose performance is among the best. A third form is learning by experimenting, a robust form of comparison and the preferred method of the scientific method. Sophisticated experimental designs may not be possible in the practical world of organizational learning, but modified experimental models such as pilot studies, and substitution or observation strategies are and should be commonly practiced.

Learning by systems thinking is Peter Senge's "fifth discipline," so called because it is pivotal to advanced learning and to forming "a coherent body of theory and practice" (1990, p. 12). Systems thinking is an antidote to tunnel vision, turfism, stovepiping, and other bureaupathologies that accrue from overspecialization of function and responsibility. Ultimately, learning by systems thinking is at the base of most contemporary management initiatives. TQM, for example, involves learning by making continuous improvements in the system, and reengineering involves learning by making radical improvements. Ironically, frontline workers and middle managers were encouraged, until recently, not to take the systems approach, which was reserved for executives and master planners. However, as classical bureaucracies' need for slow, centralized, controlled change (a virtue in a slower moving world) has become increasingly dysfunctional for contemporary needs, the need to infuse a sense of systems thinking throughout the organization has become more critical. A common example of advanced learning today is the use of cross-functional teams to bring together individuals from many departments who can arrive at new solutions that benefit all departments. This replaces the method of expecting each department to find unilateral solutions, often at other departments' expense.

Learning by competing is captured in the expression "necessity is the mother of invention" and in the underlying capitalistic belief that competition causes innovation and creativity to flourish in the long run. Competition can lead individuals to learn by requiring them to determine what they want to achieve, by driving them toward that achievement or level of excellence, and by creating both incentives for succeeding and disincentives for floundering. Goal setting can be a type of competition with oneself if the goals are beyond current levels of performance or push one to new levels of achievement. Learning by risk taking, a form of learning by competing, is a newly rediscovered quality in the public sector. Risk taking in the public sector has been considered inappropriate in the past. However, given the wide-scale policy and management reforms being promoted, modest risk taking is considered a normal part of the learning and adapting process today (Levin and Sanger, 1994). Risk taking is often associated with demonstration and pilot projects, but it can also involve new management practices or philosophical shifts that are significant departures from the past. Finally, competition generally means that not everybody is ranked first and risk taking means that not all ventures will succeed. Yet, as the quip goes, the only person who never fails or makes mistakes is the person who never does anything. So learning must allow failures; the trick is to keep failures small and successes large. Advanced forms of learning do not forestall failure, but they do work hard at understanding it through sharing, comparing, and systems thinking and going beyond failure through competition. Although the chance of failure is real in competitive environments, in most organizations there can be many winners who experience the exhilaration of learning through success.

Of all the types of advanced learning, none is more commonly discussed than *learning by suspending disbelief.* This mode of learning requires the ability to suspend our disbelief that things new to us can work—or to put it the other way around, to suspend our current beliefs about the proper way to do something, the proper way to value, or the nature of truth. We unquestioningly use our existing habits, routines, and belief systems most of the time because we have neither the time nor energy to start at the beginning or go back to first principles in everything we do. Yet some of the greatest learning comes from seeing the world afresh, discarding (at least temporarily) our mental models, and trying on new ideas, perceptions, and beliefs for size. Most great scientists and inventors are masters at this type of learning. It leads to changes in old dysfunctional routines and discovery of new patterns for doing things. Learning by suspending disbelief is undergoing a renaissance in the public sector. Quality management has many principles that encourage challenging existing mental models and playing with ideas. For example, the new emphasis on team learning requires broad-based solutions that go beyond accepted mental models. As another example, reengineering, with its emphasis on radical solutions, requires a strong discipline of challenging contemporary practices and implementing fundamentally different approaches.

CONCLUSION

An increasingly fast-changing world has vastly swelled the value of learning. People need to learn more, faster, and with heightened creativity. Because organizations are themselves changing more quickly, basic training functions must now routinely include the retraining of personnel, the refocusing of personnel, and the changing of management styles and systems. Further, those in charge of training must be ready to provide organizational assessments, in addition to the more traditional individual and department learning needs analyses. The need for such extensive learning means that training principles are only that much more important to know and master: foster participant goal setting, increase the similarity of the training to the work environment, use underlying principles, increase the organization of the material, actively involve the learner, give feedback, and use a variety of techniques and stimuli. In turn, those offering the training, whether full-time trainers or operational supervisors, must master more methods to make best use of the different training principles. Six families of methods were surveyed: lecture, discussion, print, practice and feedback, behavior shaping, and technology based. Finally, organizations need to be able to learn things better in informal settings, through helping people learn from their work experience and through prodding people to be constantly improving and, more often than ever, to learn about what is not currently known. Five types of advanced learning were discussed that all emphasize going beyond simply acquiring basic knowledge—important to contemporary organizations but no longer sufficient for the best—to transmitting, testing, expanding, and even creating knowledge.

References

Argyris, C. *Strategy, Change, and Defensive Routines.* New York: HarperBusiness, 1985.

Argyris, C., and Schön, D. A. *Theory in Practice: Increasing Professional Effectiveness.* San Francisco: Jossey-Bass, 1974.

Argyris, C., and Schön, D. A. *Organizational Learning.* Reading, Mass.: Addison Wesley Longman, 1978.

Bennis, W., and Nanus, B. *Leaders: The Strategies for Taking Charge.* New York: HarperCollins, 1985.

Benveniste, G. *The Twenty-First Century Organization: Analyzing Current Trends— Imagining the Future.* San Francisco: Jossey-Bass, 1994.

Bogan, C. E., and English, M. J. *Benchmarking for Best Practices.* New York: McGraw-Hill, 1994.

Carnevale, A. P., Gainer, L. J., and Meltzer, A. S. *Workplace Basics: The Essential Skills Employers Want.* San Francisco: Jossey-Bass, 1990.

Champy, J. *Reengineering Management.* New York: HarperCollins, 1995.

Deming, W. E. *Out of the Crisis.* Cambridge, Mass.: MIT Center for Advanced Engineering Study, 1986.

Drucker, P. F. *Innovation and Entrepreneurship.* New York: HarperCollins, 1985.

Drucker, P. F. *Managing for the Future.* New York: Penguin, 1992.

Garvin, D. A. "Building a Learning Organization." *Harvard Business Review,* July–Aug. 1993, pp. 78–91.

Hammer, M. *The Reengineering Revolution: A Handbook.* New York: HarperBusiness, 1995.

Hammer, M., and Champy, J. *Reengineering the Corporation.* New York: HarperBusiness, 1993.

Howard, A. (ed.). *The Changing Nature of Work.* San Francisco: Jossey-Bass, 1995.

Kanter, R. M. *The Change Masters.* New York: Simon & Schuster, 1983.

Kanter, R. M. *When Giants Learn to Dance.* New York: Simon & Schuster, 1989.

Kanter, R. M., Stein, B. A., and Jick, T. D. *The Challenge of Organizational Change.* New York: Free Press, 1992.

Katzenbach, J. R., and Smith, D. K. *The Wisdom of Teams.* Boston: Harvard Business School Press, 1993.

Keehley, P., Medlin, S., MacBride, S., and Longmire, L. *Benchmarking for Best Practices in the Public Sector: Achieving Performance Breakthroughs in Federal, State, and Local Agencies.* San Francisco: Jossey-Bass, 1997.

Kettl, D. F. "Managing on the Frontiers of Knowledge: The Learning Organization." In P. W. Ingraham and B. S. Romzek (eds.), *New Paradigms for Government: Issues for the Changing Public Service.* San Francisco: Jossey-Bass, 1994.

Levin, M. A., and Sanger, M. B. *Making Government Work: Issues for the Changing Public Service.* San Francisco: Jossey-Bass, 1994.

Manz, C., and Sims, H. P., Jr. *Business Without Bosses: How Self-Managing Teams Are Building High-Performing Companies.* New York: Wiley, 1993.

National Commission on the State and Local Public Service (Winter Commission). *Hard Truths/Tough Choices: An Agenda for State and Local Reform.* Albany, N.Y.: Rockefeller Institute of Government, 1993.

National Performance Review. *From Red Tape to Results: Creating a Government That Works Better and Costs Less.* Washington, D.C.: U.S. Government Printing Office, 1993.

National Performance Review. *Creating a Government That Works Better and Costs Less: Status Report of the National Performance Review.* Washington, D.C.: U.S. Government Printing Office, 1994.

Peters, B. G. "New Visions of Government and the Public Service." In P. W. Ingraham and B. S. Romzek (eds.), *New Paradigms for Government: Issues for the Changing Public Service.* San Francisco: Jossey-Bass, 1994.

Peters, T. J. *Thriving on Chaos.* New York: Knopf, 1987.

Peters, T. J. *Liberation Management.* New York: Fawcett/Columbine, 1992.

Peters, T. J., and Waterman, R. H., Jr. *In Search of Excellence.* New York: Harper-Collins, 1982.

Schein, E. H. *Organizational Culture and Leadership.* San Francisco: Jossey-Bass, 1985.

Senge, P. *The Fifth Discipline.* New York: Doubleday, 1990.

Van Wart, M. "The First Step in the Reinvention Process: Assessment." *Public Administration Review,* 1995, *55,* 429–438.

Van Wart, M., Cayer, N. J., and Cook, S. *Handbook of Training and Development for the Public Sector: A Comprehensive Resource.* San Francisco: Jossey-Bass, 1993.

Wildavsky, A. *The Politics of the Budgetary Process.* (2nd ed.) New York: Little, Brown, 1974.

CHAPTER FIFTEEN

Staffing the Bureaucracy

Employee Recruitment and Selection

Steven W. Hays

The processes by which suitable candidates for jobs are attracted and screened are referred to as *recruitment* and *selection*. Because any organization's performance is largely dependent upon the quality of its workers, those organizations that do an effective job of managing these *entry* functions are clearly the better for it. Although training and intensive supervision can transform some undesirable employees, hiring individuals who are already capable and enthusiastic is clearly preferable. Managers can save large amounts of time and aggravation by placing the right person in the right position. Among the probable benefits of a proper match of employee abilities to particular work requirements are enhanced job satisfaction, greater productivity, lower turnover, and a smaller number of "problem employees" (Vroom, 1964).

Successful recruitment and selection depend upon an adequate supply of competent or educable workers, an effective information network that reaches the appropriate population of prospective employees, an organizational environment sufficiently attractive to entice the desired job candidates, a clear sense of organizational priorities, and a reliable means of choosing the applicants who are most highly qualified. These are daunting challenges even under the best of circumstances, but they are especially problematic within the contemporary public setting.

Since the mid-1980s, a succession of reform groups, study commissions, and researchers has warned that government is losing its ability to attract and retain talented young workers. Part of the problem can be traced to the changing

298

composition of the labor pool. *Workforce 2000* (Johnston and Packer, 1987), *Civil Service 2000* (Johnston, 1988), and related studies (U.S. General Accounting Office, 1994, p. 3) predict that government confronts a "slowly emerging crisis of competence" due to a predicted decline in the quality of new hires. The public sector's need for highly skilled workers will continually increase, just as the supply of such workers is expected to diminish. Other commentators meanwhile argue that the declining pay and prestige of public employment are to blame for government's recruitment "crisis" (Rosen, 1986; National Commission on the Public Service, 1989; Thompson, 1993). Years of bashing the bureaucrats and of stingy legislatures and employee cutbacks have resulted in an inhospitable work environment that discourages job applicants. Survey results generally confirm these fears, as evidenced by reports that "government is not perceived as an 'employer of choice' among college graduates" (U.S. Merit Systems Protection Board, 1988, p. 2).

Although dire predictions about the impending doom of the public service are by no means universal (Lewis, 1991; Mishel and Teixeira, 1991), considerable quantities of empirical and anecdotal evidence support the notion that government is an ineffective recruiter and judge of talent. For this reason, public agency intake functions have recently become prime targets for reform. Many of the suggestions included in the reinventing government literature, for instance, are aimed squarely at public personnel systems generally and recruitment and selection activities specifically (National Commission on the State and Local Public Service, 1993). The application of user-friendly staffing practices is seen as a quick and efficient means of improving government performance. For this reason, public jurisdictions throughout the nation are sponsoring a revolution in the ways that their civil service systems attract, test, interview, and select public managers.

The primary purpose of this chapter is to describe the specific techniques and procedures used to staff public agencies. A significant portion of the discussion focuses on the changes now taking place in response to the crisis just described. Before commencing with the review of staffing innovations, however, I briefly summarize conditions that prevailed for much of the past century, to place the current reforms in a more understandable context.

THE MERITLESS SYSTEM: PAST AS PROLOGUE

Perhaps the most famous observation ever uttered about public personnel management and merit systems is Wallace Sayre's characterization (1948) of them as "the triumph of technique over purpose." The central point of Sayre's remark was that personnel managers were so preoccupied with applying volumes of picky rules and regulations that they neglected (or even impeded) important organizational objectives. Specific insights into this problem were provided in Savas and Ginsburg's celebrated characterization (1973) of the civil service as "the meritless system." Their description of New York City's personnel system revealed large numbers of arbitrary screening procedures. Applicants, for example, would not be considered for any agency unless they identified the exact position for which they were applying. Moreover, if a given number of applications was not received for an advertised opening, by law the job had to be readvertised, and the individuals who had responded to the first announcement were compelled to reapply. Similar conditions prevailed in most jurisdictions, leading one study commission to conclude that the "slow, unimaginative, and unaggressive" entry practices of merit systems ought to be scrapped altogether (Committee on Economic Development, 1978, p. 45).

Although these strident criticisms of public personnel systems are (we may hope) somewhat anachronistic, they still contain a grain of truth. In contrast to the private employment sector, where the hiring process is relatively invisible and unencumbered, government recruitment and selection activities are often carried out in a complex web of procedural requirements and in a fishbowl of public scrutiny. This situation reflects the undeniable fact that the means by which citizens acquire government jobs are of considerable concern in the broader community. Public jobs are public resources, to which everyone has a potential claim. Government's staffing function therefore must be performed in a manner acceptable to the community. In most public jurisdictions this typically means that intake functions are more formal and tightly regulated (at least in theory) than would be acceptable in any corporate setting.

Historical Antecedents

Much of the formalism that envelops government staffing practices has roots in public personnel administration's early history. The events leading up to the passage of the Pendleton Act of 1883, which created the nation's initial merit system, are widely known. For the first few decades after this nation's founding, the halls of bureaucracy (such as it was) were staffed by individuals selected on the basis of "fitness of character." As a byproduct of our nation's British heritage, the essential selection criteria consisted of family background, educational attainment, and reputation in the community. In effect this meant that most civil servants were from society's upper crust.

By the 1830s, the decidedly blue blood of government workers had become an irritant to the growing legions of farmers, small merchants, and laborers. Andrew Jackson gave voice to the "common man's" frustration and successfully campaigned against the elitist bureaucracy. By introducing the *spoils system,* he engineered a peaceful revolution that broadened government's base of support among the populace and, in a sense, restored democracy's balance. By parceling government jobs out to political supporters and by introducing the custom of *rotation in office* (with each election, a new crop of civil servants would be employed), the spoils system fostered the growth of political parties and exposed large percentages of the citizenry to public service.

Between the 1840s and 1880s, however, the more infamous traits of the spoils system gradually emerged. With almost no means of regulating or monitoring the qualifications of the public workforce, governments at all levels increasingly fell victim to pervasive incompetence and corruption. Large numbers of clerical workers could neither read nor write, and many employees never even showed up at their places of employment because their paychecks were simply forwarded to their homes. Meanwhile, bribery, kickbacks to contractors, and the buying and selling of public positions were commonplace. Within this milieu the public began to "associate public administration with politics and incompetence" (Mosher, 1968, p. 63).

This negative perception of the civil service received a huge boost in 1881 when President Garfield was assassinated by a disappointed office seeker. Because the assassin's imputed motive was to catapult Vice President Chester Arthur, a noted supporter of spoils politics, into the presidency, spoils became "equated with murder" (Shafritz, 1975, p. 22). Thereafter, the civil service reform movement assumed the mantle of a moral crusade.

The most enduring legacy of this chapter in U.S. history was a centurylong effort to *insulate* and *neutralize* the civil service from political influences. Politics and public administration were viewed as evil, so the shortest path to reform was to eliminate the politicians' role in public appointments.

To accomplish this feat, the reformers crafted personnel systems that had two defining features. First, in order to "lock the front door" (that is, to prevent politicians from dictating who would receive government jobs), *competitive examinations* became the norm (Van Riper, 1958, p. 101). From the start these exams tested practical (job-related) knowledge rather than the ability to produce scholarly or theoretical essays linked to academic achievement. Through this selection strategy the system designers intended to maintain a civil service that is open to all Americans, not just those privileged enough to receive university educations (as was the practice in England). And although test scores were the primary consideration in appointment, the reformers also honored some selection traditions. Preferential treatment for war veterans, for instance, had been accepted practice since George Washington's era. Also borrowed from earlier times was the norm of using public jobs as a form of welfare (Presidents Washington and Jefferson handed jobs out to the old and infirm) and the allocation of positions on a geographic basis (to ensure that no region of the country was cheated). Thus, although selection decisions were grounded in merit considerations, as reflected in the applicants' test scores, certain concessions to the still acceptable older practices were evident from the very beginning. One additional concession that also dates back to the pre–Pendleton Act era is the *rule of three*, which stipulates that candidates for positions be selected from a list of the top three scorers on the civil service exam. The intent is to give the appointing official a slight degree of discretion in hiring, rather than to compel the employment of whomever scores highest on the entry examination.

The second feature, the *civil service commission*, was initially created to ensure a fair and impartial administration of the testing program. Composed of bipartisan appointees, these commissions quickly sprung up in every state and in most large cities. Although their duties varied, they typically were responsible for all policymaking activities, and many assumed functional control over the day-to-day operations of their personnel systems.

As the science of personnel administration progressed, additional ornaments were hung on the civil service system's family tree. Technical developments during the Scientific Management era led to job classification, job analysis, much more detailed examination protocols, and quantitative forms of performance evaluation. With each innovation the civil service commissions further expanded their supervisory and monitoring roles over public personnel management. Serving in effect as civil service system police officers, the commissions took particular interest in promoting the goal of political neutrality. By propagating large numbers of procedures and safeguards aimed at insulating the civil service from corrupting influences and by adjudicating grievances lodged by civil servants against their bosses (thereby closing the so-called back door), the commissions built personnel systems that tried to resist political influence but were also unwieldy, rule-bound, and unresponsive to organizational requirements (Van Riper, 1958).

Contemporary Reforms

Given the well-deserved reputation of public-sector staffing practices for rigidity and inefficiency, it is not surprising that efforts to reform them commenced as early as 1905. In that year the Keep Committee issued the first systematic recommendations for making government recruitment and selection efforts more positive. Recognizing the flaws in a staffing system that was obsessed with the negative (that is, keeping political influences out of the civil service), the committee lobbied for a more proactive posture. The recommendations suggested that government engage in aggressive outreach programs designed to entice talented applicants into the bureaucracy. No less than ten national reform commissions, and untold numbers of state and local study groups, have echoed this sentiment during the intervening years.

By the 1990s, important facets of the public-sector staffing environment had been transformed. Civil service commissions were for the most part distant memories. Except for a few state and local examples the commissions had been abolished and replaced with *executive personnel systems,* under which the jurisdictions' chief executives control the personnel function through a direct chain of command. No longer did public managers have the intrusive commissions looking over their shoulders and second-guessing their personnel decisions. Another critical change occurred during the 1960s, when *social equity* became an important public value. The advent of equal employment opportunity (EEO) and affirmative action eventually forced the personnel profession to reevaluate its cherished techniques. Recruitment and selection practices, in particular, suffered from the scrutiny and thereby required major changes. Today the validation of civil service entry requirements and examinations, coupled with concerted efforts to open the personnel system to the chronically underrepresented, highlights the changes that have been ongoing for more than three decades.

Despite making considerable progress over the years, many merit systems continue to exhibit the negative traits that have been attracting criticism for nearly one hundred years. Civil service commissions may have disappeared, but their defensive approach to the staffing function has infected their successors, centralized personnel offices. Unable to overcome the legacy of insulation and strict neutrality, personnel departments frequently acquire a reputation for inflexibility and insensitivity to the needs of line managers (Cawsey, 1980). Instead of being encouraged by user-friendly application procedures, prospective employees are required to jump through a succession of procedural hoops that deters all but the most determined or desperate. Moreover, civil service systems are notoriously difficult to access; applicants often experience difficulties in figuring out what jobs are available and how to apply when they are lucky enough to identify a vacancy (Ingraham, 1990).

With the meteoric rise of the reinventing government phenomenon, the traditional ways of conducting the public staffing function are no longer acceptable. Pressures for reform are so intense and the chorus of reform voices so loud that fundamental changes in civil service recruitment and selection strategies are becoming almost routine. In general the reforms share three common elements. First, there is a strong drive to decentralize staffing activities. To the extent feasible, line managers are being provided with greater influence over recruitment and selection efforts. Second, government appears to be making a sincere effort to *simplify* and *invigorate* intake functions. More energy is being spent on selling public agencies to prospective workers and on easing their passage into the workforce. Finally, personnel offices are beginning to demonstrate an unaccustomed willingness to *experiment* with new staffing strategies. For these reasons the study of government recruitment and selection practices has seldom been more interesting or exciting.

THE STAFFING PROCESS: A PRIMER

Before turning to the specific techniques used to recruit and select civil servants, a short overview of the merit system *realpolitik* will help qualify and crystallize later material. The first truism that any student of public personnel administration

(PPA) must appreciate is that enormous diversity prevails in the types of staffing systems in differing jurisdictions. As a general rule, the larger the jurisdiction or agency, the more formal and sophisticated the personnel system will be. And because a large percentage of the eighty thousand plus public jurisdictions in the United States are quite small, much PPA is conducted very informally. A widely used rule of thumb is that an organization needs to have at least two hundred employees to warrant the hiring of a single full-time personnel manager. Therefore, much personnel management in small towns and rural counties is performed part-time by a city clerk, assistant city manager, or other official. Often these individuals lack any task-specific training in PPA. As a result the staffing function sometimes consists of little more than a few personnel files in someone's desk drawer. In this type of setting, recruitment and selection activities are probably ad hoc. Candidates may be identified largely through referrals from incumbent employees (a practice that, ironically, is highly regarded in the private sector); if tests are administered for selection purposes, they are likely to have been imported from other jurisdictions or purchased from examination-writing companies. In-house programs to validate tests or to engage in a well-articulated recruitment campaign will generally be quite rare in such settings.

On the opposite end of the continuum are the full-blown merit systems that function in most state and large city governments. Personnel practices vary tremendously in these systems as well, but the one likely constant is a much higher level of formality in entry procedures. Specific rules govern such topics as the method and duration of job postings, the entry qualifications for different classes of positions, and the selection protocol (for example, what tests will be required of applicants, how many must be interviewed for each position, and what level of preference will be given to candidates from within the organization?).

Another phenomenon tending to recur in formal merit systems is that different hiring strategies are available, depending upon the type of worker being sought. For positions that exist systemwide, such as clerks or secretaries, *centralized certification* may be the favored strategy. This usually means that candidates are screened through a central point of entry. A city's personnel office, for instance, will recruit and test applicants; those who are deemed to be qualified are thus referred to as *eligibles* or those who are *certified*. Their names are entered on a central roster that is termed the *job register* or the *eligibility list*. Upon hearing from an agency that a vacancy exists, the central office will then refer a given number of eligibles. Whereas the rule of three once governed this referral process, selection pools in most locations have been expanded through the adoption of a rule of ten or even a rule of twenty. Next the referred individuals are interviewed by the agency managers who will make the final hiring decision.

For positions that predominantly exist in one agency, such as police officers or air traffic controllers, *delegated examining* is often used. Here the central personnel office delegates authority to the agency to recruit and screen applicants, subject to certain guidelines. Under an even more decentralized strategy, the agency or department is given authority to receive applications directly, to examine qualifications, and to make selections. This *direct hire* format is most often used when agencies require difficult-to-find personnel, such as nurses and engineers. In recent years, however, direct hiring has become much more common in the recruitment of *all* types of employees because of its perceived speed and efficiency (U.S. General Accounting Office, 1990).

Whether they are simple or sophisticated, public personnel systems also differ in two other critical ways. The extent to which they are *centralized* or *decentralized* exerts a major influence on how they function internally. Under the most centralized format the role of line managers in recruitment and selection is highly restricted. Except for making the final determination after the interview phase, the central personnel office handles all or most of the technical aspects of the process (position definition, advertising, preliminary screening, testing). Within a decentralized framework, in contrast, line managers are responsible for writing the position description, specifying qualifications (subject to certain guidelines), and perhaps even determining how the opening will be advertised. The personnel office role under this arrangement is simply to provide technical assistance (for example, to design newspaper announcements) and to ensure that the hiring process is conducted in conformity with legal requirements.

The final operational difference among public personnel systems is the extent to which they try to adhere to the merit principle. The motto of the merit system, "the best shall serve," does not always apply. Despite all the effort that has been expended to eradicate political and personal factors from public staffing practices, many civil servants continue to enter and progress on the basis of "it's not *what* you know, but *who* you know!" Crass political motives, however, are not the primary issue. Thanks to U.S. Supreme Court decisions, politically motivated appointments are illegal in most circumstances (see, especially, *Elrod* v. *Burns,* 427 U.S. 347 [1976]; *Rutan* v. *Republican Party of Illinois,* 455 U.S. 507 [1980]). Although these appointments no doubt still occur, the far more common scenario is for public managers to circumvent merit system procedures in the pursuit of other objectives.

Where tedious requirements inhibit staffing flexibility, managers have a strong (and many believe *justifiable*) incentive to expedite matters by ignoring merit system rules. Rigid job-posting guidelines or certification standards can simply be ignored, provided that the personnel officials are not too attentive or concerned. Or, when a replacement is needed very quickly, a favored strategy is to hire someone into a *temporary* position because such jobs are almost always exempt from competitive requirements. Meanwhile, civil servants who are intent upon giving friends or acquaintances a needed boost can avail themselves of many time-honored strategies. As Jay Shafritz (1974) explains, some public managers will pressure their personnel offices to "reduce the qualifications for a specific position, or to lower the pass point on an entry exam" (p. 487). Alternatively, the position may be redesigned with the favored applicant in mind. In a process called *creative position description* a list of job requirements is drawn up that effectively excludes other applicants. Or candidates who have already been certified as eligible but who are not included on the interview, or short, list, can attempt to *wait out the register*, waiting patiently until everyone above the preferred candidate has either dropped off the register or been selected for another position, at which time the manager announces the vacancy.

In summary, public personnel systems come in an amazing assortment of shapes, sizes, and operating philosophies. What one reads in the jurisdiction's personnel manual often bears little resemblance to what is actually taking place in the public management trenches. These are useful lessons to keep in mind as the various means of recruitment and selection are described.

THE RECRUITMENT PROCESS

The central task of recruitment is to "generate a sufficient pool of applicants to ensure that there are enough people available with the necessary skills and requirements to fill positions as they arise" (Hamman and Desai, 1995, p. 90). Despite recruitment's obvious importance to the success of any organization, government has a poor track record as an effective recruiter. Agencies often tend to *satisfice* (to take the first available candidate who meets minimum qualifications) or to invest very few resources in the effort. A startling example of this problem is evident in an Office of Personnel Management (OPM) report "that nearly half of the federal agencies have no budget for recruiting" (Ingraham, 1990, p. 13).

In addition to its oftentimes haphazard approach to recruitment, government has found its ability to compete for needed human resources compromised by forces outside the control of individual public managers. Inadequate salaries, the public service's poor public image, and a noncompetitive quality of work-life discourage many applicants. At a time when most corporations offer a large variety of family-friendly niceties (such as free child care and generous cafeteria benefit plans), financial exigencies have forced many public jurisdictions to *reduce* job perquisites. Further compounding these recruitment dilemmas are such potential pitfalls as obsolete job classifications and complicated application procedures.

Obviously, a passive approach to the recruitment challenge will not suffice within this environmental context. To attract talented workers, public agencies need to be thoughtful, aggressive, and innovative.

Preliminary Considerations

Effective managers should not ordinarily be surprised by a vacancy. If they have been attentive and if their human resource planning system is functioning at a reasonable level, most turnover can be anticipated. With adequate warning the recruitment process can begin even before a critical employee vacates her post. Truly forward-thinking managers often maintain a list of talented individuals who might be lured away from their existing jobs if presented with a sufficiently appealing offer.

In addition to gaining budgetary approval to initiate a search for either a new or a replacement position, the next task facing the manager is that of *position definition.* With adequate planning and foresight this decision represents a valuable opportunity to the organization. The departure of an incumbent can prompt a needed reassessment of the vacated position and may lead to a reclassification or other significant redefinition of the job's scope and content. Organizations that have concise strategic plans, for instance, may want to use the vacancy to launch a new program, or they may decide to cannibalize the slot to meet more than one need (for example, they might hire two workers under a *job sharing* arrangement). The critical consideration is that managers need to be cognizant of the *recruitment stereotyping* syndrome. In the absence of a clear sense of purpose or in their haste to hire a replacement, agencies frequently seek someone who is "just like" the original employee. As a result the only noticeable change is a new nameplate on the office door.

Inside or Outside?

Another critical consideration early in any search process is the *inside or outside dilemma.* That is, should the organization give preference to internal candidates, intentionally seek an outsider (a process termed *lateral entry*), or declare an open search in which all candidates will be given an equal chance to compete?

There is no best answer to this question. Most organizations have a strong tendency to favor internal candidates over external ones, regardless of their relative qualifications. This predisposition is easily understandable, given the realities of organizational life. Elevating internal candidates maintains the morale of the other workers by supporting the belief that through dedicated service they too will be rewarded with promotions. And because any promotion will set off a ripple effect in which other workers move up their respective career ladders, a large number of employees can be pleased by filling just one vacancy internally. Other arguments for internal recruitment include the facts that it is cheaper (fewer costs for advertising and travel for applicants), quicker (candidates are handy), and safer (the personal quirks of internal candidates are already well known, so these insiders do not occasion the risk inherent in hiring an outsider).

Although compelling, these reasons are countered by certain important advantages of lateral entry. If an agency has not been performing up to expectations or if major changes are in the offing, the new blood provided by an external hire can be helpful. Organizations that are well managed and have a clear set of priorities are more likely to make a reasoned judgment about the relative merits of internal versus external candidates. If there is no clearly superior internal candidate, lateral entry can sidestep the bruised pride and charges of favoritism that follow upon a decision to promote a particular individual from within.

The internal-external dilemma is tempered somewhat by the requirement in many merit systems that *all* applicants be considered. Recruitment is technically an *open* process that does not exclude anyone. It is widely known, however, that public agencies commonly make no real effort to attract outside applicants. Many selections have been made *before* the job announcements are written or the vacancies advertised. This situation is exceedingly irritating to outside candidates, who, until they realize what is happening, repeatedly apply for positions for which they are never seriously considered.

The difficulties encountered in reconciling the internal-external dilemma can be reduced if an effective human resource planning program is operational and has conducted a staffing inventory before a vacancy occurs. This inventory assesses the skills, abilities, and qualities of the current workforce, compares them to anticipated staffing needs, and decides whether training or other employee development strategies are needed to enhance the promotional potential of particular candidates. A less sophisticated strategy is often employed by executives who are new to an organization but who wish to gain a quick sense of recruitment priorities. They will ask all employees to generate lists of their most significant accomplishments during the past one hundred days; these lists will then be compared to agency mission and objective statements in order to determine whether important tasks are not being fulfilled. Where gaps exist, recruitment priorities result.

Position Announcements

Depending upon how the preliminary issues are addressed (hire from the inside or outside? redefine the position or clone the departee?) the next step is to draw up a position announcement for advertising purposes. Ordinarily, the vacant position's job description is used as the centerpiece. Refinements and amendments are often made at this stage in order to accommodate changing organizational needs. The importance of consulting the individuals who will be working with the new hire is just being recognized (Ito, 1994). Because coworkers often have the best insights into task assignments and unmet needs, they represent a valuable yet underused source of recruitment information.

Position announcements typically include a description of major duties and responsibilities, a list of the requirements that candidates are expected to meet (*job specifications* or *job qualifications*), and other relevant information, such as a brief description of the agency or the employment locale. As is implicit in the earlier discussion, the design of the position announcement offers a propitious opportunity to downgrade a position that has become overclassified or to upgrade a job that has acquired additional responsibilities. Educational qualifications, in particular, need to be examined carefully because of the past tendency to *overqualify* many positions. That is, unnecessarily high educational or experience requirements were mandated for relatively menial positions, thereby excluding many candidates who were entirely capable of handling the requisite tasks.

Luring Applicants

Once the job announcement is written, the vacancy must be advertised in a manner consistent with both federal EEO guidelines and relevant policies in the agency and jurisdiction. Most merit systems operate (at least on the surface) according to the philosophy that employers should cast the widest possible net. In other words they should advertise in as many locations and outlets as possible in order to attract the greatest number of applicants. Because this is an area in which government recruitment efforts have traditionally been lackadaisical, the search (*attraction*) function is currently one of the hotbeds of experimentation.

Multiple Points of Entry. Under traditional merit systems, personnel offices would ordinarily advertise and test through the centralized certification format mentioned above. Systemwide recruitment promoted control but was not very responsive to the needs of individual agencies and departments. Recent years have seen a pronounced drift toward *multiple points of entry.* Instead of serving as a focal point for recruitment and selection, central personnel offices have delegated these responsibilities to operating units (direct hiring and delegated examining). The practical effect is that standardized entry exams and centralized job registers are giving way to agency-controlled staffing procedures. At a minimum this means that the agency becomes the source of information about jobs, the locus of decisional responsibility, and (perhaps) the designer of all screening requirements.

Attraction Innovations. In addition to experimenting with different point-of-entry strategies, public personnelists have invested considerable energy in upgrading their efforts to attract applicants. For the most part these initiatives emulate recruitment practices that have long existed in the private sector. The newly proactive approach to staffing is reflected in the appearance of *marketing plans,* in which public agencies tailor recruitment campaigns for specific audiences.

Government efforts to reach college-educated job candidates are particularly noteworthy. Many state and federal agencies now use techniques pioneered by Fortune 500 firms. Glossy brochures highlighting the agency's accomplishments and bearing an attached employment application are distributed widely on college campuses. Government recruiters are also much more evident during campus career days, working closely with college placement offices to generate interest and to identify promising candidates. And, notably, agency recruiters are being provided with special training on how to sell their organizations to applicants. Direct mailings targeted to specific classes of recipients, internship programs, and even television advertising are increasingly evident (Carnevale and Housel, 1989). Other techniques include the creation of training courses to help college placement directors better understand public employment procedures, the development of career directories as a resource guide for persons seeking job information, toll-free telephone lines for applicants to make inquiries about job openings, and much closer coordination with professional associations representing high-demand occupations (Crum, 1990).

Where the government's needs are especially intense (such as in the recruitment of some types of medical professionals), recruiters are empowered to engage in *on-the-spot* hiring (Cole, 1989–1990). One controversial program even allows government recruiters to hire applicants noncompetitively on the spot if they merely have a 3.0 college grade point average (Crum, 1990). To the best of my knowledge, public agencies have not yet begun to follow the private-sector practice of paying their employees bounties for recruiting needed workers into the organization. Some agencies pay *retention bonuses* to workers who extend their employment contracts (Ross, 1990, p. 20), but the popular custom in industry of using worker referrals as a major recruitment vehicle is not apparently widespread except in the smaller and more informal public personnel systems (Benitez, 1995). However, there *are* a few instances of paying *recruitment bonuses,* offering especially attractive candidates cash awards for accepting jobs with public agencies (Ross, 1990, p. 20).

Ongoing efforts to make the intake process more user friendly have also led to the widespread application of computer technology. Within most large public organizations, for instance, computer bulletin boards and electronic mail are used to notify potential applicants about job vacancies. This system of *job posting* is most helpful to internal candidates but is becoming increasingly accessible to outsiders as more citizens go on-line. In addition to providing applicants with vacancy information, technology helps managers identify and track people who have qualified for various types of positions. On-line access to applicants' test scores, qualifications, and professional objectives gives managers an expedient way to screen prospective employees. OPM's Automated Applicant Referral System, for example, handles 700,000 applications per year and has trimmed processing time from twelve to three days (U.S. General Accounting Office, 1990, p. 39).

This is also indicative of efforts to create a paperless application system, in which all entries and updates are made on-line. A variation on this theme—the *résumé database*—has not yet made much of an inroad in public-sector recruiting. It involves creation of a nationwide database of professional credentials that personnelists can use to prescreen thousands of applications simultaneously. The system has enjoyed such explosive growth in the private sector that it is projected to be the *primary* method of recruiting managers by the year 2005.

In summary, government's desire to lure good workers into the bureaucracy has occasioned a significant revision in traditional modes of operation. Although many public agencies still have a long way to go, recruitment has certainly become more proactive and innovative than just five or ten years ago. To the extent that government agencies continue to import private-sector techniques, their recruitment efforts are likely to experience growing success. As decentralization has become the dominant trend, some public managers worry that the advantages of greater flexibility will be counteracted by the dangers of reduced control and standardization. How does one maintain a fair and uniform personnel system when authority is exercised so broadly? This is an enduring dilemma. Each personnel system must make its own accommodations, trying to establish a workable blend of flexibility and centralized supervision. In most cases, if centrally mandated guidelines are clearly articulated for line managers and if exceptions are subjected to strict review, then most of the disadvantages of a decentralized system can be avoided (but never eliminated).

SELECTION DILEMMAS AND STRATEGIES

Once a pool of desirable applicants is identified, the next step in the staffing process is to choose those most likely to perform the job competently. Selecting workers on the basis of their *job-related ability* is one of the most sacred principles of the merit system. It means that the personnel system must determine which qualifications are necessary for job performance and then devise ways to assess those qualities competitively. Although seemingly straightforward and admirable in theory, perhaps no principle in the merit catechism has been more difficult to apply (Hays and Reeves, 1984).

The Test Validation Question

Prior to the 1970s, most of the selection and promotion examinations used in government and industry bore little direct relationship to the jobs being filled. Organizations and agencies used aptitude tests to screen applicants for menial positions, academically oriented test items that had nothing to do with job responsibilities, unrealistically high pass thresholds, and entry requirements (educational level, physical attributes, and the like) that effectively excluded many applicants who were probably capable of acceptable job performance. More often than not, the individuals disadvantaged by these exams were members of minority groups, most especially African Americans and women.

Thanks to the legal revolution inaugurated by *Griggs* v. *Duke Power Company,* 401 U.S. 424 (1971), personnel professionals have been challenged to improve their testing strategies, under threat of legal sanction. *Test validation* has thus become a major duty (and a major problem) for personnel offices everywhere. Briefly stated, the *Griggs* opinion limits employers to the use of tests that are *job-related* and that do not have a *discriminatory impact* upon any protected class of individuals (that is, any recognized minority group). Although later decisions of the U.S. Supreme Court attempted to limit the reach of the *Griggs* case (see *Wards Cove Packing Company* v. *Atonio,* 109 Sup. Ct. 2115 [1989]), passage of the Civil Rights Act of 1991 ensures not only that test validation will continue to be a critical component of all examination programs but also that the burden of proof in such cases rests with the employer. That is, if a particular test is proved to exert a discriminatory impact upon the employment opportunities of protected groups (as measured by the famous 80 percent rule), then it is up to the employer to prove that there is no discriminatory *intent.*

As a direct outgrowth of the emerging concern over test validation, the Equal Employment Opportunity Commission (1997) issued the Uniform Guidelines on Employee Selection Procedures in 1978. The nation's first attempt to establish a uniform government employment policy, the guidelines (1) provide an expansive definition of *test,* including application forms, minimum job requirements, performance tests, analyses of past training and experience, and oral interviews; (2) delineate how concepts such as adverse impact will be determined; and (3) establish a detailed set of guidelines and methods for assessing test validity (that is, the test must positively correlate with job performance). The expectations set forth in the guidelines set off stronger shock waves than even the *Griggs* decision, owing in large part to the fact that they eloquently demonstrated the pathetic quality of most civil service testing protocols. Whereas most tests had never been exposed to *any* systematic study, the guidelines led to two general strategies public agencies now can apply to establish the job relatedness of their selection strategies: criterion and content validity.

Criterion validity means that a *predictor* (a selection format or test) is correlated with a *criterion* (a measure of job performance). In other words, to establish criterion validity, the personnelist must determine that an organization's selection criteria do a satisfactory job of *predicting job performance.* This is typically accomplished by correlating employee test scores with supervisory ratings of performance (Arvey and Faley, 1988). Before conducting the studies necessary to establish criterion validity, the personnelist must clear two methodological hurdles. First, he or she must decide whether to correlate the test scores and performance ratings of *new* workers or to administer the test to *current* workers and compare their scores with available assessments of performance (Hamman and Desai, 1995). Obviously, either strategy excludes individuals who did not score well on the entry exam (unless, as some methodologists argue ought to be done, the organization has been dumb enough to hire people who scored both high *and low* on the screening criteria, thus providing a statistically accurate sample). The other methodological dilemma is even thornier. No matter how many numbers are crunched trying to establish criterion validity, the calculations will be worthless if the organization's *measures of performance* are unreliable. Given the enormous difficulties that impede the performance appraisal process, public managers cannot be blamed for putting little faith in the evaluation data that result. For these reasons, practitioners "rarely are able to show criterion-related validity" (Hamman and Desai, 1995, p. 97).

Due to the inherent difficulties in establishing criterion validity, *content validity* has essentially become the validation strategy of choice among personnel professionals in both the public and private sectors. Fortunately, the courts have endorsed this trend by confirming that content validity is "an *equally* acceptable strategy in and of itself, not just a poor second choice" (Arvey and Faley, 1988, p. 172). When establishing content validity the emphasis is placed on the test development process (see, for example, *Kirkland v. N.Y. Department of Correctional Services,* 7 FEP 700 [1974]). On the basis of a preliminary *job analysis,* the essential *skills, knowledge, and abilities* (SKAs) required for effective job performance are identified. Test items are then designed that sample these actual SKAs. Job relatedness is ensured by asking highly experienced veterans of the target position, individuals known as *job knowledge experts* (JKEs), to review the tests and to recommend alterations and additions that more accurately reflect job content. Although establishing content validity is not easy, it is certainly preferable to using selection criteria that are completely invalid.

Methods of Selection

Despite the strides made in validating examinations, the use of traditional forms of paper-and-pencil tests is subsiding in many merit systems. The difficulty (and expense) associated with validation studies and the persistent doubts about their ability to predict job performance have led to the gradual spread of alternative selection strategies. The types of exams that appear to be emerging as the new favorites among public and private users alike include unassembled examinations, performance-based tests, and assessment centers. These testing formats, along with other less popular means of acquiring information about potential employees, are briefly described in the following sections.

Unassembled Examinations. Perhaps the most widely used method of selecting managerial and professional employees, an *unassembled exam* consists of the (one hopes) *systematic* review of an applicant's education and experience. Using a résumé or job application, or both, the reviewer scores each applicant according to a consistent set of guidelines. For example, one point might be assigned for each year of general experience, three points for each year of directly relevant job experience, ten points for the appropriate professional certification, and the like. In almost all instances the candidates who rank highest on the basis of this initial review are then interviewed prior to the final selection decision.

Although quick and cheap, this examination format has been criticized as being too subjective and prone to evaluator error (Levine and Flory, 1975). Even with the most detailed of guidelines the evaluator must make an excessive number of judgments. The method also tends to overemphasize quantitative factors (years of experience, number of publications) rather than qualitative concerns that may be more relevant to job performance. In effect, unassembled exams tend to exacerbate *credentialism,* the undue emphasis on various educational and professional credentials as prerequisites to employment. Applicants, too, can undermine the reliability of unassembled exams by inflating their accomplishments. Without carefully cross-checking facts, an employer might even be fooled into hiring someone who has submitted *fraudulent credentials,* an extremely serious yet common problem.

A very different form of unassembled exam that is rarely used in government but popular in some business settings is the systematic analysis of *biodata.* Specifically, applicants are asked to respond to a set of personal history questions. They might, for instance, be asked to identify their childhood hobbies or the age at which they first held a job. Although biodata do not appear to have much face validity, research has revealed that they can often be a valuable selection tool. The U.S. Air Force, for example, has determined that one of the best predictors of success in flight training school is an affirmative response to the question, "Did you ever build a model airplane that actually flew?"

Still another form of unassembled exam is the *task inventory.* Often used in industry as a substitute form of job application, this exam asks applicants to respond to a list of items (job tasks) with such answers as, "I have never done that," "I have performed that task with supervision," or "I have trained others to perform that task." The inventory might contain such entries as, "I have written grant proposals," or "I have supervised work teams with more than six members." In order to control for lying, some task inventories contain nonsensical trap items ("operating dissimulator machines"). Even with the inclusion of traps, however, task inventories are subject to considerable applicant puffery.

Interviews. Regardless of the other screening techniques used, almost all selection procedures include an *interview* phase. The popularity of personal interviews is undoubtedly attributable to managers' desires to see applicants *in action*—to determine if they can think on their feet and to clarify any questions that may remain after the job applications and test scores have been evaluated. Because managers rely on interviews so heavily, management textbooks devote considerable time to the how-to's of interviewing. In addition to certain cardinal rules (let the applicant do most of the talking; reserve a quiet time and space to conduct the interview; be well prepared for the interview by reviewing the job description and applicant's qualifications beforehand), the most important advice is to use a *patterned interview* technique. The purpose of the patterned interview is to ensure that all applicants are asked the *same* questions in more or less the same order. Moreover, the interviewer is cautioned to know in advance (1) the specific questions that will be asked and (2) the means by which the candidates' responses will be recorded and scored. Interviewers are instructed to avoid questions that are not job related and to judiciously steer away from any topic that touches upon an applicant's race, religion, marital status, physical impairment, or other forbidden categories (except to the extent that such information may be required as a *business necessity*).

The obvious intent of the patterned interview is to increase the technique's objectivity and reliability. Although patterned interviews are a clear improvement over unstructured interviews, no interview (even when well constructed and performed by trained examiners) is as effective at assessing job competency as are certain alternative methodologies. For this reason interviews are not recommended for judging the suitability of applicants' skills and abilities or even their level of interest or job commitment. Instead, interviews serve an important (albeit misunderstood) function by evaluating candidates' *attractiveness* or *likability* (Werbel, 1995). This is undoubtedly important, because few managers are willing to hire a candidate with whom they have no comfort zone. The potential dilemma, of course, is that various kinds of prejudice will creep into the interview process.

Performance Tests. Because of their obvious connection to the job, various kinds of *performance tests* have proliferated since the 1970s. Thanks to advances in testing methodology, examiners can easily assess a candidate's competence in such areas as numerical computation (for bookkeepers, for instance), verbal proficiency (for text editors, for instance), and mechanical aptitude. Similarly, applicants for clerical positions are usually asked to demonstrate their task proficiency, just as heavy machine operators must show that they can handle a front-loader. A slightly different type of performance test, the *work sample,* is occasionally used in screening certain types of technical and clerical workers. Applicants for construction supervisor in the highway department, for example, may be asked to read a blueprint or to describe the sequence in which subcontractors should arrive at a building site.

Performance tests that emphasize physical prowess, such as those traditionally administered to prospective police and fire personnel, have been a source of continuing irritation among some groups. When, for instance, the fire department requires applicants to lift 150 pounds of *dead weight* and carry it down a sixty-foot ladder, women (and some ethnic groups) complain that they are unfairly excluded from competition. In this case the performance test resembles any *physical standard*—such as weight and height restrictions—that might adversely affect a protected ethnic or gender group. Where physical standard problems surface, the employer bears the burden of establishing their work-related necessity. Almost all selection standards based on physical ability have been relaxed in recent years; in most cases, physical requirements remain a part of the selection protocol, but they have been made more *reasonable* in the eyes of the courts.

The pros and cons of performance tests should be fairly evident. When used in the selection of most lower-level workers, they are very inexpensive to design (although they may be quite expensive to administer due to the need for proctors or evaluators to be present). They enjoy very high validity and are generally popular among applicants because they are easy to understand and feedback is immediate. If the organization is intent upon using performance tests to select managerial and professional workers, however, the scenario may be somewhat different. As is discussed in the next section, job-related screening practices for upper-level workers can be highly complex.

Assessment Centers. Because an entire chapter in this volume (Chapter Seventeen) is devoted to *assessment centers,* only a rough outline is provided here. Although assessment centers are commonly used in making promotion decisions, their use for initial selections is also expanding because they effectively simulate on-the-job tasks and activities. Assessment centers offer a battery of exercises so that candidates can demonstrate to what extent they have the skills necessary to succeed in a particular job. When used to select managerial personnel, the centers typically include in-basket simulations, oral presentations, leadership games, group discussions, and essay writing (Howard, 1974). The performance of candidates during each exercise is evaluated by two or more *assessors* who have received special training (and who probably hold positions similar to or higher than the one being sought). The resulting evaluations are pooled and analyzed, thereby yielding an overall rating for each candidate.

Assessment centers are valued for their recognized ability to gauge such elusive qualities as *leadership* and *judgment.* That is, they probe skill or behavior characteristics (such as ability to handle stress) that are often overlooked by conventional testing strategies. When carefully designed and operationalized, they enjoy very high validity and interrater reliability (Klimoski and Strickland, 1987). Their negatives include higher costs than written tests, limited applicability to mass hiring, and speculation that their results are nothing more than a proxy measure for intelligence (which, almost everyone agrees, is a very good predictor of job competence).

Computerized Adaptive Testing. Other than ongoing efforts to validate paper-and-pencil exams, the most significant innovation affecting traditional civil service testing programs is the advent of *computerized adaptive testing* (CAT).

Personnel systems that administer tests electronically often use CAT to expedite the testing process and to provide a much refined predictor of job performance. When examined via a CAT system, the applicant is first presented with questions of moderate difficulty. If those items are answered correctly, the computer poses more difficult ones; if the initial questions are missed, easier ones are provided. The point at which the applicant "proceeds from knowing generally less difficult items to not knowing more difficult ones is that individual's score" (Hamman and Desai, 1995, p. 100). In addition to its enhanced validity, CAT permits public agencies to process large numbers of applicants quickly and painlessly. Moreover, when linked with other databases (such as collections of on-line application forms or résumés), CAT offers managers an almost instantaneous ability to download eligibility lists and other applicant data.

Postexamination Considerations

Even after applicants have been recruited and examined, the selection process is not quite complete. Before any particular candidate can be appointed, *preference eligibility* (or *veterans' preference*) will probably need to be calculated and added to the applicants' scores. In most jurisdictions, veterans (and sometimes their parents, when they have become eligible as a result of the loss of sons) who receive passing scores on the relevant civil service examinations are granted an additional five points, and disabled veterans receive ten points. As a result, non-veterans are often excluded from competition for certain jobs, even when they have earned perfect scores on the entry exams.

Another preappointment requirement *should be* (but often is not) the verification of information provided by the applicant. Anyone who appoints a person to a job without checking that person's references and credentials is not only foolish but at risk legally. Fake college credentials and professional certifications have reached epidemic proportions, as has applicants' willingness to obfuscate the facts of their professional backgrounds (Barada, 1993). For positions with sensitive or highly responsible duties, a thorough *security* or *background check* might be required, involving a search of criminal records, fingerprinting, and possibly even a procedure akin to a federal *national agency check*, in which an applicant's references (and perhaps past acquaintances) are personally interviewed.

Such measures are becoming increasingly necessary because courts today recognize an employer's duty to exercise *reasonable care* in the selection of workers. Failure to comply with this requirement can result in an allegation of *negligent hiring*. Agencies that hire housing inspectors with histories of rape violations or police officers with recurrent charges of brutality will be found legally liable if the employees again engage in the unacceptable behaviors. Although rampant litigiousness has eroded managers' willingness to reveal negative information about their former employees, no employer can be successfully sued for providing information that is both factually accurate and a matter of public record.

For organizations experiencing severe turnover, *realistic job previews* are recommended before the appointment process is concluded or, alternatively, at the time applicants are first identified. The purpose of these previews is to encourage the *early* departure of those applicants who are most likely to quit at some later date, such as at the conclusion of an expensive training and orientation program. A common preview format provides the applicants with detailed and candid descriptions of job requirements, frequently including videotaped views of unpleasant aspects of the position. Prospective correctional officers, for example, might be treated to a tour of a particularly nasty cellblock and then shown a film that takes a realistic look at how their days will be spent in close proximity to one hundred–plus felons. By discouraging frivolous applications and weeding out the uncommitted, realistic job previews can save considerable training and administrative resources (Brink, 1993).

Depending upon the job being filled, drug tests and physical examinations may also be required before a candidate can be formally offered the position. Ordinarily, drug screening for selection purposes is limited to public employees in "sensitive" positions involving public health, safety, or national security (Daley and Ellis, 1994). The ability to pass a medical examination, too, is generally limited to applicants whose jobs will require unusual physical exertion. For the typical desk job an employer cannot require applicants to pass a physical exam prior to employment. In fact, unless the position clearly requires a fit individual (police and fire services, for instance), the agency has an obligation to try to accommodate applicants with physical limitations.

CONCLUSION

Recruitment and selection are the avenues by which bureaucracy acquires its most important raw materials, human resources. After a century of experience with relatively ineffective staffing practices, merit systems are finally drifting closer to private-sector approaches to the entry functions. Decentralization, flexibility, agency autonomy, and experimentation with promising new techniques are becoming the order of the day.

Although most of these developments will likely have positive effects on government staffing needs, we cannot afford to ignore the fundamental differences that separate public and private personnel administration. It would be dangerous to assume that *all* private staffing arrangements can be applied with impunity in public agencies. Business gurus, for instance, widely endorse employee referrals as their *primary* recruitment strategy. But instead of asking all employees to recommend friends and acquaintances for jobs, they ask "just the ones who have the same good values as we have" (Benitez, 1995, p. 30). Moreover, business executives "no longer believe in ads or job postings," and they "refuse to hire people who do not live nearby" (Benitez, 1995, p. 30). In the public personnel setting, these approaches obviously conflict with cherished values. Openness may not always be efficient, but it is an essential component of the government staffing philosophy. Delegation of staffing authority to line managers may be expedient now, but the long-term effect will be negative if merit considerations are buried under the weight of personal contacts and friendship. As public agencies rush to reinvent their personnel functions, a reasonable concern for some of the traditional public personnel values may not always be misplaced.

References

Arvey, R. D., and Faley, R. *Fairness in Selecting Employees.* Reading, Mass.: Addison Wesley Longman, 1988.

Barada, P. "Check References with Care." *Nation's Business,* May 1993, pp. 54–55.

Benitez, B. "Reinvention Battle Must Continue and Must Be Won." *Public Manager,* 1995, *3,* 27–31.

Brink, T. "A Discouraging Word Improves Your Interviews." *HR Magazine,* Dec. 1993, p. 49.

Carnevale, D. G., and Housel, S. W. "Recruitment of Personnel." In J. Rabin (ed.), *Handbook of Public Personnel Administration.* New York: Dekker, 1989.

Cawsey, T. "Why Line Managers Don't Listen to Their Personnel Departments." *Personnel,* Jan. 1980, pp. 11–20.

Civil Rights Act. 1991. *U.S. Statutes at Large* 105 (1991) 1071.

Cole, J. "Shoring Up Civil Service Reform." *Bureaucrat,* 1989–1990, *1,* 32–36.

Committee on Economic Development. *Improving Management of the Public Work Force.* New York: Committee on Economic Development, 1978.

Crum, J. "Building a Quality Federal Work Force." *Bureaucrat,* 1990, *2,* 30–34.

Daley, D. M., and Ellis, C. "Drug Screening in the Public Sector: A Focus on Law Enforcement." *Public Personnel Management,* 1994, *23*(1), 1–18.

Equal Employment Opportunity Commission. *Uniform Guidelines on Employee Selection Procedures. Code of Federal Regulations,* 1997, vol. 29, sec. 1607. (Originally issued 1978.)

Hamman, J., and Desai, U. "Current Issues and Challenges in Recruitment and Selection." In S. W. Hays and R. C. Kearney (eds.), *Public Personnel Administration: Problems and Prospects.* (3rd ed.) Upper Saddle River, N.J.: Prentice Hall, 1995.

Hays, S. W., and Reeves, T. Z. *Personnel Management in the Public Sector.* Needham Heights, Mass.: Allyn & Bacon, 1984.

Howard, A. "An Assessment of Assessment Centers." *Academy of Management Journal,* 1974, *17,* 115–133.

Ingraham, P. W. "Federal Recruitment Revisited." *Bureaucrat,* 1990, *3,* 13–17.

Ito, J. "Current Staff Development and Expectations as Criteria in Selection Decisions." *Public Personnel Management*, 1994, *3*, 361–372.

Johnston, W. B. *Civil Service 2000*. Washington, D.C.: Office of Personnel Management, 1988.

Johnston, W. B., and Packer, A. H. *Workforce 2000: Work and Workers for the 21st Century*. Indianapolis, Ind.: Hudson Institute, 1987.

Klimoski, R., and Strickland, W. "Why Do Assessment Centers Work? The Puzzle of Assessment Center Validity." *Personnel Psychology*, 1987, *3*, 353–361.

Levine, E., and Flory, A. "Evaluation of Job Applications: A Conceptual Framework." *Public Personnel Management*, 1975, *4*, 378–384.

Lewis, G. "Turnover and the Quiet Crisis in the Federal Civil Service." *Public Administration Review*, 1991, *51*, 145–155.

Mishel, L., and Teixeira, R. *The Myth of the Coming Labor Shortage: Jobs, Skills, and Incomes of America's Workforce 2000*. Washington, D.C.: American Enterprise Institute, 1991.

Mosher, F. J. *Democracy and the Public Service*. New York: Oxford University Press, 1968.

National Commission on the Public Service (Paul Volcker, chairman). *Leadership for America: Rebuilding the Public Service*. Washington, D.C.: National Commission on the Public Service, 1989.

National Commission on the State and Local Public Service (Winter Commission). *Hard Truths/Tough Choices: An Agenda for State and Local Reform*. Albany, N.Y.: Rockefeller Institute of Government, 1993.

Rosen, B. "Crises in the U.S. Civil Service." *Public Administration Review*, 1986, *46*, 207–214.

Ross, L. "Effective Recruiting: Lessons from Personnel Demonstration Projects." *Bureaucrat*, 1990, *3*, 19–24.

Savas, E. S., and Ginsburg, S. G. "The Civil Service: A Meritless System?" *Public Interest*, 1973, *32*(2), 70–85.

Sayre, W. S. "The Triumph of Technique over Purpose." *Public Administration Review*, 1948, *8*, 134–137.

Shafritz, J. M. "The Cancer Eroding Public Personnel Professionalism." *Public Personnel Management*, 1974, *3*, 486–492.

Shafritz, J. M. *Public Personnel Management: The Heritage of Civil Service Reform*. New York: Praeger, 1975.

Thompson, F. J. *Revitalizing State and Local Public Service: Strengthening Performance, Accountability, and Citizen Confidence*. San Francisco: Jossey-Bass, 1993.

U.S. General Accounting Office. *Federal Recruiting and Hiring*. Washington, D.C.: U.S. Government Printing Office, 1990.

U.S. General Accounting Office. *Federal Hiring Practices*. Washington, D.C.: U.S. Government Printing Office, 1992.

U.S. General Accounting Office. *The Public Service.* Washington, D.C.: U.S. Government Printing Office, 1994.

U.S. Merit Systems Protection Board. *Attracting Quality Graduates to the Federal Government: A View of College Recruiting.* Washington, D.C.: U.S. Government Printing Office, 1988.

Van Riper, P. P. *History of the United States Civil Service.* New York: HarperCollins, 1958.

Vroom, V. H. *Work and Motivation.* New York: Wiley, 1964.

Werbel, J. "A Review of Research Regarding Criteria Used to Select Job Applicants." In J. Rabin, T. Vocino, W. B. Hildreth, and G. J. Miller (eds.), *Handbook of Public Personnel Administration.* New York: Dekker, 1995.

CHAPTER SIXTEEN

Effective Job Analysis Methods

Mark R. Foster

There are many definitions of job analysis. The number is probably limited only by the number of authors who have written about and researched the subject and the number of consultants and human resource professionals who conduct such analyses. The lack of agreement on a single definition of job analysis should not, however, lead us to believe that the topic is not of importance to the human resource function within organizations. In fact, job analysis is often thought of as the backbone of the human resource function, forming the basis of almost all functions within a well-managed human resource department. Hardly any program or activity related to organizational personnel could be successful if it were not based on information generated from a thorough job analysis. This chapter provides a general definition of job analysis and describes how job analysis information can be used and why it is so important. It discusses different sources of job analysis information, and their advantages and disadvantages, and then examines the more popular techniques among the many different methods of conducting a job analysis. Finally, it addresses another source of concern in dealing with job analysis information—the legal standards. Examples and practical guidelines are provided throughout.

DEFINITION

Generally speaking, *job analysis* refers to a purposeful, systematic process that provides descriptive, important job-related information that distinguishes the job being analyzed from other jobs. A job analysis breaks the job down into meaningful components. McCormick (1976) lists several types of information that might be elicited from the job analysis process:

1. Work activities, which are broken into job-oriented activities such as what is being accomplished and procedures and processes used, and worker-oriented activities, such as human behaviors, elemental motions, and personal demands from the job

2. Machines, tools, equipment, and work aids used

3. Job-related tangibles and intangibles, such as materials processed or products made and services rendered

4. Work performance, such as standards of job performance, significance of errors, and time required to perform the job

5. Job context, such as the physical conditions, work schedule, organizational environment, social environment, and incentives to perform the work

6. Personnel requirements, such as job-related knowledge and skills, education, training, work experience, aptitudes, physical characteristics, and personality

As this list reveals, job analysis provides a wealth of detailed information about the job in question. The challenge with job analysis lies in identifying the most useful sources for the information, choosing and applying the methods for gathering it, and then organizing it in a meaningful manner. It is also important to recognize all the specific uses for job analysis information, and this concern is the one I discuss first.

USES OF JOB ANALYSIS INFORMATION

The information generated from a job analysis study has many uses. Besides satisfying a legal requirement, it forms the foundation for many other personnel practices. Some of these practices are writing job descriptions, establishing a recruitment and selection process, conducting periodic performance appraisals, establishing employees' training and development needs, and establishing the level of pay for the job.

Job Description

A *job description* and a job analysis are not the same thing, although the terms are often mistakenly used interchangeably. For example, before beginning work to develop new promotional testing materials, I always ask personnel departments if they have completed a job analysis. Many times their reply is, "Oh yes, we just finished updating all our job descriptions." This does not answer the question.

A job description is a one- to four-page summary of tasks and job requirements that are essential to the position. Job analysis is the process by which these tasks and requirements are identified. So the job description should be a brief summary of the findings from the more extensive job analysis. Often, human resource personnel assume that because they have job descriptions they really do not need to conduct a job analysis. However, job descriptions are usually not detailed enough to assist with the other human resource functions mentioned later in this section. For example, developing a selection instrument from a job description would be extremely difficult because the description lacks sufficient detail and is unlikely to meet the legal requirements for test development (discussed in more detail in a subsequent section).

Job Evaluation

The process of *job evaluation* attaches a dollar value or worth to the job. Before the pay level of a job is determined it is certainly advantageous to learn as much as possible about the job's duties and responsibilities. Additionally, once the information from the job analysis is available, comparing the pay rates in similar jobs external to the organization will be much easier and quicker.

Realistic Job Preview

A common complaint by employees new to a job is that "the job is not what I expected." Or, said another way, "The personnel office really painted a rosy picture of this job to get me to take it, but they didn't tell me about these bad things." The result most often is a discontented worker who will probably leave the job as soon as he or she has an opportunity. By adequately and accurately describing both the positives and negatives of the job, as discovered during the job analysis, this problem can often be reduced. Research examining the relationship between *realistic job previews* and tenure suggests a modest relationship (Premack and Wanous, 1985). That is, when realistic job previews are presented to applicants, these applicants are more likely to stay on the job longer if they are hired.

Organizational Analysis

Aamodt (1996) points out that you could really consider *organizational analysis* a by-product of conducting job analysis interviews and surveys. Often analysts talking to people about their jobs will uncover additional information relevant to organizations. For example, workers may not know exactly what they are supposed to be doing. Their role within the organization may not have been clearly defined for them. Or they may not understand how their performance is being evaluated. These concerns produce information on the organization's communications and leadership and reveal relevant issues to be addressed by the organization.

Legal and Quasi-Legal Requirements

Legal requirements are laws and statutes enacted by the local, state, and federal governments. *Quasi-legal requirements* are regulations adopted by enforcement agencies such as OSHA and the EEOC and also collective bargaining agreements between organizations and unions (Levine, 1983). In a subsequent section of this chapter some of these requirements—including those arising from court decisions on what adequate job analysis entails and those in the Uniform Guidelines on Employee Selection Procedures—are reviewed. Suffice it to say here that organizations can encounter costly setbacks when a job analysis is not done properly or not done at all.

The Americans with Disabilities Act of 1990 (ADA) is another and more recent legal consideration when conducting job analysis. Under ADA, employers must make reasonable accommodations for employees who are disabled. Meeting this requirement calls for focusing on essential job functions rather than marginal performance issues (Bell, 1994), and a job analysis can help satisfy this legal requirement. The Equal Employment Opportunity Commission (1992) has raised another current legal issue by stating that a job analysis should focus on the outcomes of a function rather than the manner in which the job is conducted.

Job Classification

Job classification involves grouping jobs in terms of tasks, knowledge, skills, and abilities. Factors such as difficulty, complexity, and the amount and kinds of responsibility are also considered. This information helps establish the similarity of jobs. After similarity is determined, grades, or classification levels, can be established. For example, the job of firefighter might have three classification levels, and level requirements might differ in terms of job complexity, supervisory responsibility, and training needs. Obviously, the job analysis process provides a means to gather the critical information in order to classify jobs based on similarity.

Efficiency

Job analysis information can also determine whether the work could be done in another manner with more *efficiency.* For example, maybe a workstation could be designed so that the physical demands on employees are less, thus allowing them to produce more. Or maybe the flow of the work could be altered to allow for a higher rate of production. These issues are often addressed by human factor or ergonomics specialists, who deal directly with the human-machine interface.

Safety Analysis

Many times generating information about the requirements of a job will uncover information related to *safety* concerns. For example, it might uncover job functions that require additional precautions, such as wearing safety equipment. A good example is the requirement that firefighters wear a SCBA (self-contained breathing apparatus) where they may encounter dangerous atmospheres. By looking at the job analysis information and determining how the job is being done, it is also possible to determine if there is a safer method of doing the job.

Job Design and Redesign

Job design involves establishing functions for jobs that have not previously existed. *Redesign*, or restructuring, of jobs involves making significant changes in existing jobs' functions or how these functions are carried out. Job analysis provides useful information in either case. Job analysis information from similar existing jobs is important when designing new positions with similar activities and responsibilities. In the case of restructuring, the scope of the existing activities and responsibilities may have to be enlarged or reduced in order to accomplish organizational objectives. In either case the best way to perform the job can be determined through the job analysis process.

Performance Appraisal

Another important use of job analysis information is in the construction of *performance appraisal* instruments. The more specific and job related performance appraisal instruments are, the more likely they are to be accurate. When performance appraisals are job related, they are also more likely to be accepted by the employee and by the courts in the event of a challenge. Most performance appraisal instruments require the supervisor to rate the employee on very general characteristics that may or may not be job specific—things like initiative, attitude, knowledge, interpersonal relations, or dependability. These characteristics may be only cursorily related to the performance of a job. When performance appraisal instruments are directly linked to job performance, they can serve to identify performance weaknesses for which training or counseling would be beneficial. Job analysis is critical for performance appraisals to be properly developed.

Training

Job analysis is critical to *training*. Before programs or workshops are developed, doesn't it seem reasonable to determine if they are needed? This makes common sense, but sometimes managers will leap to offer training before asking if it is the appropriate solution to a situation. Job analysis can help determine which areas will require job training by identifying critical areas of performance.

Employee Selection

Employee selection is the area that most often causes a job analysis to be conducted. It is difficult to believe that organizations would attempt to select individuals without first gaining a full understanding of the requirements for the jobs. It seems like common sense. Yet organizations often do not perform the necessary studies. By determining the needed requirements of jobs in terms of knowledge, skills, and abilities, job-related tests can be developed that will best identify candidates suitable for each job in question.

For example, one local police agency liked to ask interview questions about the death penalty. From a job-relatedness standpoint, these questions should certainly have raised some red flags. Conversely, questions likely to be job related might have included those about arrest procedures, search and seizure of suspects, criminal investigative techniques, and preservation of evidence procedures.

Career Planning

Career planning involves the mobility of workers within an organization. Job analysis can be used to determine relationships between jobs and prepare workers for natural and smooth progressions through the organization. If job analysis information is not available, then these progressions may not be smooth. The responsibilities of the next job up the ladder may not always meet employee expectations. For example, a firefighter may know that his or her next progression in the organization will be to the level of sergeant and yet may not be prepared for the supervisory responsibility or the administrative side of the job. Job analysis information would help this person plan the next move.

Vocational Guidance

Dawis and Lofquist (1988) state that the central requirements in the practice of *vocational guidance* are threefold: first, a clear understanding of the person and his or her aptitudes, interests, abilities, and ambitions; second, knowledge of the requirements and conditions of different lines of work; and third, the relationship between the person and the job. Job analysis provides the basis for understanding the specifics of different types of work. Without an understanding of these specifics, it would be nearly impossible to make a person-job fit.

SOURCES AND METHODS FOR GATHERING JOB ANALYSIS INFORMATION

Recall from the definition of job analysis that there are basically six kinds of information about jobs. The sources of these types of information include the job incumbent, the immediate supervisor of the job, human resource specialists within the organization, and perhaps clients or customers who interact with the person in the position being analyzed. In gathering information about a job, it is important to realize that job incumbents are likely to be most knowledgeable of the job requirements. Incumbents do the job day in and day out, so it makes sense that they would have the most insight. However, it is also useful to consider the input of the immediate job supervisor. Sometimes he or she will provide information as to how the job fits within the larger organization. The supervisor can also provide feedback on the incumbents' comments. At times incumbents have been known to inflate or overestimate responsibilities. The immediate supervisor can put information in perspective for the larger work unit.

Having talked about some sources of information, it is useful to now discuss generic ways of collecting job analysis data. Sometimes sources are obviously connected to particular methods.

Review of Archival Information

A *review of archival information* should be one of the very first methods of collecting information about a job. This information might include previous job analysis studies, job descriptions or specifications, performance appraisals, training materials or manuals for the job, examples of work products such as memos or other documents, and any other personnel records that shed light on the job in question. Archival information lays the groundwork for a basic understanding of the job. It is helpful to have this understanding before going to the field and conducting observations or interviews.

Observation

Observing someone perform a job is a very useful method of gathering information about that job. It allows the analyst to go to the work site and see first-hand exactly what the job involves. By viewing the work in progress the analyst can make notes about the equipment used, the work setting or environment, the people with whom the incumbent interacts, and in some cases the end product of the work. This method is especially useful when combined with other techniques like interviews and questionnaires. By observing the job the analyst can clarify notes from an interview or probe further than a questionnaire can into complex areas of the work. Seeing the job performed is especially useful because many times incumbents will not mention crucial details of the job. This may not be intentional but an oversight from having performed the job over a period of time. If they have learned their jobs especially well or have performed them for a long time, the jobs are likely to be second nature. Observation allows the analyst to see functions that incumbents may have forgotten to mention. For example, when riding with police officers an analyst may note that officers will report their location immediately when called on the radio. This constant awareness of street location is something they may neglect to report in an interview but something that will be observed when the analyst is riding with officers on the job.

Observing the job and interacting with the incumbent in his or her natural work setting has an additional advantage. It gives the analyst a chance to explain the job analysis procedure to the incumbent and describe what the information will be used for. This is especially important because it helps the analyst gain the incumbent's acceptance and gives the incumbent a chance to ask questions. Incumbents sometimes feel uncomfortable or threatened when being observed performing their jobs. They sometimes feel that the analyst will report to their boss all the things they did wrong. The main disadvantage of observing incumbents is that for most jobs the method is obtrusive; it is difficult to observe the jobs without being noticed. The analyst can never be sure the incumbents perform their jobs in the same manner when they are not being observed.

Interviews

The job analysis *interview* is one of the most common methods of gathering information about the essential functions of a job. There are several things the job analyst should do before starting the interview. He or she should first try to establish a comfortable level of rapport with the interviewee. This can be done by explaining what a job analysis is and what the information will be used for. Remember that the employee knows the job better than anyone else because he or she does it day in and day out. You will be a success as a job analyst to the extent that you can gain details about the job. This is usually not very difficult because people like to talk about their jobs when someone else shows a genuine interest.

The interview can take several different forms. First, it can be structured or unstructured. The best approach is to have some basic questions prepared in advance. This provides some structure for the person being interviewed. But too much structure can inhibit the interviewee from providing detailed answers. Remember, the idea is to get the person to talk about the things done on the job. It is best to try to strike a balance between no structure and an extensive structure.

Second, job analysts can interview individuals or groups. On the one hand, individual interviews, involving only one incumbent and the job analyst, can be costly in terms of time but can pay off in terms of information quality. Many times people are less inhibited in one-on-one situations and provide details that might otherwise go unmentioned. Also, in individual settings employees may be more open because they feel that the information will remain confidential. They may be more likely to tell the analyst the way things really get done rather than saying what the boss would want them to say. These factors may lead to more accurate information. Group interviews, on the other hand, involving several job incumbents and the analyst, can be beneficial because employees' memories may be jogged by what others say about the job. Many times, however, group interviews take the shape of one or two people doing all the talking and the others saying nothing or simply agreeing.

Because there are advantages to both approaches, when I conduct job analysis interviews, typically I will conduct individual interviews first. Then, I go back and meet with groups of incumbents to clarify certain points and make sure that I have a clear understanding of the job. The group interview also can serve as a check on the accuracy of an individual's information. If the information is inflated or exaggerated the group most often will correct it. For example, in individual interviews conducted to analyze the job of corporal in a police department, one corporal said that he had full supervisory responsibility for other officers. However, during the subsequent group interview, other corporals were quick to point out that the rank of corporal carried no supervisory functions. It also helps to let the incumbents know that their supervisor will be reviewing an aggregated list of the requirements and duties specified in the interviews.

Questionnaires

Another very common method of gathering job information is the standardized *questionnaire.* Questionnaires typically are either very specific or very general. In the case of specific questionnaires, incumbents typically are asked how frequently they perform certain job tasks, how important the tasks are to successful completion of their jobs, how difficult the tasks are, and when they learned the tasks. General questionnaires ask less-specific questions about job requirements. They are not as costly or time consuming to develop, and they allow comparisons to be made across jobs. Questionnaires receive more attention later, during the discussion of conducting job analyses.

Diaries

When workers are asked to keep *diaries,* they do not write down their innermost thoughts and feelings. Rather they write down the types of activities they have been engaged in over a period of time. A diary may require workers to write down the activities they have been involved in over the past thirty minutes. Or it may require them to make entries each time their activity changes. Workers may also be instructed to make only unique entries. For example, if a state trooper writes fifteen traffic citations during the course of an eight-hour shift, she will make that activity entry only once in the work diary.

Typically, workers are asked to keep a diary over a period of ten days to three weeks. Work diaries are especially useful for positions such as firefighter or police officer where some work activities and situations may be unique. By keeping diaries, incumbents can report these special situations. If a job analyst only conducted observations, this information might be lost. (When I have conducted job observations with firefighters, the unique situations never seemed to arise.

Indeed, firefighters have said to me that they always welcome job observers because it almost guarantees a slow shift!)

One concern with work diaries is the effort required from the incumbents. Because the work diary is one more piece of paperwork, incumbents must understand its importance and the diligent effort needed to maintain it. Diaries are useless if incumbents wait until the end of a two-week period or even just the end of the shift and try to remember and write down everything they did.

Mechanical Methods

When gathering information about jobs, it can be useful to use a audio recorder to collect worker comments. The material can be transcribed at a later date, and the recording ensures accuracy. It can also be useful to take photographs of equipment used or to capture the work setting on videocassette. Firefighters, for example, are known to carry many different pieces of equipment on their trucks. Taking pictures of the equipment and properly labeling each piece might be useful in developing training materials or constructing promotional exams.

Perform the Work

Sometimes when an job analyst wants to gain a deeper understanding of the work requirements, he or she will actually perform the job or some portion of it. For example, to understand the physical demands on a garbage collector, an analyst might perform the job for a period of time. However, this approach is rarely practical in most situations. It can be used only when the work is not particularly complex and mistakes in performance are not critical.

JOB ANALYSIS METHODS

Many job analysis methods have been professionally developed and documented in the literature. Gael (1988) has documented and offers detailed discussions of eighteen different methods of conducting a job analysis. It should also be noted that practitioners have developed variations on the established methods, largely in order to compensate for various organizational constraints that inhibit pure applications of these methods.

When selecting a particular methodology for conducting a job analysis, the practitioner generally considers several issues. Although I am sure each practitioner will find additional issues to consider, I focus on five particularly critical ones here: practicality, cost, purpose, the job analyst's experience with various methods, and of course the jobs to be analyzed. These are discussed in no particular order because all are important considerations.

Practicality. Certain methods may require the development and completion of questionnaires or the assembly of workgroups to explain or break down the job. To the extent that it is practical to conduct such activities within the organizational setting, the choice of method may be limited. For example, some organizations are spread over large geographic areas, and it simply may not be feasible to gather employees together for group meetings.

Cost. Cost is another concern usually in the forefront of an organization's decision-making process. Certain methods may elicit essentially the same types of information. If the job analysis can be done more cheaply and more efficiently by one method as opposed to another, the less expensive method will likely be chosen. Note that cost considerations might include bottom-line charges by the analyst, time to completion, chances of a legal challenge to the study, and indirect costs to the organization such as lost person-hours on the job.

Purpose. The purpose of the job analysis is probably one of the most important considerations when choosing a method. If the information gained from the job analysis is to be used for the development of selection tools, training, performance appraisals, or job classifications or for any of the other purposes mentioned here, identifying that purpose, or purposes, is one of the first tasks to be completed before the study is started. Some methods are better suited to provide certain information than others.

Analyst experience. The job analyst's experience with one or more particular methods may also be a consideration. Ideally, analysts will have experience with several different methods so that they can make the correct methodological choice for the study. They should also be familiar with the basic scientific research on particular methods, so they can foresee potential problems.

Job to be analyzed. Finally, the job to be analyzed will dictate to some extent the method chosen. For example, if the job to be analyzed is a very high level management position, the task analysis approach may not be the best method because of the difficulty of reducing the job to a list of tasks. The method chosen should give the analyst the maximum amount of information possible.

The following sections contain brief descriptions of eight of the more common methods in use. These descriptions are intended to give a basic introduction to the method. They do not provide the reader with the level of detail needed to conduct a job analysis using the method. The methods to be discussed are

- Threshold traits analysis
- Critical incidents method
- Job elements method
- Position Analysis Questionnaire
- Functional job analysis
- Fleishman Job Analysis Survey
- Job Components Inventory
- Task analysis

Threshold Traits Analysis

The *threshold traits analysis* (TTA) was developed by Felix Lopez in the early 1970s. TTA focuses on job functions and personal traits that are needed for successful completion of the job functions. A job function is a part of the total job. As defined by Lopez (1988), a *job function* consists of two separate items: a distinct activity, or task, and a working condition, or demand, under which the activity is carried out. A *task* is a discrete working unit performed by the incumbent, such as, for a police officer, reviewing a police report or handcuffing someone under arrest. A *demand* is a working condition to which the job incumbent must adjust. One example of a demand is stress. The TTA defines a *trait* as a set of observable characteristics that distinguishes one person from another. After considerable research and experimentation, thirty-three general traits have been identified and grouped into five categories: physical, mental, learned, motivational, and social. For example, the five traits associated with the physical category are strength, stamina, agility, vision, and hearing. Once traits are matched to job functions, the need for each of these relevant traits is rated by supervisors and incumbents. The end result is a list of traits and the level at which each one is required for performing the job.

Critical Incident Method

The *critical incident method* (CIT) was first developed by Flanagan (1954) as a training needs assessment device and a performance appraisal tool. The CIT is used to uncover specific behavioral examples, or incidents, of exceptionally good or exceptionally poor performance. Even though the CIT provides information on critical behaviors related to the job, the method's usefulness is limited because it does not focus on typical job requirements.

Bownas and Bernardin (1988) point out that a good critical incident has four characteristics: it is specific, it focuses on observable behaviors, it describes the context of behavior, and it indicates the consequences of behavior. Consider this example of a critical incident: "The police officer pursued a vehicle down an alley between two rows of houses. When the pursued vehicle made a turn down another alley that was too narrow for the police car, the officer tried to cut off the vehicle by taking a shortcut through a residents' backyard and smashed his car into a fence." This example meets the four criteria.

The basic methodology for the CIT involves five steps. First, persons knowledgeable about the job generate critical incidents of both good and poor performance. These incidents can be obtained thorough conferences and workshops, work diaries, questionnaires, and interviews. Usually multiple methods are used to generate critical incidents. Second, job experts decide whether the incident exemplifies poor or excellent performance. Third, the critical incidents are sorted by the analyst into the categories, or dimensions, measured by the incident. Fourth, new judges are used to confirm the dimensions chosen by the analyst. Fifth, the dimensions are reported and defined by the critical incidents they contain.

The CIT is an excellent method of capturing specific examples of job behaviors. However, it should not be used as the sole technique of conducting a job analysis in most instances because it typically does not focus on basic requirements of the job.

Job Elements Method

The *job elements method* of job analysis was developed by Primoff (1975) for use in the federal government. It focuses exclusively on worker characteristics, or traits (the *elements* in Primoff's terminology), which are needed for performance of the job. These elements take the form of knowledge, skills, abilities, and other characteristics (KSAOs).

The process requires a meeting of job experts, who generate the elements required. They might include fifty or more KSAOs. These elements are then rated by the same or a different group of job experts, using four different scales: the extent to which barely acceptable workers have the element, the importance of the element in distinguishing superior workers from average workers, the amount of trouble likely to be encountered if the element is not considered, and the practicality of requiring applicants to possess the element. The ratings from these four scales are then combined in a complex manner to form a weight for each element. Similar elements are grouped, and then their various weights help determine their use for selection, training, or other purposes.

Position Analysis Questionnaire

The Position Analysis Questionnaire (PAQ) (McCormick, Jeanneret, and Mecham, 1972, [1969] 1989) is probably the most researched job analysis instrument available. It was developed by Ernest McCormick, P. R. Jeanneret, and Robert Mecham at Purdue University. The PAQ contains 194 items that deal with worker behavior: 187 of these items deal with work activities and situations; the remaining items address compensation. The items fall into six divisions: information input, mental processes, work output, relationships with other persons, job context, and other job characteristics. Each of the items on the questionnaire is evaluated using one of several different rating scales: extent of use, amount of time, importance to this job, possibility of occurrence, and applicability. The ratings range, for example, from "does not apply" to "extreme."

The PAQ offers many advantages that other methods and instruments cannot offer. The validity of the PAQ is supported by a large research base. It is an off-the-shelf instrument, so it does not require the development of new items for each different job that is analyzed. It can be used for a wide range of jobs. Because it is a general questionnaire, it allows easy comparison of different jobs across a number of criteria. This standardization helps to ensure that different jobs are evaluated in a similar manner.

However, many of these advantages can also be turned around into disadvantages. Because it is an off-the-shelf, general instrument, the PAQ often does not provide specific details about a job, and this limits its usefulness for some purposes. For example, it may not provide the specific task requirements needed when writing job descriptions. Arvey and Begalla (1975) found that the PAQ yielded similar profiles for the jobs of police officer and homemaker. A final disadvantage of the PAQ has to do with its reading level. The PAQ and its instructions are difficult to read and understand. Therefore, people asked to complete the questionnaire should have at least a college-level reading ability. This usually means the job analyst must complete the questionnaire, based on his or her understanding of the job.

There is a basic procedure for using the PAQ. First, the job analyst becomes familiar with the PAQ instrument. This usually involves a lengthy training session in which the analyst studies the items and how they should be scored in certain circumstances. (A sample set of questions is shown in Exhibit 16.1.) Second, the analyst learns as much as possible about the job to be analyzed. This usually includes interviewing job incumbents and supervisors, observing an incumbent perform the job, and possibly reviewing documentation related to the job. The typical interview and observation period may last for several hours. Third, the analyst completes the PAQ, based on his or her understanding of the job. Fourth, the completed instrument is sent to PAQ services for computer scoring. Finally, the results are returned to the analyst with the profile of the job in question, and the results are used for the intended organizational purposes.

Functional Job Analysis

The concepts of *functional job analysis* (FJA) are based on years of research by Sidney Fine and his associates. This research began in the 1950s, and one result of it is the comprehensive *Dictionary of Occupational Titles* (DOT) (U.S. Department of Labor, 1991), which contains detailed descriptions for thousands of jobs. Associated with each of these descriptions is a DOT code that allows a relatively easy comparison to be made of various jobs. Such comparison across jobs is possible because the methods of FJA are standardized and systematic in their application.

Functional job analysis requires job incumbents, supervisors, and job analysts to write task statements that detail what is actually done by the incumbent on the job. Much emphasis is placed on adequately specifying these task statements. Each statement should answer five basic questions: Who? Performs what action? To accomplish what? With what tools? Upon what instructions? (Gatewood and Feild, 1994).

Once tasks are adequately defined, the job analyst or the incumbent rates task complexity, using worker-oriented scales. These scales provide levels of complexity for the tasks in three distinct areas: (1) *data,* the way the worker deals with information, ideas, or facts; (2) *people,* how the worker interacts with

Exhibit 16.1. Examples of PAQ Items.

D6. Types of Job-required Personal Contact

Importance to This Job

0 Does not apply
1 Very minor
2 Low
3 Intermediate
4 High
5 Extreme

This section lists types of individuals with whom the worker must have personal contact in order to perform the job.

Using the response scale at the left, indicate the importance of contact with each of the types of individuals listed below. Consider personal contact with persons both inside and outside the organization.

113. Executives/officials
E.g., corporation vice presidents, government administrators, or plant superintendents

114. Middle management/staff personnel

115. Supervisors
E.g., personnel who have immediate responsibility for a work group, e.g., first-level supervisors or some office managers

116. Professional personnel
E.g., doctors, lawyers, scientists, engineers, professors, teachers, or consultants

117. Semiprofessional personnel
E.g., technicians, drafters, designers, photographers, surveyors, and others engaged in activities requiring fairly extensive education or practical experience but which typically involve a more restricted area of operation than that of professional personnel

118. Clerical personnel
E.g., office workers, word processors, clerks, bookkeepers, receptionists, secretaries

119. Manual and service workers
E.g., skilled, semiskilled, or unskilled workers or those in agricultural, fishing, forestry, or service

120. Sales personnel

121. Buyers
I.e., purchasing agents, not public customers

122. Public customers
E.g., customers in stores or restaurants

123. The public
E.g., the public as contacted by park attendants or police officers (*Do not* include customers or persons in other categories.)

124. Students/trainees/etc.

125. Clients/patients/counselees

126. Special interest groups
E.g., stockholders, lobbyists, fraternal organizations, property owners, government and regulatory inspectors and officials, or charities

127. Other individuals
Include other types of persons not described by items 113–126 (e.g., applicants, retirees, or former employees)

coworkers, clients, or customers; and (3) *things,* the level of involvement with machines, tools, and equipment. Here are the various levels within the categories:

Data

    0. Synthesizing

    1. Coordinating

    2. Analyzing

    3. Compiling

    4. Computing

    5. Copying

    6. Comparing

People

    0. Mentoring

    1. Negotiating

    2. Instructing

    3. Supervising

    4. Diverting

    5. Persuading

    6. Speaking/signaling

    7. Serving

    8. Taking instructions

    9. Helping

Things

    0. Setting up

    1. Precision working

    2. Operating/controlling

    3. Driving/operating

    4. Manipulating

    5. Tending

    6. Feeding/offbearing

    7. Handling

In addition to specifying complexity levels for the tasks across these three broad categories, the job analyst or the incumbent must determine the extent to which a job deals in data, people, and things. A percentage is assigned to each area, and the three percentages must total 100. For example, the job of a social worker might be 35 percent data, 60 percent people, and 5 percent things. Comparing these percentages to the levels of complexity in each area suggests overall job complexity.

Fleishman Job Analysis Survey

The Fleishman Job Analysis Survey (F-JAS) is based on years of research by E. A. Fleishman. Its primary focus is on worker requirements once the job duties or tasks have been defined. That is, it is used to link tasks with worker characteristics for content validation purposes. The worker specifications consist of seventy-two abilities categorized into six groups: cognitive, psychomotor, physical, sensory/perceptual, interactive/social, and knowledge/skills. Behaviorally anchored rating scales (BARS) are used to link the job duties with the abilities and to make ratings based on the level of each ability needed to perform the job duty.

This method is fairly straightforward. It has the advantage of being usable by job incumbents or job analysts. It is particularly useful after a basic task analysis has been performed. It is also useful in identifying potential selection instruments to measure applicants for the various abilities identified as important.

Job Components Inventory

The Job Components Inventory (JCI) (Banks, 1988) is a general questionnaire that was developed in England with several purposes and uses in mind. First, it was for use primarily in lower-level and entry-level jobs. Second, it was constructed to be easily administered and not necessarily by only trained job analysts. Third, it was to be comprehensive but not too time consuming. And fourth, it was to be applicable to a wide range of jobs. It was designed for uses in curriculum assessment and development, career education, skill profiling and assessment, design of education and training content, and vocational guidance and placement. As you can see, all of the primary uses deal with vocational training of some kind.

The instrument itself contains four hundred questions covering five basic categories: tools and equipment, perceptual and physical requirements, mathematical requirements, communication requirements, and decision making and responsibility. To date there is not a wealth of research in the literature addressing various aspects of its use. It does, however, seem to distinguish reliably between different types of jobs.

Task Analysis

The final method to be discussed is the *task analysis* approach. The primary focus in this method is on the tasks that the worker performs on the job. As in some of the other approaches, a heavy emphasis is placed on ensuring that the task statements are detailed and specific in their description of the performance requirements. They contain action verbs that describe what actions are performed on the job. The task statements are then organized using general job duties as headings or categories. The number of tasks and job duties varies with job complexity but might number as many as two hundred tasks under fifteen job duties. Here, for example, is an abbreviated list of tasks under just two of the headings that might be used for the job of police lieutenant.

Criminal Investigation, Detection, and Follow-Up

- Respond to major crime scenes
- Protect, secure, and process crime scene
- Determine appropriate investigative procedures, such as requesting assistance from specialists
- Review legal statutes, codes, case decisions, and other reference material to assist in investigation preparation
- Identify and locate victims, witnesses, informants, and/or suspects
- Assist other law enforcement agencies in conducting investigations
- Assist with interrogation of suspects and record information
- Interview witnesses, informants, and victims
- Talk to victim of crime to explain investigative procedures and provide comfort
- Determine elements of a crime
- Use records to gain information
- Collect and mark physical evidence
- Ensure that lab analysis of evidence is secured
- Ensure chain of custody of evidence
- Recover stolen and lost property
- Complete or review reports

Arrest, Search, and Seizure

- Review information needed for search or arrest warrant
- Secure arrest warrants
- Determine the existence of probable cause for arrest or search purposes
- Take weapon from armed suspect
- Participate in planning and coordinating of raids
- Actively participate in execution of raids
- Arrest individuals for offenses committed in presence (that is, warrant-less arrest)
- Advise juvenile's parents of child's detainment and reason for detainment

- Search the body and clothing of persons in custody
- Execute search warrants
- Execute arrest warrants
- Apprehend suspects
- Inform suspect of charges and legal rights
- Search individuals and immediate area to locate weapons and/or contraband for protection of officers

Task statements can be developed in a number of different ways. They can be derived from interviewing, observing, and holding panel meetings with job incumbents. Work diaries maintained by incumbents are also a good source for task statement information, as is archival information. When conducting a task analysis, I like to use all of these methods as a way to gather basic information about the job in question. Usually, job analysts will also interview supervisors of the target position. By employing these methods, the analyst uses the people who perform the job as the job experts or subject matter experts. Once again, nobody knows the job better than the people who perform it day in and day out. By involving these people, the analyst also allows them to ask questions about the purpose of the study and what function within the organization it will serve. Obtaining involvement is crucial.

Once a basic task list is developed, it is a good idea to have a panel of job experts review the task statements for accuracy. At this point, tasks can be modified or added to the list. The purpose of this meeting is not to evaluate the items in terms of frequency or importance but rather to make sure that all tasks are covered. During this meeting the analyst can also obtain information on the knowledge and skill requirements for the job. Exhibit 16.2 contains a basic list of possible knowledge and skill requirements for police lieutenant. These general statements can form a basis for developing selection instruments or identifying areas for training.

After the tasks have been developed and reviewed by job experts, it is time to make task evaluations, based on several scales. Job incumbents and their supervisors generally provide these ratings. Typically, they will rate every task using two to three different scales. There are several different types of scales that can be used. The 1978 Uniform Guidelines for Employee Selection provide some direction for choosing the scales (Equal Employment Opportunity Commission, 1997). Generally, the scales should focus on frequency of task performance and on task criticality to the effective performance of the job. (Exhibit 16.3 gives an example of two such scales that might be used.) From these ratings, tasks that are determined by the incumbents not to be critical to performance are eliminated from the remaining task list. The tasks that are determined to be critical are then carried forward to the next stage of the process.

Exhibit 16.2. Knowledge and Skills for Police Lieutenant.

KNOWLEDGE AREAS

Legal Standards. This area includes state statutes, elements of crimes, state motor vehicle traffic violations, local ordinances, search and seizure, court procedures, warrants, laws regarding juveniles, rules of evidence, legal terms and definitions, case law, rights of the accused, U.S. Bill of Rights, interrogation, and civil liability.

Correct and Safe Use of Equipment. This area includes flashlights, firearms, handcuffs, batons, cameras, video equipment, crime scene kits and materials, radios, and vehicles (for example, take-home vehicles, prisoner transportation, and high-speed pursuits).

Crime Scene Search Concepts, Principles, Practices. This area includes organization of the crime scene investigation, dealing with typical crime scene problems, media relations, duties and responsibilities in crime scene investigation, infectious disease protection, types of evidence, crime scene search patterns, the chain of custody, crime scene sketching, crime scene photography, and use of video equipment to document the scene.

Physical Evidence. This area includes class versus individual characteristics; the identification, preservation, collection, packaging, marking, and transmittal of physical evidence, such as soil, fibers, impressions, residues, casting, glass, paint, cloth fragments and impressions, string, cord, rope, fingerprints, dental evidence, hair, blood, human secretions and excretions, firearms, tool marks, and questioned documents; and the laboratory conclusions that may be reached from examining such evidence (knowledge of the laboratory procedures themselves is not required).

Investigative Concepts, Principles, Methods, Procedures, and Practices for Specific Crimes. This area includes profiles of the offense, the victim, and the offender, arrest probabilities, investigative techniques, responding to the scene, tactical aspects of response, and rudimentary suggestions about prevention for the specific crime involved, such as a particular type of violent or property crime.

Modus Operandi of Criminals. This area includes information about how criminals operate in diverse violent and property crimes, such as home invasion; convenience store, taxi, and ATM robberies; carjackings; burglary; credit card fraud; stalking and domestic violence; criminal homicide and assaults; and sex crimes.

SKILL AREAS

Oral Communication. This skill involves expressing oneself orally through the use of clear, well-composed, and unambiguous statements. The quality of the speaking voice,

Exhibit 16.2. Knowledge and Skills for Police Lieutenant, cont'd.

use of facial and bodily gestures, and use of eye contact are part of the speaking component. The listening component of this dimension involves skill in picking out the most relevant aspects of what is being said by others, asking questions, giving feedback, and making demonstrable use of information gained by listening to others.

Observing and Recalling Facts, Details, Descriptions, and Related Materials. This skill involves the ability to identify and recall key elements of a situation, the importance of these elements, and their relationship to one another. It includes observing relevant details and accurately recording information.

Written Communication. This skill involves producing well-organized, logical, effective, and clearly written statements and/or orders.

Conflict Management. This skill involves sensing and correctly identifying disagreements or sources of friction among individuals or groups of individuals. Most important within this skill is the ability to objectively consider both sides of the conflict and offer reasonable alternatives or solutions. Following up with those involved to remain informed of the situation is also a key ingredient.

Making Timely Decisions. This skill involves the willingness and/or readiness to take action, or commit oneself to a course of action, and the willingness to accept responsibility for decisions made.

Making Decisions Based on Sound Logic. This skill involves integrating a wide variety of information, developing alternative courses of action, and making sound, logical decisions based on assumptions that reflect factual information.

Planning and Organizing Activities. This skill involves establishing a course of action for oneself and/or others in order to accomplish a mission or work assignment. It involves planning the proper assignments or personnel and the appropriate allocation of resources and the organization of such personnel and resources.

Analyzing Information. This skill involves understanding and making sense of information by breaking it apart into smaller components or by tracing the implications of the information step by step. It includes organizing the parts of a problem, situation, and the like in a systematic way; making systematic comparisons of different features or aspects; and identifying time sequences, causal relationships, or if-then relationships.

Exhibit 16.3. Frequency and Importance Scales.

FREQUENCY SCALE

I perform this task

5	=	About **every day** or more often.
4	=	About **once each week** or more often.
3	=	About **once each month.**
2	=	About **once every six months** or less.
1	=	About **once every year** or less.
0	=	This task **has not been required** in my assignments in the last twelve months.

IMPORTANCE OR CRITICALITY SCALE

This task is

5	=	**Critically important.** This task represents an essential function of my job and must always be performed well.
4	=	**Very important.** My performance cannot be considered successful unless this task is adequately performed.
3	=	**Moderately important.** The poor performance of this task on a few occasions will not affect my overall job performance. However, continued poor performance will not be accepted.
2	=	**Slightly important.** The poor performance of this task on most occasions will not affect my overall job performance.
1	=	**Of little or no importance.** My job could still be performed successfully even if I performed this task poorly.
0	=	**Not important.** I do not perform this task.

The next stage of the task analysis process is crucial to the effectiveness of the job analysis method. During this phase, incumbents and supervisors provide ratings that link critical tasks required for the job and the more general knowledge and skill requirements. Based on a series of statistical tests of these ratings, weights can be developed for the knowledge and skill requirements of the job. The knowledge areas can then form the basis of written examinations. And the skills can then be further analyzed to form dimensions that can be measured in performance tests such as assessment centers.

The task analysis approach has several advantages and disadvantages. The advantages are that the method focuses on specifics of a particular job. There is no translation required from a generic off-the-shelf instrument to the job being analyzed. The primary downside of this approach is the time required to complete the analysis. This includes the time of both the job analyst and the job experts needed to provide input in the process.

LEGAL VIEWS OF JOB ANALYSIS

The need to conduct job analyses is legally recognized. The evidence is contained in the many references to job analysis in the Uniform Guidelines for Employee Selection Procedures (Equal Opportunity Commission, 1997) and the many court cases in which job analysis has played a part.

The uniform guidelines have been adopted by five federal agencies: the Equal Employment Opportunity Commission, Office of Personnel Management, Department of Labor, Department of Justice, and Department of Treasury. Each agency can trace its adoption of the guidelines to one or more statutory provisions, but mainly Title VII of the Civil Rights Act of 1964 (Sparks, 1988). Levine (1983) has identified portions of the guidelines that address the issue of job analysis as it relates to test validation. These portions are detailed in Exhibit 16.4. The common thread throughout the document is the need for a demonstrated relationship between a test and the requirements of the job for which the test is being used.

A second source that demonstrates the need for job analysis is the various court cases where job analysis has been an issue. Thompson and Thompson (1982) have reviewed selected court cases in an effort to determine the criteria used by the courts in their assessment of job analyses in relation to the development and validation of selection tests. A review of cases where job analysis procedures were rejected or accepted by the courts shows the characteristics a job analysis procedure needed to withstand a court's legal scrutiny. First, a job analysis must be performed. Second, it must be on the exact job for which the selection device is to be used. Third, the job analysis must be reduced to written form, and the procedure used to conduct the analysis must be described. Fourth, data should be collected from up-to-date sources. This step might include interviews with supervisors and incumbents, questionnaires, training manuals, and observations of the job. Also, a large enough sample of data to be meaningful should be collected. Finally, tasks, duties, and activities must be identified and included in the study. The most important of these should be included on the test or selection instrument. These criteria should be obvious to the serious job analyst.

CONCLUSION

In this chapter I have shown you only the tip of the iceberg when it comes to job analysis. My hope is that this review has piqued your interest in the topic and that you will further investigate this most important area to human resource management. I have emphasized that importance by discussing various functions job analysis can serve. These include some common uses, like supporting selection and training, and some less common ones, like providing a basis for

Exhibit 16.4. Selected Excerpts from the Uniform Guidelines on Employee Selection Procedures (1978).

1607.5 General standards for validity studies

A. *Acceptable types of utility studies.* For the purpose of satisfying these guidelines, users may rely upon criterion-related validity studies, content validity studies or construct validity studies. . . .

B. *Criterion-related, content, and construct validity.* Evidence of the validity of a test or other selection procedure by a criterion-related validity study should consist of empirical data demonstrating that the selection procedure is predictive of or significantly correlated with *important elements of job performance*. . . . Evidence of the validity of a test or other selection procedure by a content validity study should consist of data showing that the content of the selection procedure is *representative of important aspects of performance on the job*. . . . Evidence of the validity of a test or other selection procedure through a construct validity study should consist of data showing that the procedure measures the degree to which candidates have identifiable characteristics which have been determined to be *important in successful performance in the job for which the candidates are to be evaluated*. . . .

1607.6 Use of selection procedures which have not been validated . . .

B. *Where validity studies . . . cannot be performed* . . . the user should utilize selection procedures which are as *job related as possible* and which will minimize or eliminate adverse impact. . . .

1607.7 Use of other validity studies . . .

B. *Use of criterion-related validity evidence from other sources.* Criterion-related validity studies conducted by one test user . . . will be considered acceptable for use by another user when . . . the incumbents in the user's job and the incumbents in the job or group of jobs on which the validity study was conducted *perform substantially the same major work behaviors, as shown by appropriate job analyses* both on the job or group of jobs on which the validity study was performed and on the job for which the selection procedure is to be used. . . .

1607.14 Technical standards for validity studies

A. *Validity studies should be based on a review of information about the job.* . . . The review should include a job analysis. . . . Any method of job analysis may be used if it provides the information required for the specific validation strategy used. . . .

B. *Technical standards for criterion-related validity studies.* . . .

    (2) *Analysis of the job.* There should be a review of job information to determine measures of work behavior(s) or performance that are relevant to the job or group of jobs in question. These measures or criteria are relevant to the extent that they represent critical or important job duties, work behaviors, or work outcomes as developed from the review of job information. . . .

Exhibit 16.4. Selected Excerpts from the Uniform Guidelines on Employee Selection Procedures (1978), cont'd.

C. *Technical standards for content validity studies....*

(2) *Job analysis for content validity.* There should be a job analysis which includes an analysis of the important work behavior(s) required for successful performance and their relative importance.... Any job analysis should focus on the work behavior(s) and the tasks associated with them....

D. *Technical standards for construct validity studies....*

(2) *Job analysis for construct validity.* There should be a job analysis. This job analysis should show the work behavior(s) required for successful performance of the job, or the group of jobs being studied, the critical or important work behavior(s) in the job or group of jobs being studied, and an identification of the construct(s) believed to underlie successful performance of these critical or important work behaviors in the job or jobs in question....

(4) *Use of construct validity studies without new criterion-related evidence*— (a) Standards for use.... [T]he Federal Agencies will accept a claim of construct validity without a criterion-related study ... only when the selection procedure has been used elsewhere in a situation in which a criterion-related study has been conducted....

Note: Emphasis in body of text added to underscore role of job analysis.

Source: Code of Federal Regulations, vol. 29, sec. 1607.

vocational guidance and realistic job previews. To some extent the goals you want to reach by gathering the information will determine the method that you employ.

I also reviewed various ways a job analyst might go about gathering information, through observations, interviews, questionnaires, diaries, and archival data. Each way has its own advantages and disadvantages. Usually a combination of information-gathering techniques is used. The brief introduction to some of the more common professionally developed job analysis techniques included, among others, the Position Analysis Questionnaire, critical incident technique, job elements method, Fleishman Job Analysis Survey, and task analysis.

Finally, I presented a brief discussion of important legal issues regarding the process of job analysis. They derive from the EEOC's Uniform Guidelines on Employee Selection Procedures and from court cases, and they emphasize the fact that job analysis must be taken seriously and conducting one must be a careful and thoughtful process. A well-prepared job analysis can often be an agency's first line of defense in justifying its actions.

Many professionals view job analysis as a tedious and boring step before the other fun things can be accomplished. I have always thought, "How can something be boring when it potentially supports and directs so many areas of the human resources function?"

References

Aamodt, M. G. *Applied Industrial/Organizational Psychology.* Pacific Grove, Calif.: Brooks/Cole, 1996.

Americans with Disabilities Act. 1990. *U.S. Code,* vol. 42, sec. 12101 et seq.

Arvey, R. D., and Begalla, M. E. "Analyzing the Job of Homemaker Using the Position Analysis Questionnaire (PAQ)." *Journal of Applied Psychology,* 1975, *60,* 513–517.

Banks, M. H. "Job Components Inventory." In S. Gael (ed.), *The Job Analysis Handbook for Business, Industry, and Government.* New York: Wiley, 1988.

Bell, C. G. "The Americans with Disabilities Act and Injured Workers." In S. M. Bruyère and J. O'Keeffe (eds.), *Implications of the Americans with Disabilities Act for Psychology.* New York: Springer, 1994.

Bownas, D. A., and Bernardin, H. J. "Critical Incident Technique." In S. Gael (ed.), *The Job Analysis Handbook for Business, Industry, and Government.* New York: Wiley, 1988.

Civil Rights Act. 1964. *U.S. Code,* vol. 42, sec. 1981 et seq. (Title VII at 2000e.)

Dawis, R. V., and Lofquist, L. H. "Vocational Guidance and Rehabilitation Counseling." In S. Gael (ed.), *The Job Analysis Handbook for Business, Industry, and Government.* New York: Wiley, 1988.

Equal Employment Opportunity Commission. *Technical Assistance Manual on the Employment Provisions (Title I) of the ADA.* Washington, D.C.: Equal Employment Opportunity Commission, 1992.

Equal Employment Opportunity Commission. *Uniform Guidelines on Employee Selection Procedures. Code of Federal Regulations,* 1997, vol. 29, sec. 1607. (Originally issued 1978.)

Flanagan, J. C. "The Critical Incident Technique." *Psychological Bulletin,* 1954, *51,* 327–358.

Gael, S. (ed.). *The Job Analysis Handbook for Business, Industry, and Government.* New York: Wiley, 1988.

Gatewood, R. D., and Feild, H. S. *Human Resource Selection.* (3rd ed.) Orlando, Fla.: Dryden, 1994.

Levine, E. L. *Everything You Always Wanted to Know About Job Analysis.* Tampa, Fla.: Mariner, 1983.

Lopez, F. M. "Threshold Traits Analysis System." In S. Gael (ed.), *The Job Analysis Handbook for Business, Industry, and Government.* New York: Wiley, 1988.

McCormick, E. J. "Job and Task Analysis." In M. D. Dunnette (ed.), *Handbook of Industrial and Organizational Psychology.* Skokie, Ill.: Rand McNally, 1976.

McCormick, E. J., Jeanneret, P. R., and Mecham, R. C. "A Study of Job Characteristics and Job Dimensions as Based on the Position Analysis Questionnaire (PAQ)." *Journal of Applied Psychology,* 1972, *56,* 347–368.

McCormick, E. J., Jeanneret, P. R., and Mecham, R. C. *Position Analysis Questionnaire. Form C, 6–89.* Palo Alto, Calif.: Consulting Psychologists Press, 1989. (Originally published 1969.)

Premack, S. L., and Wanous, J. P. "A Meta-Analysis of Realistic Job Preview Experiments." *Journal of Applied Psychology,* 1985, *70,* 706–719.

Primoff, E. S. *How to Prepare and Conduct Job Element Examinations.* Washington, D.C.: U.S. Civil Service Commission, 1975.

Sparks, C. P. "Legal Basis for Job Analysis." In S. Gael (ed.), *The Job Analysis Handbook for Business, Industry, and Government.* New York: Wiley, 1988.

Thompson, D. E., and Thompson, T. A. "Court Standards for Job Analysis in Test Validation." *Personnel Psychology,* 1982, *35,* 865–874.

U.S. Department of Labor. *Dictionary of Occupational Titles.* Washington, D.C.: U.S. Government Printing Office, 1991.

CHAPTER SEVENTEEN

A Practical Guide
to Conducting Assessment Centers

Charles R. Swanson

I n the considerable body of literature concerning assessment centers, there is
very little published research that describes how to actually conduct them.
Perhaps the main reason for this omission is that much of the assessment
center literature is written by researchers whose interests are elsewhere. A secondary reason is that the ability to provide nuts-and-bolts information is the result of extensive assessment center experience. Consultants who make their
living providing assessment center services are generally reticent to freely reveal their hard-earned insights and methods. The purpose of this chapter is to
provide a practical understanding of assessment centers and to address a gap
in the literature by presenting hands-on information.

To provide a specific context, all the examples in this chapter concern a municipal police department, the "Harborville Police Department." Similarly, although assessment centers are used for a variety of personnel functions, such
as hiring (Coulton and Feild, 1995; Pynes, 1992), promotion, and management
development, the examples all concern an assessment center used to evaluate
sergeants competing for promotion to the rank of lieutenant.

DEFINITION OF ASSESSMENT CENTER

An *assessment center* is both a process and a place. In this chapter's assessment
center example, the *process* involves evaluating the behavior of candidates
(sergeants) for a specific purpose (promotion) by providing them with multiple

independent opportunities (simulations or exercises) to demonstrate abilities and by monitoring them with multiple trained evaluators (assessors), whose individual judgments are pooled to form an overall evaluation of the extent to which the candidates have the skills necessary to succeed as police lieutenants.

As a *place,* the assessment center may occupy a physical site totally dedicated to conducting such centers, or the site may be selected as needed and may be a community college, a hotel, a civic center, a public library's meeting rooms, or other facilities at various times. The choice of place must be thought through carefully. To some extent, members of an organization use the site to gauge the importance that the employer places on the process. Dissatisfaction with the setting can create dissatisfaction with the process.

The fact that an assessment center is both a process and a place is something that must be carefully explained to those unfamiliar with the concept. Even an experienced consultant can overlook this point when explaining assessment centers to the uninitiated.

WHY USE AN ASSESSMENT CENTER?

More and more organizations are using assessment centers because

- Assessment centers can generally more accurately predict individuals' successful performance as supervisors and managers than can alternate methods.

- Participation in assessment centers, either as assessors or assessees, is a very valuable career development experience.

- Managers accept the results of assessment centers due to their rational, organized approach and the way the assessment exercises simulate an organization's supervisory and management challenges.

- Participants accept the results of assessment centers due to their face validity and the fair manner in which each participant is given the opportunity to demonstrate his or her abilities.

- Assessment centers have been shown to be equally fair and accurate in predicting the supervisory and management potential of EEOC protected group members and of those not so protected.

- Employers have successfully defended the use of assessment centers in a number of court challenges (Mendenhall, 1992). In fact, assessment centers have been mandated in a number of consent decrees, as a part of efforts to overcome the effects of past discriminatory practices.

- Assessment centers can aid in analyzing the abilities of supervisory and management personnel for the specific purpose of pinpointing areas of strengths and weaknesses. This information can then be used in making individual and organizationwide recommendations for specialized training.

- Assessment centers concentrate on the evaluation of observed behavior, and managers who serve as assessors often report an increased ability subsequently to assess the performance of their own subordinates and peers.

ASSESSMENT PROCESS CRITERIA

An assessment center is an entire process of evaluating the behavior of an individual. That process includes standardized and objective forms of evaluation that taken together, satisfy the seven criteria discussed in the following sections.

- Use multiple assessment methods
- Use multiple assessors
- Base judgments on pooled data
- Make an overall evaluation of behavior
- Use simulations (exercises)
- Require job analysis
- Assess candidate abilities related to job analysis

Use Multiple Assessment Methods

The first criterion is that the process must use multiple simulations or exercises. It is imperative that more than one simulation be used, as the assessment center process is driven by repeated independent observations by assessors.

Use Multiple Assessors

The second criterion is that multiple assessors must be used. These assessors must receive training prior to participating in the assessment center, and this training should be sufficient to enable them to intelligently evaluate the behaviors measured. *Sufficient* training will vary from one situation to another because it is a function of many factors, including

- The amount of experience an individual has as an assessor
- The recency of an individual's past participation as an assessor
- The content and extent of prior assessor training
- The methods, qualifications, and expertise of the assessment center trainer

- The assessment center experience of other members of the assessment staff

- The use of appropriately skilled professionals, such as licensed psychologists, as assessors

It is difficult to imagine assessors functioning effectively with only a one- or two-hour orientation. However, the prior training and experience of assessors; the model on which the assessment center is based; the types of assessor support, such as reference materials and well-designed forms provided by assessment center staff; the numbers and types of exercises used; the methods used to train assessors; and other logically related factors all produce variability in the appropriate length of assessor training programs. The essential goal of assessor training is attaining accurate assessor judgments (Kohlhepp, 1992).

Assessor training should include opportunities to observe mock versions of different performance levels for the exercise(s) that assessors will be evaluating. The training should also provide the assessors with an opportunity to practice all of the behaviors they will use with candidates. These include note taking, using checklists, assigning numerical values from a behaviorally anchored rating scale,[1] and participating in the consensus meeting. The use of checklists can reduce assessor training time, reduce the cognitive demands on assessors, and ensure that each candidate is evaluated on precisely the same criteria. The exercise developer prepares a checklist of items the candidate should do under each dimension being measured in the exercise. The task of the assessor, then, is to determine to what degree the candidate has satisfied each item. Writing the checklist requires good judgment. If items are written too precisely, ratings may be lowered. Conversely, if they are written too broadly, assessors will have difficulty in assigning meaning to them. The design of the exercise must be tailored with the use of the checklist in mind.

One very effective way to train assessors is to make videotapes of mock enactments prior to the time of the training. Usually, three to six mock enactments are sufficient. The next step is to have experienced members of the assessment center staff evaluate the mock performances. Their notes about each mock candidate's behaviors, their behavioral checklists, and their ratings can then be used to help "calibrate" the actual assessors during training. After showing the first mock enactment during training, allow the assessors to complete their work without having to rigorously follow any time limits. Thereafter, have them work until they can comfortably complete all assessor tasks within the time allowed. Each time the assessors complete their evaluation of a mock enactment, their ratings should be compared with those of the assessment center staff, and they should be given feedback identifying discrepancies and describing how to correct them. The final step in the training is to have the assessors acknowledge that they feel well prepared to fulfill their duties. If they cannot do so, additional training, finding a replacement, or even postponing the assessment center will be necessary. Signs that suggest that assessors are not properly trained include making relatively few behavioral observation notes, using personal judgments in the notes (for example, "This candidate just isn't Lieutenant material," or, "He just doesn't get it") and making notes that are inferences (for example, "She is a very charismatic leader") as opposed to notes that reflect the actual behaviors displayed by the candidate (for example, "She smiled and nodded her head when the role-player suggested a surveillance be placed on the defendant's place of business and then said, 'That's a great suggestion. I appreciate your initiative in coming up with this idea. Write a one-page proposal, and if we can agree on the details, we'll implement it starting tomorrow'").

Base Judgments on Pooled Data

The third criterion is that judgments resulting in an outcome (for example, a recommendation for promotion or for specific training or development) must be based on pooled or integrated information from assessors and techniques. Assessment centers typically employ one of two models for pooling data: assessment council method or mechanical/mathematical method. Although they are, strictly speaking, just methods of pooling data, they have each become associated with different assessment center practices.

The *assessment council* is the traditional assessment center method. This method typically offers five to eight exercises, often of short duration (for example, two to five minutes) and usually having a short candidate preparation period (for example, five minutes). The assessors work in pairs whose composition is systematically rotated, and this work culminates in the assessment council. After the assessors have observed all the candidates in all exercises, they convene in the council to pool their data. Initially, they record candidate scores based on each candidate's behavior in the various exercises. Once these scores are entered, the assessors share information from the notes they made while observing each candidate in different exercises. Their task at this point is to judgmentally pool or integrate all relevant information about each candidate in order to come up with the single number for each dimension that most closely characterizes the candidate's behavior with respect to that dimension. The assessors then take the data derived from their council discussion of each candidate and write feedback reports that are subsequently distributed to each candidate. The report-writing process is labor intensive and time consuming. The use of the assessment council is perhaps best suited to situations in which the reports will be used to create individually tailored development activities for candidates or high-ranking positions that do not receive close supervision.

In contrast the most common *mechanical/mathematical* method usually employs three assessors for each exercise. In this method, assessors specialize in a single exercise. Because less training time is required due to this specialization, three to four longer exercises (fifteen to forty-five minutes) are typically used, and they require longer preparation periods (twenty- to forty-five minutes). The data in this model are pooled through a consensus discussion for each exercise and are then pooled mathematically across exercises. There is some evidence that holding consensus discussions at the exercise level to generate dimension ratings and then using mathematical pooling of the dimension ratings across exercises is the most accurate method of making an overall assessment (Karl and Wexley, 1989).

Despite their variations, the methods have some similarities. In-basket exercises for both the assessment council and mathematical pooling models tend to run one to two hours and may be conducted in the traditional mode or as a multiple-choice test. In both models the preparation time for the impromptu speech is similar, ranging from one to five minutes. They both use the protocol that assessors' scores within an exercise must be within one point of each other. Finally, the assessment council and mathematical pooling models share a core technology: candidates are independently evaluated on job-relevant behaviors in different exercises by trained assessors. The limited research comparing the results obtained by using these two models indicates no significant differences in the numbers produced (Pynes and Bernadin, 1992). The most important distinction between the two methods is that the assessment council produces a greater amount of specific information about candidates.

Make an Overall Evaluation of Behavior

The fourth criterion requires that an overall evaluation of behavior be made by the assessors at a separate time from observation of behavior. This means that the evaluation is made sometime after the candidate has completed the exercise and left the room. This gives assessors time to condense the information and make judgments regarding each candidate's abilities without feeling rushed for time.

Use Simulation Exercises

A fifth requirement of assessment centers is the use of simulation exercises. A simulation is an exercise or technique designed to elicit behaviors related to dimensions of on-the-job performance. It requires the participant to respond behaviorally to situational stimuli. Examples of simulations include role-play exercises, mock press conferences, in-basket exercises, and fact-finding exercises. Simulation exercises are developed to measure a variety of predetermined behaviors and should be pretested to ensure that they provide reliable, objective, and relevant behavioral information for the organization in question. Pretesting often involves a review of the exercises and an evaluation of the checklists, which may be performed by an expert committee of three to five persons presently performing the job, a similar committee of people holding some higher-level position in the organization, or a single person with expert knowledge. To some extent the choice of people to do the pretesting will be influenced by department size and the stance that the department head takes on excluding agency personnel from any direct exposure to the exercises for reasons of test security.

It is important that agencies not overlook opportunities to use the assessment center process and especially simulation exercises to reinforce organizational change. One particular police agency had trained all its personnel on two major changes it was implementing: accreditation and community-oriented policing. The chief directed the assessment center director to come up with simulation exercises for candidates for police lieutenant that emphasized these changes. Thus, to briefly illustrate, the oral presentation involved a newly appointed precinct commander going before local merchants—role-played by the assessors—to address the merchants' concerns. These concerns were reflected in the packet of materials the candidates were given to review for forty-five minutes prior to the meeting. This packet included correspondence, crime analysis reports, newspaper articles, intelligence reports, and other documents. To do well on this exercise, candidates had to use a specific model of policing espoused in the community-oriented policing curriculum.

Exhibit 17.1 displays at length an exercise used in this department. It simulates a supervisor conducting a roll-call training session in the Harborville Police Department. Each candidate was asked to review a series of news articles and to identify actions deviating from the department's high-speed pursuit policy. Not shown in the exhibit but distributed to the candidates with the exercise was a copy of the department's actual policy on such pursuits.

Require Job Analysis

The sixth essential assessment center characteristic is that the dimensions (skills, abilities, or behaviors) evaluated be determined by an analysis of relevant job behaviors. In addition, having too many dimensions increases the cognitive demands made on assessors, and having too few may not capture important skills needed for the job. Although there is no "right" number of dimensions, their number should be carefully evaluated based on job analysis results.

Assess Candidate Abilities Related to Job Analysis

The seventh criterion requires that the techniques used in the assessment center be designed to provide information that is used in evaluating the dimensions, attributes, or qualities previously determined by the job analysis. Basically, the exercises should give the candidates ample opportunity to demonstrate their skills in the various dimensional areas. For example, if the assessors are asked to evaluate the candidates' written communication skills, then the exercises must require the candidates to write and the assessors must see this demonstration.

Exhibit 17.1. Harborville Police Department
1998 Lieutenants' Assessment Center Roll-Call Training Exercise.

Roll Call Training Exercise Packing List

Page	Description	Initials
1 & 2	Instructions to candidates	
3	Interoffice communication from Lt. T. C. Bowen	
4	Copy of newspaper article dated April 11, 1998	
5	Copy of newspaper article dated April 1, 1998	
6	Copy of newspaper article dated March 21, 1998	

I have checked the packet of information for this exercise. My initials in the right-hand column above certify the receipt of all of the pages listed.

_____   _____
Candidate Signature and   Assessment Center Representative
Candidate Number   Signature

Date: _____

ROLL CALL TRAINING EXERCISE
HARBORVILLE POLICE DEPARTMENT
1998 LIEUTENANTS' ASSESSMENT CENTER

INSTRUCTIONS TO CANDIDATES

General Scenario

In this exercise you take the role of Lieutenant C. Knox. You are assigned to Patrol Services. "Today" is April 14, 1998.

Your boss is Capt. T. C. Bowen. She is concerned about some recent events concerning pursuits. These events have been reported in the newspaper. Capt. Bowen wants you to study the attached articles about these events. Then she wants you to make a roll-call training presentation. The purpose of the presentation is to identify the actions reported that violate the HPD's pursuit policy. You are not to teach the entire policy.

**Exhibit 17.1. Harborville Police Department
1998 Lieutenants' Assessment Center Roll-Call Training Exercise, cont'd.**

You have forty-five (45) minutes to prepare for the exercise. You have a maximum of fifteen (15) minutes to make your presentation. For the purpose of the exercise, you are to present the material to the assessors in the same manner that you would to an actual group of officers at roll call. You should anticipate that the assessors may have questions regarding your presentation. However, you may *not* ask the assessors questions. Assume that all other roll-call duties have been completed before your training presentation. Your only concern for this exercise is to provide up to fifteen (15) minutes of the type of training required by the instructions for this exercise.

Things to Remember

1. You are Lieutenant C. Knox.

2. "Today" is April 14, 1998.

3. You have forty-five (45) minutes to prepare for the exercise.

4. You have a maximum of fifteen (15) minutes to make your presentation. None of your evaluation will be based on how much time you use. It is based on what you accomplish during the time you use.

5. You are to present the material as though the assessors are a group of officers at roll call.

6. The assessors may ask you questions.

7. You may *not* ask the assessors questions.

8. Assume that all other roll-call duties have been completed. Your assignment is to provide the type of training required by the instructions for this exercise.

9. You may write on all pages in this packet of information that you have been given.

10. You are allowed to take the packet of information with you while you complete the exercise.

11. You may make notes and take them into the exercise with you. You may refer to these notes and the materials in the packet of information while making your presentation.

12. All materials must be turned in at the completion of the exercise. This includes the packet of information that you were given, any notes that you made, and so forth.

13. You are *not* to discuss the contents of this exercise with anyone, except assessment center administrators and the assessors, before 5:00 P.M., April 18, 1998.

Exhibit 17.1. Harborville Police Department
1998 Lieutenants' Assessment Center Roll-Call Training Exercise, cont'd.

HARBORVILLE POLICE DEPARTMENT
INTEROFFICE COMMUNICATION

DATE: 14 April 1998
TO: Lieutenant C. Knox
FROM: Captain T. C. Bowen
SUBJECT: Pursuit of Motor Vehicles

Recent events show that some of our officers don't know or don't follow our pursuit policy. In recent weeks, there were three highly publicized pursuit events. In each of them mistakes were made. These mistakes are very embarrassing. Also, they leave us open to civil suits. Such mistakes cannot be tolerated. It is our duty to make sure that officers know and follow HPD policies.

I want you to study the three newspaper articles that are attached. In each article, you are to identify each specific violation or violations of our pursuit policy. Then, use all of these violations as illustrations in a roll-call training presentation. You are to be very specific about what mistakes were made. You are not to teach our entire pursuit policy. Teach only the portions that are related to violations of our policy as illustrated by the content of the three articles.

NEWSPAPER ARTICLES

Harborville Times
April 11, 1998

High-Speed Juvenile Escapes Police

Officer Kevin Williams was injured last night around 2 A.M. while chasing a juvenile in a 1996 Dodge Stealth. The chase reached speeds of 105 mph. It left the city and went into Pool County. It was there that Williams's car crashed into a telephone pole.

The driver of the vehicle, whom Williams knew personally and recognized, refused to stop. Williams's attempted stop was based on an outstanding warrant for a misdemeanor theft charge. Williams lost control of the police car due to the high speed and his lack of familiarity with that area of Pool County. The juvenile remains at large.

The HPD refused to comment on the incident until an investigation could be completed. However, the 911 supervisor stated that "there never was any radio traffic about a pursuit or a pursuit into the county. The first I heard about it was when a civilian with a car phone notified us of it."

Officer Williams remains in stable but critical condition at the Southeast Medical Center. *Harborville Times* reporter Sherri Hutt, riding with Williams on Police Chief Jack Sidmore's authorization, was shaken but not injured. She described the event as "enough fun for a lifetime."

**Exhibit 17.1. Harborville Police Department
1998 Lieutenants' Assessment Center Roll-Call Training Exercise, cont'd.**

Harborville Times
April 1, 1998

Fleeing Driver Nabbed at Roadblock

HPD Officer Carl Jones tried to stop a car for speeding at 4:00 A.M. yesterday on the Intercoastal Highway. That action unintentionally triggered a pursuit. It ended only when another HPD officer grabbed a tractor-trailer rig and set up a roadblock.

The speeds, according to Jones, "never got above 70 miles per hour." "But," he continued, "on narrow residential streets that's scary." Standing nearby, Fred Jackson, the HPD officer who joined the chase on his own initiative, nodded solemnly in agreement. Jackson noted that "even when I rammed the fleeing car with my patrol car, it just kept going."

The pursuit ended when HPD Officer Ben Swift commandeered a tractor-trailer. He used it and his police car to block off the road. The driver, Shirley Giddings of Bridgeport, Connecticut, hit Swift's car at the roadblock. Swift said "the impact was only at about 15 to 20 miles per hour. But without my seat belt on I got bounced around the inside of my car pretty good. I just wanted to be ready to continue the pursuit if she somehow got through the roadblock."

Chief Jack Sidmore declined comment about the incident.

Harborville Times
March 21, 1998

Rain and Traffic Hamper Police Pursuit

In what WTBS meteorologist Cindy Keller called "the most severe rain and lightning storm to ever strike this part of the coast," the HPD chased a car in heavy morning traffic across the median of Highway 17 in front of the Holiday Inn. The chase went north in the southbound lanes for about one-half of a mile. The fleeing car then cut back across the median into the correct lanes.

The vehicle apparently had no taillights. "It started to run when I hit the blue lights," Officer Jimmy Devine reported. The car was able to elude the police due to the weather and the heavy early morning commuter traffic.

PRACTICAL STEPS IN CONDUCTING ASSESSMENT CENTERS

Set the Assessment Center Schedule of Events

Police promotion rosters typically have lives of one to two years. New promotion rosters may be established according to a schedule or just on demand, when a vacancy is reasonably foreseen. In either case the first step is to examine the existing job analysis report for reliability. In the Harborville example, this step would mean convening a representative group of lieutenants, an expert panel, to review the existing job analysis report and to determine if it still accurately described the job (see Chapter Sixteen). The names of the panel members and the panel findings should be documented.

Assuming that the job analysis is found to be accurate, a date can be set for the assessment center. Civil service rules, union contract provisions, merit system regulations, department policies, labor contracts, and other sources may control how far in advance the assessment center needs to be announced. In any case, that announcement must not be made until a calender of events, much like an annual budget development calender, has been drawn up. This calendar is particularly important when the assessment center site is selected on an ad hoc basis each time.

Walk the Space and Evaluate It

If you are the assessment center director, never accept any space for an assessment center until you have personally walked through it or an experienced member of your staff has done so. This rule holds true even when you have used the space previously. For example, if you have used a particular hotel before, you may be tempted to accept its representation that "nothing has changed." However, even though the internal space might not have changed, a construction company might be noisily erecting a new building next door or remodeling might be going on elsewhere inside the hotel. The noise and other activity might directly interfere with the ability of both candidates and assessors to work.

Design the Exercise-Dimension Matrix

Table 17.1 illustrates the kind of basic relationship you need to be sure exists between assessment exercises and dimensions identified by the job analysis. Each exercise measures a different combination of dimensions. Note that each dimension should be measured in at least two different exercises. For example, the Harborville role-play exercise contained a requirement to write a report on the results of a meeting with a subordinate whose performance was deteriorating. That report was not assessed by the assessors for the role-play exercise, but by a separate panel of assessors.

Table 17.1. Harborville Police Department Tentative Dimension-Exercise Matrix.

Dimensions	Written Problem Analysis Exercise	Oral Presentation Exercise	Role-Play Exercise
Perception	X	X	X
Decisiveness	—	X	X
Judgment	—	X	X
Oral Communication	—	X	X
Written Communication	X	—	X
Leadership	—	X	X
Organizing and Planning	X	X	X

Recruit the Assessors

The right types of people to be assessors must be recruited early in the process. In business it is a common practice to use internal assessors holding a position at least two levels above the one for which candidates are competing. However, in policing, the more usual case is to use external assessors from other nonfederal law enforcement agencies, such as the state police, state patrol, or county sheriff's or police departments, or from other municipalities. To some extent the choice of assessors is a devil's dilemma for police agency assessment centers. On the one hand, if you select internal assessors, candidates will complain that the assessors selected those candidates whom they liked or knew the best. On the other hand, external assessors are sometimes seen as not knowing anything about the department or the candidates' on-the-job abilities. Candidates will sometimes complain that outside assessors should not be allowed to make such important decisions after seeing so little of the candidates. The Harborville Police Department determined it wanted internal assessors who held the rank of lieutenant or higher, who had at least two years of college, who had attended major police schools such as the FBI National Academy, who were experienced supervisors, and who had good reputations in their departments.

Assessors should be recruited from departments comparable in size to the agency conducting the assessment center. The assessor pool should also reflect consistency with community demographics such as gender and race. A different view on this matter is that assessors should at least mirror the demographics of the candidates (Lowery, 1993). As a practical matter the group of assessors you use may not meet all of the criteria noted here. For example, an assessor may be a college graduate or hold an advanced or professional degree yet not be a graduate from one of the premier *long schools* such as the FBI National Academy.

Assessment center directors must develop their own views of what constitute acceptable trade-offs in the criteria for assessor selection.

One way to recruit assessors is to select from the ranks of the high performers among the assessors with whom you have previously worked. Another way is to design a form capturing the data used to judge potential assessors and to ask other departments to use the form to make nominations. Prior experience as an assessor is usually an asset, and the nomination form should also capture when and where such experience was obtained and any associated training. Because assessors who have reputations as high performers are usually in high demand and short supply, one technique is to mix assessors with different levels of experience. This allows for the development of assessors over a period of time.

Sometimes agencies are so focused on getting their needs met by the assessors that they lose sight of the fact that the assessors also have their own needs. Thus the term *assessor abuse* has gained some currency for describing situations in which assessor needs are ignored or met in a haphazard fashion. The prime example of assessor abuse is scheduling too many candidates daily. This is unfair for the assessors and might possibly lead to inaccurate ratings of candidate abilities.

Just as people do, agencies develop reputations. An agency can get a reputation for, among other things, the type of assessment center it operates and how it treats its assessors. A failure to host assessors properly means that it will have difficulty recruiting assessors in the future.

Train the Role-Players

Properly training role-players is the key to their success. The training of a role-player starts with taking the exercise just as a candidate would. To develop the role-player further, he or she receives feedback about the performance. Then background and other information about the character and positions that the role-player will take on is given to him or her to study and is explained verbally as well. For example, a role-player might be instructed that a candidate who asks if the role-player has a drinking problem should receive a *two-knock* response: at the first question, or knock, answer, "No, I wouldn't say that," and on the second knock, reply, "You know, my wife says she is concerned about my drinking." After this, the role-player is instructed to respond accurately to all questions about drinking in accordance with the guidelines. Each time the role-player plays a part, it should be videotaped and critiqued until he or she can play it consistently. Role-players should be required to sign a security agreement that they will not divulge assessment center materials.

Select the Exercises

Exercises may be *off the shelf,* meaning that they are designed to measure the standard dimensions identified by a job analysis but will not reflect the actual practices of the department or agency for which the assessment center is being conducted. In contrast, *embedded* exercises are specifically tailored around the policies and procedures, organizational structure, shift system, resources, and conditions in the agency and community for which the assessment center is being conducted. Because embedded exercises mirror agency practices, candidates are typically more accepting of them and of the results generated by them. This means less time spent in responding to grievances and complaints.

In a police department, typically, exercise developers will sit down with a committee of lieutenants, and together they will talk about ideas and scenarios until the developer has a clear sense of what the exercises should be about. Then she or he will write the exercises and have them critiqued by the committee. Some exercise developers have the luxury of also having related work experience, publications, training, and education. Consultants with an appropriate background may elect to develop the exercises on their own and then ask the lieutenants' committee to review them. In particular, committee members must be attentive to whether the time allowed for the exercise is sufficient and whether department policies, practices, and terms or language exist as portrayed. Using department terms and language, for example, is important to making exercises acceptable to candidates. To illustrate, *roll call, reading,* and *briefing* all refer to the same event, but different agencies will prefer one or another of these terms. Similarly, *shift, tour of duty,* and *trick* all mean the same thing but are variously preferred in various departments. The best way to get feedback on accuracy is to have each of the committee members actually perform the exercises and get a realistic view of them.

Typically, it is better to schedule too much rather than too little time for the candidates' preparation part of an exercise, because that greatly obviates a common source of candidate complaints. For many police departments the minimum educational requirement for hiring and even promotion is still a high school degree or its equivalent. Commonly, people who have a high school degree actually read at about a tenth-grade level. Therefore the reading level of the exercises in agencies with the high school requirement should be kept under a grade-ten level. When you do this, you will have no or few complaints that the exercises "favor the college educated," and few or no people who call the assessment center "nothing but a reading test."

With some materials it may not be possible or even desirable to keep the reading level below grade ten. For example, the exercise packet might include copies of particular statutes. Statutes may have reading levels in excess of grade twenty. If these statutes are part of the job-related materials officers are expected to know, then the tenth-grade limit need not apply.

Once the exercises have been developed, critiqued, and modified as needed, they must be duplicated for use by assessors in training and by candidates going through assessment. Throughout this sequence of events, security of the assessment materials must be maintained. Duplication should be done by a trusted source. On site the assessors should be cautioned to maintain all materials under secure conditions. One way to help assessors do this is to issue them boxes or other containers that are sealed, like evidence envelopes, each evening.

It is also important that exercises account for other agency conditions. For example, when the Harborville Police Department hired its first chief from outside department ranks, he was greeted by agency members with some resentment and suspicion when he first arrived. One of the changes he implemented was the use of assessment centers for candidates for promotion, a process agency members knew nothing about and decried as a waste of money. To counter some of their opposition, a four-hour candidate-orientation session was held. Candidates were given numerous written handouts, and the orientation was videotaped for those who could not attend or who might want to refresh their memories at a later date. For the assessment center director, one concern was accurately evaluating the level of candidate ability. Another concern was that the project be well received, inasmuch as the chief was under scrutiny for other issues as well. To address these two concerns, the exercises were written to be hard enough to provide useful distinctions between candidates but soft enough to ensure a number of successful candidates. Additionally, ample time was provided for the candidates' exercise preparation period. These measures resulted in great acceptance by all the candidates. Several of the candidates who failed the assessment center even wrote to the chief encouraging him to continue the assessment centers because they were a practical process and all candidates were given the same opportunity to compete for a promotion.

Determine the Level of Candidate Feedback

Police departments often use the results of an assessment center only as the basis for making hiring and promotional decisions. In such schemes the feedback given to candidates will gravitate toward the minimal, and often they will receive only a letter showing how they scored on the various dimensions, what the group average was on those dimensions, and the same types of data for each individual exercise. This approach ignores the other important uses that can be made of the available data to the betterment of the candidates and their employer, such as identifying skill deficits, tailoring individual development plans, and increasing the legitimacy of the assessment process by allowing candidates to scrutinize all assessment center records pertaining to their candidacy.

Whether or not to use a *full-scrutiny* policy is a decision usually made by someone other than the assessment center director. The existence of such a policy will on rare occasions form the basis for a complaint by a candidate, due to some irregularity in the record. Although some think otherwise, this event is not justification for using a minimal level of feedback. Most often, candidates who have not done well in the assessment center will, under the full-scrutiny policy, understand where they have made mistakes and what they need to do to improve. (And candidates who have done extremely well ordinarily do not seek feedback because they have already received the most salient data of all: they are in position for promotion.)

Some departments videotape candidates' performances in the exercises before the assessors arrive. Then the assessors evaluate these performances from the videotape. Other departments videotape each candidate's performance in front of the assessors. In this latter case, the assessors refer to the tapes only to resolve disputes about particular points of a candidate's performance. In either case, when videotapes exist, it is often very helpful to show a candidate his or her videotapes as feedback. For example, I was giving feedback to a lieutenant who had failed a captains' assessment center. He came in a little hot and defensive and disagreed with the reports the assessors had written about him, particularly with respect to his lack of interpersonal sensitivity and low interpersonal communication skills. However, when I showed him the videotape of his first exercise, his entire demeanor changed, and he told me that for the first time in his career he really understood why people over the years had made some of the criticisms on his performance appraisals.

The best way to give full-scrutiny feedback is to first recruit the people who will deliver the feedback from the ranks of the people who did the assessing. Then supply training for them in how to give constructive feedback and in the protocols the host agency wants followed; this training can usually be accomplished in eight to sixteen hours. A second way to give this feedback is to recruit new people for a *feedback crew,* using the same standards used for recruiting the assessors, and to put these people through all of the exercises as well as the feedback training.

CONCLUSION

An assessment center is both a process and a place. To properly be called an assessment center, the process administered must meet certain standards. Broadly speaking, there are two methods of pooling or integrating the data generated by the assessors: the assessment council method and the mechanical/mathematical method. Each is associated with a different way of enacting an assessment center.

It is best to develop a schedule of events for an assessment center and to ensure that the selected dates are viable. The place chosen must convey that the organization takes this process seriously. To be certain the facilities are appropriate, the assessment center director should carefully evaluate them.

The dimension-exercise matrix shows the relationship between the dimensions (skills and abilities) to be measured and the various exercises. These dimensions are identified through a careful job analysis that complies with applicable standards for generating such data.

No matter how good the exercises and facilities are, it is the assessors and role-players who ultimately determine assessment center success. For that reason, the selection and training of these people, the design of assessors' forms (such as checklists), and the effort to host these people appropriately are of extreme importance. Assessor abuse should be avoided at all cost. Due to various emergencies, assessors and occasionally role-players must sometimes be replaced with little advance warning. Assessment center directors must prepare for such emergencies through contingency planning.

The exercises used in assessment centers are typically one of two types: off the shelf or embedded. The latter type meets with greater acceptance and fewer complaints from candidates because it is custom tailored to their agency. Regardless of which type of exercise is used, the reading level of the materials needs to be checked beforehand and corrected to an appropriate level if necessary. From the beginning of the exercise development process through use of the materials, the security of materials must be maintained.

The amount of feedback given to each candidate ranges from only his or her final score, to a letter identifying the dimensions and how the candidate scored as compared to the average for his or her group of candidates, to a full scrutiny, meaning that the candidate has a right to examine every paper that affects his or her promotability.

Despite an ample body of literature on assessment centers, little has been written on the practical nuts and bolts of conducting them. It is hoped that this chapter begins to fill this gap.

Note

1. There is some variety in the number of points used on assessment center rating scales. Some assessment centers use as few as five points and others as many as nine. Too many points on a scale increase the cognitive workload on assessors and may be a source of measurement error. A rating scale with an even number of points, such as six, forces the assessors to confront a fundamental issue, can the candidate do this job? This is true because in a six-point scale, levels one, two, and three are all levels of unacceptable performance and the remaining points are levels of acceptable performance. Scales with an odd number of points may cause a slight inflation of ratings.

References

Coulton, G. F., and Feild, H. A. "Using Assessment Centers in Selecting Entry Level Police Officers: Extravagance or Justified Expense?" *Public Personnel Management,* 1995, *24,* 223–254.

Karl, K. A., and Wexley, K. N. "Patterns of Performance and Rating Frequency: Influence on the Assessment of Performance." *Journal of Management,* 1989, *15*(1), 5–20.

Kohlhepp, K. "Assessor Accuracy Training: A Critical Component." *Police Chief,* 1992, *59*(6), 54.

Lowery, P. E. "The Assessment Center: An Examination of the Effects of Assessor Characteristics on Assessor Scores." *Public Personnel Management,* 1993, *22,* 487–501.

Mendenhall, M. D. "Successful Legal Defense of the Assessment Center Method." *Police Chief,* 1992, *59*(6), 61–63.

Pynes, J. "Entry Level Police Selection: The Assessment Center Is an Alternative." *Journal of Criminal Justice,* 1992, *20*(1), 41–52.

Pynes, J., and Bernadin, H. J. "Mechanical Versus Consensus-Derived Assessment Center Ratings: A Comparison of Job Performance Validities." *Public Personnel Management,* 1992, *2,* 17–28.

CHAPTER EIGHTEEN

Designing Effective Performance Appraisal Systems

Dennis M. Daley

This chapter focuses on the design of performance appraisal systems. The discussion integrates the specific appraisal instruments with the organizational and individual behaviors that are crucial to a successful performance appraisal system.

In designing a performance appraisal system an organization must answer the questions, Why do we appraise? What do we appraise? Who does the appraising? When do we appraise? and How do we appraise? Although there may be wrong answers, there are no correct or best answers to these questions. An organization must design its appraisal system around its needs and capabilities. In addition to discussing potential responses to these questions, this chapter provides an example of an objective performance appraisal process and describes a variety of rater errors that must be avoided.

WHY DO WE APPRAISE?

As a decision-making tool, performance appraisal is designed to structure the assessment process positively. By formally focusing a manager's attention solely on the objective, job-related criteria for assessing performance, an appraisal provides the manager with the means of making appropriate decisions that rationally contribute to the organization's and the individual's effectiveness and well-being (see Chapters Twelve and Nineteen).

368

The purposes for which performance appraisal can be employed are numerous. However, they can be grouped into two broad categories—*judgmental* and *developmental*. Although both developmental and judgmental appraisals have enhanced productivity as their goal, they approach it in two quite distinct fashions.

Development focuses on an individual's potential rather than on his or her current level of skills and capabilities. Hence it is essential in such assessments to consider the question, potential for what? Whether viewed from an organizational or individual perspective, the goal toward which this potential, or growth, is directed needs examination. The organizational need for developing this potential must be determined. That is, will the organization accrue some benefit from developing an individual's potential? The human resource aspects of an organization's strategic planning process should provide the answers to these questions. If an organization is to provide an employee with enhanced skills and abilities, it is important that the organization perceive what reward it expects in return.

Judgmental purposes follow the management systems, or command-and-control, model of authority. They are quite explicitly linked to extrinsic rewards and punishments (see Chapter Twenty-Seven). In fact, the degree to which a reward structure exists and is adequate is an important subsidiary question related to the effectiveness of appraising for judgmental purposes (Perry, 1986). Among public-sector agencies, the organizational reward structure has proved an important limitation on judgmental purposes. The needs to make promotions decisions and to make merit pay decisions are the two most widely known and used of the judgmental purposes.

Merit pay is especially in vogue, with many public-sector jurisdictions seeing it as a means of enhancing productivity and, at the same time, cutting costs. However, the reality is somewhat different in that governments regularly refuse to really pay for enhanced productivity (Ingraham, 1993; Perry, Petrakis, and Miller, 1989).

Promotion entails both developmental (what additional competencies does this individual need and how can they be provided for?) and pay considerations; yet it is a distinct decision. Although the criteria used in assessing performance for pay and in assessing performance for promotion overlap, they also differ. It is even suggested that a separate appraisal for promotion may be appropriate (Cederblom, 1991).

Performance appraisal can also play a significant role in other career moves, such as reassignment and demotion, and it plays a part in retention, reinstatement, and dismissal decisions. The possible negative outcomes are key ingredients in the practice of cutback management.

In addition to all these purposes, performance appraisal plays a role in the validation of personnel techniques. Tests used in the staffing and selection process are often statistically validated in terms of their ability to predict job performance. That job performance is, in turn, measured by a performance appraisal instrument.

Individuals hope to receive feedback for improving their performance from the appraisal process. They also do not generally perceive an objective assessment as threatening. To a great extent this lack of threat can be attributed to the relatively high opinion individuals tend to hold of their own abilities. There is even some evidence for managers seeking out negative comments regarding their own performance from subordinates (Ashford and Tsui, 1991).

Clearly, it may not be possible to mix judgmental and developmental purposes in the same appraisal process (Cascio, 1982; Hyde and Smith, 1982), simultaneously determining rewards and punishments on the one hand and potential on the other. Cognitive research has long indicated that managers are influenced by the purpose of the appraisal in making their judgments (Daley, 1992; Landy and Farr, 1980; Murphy and Cleveland, 1995). The purpose for which an appraisal is to be used shapes and frames how a manager assesses an individual. Even with the most objective appraisal instruments the criteria take on a subtle and specific perspective.

Multiple appraisals are one suggested solution to this dilemma (Meyer, 1991). Instead of employing one appraisal and using it for a multitude of purposes, the organization makes each specific purpose the focus of a separate appraisal process. In this case, it is important to maintain employee perceptions that the systems are indeed independent of one another. Even so, an organization establishing a performance appraisal process may have to choose between serving judgmental and developmental purposes.

WHAT DO WE APPRAISE?

The goal of performance appraisal is the enhancement of organizational effectiveness. Thus performance appraisal builds on job-specific criteria, to meet the standard of job-relatedness. Even though legal tenets currently support the use of job-specific criteria only, other measures may eventually attain correlative legal standing. For example, our growing interest in developing open or knowledge-based organizations capable of performing in constantly changing environments has focused attention on high-involvement concepts for the selection and evaluation of the *whole person*. In this case, organizational analysis is used to identify personal traits and work behaviors that although not job-specific are essential elements in the overall successful performance of the organization. The performance appraisal process has also been suggested as a means of assessing ethical behavior (Gatewood and Carroll, 1991).

Nevertheless, job-relatedness is still the chief standard by which the acceptability of a performance appraisal measurement is judged. Established through the 1978 Uniform Guidelines on Employee Selection Procedures (Equal Employment Opportunity Commission, 1997), in response to the Supreme Court's decision in *Griggs* v. *Duke Power Company,* 401 U.S. 424 (1971), the requirement for job-relatedness has been repeatedly reaffirmed and explained by the courts in subsequent rulings (*Brito* v. *Zia Company,* 478 F. 2d 1200 [1973]; *Ramirez* v. *Hofheinz,* 619 F. 2d 442 [1980]; *Zell* v. *United States,* 472 F. Supp. 356 [1979]). Job-relatedness poses a twofold requirement for organizations—appraisal criteria must enable supervisors to discriminate between employees solely in terms of their job performance, and the organization must be able to prove or demonstrate the existence of the relationship between the job and the criteria.

In choosing performance measures, care must be taken to ensure that they are reliable, practical, and controllable. To be reliable a measure must be relatively stable over time; it must produce consistent readings vis-à-vis similar performances. To be practical a measure must be readily available to those using it. In addition, it must be viewed as an appropriate measure and be accepted as such by those whose performance is being measured. Finally, to be controllable it should measure performance in behaviors or results over which the individual actually exercises substantial influence (Gatewood and Feild, 1990).

Performance standards lie at the heart of all effective appraisal systems. Performance standards are meant to anchor an appraisal system to specific, job-related tasks. It is only by adhering to job-related standards that an appraisal system can obtain objectivity and legality. Inasmuch as the standards are consistent with written position descriptions (which form the psychological contract, or expectations basis, upon which people are hired), they reinforce that contract. The failure to align a performance appraisal process with an organization's system of position descriptions introduces confusion and leads to ineffectiveness. Hence written performance standards help to communicate to the workers a clearer understanding of their jobs.

Skills, knowledge, and abilities (SKAs), personal traits or characteristics, activities or work behaviors, and results all can serve as criteria for assessing performance (Milkovich and Boudreau, 1991). However, only behaviors and results are likely to successfully meet the job-relatedness standard. SKAs, and also traits, are specific to individuals and not inherent in the jobs themselves. For this reason, satisfactorily establishing their validity poses a somewhat difficult problem. Although their use is not precluded, establishing the evidence of statistical validity necessary to support their use can be a difficult and costly task.

Skills, knowledge, and abilities include such diverse characteristics as job knowledge, physical strength, eye-hand coordination, and business knowledge and perhaps being licensed. These are the SKAs often included in position descriptions and used as a guide in recruitment and selection. They are clearly meant as a statement of competencies required to perform a given job, and if properly developed are likely to sufficiently discriminate between different performance levels. As discriminators, SKAs can serve as the focus of job analysis and basis for performance appraisal in open or knowledge-based organizations. However, SKAs often represent only the basic or minimum qualifications necessary in order to perform a job adequately.

Behaviors and results are the foundation upon which the two most objective performance appraisal instruments (*behaviorally anchored rating scales* and *management by objectives*) are built. Behaviors are the activities and tasks individuals engage in in the performance of their jobs; results are the activity outcomes (Daley, 1992; Landy and Farr, 1983; Murphy and Cleveland, 1995).

An exclusive concentration on either behaviors or results has specific disadvantages. An overemphasis on results can sacrifice long-term advantages and interests for quickly won short-term gains. In addition, an overemphasis on results can lead to the ignoring of secondary functions (such as helping customers or other employees even though that is not one's specific job) whose contributions are not so clearly seen or easily measured yet are nevertheless important to the organization's success. Furthermore, an overemphasis on results can also foster unethical conduct in reaching those results.

Equally, an exclusive focus on behaviors and processes is to be avoided. An overemphasis upon correctly performing work behaviors can lead to excessive red tape. (Indeed, in many organizations, employees find that *working to rule* is a highly effective weapon for bringing management to the bargaining table. In both the public and private sectors it is proving to be more effective than threats of a strike.) Selecting a mixture of behaviors and results tends to provide balance in the performance standards.

Whatever the criteria used, an appraisal instrument needs to discriminate, at a minimum, two levels of performance. This basic pass-fail option may be augmented with other performance levels designed to distinguish other degrees of superior performance than just those that are fully satisfactory.

A final concern is the participation of employees and supervisors in the development of performance standards. Such participation introduces a number of positive features, including employee acceptance of the performance appraisal system, a crucial element in determining whether the system will be successful. In addition to conferring legitimacy upon the appraisal system, participation affords employees an opportunity to voice their concerns, and assists in clarifying potential misunderstandings. The net result is to leave the employee with the sense of having a stake in the appraisal process. Without participation and the legitimacy it entails, the performance appraisal task is more difficult.

WHO DOES THE APPRAISING?

Traditionally, the immediate supervisor is most often the one responsible for appraising subordinates (Mohrman, Resnick-West, and Lawler, 1989). Such supervisory appraisal of subordinates is the predominate method and is widely suggested to occur in approximately 90 percent of the cases. This supervisor is the management individual deemed most knowledgeable about both the employee and the job. In fact, performance appraisal is often viewed as a key management system tool for establishing a supervisor's command-and-control authority. In contrast, from a more humanistic coach and consult perspective, the appraisal process is viewed as being designed to strengthen the employee-supervisory relationship through the encouragement of mutual understanding.

Yet there are some additional and potentially interesting answers proposed to this question of who does the appraising, answers other than that found in supervisory-based appraisal, that offer some differing insights into the appraisal process and the supervisor's role in it. These proposals (components of which are used in 360-degree feedback) fall into two general categories—the use of agency insiders (for example, self-appraisal, peer review, subordinate appraisal, and multiple raters) and the use of outsiders (for example, personnel officials, consultants and assessment centers, and clients and customers).

The self-appraisal calls upon the employee to evaluate his or her own performance. Inasmuch as the employee is the individual who most accurately knows what his or her own performance is, this can be an extremely useful assessment. Self-appraisal is a technique well suited for use in developmental appraisals because an individual is most knowledgeable about his or her own shortcomings and strengths and is also well aware of what he or she is prepared to do about them. But it is questionable when employed in a judgmental setting, as few people will honestly admit their weaknesses if doing so may lead to negative consequences (Daley, 1992; Mohrman, Resnick-West, and Lawler, 1989; Murphy and Cleveland, 1995).

Peer review is most notably employed in both military and academic settings (Landy and Farr, 1983). Although it need not be limited to professionals, theirs is the venue in which it is most often employed. Research indicates that the assessments from peer ratings are just as accurate as those provided by supervisors (Daley, 1992; Mohrman, Resnick-West, and Lawler, 1989; Murphy and Cleveland, 1995).

H. John Bernardin (1986) strongly advocates the employment of subordinate appraisal. Subordinates are especially capable of assessing those aspects of managerial job performance that focus on employee communication and development. Inasmuch as these are organizational goals, subordinate appraisals can actually support hierarchal structures. In such circumstances the subordinate appraisals become an instrument for monitoring the supervisor or manager's implementation of the prescribed organizational policy.

Subordinate appraisals can provide managers with feedback and reinforce good behavioral practices (Ashford and Tsui, 1991). In addition, they can enhance the nonmanagerial work environment within an organization, focusing more attention on subordinate concerns. This can be quite important, especially among professional establishments and in the modern client- or customer-driven organizations.

A number of different performance appraisal proposals employ upper-level managers (Daley, 1992; Mohrman, Resnick-West, and Lawler, 1989; Murphy and Cleveland, 1995) or team management concepts (Meyer, 1991). Both the superior management and team management approaches are designed to encourage familiarity with an employee's work by managers other than an employee's immediate supervisor. Organizationally, participation by these superior or team managers results in their gaining a better understanding of the interrelationships and workings within their organization.

Team management appraisal can address both development and judgment within the same appraisal process. In this approach an employee's immediate supervisor performs the developmental role of adviser, coach, and advocate; the judgmental role is fulfilled by the other team managers. In turn each supervisor presents and argues the cases of his or her subordinates, before a panel consisting of the other supervisors or managers. On the basis of these arguments and their personal knowledge of the individuals, the other panel members make the judgmental decisions. In this way, the team performs the judgmental function for the organization and the individual supervisors play the developmental role for their employees. Supervisors reap the benefits from fulfilling a developmental purpose and from the positive relationships that it helps foster. The onus of judgment is conveniently scapegoated onto the other managers.

Experts from the central personnel office and consultants can be brought in to assess employee performance. The performance appraisal process can be conducted in much the same manner as a job analysis process (Mohrman, Resnick-West, and Lawler, 1989). However, instead of evaluating the activities, behaviors, tasks, and responsibilities that go into making a position, the analysts evaluate the employee's performance level on those same items. Productivity studies, in fact, often have this process as their focus. Instead of assessing actual job performance, another option evaluates employees on the basis of their participation in an assessment center.

For external or outsider appraisals an organization may also turn to its clients or customers (Mohrman, Resnick-West, and Lawler, 1989). Because public agency customers and clients are taxpayers and voters in addition to being recipients of services, public involvement in appraisals is more commonplace among government agencies than among private-sector organizations. In fact, it may be perceived as a definitional aspect of public organizations. What is perhaps not so readily seen or accorded to is the legitimate involvement by members of the public in the specific operations of agencies and in their personnel matters.

The advantages of employing multiple raters or outside assessments are highly dependent upon the knowledge that these raters possess of the individual jobs, of the individuals being rated, and of the performance appraisal process. Information failure with its deleterious consequences (to which all methods are prone) is more readily evident in these situations. Hence, rater training is all that much more crucial.

WHEN DO WE APPRAISE?

Performance appraisals should be geared to the work cycle. In order to make judgments about an individual's performance, an assessor must see that performance in its entirety. Hence performance appraisals need to be based on a time period sufficient for the accomplishment of the job's responsibilities. Whether this period is six months or six years should be determined by the demands of the job.

In most circumstances where an annual cycle is employed, the timing decision is reduced to a choice between the *anniversary-date* and *focal-point* methods (Daley, 1992; Mohrman, Resnick-West, and Lawler, 1989). These two approaches are basically mirror images of one another, trading off their respective advantages and disadvantages.

Under the anniversary-date approach, appraisals coincide with the anniversary of each individual's date of employment. As a result the anniversary-date appraisal cycle spreads the supervisor's workload over the course of the entire year. Given the large number of employees for whom an individual supervisor may hold appraisal responsibility, this can be advantageous. Although the number of appraisals is the same under both approaches, the supervisor's ability to manage them is improved under the anniversary-date approach. With the supervisor no longer facing an avalanche of appraisals, the quality of individual appraisals should be improved. Each appraisal and each employee receive the attention they are deemed to deserve.

However, the anniversary-date method also faces a number of shortcomings. Disadvantages may flow from a lack of timely measurement information. The criteria used for assessing performance are themselves subject to work cycles and the vicissitudes of data collection. Up-to-date or appropriate measurements may just not be available for use at the time of an anniversary-date appraisal. In addition the anniversary-date method limits comparability. Supervisors find it more difficult to judge employee performances vis-à-vis one another. This is true even for employees who have virtually the same jobs.

In the focal-point approach to performance appraisal, the supervisor conducts all the employees' evaluations at the same time. Appropriate results or measurement information and data collection can then be arranged to coincide with the needs of the appraisal process or vice versa. The focal-point method addresses many of the problems discussed previously, but it does so by piling up the supervisor's workload. Therefore, even though comparability and also equity and fairness concerns can be more adequately monitored with a focal-point approach, the appraisal process itself may suffer from a lack of supervisory attention to detail. With too many employees to appraise, the individual appraisals may become perfunctory. However, in public organizations, because they often operate with smaller spans of control and consequently with more supervisors than are typically found in the private sector, this need not be a serious problem.

HOW DO WE APPRAISE?

Since the passage of the Civil Rights Act of 1964, case after case brought before the U.S. courts has led to the mandating of objective personnel practices. Although these practices had been exhaustively advocated by personnelists prior to the 1964 act, the courts in enforcing the civil rights legislation provided strong and compelling legal support for their employment. The extension of the *Griggs* decision to clearly include performance appraisal systems (*Connecticut* v. *Teal*, 457 U.S. 440 [1982]) broadens that mandate.

Current case law outlines six legal criteria for constructing performance appraisal systems. According to Shelley P. Burchett and Kenneth De Meuse (1988), these criteria require attention to

1. Job analysis
2. Job-specific work behaviors
3. Communications
4. Supervisory training
5. Documentation
6. Monitoring

Job analysis (see Chapter Sixteen) is the foundation for performance appraisal, as it is for a number of personnel practices (Daley, 1992; Murphy and Cleveland, 1995). The courts view it as essential that the performance on which an individual is to be appraised is clearly understood by both employee and supervisor (*Albemarle Paper Company* v. *Moody*, 442 U.S. 405 [1975]; *Wade* v. *Mississippi Cooperative Extension Service*, 372 F. Supp. 126 [1974]; *Patterson* v. *American Tobacco Company*, 586 F. 2d 300 [1978]; *Carpenter* v. *Stephen F. Austin State University*, 706 F. 2d 6708 [1983]). Without this mutual understanding of job requirements that an employee is expected to fulfill, it is impossible to either perform or evaluate that employee's work.

Up-to-date job analyses delineate the job duties and responsibilities; hence, they are the appropriate basis upon which to assess employees. Job analyses inform employees what is expected from them and remind supervisors what it is their employees are being asked to do. The specific evaluation factors used in an appraisal instrument are then designed to measure the performance of the tasks indicated by the job analysis.

Public administration's existing emphasis on job-relatedness, derived from the ideological value placed on the merit principle, dovetails with the employment of objective personnel management techniques such as behaviorally anchored rating scales (Daley, 1992; Latham and Wexley, 1994) and management by objectives (Daley, 1992). According to court rulings (*Brito* v. *Zia Company* and *Zell* v. *United States*), *job-specific work behaviors* are to serve as the basis for the evaluation of an employee's performance. Although subjective observations may offer certain theoretical insights, the courts are reluctant to fully sanction their use (*Zell* v. *United States* and *Ramirez* v. *Hofheinz*). The employment of subjective assessments requires careful consideration and is best used in conjunction with more objective aspects of performance appraisal.

Communication among employees and supervisors is also essential to performance appraisal. Individuals must be aware of the performance standards used to evaluate them (*Rowe* v. *General Motors,* 457 F. 2d 348 [1972] and *Zell* v. *United States*). Feedback is essential for the improvement of performance. Individuals seek out feedback on their performance. Midterm reviews add to the effectiveness of the feedback process.

Supervisory training is another criterion for acceptable appraisals. Although training in the use of complex technological equipment is readily acceded to by organizations, developing the competencies of employees and managers in the behavioral aspects of management often meets with aversion. Nevertheless, supervisors cannot be left without any guidance in the application of the performance appraisal processes (*Rowe* v. *General Motors; Harper* v. *Mayor and City Council of Baltimore,* 359 F. Supp. 1187 [1972]; and *Carpenter* v. *Stephen F. Austin State University*). Like any tool, performance appraisal requires that users be instructed in its proper and safe use.

The criterion of *documentation* addresses the somewhat more negative issue of legal defensibility. Public trials in which the accused can both confront and cross-examine the witnesses and evidence against him or her are an integral element in the American way of life. These principles are seen to adhere in court rulings on performance appraisal (*Marquez* v. *Omaha District Sales Office, Ford Division of the Ford Motor Company,* 440 F. 2d 1157 [1971], and *Turner* v. *State Highway Commission of Missouri,* 31 EPD 33, 352 [1982]). The importance attached to an individual's job is such that the courts have extended the rules of evidence to cover the employment of performance appraisal systems. Organizations must be able to produce evidence in support of their personnel decisions, especially in those incidences where severe sanctions and job loss are imposed.

The Supreme Court's ruling in *Connecticut* v. *Teal* extended the requirements of the 1978 Uniform Guidelines on Employee Selection Procedures to include performance appraisal systems. In essence, a performance appraisal is treated as just another job test. If employed by an organization, performance appraisals must be validated as job related. Hence the impact of the performance appraisal process on job changes is subject to scrutiny. All measures of discrimination, including the three-fifths or 80 percent rule as it used to test for the presence of adverse impact (that is, the pass or selection rates from two sets of similar applicants should not vary by more than 20 percent), apply to appraisals as to any other testing situations.

Due process considerations also underlie the requirement for *monitoring.* Organizations must check to see not only that their appraisal systems are up-to-date (*Carpenter* v. *Stephen F. Austin State University*) but also that they are not being abused (*Rowe* v. *General Motors*). Performance appraisal standards based on out-of-date job analyses fail to reflect current job requirements, and the employee is often left with the unenviable Catch-22 task of either doing the job correctly or following procedure correctly. In addition, liability litigation documents numerous cases involving the abuse of authority. Grievance and discipline appeal provisions can build in safeguards against managerial and supervisory abuse of the performance appraisal process.

AN MBO APPRAISAL SYSTEM

This section introduces an example of an appraisal by objectives. Management by objectives (MBO) and the related behaviorally anchored rating scales (BARS) techniques described by Latham and Wexley (1994) form the two most objective approaches to performance appraisal. The organizational introduction of objective appraisal using either approach should be accompanied by a series of training sessions and supported with supervisory and employee handbooks.

This is how a typical MBO appraisal process might evolve. The supervisor and employee initiate the objective performance evaluation process by jointly completing a job description document entitled "Responsibilities and Standards or Results Expected." This is the first of three steps in the process. It is completed at the beginning of the annual appraisal cycle, and steps two and three are written up at the cycle's conclusion.

The employee is given prior notice of and, ideally, participates in scheduling the preliminary conference. A worksheet and copies of previous evaluations are supplied to the employee for use as guides. It is specified that both supervisor's and employee's worksheets are to be filled out "in pencil" (on-line appraisal systems specify "on the wordprocessor"). This instruction is designed to remind both parties that no final decisions have been made and that the meeting is suppose to truly be participative.

The supervisor and the employee select up to eight or ten major responsibilities (four to five are the norm) and write them down in a results-oriented format, describing specific performance standards against which the achievement of the results can be measured. Each responsibility may have more than one measurable, objective standard associated with it.

Objective standards fall into three categories. *Historical standards* contrast one period in time with another (for example, they relate the upcoming year's "potholes filled" to the previous year's). *Engineered standards* focus on numbers of things in specific time frames (for example, the number of potholes to be filled in one year). *Comparative standards* measure expected results against a norm for an industry, similar work unit, or employee performing the same duties (for example, the turnover rate among municipal employees generally or in specific types of jobs).

During the employer-supervisor conference, the individual responsibilities are weighted through the use of an additive (or multiplicative) formula that factors in the time spent on each task and the evaluation of its importance or of the consequences of task error. A five-point Likert scale is used for both measures. Time is calculated as a percentage of the whole job or as hours spent on a task. Consequences encompass financial loss, client dissatisfaction, time required to correct errors, broken equipment, and psychological stress.

Should these responsibilities require modification due to changing circumstances, the supervisor and employee can prepare a new first-step statement. During the course of the evaluation period, the supervisor is also encouraged to use a critical incident approach, wherein the supervisor jots down noteworthy efforts and places them in an evaluation file. Employees can of course maintain their own list of supervisor noteworthy efforts. Both formal (with a written copy inserted into the employee's file) and informal communications between employees and supervisors are encouraged. For negative incidents it is important that a record of recommended corrective action be documented; the employee must be notified when he or she is doing something wrong, and the supervisor must indicate how the employee can correct the behavior.

At the end of the annual evaluation period, another conference is scheduled at which the supervisor and employee discuss the information that will result in the employee's formal evaluation. As with the first conference, the employee has advance notice. The employee and supervisor meet to discuss the employee's job performance in light of the responsibilities and results expected that they had outlined initially. Again worksheets are used at this meeting, with the formal written evaluation ("Performance Review or Rating") prepared only afterward. The employee will also have an opportunity to comment formally on the written evaluation.

The overall employee rating is the weighted average of the individual responsibility ratings. Each responsibility's weight has been determined at the beginning of the appraisal period by dividing its time and importance raw score (varying from 2 to 10) by the total for all raw scores and converting the result into a percentage. This percentage is then multiplied by the individual rating assigned by the supervisor to that responsibility. At the end of the appraisal period, the degree to which the employee achieved the standards for each responsibility is rated on a five-point scale: (1) unacceptable, (2) needs some improvement, (3) competent performance, (4) very good, and (5) outstanding. The rounded-up tally of the weighted responsibility ratings is then used as an overall measure, employing the same five-point scale terminology.

In the third and final step, the supervisor competes an essay entitled, "Summary of Total Job Performance and Future Performance Plans." The essay provides the supervisor the opportunity to list the employee's "areas of strength" and "areas needing improvement." The supervisor also completes "training and development plans" for correcting the areas needing improvement.

RATER ERROR

Performance appraisal is a human process. Although the tendency to focus attention on the process tools can draw attention away from this fact, it remains the essential fact of performance evaluation. The development of psychometric accuracy has produced performance appraisal instruments of complex sophistication. Yet the resultant objective BARS and MBO appraisal systems are only as good as the people who use them. For all their advantages, they are still only tools for aiding us in making our decisions. Thus the issue of rater error must be considered.

Rater errors form a topic extensively treated in the performance appraisal literature (Daley, 1992; Landy and Farr, 1980; Latham and Wexley, 1994; Murphy and Cleveland, 1995). As outlined in the following list of error sources, not all rater errors deserve that name.

Organizational Attributes Causing Error

- Lack of clarity or misunderstanding of goals
- Hidden agenda of using performance appraisal as control mechanism
- Unrealistic expectations
- Work that occurs as a group and not an individual activity

Structural Attributes Causing Error

- Supervisors not trained
- Goals not set
- Appraisals adjusted to fit predetermined decisions
- Employees that match behaviors to limited, incomplete set of criteria

True Rater Errors

- Job responsibility errors
- Contrast errors
- Unidimensional errors
- Interpersonal errors

Much of what passes under the rubric of rater error is in reality supervisory adjustment to organizational attributes and demands (Daley, 1992; Longenecker, Sims, and Gioia, 1987; Murphy and Cleveland, 1995). Although the impact of these adjustments may be deemed negative, they are neither accidental nor totally within the control of the supervisor to correct. *Goals may be unclear or misunderstood* due to communication problems. A *hidden agenda may be the desire to use performance appraisals as means of controlling employees* rather than for encouraging productivity. The *expectations may be unrealistic* in terms of what can be accomplished on the job. Finally, *results may be due to activities of groups* rather than individuals. The supervisors endeavor to coordinate workers and obtain productivity within this organizational system, and the performance appraisal becomes part of the organization's overall management control system (Swiss, 1991).

Structural problems can undermine the appraisal instruments themselves. And the failure to develop objective appraisal systems can lead to inconsistent or unreliable appraisals. Specifically, the *failure to provide adequate supervisory training* in the use of objective systems can result in a loss of consistency and reliability. An *inability to set goals* or neglect in goal setting produces similar faults. Objective appraisal systems operate only when results can be compared against expectations. The failure to establish goals and objectives leaves the system with no expectations. Because managers and supervisors take an appraisal's specific purpose into consideration in making their evaluations, using the appraisal for another, unintended purpose only confounds the process.

The performance appraisal process can be abused when *personnel decisions precede appraisals* and decision-making relationships are inverted. Instead of serving as an aid in decisions regarding employee promotion, pay, dismissal, or development, the appraisals are interpreted to justify predetermined decisions.

On a somewhat more technical level, additional problems arise when *employees match behavior to job evaluations and the criteria prove incomplete.* It is difficult to fault employees for not doing what is not asked of them; yet sins of omission can be just as deadly as the sins of commission. Ideally, an appraisal system is designed to objectively encompass all the needed tasks. In reality, important tasks are often ignored or unforeseen. Redesigning the appraisal process to be more comprehensive is essential in such circumstances.

Rater errors (falling as mentioned into the four categories of job responsibility errors, contrast errors, unidimensional errors, and interpersonal errors) in many cases are corrected through the employment of objective appraisal instruments. In other instances, more thorough supervisory training is recommended.

Job responsibility errors are committed whenever the organizational importance of the responsibilities inherent in the job is substituted for a accurate measure of the incumbent's job performance. An important and demanding job requires an individual of like stature, therefore the appraisal assumption to avoid is that the individual is necessarily of like stature. Similarly, individuals working in a critical unit may benefit from the perceived centrality or significance of their part of the organization, in that the importance of the unit to fulfilling the organization's mission is substituted for the job performance of the individual in that unit.

Contrast errors arise through interpersonal comparisons. Individuals are not assessed on their job performance in relation to a job analysis but on their performance compared to someone else's performance, or as is more often the case, their personal traits and characteristics compared to someone else's personal traits and characteristics. Personnel profiles are compiled tabulating the social and leadership traits or social, ethnic, gender, and other demographic differences of successful employees. These are then used as the norm against which others are compared. The legal liability implications of contrast errors are obvious.

Unidimensional errors abound. In these instances one item dominates the evaluation process to such an extent that other critical factors are ignored. Unidimensional errors can stem from either substantive or mechanical concerns. For example, in the substantive area, such traits and characteristics as age, longevity, or loyalty can be made the basis for an overall evaluation even when other factors are formally specified in the appraisal instrument. This is always an error even though these traits and characteristics may in many instances be desirable. For example, age and seniority can be viewed as simple indicators of experience; however, if experience is what is sought, it should be measured directly. Loyalty is the trait supervisors often value the most among employees because it is associated with a highly committed and motivated workforce; again, if those are the desired traits, direct measures of commitment and motivation should be developed. All measures of performance must be validated as specifically job related. Similarly, the vividness of one event can overshadow all other incidents: an error known as a *halo effect* occurs when a good performance in one aspect of a job becomes the basis for overall assessment, and a *horns effect* indicates that an incident perceived as negative is the basis of the overall evaluation.

Unidimensional error also occurs in appraisal mechanics. *First impression* or *recency error* is introduced when early or late events are given extraordinary weight in the evaluation. The first impression error leads later performance to be discounted. The recency error emphasizes the time period nearest the decision at the expense of earlier contributions. Critical incident files are often a means of countering this cognitive limitation.

Supervisors may also exhibit a *central tendency* (that is, they award everyone middle-range or average ratings) or a *restricted-range tendency* (that is, they do not award extremely good and bad ratings) so that they give all employees the same rating or very close and similar ratings. This problem often emerges when supervisors are required to justify only their high and low ratings. It is also likely when supervisors fear that employees will resent an individual who receives a high rating or will lose motivation if they themselves receive a low rating. Constant error occurs when supervisors exhibit tendencies toward awarding consistently high or low ratings or are overly lenient or strict in their rating evaluations.

Interpersonal errors, or biases, introduce intentional distortions into the appraisal process. The greater the extent to which a supervisor's own performance and career is dependent upon a subordinate's performance, the more likely it is that favorable ratings will be awarded to that subordinate. This interdependence creates a mutual need for maintaining a harmonious relationship.

Interpersonal biases are also often found as examples of abuse rather than of error. They may entail work site politics that cause supervisors to adjust ratings in order to support or hinder an employee's opportunity for advancement and reward. Lower-than-deserved ratings can be awarded in an effort to selfishly retain a valued and productive employee. Lower-than-deserved ratings can also be a means of taking out someone seen as a potential competitor (Longenecker, Sims, and Gioia, 1987).

Similarly, appraisal ratings can be affected by factors entirely extraneous to the working relationship. External preferences vis-à-vis politics, religion, and sex may be furthered through the manipulation of the performance appraisal process. Avoiding such abuses is one of the purposes underlying the recommendation to continually monitor the appraisal process. Requirements for the automatic review of appraisals by upper-level officials and for an appeals process are also designed with the intention to deter abuse.

Training individuals in the use of these performance appraisal instruments and thereby in the means of avoiding abuses is just as important as the development of objective appraisal techniques. Supervisory training requires care. It can encompass organizational and employee considerations as well as those related to the appraisal process itself. Performance appraisal is part of an overall performance management system. As such, it must interact with the other systemic aspects, and that interaction is just as important a part of its functioning as are the mechanics of the appraisal process itself.

CONCLUSION

Performance appraisal systems are built around a central technique. The preference is for an objective technique—behaviorally anchored rating scales and management by objectives approaches—over such subjective techniques as essays, non-task-related rating scales, and forced-choice checklists and over the ranking and forced-distribution interpersonal comparisons. Both the BARS and MBO applications of performance appraisal offer comparative advantages and disadvantages. Behaviorally anchored rating scales, on the one hand, are ideal for large organizations engaged in process-oriented tasks requiring teamwork. Management by objectives, on the other hand, can be individually tailored to specific job responsibilities. MBO also works well where individual outputs or results can be measured.

Feedback is an integral and essential part of the performance appraisal process. Through appraisal feedback, employees gain an understanding of their performance as well as an idea of what is expected of them. It is a means for correcting past behavior and encouraging motivation. Thus performance appraisal can be employed both in areas needing improvement and in areas of already proven strength.

References

Ashford, S. J., and Tsui, A. S. "Self-Regulation for Managerial Effectiveness: The Role of Active Feedback Seeking." *Academy of Management Journal,* 1991, *34,* 251–280.

Bernardin, H. J. "Subordinate Appraisal: A Valuable Source of Information About Managers." *Human Resource Management,* 1986, *25,* 421–439.

Burchett, S. P., and De Meuse, K. "Performance Appraisal and the Law." *Personnel,* July 1988, pp. 29–37.

Cascio, W. F. "Scientific, Legal and Operative Imperatives of Workable Performance Appraisal Systems." *Public Personnel Management,* 1982, *11,* 367–375.

Cederblom, D. "Promotability Ratings: An Underused Promotion Method for Public Safety Organizations." *Public Personnel Management,* 1991, *20,* 27–34.

Civil Rights Act. 1964. *U.S. Code,* vol. 42, sec. 1981 et seq.

Daley, D. M. *Performance Appraisal in the Public Sector: Techniques and Applications.* Westport, Conn.: Quorum/Greenwood, 1992.

Equal Employment Opportunity Commission. *Uniform Guidelines on Employee Selection Procedures. Code of Federal Regulations,* 1997, vol. 29, sec. 1607. (Originally issued 1978.)

Gatewood, R. D., and Carroll, A. B. "Assessment of Ethical Performance of Organization Members: A Conceptual Framework." *Academy of Management Review,* 1991, *16,* 667–690.

Gatewood, R. D., and Feild, H. *Human Resource Selection.* (2nd ed.) Orlando, Fla.: Dryden Press, 1990.

Hyde, A. C., and Smith, M. A. "Performance Appraisal Training: Objectives, a Model for Changes, and a Note of Rebuttal." *Public Personnel Management,* 1982, *11,* 358–366.

Ingraham, P. W . "Of Pigs in Pokes and Policy Diffusion: Another Look at Pay-for-Performance." *Public Administration Review,* 1993, *53,* 348–356.

Landy, F. J., and Farr, J. L. "Performance Rating." *Psychological Bulletin,* 1980, *87,* 72–107.

Landy, F. J., and Farr, J. L. *The Measurement of Work Performance: Methods, Theories and Applications.* Orlando, Fla.: Academic Press, 1983.

Latham, G. P., and Wexley, K. *Increasing Productivity Through Performance Appraisal.* (2nd ed.) Reading, Mass.: Addison Wesley Longman, 1994.

Longenecker, C., Sims, H. P., Jr., and Gioia, D. "Behind the Mask: The Politics of Employee Appraisal." *Academy of Management Executive,* 1987, *1,* 183–193.

Meyer, H. H. "A Solution to the Performance Appraisal Feedback Enigma." *Academy of Management Executive,* 1991, *5,* 68–76.

Milkovich, G. T., and Boudreau, J. W. *Human Resources Management.* (6th ed.) Burr Ridge, Ill.: Irwin, 1991.

Mohrman, A. M., Jr., Resnick-West, S. M., and Lawler, E. E., III. *Designing Performance Appraisal Systems: Aligning Appraisals and Organizational Realities.* San Francisco: Jossey-Bass, 1989.

Murphy, K. R., and Cleveland, J. N. *Understanding Performance Appraisal: Social, Organizational, and Goal-Based Perspectives.* Thousand Oaks, Calif.: Sage, 1995.

Perry, J. L. "Merit Pay in the Public Sector: The Case for a Failure of Theory." *Review of Public Personnel Administration,* 1986, *7,* 57–69.

Perry, J. L., Petrakis, B. A., and Miller, T. F . "Federal Merit Pay, Round II: An Analysis of the Performance Management and Recognition System." *Public Administration Review,* 1989, *49,* 29–37.

Swiss, J. E. *Public Management Systems: Monitoring and Managing Government Performance.* Upper Saddle River, N.J.: Prentice Hall, 1991.

PART FOUR

TOOLS FOR INTEGRATING HUMAN RESOURCES INTO THE ORGANIZATIONAL MISSION

To align HR programs and processes with mission goals and results,
HR managers must serve as a strategic partner with management.
—National Academy of Public Administration, *Strategies and*
Alternatives for Transforming Human Resources Management

The 1995 National Academy of Public Administration report *Strategies and Alternatives for Transforming Human Resources Management* seeks an expanded and invigorated role for public human resource management. Among the study's recommendations are reinforcing the role of human resource management (HRM) as a strategic organizational partner, developing new HRM skill inventories, and implementing a results orientation for the HRM function. These recommendations support the thinking in Part Four of this handbook, "Tools for Integrating Human Resources into the Organizational Mission."

This section seeks to provide the human resource manager with tools he or she can use to become more involved in the overall management of public organizations. David Ammons begins the discussion of these essential managerial tools with Chapter Nineteen, "Benchmarking Performance." Ammons defines benchmarking as simply "learning from the pros" and explains how methods such as performance measurement, performance standards, and process flow-charting can help government organizations measure their performance and set goals for overall performance improvement. Using numerous examples from state and local governments across the United States, Ammons discusses the practical applicability of benchmarks and benchmarking.

Mary Maureen Brown and Roger Brown continue the managerial theme in Chapter Twenty, "Strategic Planning for Human Resource Managers." After sketching an overview of strategic planning and its relationship to human resource management, they discuss various strategic planning methodologies and present an extensive step-by-step example for conducting a strategic planning exercise in a government setting.

Findings from employee attitude surveys often assist public managers in creating a strategic direction for their organizations. In Chapter Twenty-One, "Designing and Conducting Employee Attitude Surveys," Gary Roberts helps prepare the human resource professional to step beyond the bounds of the traditional HRM role and to become a critical partner in assessing overall organizational attitudes and climate. Roberts presents a thorough analysis, discussing the uses, types, and pitfalls of attitude surveys. He also gives specific instructions and examples for developing, administering, and analyzing an employee attitude survey. The chapter concludes with an excellent example of an employee attitude survey that can be used in a variety of organizational settings.

Perhaps the most popular management innovation of the past decade, Total Quality Management (TQM) has its share of enthusiasts and detractors. Robert Durant's "Total Quality Management" (Chapter Twenty-Two) examines the fundamental premises of TQM and assesses empirical evidence about its implementation in public agencies. Durant furnishes the reader with a map of major pitfalls experienced by government organizations in implementing TQM programs, as well as successful strategies used by agencies to avoid those pitfalls. He argues that "for TQM to fundamentally alter agency cultures and performance on the scale envisioned originally in the advocacy literature, it has to be linked in mutually reinforcing ways to an agency's organizational, responsibility, and accounting structures." Durant also maintains that "TQM's promise can never be fully realized until agencies adroitly, persistently, and clearly institutionalize TQM's values in everyday operations."

Glenn Rainey presents another key managerial tool in Chapter Twenty-Three, "Choosing and Using Human Resource Consultants: Focusing on Local Government." With the use of consultants steadily increasing in government organizations, Rainey relates practical insights for employing them effectively. He focuses on municipal organizations in cities with populations of less than 100,000 because these organizations typically lack the internal staff expertise to conduct major human resource management studies and are therefore more likely than many other agencies to use human resource consulting services. In addition to discussing the use of consultants for particular tasks, Rainey presents methods for selecting and comparatively analyzing consultants. In-depth interviews with practicing human resource managers reveal the pitfalls of choosing the wrong consultant, but Rainey also offers success stories from organizations that have hired consultants to conduct training programs, provide professionally validated assessment centers, assess differing benefit packages, and conduct major classification and compensation studies.

In Chapter Twenty-Four, "Utilizing Volunteers in the Workplace," Jeffrey Brudney describes the potential benefits and drawbacks of using volunteers in public organizations. Following an examination of the current scope of volunteerism at various government levels, Brudney discusses the need to set reasonable expectations for volunteer involvement in the public sector, drawing upon specific examples of the advantages and disadvantages realized by various government-based volunteer programs. He also provides practical advice to human resource managers faced with establishing and managing a successful volunteer program, including how to prepare the organization to accept volunteers, integrate volunteers into program activities, prepare job descriptions for volunteer positions, and develop strategies for volunteer recruitment.

In Chapter Twenty-Five, "Anticipating and Coping with Technological Change in the Workplace," James Danziger and Christopher Gianos discuss technological change as it affects the practice of human resource management in public organizations. They chart a proactive course for human resource managers, encouraging them to engage in environmental scanning (internal and external) to identify constantly evolving circumstances. Danziger and Gianos also suggest that demographic changes are easier to predict than technological ones and propose actions to help managers adopt and manage a learning organization.

Charles Coe and Catherine Reese conclude Part Four with Chapter Twenty-Six, "Budgeting Essentials for Human Resource Managers." They provide instruction to the human resource manager in how to become an integral influence in organizational budget forecasting, preparation, and execution. Coe and Reese cover a full range of issues: mandates and standards affecting staffing, calculation of compensation costs, difficulties of long-range forecasting, potential costs associated with classification and compensation studies, problems associated with unfunded pension liabilities, psychological and fiscal implications of how and when to give salary increases, strategies for presenting and justifying budget requests, and responses to executive actions concerning downsizing and privatization. Throughout they present specific examples from various government organizations to drive home the relevance of budgeting actions to the human resource management function.

All the chapters in Part Four seek to expand and enrich the role of human resource management in public organizations. Although not neglecting traditional HRM roles in employee development, recruitment, selection, and the like, these chapters outline new avenues that human resource managers may take to secure their future in a reinvented public-sector environment.

Reference

National Academy of Public Administration. *Strategies and Alternatives for Transforming Human Resources Management.* Washington, D.C.: National Academy of Public Administration, 1995.

CHAPTER NINETEEN

Benchmarking Performance

David N. Ammons

The performance improvement technique called *benchmarking* has been described most simply by devotees in the private sector as "learning from the pros" (American Society for Training and Development, 1992, p. 1). Its development as a well-defined process is relatively recent, and its application among public-sector units—at least in its most systematic and rigorous form—has been sparing. The concept that underlies corporate-style benchmarking, however, is simple, and its most general application, even by individuals in their daily pursuits and pastimes, is commonplace.

Many weekend athletes, for example, try to model their own performance after the styles and techniques displayed by their favorite professional sports heroes. By attempting to emulate the performance of a star athlete, they set their sights on a benchmark. Even if they never reach the standard represented by their model, any progress they make in that direction will improve their game. In a more formal way, organizations can improve their "game" by systematic observation and careful adaptation of practices honed by operations known for being best in the business. When pursued in a way that is deliberate, systematic, and consistent with a fairly uniform set of steps, this process is known as benchmarking.

Note: Much of the discussion in this chapter is based on *Benchmarking Best Practices in the Public Sector* (1997), a training module the author prepared for the Southern Growth Policies Board and the Southern Consortium of University Public Service Organizations as part of a larger curriculum titled *Results-Oriented Government*.

Benchmarking is a technique inspired by three notions. First, no individual, group, or organization can be the best at absolutely everything it does. Each can be improved in some facet of its activities. Second, those who achieve superior results in some aspect of their endeavors often can serve as worthy models. And third, reinventing the wheel constitutes an unacceptable waste of scarce resources. If another person or organization has already found a better way, why not adopt those practices or, more likely, *adapt* those practices with a few changes here and there to make them fit in a new setting and perhaps cause them to work even better?

Successful benchmarking relies on the choice of appropriate models, the systematic analysis of relevant processes or practices in these models, and careful adaptation for implementation back home. Benchmarking is simple in concept, but the *simplistic application* of that concept can doom a benchmarking project to failure. Careful design and faithful implementation can produce a more favorable result.

This chapter identifies three versions of benchmarking applicable to the public sector. Each version differs from the others in technique and purpose. One form emphasizes long-range vision, another features the diagnosis of operational strengths and weaknesses, and the third focuses on prescriptions for improvement. Careful choice of the version most suitable to a given purpose is a crucial first step to successful benchmarking.

DISTINGUISHING ALTERNATE VERSIONS OF BENCHMARKING

Benchmarks are points of reference from which measurements may be made. Much as surveyors use a point of known location or elevation as a benchmark from which to pinpoint other locations or elevations, organizations wishing to improve their performance on a particular dimension need a benchmark against which to measure their status and eventually their progress.

The following sections focus on three types of benchmarking found in the public sector:

- Corporate-style benchmarking
- Setting targets as benchmarks
- Comparing performance statistics to establish benchmarks

Corporate-style benchmarking is the approach introduced at the beginning of this chapter. It focuses narrowly on a single process and, through careful analysis of that process in "best-in-class" performers, attempts to extract "best practice" lessons. The second and third forms focus more broadly on the identification of benchmarks for the purposes of strategic planning, performance targeting, or evaluation.

At least initially, the second and third forms have proved to be more popular in the public sector than corporate-style benchmarking. Many public-sector units refer to benchmarks—sometimes in the form of targets, even arbitrarily established targets for future achievement, and sometimes in the form of professional standards or the performance marks of respected counterparts—and use them to inspire performance or gauge progress. Public-sector units often refer, appropriately, to this identification of benchmarks and subsequent comparisons as benchmarking. Relatively few of them, however, actually have undertaken the more rigorous process that first claimed the benchmarking label and has captured so much corporate attention in recent years.

Corporate-Style Benchmarking

Accounts of the relatively brief history of the formal process of benchmarking usually cite a few corporate pioneers that began searching for process improvement models within and outside their own industries in the late 1970s and early 1980s. The most celebrated early experience in benchmarking involved Xerox, the company credited with being the first to benchmark, and L. L. Bean, the catalogue retailer. Concerned about warehouse distribution inefficiencies, Xerox officials decided to seek clues for the development of an improved system from L. L. Bean, an acknowledged leader in distribution efficiency. Xerox looked to L. L. Bean as a model, despite the fact that the two companies represented far different industries.

Xerox was impressed by L. L. Bean for good reason: in moving requested items from inventory to the customer, L. L. Bean was three times as proficient as Xerox. Xerox sought and received L. L. Bean's agreement to cooperate and proceeded to send a fact-finding team to L. L. Bean's facility in hopes of discovering the reasons for that company's extraordinary performance. The visitors discovered two principal keys to L. L. Bean's success in prompt distribution. First was the organization of the warehouse inventory. Items were organized by frequency of sales rather than haphazardly or by a system that failed to take sales frequency into account. The most frequently ordered items were the ones most accessible. Second, L. L. Bean's computer software sorted incoming orders to allow maximum efficiency as packers went through the warehouse collecting requested items.

Neither key to L. L. Bean's distribution success had characteristics precluding its applicability beyond the catalogue retail business. Both could be and were adapted with success by Xerox.

The Xerox–L. L. Bean story epitomizes corporate-style benchmarking, but the two other forms, focusing less directly on the analysis of processes, soon began to claim the benchmarking label as well. The second form of benchmarking, often found in the public sector, usually emphasizes the establishment or identification of results-oriented targets. In many ways it is more akin to strategic planning than to the corporate-style benchmarking with which it shares a label.

Setting Targets

Oregon Benchmarks is the best-known program of the genre that identifies results-oriented targets. In 1989, the Oregon legislature created the Oregon Progress Board to help define the state's strategic vision and to monitor progress in achieving the goals embedded in that vision. The centerpiece of the board's efforts soon became the establishment of a set of benchmarks that not only converted abstract goals into tangible targets but also served as a gauge for tracking progress. These benchmarks—focusing on student achievement, housing affordability, reductions in teen pregnancy, improvements in air quality, and a host of other societal improvements—riveted the attention of Oregon's policymakers on a set of clear though ambitious targets (see Exhibit 19.1). The effort quickly gained the praise of leaders in state and local government across the country and in 1994 earned for Oregon Benchmarks the prestigious Innovations in State and Local Government Award, presented by the Ford Foundation and the Kennedy School of Government at Harvard University.

By the mid-1990s, projects similar to the one in Oregon could be found in other states as well. Minnesota's targets, Minnesota Milestones, were introduced in 1992. That same year, the governor of Florida appointed the Commission on Governmental Accountability to the People (GAP Commission), which four years later produced the *Florida Benchmarks Report* (1996). Georgia, North Carolina, and a number of other states proceeded in much the same fashion.

Several local governments pursued a similar course, selecting targets that in some cases defined a vision for their communities and in others at least focused attention on local conditions influencing citizens' quality of life. For example, the Life in Jacksonville project in Jacksonville, Florida, began in 1985 with the development of a set of quality-of-life indicators by approximately 100 local volunteers. In 1991, a second group consisting of 140 citizens under the leadership of the Jacksonville Chamber of Commerce and the Jacksonville Community Council reviewed the indicators and set targets in nine quality-of-life dimensions: education, the economy, public safety, natural environment, health, social environment, government/politics, culture/recreation, and mobility. Equally noteworthy efforts in Cleveland, Seattle, and other cities have similarly focused attention on conditions thought by local leaders to be particularly important to their communities' long-term health and well-being.

These benchmark projects of states and communities are commendable. They identify problems and opportunities; they operationalize a vision of the future by highlighting tangible features of that vision; they help mobilize action by dividing the overall vision into manageable pieces and focusing attention on what needs to be done; and by presenting measurable indicators, they offer a mechanism for tracking progress. Such projects serve an important purpose and deserve the accolades they have won. Because they measure the condition of the state or community and compare each measure with a benchmark that guides state or community efforts

Exhibit 19.1. Oregon Progress Board Definition of Oregon Benchmarks.

Benchmarks, the individual measures that collectively make up Oregon Benchmarks, are indicators of the progress that Oregon has set out to achieve in its strategic vision. Oregon wants to be a state of well-educated, competent people living in thriving communities, working in a well-paying, competitive economy, and enjoying a pristine environment. Just as blood pressure, cholesterol levels, and other such indicators serve as signs of a patient's health, benchmarks serve as signs of Oregon's social, economic, and environmental well-being. Benchmarks measure progress toward Oregon's vision of well-being in such terms as family stability, early childhood development, K–12 student achievement, air and water quality, housing affordability, crime, employment, and per capita income. Benchmarks keep Oregon's leaders, state and local government agencies, service institutions, and citizens focused on achieving those results. By staying focused on outcomes, and by keeping track of results, leaders in Oregon life can reset priorities and adapt and modify programs as they learn what works.

	Historical		Target		
Typical Benchmarks	1980	1990	1995	2000	2010
Percentage of children living above poverty	88 percent	84 percent	88 percent	92 percent	100 percent
Miles of assessed Oregon rivers and streams not meeting state and federal in-stream water quality standards	—	1,100	723	75	0
Real per capita income of Oregonians as a percentage of U.S. real per capita income	99 percent	92 percent	95 percent	100 percent	110 percent

Historical data are used to establish a baseline for various target benchmark measures. In response to each benchmark, Oregon's institutions—public, nonprofit, and private—take periodic data measures that are then collected and compiled by the Progress Board in biennial reports such as this one. This compilation of benchmarks attainment forms a foundation for determining Oregon's progress and for making policy recommendations.

Source: Oregon Progress Board, 1994, p. 2. Reprinted with permission.

or gauges the speed of progress, the use of the term benchmarking is justified. Nevertheless, projects such as these differ sharply from corporate-style benchmarking—the version of benchmarking that in recent years has earned a reputation as a powerful technique for process improvement.

Comparing Performance Statistics

A third approach that also claims the benchmarking label compares selected performance statistics of two or more organizations. Many public-sector units assemble such statistics for their own and several counterpart operations, designating the most favorable numbers to be their benchmarks. The value of such an approach is dependent upon the choice of counterparts. If a unit selects outstanding performers and sets out to meet or exceed ambitious targets, the benefits may be substantial. Unless the exercise then leads to systematic comparison of processes, however, this approach differs significantly from corporate-style benchmarking.

Therefore, despite their common label, the three types of benchmarking are remarkably different from one another. In the general differences just described we can distinguish four specific ways that corporate-style benchmarking differs from one or both of the other two forms:

• *Focus on process.* Corporate-style benchmarking projects focus on processes rather than social or economic conditions, targets or goals, or general comparisons of output or outcome measures. A process typically is selected for benchmarking because it is considered to be important or even vital to a company's success. Corporate benchmarkers try to learn how the companies that are the best in product development, customer relations, product distribution, or some other operation achieve their success. This focus on operational processes differs significantly from a project directing attention to social conditions that a state or local government hopes to influence but that often lie beyond its direct control—for example, unemployment, teen parenthood, or violent crime.

• *Identification of and comparison with outstanding or best-in-class performers.* Once corporate-style benchmarkers have selected an operational focus—as mentioned, often a key process that contributes directly to organizational success or failure—they proceed to identify organizations that achieve outstanding results in that particular operation. The most ambitious benchmarkers look for best-in-class or world-class performers, because those are the organizations from which they stand to learn the most and the performance records of those units serve as the best benchmarks. Other, less rigorous versions of benchmarking often set targets arbitrarily, rarely stacking their own performance record up against best-in-class counterparts.

• *Thorough analysis.* Many projects that establish targets or compare performance indicators for several organizations or government units include little, if any, additional analysis. In contrast, corporate-style benchmarking relies on detailed analysis of the targeted process in the organization doing the benchmarking and of the counterpart processes of benchmarking partners.

• *Depth rather than breadth.* Corporate-style benchmarkers willingly sacrifice breadth for depth. The focus is narrow—typically, a single process—and the quest is for the precise details that account for superior results among top performers. Projects that compile performance statistics for a variety of activities or that report a broad array of social indicators are valuable too, but they differ sharply from the in-depth approach that defines corporate-style benchmarking and has thrust it to the forefront of popular management techniques.

BENCHMARKS AS DIAGNOSTIC GAUGES

The fact that the three approaches to benchmarking differ from one another does not render one less worthy overall than the others or less applicable. Much as a hammer is the appropriate tool for some jobs and a wrench or drill the tool of choice for others, the setting of targets or the comparing of a broad array of performance statistics may be more appropriate in some circumstances and a corporate-style benchmarking project in others.

If the question is, What is our vision for this state or community a decade from now? or, How is this organization performing overall? or, Is the performance of that department up to par? corporate-style benchmarking is not the best choice for finding the answer. The proper focus of a corporate-style benchmarking project is necessarily narrow—too narrow for the job of answering any of these three questions. A better choice for responding to the question about vision is the Oregon Benchmarks approach. A better choice for making a general diagnosis of an organization's performance is the less detailed, less expensive examination of that performance in the context of applicable standards, performance norms, or the performance records of respected counterparts. Comparison with a broad set of performance benchmarks may be the most practical and expedient way to gain a general assessment of an organization's performance or to identify aspects of performance needing more thorough review.

Performance benchmarks of relevance to state and local governments can be found in a variety of places. Professional associations sometimes promulgate performance standards or compile performance statistics that reveal norms that can serve as benchmarks. Individual governments sometimes establish performance targets or report performance results that can be used as benchmarks by others.

Depending on the service being examined, a professional association tied to that service may be a valuable source of information. Performance statistics for public library operations, for example, are compiled and reported annually by the Public Library Association. Many state affiliates have gone a step further and have established performance standards. For instance, standards in North Carolina differentiate three grades of quality for a variety of library service dimensions, including title and subject fill rates, collection turnover rates, program attendance as a percentage of population, circulation rates per capita, and several others (*Standards for North Carolina Public Libraries,* 1988).

Similarly, performance benchmarks can be found for several other government services—sometimes from federal or state agencies. Public transit statistics, for example, are compiled by the Federal Transit Administration (1996), providing comparison information such as operating expense per vehicle revenue mile, operating expense per passenger mile, and passenger trips per vehicle revenue mile. Individual transit systems occasionally develop their own standards or compare their performance statistics with those of relevant sets of counterparts—as did the Williamsport, Pennsylvania, Bureau of Transportation (see Table 19.1).

Several reference works present extensive sets of recommended performance measures for a variety of government services (see, for example, Bens, 1991; Hatry and others, 1992; Tigue and Strachota, 1994; Ammons, 1995; and the booklet series titled *Service Efforts and Accomplishments Reporting,* by the Governmental Accounting Standards Board, 1990–1993). A smaller number of reference works provide standards and performance statistics that can serve as benchmarks (for example, Ammons, 1996; League of California Cities, 1994). The former works are extremely useful as guides for designing a performance measurement system, but

Table 19.1. Selected Performance Statistics for the Williamsport Bureau of Transportation (WBT).

Criterion	Standard	WBT Fiscal 1989	Statewide Average 1989
Percentage employee attendance	≥97 percent	98.8 percent	N/A
Vehicle-miles per employee	≥15,000	16,631	15,219
Vehicle-miles per maintenance employee	≥80,000	85,631	91,233
Vehicle-hours per operator	≥1,700	1,757	1,669
Vehicle-miles per vehicle	≥28,000	31,512	26,008
Expense per vehicle-mile	≤$2.75	$2.43	$2.75
Expense per vehicle-hour	≤$40.61	$34.57	$36.92
Vehicle-miles between road calls	≥3,500	5,596	5,024
Collision accidents per 100,000 vehicle-miles	≤3.0	0.84	2.42
Percentage on-time performance[a]			
Peak periods	≥90 percent	93.3 percent	N/A
Nonpeak	≥95 percent	100.0 percent	N/A
Percentage transfers	≤10 percent	6.5 percent	6.2 percent
Passenger trips per vehicle-hour	≥28	27.5	23.2
Net cost per passenger	≤$0.90	$0.77	$0.78
Operating ratio (revenue/expense)	≥35 percent	43 percent	51 percent

[a]Percentage of trips departing from a bus stop within five minutes of scheduled time.

Source: Poister, 1992, p. 208. Reprinted with permission.

offer little assistance, if any, in assessing performance numbers once they are collected. The latter set of references provides a context in which to judge a unit's performance results. Selected performance statistics for human resource activities, reported in *Municipal Benchmarks* (Ammons, 1996), are shown in Tables 19.2, 19.3, and 19.4. A local government may compare its own numbers to these as a general gauge of performance quality or adequacy, viewed in the context of the performance records of a set of strong performers.

A variety of factors beyond the control of a government administrator may conspire to prevent a given unit from achieving the performance marks attained by others. The blind application of performance benchmarks from other jurisdictions, therefore, may be inappropriate for rendering final judgments on managerial performance or the diligence of service workers. The use of such benchmarks, however, may be extremely useful as a means of assessing service adequacy *in a general sense* and as a diagnostic gauge for highlighting services in need of further scrutiny.

CHOOSING THE PROPER TYPE OF BENCHMARKING

If the performance question is broad—for example, How adequate is our performance on several fronts, given national standards or the performance of others? or, Is this department or that one performing up to par across all of its activities?—comparison of local performance statistics with relevant benchmarks is a practical way to get a reasonably quick answer. If the performance question is more narrowly focused—for example, Is our human resource department up to par when it comes to prompt review and referral of qualified candidates? or, What can we do to be one of the best?—corporate-style benchmarking may be the tool of choice. More specifically, a corporate-style benchmarking project may be an excellent choice in the following instances:

- When initial diagnosis draws into question the adequacy of a given service or reveals possible deficiencies in key processes

- When a given unit, despite generally adequate performance, is determined to excel at a given process and desires to learn from those perceived to be the best at it

Once an organization selects corporate-style benchmarking, there are specific steps it can follow to ensure that the project will be of value.

STEPS IN CORPORATE-STYLE BENCHMARKING

The process of corporate-style benchmarking has been described in as many as ten or eleven steps (Camp, 1989; Keehley, Medlin, MacBride, and Longmire, 1997) and as few as four steps: plan, collect, analyze, and improve (Kinni, 1994). The seven-step

Table 19.2. Benchmarks for Prompt Referral of Job Candidates.

When Eligibility List Is Not Required	When Eligibility List Is Prepared
Greenville, South Carolina	**Savannah, Georgia**
Target: referral of applications to departments within 1 day following cutoff date	Target: certify qualified applicants for civil service positions within 5 weeks of requisition
Actual: 100 percent (1990)	Actual: 100 percent (1988); 90 percent (1989); 96 percent (1990); 90 percent (1991)
Oklahoma City, Oklahoma	Target: certify qualified applicants for professional/administrative positions within 6 weeks of requisition
Target: referral of qualified applicants to departments within 3 days of vacancy closing	Actual: 75 percent (1988); 90 percent (1989); 94 percent (1990); 90 percent (1991)
Actual: 2.6-day average (1991); 3-day average (1992)	**Anaheim, California**
Oak Ridge, Tennessee	Target: recruit and provide lists of eligible applicants within 50 days after recruitment begins
Target: forward applications to hiring manager within 3 days following application deadline	**Phoenix, Arizona**
Raleigh, North Carolina	Target: establish eligibility lists within an average of 50 workdays from the recruitment order
Target: referral of applications within 5 workdays of application closing date	Actual: average of 42 workdays (estimate, 1993)
Actual: 91 percent (1991)	**Portland, Oregon**
Alexandria, Virginia	Target: 2 months to establish eligibility lists
Average number of working days between application closing date and referral of qualified applicants to departments: 5 workdays (1990); 6 workdays (1991); 9 workdays (1992); 10 workdays (1993)	Actual: 2.25 months (estimate, 1992)
	Cincinnati, Ohio
	Targets: (a) 120 days to issue eligibility lists from structured exams; (b) 60 days from unstructured exams
	Actual: (a) 75-day average with structured exam; (b) 50-day average with unstructured exam (1991)
	San Luis Obispo, California
	Target: 60 days to establish eligibility list
	Actual: 90-day average (1990)

Source: Ammons, 1996, p. 180.

Table 19.3. Benchmarks for Prompt Position Audits for Reclassification and Compensation Requests.

Oklahoma City, Oklahoma
  Target: completed within 30 days
  Actual: 100 percent (1992)

St. Petersburg, Florida
  Target: completed within 30 days

Portland, Oregon
  Target: 90 percent completed within
  30 days

Oakland, California
  Percentage completed within
  30 days: 80 percent (1991);
  74 percent (1992)

Boston, Massachusetts
  100 percent completed within 48
  days of request by department
  head or union official (1992)

Reno, Nevada
  70 percent of classification studies
  completed within 90 days; 80 percent within 120 days; 85 percent
  within 210 days (1990)

Source: Ammons, 1996, p. 181.

Table 19.4. Benchmarks for Prompt Hearing and Resolution of Employee Grievances.

City	Time Frame for Hearing Appeals	Time Frame for Resolution of Grievances
Boston, Massachusetts	93.1 percent of grievance hearings scheduled within 3 weeks of receipt (1992)	71 percent of decisions issued within 2 weeks of hearing (1992)
Raleigh, North Carolina		Targets: grievances involv-ing dismissals, demo-tions, or suspensions to be resolved within 33 workdays; all others within 75 workdays Actual: 67 percent of first category within 33 workdays; 87 percent of all others within 75 workdays (1991)
Dayton, Ohio	Target: schedule hearings within 45 days of receipt of request	
Oakland, California	Target: administrative hearing and opinion within 30 days	Target: process appeals within 60-day maximum
Cincinnati, Ohio	Target: schedule disci-plinary appeals within 2 months of request	

Source: Ammons, 1996, p. 182.

process described here (*Benchmarking Best Practices,* 1997, module 2) is generally consistent with these others, combining some of the steps in the longer models and, for the sake of clarity, dividing some of the steps in the shorter versions.

A Seven-Step Benchmarking Process

1. Decide what to benchmark
2. Study the processes in your own organization
3. Identify benchmarking partners
4. Gather information
5. Analyze
6. Implement for effect
7. Monitor results and take further action as needed

Step 1. Decide What to Benchmark

Organizations embarking on a benchmarking project often are tempted to bite off a bigger range of performance dimensions than they can easily chew. They know that they will be devoting considerable time, energy, and other resources to the project, and understandably, they want as much mileage from the effort as possible. Corporate-style benchmarking, however, is designed for achieving great depth of insights on a narrow operational process. It is much less suitable for analysis of an entire function encompassing multiple processes. In the field of human resource administration, for example, a benchmarking project could focus on the employee recruitment process, the position audit process, the grievance process, or another narrowly prescribed process in that work. Attempting to benchmark the human resource department as a whole would be unwieldy.

Whichever process is chosen for corporate-style benchmarking should be of sufficient importance to the success of the organization to justify the effort. A process that is tangential or insignificant is a poor choice.

Step 2. Study the Process Already in Place

Benchmarkers must understand the ins and outs of their own operation in order to

- Be able to explain the details of that operation to benchmarking partners
- Identify process differences that may explain superior results

Step 3. Identify Benchmarking Partners

Learning from the pros starts with identifying who the pros are—that is, figuring out which organizations are the best at the process being benchmarked. Top performers could come from the public sector or the private, but some public-sector benchmarkers find it more practical to select outstanding counterparts from their own sector, thereby avoiding concerns over the sharing of what is sometimes considered proprietary information. Furthermore, some benchmarkers have discovered that successful benchmarking does not always require the selection of partners that are absolutely best in class. In some cases benchmarking on a process that is significantly better but not light-years more advanced will produce more practical or implementable options for improvement and more attainable objectives.

Step 4. Gather Information

The information needed for a successful project will allow benchmarkers to compare in detail different approaches to performing the process being examined. Thus detailed information must be compiled on all the steps and results of the process in each of the project organizations. Although some of the needed data may be available through publications and archival sources, much is typically gathered through questionnaires, telephone interviews, and site visits.

Step 5. Analyze the Information

If proper care was taken in the selection of a process to benchmark and in the identification of outstanding partners, a performance gap between the benchmarking organization and its project partners should be discovered. The objective of the project's analysis phase is to measure the gap, estimate the benefits that would accrue from narrowing or closing it, and identify process differences that account for performance superiority. Many benchmarkers find process flowcharting (described later) to be a useful tool for identifying such process differences.

Step 6. Implement for Effect

The preparation of an action plan begins to move the benchmarking project from "just a study" toward actual performance improvement. Rarely can the processes of a top performer be adopted in toto and put in place effectively in a new setting. More often adaptation is required. In some cases new equipment and special training will be needed. These adaptations and special needs must be incorporated in the action plan, and that plan implemented conscientiously.

Step 7. Monitor Results and Take Further Action as Needed

A lot of things can still go awry, even when implementation has the benefit of a meticulously designed action plan. Careful monitoring ensures that expected results do in fact occur or, if they do not, permits midcourse adjustments—either through spotting deviations from the action plan and insisting on compliance or through revising the action plan to achieve the intended results.

The foregoing steps and brief descriptions provide an overview of the corporate-style benchmarking process. More detailed information is available in a number of recent publications (for example, Camp, 1989, 1995; Spendolini, 1992; Boxwell, 1994; Keehley, Medlin, MacBride, and Longmire, 1997). Important advice on forming a benchmarking team, securing the cooperation of benchmarking partners, benchmarking protocol, designing a questionnaire, involving operating personnel, and other relevant topics should be reviewed prior to embarking on a benchmarking project.

APPLICABLE ANALYTIC TOOLS AND TECHNIQUES

A variety of analytic tools and techniques can be applied to corporate-style benchmarking projects. Two are outlined here: *performance measurement* (the most fundamental of all tools in benchmarking) and *process flowcharting* (one of the most common analytic techniques).

Performance Measurement

Performance measurement is the art of gauging the quantity, quality, efficiency, and effectiveness of goods and services produced by an activity. Good measures can replace subjective impressions with solid information. It is by assembling reliable performance measures for each of the project participants that benchmarkers can make the meaningful comparisons that reveal variations in results and highlight relative strengths and weaknesses in alternative approaches to a given process.

Process Flowcharting

The beauty of process flowcharting is that although a fairly simple technique, it nevertheless can systematically record and categorize each step in the process being examined. Very little specialized knowledge is required for the most rudimentary forms of flowcharting, other than familiarity with the set of five symbols used to categorize the various steps in a given process (see Table 19.5). An analyst carefully observes the process or interviews someone knowledgeable about its details and lists each step in sequence on a *process flowchart,* or simply *process chart,* categorizing each step by use of the appropriate symbol.

The sample flowchart displayed in Exhibit 19.2 identifies and categorizes the steps in one local government's process for requisitioning small tools. If that government engaged in a benchmarking project focusing on this process, it would develop similar flowcharts depicting the steps in the procedures used by its benchmarking partners. By comparing the flowcharts, benchmarkers could discern both the obvious and the subtle differences among the practices and could begin to consider process adaptations based on the successes of the top performers.

Table 19.5. Process Flowchart Symbols.

Symbol	Name	Definition
○	Operation	An item is acted upon, changed, or processed.
▷	Transportation	An object is moved from one place to another.
□	Inspection	An object is examined to be sure quantity or quality is satisfactory.
D	Delay	The process is interrupted as the item awaits the next step.
▽	Storage	The item is put away for an extended length of time.

Exhibit 19.2. Process Chart: Requisitioning Small Tools.

PROCESS CHART

Present Method ☒

Proposed Method ☐

SUBJECT CHARTED _Requisition for small tools_   DATE _____

Chart begins at supervisor's desk and ends at typist's desk   CHART BY _J.C.H._

in purchasing department.   CHART NO. _R 136_

DEPARTMENT _____   SHEET NO. _1_ OF _1_

DIST. IN FEET	TIME IN MINS.	CHART SYMBOLS	PROCESS PRESCRIPTION
			Requistion written by supervisor (one copy)
			On supervisor's desk (awaiting messenger)
65			By messenger to superintendent's secretary
			On secretary's desk (awaiting typing)
			Requisition typed (original requisition copied)
15			By secretary to superintendent
			On superintendent's desk (awaiting approval)
			Examined and approved by superintendent
			On superintendent's desk (awaiting messenger)
20			To purchasing department
			On purchasing agent's desk (awaiting approval)
			Examined and approved
			On purchasing agent's desk (awaiting messenger)
5			To typist's desk
			On typist's desk (awaiting typing of purchase order)
			Purchase order typed
			On typist's desk (awaiting transfer to main office)
105		3 4 2 8	Total

Source: Haynes, 1980, p. 211. Reprinted with permission of Patricia G. Haynes, P.E.

PUBLIC-SECTOR USES OF BENCHMARKING

Relatively few of the most publicized cases of public-sector benchmarking conform to the model of corporate-style benchmarking. The most heralded projects belong to the target-setting type of benchmarking, possessing much in common with strategic planning, often focusing on goals tied to social indicators, and establishing targets called benchmarks. Undoubtedly the most common type of benchmarking in the public sector, however, is the compilation and comparison of performance statistics of several organizations.

Despite the rarity of documented cases, corporate-style benchmarking does occur in the public sector. In fact a few recent projects conform to the corporate model rather well. A tally of such projects, however, would understate the public sector's embrace of the concepts underlying corporate-style benchmarking, even if adherence to the formal steps has been spotty. Enterprising public administrators have been learning from the pros and adapting best practices in isolated cases for years—even long before the corporate-style model was formalized and benchmarking became popular.

In some cities, for example, municipal sanitation departments have lost out in competition with private contractors on some services, drawn operational lessons from the victors and other competitors, and won back the services by incorporating those lessons to improve their efficiency (Osborne and Gaebler, 1992). Municipal fire departments have adapted best practices from top-rated private fire services to improve their efficiency and effectiveness (Ammons, 1980). Municipal utility departments have studied the practices of private counterparts, modified their own operations, and underbid national and international competitors for the right to operate local plants (Syfert and Cooke, 1997; Gullet and Bean, 1997).

Some such cases have proceeded less systematically than formal benchmarking projects; some have actually predated formal benchmarking; but most have involved at least some of the steps prescribed in the corporate-style benchmarking model.

Cases of public-sector benchmarking that have explicitly followed each step of the corporate model are rare. The relative few that have been well documented include projects involving the U.S. Bureau of Printing and Engraving; the Air Force Logistics Command; the Internal Revenue Service; the State of West Virginia; and the cities of Salt Lake City, Utah; Reno, Nevada; and Arlington, Texas (Keehley, Medlin, MacBride, and Longmire, 1997; City of Arlington, 1993). The Bureau of Printing and Engraving, seeking to improve its operations in the sale of coins to collectors, benchmarked on Lenox China and Black & Decker (National Performance Review, 1995). The Air Force benchmarked on Federal Express for rapid and reliable parts delivery. The Internal Revenue Service benchmarked on American Express for billings and Motorola for accounting practices. West Virginia benchmarked with two other states to develop a system for one-stop business registration. Salt Lake City and Reno teamed up to benchmark systems for receiving and handling customer complaints and requests for information. Arlington benchmarked various parks and recreation operations with both public- and private-sector benchmarking partners.

The benefits of corporate-style benchmarking are not reserved for the private sector alone. Governments that are willing to devote the time, energy, and other resources necessary to conduct a serious corporate-style project can derive significant benefits as well.

CONCLUSION

All three forms of benchmarking have practical value in the public sector. A given form, however, must be matched carefully and appropriately to the task at hand.

Corporate-style benchmarking has a narrow focus, is process oriented, and is rather costly. It requires the gathering of detailed information, emphasizes thorough analysis, and often involves visits to the sites of benchmarking partners. If a public-sector unit wants to improve a key process or operation within its functions, corporate-style benchmarking may be a good option.

Benchmarking of either the Oregon Benchmarks or the general performance comparison variety usually has a much broader focus. Operational details are typically less important in these projects than are measures of results or indicators of social condition. If the purpose of the benchmarking project is planning, general review, or assessment, these approaches are more applicable than corporate-style benchmarking.

Project focus is one key determinant of the appropriate form of benchmarking. The expected role of the project is another. Corporate-style benchmarking is expected to reveal better ways to perform a given process or produce a given service. The expected result will be a *prescription for improvement.* Other forms of benchmarking can be expected to set targets (specifically, the Oregon Benchmarks approach) or diagnose problems (general comparisons) but are not particularly well suited for prescribing specific operational solutions.

Benchmarking in all three different varieties is applicable to the public as well as the private sector. The intended focus and role of the project will suggest the type of benchmarking that is most appropriate.

References

American Society for Training and Development. *Understanding Benchmarking: The Search for Best Practice.* Alexandria, Va.: American Society for Training and Development, 1992.

Ammons, D. N. "Taking the Best of a Private Fire Service and Making It Public." *Municipal Management*, 1980, *2*, 103–109.

Ammons, D. N. (ed.). *Accountability for Performance: Measurement and Monitoring in Local Government*. Washington, D.C.: International City/County Management Association, 1995.

Ammons, D. N. *Municipal Benchmarks: Assessing Local Performance and Establishing Community Standards*. Thousand Oaks, Calif.: Sage, 1996.

Benchmarking Best Practices in the Public Sector. A training module produced by the Southern Growth Policies Board and the Southern Consortium of University Public Service Organizations. Research Triangle Park, N.C.: Southern Growth Policies Board, 1997.

Bens, C. K. *Measuring City Hall Performance: Finally, a How-to Guide*. Denver, Colo.: National Civic League Press, 1991.

Boxwell, R. J., Jr. *Benchmarking for Competitive Advantage*. New York: McGraw-Hill, 1994.

Camp, R. C. *Benchmarking: The Search for Industry Best Practices That Lead to Superior Performance*. Milwaukee, Wis.: Quality Press, 1989.

Camp, R. C. *Business Process Benchmarking: Finding and Implementing Best Practices*. Milwaukee, Wis.: Quality Press, 1995.

City of Arlington. *Program Division Benchmarking Projects*. Arlington, Tex.: City of Arlington Parks and Recreation Department, Aug. 1993.

Federal Transit Administration. *National Transit Summaries and Trends*. Washington, D.C.: U.S. Department of Transportation, Apr. 1996.

Florida Commission on Government Accountability to the People. *The Florida Benchmarks Report*. Tallahassee: Executive Office of the Governor, 1996.

Governmental Accounting Standards Board. *Service Efforts and Accomplishments Reporting: Its Time Has Come*. [Series of booklets.] Norwalk, Conn.: Governmental Accounting Standards Board, 1990–1993.

Gullet, B. M., and Bean, D. O. "The Charlotte Model for Competition: A Case Study." *Popular Government*, Winter 1997, pp. 19–22.

Hatry, H. P., and others. *How Effective Are Your Community Services? Procedures for Measuring Their Quality*. Washington, D.C.: Urban Institute and International City/County Management Association, 1992.

Haynes, P. "Industrial Engineering Techniques." In G. J. Washnis (ed.), *Productivity Improvement Handbook for State and Local Government*. New York: Wiley, 1980.

Jacksonville Community Council. *Life in Jacksonville: Quality Indicators for Progress*. Jacksonville, Fla.: Jacksonville Community Council, Nov. 1994.

Keehley, P., Medlin, S., MacBride, S., and Longmire, L. *Benchmarking for Best Practices in the Public Sector: Achieving Performance Breakthroughs in Federal, State, and Local Agencies*. San Francisco: Jossey-Bass, 1997.

Kinni, T. B. "Measuring Up: Benchmarking Can Be Critical, but It Doesn't Have to Be Expensive." *Industry Week*, Dec. 5, 1994, pp. 27–28.

League of California Cities. *A "How to" Guide for Assessing Effective Service Levels in California Cities.* Sacramento: League of California Cities, 1994.

Minnesota Planning. *Minnesota Milestones: 1993 Progress Report.* St. Paul: Minnesota Planning, 1994.

National Performance Review. *Serving the American Public: Best Practices in Telephone Service.* Washington, D.C.: U.S. Government Printing Office, 1995.

Oregon Progress Board. *Oregon Benchmarks: Standards for Measuring Statewide Progress and Institutional Performance.* Salem: Oregon Progress Board, 1994.

Osborne, D., and Gaebler, T. *Reinventing Government: How the Entrepreneurial Spirit Is Transforming the Public Sector.* Reading, Mass.: Addison-Wesley, 1992.

Poister, T. H. "Productivity Monitoring: Systems, Indicators, and Analysis." In M. Holzer (ed.), *Public Productivity Handbook.* New York: Dekker, 1992.

Spendolini, M. J. *The Benchmarking Book.* New York: AMACOM, 1992.

Standards for North Carolina Public Libraries. Raleigh, N.C.: North Carolina Library Association/Public Library Section and North Carolina Public Library Directors Association, 1988.

Syfert, P. A., and Cooke, D. "Privatization and Competition in Charlotte." *Popular Government,* Winter 1997, pp. 12–18.

Tigue, P., and Strachota, D. *The Use of Performance Measures in City and County Budgets.* Chicago: Government Finance Officers Association, 1994.

CHAPTER TWENTY

Strategic Planning
for Human Resource Managers

Mary Maureen Brown
Roger G. Brown

Over the past two decades, human resource managers have become indispensable members of the strategic management team. Their role has evolved from personnel record keeping and position management to organizational planning and process improvement. Because human resources are critical assets that account for the largest portion of an organization's overall budget, the human resource manager often serves as an internal consultant to other units of the organization, providing training and skill building for planning exercises, serving as a resource clearing house for managers and planning teams, and researching essential data on current and future staffing needs and priorities. This chapter describes the steps of the strategic planning process, presents a model of the planning cycle, explains the role of the human resource (HR) manager in the process, and discusses opportunities and pitfalls that the HR manager must recognize and manage. Examples used to illustrate the process are taken from a recent strategic planning effort in a large metropolitan police department.

According to Perry (1993), human resource management has become "perhaps *the* most important determinant of organizational effectiveness" (p. 59). This is so because HR management focuses on acquiring and using most effectively the human capital, knowledge, skills, and experience upon which the organization depends for its success. "To manage strategically means that traditional HR objectives such as turnover or performance are superseded by organizationwide goals designed to complement a specific business strategy" (Dyer and Holder, 1988, p. 1). With such a central role in organizational success and with traditional roles expanding, human resource managers must be seen as integral to strategic management activities.

Klingner (1993) has identified five key elements in the strategic *mind-set* HR managers need to adopt in order to serve as effective consultants in the strategic planning process. First, they must recognize that human resources are critical. This includes a heightened concern for productivity and accountability and therefore requires better information systems. Second, HR managers must shift from "position management to work and employees" (p. 570), focusing on new classification and compensation systems, performance monitoring, and rewards and incentives. Third, Klingner calls for more innovation. Consulting HR managers must think and behave like entrepreneurs, which involves risk taking. Fourth, HR managers must practice simultaneously "asset development and cost control" (p. 571). Employee development goes beyond individual skill building to improving employee relationships, team building, problem solving, and retooling. Fifth, HR managers in the strategic planning process must shift from their former emphasis on equal employment opportunity and affirmative action compliance to managing workforce diversity; that is, they must move from concerns for categories and proportions dictated by compliance agencies to concerns for all employees' productivity, development, participation, and mission accomplishment.

It is with these elements in mind that following sections describe the steps in the strategic use of a planning cycle. The HR manager is ideally situated to assist in this planning process, becoming what Morrisey (1995) terms an internal "coach/facilitator . . . someone who does not have a strong personal vested interest in the outcome" but who maintains a keen concern for the organization's overall effectiveness (p. 14). The HR manager leads and supports the activities of the organization as it moves from a vision and mission to goals and objectives, from tasks and responsibilities to outcomes and solutions. He or she facilitates the development of a strategic plan that will enable the organization to achieve its mission and goals. He or she assists management in developing, implementing, and evaluating this plan. In the following discussion of the strategic planning cycle steps, each section defines the overall activities of the step, distinguishes the role of the human resource manager, and identifies some of the common tools employed in the step. The chapter concludes with a discussion of the problems that sometimes occur in the development, implementation, and evaluation of organizational plans.

THE PLANNING CYCLE

Why does management invest the energy and resources required to develop a strategic plan? In any organization, whether it is public or private, production oriented or service based, goals and activities are developed and implemented to achieve the organization's mission. On one hand goals and activities may be unspoken and unstructured. On the other they may be well documented and highly formal. Regardless of the organization's mission, every work effort has at the very least an implicit objective for achieving that mission. The *planning cycle* offers management an opportunity to examine the organization to ensure that the mission is indeed attained. Such organizational planning can be very resource intensive; it will often require several months of work from a variety of personnel across the organization. However, it acts as a device to communicate goals, reassess opportunities, and promote effectiveness and efficiency.

The planning cycle involves five steps, identified in Figure 20.1. It begins with an examination of the vision, values, and mission of the organization. The vision, values, and mission set the pace for all future efforts. The strategic planning phase in step 2 involves gathering information and exploring the alternatives and implications of current and future activities. This phase focuses on the three- to five-year goals of the organization. In step 3, operational plans are built from each of the goals identified in the strategic plan. It is these operational plans that translate the strategic goals into everyday work activities. The implementation stage,

Figure 20.1. The Strategic Planning Cycle.

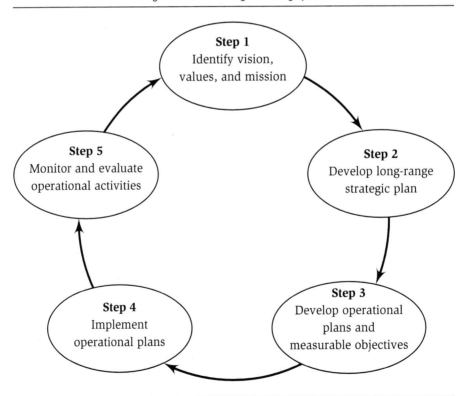

step 4, involves marketing the operational plans, solidifying support, and making the actual work changes that need to occur to support the plans. Finally, the evaluation stage, step 5, involves monitoring and evaluating the extent to which different work processes advance the values, mission, and goals of the strategic plan. For the most part, these five steps are sequential; forward progress depends on the successful completion of the previous step.

The *planning wheel* is an invaluable asset to the planning process. The wheel provides a basis for channeling energies and focusing attention on the key critical areas involved in the entire planning process. In essence the wheel comprises four concentric rings (Figure 20.2). The first ring focuses on the organization's values and vision. The second ring taps the role of the organization: for example, is it production, manufacturing, or service oriented? The third ring comprises the various arenas, or functions, that the organization employs to accomplish its goals. The final center ring focuses on the mission the organization strives to achieve. The planning wheel is a frame of reference, a starting point to direct thoughts and ideas toward developing work processes that advance the vision, values, and mission of the organization. The role of the human resource manager is to facilitate processes in which the members of the organization elaborate and develop each of the rings. It is important to recognize that the content of each ring will vary by unit or organization. (The remainder of this chapter incorporates an example of a police department using the planning wheel to assist with its planning cycle.)

Figure 20.2. The Planning Wheel.

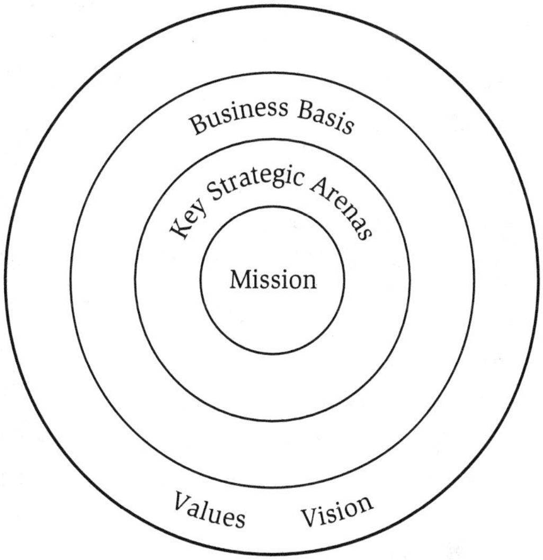

Step 1. Develop or Identify
the Organizational Vision, Values, and Mission

Developing or identifying the organization's *vision, values,* and *mission* is the first step in the planning cycle. In some organizations the vision, values, and mission are explicit. In others they are understood but perhaps not articulated. In yet others they are either in flux or not well understood across the organization. The role of the HR manager is to assist the organization in articulating the vision, values, and mission that support its activities. Efforts should focus on addressing questions such as, What is our mission? What values drive our abilities to achieve our mission? What ethics guide our actions? What is our vision for the future? What is the key to the future of our organization?

In this stage of the planning cycle the role of the HR manager is either to document or to facilitate a dialogue for crafting the vision, values, and mission. If the vision, values, and mission are apparent, the HR manager may, with management support, choose to examine the extent to which all members understand and agree with the vision, values, and mission statements as defined. If the vision, values, and mission have not been defined or are in a state of flux, the HR manager must assist management in developing and crafting these tenets.

Some of the tools the HR manager may choose to complete this step are *vision analysis, brainstorming techniques, survey analysis,* and *focus groups* (see Exhibit 20.1 at the end of the chapter). Again, the HR manager must ensure that the vision, values, and mission of the organization are well understood and agreed on before moving to the next step.

Figure 20.3 depicts how a police department began to employ the planning wheel concept. Ring 1 identifies the department's values and vision. The department values fairness, respect, courtesy, and integrity. The department vision is to develop problem-solving partnerships with the community that will ultimately influence the primary mission depicted in ring 4, to prevent and reduce the occurrence of crime. Rings 2 and 3 link the vision and values to the mission. Ring 2 illustrates the organization's primary work basis. The department does not manufacture a product but provides a service to the community. Because the focus is on solving and preventing crimes, much of the work is information or knowledge based. Thus the organization too is knowledge based. It also focuses on continuous improvement in service delivery. Ring 3 is refined in the strategic planning step discussed later.

To develop a combined mission and vision statement, the police department used a combination of top command staff brainstorming sessions and focus groups of middle-level supervisors. The command staff were asked to respond to the questions, "What is the nature of our business?" "What is community-oriented policing?" "What are our core values?" "What key results do we wish to achieve?" "What conditions and indicators will we use to gauge our success?"

Figure 20.3. A Police Department Planning Wheel (Rings 1, 2, and 4).

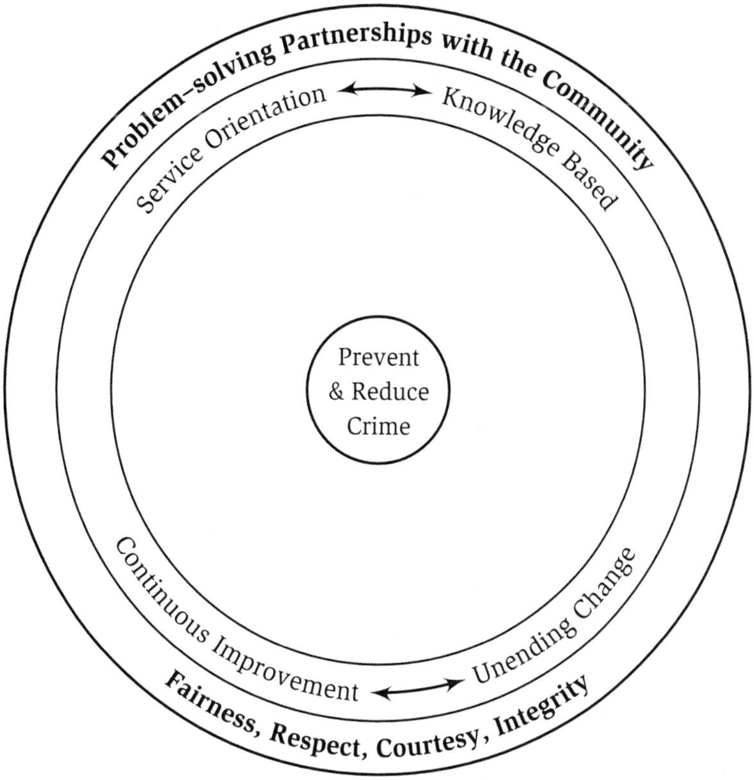

From this exercise a mission statement was drafted by a team of department managers. Then the supervisor groups were asked to identify the ways in which their respective units related to and contributed to the department's success in achieving its mission. In crafting their vision, values, and mission statements, the police executive staff relied on a number of brainstorming sessions, focus groups, and retreats. Once this foundation was set, the department shifted its attention to developing its strategic plan.

Step 2. Develop a Long-Range Strategic Plan

The *strategic planning process* is best described as an activity that ensures that the organization's mission is met. The strategic plan acts as a linking pin between the mission and how that mission is accomplished through daily activities. It serves as a bridge, providing guidance on where and how work activities should proceed to achieve goals.

In the planning cycle, managers rely on two forms of planning: *strategic planning* and *operational planning*. Strategic planning differs from operational planning in that it has a longer horizon and does not usually identify specific objectives that easily translate into daily operations. Strategic plans typically identify the three- to five-year goals of the organization. Strategic plans set the theme for the organization and help ensure that the mission is achieved. The strategic plan provides a framework for the development of operational plans; it serves as a link between the mission and daily operations.

It is the responsibility of top management to formalize the strategic plan; it is the responsibility of top management, middle management, and field operation personnel to develop the strategic plan. The importance of involving every level of the organization in the development of the strategic plan cannot be overstated. Participation across the organization is absolutely necessary to make sure that operational plans will be developed and implemented to advance success.

The strategic planning process assesses the current environment and determines where the organization needs to concentrate efforts for the coming three to five years. The central purpose of the strategic plan is to identify the goals that promote and support the organization's mission and values. The planning process includes these specific steps:

- Identify five to eight key strategic arenas where work activities should concentrate for the coming three to five years (thus the strategic plan focuses on issues that require multiyear efforts).

- Document goals of these key strategic arenas, and recruit an organizational champion to oversee the implementation process.

- Identify long-term objectives for achieving each of the goals.

- Communicate and publish the goals and objectives throughout the organization (probably with a cross-functional effort and involvement from every section of the organization; Morrisey, 1995).

Identifying and analyzing the key strategic arenas is by far the most difficult and time-consuming component of the strategic planning process. In importance it is second only to actual implementation because it sets the long-term direction for the organization. It involves conducting a critical issues analysis of all the arenas, identifying all potentially strategic arenas, prioritizing the arenas in order of importance, analyzing each of the arenas for gaps that might affect meeting the organization's mission, and finally, selecting the five to eight goals that should drive the organization's activities for the coming three to five years.

The role of the HR manager here is to facilitate the strategic planning process, to assist members of the organization in identifying the critical issues, uncovering the gaps, and prioritizing the goals. The major focus is to keep the process on track and to assist and support members as they move through the activities. As part of his or her facilitation activities, the HR manager can serve as a trainer and a data analyst.

Several tools are available to assist the HR manager in this phase. The manager may choose to conduct individual interviews, focus groups, or surveys to uncover information. Oftentimes the strategic planning process will rely on a series of retreats to develop the plan. Tools such as nominal group techniques, surveys, and elite interviews provide a good mechanism for uncovering information during retreats. Retreats are often used to confirm previously collected information and to build consensus on future directions to pursue. As the analyst begins to uncover information pertaining to the third ring, or the functional arenas, gaps between what the organization is doing and what it should be doing to achieve its mission will be identified. It is these gaps that provide the basis for the strategic plan. Organizational members should set their sights on addressing the identified gaps and bringing the arenas into closer alignment with the organization's vision, values, and mission. Once the critical issues analysis is complete and the gaps identified, then the goals can be written for the coming three to five years, and each of the goals can be assigned to an organizational champion, someone who can assist with the development of the operational plan and ensure that the goals translate effectively to work processes.

In assessing the needs of the organization, its members, and its various clientele groups, a simple principle should be followed: when you want to know what people need, ask them. The two most commonly used tools for this purpose are surveys and group analysis. Each tool consists of many techniques, and its success depends upon systematic, objective data gathering. Focus group sessions, for example, are intended to elicit in-depth views from small groups of participants (eight to twelve) about a limited number of highly focused topics (Witkin and Altschuld, 1995). Some care should be given to setting up the groups so that a representative cross section of the organization or the community is achieved by the time all groups have provided input. Within each group, however, the individuals often can share a common perspective: they can be members of the same unit within the organization or individuals who share a functional specialty for example.

The HR manager who acts as a focus group leader contacts participants well in advance to request their assistance and to inform them of the purpose of their participation. During the session the leader begins a round of introductions, warms up the group with a general question on the topic, then solicits responses from each participant in turn. An assistant records the responses in summary form in such a way that all participants can see the summaries. In the succeeding rounds of discussion the leader presents two or three more narrowly focused questions and repeats the process of clarifying and recording responses. The purpose of the focus group session is to get a range of viewpoints, not to achieve consensus. All opinions are valid, and the leader should be encouraging and supportive in order to encourage full and candid participation. Soon after each session the leader and assistant compile the responses, arrange them into any obvious themes or categories, and feed the results back to participants, stakeholders, and other interested persons in the strategic planning process.

Turning once more to the police department case study, Figure 20.4 depicts the department's planning wheel with the rings complete. Ring 3 identifies the primary arenas that affect the police department's ability to promote its values and achieve its mission. They are the most critical factors that affect the department's ability to achieve its mission. In essence these arenas reflect the resources available to the organization for achieving its mission. However, as we discuss below, the central concern is to examine how these resources align with promoting the mission. Ultimately, the human resource manager will assist management with examining the resources, or arenas, to determine if in fact the resources assist in achieving the mission or if they actually constrain mission attainment.

As mentioned, the arenas will vary by organization. For the police department the key arenas identified were information technology, human resources,

Figure 20.4. Police Department Planning Wheel (Rings 1 Through 4).

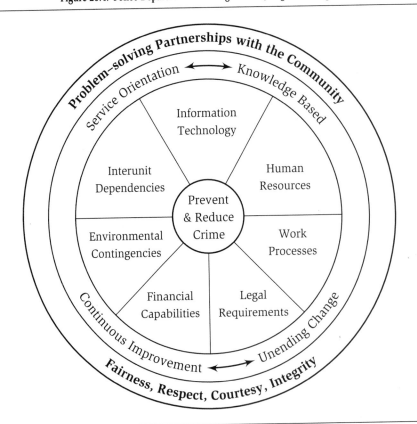

work processes, legal requirements, financial capabilities, environmental contingencies, and interunit dependencies. Each of these arenas was identified as a factor that influences the department's ability to achieve its mission.

In this setting the role of the human resource manager was to assist the department in identifying the arenas. The HR manager relied on brainstorming activities, individual interviews, and several focus group sessions to collect the information. Further, crime trends and personnel trends examinations and budget analyses were conducted to assist with the process. The human resource manager assisted the department with examining each of the key arenas to determine if there were any gaps or areas of concern that might negatively affect department values and mission. In essence the HR manager assisted management in identifying among the arenas the respective strengths and weaknesses in promoting the organization's values and mission. The planning wheel served as an important tool for focusing thoughts and crafting the strategic plan, and the process relied on input from a variety of organizational members. For example, budget analysts provided financial information, and crime analysts provided crime trends. Here the role of the HR manager was to work with management to identify what information was needed and to assist in coordinating the data collection effort. Because the arenas the police identified are common to many organizations, the following discussion elaborates on how these arenas influence mission attainment.

In sum the arenas were distinguished, their relative strengths and weaknesses for supporting the mission were assessed, and finally, the goals were identified and prioritized.

Information Technology. More and more organizations are relying heavily on information technology to support their work activities. Unfortunately, in some instances work processes and activities have evolved to fit poorly defined information technology. The extent to which technology impedes or facilitates the work efforts and the achievement of the goals of the strategic plan is of vital importance to most organizations. In the police example the existing technology was not designed to collect information on multiple suspects, and the computer system allowed the entry of only one suspect description when a crime occurred. Therefore, when a rape or homicide investigator was investigating a case with multiple suspects, it became necessary to conduct a hand search through hundreds of paper files. In this case the technology impeded attainment of the department's problem-solving vision, its knowledge-based orientation, and its mission to reduce and prevent crime.

Human Resources. The HR manager serves as a key resource to the strategic planning process. From human resource planning and forecasting to recruitment, selection, training, and development, the HR manager is involved in virtually every aspect of the effective management of people. Performance appraisal and reward systems are additional areas of expertise that the HR manager contributes to the organization's long-range strategy for enhancing effectiveness. In addition to carrying out the traditional tasks of the HR department, today's HR manager also assists in the development of organizational design and management style and in team building. The goal is to ensure that every member of the organization understands his or her roles and responsibilities and how they relate to the overall mission. The HR manager also helps diagnose and solve communication problems, both vertically across levels and horizontally among units, which is a critical prerequisite to the strategic planning effort.

Work Processes. As management examines the strategic needs of the organization, it must ask whether there is a need for redesigning current work operations. Attention should focus on the extent to which the work operation affects employee motivation, satisfaction, effectiveness, and efficiency. Attention should also focus on which aspects of each job need improvement. Process improvement focuses on the extent to which operational processes require reengineering or redesign to improve the fit between daily work and achievement of the organizational mission. Process improvement involves mapping current work processes as they are conducted and examining them for their fit with the goals of the strategic plan. Such mapping often identifies areas where the work effort does not mesh with the goals. It can also locate areas where work activities can be streamlined through new procedures or enhancements in technology.

Members of the police department had a deep sense for how work processes were conducted and believed that tremendous gains could be made in redesigning the work processes to fit their mission. For example, in one work process routine field reports were collected by one group of officers, reported to the sergeant, filed with the district captain, and catalogued by administrative personnel. Instead, investigators wanted the officers to enter the field information directly into a laptop on the scene and transmit it to a database, making the report available to all appropriate individuals in a fraction of the time.

Legal Requirements. Both public and private organizations encounter legal requirements that drive many of their daily routines. Recently, for example, the Americans with Disabilities Act of 1990 and the Family and Medical Leave Act of 1993 have changed the way the police department has approached advertising and recruitment, testing and placement, job design, and work scheduling.

All managers are encouraged to examine the extent to which the presence or absence of different legal requirements impedes mission attainment. If conflict occurs between the mission and the presence or absence of legal requirements, management may choose to incorporate into the strategic plan an action item for lobbying for legislative reform. In addition, when legislative mandates supercede agency procedures, management must consider how it can develop processes that will balance compliance with the legislative requirements and management's need to achieve the organization's mission. Turning once more to the police department case study as an example, several police agencies are actively lobbying for gun reform legislation to help reduce the occurrence of violent crime.

Financial Capabilities. The next common arena focuses on the organization's financial strengths or limitations for achieving its mission. Organizations often experience cyclical swings in the availability of financial resources. The role of the HR manager again is to focus managers' thoughts on whether the managers anticipate financial resource constraints on achieving their mission. If management foresees certain problems looming on the horizon, then the strategic plan may incorporate activities to help address shortfalls. Moreover, attention should be given to how costs are allocated. For example, an analysis of the police department budget showed that 85 percent of expenditures were in human capital. Therefore management felt that strides in streamlining work processes would assist the department in achieving its mission to reduce crime.

Environmental Contingencies. Environmental contingencies are any external factors that might influence the organization's ability to achieve its mission. For example, in the health care arena, officials might examine the annual number of births to forecast staffing requirements to meet childhood immunization needs. Although a host of external contingencies may influence the organization's ability to achieve its mission, managers are typically very astute in understanding and reacting to the external forces that drive their work activities. The role of the HR manager in this arena is to shed light on any external contingencies that might prove problematic over the coming three- to five-year time frame for achieving the organization's mission and to help managers focus on those factors. For example, if the demographic profile of the police department's community were to change dramatically, perhaps with an increase of Hispanic residents in the city, the department might add to its objectives the use of bilingual officers or interpreters.

Interunit Dependencies. Private and public agencies are often confronted with the complexities of interdependencies; this is especially true for police departments. An interdependent situation occurs when the actions of two or more units are required to achieve the mission of the organization. One of the roles of the human resource manager at this point is to help managers identify where these interdependencies occur and if they are in conflict. For example, both police and district attorney agencies play a large role in the reduction of crime. However, although each centers on reducing crime, the two agencies may conflict on how they achieve their shared goal or mission. Police are often frustrated by district attorneys who plea bargain cases, and district attorneys are frustrated by police officers who view arrest as the only recourse for solving crime-related problems. The extent to which the interdependencies conflict and therefore work to prevent attaining the mission must be identified. If management decides to focus activities on resolving the conflict, the strategic plan may dedicate resources to that effort.

The Police Department's Arenas. In sum the police department identified three arenas that demanded ongoing attention: information technology, human resources, and work processes. It noted gaps within each of these arenas and developed three- to five-year goals for addressing the shortcomings. How exactly did the department identify and collect the information and make the efforts elaborated in the discussion of the arenas?

It began with a one-day retreat whose members came from every level and unit in the organization. The retreat activities explained how to develop a strategic plan and how to identify critical issues. These activities also incorporated a brainstorming session where members were encouraged to identify the arenas and issues that support many of their activities. After this initial retreat the members split into four working teams, and each team was assigned one or more arenas. The teams were asked to meet individually over the coming months to collect information on the strengths and weaknesses of their arena (or arenas) as they related to the vision, values, and mission of the police department. Once the strengths and weaknesses were identified and documented, the draft document was circulated throughout the organization for additional comments and feedback. The police department then convened a second retreat to review the draft. It was this retreat that then identified the arenas of human resources, information technology, and work processes as the ones that needed attention. The original four teams were then mixed, and four new teams were established. Each group was assigned specific areas within one of the three arenas and was asked to meet and report back with three- to five-year goals to align these areas with the mission, values, and vision. (For example, a goal one team developed was to provide tools to patrol officers that would assist with solving community problems.) After developing the goals the teams reconvened to debate the goals and formalize them for adoption. Each goal was then assigned to an organizational champion, someone who would facilitate, nurture, and promote attainment of the goal.

Step 3. Develop an Operational Plan and Measurable Objectives for Each Goal

The *operational plans* (sometimes referred to as tactical plans) identify specific objectives for achieving each of the goals identified in the strategic plan. Operational plans provide the mechanisms for achieving the goals of the strategic plan. In its entirety the organization has identified its vision for its mission and values. The strategic plan identifies specific three- to five-year goals for achieving the mission. The operational plans identify specific concrete objectives to achieve those strategic planning goals. These concrete objectives should translate easily into work operations. The strategic plan tends to address what the organization wants to accomplish; operational plans focus on what needs to be done to achieve what the organization wants to accomplish. Operational plans also differ from the strategic plan in that they have a shorter horizon, typically one year, and they are continually monitored for the extent to which they successfully accomplish the goals of the strategic plan.

It is within the context of the one-year operational plans that an organization achieves flexibility and adaptability to both internal and external needs. The operational plans become living and breathing documents as they constantly undergo revision and modification to better promote the strategic plan and vision. The operational objectives should be measurable and verifiable. They should center on achieving the goals of the strategic plan, and managers should pay constant attention to whether the objectives are feasible. Their attention should also focus on the costs of implementation, both in time and materials. Above all, the operational plans should be consistent with the rest of the strategic plan. The daily objectives and work processes that an operational plan identifies should be those that will see the strategic plan through to completion. The role of the HR manager in this step is to assist each unit with facilitating meetings, ensure that appropriate information is collected, and provide expertise and guidance to the work teams.

As mentioned previously, in the police department case an organizational champion was assigned to each goal. This individual worked with the HR manager and various units in the department to develop objectives that would translate the goal into everyday work activities. The HR manager assisted in the development of both measurable objectives and evaluation criteria for determining if those objectives had been met. For example, to meet the goal of providing tools to the patrol officer that would assist with solving community problems, one objective was to develop a problem-solving database of the available nonprofit and government resources for addressing community problems. The database was to be developed and available to 100 percent of the officers within six months. Figure 20.5 presents an expanded view of step 3 of the police planning cycle that includes this strategic goal and its operational objectives.

Step 4. Implement the Operational Plans

The *implementation of an operational plan* will include many tasks for the human resource manager. New and revised work processes will require recruitment and selection of staff, orientation and training, and position allocation among the various units. As the new work processes are incorporated into the organization's routine, the HR manager will help revise and develop performance

Figure 20.5. Detail of the Police Department Planning Cycle.

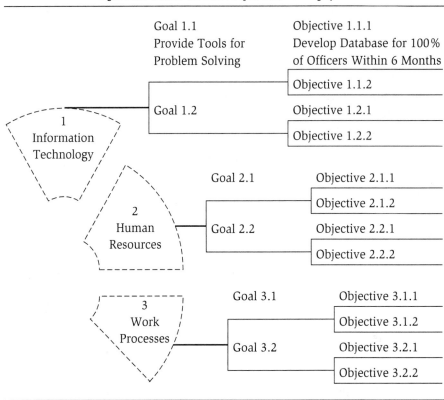

measures, monitor performance appraisals, and use the results to enhance further training and development efforts. In order to provide incentives for optimal staff performance, the HR manager will work with unit heads to implement the classification and compensation system chosen during the strategic planning phase. Many jurisdictions have moved toward broadbanding systems to allow more flexibility in managing pay scales, promoting and transferring staff, and introducing pay-for-performance incentive systems. In addition the HR manager will be a consultant to managers dealing with motivational and discipline issues as the operational plan is fully implemented.

Step 5. Monitor and Evaluate Operational Activities as They Support Plans and Goals

Finally, the HR manager will assist other managers in the organization to devise *monitoring and evaluation elements with which to regularly and systematically gauge progress* toward matching units' day-to-day activities to the objectives of the operational plans and the goals of the strategic plan. Sophistication in the evaluation processes will vary greatly, from Total Quality Management (TQM) and continuous quality improvement (CQI) process improvement measures to simple percentage change graphs and bar charts. Most important, the HR manager can help the operational managers focus on cost effectiveness as well as efficiency, quality as well as quantity. *Customer satisfaction surveys, complaint processing,* and *before-and-after comparisons* are a few of the evaluation tools especially suited for measuring effectiveness in achieving an organization's goals and objectives. Table 20.1 provides an overview of the various tools employed in different stages of the business planning cycle (a glossary defining each of the tools appears in Exhibit 20.1, at the end of the chapter).

AVOIDING PITFALLS IN THE PLANNING CYCLE

The human resource manager needs to be sensitive to the potential pitfalls and hurdles the organization may encounter throughout the planning cycle. He or she will want to identify and troubleshoot potential problems as early as possible.

Sylvia, Meier, and Gunn (1991) identify some of the major hurdles encountered in the planning process, such as difficulties in achieving consensus on strategic goals and disagreement on the relative importance of the gaps identified or on how to correct these gaps. In essence the strategic plan records how future resources will be allocated. By overtly stating that resources will be dedicated to some areas, it covertly identifies the areas that will not be elaborated. Political constraints on goal consensus often surface in the planning process. Attention must also focus on the means by which the ends or goals are achieved. The values of the organization should serve as a constant litmus test for both the end product and the means by which that product is achieved.

The tendency to oversimplify problems in order to reach consensus or to move the process along is another potential planning cycle pitfall. Managers may gloss over the complexities that will be required to implement the goals. Again, the planning group should include a broad spectrum of employees from every level of the organization so that such complexities can be called to managers' attention. Another barrier to effective planning is the desire to move through the process too fast. Managers may not dedicate adequate attention to identifying the key strategic areas or the investment required to implement the goals. The HR manager may also witness problems of cognitive nearsightedness. Management may wish to focus on short-term Band-Aid fixes rather than long-term corrections.

In some instances the HR manager may encounter information constraints. Timely, accurate, and adequate information may not be available. Budgetary or personnel requirements may not be available in the format that would fully reveal

Table 20.1. Tools Employed in the Planning Cycle.

Planning Cycle	Tools										
	Survey Questions	Elite Interviews	Focus Groups	Gap Analysis	Vision Analysis	Brainstorming	Cost-Benefit Analysis	Benchmarking	Document Analysis	SWOT	Forecasting
Step 1: Identify vision, values, and mission	✓	✓	✓		✓	✓					
Step 2: Develop long-range strategic plan	✓	✓	✓	✓		✓	✓		✓	✓	✓
Step 3: Adopt operational plan and objectives			✓	✓					✓	✓	
Step 4: Implement operational plan			✓					✓			
Step 5: Monitor and evaluate activities				✓			✓	✓			

the degree to which the organization manifests different gaps or problems. Managers may be unwilling to provide information about shortcomings because they fear a reprimand. The HR manager should be astute to these potential problems and, if they are encountered, provide a mechanism to assist the organization past the hurdle.

Finally, according to Mintzberg (1994), two primary failures of participation can derail any planning process: the first is grounded in management and the second in the organizational climate. In other words, strategic planning depends for its success on the active support of both management and the organization's broad membership.

The HR manager should be sensitive to all the issues described here and should assist organizational leaders in understanding these potential pitfalls and avoiding their occurrence.

CONCLUSION

Human resource managers play a critical role in the overall functioning of organizations. Their role as consultants to managers throughout the organization provides substantial support in planning and process improvement. Human resource managers have become integral role-players in organizational planning and in assisting managers in averting the pitfalls that threaten success. Today's human resource managers provide an invaluable service to managers as they develop and implement their strategic and operational plans for organizational success.

Exhibit 20.1. Glossary.

Benchmarking A process for systematically examining the *best practices* in the work processes of your own organization or in organizations recognized as models for your own organization's improvement. By selecting an appropriate benchmark service or process, the HR manager helps the organization establish priorities and targets for improvement. The team that evaluates each benchmark practice should include the people who will be performing the improved work processes (see Chapter Nineteen; International City/County Management Association, 1993).

Brainstorming A simple but effective data-gathering tool for needs assessment. A group of managers and employees is assembled by a facilitator such as the HR manager. The group is presented with a clear, well-worded question or issue on which the facilitator wants the group's best ideas. After a silent writing period during which participants list their ideas, the facilitator lists the ideas on a flipchart during a round-robin discussion. The participants then combine items and delete duplicate items.

Exhibit 20.1. Glossary, cont'd.

The ideas are typed, categorized, and analyzed as data gathering for the strategic planning exercise proceeds.

Cost-benefit analysis, cost effectiveness   A means of tapping the economic efficiency of a program, that is, the extent to which social benefits outweigh the social costs. All costs and benefits associated with a particular program or activity are identified and then expressed in terms of monetary units. Cost-benefit analysis often examines the cost variances associated with differing alternatives. It can provide detailed information on the costs and benefits associated with various alternatives. Cost effectiveness differs from cost-benefit analysis in that it focuses on the efficacy of a particular program or activity in terms of outcomes or outputs. In cost effectiveness analyses, inputs typically are expressed as money, but outputs are not (for example, training program A will cost about $750 for every worker trained).

Document analysis   A review, summary, and integration of various organizational documents and reports to provide an overall view of the organization. Analyzing previous reports and minutes can produce an excellent understanding of the organization. It can also produce a time line of significant events that provides a context for the organization's evolution.

Elite interview   An interview with a top manager and/or key unit head. These interviews are an important source of information for the strategic planning effort. They should be conducted by the HR manager or an experienced organizational analyst. The interview begins with a few structured questions designed to gather information about the organization, its work processes, and its mission and vision. Sufficient time should be allowed to pursue the interview in unexpected directions as the topics are developed. A transcript of the interview should be produced as soon after the session as possible.

Focus group   A session that elicits in-depth views from small groups of participants (eight to twelve) about a limited number of highly focused topics (Witkin and Altschuld, 1995). The session leader begins a round of introductions, warms up the group with a general question on the topic, then solicits responses from each participant in turn. An assistant records the responses in summary form and so that all participants can see the summaries. In succeeding rounds of discussion, the leader presents two or three more narrowly focused questions and repeats the process of clarifying and recording responses. The purpose is to get a range of viewpoints, not to achieve consensus. All opinions are valid, and the leader should be encouraging and supportive in order to gain full and candid participation. Soon after each session, the leader and assistant compile the responses, arrange them into any obvious themes or categories, and feed the results back to participants, stakeholders, and other interested persons in the strategic planning process.

Exhibit 20.1. Glossary, cont'd.

Forecasting   An examination of current and past trends to predict, or project, future occurrences. For example, future crime trends and demands on police departments can be forecast by examining past crime occurrences. Forecasting in areas such as budget allocations, employee turnover, and demands for service delivery can guide the planning cycle. Naturally, the accuracy and usefulness of forecasting depends heavily upon the quality of the available data.

Gap analysis, discrepancy analysis   An examination of clearly defined gaps between actual practice and a performance standard. The premise is that any problem is a deviation from a performance standard, whether the standard is clearly stated or not. By focusing on the performance gap, the HR manager and the planning team can determine the cause for the discrepancy and devise a solution, such as more skills training, better communication, or improved technology.

Questionnaire   A document of questions circulated to members of the organization for the purpose of collecting information. Questionnaire items may tap issues such as productivity and performance, organizational communications, morale, leadership, job satisfaction, or resource availability. Questionnaires allow the HR manager to collect information from a broad organizational spectrum, giving the HR manager an understanding of how the members of the organization perceive different work-related issues. Questionnaires also offer a relatively easy approach to tapping information from stakeholders external to the unit. Surveying customers or clients can provide valuable insight on the extent to which the organization is achieving its stated mission (see Chapter Twenty-One).

SWOT analysis   An examination of *strengths, weaknesses, opportunities,* and *threats* (SWOT). The analysis typically is conducted by a management team, but focus groups of other employees can add to the effort. SWOT analysis is conducted by an experienced facilitator who leads the team systematically through discussions of the SWOT factors facing the unit or the organization as a whole. The analysis typically lasts from two to four hours.

Vision analysis   An examination of the vision, of "where we want to be in the future" (in contrast to the mission, which states the organization's purpose and its fundamental business). The vision analysis is most often conducted by top management with the assistance of consultants, including the HR manager. After a statement of the "vision of excellence" is adopted, the role of the HR manager and top management is to share the vision with employees, customers, and community members and gain their enthusiastic support.

References

Dyer, L., and Holder, G. "A Strategic Perspective on Human Resource Management." In L. Dyer and G. Holder (eds.), *Human Resource Management: Evolving Roles and Responsibilities.* Washington, D.C.: Bureau of National Affairs, 1988.

Harrington, H. J. *Business Process Improvement.* New York: McGraw-Hill, 1991.

International City/County Management Association. *Total Quality Management: Strategies for Local Government.* Participant's Handbook. Washington, D.C.: International City/County Management Association, 1993.

Klingner, D. E. "Developing a Strategic Human Resource Management Capability in Public Agencies." *Public Personnel Management,* 1993, *22,* 565–578.

Mintzberg, H. *The Rise and Fall of Strategic Planning.* New York: Free Press, 1994.

Morrisey, G. C. *Morrisey on Planning: Vol. 2. A Guide to Long-Range Planning: Creating Your Strategic Journey.* San Francisco: Jossey-Bass, 1995.

Perry, J. L. "Strategic Human Resource Management." *Review of Public Personnel Administration,* 1993, *13*(4), 59–71.

Sylvia, R. D., Meier, K. J., and Gunn, E. M. *Program Planning and Evaluation for the Public Manager.* Prospect Heights, Ill.: Waveland Press, 1991.

Witkin, B. R., and Altschuld, J. W. *Planning and Conducting Needs Assessments: A Practical Guide.* Thousand Oaks, Calif.: Sage, 1995.

CHAPTER TWENTY-ONE

Designing and Conducting Employee Attitude Surveys

Gary E. Roberts

Employee attitude surveys are one of the primary tools of social science research (Bowditch and Buono, 1982; Stoner, 1992; Fowler, 1993). A strength of the survey method is its inherent flexibility and its relative economy in the investment of organizational resources. This chapter provides an overview of survey design, administration, and analysis, focusing on self-completed written survey questionnaires.

The literature on survey research is mammoth and ranges from in-depth texts (Bowditch and Buono, 1982) to specific applications targeting narrow methodological issues (Fowler, 1992). The challenge is to produce a concise summary of the key elements of survey design and administration. This chapter approaches that challenge through four sections discussing the uses of employee attitude surveys, survey design and development, survey administration, and analysis of survey results. Exhibit 21.2, at the end of the chapter, illustrates an attitude survey.

USES OF EMPLOYEE ATTITUDE SURVEYS

Employee attitude surveys serve three major purposes: to diagnose employee attitudes, problems, and conditions (Balch and Blanck, 1989); to assess the impact or influence of organizational change (Woodward and Williams, 1987); and to secure employee input (Standing, Martin, and Moravec, 1991). It is important to keep in mind that employee attitude surveys supplement but do not replace other forms of employee involvement. Employee attitude surveys are diagnostic tools that focus on quality of work life issues such as employee job satisfaction (Daley, 1988), work motivation (Kovach, 1987), and organizational commitment and trust (Mirvis and Kanter, 1989). Employee attitudes are important because they are associated with critical human resource processes. For example, employee job satisfaction influences employee absenteeism and turnover (Rainey, 1991), and the degree of employee motivation affects employee work efforts and productivity (Lawler, 1994).

Employee attitude surveys are extremely useful for gauging the effects of organizational interventions and are important organizational change and development tools (French and Bell, 1984). Examples of these kinds of applications include assessing employee perceptions and reactions to a new performance appraisal or merit pay system (Daley, 1988; Schay, 1988), determining the prevalence of sexual harassment (U.S. Merit Systems Protection Board, 1995), measuring the effectiveness of a gainsharing program (Hauck and Ross, 1988), and assessing the effects of a change in work design (Woodward and Williams, 1987).

Surveys are useful vehicles for enhancing employee input and organizational identification. The survey process sends a clear message that employee opinions are important, especially if the organization acts upon survey results. The very act of completing a survey can release employee tensions, facilitating organizational problem solving (French and Bell, 1984). Employees often express their appreciation of the attempt to solicit their opinions. In survey comment sections, remarks such as "this is the first time anyone from the organization has asked me what I think" are often received.

SURVEY DESIGN AND DEVELOPMENT

Plan and Schedule

The success of any survey is dependent upon coordinating a multitude of complex tasks, and that process begins with a master plan and schedule. Table 21.1 presents a prototypical schedule for completing an employee attitude survey. This survey process will take approximately six months to complete. The following sections discuss the steps in the schedule in greater detail.

Convene Task Force and Set Clear Goals and Objectives

An effective attitude survey begins with a complete understanding of the subject matter (Stoner, 1992). The critical first step is selecting the task force to oversee the project's development and administration. An effective task force consists of key stakeholders who have a strong interest in securing and acting

Table 21.1. Sample Master Attitude Survey Schedule.

	Month					
	1	2	3	4	5	6
Phase 1. Instrument development						
Convene task force	✓					
Set goals and objectives	✓					
Publicize survey	✓					
Conduct literature review	✓	✓				
Conduct interviews and focus groups		✓				
Draft questions and cover letter		✓	✓			
Conduct pretest			✓			
Make final revisions to instrument			✓			
Prepare code book			✓			
Phase 2. Survey administration						
Select sample			✓			
Print instruments				✓		
Distribute instruments				✓		
Distribute follow-up instruments				✓		
Code and enter data			✓	✓		
Phase 3. Survey analysis						
Analyze data					✓	
Complete preliminary analysis					✓	
Discuss with management					✓	
Complete final report					✓	
Distribute summary to employees					✓	
Conduct employee meetings and feedback sessions						✓
Assess the strengths and weaknesses of the survey process						✓
Make revisions to the process and instrument						✓

upon employee input. Task force members will be chief executives, managers, line employees, and union officials: for example, in a municipal police department that is completing an employee attitude survey, the chief, district commanders, first-line supervisors (lieutenants and sergeants), union officials, and selected patrol officers should be part of the task force. One of the task force's first assignments is to clearly define the survey's goals and objectives. Then, with the end results clearly defined, designate a staff member with research expertise to serve as project coordinator. Consider employing an outside consultant if the organization lacks the expertise or if high levels of conflict require a neutral third party.

Publicize the Survey

The organization should provide advance notice to employees on the survey's goals and objectives and reinforce its importance orally and in writing through memos and face-to-face employee meetings (Stoner, 1992). Top management's active participation in *selling* the survey encourages employees to take it more seriously.

Conduct a Literature Review

After the task force sets the survey's goals and objectives, the next task is learning the subject area, and this entails a literature search. There is no need to totally reinvent the wheel, however. Contact other organizations and also professional associations to obtain copies of their attitude surveys; sections of these surveys are often usable after appropriate modifications. The U.S. Merit Systems Protection Board does extensive employee attitude surveying and documents completely its survey design and development procedures including its instruments, which are public domain (U.S. Merit Systems Protection Board, 1995).

Conduct Employee Interviews or Focus Groups

After the literature review the second step is to interview selected employees or to conduct an employee focus group to gain an understanding of the major problems and issues (Judd, Smith, and Kidder, 1991). Inevitably, many employee attitude surveys fail to address key organizational issues because these surveys were not preceded by developmental research. For example, a standard job satisfaction survey may miss key factors contributing to employee dissatisfaction, such as work scheduling or overtime practices.

Develop Survey and Understand Limits and Weaknesses

A clear understanding of the survey method's limitations is essential for avoiding misapplications. The main weaknesses of survey research include various types of response bias and imprecise scaling, which reduce the reliability and accuracy (validity) of people's responses. The following list shows both the common factors that contribute to response bias and the potential solutions (Fowler, 1993). These factors are addressed in greater detail in later chapter sections.

Factors

1. Respondents fail to understand the question due to unclear or complicated directions or scaling.
2. Respondents do not know the answer.
3. Respondents cannot remember the answer, although they know it.
4. Respondents are unwilling to give the proper answer, even when they know it, as respondents lack confidence in the organization or lack interest in the subject matter.
5. Respondent answers question based on what they think the sponsoring organization wants to discover (hypothesis guessing) rather than on true feelings, out of a desire to please the organization or fear of reprisal.

Solutions

1. A thorough pretest.
2. A clear cover letter explaining the survey's goals and objectives to generate interest.
3. A clear guarantee of respondent confidentiality and anonymity.
4. Organizational receptivity to adverse feedback (no reprisals).
5. Involvement of respondent in survey design and administration.
6. An informational and educational campaign on survey benefits to stimulate interest.

The single most important step in eliminating or minimizing biasing factors is a thorough pretest.

Draft Survey Questions and Cover Letter

Upon completion of the developmental research, the organization is ready to draft questions (items). The following sections summarize the do's and don'ts of item and questionnaire development.

Survey Length and Size. As a general rule the respondent should take approximately fifteen minutes to complete the instrument (Stoner, 1992). Remember, there is an inverse relationship between the survey's length and response rates. The goal is to gather the information in the most efficient fashion possible.

Evaluate each survey item as to its importance and need, as many surveys are too long. A careful survey development process and thorough pretesting reduces instrument length by eliminating redundant, inappropriate, or inefficient questions (those answerable by other sources, such as internal records). For example, asking employees the size of their pay increase is an ineffective strategy for gathering information on compensation practices as many employees regard pay questions as invasions of privacy. It is better to consult payroll records for accurate information.

An effective employee attitude survey consists of clear, relevant, and appropriate questions. Most of the remainder of this section on drafting survey questions focuses on guidelines for item structuring and wording. It also summarizes the two major scaling formats: graphic rating scales and Likert attitude scales.

Open- Versus Closed-End Questions. There are two broad categories of questions: open-end and closed-end. Open-end questions require the respondent to provide the answer, and closed-end questions present a preselected list of response categories. The advantages of open-end questions are that they uncover answers that the developers did not foresee and that the respondent can answer the question in his or her own words, avoiding the frustration of a limited range of options (Judd, Smith, and Kidder, 1991; Fowler, 1993). In effect, open-end questions offer employees an opportunity to express themselves. These questions are also appropriate when there are many response categories (Judd, Smith, and Kidder, 1991). Disadvantages of open-end questions include uninterpretable, idiosyncratic (unique to the person) answers, ineffectiveness with employees of limited literacy levels, and greater difficulty in data analysis (Fowler, 1993; Judd, Smith, and Kidder, 1991).

Closed-end attitude questions allow the employee to choose response categories that measure strength or intensity of feeling. Closed-end questions are easier to interpret and analyze, assuming that the developer fully understands the range of responses, as a result of a complete pretest process. Most employee attitude surveys employ both open-end and closed-end questions, with the majority of questions being closed-end. Always provide at least one general open-end question asking for additional employee input, observations, or suggestions.

Literacy Levels. In writing items, there are a number of clear do's and don'ts. The work of Judd, Smith, and Kidder (1991) provides the framework for the following section.

Ensure that the respondents' literacy levels match survey requirements. Keep the wording as simple as possible.

Problem example: What are the sources
of variance in employee job satisfaction?

Terms such as *variance* and *sources of employee variance* are unfamiliar to many audiences. Use a simpler format.

Corrected example: What are the reasons
for differences in employee job satisfaction?

Jargon. Avoid jargon and acronyms unless respondents clearly understand their meaning or the survey clearly defines them.

Problem example: The procedures
that govern employee RIFs are fair.

Some employees may not understand the acronym *RIF.* Clearly spell out and explain what the term means.

Corrected example: The procedures that govern
employee reductions in force (reducing the number
of employees through layoff or attrition) are fair.

Ambiguous Wording. Clearly define all terms to avoid ambiguous wording susceptible to multiple interpretations.

Problem example: Most employees are
satisfied with the organization's compensation practices.

The key to this statement is clearly defining the term *compensation.* Does it refer to base pay, incentive systems, overtime, or benefit practices singly or in combination?

Corrected example: Most employees are
satisfied with the organization's merit pay system.

Biased Terms. Avoid using biased terms.

Problem example: Union bosses
impede effective program management.

The term *union bosses* elicits a negative response from most employees. A more neutral term enhances the item's validity.

Corrected example: Union officers
impede effective program management.

Complicating Responses. Avoid complicating the respondent's task in answering questions. If the instrument requires a considerable investment in psychic energy and external research, only highly motivated employees will respond.

Problem example: What was your after-tax family income last year?

Many employees are unable or unwilling to provide specific dollar figures. To reduce the respondent's burden, provide a range of responses.

Corrected example: Check the category that
approximates the dollar value of your pay increase.

_____$30,000 or less

_____$30,001 to $50,000

_____$50,001 to $70,000

_____$70,001 or greater

Incomplete Expression of Alternatives. Avoid incompletely expressing alternatives, as this reduces survey accuracy.

Problem example: I would eliminate the
current performance appraisal system if I were able.

This statement provides only one option, eliminating the system. The employee who disagrees with the statement is not necessarily indicating support for the current system, only an unwillingness to eliminate it. If the item's intent is to register dissatisfaction with the current system, reword the statement.

Corrected example: I would eliminate or
make major changes in the current appraisal system.

Unwarranted Assumptions. Unwarranted assumptions cause respondents to answer the wrong question(s).

Problem example: How satisfied are
you with your most recent appraisal rating?

The employee may be new and not yet formally appraised. The solution is to introduce a filter question. There is a danger here, however, as too many filter questions confuse respondents. Keep filter questions to a minimum.

Corrected example: Did you receive a performance appraisal this past year?
If yes, answer questions 1 through 4. If not, please skip to question 5.

Double-Barreled Questions. Double-barreled questions try to assess two distinct concepts within the same question.

Problem example: The performance appraisal process
increases employee motivation and satisfaction.

This question is double-barreled because satisfaction and motivation are separate attitudes and do not always vary in the same direction. Divide the question into two separate items—unless the explicit research purpose is to determine the appraisal system's influence on both satisfaction and motivation in combination.

Question Sequencing

Besides item wording, question sequencing is very important. If question sequencing is inappropriate, reduced response rates and accuracy are likely. The information here summarizes helpful question sequencing tips, based upon Judd, Smith, and Kidder (1991).

- Begin each survey with a few interesting and easy questions. This engages the respondent and increases the respondent's confidence in his or her ability to complete the survey.

- Group together questions that address the same topic. Jumping from subject to subject confuses respondents.

- Provide clear transitions and introductions explaining each section's purpose and changes in subject matter. Respondents need to know why the items are relevant.

- Place demographic (race, sex, age, and so forth) questions at the survey's end and clearly explain the need for this information in interpreting the results.

- General questions should come first, followed by more specific and detailed questions later.

- To avoid biasing a response, pay careful attention to question sequencing. For example, do not sequence a series of questions on the problems of the performance appraisal process so that this series is followed by a request for an overall assessment of the system's effectiveness. Asking specific questions before a general one creates a halo effect, biasing the response to the general question.

Scaling. All survey questions employ some type of scaling format. The most common types are graphic or itemized rating scales and Likert attitude scales (see Figure 21.1) (Fowler, 1993). In a graphic rating scale the respondent circles the response category that most reflects his or her feelings. Graphic rating scales usually include numerical anchor descriptions to denote which end of the scale is high and which low.

The Likert scaling format is the most common and assesses the strength of the respondent's feelings or attitudes toward the subject area. Likert items are easy to develop and analyze and can be combined to form indices summarizing various job-related attitudes (Judd, Smith, and Kidder, 1991). For example, six questions that deal with the appraisal process might be combined into an overall performance appraisal attitude scale, simplifying analysis. A complicating factor is the use and interpretation of the *no opinion* or (as in Figure 21.1)

Figure 21.1. Examples of Two Scales.

GRAPHIC RATING SCALE ITEM

Rate your degree of satisfaction with your present job by circling the appropriate number with 1 representing very dissatisfied and 10 very satisfied.

| Very Dissatisfied | | | | | | | | | Very Satisfied |

```
1    2    3    4    5    6    7    8    9    10
├────┼────┼────┼────┼────┼────┼────┼────┼────┤
```

LIKERT ATTITUDE SCALE ITEM

Please indicate whether you strongly agree (SA), agree (A), disagree (D), or strongly disagree (SD) with the statement below by circling the appropriate response category. Circle DK (don't know) if you are not sure.

Performance appraisal systems   SA   A   D   SD   DK
are rarely as accurate as they
claim to be.

---

don't know category. It is difficult to discern whether a respondent really does not know or is simply unwilling to provide an answer. However, in most employee attitude surveys, workers possess definite opinions on workplace conditions, and the survey can safely exclude the *don't know* or *no opinion* category from the scales on the questionnaire.

Cover Letter. The survey instrument should include a cover letter clearly explaining the survey's purpose, its importance, and the uses for the results (Stoner, 1992). In essence this letter presents a clear reason why the employee should fill out the instrument, detailing specific benefits. A well-written cover letter signed by the chief executive reinforces top-level support and commitment and signals management's receptivity to employee input (Exhibit 21.1 shows a sample cover letter). The cover letter and survey should clearly guarantee employee confidentiality and anonymity in a clear statement highlighted in bold print. One means of reassuring employees is to use a neutral third party, such as a university researcher, to receive and analyze the results (Stoner, 1992).

Exhibit 21.1. Sample Cover Letter.

Dear Mr. Jones,

Enclosed is a copy of our annual employee attitude survey. This survey gathers information on your job-related experiences and opinions concerning key workplace issues. We need your help to improve the workplace for all employees. Your participation is essential to the survey's success, and the results will make a difference.

An important point to remember is that there are no right or wrong answers. This is not a test! Answer the questions based upon your true feelings and opinions. **We guarantee that your answers and identity will remain confidential and anonymous.** No person or work group will be identified or singled out.

The survey takes approximately 15 minutes to complete. Return the completed questionnaire through interoffice mail in the sealed, self-addressed envelope.

We will present the results in a series of face-to-face meetings beginning on April 11. At these meetings we will ask for your reactions to the results with the goal of generating suggestions for improving the workplace while identifying solutions to problems. Thank you for your time and effort.

Sincerely,

Jane Smith
Chief Administrative Officer

Conduct Pretest

In developing the draft survey instrument, the most critical step is conducting a systematic pretest. This stage can save the organization from low response rates and incomplete and irrelevant information. The first step in pretesting is to select a representative sample of approximately twenty employees (Fowler, 1993). For example, for an attitude survey about employee performance appraisal system practices, the survey pretest sample should include employees who directly participate in the appraisal process, are motivated to provide accurate feedback, possess the language and literacy levels to understand the task, and typify the organization's various job classification and organizational levels.

Pretest respondents must receive clear assurances that their answers will be anonymous and confidential (no names or other identifiers on the survey instrument) and that their responses will be used only for improving the survey. They should complete the instrument in the developer's presence, and the developer should time how long it takes each respondent to complete the instrument. The pretest respondents should note unclear or confusing wording, directions, or scaling along with unreasonable or intrusive questions. Modify an item if more than 15 percent of the pretest respondents indicate some type of concern (Fowler, 1993).

Interview pretest respondents on the survey's comprehensiveness, content, and coverage (Judd, Smith, and Kidder, 1991). Are there any uncovered subjects? Should you drop, alter, or expand certain sections? Is the instrument too long? What questions should be added?

Make Final Revisions and Develop Codebook

After making the final instrument revisions, the next step is constructing a survey codebook. A codebook is critical for valid and reliable data coding and entry. It summarizes critical item information, including the numerical values assigned to each answer. To analyze the questions, assign each response a specific number. For example, a typical Likert scale item assigns a 4 for a response of *strongly agree,* 3 for *agree,* 2 for *disagree,* and 1 for *strongly disagree.* The common practice is to assign *no opinion* a zero or a missing value. The codebook is the reference guide for data entry and analysis personnel.

SURVEY ADMINISTRATION

Select the Sample

A detailed treatment of sampling is beyond this chapter's scope. Instead, the following discussion centers on two basic sampling procedures: *simple random sampling* and *stratified random sampling.*

How large should the survey sample be? The answer depends on finances, organizational size, and the nature of the issues. For small and medium-size governments or agencies (less than 250 employees), it is generally feasible to survey the entire employee population (a census). For larger organizations, a properly designed and selected sample provides valid information generalizable to the larger population.

The first step in sampling is selecting the appropriate sample size. For example, in an organization with 1,000 employees, a sample of 278 can generalize to the entire employee population (Isaac and Michael, 1981). A sample size of 400 can be representative of an employee population of 100,000 (Isaac and Michael, 1981), and the reader can discern a pattern here. From a statistical standpoint, the size of the sample assumes a smaller percentage of the whole as the size of the population increases. A clear example of this is the polling process for national political campaigns, which employs a sample size of less than 2,000 to predict election results for millions of registered voters.

The simplest sampling procedure is a random sample, where each employee's selection probability is equal. To select the proper sample size, consult a sample size table, found in most statistics or survey books (Isaac and Michael, 1981). To implement a random sampling procedure, generate an employee master list organized alphabetically or by Social Security number. Then select every nth case until reaching the designated sample size. For example, with an employee population of 1,000, select every third name for a sample of 333. To make the sample truly representative, each selected employee must respond. This is not a reasonable expectation on the first round of most employee attitude survey applications. In order to track who responds, code numbers are assigned to identify employees. Then those who do not respond can be replaced by other people, selected randomly from the remaining employees.

Another concern is that a simple random sample can mask significant differences between employee subgroups. Keep in mind that the random sampling process works best for analyzing a homogeneous group of employees and for making generalizations to an entire organization. However, organizations are frequently interested in analyzing specific subgroups as well as the complete population. A process called stratified random sampling helps to ensure that the sample generalizes to distinct subgroups. The first step in this sampling procedure is to develop separate master lists of employees by relevant occupational subgroups. Table 21.2 presents a hypothetical subgroup summary for a population of 1,000 employees.

The second step is to select every nth case based upon the required sample size for each subgroup. Note that stratified random sampling dictates a larger total sample size than does simple random sampling.

Print the Instrument

After completing the final adjustments to the instrument, the next step is printing. A professional appearance is important for maximizing response rates (Dillman, 1981). This entails an uncluttered format that is easy to follow and read. The preferred option is professional printing, but most standard word processing programs are capable of producing an attractive instrument. If available, a computer graphics program enhances the instrument's appeal.

Table 21.2. Stratified Random Sampling Example.

	Total Population	Sample Size Required
Police	350	184
Firefighters	300	169
Public works employees	350	184
Total	1,000	537

Distribute the Instrument

A healthy response rate is a basic precondition for the survey's success. With a low response rate the probability of unrepresentative results increases significantly. A key question is when and where employees complete the instrument. Generally, a captive audience produces higher response rates but at the cost of validity, as employees resent being forced to complete the instrument or fear the loss of anonymity. Several distribution options are available.

The first is to mail the instrument to the employee's home address (Stoner, 1992). Include with the survey instrument and cover letter a stamped self-addressed return envelope. A home mailing enables the respondent to complete the survey away from the pressures of the workplace, hence he or she can devote more time and thought to it. The downside to home completion is a lower response rate, as employees feel less pressure to complete the survey.

Another method of survey administration is to assemble intact workgroups and administer the instrument en masse (a captive audience method). This enhances response rates and eliminates mailing costs. The downside is the aura of compulsion surrounding such administrations. A compromise between mail and groups sessions is distributing surveys to individual employees and asking them to complete the survey sometime during their workday. Like home administration, this avoids the pressure of group administration and provides employees with opportunities for additional thought and analysis. Always provide a secure means for returning the survey, such as sealed blank envelopes returned to a locked collection box.

Distribute Follow-Up Instrument

In mail surveys, give the respondent a certain number of days to return the instrument. Nonrespondents can receive a postcard reminder or another copy of the survey (Stoner, 1992). However, employees may view this as intrusive and threatening, so a preferred solution is to issue general reminders to all employees to complete the questionnaire if they have not already done so.

Code and Enter Data

Care during the coding and data entry stage is essential, as entry mistakes introduce serious error into the analysis. Most data entry programs can limit entry codes to prespecified ranges. In addition, to ensure data accuracy, closely supervise and periodically audit the entry process. An effective auditing procedure selects 5 to 10 percent of the original surveys and compares the original responses to the coded entries.

SURVEY ANALYSIS

Nonresponse

After all the hard work of developing and administering the survey, many organizations fail to invest the requisite time and effort in data analysis. One of the first data analysis issues is the assessment of the final sample's representativeness. A truly representative final sample is one in which all respondents in the initial appropriate sample completed the survey, which is a rare occurrence. Suppose that 50 percent of the employees returned usable questionnaires. Is this still a representative sample? Unfortunately, there is no definitive statistical technique to determine sample representativeness. In certain instances, representativeness is essential, but in other cases it is not critical. For example, in a survey of employee attitudes toward benefits, if more experienced employees complete the instrument at a higher rate, this does not diminish the survey's utility as employee tenure is positively associated with benefit practice knowledge and use.

There are several means for indirectly assessing the final sample's representativeness. One strategy is to compare respondents' characteristics to overall employee norms. Characteristics suitable for comparing are

Demographic characteristics: race, gender, age, education level, degree area

Job-related characteristics: job title, organizational tenure, time in current job

If the sample's demographics are similar to the population's, this provides some indication that the sample is representative. However, there are usually unmeasured characteristics that differentiate respondents from nonrespondents. These differences often manifest themselves in the form of unmeasured attitudes, opinions, and experiences. For example, with attitude surveys assessing satisfaction with performance appraisal practices, employees who have either positive or negative experiences usually return the surveys at a higher rate than those with neutral feelings.

What is an adequate response rate? Once again, there is no magical number, but a 75 percent response rate minimizes many variables that negatively influence sample representativeness.

Basic Data Analysis Techniques

Most attitude surveys are analyzed using a computer spreadsheet or statistical package. A detailed treatment of the more sophisticated analysis techniques (regression, analysis of variance, *t*-tests) is available in relevant texts, and this discussion presents only two basic data methods, *frequency tables* and *cross-tabulations* (Isaac and Michael, 1981). Frequency tables provide the number and percentage of responses in the relevant categories and subgroups. Table 21.3, for example, is a frequency table for an item assessing employee attitudes toward older workers. Cross-tabular analysis (Isaac and Michael, 1981) analyzes group differences very effectively and easily using most types of survey data. Table 21.4 is an example of cross-tabular analysis for an item assessing pay satisfaction for firefighters, police officers, and public works employees. In this example, public works employees are more satisfied with pay (73.7 percent very satisfied or satisfied) than are police officers (63.5 percent very satisfied or satisfied) and firefighters (64.8 percent very satisfied or satisfied).

There are several statistical techniques (chi-square analysis, Somer's *D*) employed to test for statistical significance in cross-tabular analysis (see Guilford and

Table 21.3. Example of Frequency Count.

	Strongly Agree	Agree	Disagree	Strongly Disagree	No Opinion
1. On average, our older employees are less energetic than our younger employees	1 (2.2 percent)	3 (6.7 percent)	32 (71.1 percent)	9 (20.0 percent)	0

Table 21.4. Example of Cross-Tabular Data Analysis.

	Satisfaction with Pay				
	Very Satisfied	Satisfied	Dissatisfied	Very Dissatisfied	Total
Firefighters	100 (18.5 percent)	250 (46.3 percent)	120 (22.2 percent)	70 (13.0 percent)	540 (100 percent)
Police	340 (36.6)	250 (26.9)	160 (17.2)	180 (19.4)	930 (100.1)[a]
Public works employees	200 (42.1)	150 (31.6)	75 (15.8)	50 (10.5)	475 (100)
Total	640 (32.9)	650 (33.4)	355 (18.3)	300 (15.4)	1,945 (100)

Note: [a]Equals more than 100 due to rounding.

Fruchter, 1978). Statistical significance tests can be misleading, however, and the best advice is to use them with caution. A statistically significant result may be practically insignificant, especially with a larger sample size. Hence, absolute group differences are often the key factors, rather than tests of statistical significance.

Communicating the Results

After initial data analysis the analysts should prepare a preliminary report for top-level management (Stoner, 1992). Upon final analysis, prepare a summary for employees, along with the opportunity to review the final report. After dissemination of the written results, employees should have the opportunity to react to the results in a meeting or discussion group (Stoner, 1992). The discussions should focus on the survey's accuracy and relevance and also solicit specific problem-solving suggestions. These sessions can become de facto brainstorming sessions and effective avenues for employee input and participation. In addition the discussion should encourage feedback on improving the survey process for the next administration. In some cases, having an outside consultant or facilitator lead the discussion enhances perceived objectivity and employee comfort.

Further Survey Limitations

The employee attitude survey is not a substitute for genuine employee input and dialogue. Employees become quickly disenchanted and disillusioned if the organization fails to communicate survey results or takes no or few concrete actions. Management has to be very careful to avoid raising false employee hopes or expectations and must carefully select survey subjects (Stoner, 1992). Raising certain issues may exacerbate conflict if these issues are not resolvable either practically (owing to resource constraints) or politically (Stoner, 1992). The key is the clear communication of reasonable goals and objectives. The attitude survey *supplements* other more substantive methods for increasing employee-employer communication and input. It cannot function alone.

CONCLUSION

This chapter presents an overview of one of the most important tools in social science research, employee attitude surveys. The employee attitude survey is an invaluable tool in the diagnosis of human resource management problems. Used correctly, the attitude survey can identify organizational strengths and weaknesses relative to employee motivation, job satisfaction, and organizational change efforts as it also provides avenues for employee input and participation. The method's strength is its versatility and generalizability to a wide range of situations and populations. When used properly, the employee attitude survey provides a wealth of useful information to improve human resource management.

Exhibit 21.2. Kean County Employee Attitude Survey.

INSTRUCTIONS

Read each question carefully and circle the response that best represents your views and opinions. Remember, there are no right or wrong answers. Your identity and responses will remain completely confidential and anonymous.

The following questions ask for your views and opinions related to supervision, performance appraisal, organizational change, trust, organizational effectiveness, and the relationship between performance and personnel decision making. Indicate whether you strongly agree (SA), agree (A), have no opinion (NO), disagree (D), or strongly disagree (SD) with the statement by circling the appropriate response.

Quality of supervision

1. My supervisor asks my opinion when a problem related to my work arises. — SA A NO D SD

2. My supervisor encourages subordinates to participate in important decisions. — SA A NO D SD

3. My supervisor insists that subordinates work hard and do quality work. — SA A NO D SD

4. My supervisor frequently provides specific performance feedback that helps me to improve my job performance. — SA A NO D SD

5. My job duties are clearly defined by my supervisor. — SA A NO D SD

Performance appraisal practices

6. My performance rating presents a fair and accurate picture of my actual job performance. — SA A NO D SD

7. My supervisor discusses with me the specific reason for the performance rating that I receive. — SA A NO D SD

8. My supervisor considers the performance appraisal of his or her subordinates to be an important part of his or her duties. — SA A NO D SD

9. The performance appraisal process establishes a clear plan for my training and development. — SA A NO D SD

10. The performance appraisal process enhances my job performance. — SA A NO D SD

Exhibit 21.2. Kean County Employee Attitude Survey, cont'd.

Organizational change, trust, and effectiveness

11. I am told promptly when there is a change in policy, rules, or regulations that affects me. SA A NO D SD

12. In this organization, authority is clearly delegated. SA A NO D SD

13. It takes too long to get decisions made in this organization. SA A NO D SD

14. When changes are made in this organization, employees usually lose out in the end. SA A NO D SD

15. Employees do not have much opportunity to influence what goes on in this organization. SA A NO D SD

16. Overall, this organization is effective in accomplishing its objectives. SA A NO D SD

17. Employees here feel you can't trust this organization. SA A NO D SD

Relationship between performance and personnel decision making

18. In this organization, good performance enhances my chances for promotion. SA A NO D SD

19. In this organization, my work is clearly recognized. SA A NO D SD

20. In this organization, if I do a good job I am likely to receive an above average pay increase. SA A NO D SD

21. In this organization, good performance enhances my job security. SA A NO D SD

22. I have confidence that the employee grievance process adequately protects my rights. SA A NO D SD

Job satisfaction and motivation

23. My job makes good use of my abilities. SA A NO D SD

24. My job is challenging. SA A NO D SD

25. In general, I am satisfied with my job. SA A NO D SD

26. In general, I like working here. SA A NO D SD

27. Doing my job well gives me a feeling that I've accomplished something worthwhile. SA A NO D SD

Exhibit 21.2. Kean County Employee Attitude Survey, cont'd.

28. My job gives me the opportunity to use my own judgment and initiative.	SA	A	NO	D	SD
29. I work hard on my job.	SA	A	NO	D	SD
30. I care little about what happens to this organization as long as I get a paycheck.	SA	A	NO	D	SD

The work group

31. I feel I am really part of my work group.	SA	A	NO	D	SD
32. My group works well together.	SA	A	NO	D	SD
33. If we have a decision to make, everyone is involved in making it.	SA	A	NO	D	SD
34. In my group, everyone's opinion gets listened to.	SA	A	NO	D	SD
35. Coordination among work groups is good in this organization.	SA	A	NO	D	SD

Satisfaction with key job characteristics

How satisfied are you with each of the following factors? Circle VS if you are very satisfied, S if you are satisfied, SD for somewhat dissatisfied, VD if you are very dissatisfied or N if you are neither satisfied or dissatisfied.

36. Job security	VS	S	SD	VD	N
37. Fringe benefits	VS	S	SD	VD	N
38. Salary	VS	S	SD	VD	N
39. Promotional opportunities	VS	S	SD	VD	N
40. Working conditions	VS	S	SD	VD	N
41. Tools and equipment	VS	S	SD	VD	N

Employee feedback

The next series of questions asks for your views and observations on key issues.

42. What are the most serious problems confronting the organization?

43. What specific suggestions do you have for solving the above problems or improving the quality of work life?

Exhibit 21.2. Kean County Employee Attitude Survey, cont'd.

Employee demographics

Your answers to the following set of questions will help us interpret the results.

44. Please circle your gender.

Male   Female

45. Please circle your race.

 African American Hispanic White Asian Other

46. Please check your age category.

  _____ 18–25 _____ 36–45 _____ 55+

  _____ 26–35 _____ 46–55

47. How long have you worked in your current job?

  _____ years

THANK YOU FOR YOUR TIME AND COOPERATION!

Source: Modified version of the survey in U.S. Office of Personnel Management, 1979.

References

Balch, D. E., and Blanck, R. "Measuring the Quality of Work Life." *Quality Progress,* 1989, *22*(11), 44–48.

Bowditch, J. L., and Buono, A. F. *Employee Attitude Surveys.* Westport, Conn.: Greenwood Press, 1982.

Daley, D. M. "Performance Appraisal and Organizational Success: Public Employee Perceptions in an MBO-Based Appraisal System." *Review of Public Personnel Administration,* 1988, *9*(1), 17–27.

Dillman, D. A. *Mail and Telephone Surveys: The Total Design Method.* New York: Wiley-Interchange, 1981.

Fowler, F. J. "How Unclear Terms Affect Survey Data." *Public Opinion Quarterly,* 1992, *56*(2), 218–231.

Fowler, F. J. *Survey Research Methods.* (2nd ed.) Thousand Oaks, Calif.: Sage, 1993.

French, W. L., and Bell, C. H., Jr. *Organization Development: Behavioral Science Interventions for Organization Improvement.* (3rd ed.) Upper Saddle River, N.J.: Prentice Hall, 1984.

Guilford, J. P., and Fruchter, B. *Fundamental Statistics in Psychology and Education.* New York: McGraw-Hill, 1978.

Hauck, W., and Ross, T. L. "Expanded Teamwork at Volvo Through Performance Gainsharing." *Industrial Management,* 1988, *30*(4), 17–20.

Isaac, S., and Michael, W. B. *Handbook in Research and Evaluation.* (2nd ed.) San Diego, Calif.: EdITS, 1981.

Judd, C. M., Smith, E. R., and Kidder, L. H. *Research Methods in Social Relations.* (6th ed.) Austin, Tex.: Holt, Rinehart and Winston, 1991.

Kovach, K. A. "What Motivates Employees? Workers and Supervisors Give Different Answers." *Business Horizons,* 1987, *30*(5), 58–65.

Lawler, E. E., III. *Motivation in Work Organizations.* San Francisco: Jossey-Bass, 1994.

Mirvis, P. H., and Kanter, D. L. "Combating Cynicism in the Workplace." *National Productivity Review,* 1989, *8*(4), 377–394.

Rainey, H. G. *Understanding and Managing Public Organizations.* San Francisco: Jossey-Bass, 1991.

Schay, B. W. "Effects of Performance-Contingent Pay on Employee Attitudes." *Public Personnel Management,* 1988, *17*(2), 237–250.

Standing, T., Martin, J., and Moravec, M. "Attitude Surveys: A Catalyst for Cultural Change." *HR Focus,* 1991, *68*(12), 17–18.

Stoner, R. *Employee Attitude Surveys. Management Information Service Report No. 2.* Washington, D.C.: International City/County Management Association, 1992.

U.S. Merit Systems Protection Board. *Sexual Harassment in the Federal Workforce: Trends, Progress and Continuing Challenges.* Washington, D.C.: U.S. Government Printing Office, 1995.

U.S. Office of Personnel Management. *Federal Employee Attitudes.* OPM Document 127-55-8. Washington, D.C.: U.S. Government Printing Office, 1979.

Verheyen, L. G. "How to Develop an Employee Attitude Survey." *Training and Development,* 1988, *42*(8), 72–76.

Woodward, S., and Williams, A. P. "Employee Opinion Surveys in Work Redesign." *Employee Relations,* 1987, *9*(2), 17–21.

CHAPTER TWENTY-TWO

Total Quality Management

Robert F. Durant

uccessfully inculcating a customer service ethic throughout a public agency is not a task for the impatient, the miserly, or the politically unastute. Research on Total Quality Management (TQM) has consistently chronicled how agency leaders or human resource managers thinking otherwise are quickly disabused of such notions as they try to convert theory into practice. Moreover, because of the nagging implementation and research design challenges posed to assessing TQM impact, the jury is still out on TQM's independent effects, cost effectiveness, and long-run potential.

Nevertheless, empirical research on the realpolitik of Total Quality Management interventions is quite instructive. To be sure, this research genre has not yet charted a precise course for navigating the turbulent waters of TQM initiatives. Still, it does afford guidance for those determined to avoid beaching on the shoals of unrealistic expectations, premature initiatives, and strategic or tactical missteps. This chapter explores five primary lessons culled from this literature that can serve students and practitioners of human resource management well. First, TQM appears to be neither as effective as its proponents posited originally nor as ineffective as skeptics expected. Second and relatedly, the evidence on TQM's impact is mixed, and the impact appears contingent on various factors. Third, methodological conundrums in assessing TQM's independent effects still make cause-and-effect conclusions precarious at best. Fourth, the broad outlines of the obstacles implementers face and the successful strategies they use to cope with them are emerging. Fifth and finally, for TQM to fundamentally alter agency cultures and performance on the scale envisioned originally in the advocacy literature, it has to be linked in mutually reinforcing ways to an agency's organizational, responsibility, and accounting structures.

ENVISIONING PUBLIC VALUE

In deconstructing the terms of Total Quality Management, Steven Cohen and William Eimicke (1994) have afforded a most concise yet cogent definition of TQM principles. They write: "Total means applying to every aspect of work, from identifying customer needs to aggressively evaluating whether the customer is satisfied. Quality means meeting and exceeding customer expectations. Management means developing and maintaining the organizational capacity to constantly improve quality" (p. 450).

In essence the early TQM advocacy literature envisioned a *quality revolution* in private and public agencies. Organizations would focus in unprecedented ways on critical self-evaluation, constant improvement, and customer satisfaction. A quality culture would debureaucratize agencies by dissuading agency members from seeing management as *control, doers* (subordinates) as separate from *thinkers* (managers), and work tasks as isolated functions. Promoted instead would be an ethic that embraces "teamwork, coaching, listening, and leading" (Bowman, 1994, p. 134). This ethic also would focus employees on end products or services that meet or exceed customer—rather than bureaucratic—expectations (Bowman, 1994, p. 134).

How could public agencies become such *learning organizations?* Proponents of applying TQM in the public sector proffered a set of principles and a grab bag of tools that private companies were applying. The principles themselves were, and remain, straightforward. First, leaders and workers must see their work as continually needing improvements that they should call to the attention of others. Second, they must see themselves as responsible and meaningfully rewarded for constantly improving the work processes within which they labor. Third, leaders must understand that front-line workers, their suppliers, and their customers are the experts on what quality is, how to get it, and how to assess it. Fourth, front-line employees must appreciate that improving quality means anticipating and correcting problems before they occur. Finally, leaders must understand that all this depends on their being committed to, modeling, and rewarding these behaviors in persistent and compelling ways.

The straightforwardness of these principles, however, belied how much skepticism TQM would have to overcome, even among human resource managers. To begin with, TQM's postbureaucratic tenets challenged the established cultures in most bureaucracies. Thus its principles implicitly required the existence of, or the strong possibility of cultivating, trust among employees. Workers had to believe or be persuaded that TQM was not just another passing management fad. They also had to believe or observe that they would be rewarded fairly, rather than punitively, for exposing problems. Likewise they had to trust, be persuaded, or observe that improving work processes would not merely justify workforce cuts or provide fodder for traditional internecine warfare. Finally, they had to trust that the existing emotional, social, and intellectual attachments that the status quo afforded them could be reconstituted in satisfying ways.

Instrumentally, proponents of applying TQM in public agencies offered a variety of *hard* and *soft* techniques for improving quality. Among the former were such tools as flowcharts, process analysis worksheets, and tree diagrams. These would help employees determine what the flow-of-work process really was and improve it. Likewise, they offered such tools as cause-and-effect diagrams and fishbone charts to link outcomes with production processes. These were supplemented by trend, control, and Pareto charts; statistical process controls (both control charts and process capability information); and force-field analysis. Surveys of suppliers, employees, and customers also provided data necessary to inform decisions. Finally, proponents offered *reengineering* principles to promote cooperation, added value, and customer satisfaction.

Contributing to these efforts were several tools on the soft side of the prescription ledger. TQM relies on team building to *unfreeze* entrenched attitudes and to *refreeze* quality cultures. Therefore employees have had to be given the training that true empowerment requires. To these ends, a *nested* team-building approach most often has been prescribed in TQM. Using the soft techniques of brainstorming, multivoting, and selection-grid decision techniques, organizational leaders work with key resource suppliers and customers to develop a strategic vision or plan. In turn, process improvement teams comprising lower-level managerial and line employees use the hard analytic techniques discussed earlier to link those goals to day-to-day operating decisions, processes, and emphases.

THE DIFFUSION OF INNOVATION

By the early 1990s, 80 percent of Fortune 1000 companies had quality improvement programs of some type (Lawler, Mohrman, and Ledford, 1992). But was Total Quality Management transferable to public agencies? *Genericists* said yes (Wagenheim and Reurink, 1991; Perrine, 1990). *Skeptics* dismissed TQM as the latest management fad, with roots in earlier reforms that disappointed (Kronenberg and Loeffler, 1991). *Contingentists* said TQM would have to be adapted to the peculiarities of the public sector (Swiss, 1992; Radin and Coffee, 1993). *Agnostics* worried that advocates offered few strategies for determining when TQM was more likely to succeed, with what strategies, and measured in what ways (Durant and Wilson, 1993; Wilson and Durant, 1994). *Proverbialists* argued that many TQM tenets offered contradictory advice (for example, trust as a precondition for TQM and trust as a product of it). *Deliberative cynics* worried that TQM diverted attention and resources from the real sources of citizen's anomie when they looked at government: policy disputes (Linden, 1992; Frederickson, 1994).

Neither were systematic assessments of TQM's results in the private sector encouraging (Mathews and Katel, 1992; Mathews, 1993). Nevertheless, by 1992, federal quality and productivity improvement programs were alive in virtually every major executive branch department or agency, under President Reagan's Executive Order 12637 (President, 1989). Among these agencies, more than two-thirds were engaged in TQM initiatives specifically (U.S. General Accounting Office, 1992), with the Federal Quality Institute playing a lead role in diffusing TQM skills throughout the government.

Similarly, by the late 1980s, states such as Arizona, California, Michigan, and Pennsylvania had launched major TQM initiatives within their executive branches (Carr and Littman, 1990). Indeed at least forty state governments were involved to some degree with TQM (Milakovich, 1991). In turn nearly fifty county-and municipality-wide efforts had begun across the country (Carr and Littman, 1990). These efforts could be found in such functions as police protection, recreation and park maintenance, welfare services, human resource management, street maintenance, garbage collection, and emergency services (Sensenbrenner, 1991; International City/County Management Association, 1993; Walters, 1992; Kline, 1992; West, Berman, and Milakovich, 1994b).

Nor did the interest of states and localities in TQM go away during the 1990s. In the most comprehensive survey to date of TQM use and commitment in state and local government, Evan Berman (1994–1995) estimated that 8 percent of all cities with populations over 25,000 ($n = 100$) were using variations of TQM techniques. Much more impressive were his estimates of the percentage of state agencies using these techniques. On the high end he found that 65 percent of all transportation departments and 47 percent of all welfare agencies were using TQM. These were followed in frequency of use by state education (32 percent), correction (31 percent), and health (24 percent) agencies.

Overall, TQM initiatives are going on with varying degrees of scope and commitment at the state and local level. Interestingly, the South, the larger cities, and the jurisdictions with higher levels of economic growth are more involved in TQM initiatives than are their counterparts (Berman, 1994–1995; Kravchuk and Leighton, 1993; Berman and West, 1995). So too are jurisdictions that already had a history of encouraging employee participation, empowerment, and cross-functional management. In this regard, however, a history of participative management in the jurisdiction is a more powerful predictor of TQM adoption than is a commitment to postbureaucratic values.

In terms of scope of commitment, Berman and West (1995) calculate from their imaginative study of cities over 25,000 population that 11 percent have a "substantial" commitment to TQM. By this they mean that a jurisdiction applies TQM principles in at least three service areas and employs a minimum of 35 percent of the training, rewards, and resources identified as critical to TQM success. Less impressive is their calculation that the rest show only a "token" or "minimal" commitment. This may be a function of how new these programs are. Or it may be a product of limited training budgets, of a desire to start slowly and build momentum based on experience, or of knowing already where TQM initiatives are more or less likely to encounter obstacles.

Studies also confirm that more general organizational predispositions toward human resource development and postbureaucratic models of management are associated with higher levels of TQM interest (Cohen and Brand, 1993; Carnevale, 1992; West and Berman, 1993; Berman and West, 1995; Cohen and Eimicke, 1994). The most cited internal forces in Berman and West's study (1995) were city manager interest in TQM and a desire to improve productivity given reduced budgets. The most powerful external factors were public service complaints or voter demands, with TQM success stories in business a distant third. Other studies have found similar results at the state and federal levels, with the importance of top leadership commitment to TQM a common denominator (Federal Quality Institute, 1991; Mani, 1995, 1996).

WAITING FOR GODOT?

Total Quality Management proponents claimed that agencies adopting TQM would reap many benefits: material (for example, improving productivity), solidary (teamwork, empowerment, and employee commitment), and purposive (a service quality ethic). Anecdotal, case study, and multivariate evidence is now beginning to accumulate that does find successes—but also failures—on each of these three dimensions. Arguably, however, it is premature to attribute either successes or failures to TQM alone. Most likely, TQM initiatives in many agencies are too nascent to evaluate fully, have impacts that are too difficult to sort out from other factors (such as downsizing, budget cuts, and technological innovations), and are too often token efforts.

A review of the TQM literature focusing on productivity improvement tends to find a wealth of positive results in qualitative case studies of process reengineering efforts (for example, Cohen and Brand, 1993; Cohen and Eimicke, 1994; Gore, 1995; Koehler and Pankowski, 1996). Decidedly less impressive are the results of the few studies applying bivariate, multivariate, and time-series statistical analyses to assess productivity improvements. More important, however, positive results obtained by whatever method are nowhere near as significant in scope, and often in impact, as genericists in the early advocacy literature predicted. Moreover, neither are they as Lilliputian in effect as skeptics hypothesized.

Taking the claims of the genericist advocacy literature first, the most striking discrepancy is how wildly overstated the scope of TQM impacts seems to have been. As noted, proponents explicitly envisioned a *quality revolution* led by top agency officials. These leaders would tie nested team-defined strategic goals and subunit objectives to operations throughout an agency. Implicit, of course, was that all types of work would be equally amenable to TQM interventions.

To be sure, most research has found the support of top agency leadership highly welcome and beneficial in affecting the fortunes of TQM initiatives. Nonetheless, studies also make clear that it is neither a necessary nor a sufficient condition for success. Some, for example, have found that discrete work processes that are controlled by a single unit or that are distinct work projects may flourish without top leadership support and may produce that support rather than require it (Cohen and Brand, 1993; Cohen and Eimicke, 1994).

As for other factors influencing TQM success, the literature is rife with candidates. Perhaps of most interest to human resource managers are the following prerequisites: sufficient resources for training (Berman and West, 1995); personnel systems such as performance appraisal programs that support TQM philosophies (Bowman, 1994; Berman, 1997); expertise about TQM in the personnel department (Berman, 1997); and broad-based understanding and support from public officials, professional associations, political groups, and community leaders (Loveless and Bozeman, 1983).

Relatedly, the plethora of case studies touting TQM's successes shows vividly how large the gap is between what the early advocacy literature saw as its applicability across all types of processes and the actual limits to its application. Indeed, unless researchers are focusing only on particular types of TQM success stories (a dubious research approach), the warnings of contingentists and agnostics seem prescient. Most cases at all levels of government are focused on what James Q. Wilson (1989) calls *production activities*. These are processes that are noncontroversial, have inputs that are easily monitored and compared to outputs, and have agreed-on measures of success that are easily identified and measured. At the Internal Revenue Service (IRS), for example, TQM focused on such production activities as the processing of tax forms, more accurate inputting of data, and securing delinquent tax returns (Mani, 1995, 1996). In New York City, TQM initiatives focused on preventive maintenance, time card processing, and tree removal (Cohen and Eimicke, 1994). And at the Environmental Protection Agency, TQM initiatives addressed such issues as improving communication with suppliers and reducing memo response times by cutting out clearance points (Cohen and Brand, 1993).

This is not to suggest that the reported savings from these initiatives are anything to dismiss lightly. At the IRS, for example, Bonnie Mani (1995) reports that various TQM project teams in the Ogden and Fresno service centers produced savings of $3.7 million and $12 million, respectively. Likewise the Air

Force Logistics Command reports an improvement in the mission capability of its fleet from 40 percent to 76 percent and a decrease in delinquent purchase deliveries of 83 percent (Cohen and Brand, 1993). The IRS also claims that accuracy of answers to taxpayer questions improved nearly 25 percent.

Similar improvements claimed at the state and local level should not be disparaged either. For example, city managers and agency directors responding to Berman and West's national survey (1995) exhibited positive, albeit modest, impressions of TQM's material, solidary, and purposive impacts. Using a five-point scale ranging from –2 (very negative) to +2 (very positive), respondents rated gains in efficiency at .98, cost reductions at .84, and ability to cope with resource constraints at .88. Solidary gains related to empowerment and team building garnered ratings ranging from .77 (delegating responsibility), to .92 (improving group decision making), to 1.01 (improving unit communication). Finally, respondents saw the greatest gains in terms of purposive rewards: they rated service quality improvement at 1.04.

Nor is it wise to downplay Theodore Poister and Richard Harris's findings (1997) regarding the impact of long-standing quality improvement efforts by the Pennsylvania Department of Transportation. In the most statistically sophisticated and theoretically grounded assessment of such efforts to date, their path analysis reveals that maintenance backlogs were substantially reduced. Moreover, these benefits exceeded quality program costs by one-third. To be sure, the absence of experimental controls in this study admittedly reduces our ability to eliminate rival explanations for productivity improvement. Nonetheless, Poister and Harris's findings are important and encouraging to TQM supporters. They also point to the need for patience in expecting results from quality improvement efforts. They find gradual improvement over the fiscal year 1987 through fiscal year 1995 period.

What a focus on production activities does imply unequivocally, however, is that either agencies or scholars have intentionally deflected their TQM focus or assessments away from what Wilson (1989) calls craft and coping activities. One set of possibilities is that agencies are picking the lowest-hanging fruit first, are deliberately taking an incremental approach, or are constrained by training resources in the breadth of TQM coverage they can pursue. A second possibility is that scholars are—for whatever reasons (limited resources, personal interests, or a best practices approach)—inordinately focusing on only one type of TQM experience. Nonetheless, a third—and as yet empirically unsubstantiated—possibility exists. Namely, TQM may reach the limits of its competence in public agencies when it tries to go beyond routine production-oriented work processes and toward craft and coping activities.

Craft activities are bottom heavy in that they rely extensively on professional expertise, norms, and values to shape employees' behaviors. They inherently involve actions where unsupervised discretion is best, most practical, or necessary for achieving widely agreed ends (for example, when agreement exists on the need for community policing or on allowing the production of timber on public lands). Most often they involve decisions that cannot be programmed, vary by circumstance, or operate on precarious causal theories about what works best given varying circumstances (for example, disciplinary decisions made by schoolteachers or actions taken by police officers in quelling domestic disputes).

To be sure, as William Rago (1994) suggests, even these activities have support processes that can be improved by TQM and that often are. But the rub comes in the potent resistance some professionals tend to marshal when TQM requires deep changes in the core belief systems they hold about their jobs. To be effective in these instances, TQM training has to be accompanied by widespread, disruptive, and politically challenging changes in budgets, reward structures, promotional policies, and organizational structures.

Coping activities occur where disagreement or principled conflict abounds over ends and means (for example, what constitutes quality education, adequate environmental protection, or suitable occupational health and safety?). In these circumstances, external oversight of decision and implementing processes is very high, decisions are pushed to the highest levels of the agency, and empowerment of subordinates becomes more politically dangerous. Coping activities make TQM applications decidedly more challenging, less likely to take root successfully, and more in need than production activities of political hardball.

The overblown claims of the genericist advocacy literature aside, it may simply be too early to tell what the real material, solidary, or purposive effects of TQM will be in the long term. In cases where researchers find actual or perceived productivity gains modest or nonexistent in the short term, real or eventual gains may be masked. Prematurely conducting summative (that is, impact) rather than formative (that is, ongoing) evaluations of TQM initiatives may especially distort their impact.

Berman and West (1995) found, on the one hand, that 40 percent of their respondents were reacting to TQM programs that were less than four years old. Even so, many remarked that they were already seeing progress. Likewise, after eight years, Poister and Harris's research (1997) found substantial positive impact on Pennsylvania's transportation efforts. On the other hand, Mani's warning (1996) that it might take thirty years before TQM's full impact on productivity is apparent may be true but irrelevant. TQM requires substantial and costly training. Consequently, significant returns on this investment will have to come sooner rather than later for TQM to survive in other than nominal or symbolic fashion in the public sector. Still, as Mani notes, that same resource commitment can overwhelm productivity gains in the short run, thus masking TQM's potential for longer-term gains. Nor can the demonstrable gains in effectiveness noted in many studies be dismissed lightly.

Finally, perceptions by those involved in the process that solidary and purposive gains have occurred may be more important than any immediate productivity data supporting material gains. No matter how modest these solidary and purposive gains might be, their importance is verified by reams of literature lauding the gains that organizations make generally from participative and committed cultures. These gains include improved employee allegiance, morale, and sense of responsibility for the organization's fate.

At the same time, gains attributed to TQM alone may be either overestimating or underestimating its impact. TQM interventions do not take place in a vacuum. Other management improvement initiatives, actions, or events may be occurring simultaneously (for example, downsizing, investment in new technology, or changes in political leadership). Yet most research designs have eschewed multivariate or time-series analyses or counterfactual designs controlling for these factors. What is more, the few that have used them do not come to positive conclusions.

For example, Mani's time-series analysis (1996) of productivity in TQM-implementing versus pre-TQM-implementing agencies found that the only statistically significant difference between the two types was resource input. Consonant with conventional wisdom, implementing agencies were spending more money—most likely on training and staffing—to get what they produced. Otherwise no significant differences regarding productivity emerged.

If we are ever to know precisely the impacts of TQM initiatives relative to their claims, more rigorous analyses will have to take place. If it is premature presently to look at impacts with or without controlling for exogenous events, more formative evaluations will have to be conducted that do consider or control for them. Perhaps it is also true that full-blown causal models related to impact are beyond the scope of our present databases and understandings. But as Laura Wilson and I (1994) suggest and as Poister and Harris (1997) have demonstrated, more sophisticated formative evaluative models are available. Most notable in this regard are the stage-state, team-building, and two-step models of continuous process improvement.

BUILDING SUPPORT AND LEGITIMACY

If our understanding of Total Quality Management impacts has a way to go, the realpolitik of TQM interventions in public agencies is well known, well founded, and well established. Even more important, strategies for overcoming political obstacles are beginning to accumulate in the literature. TQM proponents (both within and without human resource departments) can ill afford to ignore these lessons. Consider, for example, the dilemmas dogging—and the lessons learned from—customer-based quality efforts in the federal government.

The Federal Experience

The Clinton administration's claims of productivity increases and cost savings are many, documented, and in many cases persuasive (Gore, 1995). Still, their accuracy has not gone unchallenged by neutral observers (as noted later), and they fail to avoid the methodological conundrums already described. Nor, most significantly, have these increases been as widespread in effect in any agency or department as the advocacy literature originally claimed they might.

As Beryl Radin's research (1995) shows, emphasis on effectiveness—and hence on productivity—has varied across departments, across strategies, and between political appointees and career bureaucrats. Relatedly, the U.S. General Accounting Office's latest assessment (1996) of what has been happening at 185 National Performance Review (NPR) reinventing government (REGO) labs scattered throughout the federal government is uninspiring. Nearly three years into REGO, approximately half of these efforts to inculcate a *quality ethic* and reengineer work processes were still in the planning stage or not fully established. On the plus side, 44 percent reported that downsizing had a positive effect on them; it forced them to rethink agency operations and management support systems. But again little explicit linking of policy goals, reinventing initiatives, and customer satisfaction was occurring.

Nor does one sense that the labs were truly becoming the learning organizations envisioned by TQM and reengineering proponents. For example, 53 percent reported that downsizing had actually slowed their reinvention and quality efforts and resulted in losses of institutional memory. Other labs reported that reinventing was causing high levels of fear, anxiety, and stress among employees. Meanwhile, in perhaps the ultimate irony for an exercise concerned with *outcomes* and designed to afford lessons for future efforts, most labs were not collecting and sharing data that "measure[d] improved performance" or that could "prove that the labs were making a difference" (Barr, 1996).

Similarly disappointing, the General Accounting Office found that the deregulatory components of the REGO quality and customer-focused agenda were not proceeding apace. In fact, 60 percent of the labs still had not asked for waivers from existing rules and regulations, maintaining that these waivers "were not needed to accomplish their lab's goals" (Barr, 1997). Thus either a fundamental assumption of reengineering was invalid (that is, that red tape was thwarting agency missions) or management reforms were not sufficiently targeted toward agency quality goals to make a difference. What about the 40 percent of labs that did ask for waivers? Many of them ran into staunch resistance from the Office of Management and Budget, the Office of Personnel Management, and the General Services Administration.

Finally, James Thompson and Patricia Ingraham's study (1996) of NPR reinvention labs found that "while successes have been achieved, they have been largely idiosyncratic" (p. 297). Moreover, they depend ultimately on the self-interested behaviors of individuals and are vulnerable to "deliberate obstruction" by staff and headquarters' personnel. Many of these personnel are ill disposed toward loosening the control mechanisms that are their raison d'être.

The Subnational Experience

These dynamics, of course, are hardly peculiar to federal agencies. Two of the more systematic, exhaustive, and useful conceptual and strategic frameworks to date in the TQM literature are premised on in-depth case studies of TQM initiatives in state and local agencies. Rago's work (1996) refines our understanding of TQM intervention dynamics by reporting events at the Texas Department of Mental Health and Mental Retardation (DMHMR). Similarly, Cohen and Eimicke (1994) chronicle strategic approaches taken at the New York City Department of Parks and Recreation (DPR) to overcome obstacles commonly reported in the TQM literature.

Rago used force-field analysis to document the formidable barriers to change occasioned by DMHMR's political culture. Specifically, he assessed its effects on four critical components of the TQM effort: conveying purpose, improving coordination, fostering better communication, and empowering employees. He found that the organizational and personal barriers to conveying purpose were protean and their sources mundane. Lack of ownership of values, absence of consensus about values, and teamwork problems derived from three factors: lack of time to participate in meetings, discomfort with debate, and perceptions that TQM activities were not as important as ongoing responsibilities.

Similarly unremarkable were the organizational and personal obstacles to improving cross-functional coordination, communication, and empowerment. The personal discipline necessary for making decisions consonant with strategic plans was missing, as was an organizational commitment to consensus decision making. Likewise policy communication and empowerment initiatives were shackled by personal and organizational obstacles. The most critical barriers to policy communication were not feeling responsible for carrying policies out, not trusting others to make the right decision, fear of losing power, and not being able to think beyond one's own self-interest. Organizational factors exacerbating these problems included an inability to define purpose, lack of understanding about how empowerment would work, and poor policy integration within the agency.

Cohen and Eimicke's study (1994) of New York's DPR offers strategies for overcoming the problems identified by Rago. Most interestingly, however, these strategies often challenge conventional TQM prescriptions. First, the authors make the case for project-based rather than agencywide TQM initiatives. They aver that small-scale successes, quickly reaped and widely trumpeted, are strategically the best way to get started. These projects avoid political machinations because they are less threatening than larger ones and also less costly, and they model evidence of success to others.

Next Cohen and Eimicke join others in recognizing how critical and fragile worker participation in, understanding of, and enthusiasm for TQM can be. Unconventionally, however, they advise implementers in the early stages of a TQM initiative to use only flowcharts to describe work processes. More sophisticated statistical tools are usually unnecessary in these stages, more difficult to learn, and can too easily discourage employees. Relatedly, rapid changes in standard operating procedures (SOPs) should occur. These will facilitate learning, convey TQM's importance, and presumably, catch possible opponents by surprise.

Finally, and in striking departures from conventional TQM prescriptions, Cohen and Eimicke counsel against large-scale TQM training, stand-alone quality councils, and abstract training about TQM tenets. Rather than classroom train as many employees as possible in TQM, agencies should employ small-scale, quick turnaround, and work-related TQM projects involving few employees at a time. What is more, projects that are totally within the control of a single organizational unit are the ideal. They dramatically increase the chances of success, make training more manageable and customer oriented, and cut training costs considerably. At the same time, work-related projects attenuate employee impressions that TQM efforts are tangential to, and draining resources away from, employees' "real work." Finally, these projects reduce the need for, and thus the political complications inherent in, cross-unit collaboration.

Where Cohen and Eimicke do not differ appreciably from conventional wisdom, however, is in the importance they attach to TQM training of some sort, to ensuring that personnel policies are consistent with TQM practices, and to persistently monitoring and heralding TQM results (see Hyde, 1993; Carnevale, 1995; West, Berman, and Milakovich, 1994a; Brelin, Davenport, Jennings, and Murphy, 1994; Bowman, 1994; Koehler and Pankowski, 1996; Milakovich, 1995). Personnel policies must adhere to TQM precepts, and personnelists must become TQM experts in order to train line operatives and staff. Moreover, human resource departments must switch from a "gotcha" mentality premised on rule monitoring to a facilitator mentality premised on serving department needs (also see Barzelay, 1992).

The Human Resource Management Conundrum

How well are human resource departments and elected officials fostering these ends? Berman's earlier survey (1994–1995) of city managers and state agency directors found that some of the most stubborn barriers to TQM initiatives involved inadequate training. Funds for teaching employees analytic, team-building, interpersonal, and empowerment skills were decidedly wanting. Inadequate as well were rewards for quality improvements. But most lacking was a widespread commitment by human resource departments to TQM principles in their own operations. Indeed, West and his associates (West, Berman, and Milakovich, 1994a) found that only 8 percent of personnel departments in cities over twenty-five thousand in population were using TQM. And Berman (1994–1995) found that of these users of TQM in the four types of agencies he surveyed, fully 40 percent lacked full-fledged programs. Still, all does not appear lost. Many human resource departments increasingly are moving to become just-in-time service providers to departments and facilitators of quality programs agencywide (Berman, 1997).

Overall, however, one of the most stubborn, debilitating, and widely recognized human resource obstacles to TQM initiatives in public agencies is the realpolitik of the performance appraisal process (Moen, 1989; Berman, 1997; Bowman, 1994; Daley, 1992). TQM proponents such as Juran (1988) and Deming (1986) argue that it is the traditional work system, not the people within it, that debases quality. Moreover, while traditional management models stress individual performance evaluations, TQM's emphasis on team building, group participation, and facilitative coaching requires a focus on group rewards. The rub, of course, is that both managers and employees tend to cling to individual rather than group performance appraisals despite ongoing TQM efforts in their agencies (Bowman, 1994).

Fears that team appraisals will breed free-riding, rating uncertainty, and placing one's financial destiny in the hands of coworkers are real, realistic, and not easily assuaged. But if systems and not people are the problem and if collaborative teams are responsible for improving those systems, why evaluate individuals? Juran and Deming say not to. James Bowman (1994, p. 134) puts the argument and its stakes best: "to apply measurement criteria from the old paradigm to the new one . . . only makes things worse." Still, one is left wondering how to get there from here strategically. Puzzling as well is why individual and team evaluations cannot coexist—weighted and merged appropriately—in any performance appraisal.

Finally, even though the realpolitik of quality improvement within individual public agencies affords tremendous challenges to TQM reformers, these challenges pale in comparison to those provoked when work processes require different agencies to cooperate. Such challenges, of course, grow increasingly common as government becomes a catalyst for getting others to deliver services that it traditionally provided. Nor does devolution of responsibilities to states, localities, and the private sector in the 1990s attenuate these problems.

No one doubts that public managers increasingly must craft strategies for and operate successfully in nonhierarchical and alliance-based networks. They stretch across levels of government, within each level, and out to the private sector. Yet TQM practice and research is largely silent about how to deal with these networks as they affect craft and coping activities and the subprocesses that support them. One thing can be confidently predicted, however. The obstacles to implementing TQM in single agencies will be compounded exponentially in interorganizational networks with multiple independent actors.

Some Rules of Thumb for Political Management

Certainly, the depth, breadth, and commonality of the obstacles to TQM that require political management skills are formidable. Nor is it clear that overcoming or finessing these obstacles in discrete parts, projects, or processes will launch quality initiatives throughout an agency. Indeed, if successes result from picking the lowest-hanging fruit first, no guarantee exists that they will be replicable under more difficult circumstances.

But success is success. Any improvements in productivity, customer satisfaction, and cost savings that do occur are welcome in an era of doing more with less and citizen cynicism about government. Consequently, it is useful to know what the obstacles are to success, how much resistance TQM is likely to encounter, and when resistance is more or less manageable. My review of the literature suggests, first, that TQM's value more easily is established when

- Initiatives target discrete production tasks or projects.
- Initiatives have noncontroversial means and ends.
- Initiatives are carried out at the operating levels of a single agency.
- Employee performance awards are related to TQM precepts.
- SOPs, bureaucratic routines, and regulations are consonant with TQM values.
- If not, SOPs, bureaucratic routines, and regulations are changed quickly.

Second, proponents of TQM are likely to be more successful when their political management initiatives result in TQM training that is

- Adequately funded
- Linked to work
- Adroitly synchronized to implementation stages
- Aggressively conveyed to department personnel by the human resource department
- Consistently and broadly applied to the human resource department's own activities

Third, public managers can expect more difficulty with TQM initiatives when the changes they entail or the results they may produce

- Will involve massive shifts in goals and mission
- Will result in nonincremental shifts in operations affecting many units
- Will result in internal or external redistribution of power, resources, or services

- Will require legislative approval
- Are attempted without courting public and media support for TQM generally
- Are not accompanied by broadly participative planning and management
- Are attempted by agencies with weak, unsupportive, or divided clienteles
- Require high levels of trust among employees and managers where none exist

CONCLUSION: INSTITUTIONALIZING A QUALITY ETHIC

As management experts routinely counsel, an organization's strategy should determine its structure (Thompson, 1967). *Strategy* is the pattern of purposes and policies that defines an organization's mission and market niche, and *structure* is conceptualized as having three distinct but related components: administrative, responsibility, and account (or control) structures. Respectively, the latter tell who does what, who is responsible for achieving what, and how these persons' performance is measured.

More important, protean research evidence suggests that organizations, and human resource managers within them, that successfully realize their quality goals do so by adroitly meshing these three structures with quality values in mutually reinforcing ways (for example, Hall, Rosenthal, and Wade, 1993; Denhardt, 1993; West, Berman, and Milakovich, 1994a). All of this, of course, raises several questions. How can present attachments to the status quo be best unfrozen? How might administrative and responsibility structures be best recast? How can accounting structures be best revamped?

The literature on cultural change in organizations is voluminous and cannot be treated comprehensively in this chapter. More manageable is a brief synopsis of three major tenets culled from research on quality improvement. First, the focus on customers is by itself a most powerful lever for cultural change in an organization. As such, it is also quite threatening initially to everyone within the organization.

As business consultants Gene Hall, Jim Rosenthal, and Judy Wade (1993) note, a crucial way to change organizations is to alter their vocabularies. The words employees use in daily organizational life pattern the way they think and act. Thus if terms like *customer satisfaction, quality,* and *value-addedness* become part of agency managers' everyday speech, employees acquire new understandings about what is valued and what is less important. Moreover, if the values are institutionalized and rewarded in responsibility, accounting, and budget structures, employee behaviors tend to shift toward them.

By the same token, however, focusing on customer needs initially can put feelings of safety, sinecure, and financial security decidedly at risk. As Deborah

Smith Cook (1996) notes, even change of the most positive kind leaves employees temporarily "grieving" for old ways. Moreover, because TQM's emphasis on continuous process improvement means that employees must identify past or ongoing errors, a period of "defensiveness" is typical as well. The resulting angst may manifest itself in anger, missed TQM deadlines and meetings, or even outright sabotage.

To cope with these events, researchers have suggested a variety of unfreezing strategies. Included prominently among these are "assembling a critical mass of stakeholders," "positive reminiscence" (Hall, Rosenthal, and Wade, 1993), "creating a sense of urgency" (Goss, Pascale, and Athos, 1993), creating an "amnesty" policy (Cohen and Brand, 1990), and confronting resisters directly after a reasonable period of adjustment (Cohen and Eimicke, 1996). The only nonobvious strategy among these is positive reminiscence. Here, every meeting is opened by encouraging employees to talk about what they did right in the past and to relive past successes. Talk will soon transition into a recognition of how they could have done better, what obstacles they faced, and how these might be changed.

When it comes to revamping administrative and responsibility structures, the most striking feature of TQM research in the private sector, and the second tenet for quality improvement, is the consensus growing around reorganizing on the basis of flow-of-work principles. Known as a *process-complete department* (PCD), this type of responsibility structure organizes work by incorporating all the cross-functional steps or tasks necessary to meet customer needs in a single work unit. In the process, common purpose replaces cross-functional competition as cooperation rather than conflict becomes in everyone's interest. Indeed, so powerful has this logic become that major corporations have created PCDs by the thousands.

Looking at this conventional wisdom, some public managers may assume that creating quality cultures is beyond their ken. Agency leadership or elected officials may be either unwilling or unable to change administrative and responsibility structures on this scale. Thinking that PCDs are a prerequisite for success, they may write off the feasibility of TQM in their agencies. Such might not be the case, however, if they take the findings of recent empirical research on PCDs into account. Some PCD efforts are associated with increased customer satisfaction, higher productivity, and shorter cycle times for producing products and services. Many others, however, are associated with quality outcomes that are no better, or are even worse, than those of conventional structures. Moreover, if the right things are done within conventional functional structures, the results may be just as positive (Majchrzak and Wang, 1996).

As Ann Majchrzak and Qianwei Wang (1996) persuasively argue, getting employees to assume collective responsibility for improving customer satisfaction requires more than reorganizing functional units into PCDs. Indeed, their research indicates that trying to develop a quality ethic in this fashion may be counterproductive and cost ineffective. Most telling, if managers are unwilling to create a collaborative culture within PCDs, the PCDs ultimately will fail. Studying thirty-one PCD efforts and comparing their performance with that of fifty-five more traditional functional departments, these researchers found that high-performing functional departments were just as quality and customer focused as PCDs under certain circumstances. Thus, whether or not public managers are disposed or able to move toward PCDs, they should consider doing four things that will adroitly link strategy with structure. First, they should assign cross-functional responsibilities to employees. Second, they should create information networks among employees that stress timely sharing of process and quality data in user-friendly formats. Third, they should introduce outcomes-based performance evaluation measures that are clear, stress collaborative and quality values, and are consequence laden. Finally, they should create customer satisfaction milestones, hold meetings to assess progress toward them, and include members from all relevant functions in these meetings.

Interestingly, some within the business community aver that if TQM is pursued within such a framework for linking strategy with structure, a corporation is well on its way toward a strategic management system as well. This is the third tenet for quality improvement. Robert Kaplan and David Norton (1996), for example, show how this approach works in an accounting structure they call the *balanced scorecard*. Here, scores on four critical and interlocking processes are used to overcome a common dilemma in private and public entities: "lofty vision and strategy . . . don't translate easily into action" at the lower levels of an organization (p. 76).

The first critical process—communicating and linking—comprises setting production and quality goals, communicating them to and training employees, and linking performance rewards to these goals. The second process—planning—involves setting precise targets consonant with these goals. Strategic initiatives are aligned, resources are allocated to advance them, and milestones are established to track progress toward them. Subsequently, the third and fourth parts of the scorecard focus on performance feedback acquired from the first two processes. Adjustment of processes, tactics, or goals takes place premised on what has been learned.

Would the balanced scorecard approach blossom within public agencies? No doubt the obstacles to applying it are more formidable in the public than the private sector. Still, recent research sees movement toward variations on it (Berry and Wechsler, 1995). Much as with TQM, implementers would have to adapt the model to public-sector peculiarities, contingencies, and realpolitik.

But whether the balanced scorecard approach is adopted or not, the principle underlying the model is inviolable if TQM is to succeed widely and realize the potential its proponents see for it in public agencies. Structures must follow strategy by mutually reinforcing TQM values. TQM's promise can never be fully realized until agencies adroitly, persistently, and clearly institutionalize TQM's values in everyday operations. Doing so requires nothing less than meshing an agency's administrative, responsibility, and accounting structures with TQM tenets.

What is more, these efforts must be tethered tautly by agency leaders and human resource managers to TQM initiatives that

- Are clearly focused

- Involve modest aspirations

- Anticipate and cope strategically with employee indifference, skepticism, and (sometimes) subterfuge

- Take time to build support and alliances for this effort with key internal and external stakeholders

- Are heavily invested in training programs linked to specific tasks

- Can be leveraged as exemplars to others in the agency

- Provide clearly understood performance measures that routinely stimulate periodic feedback and evaluation capable of changing the agency's vocabulary (that is, what it values)

- Send signals through employee reward structures that a quality philosophy is valued

References

Barr, S. "GAO Report Details Quiet Efforts of Gore's 'Reinvention Labs.'" *Washington Post*, Mar. 25, 1996, p. A15.

Barzelay, M. *Breaking Through Bureaucracy: A New Vision for Managing in Government*. Berkeley: University of California Press, 1992.

Berman, E. M. "Study Looks at Prevalence of TQM in State and Local Personnel Operations." *Periscope*, 1994–1995, *15*(3), 6.

Berman, E. M. "The Challenge of Total Quality Management." In C. Ban and N. M. Riccucci (eds.), *Public Personnel Management: Current Concerns, Future Challenges*. (2nd ed.) New York: Longman, 1997.

Berman, E. M., and West, J. P. "Municipal Commitment to Total Quality Management: A Survey of Recent Progress." *Public Administration Review*, 1995, *55*(1), 57–66.

Berry, F. S., and Wechsler, B. "State Agencies' Experience with Strategic Planning: Findings from a National Survey." *Public Administration Review*, 1995, *55*(2), 159–168.

Bowman, J. S. "At Last, an Alternative to Performance Appraisal." *Public Administration Review*, 1994, *54*(2), 129–136.

Brelin, H. K., Davenport, K. S., Jennings, L. P., and Murphy, P. F. *Focused Quality: Managing for Results.* Delray Beach, Fla.: St. Lucie Press, 1994.

Carnevale, D. G. "The Learning Support Model: Personnel Policy Beyond the Traditional Model." *American Review of Public Administration,* 1992, *22*(3), 19–34.

Carnevale, D. G. *Trustworthy Government: Leadership and Management Strategies for Building Trust and High Performance.* San Francisco: Jossey-Bass, 1995.

Carr, D., and Littman, I. *Excellence in Government: Total Quality Management in the 1990s.* New York: Coopers & Lybrand, 1990.

Cohen, S., and Brand, R. "Total Quality Management in the U.S. Environmental Protection Agency." *Public Productivity and Management Review,* Fall 1990, pp. 99–133.

Cohen, S., and Brand, R. *Total Quality Management in Government: A Practical Guide for the Real World.* San Francisco: Jossey-Bass, 1993.

Cohen, S., and Eimicke, W. "Project-Focused Total Quality Management in the New York City Department of Parks and Recreation." *Public Administration Review,* 1994, *54*(5), 450–456.

Cohen, S., and Eimicke, W. "Roundtable on TQM." Paper presented at the National Conference of the American Society for Public Administration, Atlanta, Ga., June 29–July 3, 1996.

Cook, D. S. "An Education in Managing Change Includes Analysis and Creativity." *Warfield's,* Aug. 5, 1996, p. 15.

Daley, D. M. "Pay for Performance, Performance Appraisal, and Total Quality Management." *Public Productivity and Management Review,* 1992, *16*(1), 39–51.

Deming, W. E. *Out of the Crisis.* Cambridge, Mass.: MIT Center for Advanced Engineering Study, 1986.

Denhardt, R. B. *The Pursuit of Significance: Strategies for Managerial Success in Public Organizations.* Belmont, Calif.: Wadsworth, 1993.

Durant, R. F., and Wilson, L. A. "Public Management, TQM, and Quality Improvement: Toward a Contingency Strategy." *American Review of Public Administration,* 1993, *23*(3), 215–243.

Federal Quality Institute. *Introduction to Total Quality Management.* Washington, D.C.: Federal Quality Institute, 1991.

Frederickson, H. G. "Total Quality Politics: TQP." *Spectrum,* 1994, *67,* 13–15.

Gore, A., Jr. *Common Sense Government: Works Better and Costs Less.* New York: Random House, 1995.

Goss, T., Pascale, R., and Athos, A. "The Reinvention Roller Coaster: Risking the Present for a Powerful Future." *Harvard Business Review,* Nov.–Dec. 1993, pp. 97–108.

Hall, G., Rosenthal, J., and Wade, J. "How to Make Reengineering Really Work." *Harvard Business Review,* Nov.–Dec. 1993, pp. 119–131.

Hyde, A. C. "Rescuing Quality Measurement from TQM." *Bureaucrat,* Winter 1990–1991, pp.16–20.

Hyde, A. C. "Barriers in Implementing Quality Management." *Public Manager,* 1993, *22,* 33–37.

International City/County Management Association. "State of the Profession Survey." *ICMA Newsletter,* July 1993 (special feature supplement).

Juran, J. *Juran on Planning for Quality.* New York: McGraw-Hill, 1988.

Kaplan, R. S., and Norton, D. P. "Using the Balanced Scorecard as a Strategic Management System." *Harvard Business Review,* Jan.–Feb. 1996, pp. 75–85.

Kline, J. J. "Total Quality Management in Local Government." *Government Finance Review,* Aug. 1992, pp. 7–11.

Koehler, J. W., and Pankowski, J. M. *Quality Government: Designing, Developing, and Implementing TQM.* Delray Beach, Fla.: St. Lucie Press, 1996.

Kravchuk, R. S., and Leighton, R. "Implementing Total Quality Management in the United States." *Public Productivity and Management Review,* 1993, *17*(3), 71–82.

Kronenberg, P. S., and Loeffler, R. G. "Quality Management Theory: Historical Context and Future Prospect." *Journal of Management Science and Policy Analysis,* 1991, *8,* 204–221.

Lawler, E. E., III, Mohrman, S. A., and Ledford, G. E., Jr. *Employee Involvement and Total Quality Management: Practices and Results in Fortune 1000 Companies.* San Francisco: Jossey-Bass, 1992.

Linden, R. "Meeting Which Customers' Needs?" *Public Manager,* Winter 1992, pp. 49–52.

Loveless, S., and Bozeman, B. "Innovation and the Public Manager." In W. B. Eddy (ed.), *Handbook of Organization Management.* New York: Dekker, 1983.

Majchrzak, A., and Wang, Q. "Breaking the Functional Mind-Set in Process Organizations." *Harvard Business Review,* Sept.–Oct. 1996, pp. 92–99.

Mani, B. G. "Old Wine in New Bottles Tastes Better: A Case Study of TQM Implementation in the IRS." *Public Administration Review,* 1995, *55*(2), 147–158.

Mani, B. G. "Measuring Productivity in Federal Agencies: Does Total Quality Management Make a Difference?" *American Review of Public Administration,* 1996, *26*(1), 19–39.

Mathews, J. "Total Quality Management." *Washington Post,* June 6, 1993, pp. H1, H16.

Mathews, J., and Katel, P. "The Cost of Quality." *Newsweek,* Sept. 7, 1992, pp. 48–49.

Milakovich, M. E. "Total Quality Management in the Public Sector." *National Productivity Review,* 1991, *10*(2), 195–213.

Milakovich, M. E. *Improving Service Quality.* Delray Beach, Fla.: St. Lucie Press, 1995.

Moen, R. D. "The Performance Appraisal System: Deming's Deadly Disease." *Quality Progress,* Nov. 1989, pp. 62–66.

Perrine, J. L. "The Quest for Quality." *Bureaucrat,* Summer 1990, pp. 47–48.

Poister, T. H., and Harris, R. H. "The Impact of TQM on Highway Maintenance: Benefit/Cost Implications." *Public Administration Review,* 1997, *57*(4), 294–302.

President. "Productivity Improvement Program for the Federal Government," Executive Order 12637. *Code of Federal Regulations,* 1989, vol. 3 *(The President: 1988 Compilation).*

Radin, B. A. "Varieties of Reinvention: Six NPR 'Success Stories.'" In D. F. Kettl and J. Di Iullio Jr. (eds.), *Inside the Reinvention Machine: Appraising Governmental Reform.* Washington, D.C.: Brookings Institution, 1995.

Radin, B. A., and Coffee, J. "A Critique of TQM: Problems of Implementation in the Public Sector." *Public Administration Quarterly,* 1993, *17*(2), 43–53.

Rago, W. V. "Adapting Total Quality Management (TQM) to Government: Another Point of View." *Public Administration Review,* 1994, *54*(1), 61–64.

Rago, W. V. "Struggles in Transformation: A Study in TQM, Leadership and Organizational Culture in a Government Agency." *Public Administration Review,* 1996, *56*(3), 227–234.

Sensenbrenner, J. "Quality Comes to City Hall." *Harvard Business Review,* Mar.–Apr. 1991, pp. 64–75.

Swiss, J. E. "Adapting Total Quality Management (TQM) to Government." *Public Administration Review,* 1992, *52*(4), 356–362.

Thompson, J. D. *Organizations in Action.* New York: McGraw-Hill, 1967.

Thompson, J. R., and Ingraham, P. W. "The Reinvention Game." *Public Administration Review,* 1996, *56*(3), 291–298.

U.S. General Accounting Office. *Quality Management: A Survey of Federal Organizations.* Washington, D.C.: U.S. Government Printing Office, 1992.

U.S. General Accounting Office. *Management Reform: Status of Agency Reinvention Lab Efforts.* Washington, D.C.: U.S. Government Printing Office, 1996.

Wagenheim, G. D., and Reurink, J. H. "Customer Service in Public Administration." *Public Administration Review,* 1991, *51*(3), 263–269.

Walters, J. "The Cult of Total Quality." *Governing,* May 1992, pp. 38–42.

West, J. P., and Berman, E. M. "Human Resource Strategies in Local Government: A Survey of Progress and Future Directions." *American Review of Public Administration,* 1993, *23*(3), 279–297.

West, J. P., Berman, E. M., and Milakovich, M. E. "HRM, TQM, and Organizational Policies: The Need for Alignment." In *Proceedings of the Academy of Business Administration: Public Sector Studies.* London: Academy of Business Administration, 1994a.

West, J. P., Berman, E. M., and Milakovich, M. E. "Total Quality Management in Local Government." In *Municipal Yearbook, 1994.* Washington, D.C.: International City/County Management Association, 1994b.

Wilson, J. Q. *Bureaucracy: What Government Agencies Do and Why They Do It.* New York: Basic Books, 1989.

Wilson, L. A., and Durant, R. F. "Evaluating TQM: The Case for a Theory-Driven Approach." *Public Administration Review,* 1994, *54*(2), 137–146.

Choosing and Using Human Resource Consultants

Focusing on Local Government

Glenn W. Rainey Jr.

Consultants are used to address a wide range of needs in public-sector human resource management, and their use has been growing. Indeed, the problems that human resource management must address are too complex and changeable and the factors that condition the design and choice of solutions are too varied to permit a comprehensive prescription for the use of consultants. It is possible, however, to describe in general terms the political and administrative conditions that affect the development and implementation of consulting projects, the most salient purposes for which consultants are employed, some sources of information about consultants, and some key considerations in selecting and managing them. That description is the purpose of this chapter.

To keep the subject manageable, attention is restricted to consulting practices in small and medium-size communities—those large enough (5,000 to 10,000 in population) to assign the human resource (HR) function to a particular office or staff member full time or part time, but small enough to be unable to afford a highly differentiated HR department containing specialists in a wide range of HR functions. Attention is also concentrated on project consulting as opposed to contracts for recurring services—that is, on consulting agreements resulting in the solution of specific problems or development of a new administrative system rather than the provision of services such as benefits administration, drug and alcohol testing, applicant testing, or employee training.

Larger jurisdictions will have HR problems that parallel those of small and medium-size jurisdictions and should be able to find analogues to the strategies and tactics suggested for use of consultants. Naturally, it is hoped that managers in larger jurisdictions will find this chapter informative, even if they must make allowances for some substantively different types of problems and adapt the information to environments characterized by greater differentiation and internal resources.

The literature on general management consulting and the more limited literature on HR consulting reflect the complexity of the subject matter. Both, with occasional exceptions, address problems and solutions in general terms, tending to invoke inductive and experiential rather than deductive and experimental knowledge. The result is large doses of subjective wisdom and arguments that are at times internally inconsistent.

To augment the available literature, detailed and confidential interviews were conducted with a small number of HR managers and consultants. Five managers, in California, Ohio, Kentucky, Virginia, and Georgia were interviewed concerning their experiences with HR consultants. (The interview with one was quite brief—her city would not allow her to hire consultants at all; the attitude was "that's what we pay you for.") Four interviewees were HR directors; the other was a city manager with a one-person personnel department. The cities represented range in size from populations of 20,000 to 90,000, the largest having a merged county-city form of government. The total HR staff under the HR managers ranged from none to nineteen employees. Although an effort was made to spread the interviews among varied communities, a principal consideration was access to individuals willing to engage in a lengthy interview and discuss sensitive matters explicitly. This resulted in reliance on referrals and personal acquaintance to recruit the participants. As a result, the individuals interviewed work in communities that have relatively strong economies and large middle-class populations and would therefore tend to support professionalism in administration.

A senior representative of a large national consulting firm and an individual who has operated a successful personal consulting office focused on local government for over ten years were also interviewed concerning a variety of problems in consulting with local governments.

THE USES OF CONSULTANTS

Several reasons are commonly cited for employing consultants: (1) to gain access to specialized expertise; (2) to save on recurring personnel costs; (3) to obtain an objective, external perspective on problems; and (4) to obtain leadership or inspiration through the reputation or charisma of an external change agent. General management consulting experienced a surge in growth beginning in the 1960s and 1970s, with the number of consultants increasing from about 60,000 in 1960 to over 400,000 in the late 1980s. The growth was fueled by the pace of technological change and the generally increasing importance of technical knowledge, increasing complexity and growth in the economy, increasing regulation, and increasing reliance on outsourcing (Tompkins, 1995; Fitzsimons, 1993; Shenson, 1990). Although specific figures on HR consulting could not be found, it has probably grown apace and for similar reasons.

Use of consultants affords the HR manager access to specialized knowledge and skills in such varied arenas as design of compensation systems, content of personnel policies and regulations (concerning, for example, substance abuse and lawful discipline or dismissal), and application of new technologies (such as computer hardware and software). Through hiring consultants, the HR manager can overcome a lack of specialized staff and still accomplish important functions on an occasional basis. Consultants can, for example, design and run an assessment center, recruit a new police chief, or design a new classification and compensation system. In addition, they can offer an independent perspective on internal problems and thus restrict controversy—for example, an HR manager can bring in an external specialist to evaluate the compensation of a particular position. Finally, they can provide inspirational leadership, and their recommendations may carry influence with political officials and employees that would not be accorded to another member of the city workforce.

The feasibility, specific design features, and cost of a given consulting project depend upon the interaction of the city's political and social environment, the type of problem to be solved, and the consulting resources available to the city through the market. For example, communities will differ in the prevailing interest and support expressed for professionalism, managerial efficiency, and equity in HR management. Similarly, both the demands that HR managers must meet and the resources available to meet them will vary with technological and administrative infrastructure, state legal and institutional environments, economic markets, and cultural and social environments (embodying, for example, factors such as economic wealth and growth, urban-rural environment, or ethnic diversity).

PROBLEMS FOR WHICH CONSULTANTS ARE EMPLOYED

Problems that consultants may be employed to address tend to fall into two basic classes: systems development and problem solving. (For a more detailed discussion of different types of general managerial consultants, see Shenson, 1990, chap. 3.) *Systems development* refers to the design and implementation of major processes and infrastructures for long-term use, such as classification and compensation systems, computer networks and general data processing systems, personnel records systems, and general health and safety systems. *Prob-*

lem solving describes the myriad ways of providing specific ideas or advice or administering a particular service within a relatively delimited time frame and cost. Examples include specific training services, software consulting, advising and counseling to resolve a particular problem in discipline or dismissals, recruitment of a new department head by a headhunter, and health and safety consultants resolving particular problems in employee behavior.

Both systems development and problem solving efforts may be obtained from a variety of sources. Commercial providers include large diversified firms, small firms consisting of an individual or small group of associates, and teams or individuals running a private office or doing consulting as a second career. In turn, the small offices and individuals may be divided into specialists, who apply personal expertise to specific types of problems such as testing or computers, and generalists, who usually have a career background with extensive experience in HR policy or administration and who are willing to take on a range of responsibilities for HR system development and administration (especially for smaller cities). The types of problems for which consultants are likely to be employed are reviewed in the rest of this section, and then the sources of consulting services are reviewed in greater detail.

Although consultants are employed to attack problems related to every HR function, interviews and experience with HR managers and consultants suggest that as a practical matter certain types of problems are particularly likely to be addressed with the help of consultants, and in particular ways. The system development project for which HR managers seemed most likely to hire consultants was the design or redesign of classification and compensation systems (class and comp), frequently but not always accompanied by the redesign of performance evaluation systems. Other uses for consultants primarily involved the following problem-solving activities:

- *Recruitment and testing.* Examples: running an assessment center for protective services promotion candidates; recruiting and assessing applicants for police chief or head of the transportation department; purchasing testing packages and supplying supporting advice on their application.

- *General counseling on HR problem resolution.* Examples: identifying and implementing options to correct an unlawful dismissal; preparing action on a case of sexual harassment; recommending changes in compensation policies to resolve a specific equity problem.

- *Training and development.* Services provided by generalists: performing climate assessment (done by a professor on a retainer); serving as a meeting facilitator; providing counseling services for such needs as employees desiring career improvement. Services provided by personnel from the state employee relations board: training on interest-based bargaining. Services provided by external specialists: ethics training; directing quality management teams. Services provided by representatives from an employee assistance plan (EAP) or third-party workers' compensation administrator: supplying targeted advice and training on workers' compensation costs and cost control; resolving particular behavioral and disciplinary problems; training on such subjects as stress management, violence in the workplace, and detection and control of drug abuse. Services provided by a consultant or under contract with an institute: regular training programs such as quarterly management training courses.

- *Employee health, safety, and wellness issues.* Services provided by an insurance consultant: performing risk and loss control reviews; reviewing an accident scene.

- *Targeted research or evaluation projects.* Services provided by an external compensation specialist or HR administrator: reviewing compensation for a particular classification so that an independent opinion can be generated. Services provided by a professor: conducting a survey and doing comparative analysis on a particular compensation problem, such as salary differentials between county and city employees involved in a merger.

- *Preparation or modification of employment regulations and policies.* Services provided by a local physician with a law degree: preparing a drug and alcohol testing policy. Services provided by a local attorney: assisting in writing general personnel policies.

- *Labor-management relations (LMR) representation.* Services provided by a labor lawyer: supplying representation during union negotiations.

- *Development of computer systems.* Services provided by a computer specialist or consultant: developing software and related processes for specific functions such as applicant tracking or compensation analysis and revisions.

THE PUBLIC SECTOR AS A CONSULTING ENVIRONMENT

In a number of important respects, local government presents a distinctive operating environment to the consultant. The detailed and multiple lines of oversight that usually accompany political accountability create an environment that may be quite different from the corporate environment. Among other potential effects, this difference has major implications for project time frames and communication requirements. For example, a major project in a government HR agency may require multiple presentations that would not be required in a private company—to the HR staff, then to the city manager or chief executive officer, then to the mayor, then to the city council members—possibly individually, then collectively, and then in formal session.

Moreover, public-sector agencies often have HR staff (usually below the HR director level) that are, relatively speaking, not well versed in general HR functions. First-line supervisors are often not extensively trained and may be accustomed to operating in nonconfrontational modes when the implementation of important changes requires authoritative decision making. Council members may not be well experienced in specific HR practices. For example, business persons used to paying minimum wage in a personal business or a small local firm may bring a limited perspective on compensation to political oversight.

From the consultant's standpoint, moreover, dealing with elected officials can be frustrating. When costly or controversial decisions are to be made, as one consultant put it, these officials are often "unwilling to do anything that is a strong statement in any direction." Even when a consensus appears to be emerging, the prospect of controversial decisions and unpleasant impacts may elicit second thoughts and the declaration, "I didn't understand that!"

Conversely, because not all elected officials are wishy-washy, it is not unusual to find one or more council members who have positioned themselves as advocates for city employees and who allow the employees to make end runs around a consultant to complain about the effects of a new system. Changes in administration can also remind consultants and HR directors alike that political officials may have their own strongly held views—the support for given projects may depend upon the administration in power. It is not unheard of for a particular mayor or city council to strongly support the development of a new compensation system incorporating pay-for-performance and to spend considerable time and money on a contract for it, only to be followed by another administration in which key officials have seen all the evidence on the other side of the issue and decide not to implement the system.

While creating difficulties for consultants, the foibles of elected officials also create the need for their services. Consultants may have to be employed to correct or guard against ill-advised and possibly illegal actions by the officials, such as unlawful discipline or promotions or behavior that runs afoul of affirmative action guidelines.

Finally, municipal governments present consultants with certain distinctive HR problems that can include some unpleasant surprises for the inexperienced or unprepared consultant. One example is the relatively rigid and inflexible classification systems that have emerged from traditional civil service policies. Another is the unique niche that protective service workers occupy in the municipal workforce. They are often formally or informally organized when the rest of the workforce is not. They also may have been granted variations in employment practices, such as a strong emphasis on seniority in promotions, that prevent their classifications from being treated independently with regard to time in grade, as may be the case for other municipal workforce positions. And they may draw the consultant into the widespread and recurring arguments over parity between police officers and firefighters.

Public-sector clients can present to the consultant other characteristic problems that grow out of today's intensified concern with political accountability and cost control. They may, for example, use rigid bidding practices appropriate for purchasing supplies or equipment. The intent of these practices, of course, is to guard against favoritism or political capriciousness and ensure objectivity and efficiency in awarding contracts. However, if they require a fixed figure bid within detailed specifications for type of system to be delivered and time frames and if they limit the bidder's opportunity to ask questions and propose specification variances, the effect may be to prevent advantageous exploration, negotiation, and adaptation. For example, in classification and compensation studies, the consulting firm may not be able to clarify the city's compensation goals and philosophy in advance—that is, against what compensation standard does the city wish to compete: middle of the road, high, or low? As a result, the contractor may encounter unexpected communication or design problems while executing the contract, and when the study is completed the city may find that it has contracted for a new pay plan that it does not feel it can afford.

Communication or design problems also result from short-term concerns with cost savings on big projects. Public-sector officials often focus their primary attention on project costs and may be inclined to try to save money by cutting out communication and training expenses. They may also be inclined to focus attention on project costs to the exclusion of implementation costs. They may, for example, try to reduce project design expenditures to save some hundreds or thousands of dollars as they back unprepared into a new compensation system that might cost the city anywhere from 3 percent up to as much as 10 or 12 percent of payroll!

The effects of these considerations can be to triple the budget a commercial consultant will allow for the communication portion of a public-sector project. The additional risks associated with public-sector practices, such as those just described, may also lead to higher bids, because the consultant must cope with the increased uncertainty over the actual work that will be required to execute the contract. It is entirely possible that a public-sector client may have to pay more than a private-sector client for a given project carried out by a commercial consultant, all other things being equal, simply because the administrative costs of execution are greater.

SOURCES OF CONSULTING SERVICES

Consulting services and support are potentially available from a variety of sources, including the following:

- *Commercial firms and professional consultants* include large firms, often with specialized divisions and often organized with offices in a number of states, and small firms of a few employees or simply one individual operating a personal consulting business, perhaps with associates involved in projects on an ad hoc basis. The smaller firms and individuals may be generalists, or they may specialize in particular types of problems.

- *State agencies for local government* in some states provide technical support for local governments in the area of personnel administration.

- *Councils of governments,* professional associations, and associations of governments include such entities as the Kentucky League of Cities or the Georgia Municipal League; the International Personnel Management Association (IPMA); consortia organized by groups of local governments within a state, which may have some staff devoted to HR-related problems; and multicounty councils of governments, which offer technical support staff for local government.

- *University-based institutes or centers for government*—either formally organized under state mandates supported by state appropriations or semiformal service units created by universities on the basis of grants and contributed time—may have extensive specialized staffs or may provide brokerage services, arranging contacts between jurisdictions with specific needs and other resources available in their areas; they may generalize their services or may specialize in a particular need such as legal advice and training.

- *Moonlighters* include professionals such as lawyers, physicians, engineers, college professors, or other people in specialized vocations who take on part-time consulting activities. They may work as teams of two or more people who regularly seek contracts to provide particular types of services in which they have expertise (such as running assessment centers or designing examinations) or as individuals who volunteer to provide services out of civic generosity (such as a lawyer who agrees to provide some training or a physician who volunteers to advise on a substance abuse policy).

- *HR managers may call upon each other* to obtain advice about resolving particular problems; to share policies, knowledge, and instruments; and to obtain information about other consultants who may be available.

TRADE-OFFS AMONG SOURCES
Large Commercial Firms

Availability of particular types of commercial services varies widely according to the political, demographic, economic, and social environment of a city. Large firms are particularly suited for the development of major systems such as classification and compensation systems, although the smaller firm and the individual commercial consultant may be able to provide perfectly adequate service for smaller jurisdictions. Urban environments will naturally tend to have an enhanced market, with more small firms and individual consultants, more specialists, and ready access to the offices of large firms.

Large commercial firms offer certain obvious advantages, including a varied staff with multiple talents. These firms may be experienced in a variety of environments, including various types of businesses. Specialization appears to be generally increasing in consulting, and even within large commercial consulting firms, generalists have been declining in favor of specialists on given technical subjects such as broadbanding or competency-based performance appraisal. When combined with large firm mergers designed to increase market access, specialization in large firms may have the effect of reducing local offices' autonomy as it increases structural differentiation and administrative control, together with related overhead costs. (Issues related to cost are treated in further detail in a later section.)

As a consequence, large firms may avoid small cities altogether, or they may operate a subsidiary to pick up municipal business. Some vary their operations by region, taking on more municipal contracts in relatively nonurbanized areas that have cities over 50,000 or so in population but focusing on large metropolitan centers in states that have them.

When large management consulting firms *are* available, they tend to focus on the development of HR systems—policies, recruitment, assessment, selection, class and comp, benefits and investment, performance appraisal, computers and software, training and development, and research and statistical analysis. Other, special needs (for example, legal advice, especially on discipline; wellness or employee assistance programs; and labor-management relations support) may be met by special firms—such as health providers who administer EAPs or drug-testing programs and can also provide design and training services related to employee health and wellness.

Small Firms and Individual Commercial Consultants

Small consulting firms and individual consultants range from generalists providing assistance in solving specific problems or implementing small-scale general systems to specialists such as the psychologist who designs assessment and testing procedures or the computer consultant who designs and adapts software and small computer networks. The literature on consulting includes the detailed argument that small firms have lower overhead than large ones, tend to cost less, and often provide more carefully tailored and conscientious attention to a client's needs (Shenson, 1990, pp. 25–26). At the same time, however, the smaller office must devote a large amount of time—perhaps as much as a third of the work year—to the development of new business (Shenson, 1990; Tompkins, 1995). In addition, small consultants may not advertise at all but obtain manageable numbers of clients through referrals and word of mouth. A significant amount of their time may be spent attending association conferences and meetings or meeting with prospective clients to discuss problem situations that do not generate paid business.

The small city with a big project often finds small consultants more adaptable and reliable. By the nature of their business, they are usually interested in repeat customers. Moreover, if they are located within driving distance of the client city, they are better positioned to become involved in the ad hoc meetings, discussions, and problem-solving activities associated with open-ended problems.

For example, consider the situation in which elected officials have carried out an unlawful dismissal or promotion and need to rectify the situation. The consultant is the individual who may be able to (1) command the respect of the elected officials by dint of professional status and background, (2) work out a resolution of the immediate problem through appropriate and legal measures (such as reinstatement with appropriate compensation), (3) progress as necessary to the design or modification of appropriate promotion or dismissal procedures for future application, and (4) pursue implementation and adoption of these procedures through a series of meetings, negotiations, and formal approvals. Another example is the computer consultant who is able and willing to work through the problems involved in adapting a particular software package such as an applicant tracking system to a city's particular administrative situation. The need for such customized and attentive services is difficult to capture in a request for proposals (RFP), and in fact individual freelance consultants often work without contracts, expecting to bill for hours used.

The particular disadvantage of small firms is their inability to provide multiple specialties. By way of illustration, it is the larger general management firms that will typically be able to not only provide a new class and comp system but also provide a software package specifically adapted to modify the classifications and salary ranges over time (*if* the system is properly designed and functions as expected). It is the larger health services firm that may be able to augment an EAP contract with support from specialists in the subfields of psychology, counseling, and rehabilitation.

Moonlighters, Associations and Councils, Consortia, and Institutes

Moonlighters, associations and councils of governments, local government consortia, university institutes and centers, and state agencies for local government may be cheaper than commercial consultants, or free (depending upon fee structures and inclinations to civic volunteerism), and may have particularly refined expertise for dealing with certain types of problems. Again, however, availability of these sources and the appropriate expertise depends on local circumstances and chance. If councils or agencies of local government with technical support staff are available at all, they tend to have limited resources and to be preoccupied with basic needs in the smallest or most underdeveloped communities. Moonlighters are likely to include individuals carrying multiple career responsibilities, such as the psychologist operating a general practice who agrees to provide training on supervision but who delivers a wholly boilerplate training package on interpersonal styles. The package may be very useful in developing needed general skills among supervisors, but the problem must be adapted to the package rather than the package to the problem. Local government consortia may maintain ongoing contracts for services with consultants or may employ permanent staff, but in either case the services provided are likely to fill a particular technical niche, such as analysis and reporting or legal services.

HR Colleagues

When HR managers were asked to rate the usefulness of their "sources of consulting support," all gave particularly strong ratings to their colleagues and local HR management associations. Other sources identified earlier in this chapter, with the exception of commercial consultants, received much lower ratings, based on a variety of factors, including lack of availability (for example, of a university institute), resources (for example, very limited and overcommitted staff in state agencies or councils of government), and relevance or appropriateness (lacking skills or knowledge that were particularly needed). The managers were not asked to rate commercial consultants as a single group because there are so many types performing so many different functions. Instead, they were questioned about specific contracts and services and their reactions to each one. Their responses are an important component in the discussions of the selection and management of consultants that follow.

IDENTIFYING CONSULTANTS

Asked what sources they used to identify qualified consultants, HR managers again placed high value on informal contacts with fellow HR professionals, including contacts through the professional associations. Other sources identified by some as potentially useful included professional and trade journals (*if* the managers got a chance to read them), and contacts with a chosen state agency, association of governments, or university institute. The usefulness of these sources depended very much upon their individual accessibility and expertise. Solicitations from consultants were generally not considered very useful, except as entries for a mailing list for solicitation of bids. Directories of consultants, such as those published by some of the trade and professional journals were also generally not considered very useful. However, here are three such directories readily found in HR journals.

Directories of Consultants

"HRMS" (Human Resources Management Systems, advertising supplement), *Personnel Journal,* 1995, *74*(4), 95–110.

"1995–1996 *HR Magazine* Directory of Consultants," *HR Magazine,* July 1995, pp. 107–140. Organized by type of service with state listings for each type. This issue of *HR Magazine* also includes "The Yellow Pages: Guide to HR Products and Services," pp. 93–98.

"1990 Directory of Human Resources Services, Products and Suppliers." *Personnel,* Jan. 1990, pp. D1–D38. Organized by type of service or business.

BIDDING, CONTRACTING, AND COSTS

There are no fixed guidelines or standards for whether contracts of a certain type should be put out for bids, whether and how contracts should be written, and what given projects should cost. The general literature does address customs, conventions, and advice about bidding and contracting, and some detailed consideration given to cost factors and market trends can be incorporated into a determination of reasonableness (Shenson, 1990), but often the literature simply kicks the issue of price of services back into the lap of the consultant as a marketing judgment or even a matter of "feelings" (Weinberg, 1985, pp. 183–192).

Bidding and Contracting

Typically, cities request bids only when a contract can be expected to involve a sizable cost usually in excess of $5,000 to $10,000, the threshold depending in part on state contracting laws. Discussions with HR directors suggested that $10,000 is the norm, but bids may also be sought at lower costs if project circumstances warrant. The discussions further revealed that these directors did not keep standard requests for proposals on hand—the general practice was to have an RFP prepared as needed for each individual project, either by the HR department itself or by some other department designated to carry that function (such as the finance department).

The process of writing RFPs, reviewing bids, and managing contracts could easily be the subject of several books. Topics in need of attention in the literature include designing project specifications; advertising and distributing the RFPs; determining required content for proposals; designing the review process, including the selection and management of review committees; negotiating the details of contracts; implementing recommendations and systems; modifying contracts during implementation; and terminating contracts or services.

Unfortunately, no major works could be found on bidding procedures for HR services in particular. One source published in England (Bailey and Sproston, 1993) includes a discussion of RFPs and a sample RFP for recruiting training consultants. Books on general management consulting do include general chapters on recruiting, selecting, and managing consultants (for example, Holtz, 1989; Shenson, 1990; Kibbe and Setterberg, 1992). One important source of sample RFPs and advice about the process is, of course, other HR practitioners.

A particularly important subject for which both additional research and technical support for management are needed is the identification of alternative solutions—for example, how to find the cheaper, simpler software system that meets the needs of the jurisdiction for $2,000 instead of $20,000. Given the present state of knowledge about HR consulting, the search for alternatives and optimal solutions is likely to take the form of opportunistic inquiry—that is, directing a lot of questions at consultants, fellow HR professionals, publications, data banks, or any other readily available sources that might produce useful ideas. Any alternatives identified, however, must still be evaluated for their applicability and cost effectiveness. Effective evaluation of alternatives, in turn, will usually require detailed knowledge about the compatibility between specific attributes of alternatives and the HR needs of the jurisdiction.

The dilemma for the HR director may be illustrated through an endemic concern in the use of all consulting services: the provision by consultants of materials and solutions that are either completely predesigned ("canned") or partially adapted to the needs of a particular client. Canned solutions may include predesigned classification and evaluation systems, training materials, computer systems, personnel policies, testing and assessment procedures, and disciplinary procedures. But there is no hard and fast rule about the utility of canned solutions. If they do in fact meet the needs of the jurisdiction and if the consultant is willing to pass along the savings of providing a canned service, they may be the cheapest and most efficient solutions for a variety of problems. If, however, the consultant provides a canned solution in lieu of spending adequate time studying and specifically addressing a client's unique needs, the jurisdiction may suffer. The only way to know whether the solution offered is the best is to conduct a detailed analysis of a kind that the consultant may have been employed to provide in the first place! Thus there is no substitute for informed judgment—not because informed judgment is necessarily reliable but because information technology has not yet advanced to the point of offering a better approach.

Costs

The available literature stresses that the costs of commercial consultants (1) are determined by the market and (2) must, in addition to allowing for profits and benefits, cover all of the consultants' overhead expenses—office costs, communication costs, staff salaries and benefits, materials, travel, and so forth. These costs can be highly variable and may be difficult to predict; for example, travel costs in particular may depend on how much airline travel is necessary and the extent to which the consultant is able to arrange for reduced fares. Consultants must also somehow recoup the costs involved in preparing or negotiating unsuccessful bids and proposals as well as costs of time devoted to outreach and networking and to pro bono activities such as conference presentations or answering incidental follow-up questions to a project. Finally, if the contract is a fixed-fee agreement, the consultant must hedge against the risk of underbidding, and in any event must pass on to some other client the loss incurred when a project is underbid or undercharged. Estimating the costs of a project carried out by a consultant by calculating the direct costs the jurisdiction would have to pay to do the same project can therefore be highly misleading.

Shenson (1990) reports that daily billing rates for management consultants range from as low as $300 per day to as high as $1,500. Reporting the results of a survey of consultants conducted in March 1989, he found that the median daily billing rate for personnel or HR consultants in general was at that time $769. The respective rates for training consultants and insurance consultants were $790 and $734 (p. 64). In general, costs should probably be expected to be lower for consultants in small town and rural environments than those in metropolitan centers and for those specializing in the public sector than those covering the corporate market. Large general consulting firms, however, are likely to use standard billing formulas, based on such factors as compensable hours, that are not adjusted to sector or location.

In judging the reasonableness of cost, the old adage that "you get what you pay for" is relevant but simplistic. A costly consultant may or may not provide what you need; a consultant being financially pressured by a contract is particularly unlikely to do so; and a consultant with a demonstrated record of reliability and advanced expertise can generally charge more within his or her market environment and is likely to be worth it if properly used.

Moreover, excellent assistance can often be obtained free of charge for some relatively limited problems, such as specialized training or advice on technical problems. Sources include doctors, lawyers, or professors who are willing to provide some pro bono training time as a public service and commercial consultants who are willing to answer technical questions on compensation or discipline problems as part of an ongoing client relationship.

PROBLEMS IN USING CONSULTANTS

The existing literature on consultants includes some treatments of problems that clients may experience with consultants they hire. There are, for example, general statements about poor project design and ethical concerns (Holtz, 1989) and discussions of more specific problems in particular markets (Menagh, 1993; van Kirk, 1992, on computer consulting; Luden, 1992, on executive search services; Kibbe and Setterberg, 1992, on consulting to nonprofits). A systematic examination of performance problems in public-sector HR consulting could not be found and is beyond the scope of this chapter. The following sections, however, review some problems that seem prominent in the experience and comments of HR directors, and consider some options for addressing them.

Small Projects

Discussions with HR managers yielded a striking pattern. They seemed to have few complaints about the smaller projects with which they had experience. The complaints mentioned included consultants who had pandered to elected officials' interests in contemporary fads such as privatization or quality management and, in the process, overpromised results. Some HR directors and municipal department heads also concluded, or at least suspected, that they might have achieved just as good a result through their own methods as they did by hiring the consultant and executing the contract—in one case, for example, the personnel results achieved through an assessment center matched closely the choices the manager would have made anyway. If trust in the judgment of the selecting officials is not a problem and the objective perspective of the consultant is not an advantage in choosing personnel, an assessment center may indeed be unnecessary.

Large Projects

Of the four managers with whom in-depth discussions were conducted about consulting, three had undertaken a class and comp project within the past five years, and it was their primary or only large externally bid contract. These class and comp projects were undertaken for a variety of reasons: to update classifications that had been patched together by operating departments over a period of years and that used inconsistent language; to obtain a state-of-the-art system incorporating pay-for-performance; and to reintegrate and standardize personnel positions after a merger.

As noted earlier, the most expensive and difficult HR project in which most small and medium-size cities are likely to engage—and often the most traumatic—is the development of a new class and comp system. As one HR director put it, two fellow HR directors had "warned me that class and comp would be the most difficult thing I ever did, and I wouldn't believe them; now I know."

Many of the frustrations and challenges in class and comp projects are inherent in the process of reviewing and changing the criteria by which employees are paid. Controversy may arise from the contracting and design process itself, from technical issues, and from the processes of organizational politics, communication, and accommodation. Thus the city must resolve such technical issues as identifying its compensation goals (will pay be set at high, medium, or low market standards?), resolving the form of its reward structures (will it emphasize seniority? pay-for-performance?), and even choosing its basic managerial climate and philosophy (implemented with broadbanding?). And choices on these issues carry assumptions with them. For example, a decision to adopt broadbanding carries the assumption of reduced numbers of hierarchical levels and enhanced discretion at operating levels. Moreover, because no city is exactly like another in organization and functions, specific adaptation of any boilerplate material used is particularly important in class and comp studies.

Adding to the challenge is the simple fact that compensation issues are inherently explosive: employees tend to assume that they are underpaid and that an objective review should produce higher wages. Also, when attention to compensation is aroused, issues in equity provide rationales for political and managerial maneuvering and gamesmanship. Tensions may be heightened by environmental factors such as the degree of unionization and the labor relations climate or the political climate. Members of a city council, for example, may attempt to intervene in the process of developing a new classification system in order to ingratiate themselves with the workforce or to embarrass a mayor or administrator they do not like. The council must accept the compensation standards and philosophy that undergird any new pay system, and it is important to ensure that the council is sufficiently informed and supportive during the system's development so that an unexpected curtailment or rejection does not occur when the system is ready to implement.

All of the three projects specifically discussed with managers presented serious problems, and for all the same core issue arose during the stage of the design process in which job evaluations were conducted and new job descriptions written. In all cases the job descriptions were too canned, poorly or inconsistently written and worded, or simply full of errors. In all cases the process took longer than expected—up to several years longer. The immediate consequences were extensive delays in completing the system and the loss of legitimacy for the entire process in the eyes of the employees. The problems had to be resolved through such means as applying intensive backstop work by the HR staff, bringing in a second contractor, or suspending parts of the project, such as the implementation of the new compensation scales or the design of a new performance appraisal system. The backstopping work by the HR staff might involve completing the job descriptions themselves, carrying out the compensation plan themselves, suspending performance appraisals for an extended period of time because the old ones were outdated and the new ones were not ready, and terminating the original contract or negotiating a follow-up contract with a different contractor to complete the lagging stages of the project.

It is perhaps not surprising that a litany of problems tends to recur naturally in something as complicated as class and comp studies. Here are a few more examples, drawn from the comments of both municipal managers and consultants:

- A contractor can lead employees to believe that everyone will be interviewed during the job evaluation process or that dissatisfaction with a new compensation system can be alleviated because every employee can appeal his or her classification.

- The advance representative of the consulting firm who negotiated the details of the contract can turn out not to be the project director, and the actual project director does not succeed in winning the trust of the municipal staff.

- The consulting staff that conducted the job evaluation process on site can be clearly overworked with too many project assignments, can be inexperienced, or can spend all the promised time doing the on-site interviews but then hand off the results to other staff who do not use them effectively.

- Some municipal managers or employees can succeed in snowing the consulting staff—persuading the consultants that they are actually doing more, and more responsible, work than is the case.

- An employee committee conducting the initial audit and the planning leading up to the project can be too large (twenty members is a realistic maximum). Having too large a committee can lead to such problems as factionalism, difficulty in arranging meetings, uneven productivity among members and subcommittees, and the need to ensure that all members have the minimal understanding needed to participate effectively. The committee may also have few or no people with direct HR experience. It can include people who think they know more about compensation than the consultants. It can decide to force the contract review away from a consultant with which the city has experience because the committee members want to try somebody new, perhaps hoping for compensation more to their liking.

- Employees or employee groups can challenge the consulting staff's expertise or findings, seek intervention from elected officials, or even conduct their own independent salary surveys.

- Members of an employee or management committee can assume that they are experts on compensation and can pass over previous consultants in reviewing bids, not because the consultant did poor work but because committee members do not like the results of previous compensation studies and refuse to believe those studies were valid.

EVALUATING CONSULTANTS AND PROPOSALS

Such problems lead naturally to the desire for systematic methods of consultant and project evaluation and selection that can ensure their effectiveness. Alas, there aren't any. Prevailing methods of trying to ensure successful outcomes include the use of carefully selected review committees to consider proposals, the use of references, and attempts to carefully negotiate details of implementation (using the negotiation process as an opportunity to probe for information).

Committee Reviews

In reviewing, say, a class and comp proposal, a normal practice is to establish a review committee, representing several departments and using experienced managers and department members with extensive HR experience if at all possible. As already noted, however, the larger a committee is, the more factionalism is likely to surface. Loading a committee with large numbers of rank-and-file employees who believe they are underpaid and who may or may not understand the technical aspects of compensation is probably begging for trouble.

Consultants' References

Checking consultants' references is considered essential by HR managers and by responsible consultants too. ("I begin to get worried when they don't even call the references," said one consultant.) Unfortunately, there are as many problems in using references to evaluate consultants as there are in using them to evaluate job applicants. In all the class and comp projects described earlier, references were either formally or informally consulted. The references were positive—the firms were reputable and experienced, either in class and comp specifically or in general management. Problems occurred anyway.

Attempts to refine and target the reference process lead naturally to efforts to get more and more detailed information. One way to do this is to ask for a complete list of all similar projects that a consulting office has conducted in a specified prior time period, together with contact people, in the hope of avoiding bias in the selection of references. A naturally attractive next step is to ask for samples of work, but this can be a major problem for commercial consultants—the work product may contractually be the property of the client, not the consultant. (And jurisdictions should remember that consultants, too, have to deal with a certain amount of potential client gamesmanship—for example, a jurisdiction may use the bidding process to acquire ideas and samples for its own use and then stiff the contractor.) Of course, HR directors can ask a consultant's other *clients* for work samples directly.

Attention to Details

Negotiating details of contracts is easiest for simple and short-term projects where the need is least pressing, such as projects for training or for the development of testing instrumentation. Implementation of a complex project such as a class and comp study, however, is an evolutionary and developmental process, the outcomes of which will depend on the combined effects of many factors, and the contract will be correspondingly more complex.

In the case of the class and comp study, the ideal objective might be summarized as timely completion of an accurate and carefully designed classification plan, followed by implementation of a precise and internally consistent compensation plan, with a reasonably high level of acceptance by the employees. The opportunity to achieve such outcomes will be affected by the interaction of such factors as the size of the city, the time and effort invested by the consultant, the managerial competence and objectivity of the city, and the technical requirements of the process itself.

As city size increases, the city workforce becomes more differentiated—for example, the police department expands to include multiple layers of command, specialists such as detectives, and then specialized divisions. In smaller jurisdictions with workforces of no more than three hundred or so a consultant can achieve a high degree of natural visibility and interaction during the process of administering position description questionnaires and conducting desk audits. It is easier to talk with at least one incumbent in every type of position, and the contact is likely to have ripple effects throughout the workforce. Even supervisors are more likely to be effective vectors for transmitting a sense of involvement and objectivity to the workforce. As one consultant put it, "Some of those department heads spend more quality time with their employees at work than they do with their families!"

As the workforce becomes larger and more specialized, contact and interviewing become perforce more selective, and more reliance is likely to be placed on paper communication. One conventional practice is to rely more on committees—for example, to train a committee of employees and supervisors representing a range of units to use a position evaluation methodology, and to involve them extensively in the process of developing the new classification plan out of the position survey data. If the committee is effective, its members can assist in developing legitimacy for the new plan, and the necessity and cost of bringing consultants on site may be reduced.

Discussions with HR managers and consultants suggest that two basic city-consultant mixes are likely to be found in class and comp studies: the relatively small community relying on an individual consultant or small firm, typically staffed by one or a few experienced generalists, and the larger community employing a regional or national firm. In both cases the prevailing approach to compensation seems to be a point-factor system anchored on both local markets and the city's own tolerance for compensation costs. Also, in both cases, a relationship of mutual trust and respect between the elected officials and the city's workforce on one hand and between managers and employees on the other hand can make a major contribution to a systematic and reasonable process.

In the first case, however, an energetic consultant will invest considerable personal time in on-site contact and research during the development of the classification plan, using previously developed material but building trust and adapting the material through extensive personal interaction. By the time the process is completed the resulting point assignments may be largely understood and anticipated by the workforce as a whole, promoting better acceptance among the employees.

The large firm working in the larger city will follow a more formalized process in which the classification plan may be developed with the cooperation of an employee committee and/or with a series of planned survey and interview cycles. The plan itself may be developed through a series of three or four iterative analytic steps in which the results of the position surveys are projected into the point system, possibly using multivariate computer analysis to measure contributions of different factors to the content of a position. At each step the results of applying the point system may be reconsidered, and the allocations tightened and made more consistent. As the compensation plan is then applied to the classifications and becomes formal policy through adoption by the city council or legislative body, hard statements of dollar value are made. Some significant degree of tension and conflict is inescapable at this point in the process. This is true not only because employees must often accept less compensation than they would have wished but also because the process of developing the new system will inevitably create anomalies or disparities in rewards. One example is the senior employee who is found to be earning a salary already higher than the top of his or her new classification, confronting the city with the specter of reducing the compensation of an employee of long, devoted, and competent service. There are no perfect solutions to such a problem; a compromise must be found, such as grandfathering the higher salary into the new system but redlining all raises for employees who are above the maximum compensation for their classification.

A certain number of complaints and appeals are also inevitable at this stage of the process (although a large number of appeals—coming from 30 percent of the workforce, for example—would certainly be regarded as an unacceptable outcome by most HR managers). In the small city that has employed an individual consultant, the consultant may be willing to meet with employees who have complaints, either individually or in groups, to explain the process and the results, before the appeal is carried forward for formal resolution. This intervening consultation can be an important factor in educating employees and promoting their realistic understanding of the employment market. Formal adjudication may involve a committee, but smaller workforces are, if anything, perhaps more likely to exhibit avoidance of conflict than larger ones, and it is often the legislative body that hears the appeal.

The larger jurisdiction that has employed a large firm is more likely to rely on an appeals committee. A relatively small appeals committee, which has members competent to understand and address technical issues in compensation (managers or technically competent employees, for example) and which takes appeals only on paper and not in person, is likely to be most effective in maintaining the objective consistency of the system. The natural hope is that in the more impersonal and administratively systematic environment of the larger jurisdiction, the committee will be able to confront conflict and enforce the new system more assertively than elected officials or a complainant's fellow employees could in the very personalistic environment that often characterizes small jurisdictions.

CONCLUSION: TWO GRAINS OF ADVICE

Although no perfect formula can be prescribed for success in all consulting situations, my review suggests at least a couple of ways in which HR managers in local government can strengthen themselves for the process, particularly when they must handle the large projects. The first is to prepare carefully to investigate and understand the technical details of projects; the second is to network.

Be Prepared to Handle Details

By educating themselves and being prepared to negotiate and manage the details of projects, HR managers may increase their chances of detecting and avoiding not only basic lack of expertise in a consultant but also such problems as inadequate commitments of resources, inadequate provision for employee communication and education, and misplanning or neglect of technical details. This preparation process will be time consuming. It may also seem ironic, because the time goes to acquire expertise that the consultant is expected to provide.

Adding to the difficulty is the fact that each process is likely to have a number of unique elements. In class and comp the key challenges have to do with timely and precise completion of specifically relevant job descriptions, design of a compensation plan adapted to specific local needs, and design of specific provisions for addressing resulting anomalies and maximizing employee acceptance. For other large projects, the challenges will be different. In the development of a new computer system, for example, the key considerations to watch for will be realistic training provisions, postimplementation technical support, consultant biases toward specific products, needs for interfacing equipment and software, and ability to meet the specific analytic needs of the HR department. Self-education has been recognized as an important safeguard in computer systems contracting (van Kirk, 1992) and is equally appropriate for other technical HR functions.

Educated and prepared, an HR manager is better able to ask specific questions about project design and implementation. For example, my review suggests that HR departments beginning class and comp projects might ask consultants the following questions, above and beyond the standard ones dealing with consultant experience and credentials, the basic work plan, and the budget:

- What specific plans does the consultant have to promote employee understanding and acceptance of the new system? What prior experience has he or she had in doing so?

- What recommendations will be made for handling the appeals process? What role does the consultant expect to play in that process?

- Who will be the project director? Can he or she be interviewed before the project begins?

- What staff will be involved on site to conduct the position analysis? Will the same staff or different staff write the position descriptions? What other projects will the staff be working on at the same time as they work on our project?

- Is the consultant willing to furnish a complete list of references, including those for projects that were terminated or considered unsuccessful?

Be Prepared to Network

Most HR professionals probably do not need to be told of the importance of maintaining a strong professional support network; many, however, seem not to act on this intelligence, either because of some personal constraint or because they are restricted by unsupportive attitudes among higher managers or elected officials. HR professionals with whom consulting was discussed clearly placed great importance on networking. Among its other benefits, it provides a primary source of reliable referrals to and information on consultants and consulting firms. It can also provide access to ideas and solutions for a variety of technical problems (with the natural caveat that a system or procedure specifically adapted for one municipal environment cannot be casually expropriated and implemented in another without great risk). With these and other benefits, professional networking among human resource managers is worth considerable cost in time, travel, and communication.

References

Bailey, D., and Sproston, C. *Choosing and Using Training Consultants.* Hants, England: Gower House, 1993.

Fitzsimons, D. J. "Marketing the Human Resources Function." *Journal of Compensation and Benefits,* Sept.–Oct. 1993, pp. 81–84.

Holtz, H. *Choosing and Using a Consultant: A Manager's Guide to Consulting Services.* New York: Wiley, 1989.

Kibbe, B., and Setterberg, F. *Succeeding with Consultants: Self Assessment for the Changing Nonprofit.* New York: Foundation Center, 1992.

Luden, B. V. "HR vs. Executive Search." *Personnel Journal,* May 1992, pp. 104–109.

Menagh, M. "Hi! I'm Your Consultant from Hell." *Computerworld,* Dec. 6, 1993, pp. 79–80.

Shenson, H. L. *How to Select and Manage Consultants.* San Francisco: New Lexington Press, 1990.

Tompkins, N. C. "Specialization Fuels Growth of Consulting." *HR Magazine,* July 1995, pp. 110–113.

van Kirk, D. "Can You Trust Vendors as Systems Integrators?" *Infoworld,* Nov. 16, 1992, p. 106.

Weinberg, G. M. *The Secrets of Consulting: A Guide to Giving and Getting Advice Successfully.* New York: Dorset House, 1985.

Recommended Reading

"Consultants No Substitute for In-House Personnel, Says Curnow." *Personnel Management,* Dec. 23, 1991, p. 15.

Cooley, M. S. "Selecting the Right Consultants." *HR Magazine,* Aug. 1994, pp. 100–103.

Famularo, J. T. *Handbook of Human Resources Administration.* New York: McGraw-Hill, 1986.

Kubr, M. (ed.). *Management Consulting: A Guide to the Profession.* Geneva: International Labor Office, 1976.

Laabs, J. J. "HR for Profit: Selling Expertise." *Personnel Journal,* May 1995, pp. 84–92.

Nadler, L. (ed.). *Handbook of Human Resource Development.* New York: Wiley, 1984.

Richards-Carpenter, C. "The Essential Skills of the Personnel Systems Consultant." *Personnel Management,* Oct. 22, 1990, pp. 103, 105.

Scheer, W. E. *Personnel Administration Handbook.* Chicago: Dartnell, 1985.

Tompkins, N. C. "How to Become a Human Resources Consultant." *HR Magazine,* Aug. 1994, pp. 94–98.

CHAPTER TWENTY-FOUR

Utilizing Volunteers in the Workplace

Jeffrey L. Brudney

In the decade of the 1990s, perhaps no other occupational specialization in government has confronted a greater number of important challenges than the field of human resource management. Virtually all of the demands and complaints that have been visited on the public sector over the decade have come to rest in the office of the human resource manager. Public personnel administrators have had to respond to cutbacks in government funding and paid staff, legislative mandates to accommodate diverse personnel and extend the rights of employees, court decisions to validate testing procedures and criteria for promotion, exhortations to emulate compensation systems used by profit-making businesses and to achieve gains in productivity, and pressures to decentralize operations and empower employees and at the same time maintain control and accountability over the workforce.

In a decade that has witnessed growing constraints on the employment and use of human resources, the prospect of drawing on a new source of labor that could be tapped without benefit of monetary compensation has very great appeal, especially to financially strapped governments. The involvement of volunteers in government holds out considerable promise for containing costs and enhancing agency capacity, but the effort also requires planning, organization, coordination, and management. Just as with the other challenges mentioned above, these demands will likely fall at the door of the human resource manager. This chapter explains how human resource professionals can create and sustain a thriving volunteer program that will serve clients, paid staff, volunteers, and the organization. After defining volunteers to government, the chapter discusses five challenges for successful volunteer programs: acceptance by paid employees, recruitment of volunteers, accountability to the larger agency and its purpose, management, and evaluation.

WHO IS A VOLUNTEER?

Although defining who is a volunteer might seem an abstract, theoretical exercise, it is with this question that the design of an effective volunteer program begins. Without a clear conception of the volunteer, the human resource manager is apt to draw very misleading conclusions about the magnitude of the pool of volunteers available and the possibilities for attracting them to government service and using them effectively.

Reviews of the volunteer concept expose a surprisingly broad array of definitions and constituent dimensions (Cnaan, Handy, and Wadsworth, 1996; Cnaan and Amrofell, 1994). Ram Cnaan, Femida Handy, and Margaret Wadsworth (1996) find that underlying the various definitions are four principal dimensions: the extent to which the decision to volunteer is free or uncoerced, the extent to which the volunteer receives remuneration (for example, a stipend or reimbursement for expenses), the degree of structure to the volunteer activity (whether it takes place inside or outside an organized setting), and the intended beneficiaries of the activity (other people such as agency clients or the volunteers themselves). Cnaan and Laura Amrofell (1994) are more specific. They show that volunteer activity can be usefully categorized or *mapped* according to ten broad facets, including who the volunteers are (demographic characteristics), what they donate (for example, time or services), how often or regularly the action occurs (for example, once per year versus once per week) and for how much time per episode, the beneficiaries of the donations, the management aspects of volunteering (such as who, if anyone, manages the activity and what functions that manager performs), and the rewards sought and received by the volunteers. Similarly, Nancy Macduff (1996) has proposed a *volunteer taxonomy* that classifies volunteer positions according to type (for example, elected or mandated), function (direct service, administrative, or leadership), kind of activity performed, and time and duration of commitment (for example, continuous or episodic).

Each combination of the Cnaan and Amrofell (1994) facets or application of the Macduff (1996) taxonomy will produce very different volunteer profiles with important implications for design of the volunteer program. Or as Cnaan and Amrofell (1994) put it, "only the combination of all facets forms a volunteer profile that is distinctive enough to warrant generalizations" (p. 349). For example, an annual job fair organized by a municipal personnel department and staffed by volunteers will call for a very different program than an effort to place service-learning participants in city government or a volunteer task force charged with examining municipal operations and making recommendations for improvement or a citywide beautification project coordinated by the human resource office relying on labor supplied by neighborhood and civic groups. Although each of these programs uses volunteers, these volunteers will differ greatly with respect to recruitment, screening, management, beneficiaries, and rewards.

A poignant illustration of the potential scale of the differences comes from the 1996 Summer Olympic Games, sponsored by the city of Atlanta (Schwed, 1996). As might have been expected, organizers had no problem attracting the more than forty thousand volunteers needed to stage the grand, sixteen-day event, and the large number of people from highly professional occupations drawn to that world stage facilitated volunteer management. The rewards were also on a special scale. A Dalton, Georgia, native described the enjoyment and thrill generated by volunteering in the envoy program with the country of Burundi (a small African nation located next to Rwanda) for that country's first Olympic Games. Crowded near the finish line of the men's 5,000-meter event, the volunteer shared the honor of passing the nation's flag to the winning Burundian runner for a victory lap and "will always remember helping to find a flag for my adopted country" (Light, 1997, p. H3).

The typical volunteer assignment cannot match such stimulation. "Most volunteer work does not convey a sense of completion in days or weeks, much less provide prestige, one hot meal a day and a spiffy uniform. Those laboring in the volunteer trenches sometimes go years without seeing much benefit from their labors" (Schwed, 1996, p. B1). Lacking the bright glare of publicity, the heady chance to mix with interesting people from around the globe, and the opportunity to witness or even play a part in the dramatic action, recruitment to more prosaic volunteer opportunities in Atlanta has returned to the levels experienced before the Olympics by that city—as well as by other cities and towns that count on volunteers to assist in public health, education, crime prevention, recreation, and so forth. Sustaining even the present participation over the long haul remains a daunting problem.

Although the Cnaan-Amrofell typology demonstrates the great diversity of volunteer-based projects, this chapter focuses on the programs that are most common and that have sparked the most interest in the public sector: those that enlist volunteers to serve governments in dedicated positions—ombudsperson, recreation assistant, library docent, emergency medical technician, teacher's aide, museum guide, family counselor, police auxiliary, court advocate, firefighter, and a host of other jobs. Citizens in these positions labor in relative obscurity, usually in social problem areas that do not yield easily to the quick fix. These volunteer programs have the following main characteristics:

- They are sponsored and housed under the *auspices of a government agency.*

- As implied by the first characteristic, the volunteer activity occurs in formal setting, that is, *an organizational context.*

- Participants receive *no monetary compensation* for their labor. The most authoritative surveys probing this behavior—a series of biennial surveys commissioned by the Independent Sector organization and conducted by the Gallup Organization—as well as many other surveys, operationalize volunteering as "working in some way to help others for no monetary pay" (see Hodgkinson and others, 1996b).

- Nevertheless one should not have to pay financially for the privilege of volunteering. Thus volunteers are entitled to *reimbursement for out-of-pocket expenses* incurred in their activity, such as mileage, meals, and parking.

- Volunteers' *time should be given freely,* rather than mandated (for example, court-ordered community service or restitution lies outside the present definition); compulsion alters significantly the character of the endeavor (Van Til, 1988).

- The volunteers perform jobs with ongoing responsibilities for service delivery (for example, client contact) or organizational maintenance (for example, assisting paid staff). For volunteers just as for paid employees, *a regular investment of time* (rather than one-time-only or sporadic efforts), albeit at a dramatically reduced level compared to paid staff, is necessary for effective job performance.

Human resource managers should be aware that not every volunteer program in the public sector has these characteristics (for a discussion of the range of programs, see Brudney, 1990b, 1995b). However, these provisions delineate the type of program—and the type of volunteer—most often desired by government organizations to assist in agency operations and the delivery of services.

CHALLENGES OF GOVERNMENT-BASED VOLUNTEER PROGRAMS

Volunteer programs in the public sector constitute examples of *coproduction:* the active involvement of lay citizens with paid service agents in the planning and especially the delivery of publicly supported goods and services (Ferris, 1984; Percy, 1984; Brudney and England, 1983; Parks and others, 1981). Although citizen-government collaboration is common and takes a variety of forms (see Sharp, 1980; Whitaker, 1980), in this one, citizens are assigned to designated positions in government programs and departments where they work hand-in-hand with public employees to carry out agency missions (Brudney, 1990b). For the human resource manager responsible for the coproduction effort, designing, implementing, and managing a volunteer program raises five interdependent challenges (Brudney, 1996):

- *Acceptance challenge.* Paid employees must learn to accept and accommodate volunteers on the office floor and in the government workforce.
- *Recruitment challenge.* Volunteers must be attracted to the agency and placed in positions where their backgrounds, skills, interests, and energies can be put to best use.
- *Accountability challenge.* The sponsoring organization must have mechanisms in place to ensure that the volunteer program is operating in a manner consistent with agency values and goals.
- *Management challenge.* The volunteer program must be administered in such a way that despite the absence of monetary incentives, citizens are competent in their duties and perform in a professional manner.
- *Evaluation challenge.* At regular intervals the volunteer effort and individual participants should undergo assessment to monitor the operation and results of the program.

A successful volunteer program must surmount these challenges. Because each challenge spills over into the other challenges, addressing each one is particularly important. For example, a volunteer program faces no more crucial challenge than recruitment. Without citizen involvement, coproduction is stymied, and all other challenges become meaningless. Successful recruitment depends, in turn, on gaining employee acceptance for the volunteer program. Unless employees can be won over, volunteer recruitment (and retention) will be problematic. Recruitment depends as well on creating and offering jobs within the agency that stimulate the interest and service motives of volunteers, key management functions. Thus should the program fail to meet either the acceptance or the management challenge, recruitment will suffer as well.

Winning the acceptance of paid employees for the volunteer program hinges on involving them in decisions on how to share the workplace with citizens. These agreements provide the foundation for job descriptions for volunteer assignments, a critical management challenge. Employees need reassurance concerning not only the jobs volunteers are to perform but also the training and orientation volunteers are to receive in preparation for agency work roles. Programs that falter in providing such background knowledge and training jeopardize not only employee acceptance of volunteers but also program accountability to agency values and objectives. Finally, the accountability and evaluation challenges are closely intertwined. A goal in the evaluation of any program (volunteer or otherwise) is to generate the information that can be used to gauge the extent to which authority and funding have been applied appropriately and effectively toward public purposes and accountability has been met.

Given the interrelationships among the challenges, a lapse in addressing any one of them could have far-reaching implications for the success of the volunteer program. Each challenge is discussed in detail in the following sections.

Meeting the Acceptance Challenge

Successful volunteer programs in government constitute a partnership between employees and volunteers. Coproduction relies on the labor and cooperation of both parties in meeting organizational objectives. Without the support of paid staff for a volunteer program, or at the least their tacit acquiescence, the promise held out for these ventures—for example, increasing agency productivity, responsiveness, and community representation—will not be realized. Conflicts and antagonisms between paid and nonpaid staff sap the volunteer effort of vitality, impair organizational performance, and ultimately jeopardize client welfare. Even subtle forms of resistance can undermine volunteers on the job and retard recruitment and retention of citizens.

Writing in 1977, volunteerism expert Ivan Scheier was already labeling the often indifferent or antagonistic reception of paid staff to the inception and operation of a volunteer program an "old failure" (p. 32). In spite of escalating demands for services and diminishing resources to meet them in the ensuing two decades—conditions that should have opened public and nonprofit agencies to assistance—the problem of acceptance has persisted well into the 1990s (Lafrance, 1996). In some cases, unfortunately, insufficient attention to program implementation has given employees reason for distrust and suspicion. When top officials introduce volunteers without an underlying foundation for collaboration—consisting of job protections for employees, adequate orientation and training for volunteers, jobs designated expressly for citizens, and a program structure that renders use of nonpaid personnel easy and advantageous for paid staff—opposition can be anticipated. The blame cannot be placed on agency leadership alone, however. Even with the proper foundation in place, in other cases employees have resisted introduction of what could be a valuable citizen resource, offering not only help on the job but also support in the political system (Brudney, 1990b).

The key to surmounting the acceptance challenge lies in involving all parties—top-level organizational officials, paid staff members, and citizen volunteers—in planning the volunteer program and in making the crucial decisions on sharing the workplace (Brudney, 1990b). Speaking of social work, Jean Lafrance (1996) has described the urgency of this task: "A new alliance must be forged between social workers and volunteers to help people in need. The alliance will not come from a paradigm of domination by one of the other, but from a spirit of equality that respects and values the unique contribution each has to offer. The opportunities for service are many. . . . [The alliance] must call forth the best that both professionals and volunteers have to offer" (p. 7). The charge is no different in the other public service domains.

Thus top officials should not unilaterally impose volunteer involvement but work with paid staff to earn their approbation and backing. Employees deserve input into decisions and changes that can so dramatically affect the workplace and the welfare of clients; the paid workforce is more knowledgeable than any other group concerning the service demands that it can accommodate and, conversely, those areas where additional assistance is most necessary and welcome. Conversely, citizens are in a position to offer fresh insights into agency operations and relations with the community and, of course, the job responsibilities within the agency that volunteers would be most likely to embrace. They, too, deserve a say.

Gaining the acceptance of employees for the volunteer program rests on their participation, along with volunteers and high-level organizational officials, in meetings intended to come to agreement on the goals underlying volunteer participation in the agency, the job tasks to be allocated to citizens (and those to be retained by employees), and the overall philosophy guiding the volunteer effort. This process should culminate in formal policies and guidelines governing volunteer involvement in the agency. The most important set of decisions is the designation of jobs that might be assigned most productively to volunteers. The respective job tasks for nonpaid and paid workers should be codified in formal job descriptions, with the stipulation that neither group will hold the positions reserved for the other. Although no task is inherently volunteer or paid, prime candidates for delegation to volunteers are tasks with the following characteristics (Ellis, 1996, pp. 103–105):

- They can be performed on a part-time basis.
- They do not require the specialized training or skills of paid personnel.
- They cannot be accommodated by in-house expertise.
- They are tasks for which the current position occupant feels uncomfortable or unprepared.

Nearly always, successful implementation of the volunteer program necessitates organizational changes requiring the approval of top agency leadership. Leaders' endorsements are essential to signal the importance of volunteerism to the agency and to lend authority to the initiative. In addition, legislation may have to be introduced or amended to permit the use of nonpaid personnel in government; paid positions in volunteer administration created, posted, and bid; job descriptions changed to incorporate responsibilities for citizen participation;

volunteer policies and procedures approved and disseminated; and resources committed to the program.

Not only paid staff but also top agency management must accept the citizen participants. Human resource managers can work to meet the acceptance challenge by involving employees in volunteer program design and by laying the foundation for a collaborative effort that furthers the interests of paid staff, volunteers, and ultimately agency clients.

Meeting the Recruitment Challenge

As discussed earlier, coproduction involves a mixing of the productive labor and talent of citizens and paid staff. For the human resource manager committed to establishing and maintaining a volunteer program, the combining of effort raises two interdependent challenges: employees must come to accept (or tolerate) working with volunteers (the acceptance challenge just discussed), and citizens must be attracted to nonpaid positions in public agencies. No less than on gaining employee acceptance, the success of the volunteer program depends on meeting the recruitment challenge to enlist volunteers in attractive and worthwhile service in the public sector.

Government is not the sole outlet for volunteers' contributed time and labor but must compete for this time and labor with nonprofit organizations. In fact the nonprofit sector is far and away the leading employer of volunteer labor, accounting for about two-thirds of all volunteer work assignments (66 percent) and hours donated (68.1 percent), compared to roughly one-quarter for government agencies (26.6 percent of work assignments and 25.3 percent of hours). The remainder of the vast pool of donated labor is directed to for-profit organizations that sponsor volunteer programs, frequently staffed by their own employees. Although the Fair Labor Standards Act of 1938 proscribes for-profit firms from enlisting or otherwise using volunteers, a business may establish a nonprofit organization or foundation to house a volunteer effort, as do many private hospitals and museums. According to national surveys, as many as 7.5 percent of all volunteers may donate time to business-supported volunteer programs, which account for 6.5 percent of all hours volunteered (Hodgkinson and others, 1996b, pp. 75–76, 105).

Human resource managers confronted with the recruitment challenge might take comfort in the fact that over the past decade the percentage of Americans eighteen years of age or older who claim in national surveys that they have volunteered over the past year has hovered at around half the population. The latest estimate, from a 1996 survey conducted by the Gallup Organization, puts the figure at 48.8 percent (Hodgkinson and others, 1996a, pp. 2, I–30). According to the survey, 93 million citizens volunteered an average of 4.2 hours per week to organizations and causes (that weekly figure has remained stable over the decade), generating a total of just over 20.3 billion volunteer hours in 1995, the equivalent of 9.23 million full-time employees. The donated labor was valued at a staggering $201.5 billion. Because national surveys routinely demonstrate such impressive statistics regarding the generosity of the American people (for example, Hodgkinson and others, 1996b), observers might reasonably question whether recruitment poses a genuine challenge to a volunteer program.

Yet close examination of the surveys reveals that with respect to the aims of building and sustaining volunteer programs in government, the estimated rate is quite misleading: it includes all acts of volunteering—both formal (within an organization) and informal (outside of organizational auspices), regular (on a continual basis) and sporadic (one-time-only or episodic), and requiring large and small amounts of time per episode, and to all types of institutions (secular and religious, government and nonprofit). Applying the definition of volunteer program elucidated previously as a means of correcting for these and other survey features, the effective pool of volunteers potentially available to government agencies is probably only about one-third the size suggested by the national surveys (see Brudney, 1990a, for a complete analysis). This group is highly prized, moreover, not only by government agencies but also nonprofit organizations.

Other studies, too, dispel the notion of a ready pool of volunteers eagerly awaiting the call from government and other agencies to lend a hand. A small army of social scientists, led by Robert D. Putnam (1995), laments an erosion in "social capital" over the past twenty to thirty years, a weakening of norms of personal trust and community participation. The trend is exemplified by steep declines in membership in and volunteering for such mainline civic and fraternal organizations as the Boy Scouts, Red Cross, League of Women Voters, Lions, Elks, Shriners, Jaycees, and Masons. Due to such factors as increased residential mobility, the movement of women into the labor force, the transformation of leisure into a more solitary activity by technology (such as the television, VCR, and Internet), and other demographic changes, traditional sources of volunteers and stimuli for volunteer participation are likely eroding.

These changes have not been lost on human resource professionals responsible for government-based volunteer programs. Surveys of this group confirm that recruitment poses a serious challenge (for example, Brudney, 1990b; Duncombe, 1985). On the one hand, some organizations, such as volunteer fire departments, have begun to rely more heavily on paid than nonpaid staff (Brudney and Duncombe, 1992). On the other hand, human resource managers have used a variety of novel strategies to recruit citizens effectively. To attract volunteers, these officials:

- *Practice outreach.* No matter how commendable their volunteer programs, human resource managers should not assume that citizens will take the initiative to learn about them and to commit their time. Most people who volunteer have been asked to do so.

- *Publicize the volunteer program.* Citizens have many fulfilling avenues to take in donating their time. Human resource managers should make every effort to publicize the volunteer program and its opportunities for service at the workplace, school, church, synagogue, neighborhood group, civic and other associations, and so forth.

- *Design positions for volunteers that appeal to their motivations.* The content and variety offered by the job, as well as possible progression in responsibility, are important factors to many volunteers.

- *Invest in human capital.* At least some volunteer positions should enable participants to acquire contacts, training, and references that increase their marketability for paid employment.

- *Exercise flexibility in job design.* Consider having some jobs for volunteers that might be performed outside the agency (for example, in the home or automobile), some tasks and assignments that are conducive to group-based volunteering (for example, by the family, religious congregation, or work unit or organization), and some fixed-term (rather than open-ended) volunteer appointments.

- *Facilitate volunteer involvement.* When possible, extend the opportunity to volunteer beyond the traditional working hours to evening and weekends, provide transportation and all necessary equipment and supplies for volunteers, and reimburse participants for all out-of-pocket expenses (for example, mileage, parking, meals, and child care).

- *Celebrate volunteer participation.* Give volunteers the chance to affiliate with important policymaking bodies (commissions, boards, and other institutions), meet elected officials, and receive public recognition for service.

Finally, managers can strive to build an organizational culture receptive to volunteer involvement. This step begins with gaining employee acceptance for volunteers, as discussed earlier.

Although none of these strategies alone is likely to prove sufficient, together they can surmount the recruitment challenge (Brudney, 1995a).

Meeting the Accountability Challenge

In third-party arrangements for the delivery of public services—such as contracting out, public-private partnerships, and franchise and voucher systems—the accountability challenge lies in ensuring that the goals and effort of nongovernment service providers remain focused on and consistent with the values and purposes of the host agency. Engaging volunteers in the front lines of public service delivery or in support roles is another form of this *indirect administration,* in which government organizations grant authority to citizens to assist in carrying out the public's business. As with any such grant, the challenge is to establish mechanisms to maintain the accountability of the third parties.

The accountability challenge is all the more pressing with respect to volunteers because the scope of their involvement in the public sector has become so wide. A 1996 survey conducted by the National Association of Counties (Lane and Shultz, 1996) finds that an astonishing 98 percent of counties involve volunteers in government operations (including advisory boards, firefighters, and other direct service roles) (p. 1). As might be expected, the area in which counties use volunteers most often is firefighting and emergency medical services (73 percent); however, volunteers are also common in many less traditional service domains, including programs for the aging (64 percent), libraries (50 percent), parks and recreation (49 percent), youth services (48 percent), social services (43 percent), education (42 percent), environment and recycling (41 percent), sheriff and corrections (40 percent), community and economic development (37 percent), public safety (35 percent), and public health (33 percent) (p. 5). Although survey research pertaining to the use of volunteers by city governments is more dated (Morley, 1989), findings likewise show very broad participation by nonpaid citizens in service areas such as culture and the arts (41 percent of cities), food programs (37 percent), museum operations (34 percent), recreation (26 percent), homeless shelters (26 percent), and programs for the elderly (25 percent) (pp. 42–43). The county survey, moreover, suggests dramatic increases in government involvement of volunteers in the 1990s (Lane and Shultz, 1996, p. 2).

Given the breadth of the delegation of public functions and obligations to volunteers, accountability for processes and results is a salient issue. Human resource managers must see that the application of citizen effort remains consistent with public-sector norms and goals. Two primary methods can help them to do so.

First, organizational leadership should establish a position bearing overall responsibility for volunteer management and representation. This volunteer director or coordinator position should lodge accountability for the program squarely with the incumbent, link this official with the program performance and thereby provide incentives for effective oversight and supervision, serve as the focal point for all contact with the volunteer operation (for example, inquiries, complaints, requests, and referrals), and require this official to implement a core structure for program administration. The coordinator should work with department and other organizational officials to ascertain workloads and requirements for voluntary assistance, and be the in-house expert on all facets of volunteer involvement and management, including orientation and training. As spokesperson for the volunteer program, he or she should endeavor not only to express the perspectives and views of the volunteers but also to allay any apprehensions of paid staff and to facilitate collaboration between these two groups.

Despite ample justification to create and maintain a position with responsibility for volunteer programs, relatively few public agencies appear to have done so. According to the National Association of Counties survey, well over half the counties (60 percent) do not have a volunteer coordinator (Lane and Shultz, 1996, p. 7). As unsettling as this rate may be, it appears to surpass the rates in other jurisdictions. In a national survey, only about one in five cities with volunteer programs had an official designated as program head (21.9 percent); in many instances the municipality had simply appended this function onto an existing job description (Duncombe, 1985, p. 363). Similarly, a survey administered to all Georgia cities and counties found that just 12 percent of local governments that engaged volunteers in service delivery had a "volunteer coordinator or other official with recognized responsibility for volunteer programs" (Brudney and Brown, 1993, p. 14). A large study of school districts in the western United States reported that 30 percent had a volunteer coordinator to manage citizen activities in the school district (Harshfield, Peltier, Hill, and Daugherty, 1996, p. 10). By dedicating resources to this position, human resource managers can increase accountability in the administration of the volunteer program.

A second method the human resource manager can use to achieve this goal is to institute and disseminate policies governing the volunteer program. A compact manual or booklet summarizing policies and procedures should be distributed at orientation sessions for volunteers and should be readily available to all staff, nonpaid and paid alike. Policies should address all important aspects of the volunteer program, including public-sector norms (for example, equal treatment, confidentiality, record keeping), application procedures, probationary acceptance period (if applicable), general standards of conduct, attendance and absenteeism, task assignment and reassignment, performance review, benefits and duties, grievance procedures, reimbursement of expenses, use of agency equipment and facilities, and suspension and termination (McCurley and Lynch, 1989). Although the provisions established may dissuade some potential volunteers, Brudney (1990b) argues that it is far better to set the appropriate tone and standards for the program prior to acceptance of volunteers than to court possible management, morale, and liability problems later from citizens who inadvertently receive the message that any behavior will be countenanced (compare Fisher and Cole, 1993). Policies for the volunteer program should normally be inaugurated at the acceptance stage (as described previously) but will need to be elaborated, amended, and expanded during implementation and operation.

Although published standards of organizational policy and procedures for volunteers may strike some observers as inimical to the spirit of help freely given, this step is highly constructive for the agency, employees, and volunteers. Explicit policies demonstrate that the agency takes seriously the participation of volunteers, values their contribution to the organizational mission and goals, and seeks to maintain collaborative working relationships. Equally important, formal guidelines greatly help in defusing potential conflicts, handling problem situations on the job, protecting volunteer and employee rights and prerogatives, and managing for consistent results. Steve McCurley and Rick Lynch (1989) advise human resource managers that agency guidelines for volunteers should be comparable to the respective policies for employees: "If you have a question about the content of a policy or procedure, refer to the agency policies and procedures for paid staff. The rules should be as similar as possible" (p. 23). By setting standards as high for volunteers as for paid staff, an agency engenders trust and credibility, increased respect and requests for volunteers from employees, a healthy work environment, and, perhaps most important, high quality services.

In short, to enhance the accountability of volunteer-based services, human resource managers should, first, insist on the establishment of a volunteer coordinator or director position. Second, they should see to the creation and distribution of a volunteer handbook that communicates the norms and values of public agencies and states in relevant policies and procedures. These steps appear to be interrelated. A study of school districts in the western region of the United States found that those that employed a volunteer coordinator differed significantly from those that did not with respect to the importance they attached to various components of volunteer policy and management such as recruitment, recognition, confidentiality, and legal issues (Harshfield, Peltier, Hill, and Daugherty, 1996). The larger school districts were more likely both to employ volunteer coordinators and to place greater importance on these provisions.

Meeting the Management Challenge

In addition to the challenges of gaining employee acceptance, securing adequate volunteer recruitment, and increasing program accountability, human resource managers must provide a sound underlying structure for managing the volunteer effort. Simply introducing volunteers without consideration for the managerial task thus created will not solve but exacerbate the problems facing public agencies. Although agency leaders may find the potential advantages offered by volunteers persuasive, they should resist introducing citizens until a structure to maintain and direct volunteer involvement has been put in place. The management challenge consists of designing and implementing a program structure that develops, channels, and sustains volunteer talents and energies toward the achievement of organizational objectives. A well-structured program has the following main characteristics:

- It gives orientation to its citizen participants (see the earlier discussion).
- It interviews and screens prospective volunteers to ascertain competencies, background, experience, and aspirations.
- It offers a range of volunteer jobs to aid citizen recruitment and to offer continuing motivation to volunteers; relevant job descriptions are developed, codified, and amended as necessary.

- It places citizens in work assignments crucial to the agency, also allowing these citizens to meet some of their own needs for, for example, personal growth, esteem enhancement, career exploration, and community benefit.

- It furnishes training for volunteer positions as these assignments warrant.

- It provides support and technical assistance to paid employees who work directly with volunteers; orientation and training for these employees are desirable.

- It assesses the performance of volunteers and the volunteer effort as a whole and provides appropriate recognition.

The essential building block of a successful volunteer program is the job description. It is the primary vehicle for recruiting volunteers, reassuring employees, and meeting organizational and client needs. "The importance of a volunteer job description cannot be overstated," writes McCurley (1994). "The job description is the agency's planning tool to help volunteers understand the results to be accomplished, what tasks are involved, what skills are required, and other important details about the job" (pp. 515–516). All other aspects of volunteer management—recruitment, interviewing, screening, placement, supervision, training, evaluation, and recognition—are based on the job description.

Despite the significance of this component, no intrinsic basis exists to create a position, or classify an existing one, as paid or volunteer. As a result the *process* by which work responsibilities are allocated between paid and nonpaid personnel is the crucial element in job design (Brudney, 1990b). As elaborated earlier, this process begins with meetings among top agency officials, employees, and if possible, volunteers to work out in advance of program implementation an agreed-upon rationale for involvement of volunteers, the nature of the jobs they are to perform, and the boundaries of their work. The result should be a general agreement that designates (or provides the foundation for distinguishing) the jobs assigned to volunteers and those held by paid staff.

In the next step of the job design process the human resource manager should query employees (for example, through a survey or personal interviews) to ascertain key factors about their jobs and to make them aware of volunteers' potential contributions. Surveys or interviews should seek to identify those job aspects that employees most enjoy performing, those that they dislike, and those for which they lack sufficient time or expertise. The manager should also probe for areas in which employees feel the organization should do more, client needs remain unmet, staff support would be most welcome, and novel or different organizational goals could be undertaken were greater time and skills available. Because employees often lack background information regarding the assistance that volunteers might lend to them and to the agency, the survey or interview (or alternatively in-service training) should provide resource material about typical volunteer tasks, such as a listing of the jobs or functions that nonpaid staff are already performing in the agency or in similar organizations (compare Ellis, 1994; McCurley and Lynch, 1989).

What information should the job description contain? The International City/County Management Association advises local governments that "volunteer job descriptions are really no different than job descriptions for paid personnel. A volunteer will need the same information a paid employee would need to determine whether the position is of interest" (Manchester and Bogart, 1988, p. 59). That advice applies equally to any organization seeking volunteers. A useful job description will specify job title and purpose, qualifications and duties, examples of activities to be performed, time commitment (for example, hours per week), job site or location, proposed starting date (and ending date if applicable), authority invested in the position, reporting and supervisory relationship, and benefits to the occupant.

The management structure of the volunteer program must also see to the legal and liability aspects of donated labor, a complicated and sometimes conflictual area of labor law. Although the Fair Labor Standards Act (FLSA) specifically distinguishes volunteers from employees and would thus seem to exempt volunteers from its provisions, litigation has nevertheless erupted over the use and implications of contributed labor. In a 1993 case brought by paid firefighters in Montgomery County, Maryland, and based on the FLSA, for example, the Department of Labor ruled that professional firefighters could not donate their spare time to help combat fires in their own communities because the donations suppressed the overtime wages of paid firefighters (Walters, 1996).

One reason for the legal thicket surrounding volunteer involvement in government and nonprofit agencies had been variations in state laws and sometimes even in local provisions that dealt with such matters. Culminating a decade of lobbying and promotion from nonprofit organizations and groups, some uniformity has recently been brought to the issue of volunteer liability. On June 19, 1997, President Clinton signed into law the Volunteer Protection Act of 1997 (P.L. 105–19), intended to provide volunteers with some protection from lawsuits; encourage people to volunteer for nonprofit civic, charitable, government, and other organizations; and bring down the high cost of liability insurance. Three aspects of the new law are particularly significant for volunteer management: the act protects volunteers from lawsuits in civil cases only, not criminal cases; the volunteer must have been acting within the scope of her or his responsibilities at the time of the act or omission; and the protection extends only so long as the volunteer does not engage in willful or criminal misconduct, gross negligence, reckless misconduct, or conscious, flagrant indifference to the rights or safety of others.

The Volunteer Protection Act does not provide blanket immunity from lawsuit to volunteers but instead places even greater emphasis on the elements of volunteer management discussed here. The requirement that volunteers must have been acting within the scope of their responsibilities for the law to apply means that a program must provide current, accurate job descriptions for each volunteer. Without these documents, the organization cannot demonstrate what any volunteer's "job" was supposed to have been and thus puts itself and the volunteer at legal risk. The exceptions in the law for willful or reckless misconduct, gross negligence, and flagrant indifference on the part of the volunteer send a similar message and warning: to avoid such counterproductive and potentially dangerous behaviors—and to provide quality services for clients—the volunteer program must satisfy the elements of successful management, especially proper screening, orientation, training, and policies and procedures.

In sum, to the degree that the volunteer program can facilitate the work of paid staff, agency leaders can anticipate not only employees who are more likely to accept it but also higher levels of organizational performance. The key is a management structure that attends to the major elements of effective volunteer participation. As suggested by the recent growth in the number of colleges and universities that offer courses in volunteer administration and management, supported by specialized textbooks (for example, Fisher and Cole, 1993; McCurley and Lynch, 1989), program management is becoming increasingly professionalized. If management duties are left, instead, to employees to perform (or to ignore), the prospects for successful volunteer involvement dim considerably.

Meeting the Evaluation Challenge

The final challenge, evaluation, entails collecting systematic information on the processes and results of the volunteer program and applying these data toward program assessment and, one hopes, improvement. Evaluation of the volunteer program should focus on its consequences for three target audiences: the clients or intended beneficiaries of the volunteer program, paid employees and other components of the sponsoring agency, and the volunteers themselves. Ideally, a volunteer program attempts positive results for all three constituencies. Evaluation is necessary to appraise both accomplishments and limitations of the program and, on this foundation, to present recommendations.

Research shows that the evaluation function is carried out less often and less well than are many of the other central elements of the volunteer program. Findings from the 1996 National Association of Counties survey are indicative. Of a listing of eleven administrative components, or tools, "Most often, the component the volunteer program did not include was the program evaluation or the volunteer evaluation" (p. 4). Program evaluation was conducted by just 18 percent of counties, and volunteer evaluations by staff by just 17 percent. Only 31 percent of counties had prepared an annual report summarizing volunteer efforts (p. 8). Other studies confirm these results. In a national sample of cities over 4,500 in population that used volunteers in service delivery, only 11.6 percent had made an evaluation study (Duncombe, 1985, p. 363). And just 5 percent of a representative sample of Georgia cities and counties with volunteer programs had conducted an evaluation (Brudney and Brown, 1993, p. 14). When government officials pay so little heed to volunteer program monitoring and oversight, not only the evaluation challenge but also the accountability challenge is imperiled.

Reluctance to evaluate is understandable, if lamentable. Organizations that rely on the goodwill and donated labor of volunteers may be loath to question through evaluation the worth or impact of such helping efforts. In addition, officials may be apprehensive about the effects of an evaluation policy on volunteer recruitment and retention, and on public relations. Nevertheless, evaluation is essential to keep the volunteer effort focused on the objectives of the program and the goals of the sponsoring agency and to assess results.

The fears of organizational leadership notwithstanding, volunteers have good reason to view personnel appraisal in a favorable light. A powerful motivation for volunteering is to achieve worthwhile and credible results; evaluation can guide volunteers toward improvement on this dimension. Susan Ellis (1996) explains that evaluation of performance is actually a form of compliment to the volunteer: a sincere effort at appraisal indicates that the work merits review and that the individual has the capability and will to do a better job. Moreover, for many who contribute their time, volunteering is an opportunity to acquire or hone desirable job skills or to build an attractive résumé for purposes of paid employment. To deny constructive feedback to those who give their time for organizational purposes and who could benefit from this knowledge and often hope to do so is both unethical and a disservice to the volunteer.

Volunteer-based services normally require the participation of not only volunteers but also paid staff. If organizational officials are committed to having employees and volunteers work as partners, evaluation should apply to both members of the team. Although this function is frequently overlooked in job analysis, employees expected to work with volunteers should have the pertinent responsibilities written into their formal job descriptions, and performance appraisal should assess employees' requisite skills in volunteer management. Just as demonstrated talent in this domain should be encouraged and rewarded, an employee's resistance to volunteers or poor work record with them should not go overlooked and therefore implicitly condoned. As necessary, the organization should support training activities for paid staff to develop competencies in volunteer administration.

Finally, agencies that mobilize volunteers for public purposes should periodically conduct an evaluation of program outputs or impacts. Too often what passes for evaluation is a compilation of the number of volunteers who have assisted the organization, the hours they have contributed, and the total client contacts they have made. Some agencies calculate the *equivalent dollar value* of the services donated by volunteers, based on the wage rates the organization would otherwise have had to pay. Although such statements routinely document tremendous levels of contributed effort and monetary value across both public and nonprofit institutions, they almost always neglect the costs of volunteer involvement. More important, they tap the volunteer program's inputs or resources rather than its accomplishments.

Human resource managers should call for two additional kinds of program evaluation. First, just as they are expected to do for any other operational unit, at regular intervals agency officials should assess the outcomes of the volunteer program against its stated goals or mission. Officials need to review the aggregate performance of the volunteers in assisting clients, addressing community problems, expediting agency operations, and meeting other objectives. For example, a volunteer program organized by a city recreation department to help meet the vision of having all children in the community participate in at least one sports activity might be assessed on such relevant criteria as the numbers of leagues and teams organized, the numbers of children and of adult coaches involved, and the numbers of children and of coaches who are new or repeat users of recreation department services. A volunteer program intended to attract disadvantaged youths to the library might be evaluated on the basis of outreach efforts (bookmobile trips, talks at schools, preschools, and day-care facilities), special activities for this audience (cultural awareness programs, reading clubs), new library cards issued to the target group, and repeat uses of library privileges. A volunteer program sponsored by the municipal personnel department with the mission of placing unemployed workers in jobs (public or private) might be expected to hold training sessions on such relevant topics as preparing a résumé, finding a job, interviewing for a position, and instilling effective job habits and attitudes and might be held accountable for such results as session attendance, training program completion, and ultimately, job placement rates. Not only does this kind of assessment against goal-related criteria yield information that can improve program functioning but it also reinforces the importance attached by the organization to the volunteer component.

The second additional type of evaluation assesses volunteer program processes. Officials should determine that procedures to meet essential program functions such as recruitment, orientation, screening, placement, and recognition are in place and operating effectively and should identify any areas needing improvement. The evaluation should also attempt to gauge the satisfaction of volunteers and paid staff members with the program and determine their perceptions of the program's impact on clients and the external environment.

CONCLUSION

As government agencies move increasingly to incorporate volunteers, human resource managers are likely to inherit new responsibilities. A volunteer program engages the assistance of citizens who donate their time to public programs or services in an organizational context. This behavior is not mandated or coerced but undertaken willingly. Although volunteers do not expect monetary compensation, they are entitled to reimbursement for out-of-pocket expenses and other costs associated with this activity. A volunteer program places citizens in positions that require a regular expenditure of their time and talents.

These volunteer programs can offer definite advantages to government agencies, including expansion of services, containment of costs, and improvements in responsiveness and community relations. To achieve these benefits the program must be designed and organized to meet five interdependent challenges. Human resource managers must work to gain the acceptance of employees for volunteer involvement, recruit citizen participants for designated positions, ensure accountability of the program to public values and goals, establish a program structure that facilitates management, and evaluate the program with an eye toward improvement. This chapter has elaborated each challenge and discussed strategies to surmount it.

Human resource managers charged with responsibility for volunteer programs will find that even though effectual, these strategies normally exact costs, for example, for the manager's own time and effort and for the organizational resources that must be devoted to such activities as orientation and screening of prospective volunteers, training for citizens and paid staff, supervision of participants, reimbursement of out-of-pocket expenses, distribution of program policies and other information, provision of materials and supplies, and so forth. Volunteer labor may be donated, or free, but volunteer programs are not. Michael Connelly (1996) warns: "Almost magically, it seems, volunteers will step into otherwise vacant areas of need with the knowledge, training, and ability to perform many necessary functions previously left undone. The theory is that this will allow fiscally strapped governments to do as much, or more, for public services even as their funding decreases. . . . The increasing demands on tax dollars may force us to consider a greater deployment of volunteers for service delivery, but only if there is an in-place and functioning infrastructure for effective volunteer involvement" (p. 21). Providing this infrastructure is the job of the human resource manager.

References

Allen, N. J. "The Role of Social and Organizational Factors in the Evaluation of Volunteer Programs." *Evaluation and Program Planning*, 1987, *10*, 257–262.

Brudney, J. L. "The Availability of Volunteers: Implications for Local Governments." *Administration and Society*, 1990a, *21*, 413–424.

Brudney, J. L. *Fostering Volunteer Programs in the Public Sector: Planning, Initiating, and Managing Voluntary Activities.* San Francisco: Jossey-Bass, 1990b.

Brudney, J. L. "The Involvement of Volunteers in the Delivery of Services: Myth and Management." In S. W. Hays and R. C. Kearney (eds.), *Public Personnel Administration: Problems and Prospects.* (3rd ed.) Upper Saddle River, N.J.: Prentice Hall, 1995a.

Brudney, J. L. "Volunteers in the Delivery of Public Services: Magnitude, Scope, and Management." In J. Rabin, T. Vocino, W. B. Hildreth, and G. J. Miller (eds.), *Handbook of Public Personnel Administration.* New York: Dekker, 1995b.

Brudney, J. L. "Designing and Implementing Volunteer Programs." In D. F. Kettl and H. B. Milward (eds.), *The State of Public Management.* Baltimore: Johns Hopkins University Press, 1996.

Brudney, J. L., and Brown, M. M. "Government-Based Volunteer Programs: Toward a More Caring Society." Paper presented at the Independent Sector Spring Research Forum, San Antonio, Tex., Mar. 1993.

Brudney, J. L., and Duncombe, W. D. "An Economic Evaluation of Paid, Volunteer, and Mixed Staffing Options for Public Services." *Public Administration Review,* 1992, *52,* 474–481.

Brudney, J. L., and England, R. E. "Toward a Definition of the Coproduction Concept." *Public Administration Review,* 1983, *43,* 59–65.

Cnaan, R. A., and Amrofell, L. "Mapping Volunteer Activity." *Nonprofit and Voluntary Sector Quarterly,* 1994, *23,* 335–351.

Cnaan, R. A., Handy, F., and Wadsworth, M. "Defining Who Is a Volunteer: Conceptual and Empirical Considerations." *Nonprofit and Voluntary Sector Quarterly,* 1996, *25,* 364–383.

Connelly, M. "The Catch-22 of Reinventing Corrections: Training Volunteers to Offset Costs." *Journal of Volunteer Administration,* Summer 1996, *14,* 21–27.

Duncombe, S. "Volunteers in City Government: Advantages, Disadvantages and Uses." *National Civic Review,* 1985, *74,* 356–364.

Ellis, S. J. *From the Top Down: The Executive Role in Volunteer Program Success* (revised edition). Philadelphia: Energize, 1996.

Ellis, S. J. *The Volunteer Recruitment Book.* Philadelphia: Energize, 1994.

Fair Labor Standards Act of 1938. U.S. Code, vol. 29, sec. 201 et seq.

Ferris, J. M. "Coprovision: Citizen Time and Money Donations in Public Service Provision." *Public Administration Review,* 1984, *44,* 324–333.

Fisher, J. C., and Cole, K. M. *Leadership and Management of Volunteer Programs: A Guide for Volunteer Administrators.* San Francisco: Jossey-Bass, 1993.

Harshfield, J. B., Peltier, G. L., Hill, G. C., and Daugherty, R. F. "How Public Schools View Selected Components of Volunteer Management." *Journal of Volunteer Administration,* Fall 1996, *15,* 9–14.

Hodgkinson, V. A., and others. *Giving and Volunteering in the United States: Findings from a National Survey, 1996 Edition.* Washington, D.C.: Independent Sector, 1996a.

Hodgkinson, V. A., and others (eds.). *Nonprofit Almanac, 1996–97: Dimensions of the Independent Sector.* San Francisco: Jossey-Bass, 1996b.

Lafrance, J. "Social Work and Volunteers: A Case of Shifting Paradigms." *Journal of Volunteer Administration,* Fall 1996, *15,* 2–8.

Lane, P., and Shultz, C. *Volunteerism in County Government Survey Results.* Washington, D.C.: National Association of Counties, 1996.

Light, J. "Bearer of Burundi's Flag." *Atlanta Journal-Constitution,* July 13, 1997, p. H3.

Macduff, N. "A Volunteer Taxonomy." Paper presented at the annual meeting of the Association for Research on Nonprofit Organizations and Voluntary Action, New York, Nov. 1996.

Manchester, L. D., and Bogart, G. S. *Contracting and Volunteerism in Local Government: A Self-Help Guide.* Washington, D.C.: International City/County Management Association, 1988.

McCurley, S. "Recruiting and Retaining Volunteers." In R. D. Herman and Associates, *The Jossey-Bass Handbook of Nonprofit Leadership and Management.* San Francisco: Jossey-Bass, 1994.

McCurley, S., and Lynch, R. *Essential Volunteer Management.* Downers Grove, Ill.: VMSystems and Heritage Arts, 1989.

Morley, E. "Patterns in the Use of Alternative Service Delivery Approaches." In *Municipal Year Book, 1989.* Washington, D.C.: International City/County Management Association, 1989.

Parks, R. B., and others. "Consumers as Coproducers of Public Services: Some Economic and Institutional Considerations." *Policy Studies Review,* 1981, *9,* 1001–1011.

Percy, S. L. "Citizen Participation in the Coproduction of Urban Services." *Urban Affairs Quarterly,* 1984, *19,* 431–446.

Putnam, R. D. "Bowling Alone: America's Declining Social Capital." *Journal of Democracy,* 1995, *6,* 65–78.

Scheier, I. H. "Staff Nonsupport of Volunteers: A New Look at an Old Failure." *Voluntary Action Leadership,* Fall 1977, pp. 32–36.

Schwed, P. "After the Olympics: The What-Next Syndrome." *Atlanta Journal-Constitution,* Aug. 25, 1996, p. B1.

Sharp, E. B. "Toward a New Understanding of Urban Services and Citizen Participation: The Coproduction Concept." *Midwest Review of Public Administration,* 1980, *14,* 105–118.

Van Til, J. *Mapping the Third Sector: Voluntarism in a Changing Social Economy.* New York: Foundation Center, 1988.

Volunteer Protection Act of 1997. U.S. Code, vol. 42, sec. 14501 et seq.

Walters, J. P. "A Wet Blanket for Volunteer Firefighters." *Policy Review,* May-June 1996, pp. 6–7.

Whitaker, G. P. "Coproduction: Citizen Participation in Service Delivery." *Public Administration Review,* 1980, *40,* 240–246.

CHAPTER TWENTY-FIVE

Anticipating and Coping
with Technological Change
in the Workplace

James N. Danziger
Christopher L. Gianos

I visited a school district that had made a large investment in technology. My enthusiasm with their initiative quickly faded, however, when the school executive who was explaining the project remarked, 'Now that we've got the technology, we need to get someone in here to get our teachers up to speed.' To my disappointment, this district had indeed put the cart before the horse. It had made the critical mistake of launching a major school improvement initiative without the direct involvement of those who were now expected to 'get up to speed.'"

Daniel Kinnaman (1994, p. 62) recounts this telling example of the failure of a manager to grasp the critical relationship between information technology (IT) and the organizational personnel who are the end users of that technology. The leitmotiv of human resource management (HRM) is that people are an organization's greatest asset. However, people are also the organization's greatest cost factor. Thus many organizations have pursued strategies that aggressively manage their human assets, such as downsizing and outsourcing. And as reflected in Kinnaman's comments, some organizations focus particularly on investment in technology as a means to increase their employees' productivity and efficiency. Therefore, with the astonishing recent expansion of the role and significance of information technology in the workplace, this premise about the primacy of the organization's people is now at least subject to debate.

There is no question that IT penetrates and has impacts on every activity in an information-based work environment. IT can be such a compelling force within an organization that managers, like the one in the school district, might give it primacy in their strategic thinking. Ideally, however, managers should look for strategies that maximize the contributions of both knowledge workers and IT. This chapter asks, How can this joint maximization be accomplished?

One key strategic challenge facing many managers in both public- and private-sector organizations is the continuing (r)evolution of information technologies in the workplace. Because each rapid advance in IT changes the way many knowledge workers and managers do their jobs, successful integration of new technologies into the workplace can pay substantial dividends through increased productivity and effectiveness. Achieving these benefits requires active involvement and understanding by managers (Davenport, 1994). On the negative side, failure to manage IT can undermine these central organizational goals.

Demographic changes also constitute an important strategic challenge to which managers must respond. Like technology, the people in the white-collar workforce are characterized by significant, if more predictable, changes. The manager must understand whether strategic implications result from the way he or she guides this workforce, which is older, better educated, and more diverse than in years past (Coates, Jarratt, and Mahaffie, 1991). Some of these demographic changes are closely tied to technological issues, because age, education, and gender are associated with differential levels of both use of and competence with information technology (Hoffmann and Novak, 1996).

How are these IT and demographic issues particularly shaped by the HRM perspective? HRM is a series of concepts and strategies whose central goal is the effective and efficient use of an organization's human resources. HRM involves such concerns as employee recruitment, placement, evaluation, compensation, and professional development. Three critical HRM components are associated with the issues of technological change facing public managers: (1) planning to meet the personnel needs of the organization, (2) developing employees to their full potential, and (3) controlling personnel policies and programs (Beaumont, 1992; O'Brien, 1993).

An overall challenge for managers is to ensure that the fit among human resources, technology, and organizational needs is maximized. Managers are in a strong strategic position to link these three elements because they are able to understand their employees' needs and abilities, the changing technology available to their unit, and their unit's responsibilities within the broader context of the organization's culture, history, and goals. Managers can use incentives that motivate employees to commit themselves to organizational goals and encourage innovation in the workplace, rather than attempt to force employee compliance with technological change. They can also develop creative approaches to ensure that employees are provided with rewarding work and with appropriate training and support so that they can be successful in their jobs. Traditionally, HR specialists had the responsibility to ensure that new technologies were implemented effectively (Long, 1987). However, meeting all these challenges in the current technological workplace is more likely if line managers are primarily responsible for human resource management (Storey, 1992).

This chapter is organized into three sections. The first examines key issues for public managers regarding the linkages between information technology and the organization's human resources. Section two evaluates the consequences of demographic trends on the human resource management–information technology nexus. The final section explores the role of managers who are committed to HRM within an information-centered workplace.

The core argument of this chapter is that with the widespread penetration of information technologies into the workplace, managers must be familiar with what IT can provide in productivity benefits and with how IT affects the work of individual employees, individual workgroups, and the entire organization. Managers must understand key technical issues associated with the efficient application of IT; grasp how IT can influence job domain, work routines, information flows, and worker morale; and be aware of the ways in which IT either supports or changes a manager's own responsibilities. Such understanding will significantly improve the manager's strategic approach to more effective integration of IT into the behavior of the organization's workforce.

ENHANCING EMPLOYEE PERFORMANCE WITH CHANGING TECHNOLOGIES

It is evident that information technology substantially enhances the information power available to many knowledge workers. IT increases the richness of the information they can access, the speed with which they can select relevant information, the sophistication with which they can analyze and present information, and the ease with which they can share that information in intra- and interorganizational channels. Current planning for IT begins with the dual assumptions that computer hardware will continue to get faster and cheaper and that software will continue to present new information-handling capabilities (Howard, 1996). Planning must also adapt to the fact that the scale and breadth of relevant, available information resources, both within and outside the organization, are expanding at a very rapid rate.

Ideally, the manager should be aware of how IT is evolving and of the possible effects of new capabilities and resources. Realistically, continual technological change, the complex interplay between technological change and other elements of organizational change, and sporadic step-level advances in individual employees' patterns of IT use make it difficult for managers to anticipate either the evolving patterns or the impacts of changed information systems on employees (Zuboff, 1988).

Moreover, there is still much discussion of the "productivity paradox": in many organizations it is difficult to establish that the net benefits from IT outweigh the complex set of costs associated with the acquisition, upgrading, and maintenance of hardware and software, the hiring and retention of technical personnel, end-user training, disruptions in standard operating procedures (SOPs), and so on. There is no question that most public organizations in postindustrial societies have now applied IT to many of the basic information processing tasks and that some dramatic efficiency increases have occurred (Frissen and Snellen, 1994). But organizations continue to develop new applications and modify existing ones, with all the attendant costs just noted.

At this point the question for most key organizational functions in the public sector is no longer to automate or not to automate. Rather the real puzzle for managers centers on the attempt to answer two key questions: (1) Which opportunities to change IT are sufficiently beneficial to cause managers to alter their existing IT systems and/or their employees' work routines? and (2) How should those IT changes be implemented to achieve increased productivity and/or greater worker satisfaction at an acceptable cost?

Technical Considerations and HRM

Given the changes in and diversity of the information technology available to most knowledge workers, managers must monitor whether the technology in use is technically well suited to the work that employees must perform. Considerable empirical research has examined the linkages between the computer end user and his or her *package* of IT hardware, software, and technical support staff—an array of relationships that is termed the *sociotechnical interface* (STI) (Kraut, Dumais, and Koch, 1989). Due to the HRM focus on establishing conditions that facilitate the full potential of employees, managerial concern for the sociotechnical interface is extremely important. Managers should attend to four areas.

First, although the desirability of *ergonomically appropriate IT arrangements* might seem evident, most managers pay little or no attention to this dimension. *Ergonomics* particularly refers to the physical aspects of the worker's space, tools, and equipment. For knowledge workers, computer ergonomics address seating, lighting, monitor location, wrist support, and so on (Perrolle, 1987). Decisions about ergonomic elements currently tend to be made ad hoc, often by the individual worker. Few organizations provide their workers with guidance about, let alone support for, brief exercises and other actions that can decrease the physical problems sometimes associated with extended computer use. Managers should designate a staff person (for example, a member of the information systems department) to assess periodically the IT-related ergonomics of each employee's work space and implement appropriate corrective measures.

A second aspect of sociotechnical interface is the *design of the IT applications* used by the employee. Unless the individual end user has a high level of computer competence, he or she is unlikely to make many significant modifications in the software provided (whether off-the-shelf or designed in-house), even though such changes might substantially improve the ease of use or the goodness of fit between a work task and a particular system. Rather, many end users simply accept the information systems they are given, and they adapt their own work routines to those systems, even when a system's design features make use more difficult and lower worker effectiveness.

Although a concern for these elements of the work environment might seem obvious, information systems (IS) staff who do applications design and modifications are not generally rewarded by the organization for giving primary attention to ease of use for the end users. Within their peer professional group, IS staff gain greater recognition for elegance of technical design and for working on sophisticated applications. And when evaluation is by central managers, IS staff are more commonly assessed for outcomes such as delivery of the IT products on time, within budget, supportive of standard operating procedures for the task, and integrated with the organization's overall information system needs. Managers need to implement clear incentives that reward IT modifications that increase end users' ease of IT use.

These points relate to a third element of the sociotechnical interface: *the quality of the working relationships between the end user and the organization's technical support staff.* Despite increasing managerial awareness of the value of effective communication between end users and "tekkies," the two cultures remain quite separate in many organizational environments. Technical support staff who understand end-user work needs and who can discuss IT issues in the lexicon of the end user can have an extremely positive effect on the effectiveness with which IT is used (Danziger and Kraemer, 1986). Technical support staff perceived to be available, understanding, and responsive to the end users' needs will overcome most users' reluctance or anxiety about bringing their questions and concerns to those with high technical competence. When the technical support staff are not perceived as user friendly, many end users either attempt to get advice from their peers (which might or might not be of high quality) or soldier on without the kinds of guidance that could make them more competent and satisfied IT users.

Fourth is the sociotechnical interface question of *centralized versus decentralized provision of IT services.* There has been extensive debate about the relative merits of each approach, and although each has its advocates, empirical evidence from U.S. local governments suggests that this issue is less critical than it once seemed (Danziger, Kraemer, Dunkle, and King, 1993). The delivery of high-quality IT services to units and end users is very important. However, the quality of provision is more contingent upon other factors, such as handling of the other three STI issues listed here and the organization's overall approach to information resources management, than it is upon the institutional locus of IT services.

Human Resource Information Systems

In considering the linkages between human resource management and the organization's information systems, many managers overlook a very direct way in which the latter can support the former. Most organizations have implemented some elements of a *human resource information system* (HRIS).

James O'Brien (1993, fig. 12.13) identifies four major functions of HRM that can be directly supported by a computer-based HRIS:

1. *Staffing.* An HRIS can support a personnel database that records and tracks human resources, personnel requirements forecasting systems, and automated employee skills inventories.

2. *Training and development.* An HRIS can support applications that plan and monitor recruitment and training programs, on-line training courses, automated employee performance evaluation systems, and career development activity tracking.

3. *Compensation analysis.* An HRIS can support systems that analyze and monitor employee wages and compensation packages, including fringe benefits and incentive pay, as well as on-line self-access benefits systems.

4. *Employee-related records and reporting requirements.* An HRIS can especially support the record keeping and reporting activities mandated by government agencies, regarding such matters as worker health and safety, equal opportunity hiring practices, workforce statistics, and grievance handling.

Table 25.1 indicates some of the specific ways in which an HRIS can support many aspects of the HRM function. In most public organizations only a few of these applications are well developed.

Information Network Issues

Scott McNealy, the founder of Sun Microsystems, has observed that "the network is the computer" (Samuels, 1996, p. 98). The goal of any network, regardless of its scope, is to increase the ease with which information is shared between users. The development of such computer networks and the resulting capacity for extensive *information sharing between individuals and units* is one of the most critical recent IT developments, providing new opportunities for productivity enhancements and workplace synergies (Levine and Tyson, 1990).

From LANs (local area networks) to WANs (wide area networks), from the Internet to the intranet (that is, the adaptation of Internet standards to internal

Table 25.1. Examples of Human Resource Information Systems
That Support the Human Resource Management Function.

	Staffing	Training and Development	Performance Review	Compensation
Strategic	Personnel planning		Appraisal planning	Salary forecasting Benefits tracking
Tactical	Budget analysis Turnover costing	Training effectiveness Career matching		Benefits preference modeling
Operational	Workforce planning Scheduling Recruiting	Skills assessment	Computer-based evaluation programs	Equality-of-compensation analysis

Source: Adapted with permission from Meinert and Davis, 1989, p. 45.

networks), new forms and new applications of network connectivity are widespread. Users of an intranet can, like the Internet, use World Wide Web (WWW) standards and many existing software packages, making employees' access to and exchange of information easier and less costly, even among computers with different standards (Ayre, 1996).

Through richer connections to the organization's information flow, individual employees are more likely to develop a better awareness of the organization's processes, needs, and goals, leading to feelings of inclusion and identity with the organization. Citizens can also benefit from the ease with which they can obtain information electronically from various government sources (Dutton and Guthrie, 1991). Interdepartment and other intraorganizational information networks make it easier and less costly for public employees to access information from other government agencies at the local, regional, state, and national levels (Danziger, 1991).

Although network advances make computers more powerful and information exchange and sharing easier in principle, a variety of HRM issues are raised. Sharing information electronically is limited by the weakest link in the information system. Although the weak link could be a technical problem, managers'

HRM considerations primarily address worker-based behaviors associated with information sharing.

At the between-unit level of the organization's information systems, units must have a willingness to enter and share data that are useful to other units, in formats that those units can use. In many information systems, meeting other units' data requirements entails changes in standard operating procedures and thus additional work for the data-providing unit. The result is increased costs to that unit and to those individuals modifying their behavior, costs for which there are not always corresponding benefits.

More broadly, as additional data are captured in a shared system, others gain greater access to and knowledge about the operations of the data-providing unit. This development is seldom perceived as an advantage by the data-providing unit. In such situations it is often necessary for top managers to engage in reasoned and diplomatic discussions with all affected units, so they develop willingness to participate in data sharing. Top-down directives mandating that data must be shared because they serve overall goals can provoke worker resentment, resistance, and even sabotage.

A recent example of these organizational difficulties occurred in Los Angeles County, where department heads make the information technology decisions for their individual units (Richter, 1995). Although the county's telecommunications planning department has developed a countywide networking strategy and a large network infrastructure, each department has the option to determine its level of connectivity to the network. In fact, many departments use only portions of the county network, and then only to link their numerous internal networks. As a consequence, electronic communications within each department are easy, but it is often impossible for one department to share information electronically with another. In contrast, New York City has established a special department with strong oversight powers to facilitate connectivity and to negotiate shared information practices between units (Richter, 1995).

The introduction of information sharing and extensive networking capabilities has additional implications at the level of the individual employee. The issue of *information privacy* in the workplace has become vastly more complicated. First, anyone with access to the organization's network can, with enough persistence and skill, obtain confidential information from that network. Second, in a development with far-reaching implications, most organizations have insisted upon their proprietary rights over *all* information transmitted through corporate systems. In the United States, a series of court decisions, centering in the Electronic Communications Privacy Act of 1986, has generally upheld the principle that the organization owns all such information. This includes not only work-related correspondence that the sender might assume is private but also personal communications that have no bearing on the organization's activities.

Thus the information access policy in most organizations holds that *any* information transmitted via its systems can be accessed and that the sender is accountable for the content of all such information. There are a growing number of contentious staff grievances because personnel in many organizations have not grasped or do not accept this critical policy and continue to act as though some of their electronic activities are private. The issue of information privacy is especially problematic for public-sector employees, because key freedom-of-information statutes allow any citizen to claim access to many of the public organization's files.

An associated issue is employees' understanding about their *responsibilities as communicators* (senders and receivers) of electronic information. A complex mix of benefits and potential pitfalls has been identified in the research on electronic communications within organizations. On the one hand, the efficiency benefits from asynchronous electronic communication compared to face-to-face, paper, or telephonic modes are well understood. Moreover, certain individuals (for example, some women, some less aggressive talkers) also feel more competent in electronic communication than in face-to-face communication (Sproull and Kiesler, 1986).

On the other hand, certain problems can emerge from electronic communications. First, electronic information tends to be more formal, less affective, and less interactive than other modes of communications between employees, and thus it can reduce the employees' shared identity and ability to work collectively. Second, the content and tone of some employees' communications tend to be substantially more intemperate in electronic modes than in other modes.

Third, the implied privacy and impermanence of verbal communications are lost with electronic communications, which become permanent records, easily forwarded to others. Such communications can ultimately be circulated and have impacts that neither the sender nor the original receiver intended (Peyser and Rhodes, 1995). For some employees this has produced extremely embarrassing or damaging outcomes. Others have adapted to this new world of organizational communication by engaging in extraordinarily formal and cautious "cover your ass" modes of electronic interaction (Markus, 1991). Few organizations have been particularly attentive to sensitizing their employees about this array of issues, leaving individuals to learn, in their roles as sender, receiver, and forwarder, how to use the networked communications systems by trial and, too frequently, by error.

End-User Competence Issues

Recall the example at the beginning of the chapter of the school executive who assumed that making good use of the school's new information technology meant simply that the teachers had to "get up to speed." One obvious point is that there are huge potential problems when new applications of IT are introduced without an appropriate strategy for user training and implementation. Indeed, such action could even cause a productivity decrease because personnel have not contributed their insights to the development and implementation stages, and the new IT applications might not perform the tasks end users require. Many managers do not insist on adequate user involvement in these early stages. Perhaps even more important, ad hoc approaches to end-user training can squander the payoffs expected from a new system. At best they mean users take much longer than necessary to discover and routinize good IT practice. At worst, mastery might never be realized.

There is strong empirical evidence that as end users feel more competent with IT, there are many positive work-related impacts. Users report higher levels of job satisfaction, their levels of IT use increase, and they are substantially more open to IT innovations. Moreover, as their information technology competence increases, end users credit IT with greater increases in the scope and effectiveness of their work (Danziger and Kraemer, 1986).

IMPLICATIONS OF CHANGING DEMOGRAPHICS FOR MANAGERS

In the postindustrial society the demand for highly skilled, technically competent workers in the information-based workplace might outstrip the supply, creating a gap between the technical skills required and the skills available. The need for knowledge workers with IT skills is expected to be particularly high in the government workforce (Wooldridge, 1994). So this gap is especially challenging for public-sector managers, who must attract and retain the appropriate mix of technically skilled workers while coping with civil service and salary constraints.

As one element of the strategy to secure a technically skilled workforce, the manager must evaluate the implications of changing worker demographics for the role of new workplace technologies. Given a workforce that is becoming older, more diverse, and better educated (Coates, Jarratt, and Mahaffie, 1991), some specific IT considerations are relevant. First, a common stereotype holds that the more capable IT user tends to be male, white, and young (Gattiker, 1994). This stereotype does have some support in the empirical research, which indicates that males and younger workers do tend to have more favorable attitudes toward computers and have more competence in using them than females and older workers, controlling for other key traits (Ogletree and Williams, 1990; Williams, Ogletree, Woodburn, and Raffeld, 1993).

However, managers should also be aware that although some (primarily male) users do believe that they are more IT competent than others, the fact remains that computers have become well integrated into most white-collar office environments, regardless of the demographic profiles of the employees. In fact, the levels of IT usage and the effectiveness attributed to IT in the workplace are more often dependent on job traits, experience with IT, and the quality of end-user support than on such factors as workers' age and gender (Dunkle, King, Kraemer, and Danziger, 1994).

Lower levels of acceptance and adaptation to new technologies have also been attributed to female and older workers. Yet female workers in the public sector actually seem more open to the introduction of IT into their work than their male peers (Dunkle, King, Kraemer, and Danziger, 1994). And, although older workers tend to lack initial confidence in their ability to master new technologies, they are very capable of learning to use these technologies effectively (Wooldridge, 1994). To facilitate such learning, IT training for older workers should take their lack of confidence into account. An approach that balances an emphasis on user training with one on confidence building is arguably the most successful means of training older workers (Gist, Rosen, and Schwoerer, 1988). Younger workers generally have more initial IT competence, are more adaptable to innovation, and have higher expectations about what can and should be accomplished with new technologies.

The differences in IT skills and expectations across cohorts require more complex HRM practices within organizations. While reaching out to workers with initially low competencies, the opportunities for IT use and end-user support must also be rich enough to challenge and engage those cohorts with high competencies. Diverse modes of continuing staff development and attractive incentives to innovative practice are of critical importance. And the training for and use of IT among the less competent must encourage personnel to attempt new approaches to work and must provide a particularly nurturing context of end-user support.

Because cohorts with different competencies often work together or in close proximity, it can be extremely difficult for managers to create a supportive work environment that fully integrates everyone into the IT-based workplace. Nonetheless it is desirable to tailor IT training so it is compatible with the substantial differences among personnel in their IT competence, confidence with the technology, and modes of learning. The manager must reject uniform, one-size-fits-all approaches to training the diverse workforce, and must evaluate training options to ensure that IT training is sensitive to employee differences, whether based on IT competence or other personal characteristics. Similarly, it is essential that those providing end-user support are extremely sensitive to the differences in comfort and competency with the technology among the various individuals to whom they provide that support.

MANAGERS' ROLE IN AN
INFORMATION-CENTERED WORKPLACE

The previous sections have identified some of the strategies by which public managers can establish more effective linkages between their organization's personnel and information technologies when both elements are undergoing substantial change. Clearly, it is useful for managers to keep current on IT developments and to implement a strategy that aims to maximize the IT benefits to the organization. A rich awareness of current IT conditions and of the nature of the workforce allows a manager to integrate computing into the overall organizational goals and to determine how to match employees' competencies with the rapidly changing IT package.

Both the HRM and the IS management literature frequently refer to the need for managers to engage in such strategies as *environmental scanning* and *constant vigilance* (Janis, 1989; Schuler and Walker, 1991). These strategies support the manager's fuller understanding of both technological developments and workforce changes and thus provide the manager with increased capacity to evaluate how such changes translate into opportunities and constraints. Scanning is also useful for assessing the political and fiscal conditions that can affect managerial action.

These managerial strategies are clearly desirable. However, as a practical matter most public managers are quite constrained by personnel regulations and other limits on their flexibility regarding the short-term personnel choices they can make in relation to changing workforce demographics. Even more significant, few public managers have the time and the expertise to understand the rapid changes occurring in information technologies. Indeed, most managers are hard-pressed to maintain their own competence as effective end users of computing resources. Hence one of the most important actions a manager can take to be more effective in guiding the organization's use of IT is to become a more active and competent IT end user.

Thus the realistic challenges to which the manager must respond are associated with many practical questions about both the organizational processes for which changes in information systems seem merited and the level of benefits and costs, human and fiscal, associated with making such modest changes. These are very tough questions, and they have broad-ranging implications for many domains, including human resource management. How is the manager to achieve sufficient understanding to make these IT change decisions? From whom should the manager obtain information and assistance? What criteria should be applied in assessing whether and how to modify the IT environment?

IT Information Sources

The most common sources of managerial information and assistance are the IT experts within the manager's own unit, the technical specialists from the IS unit, a peer group of managers, or an IS committee. Each alternative has certain benefits and shortcomings.

- In general, the IT experts, whether in the manager's own unit or in a central IS unit, are useful sources of information about the state of IT. They tend to have the best understanding of the overall configuration and integration of the organization's existing information systems and of the capabilities of emerging technologies. On the negative side, they can lack a sensitive appreciation of end users' needs and they tend to be intrigued with advanced hardware and new applications. Thus they might push for IT changes at too high a rate and too sophisticated a level.

- Peer managers have the advantage of shared perspectives and comparable needs from IT, but they can be insufficiently knowledgeable about key technical and operational aspects of IT, and they usually lack sufficient time to communicate fully with each other.

- An IS committee can be a manager's most effective source of guidance about technological developments. However, such a committee must be kept clearly focused on an agenda and priorities set by the managers because these committees are subject to logrolling and groupthink. The manager must be vigilant against such group dysfunctions. It should also be a rotating committee, composed of a mix of supervisors, knowledgeable end users, and technical specialists who can communicate with nonspecialists. Meeting regularly, it should engage in assessments and recommendations regarding proposed IT developments and also in longer-term strategic discussion of the desirable evolution of the organization's overall implementation and use of IT. The ongoing evaluation of end-user training and support should also have high priority.

Applying IT Cost-Benefit Criteria

Whether acting individually or within a collective decision-making group such as an IS committee, a manager must establish appropriate criteria for decision and action on technological changes. The standard four-stage policy analysis process is a relevant prescriptive framework for IT policy (Janis, 1989): (1) the problem is formulated and placed in the context of the organization's strategic goals, (2) relevant information about opportunities and constraints is gathered in order to ground the decision in a realistic framework for action, (3) alternative actions are specified and analyzed, and (4) a course of action is selected and, if feasible, is implemented.

The ramifications of a change in information technology can be substantial for a public-sector organization, its managers, and its workers, especially when the change involves either major alterations of organizational processes or the development of large-scale automated systems. A recent, dramatic example of IT policy analysis failure is the attempt to use IT to modernize and simplify the operations of the California Department of Motor Vehicles (DMV). A $27 million project was initiated to upgrade the DMV's computing capacities (Gurwitt, 1996). By late 1993, $44 million had been spent and there was no operational system. Analysts then estimated that it would cost an additional $100 million to achieve the system's original goals. In 1996, managers decided to scrap the program and start from scratch. Failure was largely attributed to policy analysts' gross underestimation of the complexity of the crucial database at the heart of the system. Although the DMV example is extreme, it accentuates the importance of adequate policy planning and rich understanding of end users' information environments when an organization considers implementing new information technologies.

Because continual IT advances offer frequent opportunities for change, it is critical that the manager be guided by an analytic assessment of whether the change in standard operating procedures or the implementation of new technology has high priority and will generate net benefits. It is these priorities and payoffs, rather than the attractive technological possibilities, that should drive the decision to introduce a change in IT. Clearly, the costs and benefits of any such change should be estimated as precisely as possible. IT changes typically require far more investment in money and personnel time than is initially expected. Indeed, personnel costs will dominate hardware and software costs by at least three to one. Moreover, the ongoing costs of maintaining most systems will outstrip development costs.

Human Resource Criteria

Although such an analytic perspective on IT costs and benefits is useful, it is equally important from an HRM perspective to evaluate the internal conditions of the organization's workforce to determine how IT changes might affect those workers. In some cases, changes in IT produce significant enhancements in employees' work environment and job satisfaction. However, the impacts of changes in IT on employees can be extremely complex and might not result in net benefits for the organization, even when the information system works exactly as specified. The manager should assess a variety of issues and ask a number of questions before acting.

- To what extent will the employees' current levels and patterns of IT use be changed?
- Are most staff supportive of expanding IT in their work? Do staff have the IT competence to adapt to changes without extensive training or disruption?

- Will the proposed changes result in job enhancement or will employees perceive that the changes lead to deskilling or a reduction in the quality of their work environment?

- Will the change cause alterations in information flows that might influence or impede provider-client interactions, supervisory relationships, information sharing, or the boundaries between units or functions?

In an ideal setting, where personnel were viewed as the public organization's major asset, such questions would be carefully assessed. But in most real-world situations neither managers nor their support staff systematically consider such personnel issues. This is attributable, first, to the time pressures associated with decision and action; second, to the continuing advances in available information technology that seem to make change inevitable; and third, to the typically incomplete and imprecise information at hand for assessing IT impacts on personnel and their work environments. Decisions about hardware and applications software seem more tractable and engaging than those about the subtle and complex impacts of IT on staff. Yet effective constant vigilance by managers should be as concerned with understanding human resource factors as with knowledge of IT changes.

Many employees lack sufficient training and support to take full advantage of the technological capabilities already on their desktops. U.S. businesses are investing more than ever in formal training for their employees ($52.2 billion in 1995, a 3 percent increase over 1994), particularly on technology skills (Oldham, 1996). Yet most organizations still allocate far fewer resources to upgrade their personnel's IT competence than to upgrade hardware and applications. Such organizations could make a wise investment by improving their IT consulting staff, IS customer service centers, and IT training programs. Other useful tools include providing rewards for end users who assist or train their coworkers and also conducting performance audits to determine end users' actual current levels of effective IT use.

CONCLUSION

Many public and private organizations are still characterized by insufficient understanding of and inadequate techniques for the provision of effective end-user training and support to a changing population of knowledge workers. These shortcomings are evident in the strategic approaches to end-user support that are mandated by managers, in the actual services provided by professional trainers, and in the limited findings on end-user training and support produced by policy-oriented empirical researchers (Northrop, Kraemer, Dunkle, and King, 1994). Although this is the bad news, it can also be viewed as good news. With a greater commitment to supporting end users, most public-sector managers can devise actions that will generate benefits, by enhancing the job satisfaction, work effectiveness, and work environment of their knowledge workers.

In sum, to take greater advantage of knowledge workers' capabilities in a technology-intensive context, managers' constant vigilance should be directed less toward the question of what IT applications and equipment to acquire next. Rather managers should first assess how well their employees are managing with the technology that already pervades their work environment and determine what can be done to help those employees make better use of that existing technological base. A second imperative for managers is to undertake cost-benefit analyses that indicate what work processes and outputs are amenable to changes and improvements via technological innovation. In this effort, input should be solicited from multiple sources, such as technical specialists, peers, and IS committees. Such actions will support the public manager, positioning him or her to take the next steps in using the evolving workforce and new information technology applications in ways that enhance workers' performance and job satisfaction as well as the organization's broader goals.

References

Ayre, R. " Setting Up Shop." *PC Magazine,* 1996, *15*(8), 151–156.

Beaumont, P. B. "The U.S. Human Resource Management Literature: A Review." In G. Salaman and others (eds.), *Human Resource Strategies.* Thousand Oaks, Calif.: Sage, 1992.

Coates, J. F., Jarratt, J., and Mahaffie, J. B. "Future Work." *Futurist,* 1991, *25*(3), 9–15.

Danziger, J. N. "Management Information Systems and Interorganizational Relations with the American Governmental System." *Informatization and the Public Sector,* 1991, *1,* 169–187.

Danziger, J. N., and Kraemer, K. L. *People and Computers: The Impacts of Computers on End Users in Organizations.* New York: Columbia University Press, 1986.

Danziger, J. N., Kraemer, K. L., Dunkle, D. E., and King, J. L. "Enhancing the Quality of Computing Service: Technology, Structure and People." *Public Administration Review,* 1993, *53,* 161–169.

Davenport, T. H. "Saving IT's Soul: Human-Centered Information Management." *Harvard Business Review,* Mar.-Apr. 1994, pp. 121–131.

Dunkle, D. E., King, J. L., Kraemer, K. L., and Danziger, J. N. "Women, Men, and Information Technology: A Gender-Based Comparison of the Impacts of Computing Experienced by White Collar Workers." In U. E. Gattiker (ed.), *Women and Technology.* Hawthorne, N.Y.: Walter de Gruyter, 1994.

Dutton, W. H., and Guthrie, K. "An Ecology of Games: The Political Construction of Santa Monica's Public Electronic Network." *Informatization and the Public Sector,* 1991, *1,* 1–24.

Electronic Communications Privacy Act of 1986. U.S. Code, vol. 18, sec. 1367 et seq.

Frissen, P.H.A., and Snellen, I.T.M. (eds.) *Informatization Strategies in Public Administration.* Amsterdam, Netherlands: IOS Press, 1994.

Gattiker, U. E. (ed.). *Women and Technology.* Hawthorne, N.Y.: Walter de Gruyter, 1994.

Gist, M., Rosen, B., and Schwoerer, C. "The Influence of Training Method and Trainee Age on the Acquisition of Computer Skills." *Personal Psychology,* 1988, *41,* 255–265.

Gurwitt, R. "Technology Overload." *Governing,* Aug. 8, 1996, p. 16.

Hoffman, D., and Novak, T. P. "Marketing in Computer-Mediated Environments: Research Issues and Challenges." Paper presented at the Center for Research on Information Technology and Organizations, University of California, Irvine, May 1996.

Howard, B. "PC Predictions for '96." *PC Magazine,* 1996, *15*(1), 95–96.

Janis, I. L. *Crucial Decisions: Leadership in Policymaking and Crisis Management.* New York: Free Press, 1989.

Kinnaman, D. E. "Remember the Human Element in Your Technology Planning." *Technology and Learning,* 1994, *14*(5), 62.

Kraut, R., Dumais, S., and Koch, S. "Computerization, Productivity and the Quality of Work Life." *Communications of the ACM,* 1989, *32,* 220–238.

Levine, D. I., and Tyson, L. D. "Participation, Productivity, and the Firm's Environment." In A. S. Blinder (ed.), *Paying for Productivity: A Look at the Evidence.* Washington, D.C.: Brookings Institution, 1990.

Long, R. J. *New Office Information Technology: Human and Managerial Implications.* London: Croom Helm, 1987.

Markus, M. L. *Is Information Richness Theory Rich Enough? or How Managers Using E-Mail Cope with Lack of Richness.* Unpublished manuscript, Anderson Graduate School of Management, Los Angeles, 1991.

Meinert, D., and Davis, D. "Human Resource Decision Support Systems (HRDSS)." *Information Resources Management Journal,* Winter 1989, pp. 41–52.

Northrop, A., Kraemer, K. L., Dunkle, D. E., and King, J. L. "Management Policy for Greater Computing Benefits." *Social Science Computer Review,* 1994, *12,* 383–404.

O'Brien, J. *Management Information Systems: A Managerial End User Perspective.* (2nd ed.) Burr Ridge, Ill.: Irwin, 1993.

Ogletree, S. M., and Williams, S. W. "Sex and Sex-Typing Effects on Computer Attitudes and Aptitude." *Sex Roles: A Journal of Research,* 1990, *23,* 703–712.

Oldham, J. "Wanted: New Skills." *Los Angeles Times,* July 30, 1996, p. A14.

Perrolle, J. A. *Computers and Social Change.* Belmont, Calif.: Wadsworth, 1987.

Peyser, M., and Rhodes, S. "When E-Mail Is Oops-Mail." *Newsweek,* Oct. 16, 1995, p. 82.

Richter, M. J. "A Guide to Networking: Government Connects the Dots." *Governing,* July 1, 1995, pp. 48–56, 63–67.

Samuels, G. "Computers and Communications: Is the Whole World Ready to Surf the Internet?" *Forbes,* Jan. 1, 1996, pp. 98–101.

Schuler, R. S., and Walker, J. *Managing HR in the Information Age.* Washington D.C.: Bureau of National Affairs, 1991.

Sproull, L., and Kiesler, S. "Reducing Social Context Cues: Electronic Mail in Organizational Communication." *Management Science,* 1986, *32,* 1492–1512.

Storey, J. "Human Resource Management in the Public Sector." In G. Salaman and others (eds.), *Human Resource Strategies.* Thousand Oaks, Calif.: Sage, 1992.

Williams, S. W., Ogletree, S. M., Woodburn, W., and Raffeld, P. "Gender Roles, Computer Attitudes, and Dyadic Computer Interaction Performance in College Students." *Sex Roles: A Journal of Research,* 1993, *29,* 515–526.

Wooldridge, B. "Changing Demographics of the Workforce: Implications for the Use of Technology as a Productivity Improvement Strategy." *Public Productivity and Management Review,* 1994, *17,* 371–386.

Zuboff, S. *In the Age of the Smart Machine: The Future of Work and Power.* New York: Basic Books, 1988.

CHAPTER TWENTY-SIX

Budgeting Essentials for Human Resource Managers

Charles K. Coe
Catherine C. Reese

S alaries and benefits constitute a significant share of government budgets. Salaries and benefits generally average 65 percent of state and local budgets and 40 percent in the federal government. In some types of agencies, such as schools, they are more than 80 percent of the budget (Hildreth, 1995, p. 389). However, current public personnel literature seldom mentions public budgeting. Public personnel processes and public budgeting processes are often treated separately, except for the usual discussion of forecasting personnel service needs in public budgeting texts.

Our goal in this chapter is to help bridge this gap by providing an overview of public budgeting from the perspective of a public personnel manager. By organizing the chapter according to the four phases of the budgetary process, we use a framework commonly employed in the field of public budgeting. Specifically, we review budgeting essentials in the budget preparation, legislative review, budget execution, and audit stages of the public budgeting process.

BUDGET PREPARATION

Deciding How Many Regular Positions to Hire

Determining appropriate staffing levels is often an inexact, subjective art. Agencies can show their workload is increasing but how do budget analysts know if personnel are being properly managed? Analysts must ask if more work could be done with the same numbers if personnel were better equipped, better organized, more motivated, or better managed. Public policymakers ideally should decide what service levels they want and how many people are needed to meet these levels. Unfortunately, few public services lend themselves to precise measurement and planning. Therefore considerable debate exists over what constitutes appropriate staffing levels. For example:

- How many firefighters should initially arrive at a fire scene?
- How many patrol officers are needed when research shows little relationship between the number of police officers on the street and the crime rate?
- What is the appropriate class size?
- What are reasonable caseloads for social workers and mental health professionals?
- How many armed forces do we need to be secure?

Another area of debate centers on what constitute appropriate spans of control for supervisors. The private and public sectors alike are moving from the Weberian notion of tight, small spans of control to larger spans and to flatter organizations. An "empowering" management style presumably enables workers do work formerly done by middle managers; however, in any attempt to rightsize, at what point are personnel stretched too far?

A host of factors, both objective and subjective, influence staffing decisions. Sometimes staffing becomes institutionalized: that is, decisions are based on already agreed-upon criteria. For example, staffing decisions may be influenced or determined by mandates of federal and state legislatures, by norms of professional associations, by staffing ratios for states or regions, by standards engineered by the government, or by service level norms adopted by elected policymakers. Let us discuss each.

Mandates. The U.S. Supreme Court has decided cases in ways that effectively impose mandates on the budgets of state and local governments. Likewise, Congress passes acts requiring certain standards in the recruiting, hiring, and disciplining of employees. Some state governments mandate pension benefit levels for police officers and firefighters.

The fiscal effects of mandates vary (Dearborn, 1994; McLaughlin and Lehman, 1996). Dearborn (1994), for example, found that the fiscal impact of federal mandates on cities was less than 3 percent of the budget. Nonetheless the "M" word to many local policymakers is a fighting term. The principal frustration stems from the fact that mandates—although usually noble in purpose—typically have no funding attached to them. A second major objection is the one-size-fits-all mentality that restricts local officials from tailoring federal and state regulations to their community's particular needs.

In response to protestations against the cost of unfunded mandates, Congress passed the Unfunded Mandate Reform Act of 1995. This act requires that a cost-benefit analysis be made of all bills having a fiscal effect of more than $50 million and that Congress raise taxes to pay for the cost of mandates.

Table 26.1 itemizes some federal mandates affecting public human resource management. Of note is the application of the Fair Labor Standards Act to state and local governments following the U.S. Supreme Court decision in *Garcia* v. *San Antonio Metropolitan Transit* (1985), which reinstated provisions on wages and hours applicable to the public sector. Passed in the middle of most state and local governments' fiscal years, the decision resulted in the first year in unbudgeted costs of about $3 billion (Johnston and Kurtz, 1986).

Table 26.1. Federal Legislation Affecting Employment.

The Age Discrimination in Employment Act of 1967	Prohibits discrimination in pay, benefits, or continuous employment for employees over the age of forty, unless an employer can prove that age is a bona fide occupational qualification (BFOQ) for the job in question.
The Vietnam-Era Veterans Readjustment Act of 1974	Federal contractors and subcontractors must take affirmation action to ensure equal employment opportunity for Vietnam-era veterans.
Title VII of the Civil Rights Act of 1964	Prohibits discrimination on the basis of race, color, religion, sex, or national origin.
Fair Labor Standards Act of 1938	Fair labor standards apply to all public employees thereby increasing overtime pay (see *Garcia* v. *San Antonio*, 1985).
The Immigration Reform and Control Act of 1986	Employers may not hire "unauthorized aliens."
Americans with Disabilities Act of 1990	Workers for employers with fifteen or more employees are protected from discrimination in employment, transportation, and public accommodation.
Family and Medical Leave Act of 1993	Employers with more than fifty employees for at least twenty weeks per year must provide up to twelve weeks leave based on (1) medical condition, (2) birth or adoption of a child, or (3) need to take care of a child.

More recently, Congress passed the Americans with Disabilities Act of 1990 (ADA), which states that organizations with at least twenty-five employees are liable for their employment practices with respect to qualified individuals with disabilities. In response employers had to adapt their testing procedures (Hayes, Citera, Brady, and Jenkins, 1995).

On the judicial front, Straussman (1986) makes the point that judges make budget decisions for agencies. For example, the federal courts have been particularly active in the area of prison reform. At least thirty-six states have faced litigation against their prison systems, and spending for corrections as a percentage of the total state budgets increased after court orders.

Professional Associations' Standards. Public managers sometimes try to use their professional organization's standards to secure funding for positions. Such standards, briefly described in Table 26.2, are depicted in detail by Ammons (1996). As Table 26.2 shows, the adoption of professional standards may affect staffing directly or indirectly. The International Association of Fire Fighters, National Fire Protection Association, Public Library Association, International Association of Assessing Officers, and American Correctional Association recommend staffing levels either as a blanket amount (for example, number of firefighters per responding engine company) or according to work load (for example, number of librarians per patrons or number of parole officers per prisoners supervised). Other standards simply imply staffing levels when they recommend standards for the frequency of property assessments, the number and size of parks, the size and operation level of animal shelters, and so forth.

The empirical questions raised by such standards relate to both their validity and the degree to which they influence staffing and other budgetary decisions. Some staffing standards are useful budgeting guides; others are self-serving (Ammons, 1994) and have been labeled *pseudo-measures* of performance (Hatry, 1980).

Staffing Ratios. To ensure staffing stability, some agency heads try to get their elected board members to adopt, either formally or informally, policies that ensure specific staffing ratios. Police, fire, and emergency medical departments have been particularly successful at this. The Bureau of Justice Statistics of the U.S. Department of Justice annually reports by region full-time law enforcement employees per 1,000 inhabitants. Likewise, the National Fire Protection Association (NFPA) periodically reports by region career firefighters per 1,000 inhabitants. Some agencies convince their elected decision makers to staff based on these ratios. For example, most cities in North Carolina with populations larger than 50,000 have committed to a staffing ratio of two police officers per 1,000 people. So, as population grows, departments are assured of staffing increases.

Local governments should, however, be cautious and not adopt such ratios without careful analysis. A relationship between population size and staffing may exist, but each community should examine other factors such as the amount of

Table 26.2. Standards of Professional Organizations.

Professional Organization	Standards
Humane Society of the U.S. (HSUS)	Standards for animal control operations, including animal shelter operating hours, estimated kenneling needs, and recommended spaying, neutering, and mandatory sterilization programs.
Commission on Accreditation for Law Enforcement Agencies (CALEA)	Four hundred and thirty-six standards covering every aspect of law enforcement operations. Of these about 325 are mandatory standards dealing with matters in which liability is a substantial issue, such as training, police pursuit, and personnel.
International Association of Fire Fighters (IAFF); National Fire Protection Association (NFPA)	Among many recommended standards regarding equipment, training, fire ground operations, and communications, both organizations recommend minimum response strength of firefighters to a fire scene.
National Recreation and Park Association (NRPA)	Recommends appropriate mix of parks (for example, neighborhood parks, miniparks, and community parks), sizes, service areas, and acreage per 1,000 population.
Public Library Association (PLA)	Prescribes staff credentials, travel time for library patrons, library operating hours, collection size and quality, library staffing levels, collection maintenance practices, and physical characteristics of the library.
International Association of Assessing Officers (IAAO)	Recommends that property be reinspected at least every six years and that staffing equal at least 1.5 percent of property tax collection; describes standards for appraising property.
National Arborist Association (NAA)	Recommends tree care maintenance practices, including frequency and amount of fertilizer application.
American Public Health Association (APHA)	Recommends national public health goals, for example, at least 90 percent of all pregnant women should receive prenatal care in the first trimester.
Illuminating Engineering Society of North America	Recommends roadway and walkway illumination levels for specific types of commercial, intermediate, and residential areas.
American Correctional Association (ACH)	Accredits state correctional operations, recommending caseload ratios and probation and parole procedures.
American Humane Association (AHA)	Recommends staffing levels in child protective services, covering investigations and intakes per month, ongoing cases per caseworker, combined investigation and ongoing cases per caseworker, and the number of caseworkers per supervisor.

free patrol time that officers have, the caseload of investigators, and the desired response time to reported crimes.

Engineered Standards. Using industrial engineering techniques, some governments conduct time and motion studies to set the optimal mix of labor, equipment, and materials to perform a task. These engineered standards also establish an average amount of time to perform the job. Maintenance services readily lend themselves to engineered standards. Ammons (1996) found that local governments most commonly have engineered standards for inspections, street, water, and sewer maintenance services.

For some services, national standards exist. For example, the *Chilton Guide* and the *Mitchell Manual* are two widely accepted manuals setting standards for garage mechanics. Likewise, the Building Service Contractors Association International suggests time standards for custodial services including basic service, restroom service, floor service (carpets), floor service (hard and resilient), and stain service (Ammons, 1996, p. 258).

Service Norms. Sometimes staffing decisions are based on customer service norms. Included in this category are times for police and fire response, times for clerks to prepare minutes, times to set cases on dockets and try cases, times for data processing systems to respond to users, times to review developers' construction plans, times to process purchase requests, and times to respond to citizen complaints.

Hiring Temporaries

Hiring temporary rather than regular employees has budgetary implications because temporary employees do not qualify for the costly fringe benefits of health insurance, retirement, and merit increases. Temporary employees should be hired

- To staff workload peaks: for example, hiring recreation and street maintenance employees during the summer
- To fill positions for which future workloads and funding are doubtful
- To fill vacancies in a service about to be contracted out

The use of temporaries in the private sector is dramatically increasing. In contrast, at the federal level from 1983 to 1993, temporary employees remained constant at 6 to 7 percent of the civilian workforce. At the local level, however, use of *temps* is increasing due to currently more severe fiscal conditions (Hildreth, 1995, p. 397).

Public organizations should take care not to abuse the use of temporaries. An egregious example is that of the U.S. Postal Service employing a temporary worker for twenty years without any employment rights (U.S. Merit Systems

Protection Board, 1993, p. 7). The U.S. Merit Systems Protection Board (p. 4) has found that although this is an extreme case, federal agencies show a pattern of abusing the use of temporaries in these ways:

- Hired to avoid employee benefits
- Used as *tryouts* before regular appointments
- Hired to avoid the competitive selection process
- Refilled with the same persons beyond the period that temporaries are supposed to work

Budgeting for Overtime

Overtime should be paid only for emergencies and when the cost of overtime is less than the cost of full-time positions. Budget analysts should carefully scrutinize overtime budget requests because a potential for abuse exists. Either through oversight or intent, overtime may be requested that is unnecessary or is for work more economically done by hiring more employees working a forty-hour week at straight time.

Governments commonly underestimate overtime during budget preparation (Hildreth, 1995), which can negatively affect services during the fiscal year. To avoid this poor planning, governments should adopt overtime policies that guide budgetary decisions.

Determining Employee Benefits

Employee benefits are a significant part of budgets, ranging from 20 to 40 percent of total compensation. The following list shows possible benefits. Some are a direct cost (for example, health insurance and pension plans). Others (such as sick leave, vacations, and holidays) are an indirect cost.

Security and health benefits
- Retirement and pensions
- Life insurance
- Workers' compensation
- Disability insurance
- Health insurance
- Health maintenance organizations (HMOs)
- Sick leave
- Social Security

Compensation for time not worked

Earned time off

- Vacation

- Holidays

- Compensatory time off

Paid time away from primary duties

- Coffee breaks

- Training and employee development

- Maternity and paternity leave

- Military leave

- Educational leave

- Civic duty leave (jury duty, and so forth)

Employer services

- Tuition

- Fitness and wellness programs

- Transportation and parking

- Career clothing

- Child care

- Employee assistance programs

Employees are often unaware of the value of either direct or indirect benefits. Valuing pay more, employees often underestimate the dollar value of fringe benefits. Knowing this, government agencies should annually inform employees of the value of their total compensation packages, including pay and both direct and indirect benefits.

The following sections examine budgeting issues associated with a number of employee benefits.

Security and Health Benefits. State and local employees have extensive fringe benefit coverage. As of 1990, retirement plans covered 96 percent of full-time state and local employees. In addition, 93 percent were covered by medical insurance, 88 percent by life insurance, 62 percent by dental insurance, and 95 percent by paid sick leave (Hildreth, 1995, p. 405). The most expensive benefit over which governments have some influence is health care. In all sectors of our economy, health care costs far outpace inflation. Cost containment is therefore now a prime objective, and it has led to various managed-care options—such as health maintenance organizations (HMOs)—as alternatives to the usual fee-for-services approach.

To reduce health care costs, public organizations should also establish wellness programs that encourage healthy behaviors and teach stress reduction. Stress is a major contributor to physical illness, including heart disease and stroke. Employee assistance programs provide counseling and support to individual employees in such areas as drug and alcohol treatment, weight control, stress reduction, and career counseling.

An often abused health benefit is sick leave. Researchers estimate that absenteeism costs the U.S. economy $38 billion annually (Scott and McClellan, 1990).

Sick leave is more often abused by younger and nonprofessional employees (Rogers and Herting, 1993) and by employees with lower salaries (Kroesser, Meckley, and Ranson, 1991). However, employees who have more control over their work procedures are much less absent than those with less control (Kroesser, Meckley, and Ranson, 1991). Moreover, short-term monetary rewards for nonuse of sick leave reduces excessive sick leave (Rogers and Herting, 1993). These research findings aside, from 1990 to 1995 the percentage of cities paying for unused sick leave fell from 44 percent to 37 percent (International City/County Management Association, 1996).

Like health plans, retirement and pension programs can be designed to improve public services and achieve budgetary ends. Police work and firefighting are physically demanding professions that take their toll on older women and men. To encourage turnover, governments provide bonuses to employees retiring after a reasonable work period (Tvedten, 1993). Similarly, to encourage early retirement and avoid painful layoffs during periods of fiscal stress, employers may offer monetary inducements to take early retirement. Twenty-five percent of governments mandate such a program, and 52 percent optionally offer it (Siegel, 1994).

Compensation for Time Not Worked. Governments compensate employees for time not worked (see the earlier benefits list). Pay for time not worked is increasing in the public sector, perhaps because such compensation is sometimes improperly perceived as an indirect cost (Woska, 1988).

Such benefits have a direct and significant effect on budgets. For example, fire departments commonly must maintain minimum staffing levels as part of labor agreements. When staffing falls below the established minimum due to vacations or other instances of time not worked, off-duty employees work at overtime rates.

When employees are trained, they are being compensated for time not worked. Effective training improves the knowledge, skills, and attitudes of employees. Conversely, inadequate training damages an organization's service mission. During times of fiscal stress, public organizations often substantially reduce training funds. Failing to train can lead to tort legal actions and sizable dollar damages against governments (Leazes, 1995).

Setting Pay

Pay levels tremendously affect budgets. Government decision makers must answer such questions as

- What are appropriate pay levels?
- Should merit pay be given, and if so, based on what criteria?
- Should longevity pay be granted?
- What is the government's position regarding pay and benefits when bargaining units exist?

We will discuss each question.

Pay Levels. Employee pay reflects external and internal labor markets. Internally, position classification systems arrange jobs according to similar duties and responsibilities. Generally, classification systems remain constant, until agencies attempt to reclassify positions or internal staff or external consultants make a classification and compensation review. Agencies may try to reclassify positions (usually upwards) when they think the duties and responsibilities of the positions have changed. Sometimes, agency managers are mistaken in their belief and really want only to reward diligent employees stuck at the last step of their pay range. Personnel departments look askance at such attempts.

State governments usually use their own staff to conduct classification and compensation studies, and local governments normally employ consultants. The process is to compare the pay ratios of the government under study to those of comparable local governments and to comparable private-sector positions. Deciding which governments are comparable is part art, part science, and a key determinant of pay levels. Naturally, all things being equal, employees would like to be compared with larger, more affluent communities with higher pay structures.

As the chief executive ponders what pay increases, if any, to recommend to the governing board, he or she considers several factors: the pay rate compared with like public-sector governments, the effects of pay rate changes on taxes and other revenues, the public's view of compensation levels, and the wants of the governing board.

Merit Pay. Public agencies have traditionally taken one of two options in designing merit systems: *step plans* and *range plans.* Thirty-seven states have step plans. Each step has a salary range represented as a pay grade with the number of steps in each pay grade ranging from four to eighty-one (Kearney and Morgan, 1990). Thirteen states have range plans that contain no steps, just minimum and maximum salaries for each pay grade.

Longevity Pay. Governments award longevity pay as an incentive to reduce employee turnover and to reward continuous service. Longevity pay is normally awarded after anywhere from five to twenty years of service. Sixty-one percent of cities (International City/County Management Association, 1996) and twenty-six states award longevity pay (Kearney and Morgan, 1990). Longevity pay contradicts the notion that employees be paid for performance. Still, as Kearney and Morgan (1990) point out, pay-for-performance has failed in public settings because of the difficulty of measuring public-sector performance.

Using Volunteers

Using volunteers reduces personnel costs, but volunteers are objectionable to unions when volunteer efforts replace union members. Yet, clearly, volunteers are absolutely essential for some public services. For example, the vast majority of fire departments consist of either all volunteers or a combination of volunteers and full-time firefighters. Likewise, recreation departments depend heavily on volunteers. Moreover, the number of volunteers has markedly increased in police departments experiencing management problems. As would be expected, volunteering is also greater in police departments serving more affluent populations that have more spare time (Siegel and Sundeen, 1986). In some communities, getting volunteer support is becoming more difficult as the work week lengthens and more spouses work. To attract and retain volunteers, government agencies should provide adequate training and pension benefits to those who work for extended and substantial periods (Hinton, 1995).

Costing Government Services

During budget preparation, analysts face a number of costing questions about labor costs, including these:

- Should particular services be privatized?
- How much labor should be budgeted for construction projects?
- How well is the government performing compared to like governments?

The literature on privatization is especially replete. The purpose here is not to summarize this research but to discuss costing issues that must be dealt with in any costing analysis.

Methods of Costing. *Cost accounting*—also called *managerial* or *activity-based costing*—is an ongoing process that collects, classifies, analyzes, records, and summarizes *cost* information. Costs are different from *expenditures,* for costs include depreciation, debt, and overhead (indirect) charges. Governments use cost accounting to budget and then track the costs of construction and maintenance jobs. These are called *job-order* costs because they are charged to discrete jobs. Governments also use cost accounting to record costs charged to a cost center performing repetitive, routine work with measurable output. This is called *process costing* because costs are associated with uniform, continuous (not job-by-job) work.

Cost accounting is a sine qua non in the private sector, where accurate product pricing and work scheduling are critical to a company's success. In sharp contrast to the private sector, most governments do not perceive that the benefits of cost accounting outweigh the costs of establishing a cost-accounting system. To account for costs, governments must be able to record the directs costs of time, equipment, and materials and also indirect costs on a daily basis. Few governments have such a capability. Coe and O'Sullivan (1993) found that only 4 percent of cities were able to collect indirect costs to enable accounting.

Short of cost accounting, governments may use *cost finding*. Cost finding entails converting expenditure (or expense) data to cost data by assigning all costs to the period in which they occurred. Although less accurate than cost accounting, cost finding enables managers to determine reasonable cost estimates.

Still less accurate than cost finding are *ballpark estimates,* which may either exaggerate or understate costs. Savas (1979) found that in sixty-eight jurisdictions actual service costs were 30 percent greater than the figures shown on their budget pages. Similarly, Martin (1992) found that governments often underestimate the costs of administering contracts with private firms providing public services.

Methods of Handling Indirect Costs. In deciding whether to contract out a service, how much to pay a contractor for a service, or how to price a service, governments must face the question of how to handle indirect costs, including

- Department costs that cannot be charged directly to the daily work (for example, supervisory time, fringe benefits, office supplies, utilities, and capital purchases for equipment)

- Depreciation of fixed capital assets like buildings

- Organizationwide overhead services provided to line departments by such staff agencies as the personnel, purchasing, accounting, auditing, and legal departments

The first task is to be able to collect such indirect costs. The use of internal service funds (ISFs) for equipment and supplies permits the motor pool and central stores departments to charge these costs to using departments, who in turn can charge them to jobs and cost centers. Governments use *cost allocation plans* to allocate organizationwide indirect costs and to get reimbursement from the federal government for indirect costs expended on federal grants.

All indirect costs are clearly real costs of doing business and should be fair game in pricing a service. However, when a government contracts out a service, some of these costs are *avoidable* and others not. For example, the government may still have the same depreciation and departmentwide and organizationwide indirect costs after a small service is privatized. However, eliminating a major service such as garbage collection might reduce all types of indirect costs. Therefore, governments should determine which costs they can avoid when contracting out.

Cost Comparisons. Governments often use intergovernment cost comparisons as a guide to allocating resources during budget preparation. Comparing costs per regular staff member gives some direction about the relative size of staff in comparable local governments. Likewise, costs per service output or outcome offer a point of comparison. Although at first glance useful methods, cost comparisons should be applied with great care, so governments can be sure they are comparing apples to apples and not apples to oranges.

Here is a partial listing of cost factors that may confound intergovernment cost comparisons:

- Wide variability in the use of ISFs (Coe and O'Sullivan, 1993)
- Variability in the extent to which offsetting revenues are charged
- Variability in how a public service is defined and measured
- Variability in whether and how indirect costs are measured

LEGISLATIVE REVIEW

In governments that use an executive budget system—this includes most U.S. government entities—the executive's budget is reviewed and ultimately approved by a legislative body. The state legislature, city council, or county commission does not generally have to adopt the chief executive's budget proposals as given. Funding levels, revenue systems, and programming priorities may be revised, although this may be more difficult to do in those local governments where the chief executive has greater legal power.

In most states today the governor is responsible for preparing a budget proposal, although that power is still shared with the legislature in several states. Also in most states today the legislature has the authority to substantially alter the executive budget proposal as long as various legal constraints—including balanced budget requirements—are not abridged. More specifically, the joint legislative appropriation committees that exist to iron out differences between house and senate versions of budget bills often are extremely powerful, sometimes even substantially altering the versions of the bills referred by each house and returning only compromise versions to the legislative body in a take-it-or-leave-it bid for power on the last day of the legislative session, forcing quick action in terms of a vote. Most local governments also use some variation of an executive budget system, although the budget ordinance as passed generally contains plans for both revenue and expenditure and is often enacted with far less friction than at the state or federal levels, in part because the chief executive of a local government often has more power relative to the legislative body than the governor has at the state level (see Thurmaier, 1995).

Aaron Wildavsky (1979) once wrote that budgeting takes place "in a twilight zone between politics and efficiency" (p. 143); thus public budgeting is inherently political and any discussion of the budgetary process needs to address both the administrative and political aspects of budgetary decision making.

Decision-Making Contexts

Administrative Context. The kinds of decisions reached during the legislative review process involve trade-offs among competing interests for scarce dollar resources. Both decisions made by human resource managers about the appropriations to request and some of the subsequent analysis, review, and modification of those requested figures by executive (and possibly legislative) staff members will have been completed by the time legislative review occurs. The greatest decisions in the legislative review process are made by the members of the legislative body. However, the human resource manager is responsible at this time for justifying his or her decisions, as requested by the legislature. In effect the legislature is in a proactive decision-making mode and the human resource manager—or any staff agency manager called to testify—is in a reactive decision-making mode during this phase of the process.

Political Context. The decisions made during legislative review are not, however, merely administrative; in fact, budgeting is a subsystem of politics, not the other way around (Wildavsky, 1988). Thus the trade-offs made among competing groups for scarce dollars are not always based solely on the competing groups' relative merits. Rather, some legislative decisions are made—at least partially—on the basis of knowledge of the degree of support a particular option has and similar factors. In fact, decisions may be made strategically to benefit or discredit the requests of a particular agency, program, or group due to its association with a particular sponsor or leader. Some of the strategies that both legislatures and human resource managers might use in the political arena of the legislative review process are discussed later.

Budget Format. How are positions shown in the budget? The answer to this question depends largely on budget format. Although many jurisdictions employ some sort of hybrid format, the evidence is that most still favor exercising ultimate legislative control over subsequent executive and agency spending and therefore use a line-item budget.

The Government Finance Officers Association (GFOA), which gives annual awards for distinguished budget presentations in local governments, strongly encourages the role of the public-sector budget as a tool of communication between the government and the public. Although guidelines for award qualification stop short of advocating a particular budget format, GFOA criteria emphasize organizational clarity, including the provision of clear, easily understandable material that summarizes past and projected budget activities (see Lynch, 1995).

Legislatures as Guardians of the Public Purse

Several different types of decisions are made by, first, the executive or the legislative budget office and then the legislative body (or committees and subcommittees thereof) during the legislative review process; presumably the legislative body has the benefit in its decisions of seeing total revenue and expenditure projections for the government entity. The following information refers to both legislative and central budget office review processes because they have several features in common. Its purpose is to illustrate common legislative decision-making methods and strategies.

Deciding Whether to Increase or Decrease Positions. The bad yet well-known news for human resource managers is that the number one decision rule for budget authorities—discovered by Arnold Meltsner (1971) in his analysis of Oakland, California, budget review methods—is to cut all increases in personnel. Simply put, the budget category that is the largest in terms of public-sector direct spending is also the most obvious and most vulnerable choice for budget reductions. More specifically, a common managerial position in times of fiscal stress today is to impose a hiring freeze. As W. Bartley Hildreth (1995) points out, a hiring freeze is a common announcement from incoming chief executives at all levels of government. Legislatures and budget analysts must take the financial status of the government into account when making decisions about allotted personnel positions. Aside from areas involving major new policy innovations, and assuming no severe fiscal crisis, the position of the legislature is likely to lean toward allowing the previous fiscal year's personnel allotment to continue (Thurmaier, 1995).

The number of personnel positions allowed or directed to remain unfilled can generate substantial savings for a large government, at least on paper. The number of positions unfilled can thus be manipulated within the context of a balanced budget to make the expenditure picture appear rosier than it actually is. For example, it was the practice of Governor Ray Blanton of Tennessee to provide some flexibility in the annual appropriation bill by budgeting all personnel positions at 100 percent in order to guarantee a revenue cushion during the fiscal year. Specifically, this was a way of overappropriating expenditures—or underspending revenues, because in a given year, turnover among state personnel ensured that appropriated position costs would be less than actual position costs.

Reviewing the Adequacy of Benefits Packages. Personnel benefits include insurance, pension plans, and the like and may be protected from budget reductions by various laws and standards, as discussed earlier in the chapter. However, the adequacy of pension plan management should be monitored by the legislature using such common standards as those provided by the GFOA. Specifically, investment standards require a three-part test for investments: creditworthiness, appropriate liquidity, and appropriate market rate of return (see Mikesell, 1995). Mismanagement of pension plans, including the misuse of invested funds to achieve budget balance, has in the past resulted in severe costs and legal action for a variety of state and local governments.

Deciding Whether to Increase or Decrease Pay. It is more likely that a legislature would decide to cut or freeze wage raises than that it would reduce the actual pay scale. The use of raises—whether in part merit based or not—as motivators for employees is well established. Conversely, the elimination or reduction of, for example, cost-of-living adjustments (COLAs) can have the opposite effect and thus be a disincentive to good work performance and result in lowered employee morale, a less effective workforce, and even legal action against the government (Hildreth, 1995). Thus, in the long run, these kinds of decisions are probably not wise but still are very common.

In times of drastic fiscal stress even wage freezes and cuts may not be seen as adequate by policymakers. For example, several years ago the state of Georgia was experiencing a severe fiscal crisis, and the legislature and governor imposed a mandatory furlough—one or two days of enforced leave without pay per month—for many state positions. This action (widely protested and eventually found to be illegal via a court challenge) is just one example of the lengths to which policymakers may feel required to go in order to avert a budget in the red.

Reviewing Chief Executive Recommendations for Contracting Out, Downsizing, or Reorganizing. The legislature must also make decisions upholding or altering the chief executive's position on the contracting out of services. The importance of complete cost data, including information on the indirect costs of service provision, to making appropriate decisions cannot be overemphasized. Specifically, members of the legislative body must be as careful in comparing total costs for in-house versus privatized service provision as the members of the executive budget staff are when preparing the initial budget document. Legislators and their staff members should be able to either evaluate cost data provided by the executive branch or develop their own measures in order to assist with this type of decision. Of particular consideration to the human resource manager is the effect a decision to contract out a service will have on the configuration of personnel required to conduct noncontracted activities; that is, how will the personnel who formerly performed the proposed contracted-out function be used? Can the human resource manager make the case that the personnel presently performing the tasks in question are working efficiently and effectively? The human resource manager has to deal with reductions-in-force and similar actions through restructuring work for those who survive.

The overall reorganization of government through executive order is a power afforded either informally or, more commonly, through constitutional or statutory provision to the governors of twenty-four states (Council of State Governments, 1991). In other cases, however, and in cases of disagreement over the means of reorganization, full-scale political war may break out between the legislative and executive branches. It is highly likely that some personnel positions will be casualties in such a war. Governor Jimmy Carter of Georgia used his line-item veto power more frequently than any other governor of the state when in a major policy disagreement with the legislature over a proposed reorganization (Lauth and Reese, 1993).

Downsizing and reorganization are sometimes combined in actions that may also detrimentally affect personnel and human resource managers. For example, when Governor Ned McWherter of Tennessee first took office in 1987, he instituted a massive reduction in force and restructured many major departments in state service. In the department of human services, for example, supervisors who had not held their positions long were demoted back to the level of caseworker, and many caseworker positions were eliminated as well.

Now that we have reviewed some basic decisions that legislatures and budget analysts make during the legislative review process, let us turn to a review of the various response strategies human resource managers can employ during the legislative review process.

Human Resource Managers as Advocates for Personnel Functions

The ability of the human resource manager to successfully respond to or challenge the various legislative decisions and strategies just discussed is of paramount importance. The discussion that follows is more applicable to a staff than a line agency and could be generalized to other staff agencies as well but is particularized to a human resource agency here. Some of the factors that make personnel concerns likely to be the center of administrative or political budget reduction decisions are, in fact, relatively particular to human resource organizations.

For example, the services provided by human resource departments are not high-profile, politically popular services that legislators are especially keen to provide to their constituents. In fact, public perceptions of government size and the consequent development of campaign platforms along the lines of government reduction may make human resource agencies even more likely to be cut. Therefore, human resource managers need to be especially skilled and adept at the presentation and justification of budget requests in order to ensure that their services will continue to be provided. Moreover, the strategies given by budgetary scholar Wildavsky (1988) for agency acquisitions do not apply equally to human resource agencies and other agencies. For example, Wildavsky suggested that agencies develop a clientele, but the clientele of a human resource agency is already defined by the workforce. The following sections offer a brief series of justification suggestions for human resource managers, classified by the major functions served by typical state and local human resource agencies that were identified through a review of several state, county, and city budgets: employee training, technical support, and safety and workers' compensation coordination.

Justifying Employee Training. Because employee training is extremely future oriented and its results are not easy to demonstrate to the public, it is one of the first areas cut in times of fiscal stress. The long-range benefits of employee training to both employees and citizens must therefore be emphasized. In areas such as fire protection, the need for employee training directly relates to public safety; in some other areas, such as foster care, training directly relates to the propensity for citizen lawsuits against the government.

Justifying Technical Support. The maintenance of a civil service system for all government employees requires a great proportion of any human resource program budget. Specifically, the administration of civil service examinations and performance evaluations, required to ensure the selection and retention of quality personnel, is virtually a mandated function of human resource managers. Of course legal action resulting from a poorly run personnel system is also a threat, and this fact can be used in justification as well.

Justifying Safety and Workers' Compensation. The complexity of workers' compensation and ongoing concerns for the safety and well-being of public employees combine to create a specific need for human resource managers to be clear in justifying their budgets. State-level workers' compensation data can be used both to identify risks to personnel and to demonstrate the effectiveness of safety programs in reducing costs for the indemnification of work-related injuries and deaths (see Pine, 1994). One of the major prerequisites for the establishment of a risk management program is a good record-keeping system; the main steps for conducting such a program are (1) risk identification, (2) risk control, and (3) ongoing risk management evaluation (Coe, 1989). If these conditions and steps are followed, the human resource manager should be able to readily produce the data required for safety program justification.

Overall, strategies for presentation and justification before the legislature are similar for human resource managers and other staff agency managers. That is, program goals and objectives should be linked explicitly to particular expenditures in a way that is easy for members of the legislative body and the general public to understand. For human resource functions in particular, the long-term effects of neglecting areas such as employee training should be emphasized. Any information regarding the past and current efficiency and effectiveness of department operations should be presented as well. Finally, the findings of a recent study of central budget office tactics and decision-making processes (Thurmaier, 1995) suggests that political imperatives are of a high level of importance to budget analysts; thus it is certainly to the advantage of the human resource manager to cultivate relationships with important political figures in his or her government.

BUDGET EXECUTION

Generally, the budget execution, or administration, phase of the budget cycle refers to the period of time corresponding to the fiscal year. It is the period of time when the appropriated monies are actually spent. During this time the budget document itself serves as a managerial tool for charting and monitoring expenditure as the expression of legislative intent and, ultimately, the will of the people. The execution phase is when the human resource manager, like the managers of other staff agencies, must document expenditures over time, account for personnel transactions, manage interim personnel needs, and respond to various executive actions.

Documenting Expenditures over Time

The human resource manager must document expenditures throughout the course of the fiscal year. A regular comparison—monthly or quarterly—of budgeted versus actual expenditures in all service categories needs to be maintained. Particular to the position of human resource manager is the need to demonstrate efficiency and effectiveness in current operations as a means of averting potential future revenue cuts due to the tendency of lawmakers to cut personnel items first in a crisis.

Accounting for Personnel Transactions

Furthermore, along with his or her regular responsibility of maintaining complete expenditure data for the department, the human resource manager must also ensure the integrity of the maintenance of all personnel transaction records for the entire government entity during the budget service period. Controls implemented during the budget execution phase may include a requirement that personnel transactions such as the hiring of new positions be cleared through the central finance office of the government, necessitating that human resource and financial managers work together. Another area in which personnel and financial managers must coordinate work processes is payroll processing. As Hildreth (1995) states, human resource managers "face a steady encroachment in their functional responsibilities" from financial managers (p. 421).

Responding to Various Executive Actions

Sometimes during the fiscal year the chief executive may announce budget restrictions or reductions beyond those anticipated either during the budget preparation or the legislative review stage of the public budgeting process. Reasons for such further actions are most commonly related to projected revenues having declined since the passage of the budget or, similarly, to the discovery of inaccurate revenue forecasts. Again, in the face of a drastic fiscal crisis, the likely first target of reductions will be personnel. Executives most commonly respond to such financial pressures by implementing hiring, promotional, or wage freezes (Hildreth, 1995). Possible strategies for human resource managers in response to these kinds of decisions have already been reviewed.

However, as a proactive measure, human resource managers need to maintain and monitor data that will, when necessary, demonstrate that their activities are having an effect or outcome that is important to the government's employees and to the general public. For example, the human resource manager needs to develop data showing the impact of employee training. And he or she needs to be able to show that the workers' compensation administration is saving the community money in the long run.

In short, the human resource manager must be actively preparing to justify the efficacy of specific managed activities and programs, both in order to protect against threats of proposed reductions and in anticipation of the audit phase of the budget cycle, during which not only financial and compliance audits but also performance audits to guide future program planning may be conducted. It is to the audit phase of the budgetary cycle that we turn next.

AUDIT

During the audit phase of the budgetary cycle, which occurs after the end of the fiscal year, the government evaluates, at a minimum, fiscal compliance with budgetary goals and spending stipulations. This *financial audit* may either be performed in house or by an external auditor. A more specific type of audit is the *performance audit,* usually performed by personnel internal to the government and concerned with efficiency and effectiveness of government operations (Coe, 1989). The human resource manager will be asked such questions as whether agencies lived within their budgeted personnel service allotments, whether overtime was contained, and sometimes what were the unit costs of service provision. Generally, however, as long as adequate, complete records of all personnel matters have been kept during the budget execution phase, the human resource manager need mainly be concerned with producing the appropriate documentation as requested by auditors. One other specific and yet ongoing duty of the human resource manager, which may not occur during the audit stage itself but over the course of the forthcoming fiscal year, is to work with other agency managers in ensuring that audit recommendations are implemented (Pariser and Brooks, 1994). That is, if audit findings in a human resource area are or may prove detrimental to the fiscal health of the organization in terms of subsequent bond ratings, it is the responsibility of the human resource manager to assist in the resolution of these findings.

CONCLUSION

We have identified several functions and decisions that occur within each stage of the public budgetary cycle, both generally and as they pertain to human resource managers. By employing the framework of the budgetary process for our discussion of human resource management concerns, we hope to have shed some light on the often neglected connection between public personnel processes and budgeting processes.

References

Age Discrimination in Employment Act of 1967. U.S. Code, vol. 29, sec. 621 et seq.

Americans with Disabilities Act of 1990. U.S. Code, vol. 42, sec. 12101 et seq.

Ammons, D. N. "The Role of Professional Associations in Establishing and Promoting Standards for Local Governments." *Public Productivity and Management Review,* 1994, *17,* 282–298.

Ammons, D. N. (ed.). *Municipal Benchmarks: Assessing Local Performance and Establishing Community Standards.* Thousand Oaks, Calif.: Sage, 1996.

Civil Rights Act of 1964. U.S. Code, vol. 42, sec. 1981 et seq. (Title VII at 2000e.)

Coe, C. K. *Public Financial Management.* Upper Saddle River, N.J.: Prentice Hall, 1989.

Coe, C. K., and O'Sullivan, E. A. "Accounting for the Hidden Costs: A National Study of Internal Service Funds and Other Indirect Costing Methods in Municipal Governments." *Public Administration Review,* 1993, *53*(11), 59–64.

Council of State Governments. *The Book of the States.* Vol. 28. Lexington, Ky.: Council of State Governments, 1991.

Dearborn, P. M. "Assessing Mandate Effects on State and Local Governments." *Intergovernmental Perspectives,* 1994, *20*(3), 22–26.

Fair Labor Standards Act of 1938. U.S. Code, vol. 29, sec. 201 et seq.

Family and Medical Leave Act of 1993. U.S. Code, vol. 29, sec. 2601 et seq.

Hatry, H. P. "Performance Measurement Principles and Techniques: An Overview of Local Government." *Public Productivity Review,* 1980, *4,* 312–339.

Hayes, T. L., Citera, M., Brady, L. M., and Jenkins, N. M. "Stopping for Persons with Disabilities: What Is 'Fair' and 'Job Related'?" *Public Personnel Management,* 1995, *24,* 413–428.

Hildreth, W. B. "Budgeting Human Resource Requirements." In J. Rabin, T. Vocino, W. B. Hildreth, and G. J. Miller (eds.), *Handbook of Public Personnel Administration.* New York: Dekker, 1995.

Hinton, K. L. "Perceived Training Needs of Volunteers in Government Service." *Public Personnel Management,* 1995, *24,* 531–534.

Immigration Reform and Control Act of 1986. U.S. Statutes at Large 100 (1986) 3359.

International City/County Management Association. *The Municipal Yearbook.* Washington, D.C.: International City/County Management Association, 1996.

Johnston, V. R., and Kurtz, M. "Handling a Public Policy Emergency: The Fair Labor Standards Act in the Public Sector." *Public Administration Review,* 1986, *46,* 414–422.

Kearney, R. C., and Morgan, K. S. "Longevity Pay in the States: Echo from the Past or Sound of the Future?" *Public Personnel Management,* 1990, *19,* 191–200.

Kroesser, H. L., Meckley, R., and Ranson, J. T. "Selected Factors Affecting Employees' Sick Leave Use." *Public Personnel Management,* 1991, *20,* 171–180.

Lauth, T. P., and Reese, C. C. "The Line-Item Veto in Georgia: Incidence and Fiscal Effects." Paper presented at the Georgia Political Science Association annual meeting, Savannah, Feb. 1993.

Leazes, F. J., Jr. "'Pay Now or Pay Later': Training and Torts in Public Sector Human Services." *Public Personnel Management,* 1995, *24,* 167–180.

Lynch, T. D. *Public Budgeting in America.* (4th ed.) Upper Saddle River, N.J.: Prentice Hall, 1995.

Martin, L. L. "A Proposed Methodology for Comparing the Costs of Government Versus Contract Service Delivery." In International City/County Management Association, *The Municipal Yearbook.* Washington, D.C.: International City/County Management Association, 1992.

McLaughlin, M., and Lehman, J. "Mandates to Local Government: How Big a Problem?" *North Carolina Insight,* 1996, *16*(3), 42–75.

Meltsner, A. J. *The Politics of City Revenue.* Berkeley: University of California Press, 1971.

Mikesell, J. L. *Fiscal Administration: Analysis and Applications for the Public Sector.* (4th ed.) Belmont, Calif.: Wadsworth, 1995.

Pariser, D. B., and Brooks, R. C. "Audit Recommendation Follow-Up Systems: Getting Audit Recommendations Implemented Effectively." In A. Khan and W. B. Hildreth (eds.), *Case Studies in Public Budgeting and Financial Management.* Dubuque, Ia.: Kendall/Hunt, 1994.

Pine, J. C. "Analyzing Workers' Compensation Risks." In A. Khan and W. B. Hildreth (eds.), *Case Studies in Public Budgeting and Financial Management.* Dubuque, Ia.: Kendall/Hunt, 1994.

Rogers, R. E., and Herting, S. R. "Patterns of Absenteeism Among Government Employees." *Public Personnel Management,* 1993, *22,* 215–236.

Savas, E. S. "How Much Do Government Services Really Cost?" *Urban Affairs Quarterly,* 1979, *15*(1), 23–42.

Scott, K. D., and McClellan, E. "Gender Differences in Absenteeism." *Public Personnel Management,* 1990, *19,* 229–253.

Siegel, G. B., and Sundeen, R. A. "Volunteering in Municipal Police Departments: Some Hypotheses on Performance Impacts." *Public Productivity Review,* 1986, *10,* 77–92.

Siegel, S. R. "A Comparative Study of Preretirement Programs in the Public Sector." *Public Personnel Management,* 1994, *23,* 631–643.

Straussman, J. D. "Courts and Public Purse Strings: Have Portraits of Budgeting Missed Something?" *Public Administration Review,* 1986, *46,* 345–351.

Thurmaier, K. "Decisive Decision Making in the Executive Budget Process: Analyzing the Political and Economic Propensities of Central Budget Bureau Analysts." *Public Administration Review,* 1995, *55,* 448–460.

Tvedten, J. "The City of Kansas City's Firefighters Pension Bonus Plan." *Public Personnel Management,* 1993, *22,* 345–362.

Unfunded Mandate Reform Act of 1995. U.S. Statutes at Large 109 (1995) 48.

U.S. Department of Health and Human Services. *Source Book of Health Insurance Data.* Washington, D.C.: U.S. Government Printing Office, 1984–1985.

U.S. Merit Systems Protection Board. *Temporary Federal Employment: In Search of Flexibility and Fairness.* Washington, D.C.: U.S. Merit Systems Protection Board, 1993.

Vietnam-Era Veterans' Readjustment Assistance Act of 1974. U.S. Statutes at Large 88 (1974) 1578.

Wildavsky, A. *The Politics of the Budgetary Process.* (3rd ed.) New York: Little, Brown, 1979.

Wildavsky, A. *The New Politics of the Budgetary Process.* New York: Little, Brown, 1988.

Woska, W. J. "Pay for Time Not Worked: A Public-Sector Budget Dilemma." *Public Administration Review,* 1988, *48,* 551–556.

PART FIVE

MOTIVATING AND COMPENSATING EMPLOYEES

*Managers find a confusing array of regulations and procedures
standing in their way when they seek to reward good performance.*
—Alan K. Campbell, congressional testimony on
civil service reform and organization, 1978

Finding new ways to motivate and compensate employees is a major priority, as Alan Campbell, then head of the U.S. Civil Service Commission, testified before the House Post Office and Civil Service Committee prior to passage of the Civil Service Reform Act of 1978. Campbell's experiment with merit-based compensation was to find a rocky road ahead (see Chapter Thirty), yet despite the pervasive difficulties encountered by all public HR managers, the desire to fairly motivate and reward public employees for better performance is a recurring and consistent theme of public human resource management literature and practice.

The methods that public organizations employ to motivate and compensate their members have long-term consequences for organizational health and viability. This part of the handbook, "Motivating and Compensating Employees," synthesizes the literature on these two important topics and gives specific guidance about the efficacy of varying reward systems, position classification and compensation strategies, pay-for-performance compensation systems, and a wide range of employee benefits.

Arie Halachmi and Theo van der Krogt begin Part Five with Chapter Twenty-Seven, "The Role of the Manager in Employee Motivation," an overview of different theories and methodologies for motivating and rewarding public employees. These authors also discuss monetary and nonmonetary rewards and their use in the public sector and suggest the central elements of a nonmonetary employee incentive plan.

In Chapter Twenty-Eight, "Work Management and Job Evaluation Systems in a Government Environment," Gilbert Siegel uses his extensive academic and consulting experience in explaining how HR managers can employ job evaluation methodologies to create an effective position classification system. Siegel discusses such public-sector job evaluation methodologies as point rating, factor comparison, point factor, and other popularly used systems. He presents an instructive section on broadbanding, perhaps the most discussed but least used system for organizing and compensating public-sector positions, and he also provides an example of a point-factor job evaluation methodology. He notes that after reading this chapter, "The reader should have gained sufficient understanding to be a critical consumer of such [position classification] systems and should be able to judge organizational requirements for job evaluation."

Siegel continues his practical advice in Chapter Twenty-Nine, "Designing and Creating an Effective Compensation Plan." Here he discusses such issues as market value, comparable worth, merit pay, skill-based pay, and group performance systems. He again provides specific guidance to the practicing manager on how to construct and maintain an effective salary structure by merging job evaluation and salary survey data. Siegel stresses the need for management to consciously decide upon its compensation objectives, recognizing the clear advantages and disadvantages of the compensation philosophy it adopts.

Probably the most touted private-sector compensation technique to take hold in the public sector is merit- or performance-based pay. Gerald Gabris provides an extensive treatment of this phenomenon in Chapter Thirty, "Merit Pay Mania: Transforming Polarized Support and Opposition into a Working Consensus." Gabris states that "attitudes surrounding merit pay can often be described as manic. Advocacy or rejection of merit pay can reflect extreme enthusiasm or disenchantment that is extreme but also frequently transient." Gabris's aim is to bring some measure of rationality and balance to the subject of public-sector pay-for-performance compensation systems. Despite system failures, he predicts that "merit pay will not become extinct"; thus human resource managers should become keenly aware of the promise and reality of merit-based compensation systems.

Joseph Cayer concludes Part Five with Chapter Thirty-One, "Employee Benefits: From Health Care to Pensions." Cayer notes the increasing importance of benefit packages in attracting and retaining employees, observing that although "referred to as fringe benefits in the past, benefits now represent a central part of compensation systems." He states that "contemporary approaches provide benefits that change with employees' life cycles . . . addressing employees' differing needs as they move through educational opportunities, parenting, and retirement." Cayer thoroughly discusses the varying types of mandatory and discretionary benefits afforded public employees and also addresses how organizations can contain costs yet still strive to offer an attractive benefits plan to employees.

Human resource management's quest for the reward structure that strikes the perfect balance between employee needs and public responsiveness will no doubt remain elusive. However, as the array of motivation, compensation, and benefit alternatives continues to expand, it is crucial that the public human resource manager be prepared to provide strategic advice and counsel about these essential activities to key organizational actors.

Reference

U.S. House of Representatives, Committee on Post Office and Civil Service. *Civil Service Reform.* Washington, D.C.: U.S. Government Printing Office, 1978.

CHAPTER TWENTY-SEVEN

The Role of the Manager
in Employee Motivation

Arie Halachmi
Theo van der Krogt

The *industrial revolution,* the "second wave" in Toffler's terminology (1970, 1980, 1990), had important implications for the division of labor and for organizing the means of production of goods and services. Henry Ford's assembly line, where employees specialized in carrying out smaller and smaller tasks but in the most efficient way, and Charlie Chaplin's *Modern Times* are two examples of implications of the industrial revolution for the human side of the enterprise. The *information revolution,* the "third wave" (Toffler, 1980, 1990), led not only to changes in the way work is organized but also to corresponding transformations in what Mintzberg (1973) calls the decisional, informational, and interpersonal roles of managers (Halachmi, 1991).

Early in the twentieth century another change was taking place influencing the operations of organizations in the private sector and facilitating the evolution of the corporate structure as we know it today. That change was the separation of ownership (holding shares) from management in running daily operations. The ability to sell and publicly trade the stocks of a company not only allowed the separation of ownership and management but changed the role of managers in the private sector and also how we evaluate the performance of those managers. These changes—the separation of ownership from management, the transformation of managers' organizational role, and the alteration in evaluating managerial performance—made the administration of the private sector more similar to the administration of the public sector. The resulting growth in the number and size of nongovernment organizations that assumed a corporate structure and the occasional call for the public sector to become more like the private sector contributed further to increased similarities between the roles of managers in the public and private sectors. The implication of this growing similarity is that any attempt to study, understand, or influence the performance of organizations in one sector may benefit from a corresponding study of management and behavior of organizations in the other sector.

In the second half of the twentieth century, managers in both sectors experienced growing pressures from their respective stockholders or stakeholders to get the most out of the resources available to them. As labor costs increased at a growing pace relative to the cost of other production process elements, greater attention was given to the need to "optimize" or, as it is seen by organized labor, to reduce the use of manual labor. In one report about improving state government we read: "State employees are our most valuable asset—and largest expenditure. The state spent close to $1 billion on salaries in fiscal year 1995, and an additional $429 million on benefits. We believe we can maximize these resources by reforming our personnel system" (State of Oklahoma, 1995, pt. 4, p. 1). The report goes on to say that "to turn challenges into opportunities for a better future, Oklahoma state employees must be better led, motivated, rewarded, trained and equipped than they have been. Today they are trapped by many outdated and ineffective systems that put unintended roadblocks in the way."

Toward the end of the twentieth century, managers are encountering additional challenges to the ways they used to play their organizational roles. These challenges arise from changes in the demographic characteristics of the workforce such as the increase of the median age, the increase in the years of formal education and in the accompanying phenomenon of professionalization, and the greater diversity in terms of ethnic origin, gender, and domestic status (U.S. General Accounting Office, 1992). Even more important, such workforce changes have been augmented by (related) changes in employees' expectations about three important issues: (1) having working conditions that are more family (and single-parent) friendly: for example, access to benefits such as maternity leave, child care, and parent care; (2) having a say about decisions that affect the way employees carry out their work and about the roles of employers and immediate supervisors who may act as mentors and coaches; and (3) especially for professionals, having authority, responsibilities, and autonomy in their work. Thus, for example, managers are expected not only to provide the necessary physical conditions for carrying out the job but also to help employees develop a career, to ensure a friendly atmosphere conducive to employee participation in decision making, and to keep the workplace free of pressures that have to do with gender, race, sexual orientation, religion, disabilities, age, and so forth.

It does not take much effort to see that the roles managers are expected to play within the organization have grown in complexity since the turn of the century. This change has been augmented by the changes in the roles managers are expected to play as they also deal with the external environment. The growth in role complexity is commensurate with the increase in the possibility that any effort by a manager to meet the demands or needs of one stakeholder may come at the expense of meeting another stakeholder's needs. This complication, in turn, may lead to countless reactions and counterreactions that put additional pressures on the involved individuals, diminishing their abilities to carry out their other managerial roles.

The purpose of this chapter is to explore a subset of the roles managers are expected to carry out in order to maintain a productive, satisfied, and highly motivated workforce. This subset of roles cuts across Mintzberg's classification (1973) of managerial roles, but all managerial roles require managers to encourage employees, an important resource and group of stakeholders, to make better and greater contributions to the organization so that it can meet the demands of other stakeholders.

The chapter begins with a general, but brief, review of several models and theories of motivation that provide the rationale for urging greater employee productivity. As noted by the U.S. General Accounting Office (1990), "Individual motivation is a key factor in dealing with poor performers. Therefore, agency management must focus on creating an environment within which supervisors are encouraged and are motivated to identify poor performers and are properly trained and supported when they attempt to deal with them" (p. 3). The chapter then goes on to examine some issues in the use of economic incentives and in the demise of the system known as *quality of working life*. It concludes with some thoughts about the emergence of ad-hocracy and the shift of responsibilities for motivation and self-actualization from the organization to the individual.

IMPORTANCE OF MOTIVATION

Effective employee motivation has long been one of management's most difficult and important duties. Success in this endeavor is now becoming even more of a challenge due to the current fashion of downsizing and the difficulties associated with managing a diverse workforce (Kreitner and Kinicki, 1995). Downsizing, because it reduces the size of the workforce and thus leaves sharply fewer opportunities for upward career mobility and less job security for the future, is a prospect that can cool the heels of any aspiring employee. Increased workforce diversity in turn increases the variety of issues managers must address successfully to avoid demotivation among employees. With growing attention to political correctness (a.k.a. PC) and increased sensitivity to the ways people should be addressed and treated, it does not take much to alienate some employees by comments, looks, or gestures, behaviors that might have been barely noticed in the past or at least not openly challenged. The ensuing unpleasant atmosphere, including the prospects of lawsuits under Title VII of the Civil Rights Act of 1964 for subjecting people to adverse working conditions, can have dire consequences for productivity. Today's manager must be prepared to work with employees who are single parents, who have dependent older parents, who have physical and mental impairments, who represent more than one sexual orientation, and who represent a variety of cultural and ethnic backgrounds. This kind of diversity increases the odds for human relations mistakes with dire motivational consequences and quite naturally complicates efforts to encourage employees to be more productive.

Understanding motivation has always been a tall order, even before the recent organizational turmoil. The inconclusive nature of past inquiries into how the roles of managers and organizations help or hinder employee motivation and productivity has been made evident by the continuing publication of new and alternative motivation models as additions to a very rich body of literature. Several reasons explain why the hunt for the ultimate motivation theory is so difficult. They include the prospect that (1) personality differences may cause various individuals to react in different ways to possible motivators, and (2) changes in popular culture and societal values eventually alter the attractiveness of traditional inducements or, similarly, alter people's urge to satisfy certain needs. It is not surprising that there is no one theory or model that can help managers motivate all employees at all times. Yet, as noted by Gordon (1996), when a workforce becomes more diverse, recognizing the individuality of motivational needs becomes paramount. The employee's position in the organization, age, gender, education, marital status, or any other socioeconomic characteristic can be an important variable that reinforces or mitigates other forces that shape behavior. Thus it is suggested (Kreitner and Kinicki, 1995) that managers use a contingency approach, that is, that they attempt to match what they know about the individual, the situation, and the issue at hand with the strengths and weaknesses of various motivation theories, before deciding which one to follow. Understanding of and familiarity with the leading theories of motivation can therefore be instrumental when a manager feels the need to encourage stronger motivation in a particular individual.

The next part of this chapter provides the reader with a brief but critical review of some theories and models that have influenced the direction of thinking and research about motivation in the workplace.

MODELS OF MOTIVATION

Barnard (1938) and Homans (1961) attempt to explain the relationship between employees and the organization by refereeing the balance between the contributions employees make to the organization and the inducement they get from the organization. The exchange that takes place between the two parties allows us to view the relationships between employees and the organization as a kind of *psychological contract* (Rousseau and Parks, 1993). This contract may have attributes different from the legal document that reflects or guides the formal relations between the two parties but is likely to be more detrimental to employees' moral satisfaction, loyalty, and productivity. The parties to the psychological contract have specific expectations of each other. However, unlike the parties to a formal employment contract, the parties to the psychological contract may not share their understanding of the contractual relations, update each other when they change their understanding, or expect a change in the relations in order to keep the formal employment contract in place. When the expectations of the two parties to the psychological contract are met, the two parties are satisfied. When one of the parties feels an inequity in the contract, that party may initiate a change expressed as a request for a modification of the employment contract, the formal document that is open for scrutiny by outsiders. Thus unhappy employees may ask for a raise or better career opportunities. If they cannot get them, they may start looking for employment elsewhere or find ways to adjust their contributions and to bring them to the level of the perceived inducements they get from the organization. This point will be visited again later on in connection with the equity theory of motivation. Here it should be noted that the organization, too, may sense imbalance between the inducements it provides and the contributions it gets back from a given employee or subgroup of employees. The organization may seek to correct the imbalance by asking employees to improve the observed level of performance, by adjusting compensation—for example, by relating compensation more directly to the output produced—and by offering other tangible and intangible inducements. Managers can replace subperforming employees or they can get rid of the problem of poor performance in a given area by contracting out. Thus Moorhead and Griffin (1995) conclude that "a basic challenge faced by the organization, then, is to manage psychological contracts. The organization must ensure that it is getting value from its employees. At the same time it must ensure that it is providing employees with appropriate inducements" (p. 53).

Many factors may influence the extent to which either the employee or the organization feels that the psychological contract is fair. However, a good fit between the employee and the job, as a result of proper placement efforts, can go a long way toward facilitating such a mutual feeling. Selection-placement processes give the organization the opportunity to identify some important things about individual employees, such as personality traits and abilities. Hiring people whose personalities mesh well with the existing organizational culture and with the tasks they will be expected to carry out increases the odds that they will be successful and satisfied employees. Matching personalities, skills, and abilities with the right jobs increases the likelihood of meeting the employees' expectations while also ensuring that their assignments capitalize on important employee qualities for meeting organizational goals.

A textbook on organizational behavior (Kreitner and Kinicki, 1995) suggests that most contemporary theories of motivation are rooted partially in the principle of hedonism, which states that people seek pleasure and avoid pain. Other writers (Moorhead and Griffin, 1995) suggest that the drive to satisfy some important needs is the common denominator among various theories of motivation. Although the two claims are not mutually exclusive, it should be noted that too much emphasis on hedonism as a key to motivation implies an unflattering and extremely narrow view of human behavior and of the complexity of the relationships with fellow workers (Erez and Somech, 1996) that people experience at work.

Given the enormous amount of published research on motivation and the lack of consensus about this important subject, it is not surprising to find a variety of attempts to classify various theories of motivation. One of the more common ways is to classify motivation theories according to content—*what* motivates the individual—and process—*how* one gets motivated. The discussion that follows starts with a brief description of some of the leading theories in the content group before going on to describe some process theories.

Content Theories

Maslow's Hierarchy of Needs. The work of Abraham Maslow (1954) provided the key to a whole family of theories formulated to explain behavior as an effort to satisfy needs. At the bottom of Maslow's hierarchy of needs are the physiological needs. Any deficiency in these needs must be satisfied and the individual must be fundamentally comfortable before he or she will be in a position to meet a higher need. The security needs, shelter and protection, come second, followed by belonging needs. At the top of the hierarchy are the psychological needs (self-esteem and respect) and self-actualization needs.

Maslow's needs theory does not provide managers with much of a challenge for the most part. Managers can help employees meet the basic physiological needs by paying them reasonable wages and providing a comfortable physical environment. They can meet employees' security needs by offering life employment, a grievance and mediation system, and insurance and retirement benefits. By fostering the necessary conditions for successful teamwork (Erez and Somech, 1996) and by rewarding performance, managers can help employees meet their needs for belonging and self-esteem. The most difficult need to satisfy and a great challenge to managers and the employees themselves, seems to be the need for self-actualization. The magnitude of this challenge should be assessed in the context of the emerging new reality of the workplace. This new reality offers an interesting paradox. On the one hand, government regulations such as those that set standards about accommodations for workers with disabilities, maternity leave, the minimum wage, the maximum number of working hours, protection from work hazards, Social Security, pensions and retirement, unemployment compensation, medical insurance, and adverse working conditions arising from biases against age, gender, race, religion, or ethnic origin make the satisfaction of most needs easier than it was in earlier generations. Managers are left with less of a task when they must find ways to help employees satisfy the lower needs on the hierarchy because government regulations prescribe most of what they have to do as employers. Employees, too, find it easier in the 1990s to meet their basic needs, for two reasons: (1) because these same government regulations provide them with benchmarks that assist them in deciding when they have met a need and (2) because whatever is not provided or facilitated by employers (for example, child day care) is provided or facilitated by governments as a social service. It should be noted that many government services that are part of the so-called welfare state have since the mid-1950s made a deliberate effort to reduce the likelihood that the service recipient will feel a sense of humiliation and thus a possible threat to his or her self-esteem. The paradox is that at the same time as it has become easier for employers to meet employees' basic needs, organizations have reduced their workforces and turned more of their employees into self-employed contractors, an act that threatens people's sense of security about meeting their basic needs in the future. In fact, these changes in employment practices are shifting the responsibility for facilitating the necessary conditions for meeting the basic needs to the individuals themselves or the taxpaying public. This transformation that is taking place with contracting out and the emergence of the *hollow corporation* and *hollow government* (Halachmi and Holzer, 1993; Goldstein, 1990) means each individual now has the task of motivating himself or herself to secure and to carry out the contract(s) for mobilizing the means to meet basic needs. Yet as this transformation takes place, governments are starting to cut back on the scope of social services and the eligibility for them, burdening more people with the task of devoting their energies to meeting the lower rather than the higher survival needs.

For those who are still meaningfully employed, either by other organizations or on their own, the illusive need to be satisfied is still the need for self-actualization. Satisfying this need continues to be a challenge, as it ever was, for several reasons. It is not content specific. It does not lend itself to simple measurement or monitoring so that the individual or the manager can assess whether exerted efforts are making progress toward achieving it. In addition, once achieved, the sense of self-actualization may be temporary and may not even be recognized as self-actualization until after the fact. Even assuming that there were no questions about the validity of the Maslow hierarchy, it is not hard to see that at best it can help managers deal with the challenge of motivation when the needs to be satisfied are relatively low on the scale. Conversely, managers are left with little help from Maslow when it comes to the ultimate need, self-actualization. This need that is hardest to satisfy is also the need that is most likely to be experienced by the better-educated workforce in general and professional employees in particular. These employees, whose motivation may be particularly important to the organization due to the significant cost of their contributions and inducements, are more difficult to please than others. One reason is that they have more and higher expectations about the work they perform and thus a more complex relationship with their place of work. For example, for such employees doing what they were trained for may not be enough. Also the general reputation of the employer may be one of the variables that contribute to how they feel about their jobs and whether or not they experience self-actualization. Some employees may feel self-actualized working for an excellent agency while employees with similarly or even more challenging jobs at an agency that does not have a great reputation may not be as satisfied or motivated and may never experience self-actualization. Moreover, the conceptual and functional problems with the notion of self-actualization are not the only weakness of the Maslow hierarchy as a theory of motivation and a guide for managers.

In spite of the intuitive logic of Maslow's hierarchy of needs, there is little research to support the validity of many of the assumptions a manager must make in order to accept it. For example, a manager must assume that all individuals, regardless of age, attempt to satisfy physiological needs before proceeding up the hierarchy to satisfy psychological needs. A manager must accept the notion that satisfied needs do not motivate and at the same time assume that if lower needs become once again unsatisfied, the individual will give up the effort to satisfy higher needs until those lower needs can be satisfied again. In the same vein a manager must assume that all people experience the need to develop and reach self-actualization or to reach the same level of self-actualization. It does not take elaborate research to question some of these assumptions. One just has to think, for example, about the numerous examples of artists or scientists who in their striving to achieve artistic or scientific self-actualization compromised many of Maslow's lower-level needs: food, shelter, companionship, or the respect of others.

Herzberg's Two Factors Theory. Herzberg's *two factors theory* (1959) suggests on the one hand that *hygiene factors* (for example, pay, job security, working conditions, status) cause dissatisfaction when they are absent but do not finally satisfy or motivate employees when they are present. On the other hand, *intrinsic factors,* or *motivators* (for example, recognition and possibilities for growth and advancement), when present can satisfy employees and motivate them. However, when these motivators are absent, they do not greatly dissatisfy. The two factors theory does offer managers some guidelines for making employees more content on the job and more productive. However, there are questions about the methodology Herzberg used for collecting the empirical data to support his claims. According to some writers (Moorhead and Griffin, 1995), Herzberg's work has been scientifically scrutinized more often than other theories because it gained popularity so quickly. For our purposes here, it is important to note that Herzberg's division of aspects of the work situation into hygiene factors and motivators influenced a lot of subsequent discussion about the use of incentives, like performance-related pay, to induce higher performance (Halachmi and Holzer, 1987).

McClelland's Needs Theory. McClelland (1961) asserts that many needs are learned from culture but that there are three primary needs, and any one of them may explain most of any observed behavior in a given individual. The three primary needs are the need for achievement (nAch), the need for affiliation (nAff), and the need for power (nPow). Note that without much effort these three primary needs can be related to the clusters of needs used by other theories, as illustrated in Table 27.1.

According to McClelland, at any point in life one of these needs may be more dominant than the other two in influencing the individual's perception of reality. Thus an employee motivated by the power need will read a given situation as an opportunity to exercise power, to gain power, or to challenge power. The employee with a strong affiliation need will perceive the same situation in terms of social interaction and the relationships among all involved. The employee that has a stronger need for achievement will see in the same situation opportunities for feedback on performance, job-related problem solving, and so on.

According to McClelland, these needs are learned from the experience of coping with the environment; rewarded behaviors reoccur more often than unrewarded ones. To establish which need is dominant at a given time, McClelland used a projective test called the Thematic Apperception Test (TAT). Looking at a series of pictures, the individual taking the test is asked to tell in his or her own words what is going on in each picture, what led to that event, and what is

Table 27.1. Three Sets of Motivational Needs.

Maslow	Herzberg	McClelland
Physiological needs	Hygiene	
Safety and security		
Belongingness		Affiliation need (nAff)
Self-esteem	Motivator	Achievement need (nAch)
Self-actualization		Power need (nPow)

going to result from it in the future. The strongest need manifests itself and can be recognized through the individual's consistent choice of words and the similarity of the scenarios the individual uses to describe the pictures.

McClelland's needs theory has interesting implications for management in the context of efforts to enhance productivity through Total Quality Management (TQM). TQM empowers employees to make suggestions and to introduce changes that may improve performance, and this can provide some individuals with a method for meeting needs for achievement and affiliation. Participation in team efforts and the TQM process gives employees influence over their own work situations and the way work is performed by others, and for some individuals this may prove an opportunity to exercise power. Though TQM does not provide opportunities for exercising raw power over others, it nevertheless puts employees in positions where they can influence others more than they could expect to under other circumstances. In other words, TQM can give individuals with different needs the various opportunities to satisfy them.

Although the promise of McClelland's work has yet to be fully explored, there are some questions about the theory. The projective technique identifying the stronger of the three needs produces several challenges. From a methodological point of view, it is easy to see that it is hard to control for bias among the testers, who are likely to perceive an individual's responses in the context of their own needs. By the same token, it may be difficult to assess the exact point when the use of certain words or the perception of relations changes as a result of differences in an individual's cultural or societal norms. Two further examples of difficulties with the methodology may illustrate this point. First, it is hard to establish in a way that is not susceptible to differences in social mores the point at which an individual's drive to achieve becomes an instrument for getting acceptance, that is, a way of meeting the need for affiliation (or the other way around). Similarly, at what point does the individual's drive to achieve become a mask for the search for power, possibly as the individual is gaining recognition for being an expert on some subject? Second, in a picture of a room filled mostly with men and only one woman, what is the role or the position of the female? Depending where, when, and of whom the question is being asked, reaction to the picture may be very different: is she the boss, one of the guys, or a secretary? Interpretation of this image may have gone through many changes in the United States since the 1960s when McClelland introduced his ideas. In some countries even today, most respondents over a certain age are not likely to consider the prospect that the lady is the boss or a highly skilled professional.

Process Theories

Vroom's Expectancy Theory. Vroom's *expectancy theory* (1964) is one of the better known efforts in the process theory category. Vroom defines motivation as a process governing choices among alternative forms of voluntary activity, a process controlled by the individual. That is, the individual makes choices based on estimates of how well the expected results of given behavior are going to match up with or eventually lead to desired results. Motivation is a product of the individual's expectancy that a certain effort will lead to the intended performance, the instrumentality of this performance to achieving a certain result, and the desirability of this result for the individual. For example, a student will be motivated to study for an SAT exam if studying is likely to increase the odds for a higher score on the test, if getting a better score is seen as the most important factor in securing admission to the college the student prefers. A student will be less motivated if he or she is uncertain whether studying for the exam can in fact improve the score or whether the score is the most important determinant for college admission (low instrumentality) or if he or she is not enthusiastic about going to any particular college (valence). In short, motivation is determined by beliefs about the relationships among effort and performance and the attractiveness of the end result when it is perceived as a direct function of that performance. The weakness of the theory is in its hidden assumptions, such as these two: first, that the individual is a rational actor whose entire behavior is purposeful; second, that the attractiveness of the end result, rather than the opportunity to indulge in a certain behavior, induces the choice of behavior.

Expectancy theory has several implications for management. It suggests that managers should make an effort to help employees see the relationship between the various job activities they are expected to perform and the desired outcomes. To help employees avoid the frustration that results when the intended outcomes fail to materialize, managers should work with employees to establish realistic expectations. They need to find out the desired outcome an employee is seeking and to work with that employee to establish the necessary efforts to effect that outcome, given the employee's ability. In particular, managers can help employees develop a realistic assessment of their own abilities, and can point to ways of factoring that assessment into the effort needed to effect a desired outcome. To induce employees to make such an effort, management must present employees with reasonable odds for getting attractive rewards from the organization.

Adams's Equity Theory. *Equity theory* (Adams, 1965) attempts to explain the dynamics of the process used by employees to relate their perceived contribution to the inducements they get in return. The equity theory of motivation asserts that employees compare their efforts and rewards with those of their peers. Following such comparisons, individuals seek to restore equity, if necessary, by adjusting the effort they put forth or by trying to adjust what they get from their employer in accordance with what they think is fair. Equity is felt to exist when the individual's ratio between effort and reward equals the effort-reward ratio of the comparison target. When a disparity is sensed, the individual takes action to restore equity by increasing or decreasing work effort or, theoretically, reward as needed. Although the theory has serious limitations (for example, why would the comparison be made with one employee and not with another?), it has potential for explaining attitudes toward pay and compensation in general. The theory illustrates the salience of fairness as an American value, and the feeling of U.S. behavioral scientists that fairness is a factor that influences behavior in the workplace. So far there is little research to suggest that the U.S. notion of what constitutes fairness is an important variable in other than Western cultures.

Equity theory has several implications for managers. To start with, managers can help individuals make a more educated comparison of what they get for their efforts in comparison to others. They can provide employees with proper feedback on their performance and adjust the inducement package (that is, salary, status symbols, public show of appreciation) they offer the employee accordingly. When supervisors maintain one-on-one relationships with employees, they may be able to sense when a given employee starts to feel a sense of inequity, and deal with it before the employee takes a corrective measure that involves reduction of effort or a move to another job. Experienced supervisors may be in a position to help employees reassess their contribution to the organization more realistically, to help them overcome any underestimation of the contributions made by the employees to whom they compare themselves, or to take the necessary steps to get the organization to improve the inducement package. A consistent effort to document and study instances of concern with equity across the board may help the organization to identify those areas where not enough is being done to educate employees about the merit of each contribution and about the organization's way of relating inducements to effort. Equity theory should also remind managers that perception is reality and that the *appearance* of what they do, of how they treat different employees, has implications for employee motivation.

For public organizations, equity theory poses a specific problem. If public employees (especially managers) must perform like their colleagues in the private sector (as is more and more the case) and at the same time labor relations are "normalized" to resemble those common in the private sector (no lifetime employment, strict performance measurement, and so on), it can be expected that these public employees will judge their jobs and salaries in comparison to those of private employees also. But if public managers ask for more authority, greater responsibilities, or better compensation, politicians get upset because they do not want to give up their own influence. What politicians want, as Vice President Al Gore put it in his report for the National Performance Review (1993), is a government that "works better and costs less."

Goal Setting Theory. Locke and Latham (Locke, 1968; Latham and Locke, 1979; Locke and Latham, 1990) assert that the primary determinants of behavior are the individual's conscious goals and intentions. Important attributes of goals are goal specificity (degree of goal clarity); goal difficulty (performance level required to achieve the goal); goal intensity (process of setting the goal and determining how to achieve it); and goal commitment (amount of effort expended to achieve the goal). In this *goal setting theory,* individuals begin to be motivated when they have clear goals, when achieving the goals presents a challenge but is not hard enough to discourage an effort, when what should be done to achieve goals is clear, and when the individual is in a position to make the necessary effort.

Clear goals are necessary but not sufficient for motivating employees. The right kind of feedback on performance is equally important. This feedback can come from different sources: from managers, colleagues, and service recipients and also from the employee's own assessment of the work performed in comparison to such benchmarks as past performance, performance of others, work plans, or professional standards. Another important aspect of motivation is the work environment (that is, the availability of resources; the physical setting; the proper tools, including IT; and the like).

Building on their goal-setting theory and elements of other theories, Locke and Latham (1990) have also developed the *high performance cycle.* Although this theory has some interesting implications for managers, there is currently not enough research to support it.

Reward Systems. Rewards are important motivators, and a total reward system includes both monetary and nonmonetary compensation (Schuler and Jackson, 1996). Monetary compensation requires an assessment of the employee's contribution to the organization. The core parameters of direct monetary compensation are derived from sources such as job descriptions, job classifications, performance appraisal records, and longevity with the organization. However, the influence of these parameters on the actual compensation is particularly sensitive to the prevailing conditions in the business environment, that is, the general state of the economy and the relative cost or difficulty of replacing the employee under consideration. Nonmonetary rewards such as recognition or job security may have no cash value to employees (although they are not likely to be free to the employer), yet they may be as important to employees as those rewards that contribute to their net worth when they go out to secure a loan for a new house or car. As a matter of fact, under some conditions, nonmonetary rewards may be more important than monetary rewards, as may be the case when employees choose to take a job with another organization or opt for early retirement. As noted by Schuler and Jackson (1996), job security became an important nonmonetary reward during the 1990s. Other important nonmonetary rewards are recognition and more autonomy and more responsibilities in the job.

Inner Satisfaction and External Inducements. Although internal satisfaction was recognized long ago as an important source of motivation, the question of whether employers can influence it at will has yet to be settled.

As reported by Kohn (1987), creativity and intrinsic interest can diminish when carrying out an assignment that involves the winning of a tangible reward. Because this proposition is not self-evident or intuitive, it is worthwhile to examine the argument and the examples that Kohn offers. It is an article of faith for many managers that rewards promote better performance. Indeed, to most people the term reward itself means that a desired result was attained. To those who have been superficially exposed to various motivation theories, bestowing an award as a measure of encouraging a given behavior is consistent with Skinner's concept of *operant conditioning* ([1953] 1965). Yet Kohn finds that a growing body of research suggests that this law is not nearly as ironclad as was once thought. He notes (Kohn, 1987, 1992) that several research findings suggest that rewards can lower rather than promote performance levels, especially when the desired performance involves creativity. For example, one study showed "that any task, no matter how enjoyable it once seemed, would be devalued if it were presented as a means rather than an end" (Kohn, 1987). Still other studies showed that intrinsic interest in a task—the sense that something is worth doing for its own sake and an important element in not-for-profit and public organizations—typically declines when a reward is attached for doing the task. Similarly, young children who are rewarded for drawing are less likely to draw on their own than are children who draw just for the fun of it, teenagers offered rewards for playing word games enjoy the games less and score more poorly on them than those who play with no rewards, and employees who are praised for meeting a manager's expectations of them rather than for doing a good job suffer a drop in motivation.

Thus Kohn (1987, 1992) goes on to conclude that if a reward—money, awards, praise, or winning a contest—comes to be seen as the reason one is engaging in an activity, that activity will be viewed as less enjoyable in its own right. And if Kohn and the studies he uses are correct, it is possible that managers may unwittingly be squelching interest and discouraging innovation among workers, students, and artists when they take certain paths of action intending to encourage these aspects of productivity.

Motivation Factor Summary

Content and process theories taken together, the most important factors that influence motivation are characteristics of the individual with respect to his or her needs, expectations of the individual with respect to his or her capacities, the job content, and the characteristics of the organization in which the individual has to work. Yet the debate about the functional and dysfunctional effects of external incentives has not been settled, and that is one reason why the next section of this chapter provides a brief survey of common approaches to the management of incentive plans.

and avoid frustration at work" (p. 146). Toward that end employers must foster such specific conditions as

- A pleasant physical environment where the job is performed
- Job designs that allow employees to use all their abilities in ways that allow personal and professional growth
- Flexible schedules that are family-friendly and conducive to the professional and social life of the individual
- A work environment where individual rights are protected and many employee idiosyncrasies are tolerated if not facilitated
- Teamwork and communication that allow employees to be aware of what is going on and to participate meaningfully in decisions that shape organizational goals and their own compensation and careers

The *job characteristics model* (Hackman and Oldham, 1975) points to the same conditions. According to this model, positive behavioral results—high motivation, high satisfaction, better performance, and lower absenteeism and turnover—are caused by three elements of the task experience: employee experience of usefulness, employee experience of responsibility for the end result, and employee knowledge about the results of the effort. These three task elements in turn are influenced by five job characteristics. The alternation of activities in the job, the extent to which the job consists of a series of coherent tasks that lead to visible results (task identity), and the significance of the task for others and the organization influence employee experience of usefulness. Autonomy in the job to make decisions about job planning and job execution influences employee experience of responsibility for the end result, and the feedback of job results influences employee knowledge about the results of the effort. Because not every individual reacts in the same way to a job with high motivational potential, the model supposes that the need for personal growth will intervene in the relationship between the job characteristics and the three elements of job experience, and in the relationship between the job experience and the behavioral results.

Organizational responses to employees' QWL expectations include the introduction of flextime work schedules and of benefit plans that allow employees to select the times and the kinds of benefits most suitable to their needs. Sponsoring quality circles (QC) and introducing TQM is a way for the organization to allow many employees to have a greater say about organizational goals and work practices. Provision of day-care and parent-care facilities in close proximity to the workplace and of tuition assistance programs allows employees to meet family needs and professional and personal growth needs more easily.

However, QWL plans have never been especially common in the public sector. The private sector has adopted them as part of collective bargaining agree-

INCENTIVES IN THE WORKPLACE

The Scanlon Plan

The Scanlon Plan was introduced in the private sector by Joseph Scanlon, a leader in the United Steelworkers of America in the 1930s. The plan is based on a collaborative effort between management and employees to improve organizational performance and to share the benefits realized from such improvement. A key element of the plan is therefore the element of cooperation, which is fostered by offering workers an active role in the organization through an exchange of information, the introduction of a suggestion system designed to increase efficiency and to reduce cost, and the use of an agreed-upon formula for the distribution of cash bonuses based on increases in productivity. The plan is likely to be at its best when the participating workforce is small enough for employees to see the relationship between a suggestion for a modification of the way work is carried out and a reward that recognizes the resulting improvement in productivity. It is of special interest that the concept of the Scanlon Plan, introduced in the 1930s, was promoted with such benefits as "elimination of repetitive work to correct mistakes" or "elimination of nonproductive/unnecessary work" and "teamwork" or "management-employee cooperation," benefits attributed in the 1990s, in much the same language, to Total Quality Management (TQM), reengineering, and the learning organization. The Scanlon plan has also been presented as an option for making government agencies work smarter through cooperation of management and employees to improve quality control, for eliminating unnecessary and nonproductive work, for improving communication, and for "developing a greater sense of responsibility for completing work in a timely and cost effective fashion" (Institute of Public Performance, 1980, p. 3).

Although on its face the Scanlon Plan has a lot to offer, its implementation across the board is not a simple matter, and its long-term contribution to real productivity gains is not certain for several reasons (Institute of Public Performance, 1980). First, the plan assumes voluntary acceptance of plan participation due to the attractiveness of a future monetary bonus. It further assumes that because other members of each group (employees or management) will have a stake in winning the award, individuals will be encouraged, if not pressured, by the dynamics of the group relations to come up with suggestions to improve work and generate savings that will translate into bonuses. These two assumptions may not be valid when some members of the group (designated as such by the organization) are professionals who are concerned about keeping their professional autonomy or about a possible conflict between productivity gains and maintenance of professional standards. The paring of the workforce in many public and private organizations in the 1990s increased the sense of *us* versus *them* among nonmanagerial employees on the one hand and members of the executive ranks on the other. A kind of paranoia also increased that encouraged the belief that additional increases in productivity might be reached only by further paring of the nonmanagerial ranks. Consequently, the incentive to cooperate with other employees on productivity improvement is not as strong as it used to be, and the promise of a bonus (a practice employees may associate with previous layoffs) may not be as attractive as it used to be.

A second reason for doubting the effectiveness of the Scanlon Plan is that even though an employee suggestion may contribute to improvement in productivity, such gains may be offset by adverse conditions outside the organization. When the organization as a whole is not doing well, it is hard to justify any allocation of bonuses, particularly in the public sector. Attempts to recognize the contributions of individual employees in the U.S. Department of Defense (DOD), for example, resulted in loud public criticism, because the public was cognizant only of overpriced DOD purchases and was not able to consider the contributions of single employees outside that context. As far as the public is concerned, a civil servant's job description *requires* being alert for ways to avoid wasting resources and being creative in not spending unnecessary tax dollars, and therefore these are not matters to be singled out for special reward. Popular reactions to rewards received by federal employees parallel the U.S. General Accounting Office (1993) finding of a "perception that the results of an effective performance management system—improving employee performance, establishing accountability, and promoting employee trust—are not being achieved" (p. 2).

Another problem with any Scanlon-like plan is the difficulty of arriving at an agreed-upon formula for measuring productivity gains, ensuring that all employees understand it, and carrying out the measurement to the satisfaction of all the concerned parties. Here one of the concerns is always the prospect that employees will do what is necessary to score right on the formula and suppress or manipulate data that might interfere with it. In other words, employees will do what is demanded of them by the conditions of getting the bonus instead of doing things right from a professional or civic point of view.

Employee Stock Ownership Plans

Employee stock ownership plans (ESOPs) share some of the assumptions behind the Scanlon Plan and other profit-sharing programs that exist mostly in the private sector. Here too the idea is to motivate employees by giving them a stake in the success of the organization. Employee ownership can be accomplished in a variety of ways. Employees can buy stock directly, be given it as a bonus, buy stock with the benefit of stock options, or purchase stock at a discount through profit-sharing plans. Employees may own shares as a cooperative, with each person having a single vote, or they may own individual portfolios of different sizes. Although the ESOP concept can be very attractive when applied in a consistent manner across the board, it has the potential of backfiring if some groups of employees, for example, salaried employees or managers above a certain rank, get

preferential treatment. The stock options made available to top corporate America in the 1990s but not to their subordinates at media attention and criticism. For example, CBS News broadcas 1996 a series of reports highlighting the bonanza experienced by who got stock options as part of their employment contracts ployees were taking cutbacks in salary or facing layoffs.

Although plans like the Scanlon Plan or ESOPs may not be re to managers in the public sector, the attractiveness of such sche steadily growing in the 1990s. This development reflects the tren able pay programs tied to individual, team, subunit, or organiz, mance. In other words, managers like to use these plans becaus employees with financial incentives to work harder and at the san rectly related both to employees' performance (as individuals or teams) and to the performance of the organization as a whole. E tant, and in some cases even more important, the use of variable plans allows managers to reward employees without saddling the with the future financial obligations that result from merit raises by Lubin (1997), "Routine salary increases for nonunion empl headed for extinction." Yet she goes on to say that "the shift away merit raises could lower morale and lessen loyalty in an already a force" (p. B1).

The renewed interest in variable compensation plans in the 1 serves close attention because it represents a move away from cc forts to provide employees with a *wholesome* work environm something more than economic, that is, external, incentives. T which were very common in the late 1960s and in the 1970s, invo cept of quality of working life.

QWL: The Concept and the Promise

The basic premise of *quality of working life* (QWL) programs is th who feel better about their jobs are likely to be more productive. Carrell, Elbert, and Hatfield (1995), one is likely to have a better Q work meets more and more personal needs, such as security, respo self-esteem" (p. 31). Making work more rewarding, reducing emp eties, encouraging more participation in decisions relating to w ployment, and team building are examples of QWL approache intuitively the QWL premise seems to be true, closer examination r questions about its validity. This section describes some basic QW fore going on to examine those questions.

According to Glueck (1982), "To attract and retain competent em ployers must offer high quality jobs and working conditions beca ees wish to maximize the satisfaction of needs, use their abilities t

ments with unions and to retain talented employees or to attract them from the competition. In the public sector many of the elements of QWL are seen as extravagances by legislators, who are reluctant to raise taxes to fund them. Mere talk about them seems to play into the hands of government critics who, from lack of understanding, claim that public employees are overcompensated.

These attitudes were not helpful, yet the demise of QWL as an approach to organizing public-sector work and human resource management was the result of two other factors. One had to do with the assumptions about motivation satisfaction and productivity. The other had to do with the evolution of the global village and its implication for competitiveness.

Although motivated employees may be more productive than unmotivated employees, job satisfaction is not a sufficient condition for motivation or productivity. Content employees may be too slow to search for innovations. Some frustration can be a source of motivation, and unhappy employees may be very productive as they try to resolve their frustrations or make themselves attractive to other employers.

In addition, the workaholic culture of the baby boom generation changed some of the significance of the family-friendly work schedule. And the pressure to become lean and mean in order to survive global competition required employers in the early 1990s to contract out services, lay off employees, and reduce overhead expenses. Under these circumstances job security and employability became more important than workplace ambiance and being snubbed and excluded from participation in decision making. Though a culture of fear and uncertainty is not healthy or desired in the long run, it seems to serve corporate managers in their efforts to minimize the cost of labor. Due to recent developments in information technology, work can be shifted from localities with high labor costs to places where pay is low, from places where employees insist on collective bargaining to places where pay is by the piece and minimum wages or maximum hours of work per week do not exist. Because of these realities QWL is a thing of the past in the corporate world, and given its demise there, it is likely to be impossible for managers to retain it, let alone to expand it, in the vulnerable public sector, which is already constantly under attack for not being as efficient as the private sector.

MANAGEMENT OF PERFORMANCE: EMERGING TRENDS

The growing pressures to contract out and the emergence of the hollow corporation and hollow government along with the developments in information technology suggest that the classic roles of the manager, as identified by Mintzberg (1973), may not exist in the future. The motivational and leadership roles of the manager may shrink and the responsibility for overall coordination and strategic planning may increase. As *ad-hocracy* (Toffler, 1970; Halachmi, 1989) replaces bureaucracy, the responsibility for creating the necessary conditions for external and internal motivation, incentives, and satisfaction is being shifted from organizations to individuals themselves. As the contractual nature of the relationship between the individual and the organization changes—and the individual moves from being an employee to being a vendor of goods and services—compensation and bonuses become a function of the individual's management of his or her own affairs. Professional growth and self-actualization, under the new conditions of the ad-hocracy, are likewise left to the individual's discretion and initiative. Under these conditions success is likely to be more a function of the individual's own decisions and willingness to make an effort and less a matter of longevity with the organization or of socioeconomic characteristics that might once have given the individual preference. Under these conditions maturity and natural talent may result in many rewards to individuals that are denied, especially to public employees, under current legal regulations. At the same time, issues of social justice and a sense of civil unrest among those who do not advance due to lack of talent or willingness to make the effort may raise new questions about the proper role of managers and organizations in society.

CONCLUSION: WHAT CAN A MANAGER LEARN FROM A GOOD THEORY?

A good theory of motivation is one that allows managers to understand what makes individual employees tick and which options are the most promising for influencing what makes employees tick. Yet, because there is no one theory of motivation that is most useful across different groups of employees and across individuals with different personalities and socioeconomic characteristics, managers need to familiarize themselves with many theories and be cognizant of their strengths and weaknesses. Also managers should remember that in many cases they cannot motivate subordinates because only they can motivate themselves. However, even in these cases, managers can foster the conditions in which it is easier for people to motivate themselves. From the theories presented here, we distill these recommendations:

- Charge employees with challenging, but attainable, goals.
- Give them honest feedback on their performance; aim to help them learn and to reinforce their self-efficacy.
- Enlarge their competencies and responsibilities (create challenges) and facilitate the development of each employee's vision of a future and a career with the organization.

- Create good working conditions (effective and efficient work processes, sufficient and effective tools and means, good group atmosphere and culture, sufficient participation).

- Tune your interventions to the needs of the individual employee (tailor-made management).

- Prevent the negative spiral in which insufficient performance leads to more managerial control and less employee autonomy, which leads to decreasing employee commitment, which leads to decreasing employee performance, and so forth. (Avoiding this spiral is especially important.) Two other dangers to avoid are, first, excessive work pressure that leads to stress and burnout and so to decreasing performance (another negative spiral can start from here), and second, the presence of an incorrect self-image in people about their capacities and potentials. Incorrect self-image can lead people to unrealistic career expectations, for example, and to frustration when these expectations are not met.

- Do whatever you can to ensure that employees feel they are treated fairly. That means taking all the necessary actions to ensure that justice is not only done but is seen (by everyone) to be done.

- Demonstrate to employees that you and the organization care about them and their welfare as much as you care about managers' perks, the operation's financial health, and all the organization's nonhuman assets.

References

Adams, L. S. "Injustice in Social Exchanges." In L. Berkowitz (ed.), *Advances in Experimental Social Psychology.* Orlando, Fla.: Academic Press, 1965.

Barnard, C. I. *The Functions of the Executive.* Cambridge, Mass.: Harvard University Press, 1938.

Carrell, M. R., Elbert, N. F., and Hatfield, R. D. *Human Resource Management.* (5th ed.) Upper Saddle River, N.J.: Prentice Hall, 1995.

Civil Rights Act of 1964. U.S. Code, vol. 42, sec. 1981 et seq. (Title VII at 2000e.)

Erez, M., and Somech, A. "Is Group Productivity Loss the Rule or the Exception? Effects of Culture and Group-Based Motivation." *Academy of Management Journal,* 1996, *39,* 1513–1537.

Glueck, W. F. *Personnel.* (3rd ed.) Plano, Tex.: Business Publications, 1982.

Goldstein, M. L. "The Shadow Government." *Government Executive,* 1990, *22*(5), 30–31.

Gordon, J. R. *Organizational Behavior.* (5th ed.) Upper Saddle River, N.J.: Prentice Hall, 1996.

Hackman, J. R., and Oldham, G. R. "Development of the Job Diagnostic Survey." *Journal of Applied Psychology,* 1975, *60,* 159–170.

Halachmi, A. "Ad-Hocracy and the Future of the Civil Service." *International Journal of Public Administration,* 1989, *12,* 617–650.

Halachmi, A. "Information Technology, Human Resources Management, and Productivity." In C. Ban and N. M. Riccucci (eds.), *Public Personnel Management: Current Concerns, Future Challenges.* New York.: Longman, 1991.

Halachmi, A., and Holzer, M. "Merit Pay, Performance Targeting and Productivity." *Review of Public Personnel Administration,* 1987, *7*(2), 80–91.

Halachmi, A., and Holzer, M. "Towards a Competitive Public Administration." *International Review of Administrative Sciences,* 1993, *59,* 29–45.

Herzberg, F. *The Motivation to Work.* (2nd ed.) New York: Wiley, 1959.

Homans, G. C. *Social Behavior in Its Elementary Forms.* Orlando, Fla.: Harcourt Brace, 1961.

Institute of Public Performance. *Possible Application of the Scanlon Plan in State Government.* Report to the New York State Joint Labor Management Committee on Work Environment and Productivity. Albany, N.Y.: Governor's Office of Employee Relations, 1980.

Kohn, A. "Studies Find Reward Often No Motivator." *Boston Globe,* Jan. 19, 1987, p. 43.

Kohn, A. *No Contest: The Case Against Competition.* Boston: Houghton Mifflin, 1992.

Kreitner, R., and Kinicki, A. *Organizational Behavior.* (3rd ed.) Burr Ridge, Ill.: Irwin, 1995.

Latham, G. P., and Locke, E. A. "Goal Setting: A Motivational Technique That Works." *Organizational Dynamics,* 1979, *8*(2), 68–80.

Locke, E. A. "Toward a Theory of Task Performance and Incentives." *Organizational Behavior and Human Performance,* 1968, *3,* 157–189.

Locke, E. A., and Latham, G. P. *Toward a Theory of Goal Setting and Task Performance.* Upper Saddle River, N.J.: Prentice Hall, 1990.

Lubin, J. S. "Don't Count on That Merit Raise This Year." *Wall Street Journal,* Jan. 7, 1997, pp. B1, B6.

Maslow, A. H. *Motivation and Personality.* New York: HarperCollins, 1954.

McClelland, D. C. *The Achieving Society.* New York: Van Nostrand Reinhold, 1961.

Mintzberg, H. *The Nature of Managerial Work.* New York: HarperCollins, 1973.

Moorhead, G., and Griffin, R. W. *Organizational Behavior: Managing People and Organizations.* (4th ed.) Boston: Houghton Mifflin, 1995.

National Performance Review. *From Red Tape to Results: Creating a Government That Works Better and Costs Less.* Washington, D.C.: U.S. Government Printing Office, 1993.

Rousseau, D. M., and Parks, J. M. "The Contracts of Individuals and Organizations." In L. L. Cummings and B. M. Staw (eds.), *Research in Organizational Behavior.* Vol. 15. Greenwich, Conn.: JAI Press, 1993.

Schuler, R. S., and Jackson, S. E. *Human Resource Management: Positing for the 21st Century.* (6th ed.) Minneapolis, Minn.: West, 1996.

Skinner, B. F. *Science and Human Behavior.* New York: Free Press, 1965. (Originally published 1953.)

State of Oklahoma. *A Government as Good as Our People.* Norman, Okla.: Governor's Commission on Government Performance, 1995.

Toffler, A. *Future Shock.* New York: Random House, 1970.

Toffler, A. *The Third Wave.* New York: Bantam, 1980.

Toffler, A. *The Power Shift.* New York: Bantam, 1990.

U.S. General Accounting Office. *Performance Management: How Well Is the Government Dealing with Poor Performers?* GAO/GGD-91–7. Washington, D.C.: U.S. General Accounting Office, 1990.

U.S. General Accounting Office. *The Changing Workforce.* GAO/T-GGD-92–61. Washington, D.C.: U.S. General Accounting Office, 1992.

U.S. General Accounting Office. *Federal Performance Management.* GAO/GGD-93–57. Washington, D.C.: U.S. General Accounting Office, 1993.

Vroom, V. H. *Work and Motivation.* New York: Wiley, 1964.

CHAPTER TWENTY-EIGHT

Work Management
and Job Evaluation Systems
in a Government Environment

Gilbert B. Siegel

This chapter discusses concepts, methods, and uses of job evaluation. Among areas considered are the evolution and importance of job evaluation, components of job evaluation systems, and various evaluation methodologies. Attention is given to the comparatively new concept of broadbanding, which fuses such constructs as career, job evaluation, compensation, and workforce management. The chapter closes with a description of system development using in-house staff or consultants or both, and a procedural example of the application of one methodology: the factor-point system.

IMPORTANCE OF JOB EVALUATION
SYSTEMS IN GOVERNMENT

Historical Evolution: The Title's the Thing—
the Job's the Thing—the Person's the Thing

When civil service reform first began at the federal level in the United States during the late nineteenth century, it emphasized candidate selection and the prohibition of political influence in that selection. However, it was not long after initial reforms were installed that the vagaries of compensation levels also became an issue. Congress heard complaints from civil servants about disparities between titles of assignments and pay. Persons doing the same thing were compensated differently, sometimes significantly so. This no doubt was a hangover from the spoils system that the reforms were to correct.

As the Industrial Revolution matured in the United States, some of its organizing principles also influenced government, especially Frederick W. Taylor's concepts of job analysis and Hugo Musterberg's ideas on industrial psychology, particularly selection. Though Taylor's chief concern was increasing efficiency, he pioneered the use of job analysis for describing an individual's work in component elements, and he also advocated and used standardizing of positions. These techniques led to the first job evaluation system in history based on the standardized position clustered into series, classes, and grades. Installed in the city of Chicago early in the twentieth century, the system was then adopted by other jurisdictions and was established in the federal government by the Classification Act of 1923. Thus the idea became firmly established of the job as the object of compensation, rather than the incumbent.

As the close of the twentieth century approaches, the design principles of the Industrial Revolution have been found to be inadequate. Indeed, people have railed against them for many years as organizational environments have come to require more flexible and adaptable workforces only to be frustrated by the organization and management principles of *scientific management*. Thus the traditional concept of *rank in person* (in contrast to *rank in position* or *rank in corps*), rejected for the most part by civil service reformers in the nineteenth century, has now been resurrected, though perhaps unconsciously so, through broadbanding. Also new to compensation practice and gaining some currency are various versions of team performance and reward systems. From the standpoint of management and compensation these concepts are emphasizing the worth and reward of the individual more than the job.

Job Evaluation, Work Design, and the Job Hierarchy

From the perspective of scientific management, executives create organization through a process of division of labor and task specialization. At higher and intermediate levels this means factoring organizational goals into means for carrying out objectives and results in an ends-means hierarchy. For example, an overall organizational goal might be to promote the health and welfare of military veterans. This is carried out through the means of providing various benefits (for example, insurance, burial, disability, and educational) and delivering health services. The benefits and services then become subgoals, which are carried out through means such as disability payments and hospitals—and so forth, hierarchically. Various principles are applied in specializing or departmentalizing. These so-called classical principles of organization include various bases for organizing work into department units (for example, by major processes applied, such as engineering; geographic location; or clientele served) and other traditional concepts such as span of supervision, unity of command, and hierarchical coordination.

At operating levels, work is not viewed as units of specialized management; work is organized in flows, a series of work segments linked in processes. Segments in turn are clustered, also based on principles of specialization, and standardized to create *positions*—each position the work of one individual.

From a traditional management perspective, positions have to be grouped into abstract categories known generically as *jobs,* or *classes.* These groupings allow organizations to manage variety through fewer categories. Jobs similarly classified have common titles, similar duties and responsibilities, and similar pay ranges and qualification requirements—all of this reflected in the job description and specification.

Job evaluation creates a hierarchy—the organization's *value system for jobs.* Usually, this value system uses various criteria that relate to the nature of the work and the worker qualifications required. It may also be modified by the realities of the marketplace for particular jobs.

Contemporary concepts have emphasized fewer hierarchical levels and have broadened performance categories, looking at the ability to perform the requirements of entire processes or to fill nearly open-ended *virtuoso* jobs. Job evaluation must of course be adapted to such changes.

Uses of Job Evaluation in Government

The place in the value system of a given job's worth is reflected in compensation, particularly in the form of a base rate or range of pay. Thus the value system is usually important to employees as well as to management because it establishes the basis for equity, at least it has traditionally. Other factors may be influential in actual rates of pay. Modern compensation concepts emphasize the tailoring of pay to the individual in a variety of ways. Some of these will be considered later.

The job hierarchy is used for more than determining compensation, particularly in public organizations. It serves as a general guide in recruitment and selection; it is a tool for redesigning organizational processes; and it assists in the management of career planning, training and development, assignments, and reductions in force. It also forms the basis for personnel system planning and controls. For example, in planning, the job hierarchy plays a part in determination of future staffing needs and costs in terms of both existing and different occupations; it bears on reorganizations in which decisions about responsibilities and assignments are influenced by job descriptions and specifications; and it has a role in the various personnel research studies that use occupational categories to generalize findings (as in human resource forecasting). In the area of control the job hierarchy influences average grade-level ceilings; although based on pay standardization, they are rooted in the job hierarchy, budgetary controls on positions (which limit authority to employ and pay), and audit controls to verify that positions are appropriately allocated and that they are authorized.

COMPONENTS OF A JOB EVALUATION SYSTEM

A distinction inherent in this discussion is that between crafting a job evaluation system and operating under one. This chapter emphasizes system development. However, in either case a manager has to grasp design components in order to understand the applicable concepts. Once the system(s) is developed, then all positions involved are allocated to the system(s).

Objectives

Not all job evaluation systems have the multiple uses and objectives just described. In fact it has been argued that these secondary uses complicate the basic mission of job evaluation, which is to create the organizational value system for jobs—value in turn being reflected in pay. For example, it would be possible to use very general criteria for allocating positions to jobs, or classes, if compensation was the only purpose. However, greater precision is required when the description is to be used as the basis for testing in promotions and for making other career decisions while adhering to civil rights law.

Scope of the System: Who Is Covered?

Will the job evaluation plan integrate all positions from janitor to chief executive officer, or will there be separate systems for, say, professionals, managers, office clerical and technical personnel, trades, and so on? It has been argued that different ranking criteria are needed for different positions. Although a common set of criteria might be applied to all types of positions, separate pay standardizations will prevent *grade creep,* an affliction particularly of public bureaucracies. Grade creep will be discussed here and in the next chapter.

Evaluation Factors

The essence of job evaluation is the rating or ranking of jobs by their relative worth. The value system used is composed of *job evaluation factors* (also called *allocation factors, classification factors,* or *compensable factors*). Technically, these factors need to be present in different amounts in various jobs, to be minimized in number (fewer is better), to be discrete in meaning to avoid double weighting, to be agreed to by employees, and to be found to some degree in all positions in the system. Also, from the traditional job evaluation perspective, it can be added that each factor must measure aspects of jobs, not incumbents. The following factors are commonly used: job requirements, responsibility, working conditions, physical demands, difficulty of work, personal relationships, and leadership and management.

Methodologies

Later, I discuss whole job ranking, position classification, point rating, factor comparison, and factor-point ranking. All of these systems are found in some form in organizations. Three additional hybrid approaches are also briefly considered: equitable payment, the Paterson method, and the Hay Guide Chart Profile. Among the latter only the Hay method, which is proprietary, is extensively applied.

Data-Gathering Activities

Management and employees should be trained to participate in the job analysis. Usually, expense dictates that questionnaires be used and that a limited sample of interview audits be conducted to verify questionnaire data. *Position description questionnaires* (PDQs), as the basic data-gathering instruments are known, and audits focus on three types of data. First are general data about the respondent (position title, location information, supervisor, salary). Second are data about the work of the individual, that is, the position (duties and responsibilities) and the qualifications required (knowledge, skills, abilities, and minimum requirements). In addition, the Americans with Disabilities Act of 1990 imposes a more contemporary requirement. Tasks must also be identified by whether or not they are essential to the work of the position. An essential task or duty is one that could not be reallocated to another position as a reasonable accommodation for a disabled person assigned to the position. Third are data about the individual's work in terms of the several job evaluation factors. PDQs are gathered from all employees.

Benchmark Positions

Key or *benchmark positions* serve as another part of the database for development of the job evaluation system(s). They are also important in developing salary standardization and in surveying labor markets. These benchmark positions are usually few in number—1 to 10 percent of all the positions covered by an evaluation plan. These positions may be treated as jobs (remember the distinction between jobs and positions) because they usually represent a range of positions involving large numbers of employees and because they are important in the organizational structure, may be used often in collective bargaining, are well known by executives and labor leadership, are relatively stable in content, are good reference points for levels of difficulty and responsibility, and are susceptible to precise definition.

JOB EVALUATION METHODOLOGIES

Perhaps the simplest form of job value differentiation is not a system: it is simply that the boss pays some jobs more than others. This is a type of whole job ranking, in which jobs compensated at different levels yield a de facto job evaluation system. Alternatively, the boss may value certain jobs or people more than others without awarding differential compensation. Later this chapter discusses a method of allocating positions to broad bands, in which job evaluation, career paths, personal rank, and pay levels are combined, and one method of broadband allocation is to rank whole positions relative to limited criteria. Usually, however, job evaluation requires considerably more rationalization. Most methodologies share some common elements: differentiation of occupational families, rating or ranking of positions, and allocation criteria or some type of standards. I begin the discussion of methodologies with position classification, the granddaddy of all such systems.

Position Classification

Position classification differentiates all positions as to kind of work and level of work. The former refers to the general nature of the work performed, the latter to factors such as level of complexity, supervision received or given, and technical knowledge required. Thus clerks and scientists perform different kinds of work, but both kinds have various levels. Certain clerks must have a detailed knowledge of regulations that is not expected of others, and some scientists perform routine tests while others devise completely new methodologies. Usually kind and level of work are divided by several lines of differentiation. When there are few distinctions, broad classes tend to result; whereas when there are many, the class structure is narrow. (Class, as already indicated, has the same meaning as job, but class is the term commonly used in the methodology of position classification.)

Classes are ranked within occupational series, and positions are ranked within classes, based on their standing relative to the classification factors used. When this type of system was first initiated it used verbal standards and factors to determine rank both within an occupational series and within a class. Later various quantification aids were introduced.

The positions in each class are sufficiently alike that they can be clustered under the same broad qualification requirements, the same tests of fitness, and the same scale of pay. Classes are described by standards. A class standard usually consists of an official title, a brief statement of the kind and level of work, identification of the factors that distinguish this class from others, examples of duties and responsibilities, and employee qualification requirements.

From Point Rating and Factor Comparison to Factor-Point Systems

The only objective of both point rating and factor comparison is compensation, in contrast to the several purposes of position classification.

Point Rating. Instead of being a global system, as position classification was first envisioned to be, *point rating* is applied to positions differentiated by general criteria into such groups as office clerical and technical workers, blue-collar workers, and professionals. Factors to be compensated must meet the criteria previously listed in the evaluation factors section. For each evaluation plan the factors are defined and then ranked quantitatively so that each factor has a point value. Based on empirical differences among the benchmark positions used to construct the system, each factor is then divided into defined levels or degrees. Degree levels represent portions of the factor's total numeric value. Positions can then be graded, or allocated to a system, by comparing their position descriptions factor by factor and level by level until total points can be allocated for each and all factors and totaled.

Factor Comparison. When *factor comparison* was first developed, it was envisioned that universally applicable factors (usually no more than five) would be applied to all jobs in the organization, much as in position classification. In this system, because they are based on job analysis, position descriptions are written in terms of the factors. The factors are described verbally by the organization before position descriptions are written. In developing this system, the organization ranks each benchmark position twice: factor by factor, to determine factor importance in the position, and by units, such as points or money, to determine how a salary or wage is distributed among factors. The result for each benchmark position is two rankings (importance and units), which must be reconciled. As a result, some benchmarks may have to be discarded from system development if the two ranks do not correspond.

The factor comparison evaluation system produces two artifacts. One is a matrix with factors heading the columns (horizontal axis) and points or monetary values heading the rows (vertical axis). After reconciliation of the two rankings, benchmark positions can be matched up with the appropriate cells in the matrix for each factor and the benchmark position titles placed in those cells. When positions are to be allocated to the system, their job analysis data, or job descriptions, are examined factor by factor for a relationship to the benchmark positions in each factor column. This examination is assisted by the second artifact of the system, the benchmark position descriptions that describe the position factor by factor and assign point or monetary values. Points or dollar amounts are assigned for all factors, and their total value is summed for either total salary or total points. When points are used, they have to be related to salary levels.

Factor-Point System. In 1971, the developmental work of the federal group known as the Job Evaluation and Pay Review Task Force, under the leadership of Philip M. Oliver, produced a unified approach to job evaluation. The task force had been charged to establish a system that would rectify the "universal complaints about existing job evaluation and pay systems" in the federal service (Richter, 1972, p. 1). In response it developed the *factor-point system*, a hybrid of the point rating and factor comparison systems.

Among the greatest problems with position classification have been that class standards are developed as composites of many positions, are stated in general terms, and being nonquantitative, eventuate in multiple interpretations and organizational conflict. These problems have been exacerbated by the hidden agenda of personnel departments to prevent *pay grade escalation,* or grade creep, through either initial position allocations or reclassifications.

The Oliver task force sought to overcome such problems through a series of design features. In this system (as in factor comparison) the counterparts of class standards are the actual occupied positions that have served as benchmarks during system development. This use of benchmarks is similar to the factor comparison approach. The factors used in this system are the same as many of those discussed earlier, however not all factors will apply or will apply to the same extent in all job evaluation plans. So in the factor-point system, guide charts are developed to aid managers in assessing positions for the various factors. Each factor is defined and consists of various degrees, or levels, and each level is also defined. Job families that are alike in kind of work performed but vary in terms of knowledge and qualifications are usually supposed to have no more than four levels (entry, journeyman, senior, specialist). The concept of separate systems or subsystems was also adopted by the task force. Again the idea is to militate against the organizational tendency to create multiple layers of middle and upper management, each layer of course requiring a separate job or class. Another problem the factor-point system is meant to address is the tendency on the part of departments and agencies to establish positions within narrow criteria, partly for status, partly to recognize narrow professional and occupational differences. Both tendencies put pressure on pay.

In allocating positions to the system, one first identifies the kind of work (for example, civil engineering, accounting) from job analysis data or an accurate position description. If a benchmark standard exists that matches the position being allocated for each factor, the factor points for that benchmark are adopted. If a match is not found, the position is bracketed, factor by factor, between related benchmarks. Interstitial point values are determined by referring to guide charts for point allocations. Total points are summed. Based on this total the position is also allocated to a pay range that corresponds to points-to-range conversion standards. Constructing a factor-point system is discussed with an example later in this chapter.

Other Systems

Jaques's Equitable Payment. Elliot Jaques's system (1961, 1964) of job evaluation is based on three interrelated factors: the level of work, as measured by a *time-span of discretion;* the comparison of pay with an *equitable payment* figure, which, Jaques claims, represents one of the "common norms of payment" that individuals in jobs with similar time-spans feel are appropriate for their tasks; and *capacity—* the amount of an individual's job-related abilities at a given point in time.

Time-span of discretion is defined as "the longest period which can elapse in a role before the manager can be sure that his subordinate has not been exercising marginally substandard discretion continuously in balancing pace and quantity of his work" (Jaques, 1964, p.17). For multiple-task jobs (in which the individual carries through a number of different tasks concurrently), time-span of discretion is determined by analysis of the task that has the longest completion time. Jaques recommends that managers use the technique of *successive approximations* to identify the time limits of subordinates' task completion (time being a surrogate for productivity). This technique forces managers to attend solely to productivity—estimating too high, then too low, and finally bracketing a reasonable figure. The level of work is determined by managerial appraisal of tasks (difficulty, complexity, and so on) rather than content.

Jaques uses a so-called social-analytic method to determine people's norms of equitable payment. It employs confidential interviews to help individuals clarify feelings, judgments, and attitudes that they may not have recognized themselves.

Literature reviews of this method have produced little support for any but the idea of time-span of discretion as ideas that might be used in job evaluation (Hellriegel and French, 1969).

Paterson Decision Band Method. The Paterson *decision band method* (Paterson and Husband, 1970; Paterson, 1972) is a single-factor job evaluation method that emphasizes level of decision making as the factor that differentiates all jobs. Paterson identified thirteen decision grades according to which jobs can be analyzed and graded. The higher the grade, the greater the value of the job to the enterprise, and therefore the greater the reward. The decision grades fall into seven bands that correspond to organizational levels. Beginning with the highest, A and B band decisions involve *policymaking* to guide the organization; decision choice is unlimited or constrained only by law. In bands C and D, *programming* decisions are made, typically by senior managers within the limits of policy. In band E, *interpretive* decisions are the purview of middle managers, who act within programmed limits. The *routine* decisions of band F are made by first-line operatives to execute interpreted policy decided at band E. Finally, band O comprises *defined* decisions, made by unskilled workers. Here only the most limited decision discretion is possible, such as the speed of working. At each level except band O, *coordination* decisions are considered higher level than other types of decisions, thus creating the thirteen grades. Because this method provides only a framework within which differentials may be applied, the factor-point system can be used for various employees.

Paterson claims he has data from more than seventy firms, involving nearly sixty thousand employees, that establish a logarithmic relationship among the existing wage rates paid to different decision grades as defined by this method. Plotting current pay rates on a log scale against thirteen job grades demonstrates this relationship. Paterson interprets this result as showing an unconscious tendency by companies to reward decision makers according to this specific logarithmic relationship. Organizations studied that did not follow the logarithmic-differential compensation pattern tended to suffer from poor morale, a high incidence of industrial relations problems, and related difficulties.

Hay Guide Chart–Profile Method. The *Hay guide chart–profile method* (Patten, 1988) is similar to point-factor ranking and is one of the methods that influenced the Oliver task force in developing the federal evaluation system. The content of each position is studied within a framework of four major dimensions and eleven factors, and then point values are assigned to each aspect of job content. The four dimensions and their factors are as follows:

1. *Know-how.* Technical knowledge requirements; leadership or supervisory demands; quality of human relations skills needed.
2. *Problem solving.* Problem-solving challenges and procedural constraints in problem solving.
3. *Accountability.* Levels of freedom to act to fulfill job objectives; impact of actions on the organization as a whole.
4. *Working conditions* (used with blue-collar and certain specialized occupations). Environment in which the job is performed; level of physical effort involved; hazards presented in the job.

These dimensions are organized and described in guide charts that assist raters in evaluating job content. Multiple raters evaluate benchmark positions, in terms of the factors, on a geometric scale with a ratio of approximately 15 percent between increments in the series.

A third judgment on job aspects is then made by *profiling.* Jobs are often typed: for example, a researcher might be said to hold a *think job.* A job profile describes the proportion of know-how, problem solving, and accountability that make up the total job. Further, profiling adds numerical values, judging a job as x percent know-how, y percent problem solving, and z percent accountability.

BROADBANDING

Basically, broad bands come in two designs. In one, *career bands,* there are subranges of pay, which make personal rank possible as a pay level, but usually there are no more than four or five job levels (entry or trainee, development, full performance, and senior expert or supervisor). Career bands also have specific but greatly simplified classification criteria. In the federal government the four to five bands can replace as many as fifteen General Schedule pay grades.

Alternatively, the bands can be broad ranges to which positions are allocated based on traditional job evaluation criteria. The latter model might be called a *broad grade system* ("Study Identifies Two Broadbanding Approaches," 1995).

Figure 28.1 is a structural example from a broadbanding system developed under the U.S. Navy Demonstration Project. Shown are career paths, job levels, and several General Schedule (GS) levels (pay ranges) collapsed into different bands. The experimental Navy laboratories used two simplified approaches to classification, or allocation, of positions (Schay, 1993). One was whole job comparison based on a limited number of benchmark position standards. In the second approach, or system, the manager made a tentative career path and level determination, then reviewed a menu for the path and level and selected appropriate description statements from a list of job factors similar to ones discussed earlier in this chapter. At least one statement was selected for each factor. These systems were carried out with the aid of a computer program that then produced position descriptions.

Although the structure of these systems has important implications, it is the implicit organizational culture changes that are most important. Federal personnelists acknowledge three roles that comprise the new human resource management authority of managers under broadbanding: compensation management, job evaluation management, and performance management (Schay, 1995). The U.S. Merit Systems Protection Board (1989) has spelled out the implications of this cultural change for the federal government, where the most extensive broadbanding interventions are taking place: the definition of *equal pay for equal work* becomes elastic because base pay for similar jobs can vary considerably; the accuracy and credibility of performance appraisals become critical to system success; and once an incumbent gets into the full working (rather than trainee) band for an occupation, the determination of type of work assigned and amount of pay is no longer affected by personnel department actions or control—it is the manager's responsibility. Thus the career band approach has caused a significant shift in human resource management focus—from the job to the person. (Broadbanding is discussed further in Chapter Twenty-Nine.)

Before moving to a detailed example of techniques in system implementation, we can look at ideas about who ought to do the work of applying these techniques.

STAFF- VERSUS CONSULTANT-DEVELOPED PLANS

This section looks at three alternatives for accomplishing the job evaluation project (the reader may want also to refer to Chapter Twenty-Three, on using consultants). However, first, a caution: no matter who does the work, the importance of management support for the project cannot be overstressed. Support means

Figure 28.1. Career Path Identification by Classification and Current Grade.

Classification	GS Grade Level															
	1	2	3	4	5	6	7	8	9	10	11	12	13	14	15	16–PL[a]
Clerical career path	I (NCM)	II (ACM)		III (FCM)		IV (SCM)			V (CE)[b]							
Technical career path				I (NTM)		II (ATM)			III (FTM)			IV (STM)		V (TE)[c]		
Administrative career path						I (NAdM)			II (AAdM)		III (FAdM)			IV (SAdM)		V (AdE)[d]
Professional career path						I (NFM)			II (APM)		III (FPM)			IV (SPM)		V (PE)

Note: N = New; A = Associate; F = Full; S = Senior; C = Clerical; T = Technical; Ad = Administrative; P = Professional; M = Member; E = Exceptional.

[a]Public Law.

[b]Reserved for agency-level position.

[c]Reserved for managerial position.

[d]Reserved for managerial or expert position.

Source: Naval Ocean Systems Center, 1979, p. 23.

that management, at the least, endorses the system being developed and communicates that endorsement throughout the organization, finds the time to work with responsible staff and consultants developing the system, and facilitates whatever workforce participation is needed.

The three alternative approaches to job evaluation system development are a plan entirely developed by in-house staff, a plan developed by in-house staff with assistance from one or few consultant advisers, and a plan almost entirely developed by a consulting organization.

Alternative 1. In-House Staff

Several advantages can accrue from in-house staff development. The project will be carried out by people who know and understand the organization. If it is not rushed, the experience can result in considerable learning for the human resource management staff, department management, unions, and even policymakers. The project may extend beyond the objective of developing the system to objectives such as changing the organizational design. Theoretically, it is cheaper to do the project in-house because it avoids the consulting costs. These savings may be illusionary, however, because of the trial and error inherent in learning while doing. Finally, the plan can be tailored to perceived special organizational needs.

The major disadvantage to attempting system development in-house is lack of expertise. As previously mentioned, learning while doing can be costly, and the time required to learn the appropriate technology may be too great given the usual desire to install the new system quickly.

Alternative 2. In-House Staff
with Minimum Consultant Assistance

The advantages of using in-house staff with minimum consultant assistance are more or less the same as those in alternative 1, and this method may avoid the primary disadvantage found in the first one. In this alternative the educator role of the consultant is most important. However, the disadvantages of having to take time for learning and, as in alternative 1, of slow project accomplishment may make this alternative impractical.

Alternative 3. A Consulting Organization

In the third alternative all the components of the job evaluation system are under the control of a consulting group. Naturally, at various stages of the project there will be considerable involvement of the human resource management staff, organizational management, employees, and unions or employee associations.

There are many advantages and disadvantages to hiring a consulting organization. Some are counterparts of those in alternatives 1 and 2. Here are the advantages. Use of the consultants gives the appearance of an independent point of view on organizational requirements. This may also be possible in alternative 2 if the consultant is highly reputed. However, the consultant in alternative 2 is usually viewed as ancillary to in-house staff. By using a consulting organization for most of the work in alternative 3, the jurisdiction buys expertise that has been extensively applied in a variety of organizations. This alternative is generally the most expeditious approach where management is concerned about minimizing installation time. The consulting organization usually has well-developed employee communication and training plans to accompany a project. A reputable firm will continue to support an installation until problems are solved, and the customer is satisfied. The minimization of problems can compensate for contract costs.

Then there are the disadvantages. To begin with, the cost is usually high. Moreover, consulting firms tend to specialize in one approach and methodology that they have adapted and perfected. It may be difficult, or result in additional expense, to change the consultant's standard approach. Finally, a jurisdiction is likely to get itself into trouble when it neither has developed selection criteria to choose among competitive bidders for the project nor has the ability to write a performance contract appropriate for this type of consulting. It can then end up hiring low-cost, low-competence contractors over whom it has no management process and progress controls.

FACTOR-POINT METHODOLOGY: A PROCEDURAL EXAMPLE

This section is designed to provide a nuts-and-bolts illustration of how a factor-point system might be developed and installed. Irrespective of which of the three alternatives is chosen to implement a project, it is important for management to grasp the fundamental steps described here. The use of job evaluation in compensation system design and allocation of positions to pay ranges is discussed in Chapter Twenty-Nine.

Step 1. Select Evaluation Factors

Unless you believe that unique evaluation factors are required you probably will want to adopt commonly used ones. In any case, factors are defined so that a person describing his or her position with them will understand what is meant. Factors are usually described in terms of levels or degrees. Exact level descriptions can be distilled from PDQ data, as discussed later in this procedure, or can be pre-positioned in the PDQ under each factor and then summarized for degree statements in guide charts.

The following are commonly used factors. First are job requirements, stated as various areas of knowledge, skills, and abilities. Knowledge, skills, and abilities vary in type and depth required to perform the work—basic skills, for example, are needed to perform a single task, but skills go through several levels, to high degrees of expertise. Second are complexity and creativity, stated as complexity of analysis, independent thought, resourcefulness, and judgment. Again, several levels are used to describe complexity and creativity, from minimal abilities to high degrees of creative thought, judgment, and the like.

Third are leadership and management, stated as planning, directing, and integrating the work of others. These factors too are scaled, from no direction provided to others to setting the direction of the mission, goals, and objectives for an entire independent organization. Fourth is communication. Here evaluation is concerned with the functions of interpersonal transactions, and degrees may vary from routine factual communication to motivational leadership.

Fifth is latitude of authority, stated as independence and freedom to take action. It can vary from limited freedom to unrestrained decision making in unprecedented situations. Sixth is scope of impact, stated as the effects of independent decisions or actions. Levels can vary from impact on a small subgroup to impact on an entire independent organization.

Seventh are working conditions. This factor might be subdivided as follows (or these subdivisions might be used as separate factors, depending on the organizational structure of occupations): (1) the environment of work (varying from working in a normal office to working with machinery, out of doors, in difficult work spaces, on heights, with risk of injury, and with exposure to such hazards as odors, dust, cold, disease, and so on); (2) the work schedule (which might involve travel, shift work, being on call, holiday work, unpredictable schedules, and so on); and (3) the work demands (time constraints, productivity demands, need for extended visual concentration, need to handle highly confidential information).

Step 2. Design Position Description Questionnaire

The PDQ must be designed to obtain desired information. Data must be scaled in terms of attributes, such as degrees or levels of importance. Wherever possible, data are gathered in categories and pre-positioned formats. Supervisors are allowed space to comment in each section. Specific work examples are provided for each factor. Each task or duty and responsibility statement is rated or scaled for importance (for example, 5 = least important). Each is rated for percentage of the position's time it consumes (100 percent being the time for all tasks). The number of other employees who can perform the task is indicated, as is whether the person must be an expert in the task. Finally, as mentioned earlier, tasks must be rated for whether or not they are essential, in accord with the Americans with Disabilities Act. The performance of an essential task is inherent in the nature of the position (for example, driving an automobile is essential to working as a highway patrol officer).

Step 3. Train Staff and Administer PDQs

Whoever is to administer and certify the accuracy of data must be trained. If human resource staff exist, they might be trained as trainers who will later instruct managers and line personnel.

After PDQs are completed, reviewed, and signed by both employees and supervisors, they are reviewed for completeness, clarity, and consistency of data by central staff. Human resource department personnel might be trained to do this also. Completeness and clarity of data are self-evident; consistency means that factorial ratings make sense in terms of task data. For example, task statements that document decision making based on application of programmed rules probably do not adequately describe tasks that involve complex analysis and judgment. Problem cases are followed up with interviews. PDQs are prepared by or for all employees.

Step 4. Decide on Subsystems and Benchmark Positions

The purpose of subsystems is to inhibit the phenomenon of grade and class creep, as previously defined. Limiting the number of levels of an occupational specialty to four or five also helps to thwart grade escalation. Further, analysis is facilitated because a common set of factors is relevant in each subsystem. A review of PDQs will suggest a provisional set of subsystems, such as managers and supervisors, professionals, administrative and higher positions, protective positions, clerical and office operation personnel, trades and crafts positions, and perhaps semiskilled and unskilled personnel. Ultimately, the number of personnel, differentiated into occupational specialties that might fall into combinations of these categories, help determine the subsystems.

Once the definitional decision is made on subsystems, benchmark positions are selected for each subset, using the criteria described previously in discussing components of a job evaluation system. Draft position descriptions are prepared for benchmarks using this format: title, narrative statement of duties, employee qualifications, description of the position in terms of each factor. Duties or task statements are written in *functional job language.* Each statement includes an action verb, object, objective, perhaps standards or guides for performance, and any tools or equipment needed (see Exhibit 28.1).

Step 5. Prepare Guide Charts

Assemble advisory groups, each group consisting of individuals who are familiar with the positions in a particular subsystem. Each advisory group ranks all benchmark positions for each subsystem factor by factor, using the technique of paired comparisons or some other multiattribute ranking algorithm. In paired comparisons each benchmark is compared with all others in a matrix. When one benchmark is higher than another on a given factor, a 1 is placed in the interfacing cell.

Exhibit 28.1. Sample Job Description.

Job title   Policy Analyst–Special Projects

Department   Operational Support and Development, Office of Planning and Budget

Job summary   This position is responsible for providing technical support to the Division Director and other agency staff for a variety of special research projects.

Major duties:

- Provides technical research support to the Division Director and other divisional staff for a variety of special projects

- Responds to requests for information from other divisions

- Develops a database of information possessed by different state agencies, including a list of contact persons for obtaining needed data

- Maintains a central library of data for the agency

- Analyzes proposed legislation for policy and financial implications in assigned program areas

- Prepares responses to correspondence directed to the Governor and Director as assigned

- Serves as member of various committees related to assigned program areas or department operations as assigned

- Performs other related duties as assigned

I. Job Requirements
Knowledge, skills, and abilities required by the position:

- Knowledge of public administration principles and practices

- Knowledge of state government operations, including legislative and budgetary processes

- Knowledge of state agencies and programs

- Knowledge of agency policies and procedures

- Knowledge of generally accepted government accounting standards

- Knowledge of relevant state and federal laws

- Knowledge of state and national issues and trends within assigned areas of program responsibility

- Skill in mathematics, basic research, and statistical analysis

- Skill in policy analysis

- Skill in oral, written, and interpersonal communication

- Skill in using a personal computer and various spreadsheet and word processing software programs

Exhibit 28.1. Sample Job Description, cont'd.

II. Latitude of Authority

The Division Director assigns work in terms of general instructions. Completed work is reviewed for accuracy and compliance with procedures.

Guidelines include the Official Code of the state, relevant state and federal laws, and agency policies and procedures. These guidelines require judgment, selection, and interpretation in application.

III. Complexity and Creativity

This position consists of tasks in basic research and statistical analysis. The need to gather information from a variety of sources and legislative time constraints contribute to the complexity of the work.

IV. Scope of Impact

The purpose of this position is to provide technical research support to the division and agency. Successful performance helps ensure the effective and efficient operation of the division and agency.

V. Communication

Contacts are typically with coworkers, representatives of agencies, auditors, legislators, and legislative staff members. Contacts are typically to exchange or obtain information, resolve problems, and provide services.

VI. Working Conditions

The work is typically performed with the employee sitting at a desk. The employee frequently lifts light objects and uses tools or equipment requiring manual dexterity.

Work environment   The work is typically performed in an office.

Leadership and management   None

ADA Limitations   None

Minimum qualifications:

- Knowledge and level of competency commonly associated with the completion of a master's degree in a course of study related to occupational field
- Sufficient experience to understand the basic principles relevant to the major duties of the position: experience of tasks similar to tasks performed by an Associate Policy Analyst or experience of having held a similar position for one or two years

Factor	Point Value	Guide Chart Scale
I	75	C
II	40	J
III	100	T
IV	60	B
V	30	A
VI	0	
Total	305	

All 1's are totaled for a column or row for a total rank value. Benchmarks with similar scores form clusters. These clusters result in a number of degrees or levels for each factor used in the subsystem.

Degree definitions are written by reviewing and synthesizing benchmark draft position descriptions, cluster by cluster and factor by factor. The scales and level definitions in the PDQs may assist.

Each advisory committee weights the factors by allocating 100 points among the factors in terms of importance. The points given to each factor become the lowest degree for that factor. Higher levels are then arithmetically extrapolated. For example, if a factor is weighted 40 and there are three levels (because there are three clusters of benchmark positions) the factor levels will be 40, 80, and 120. The benchmark positions for each subsystem are evaluated on all factors with the aid of guide charts. Points for all factors are added up and summarized on the final draft of each benchmark position description (Exhibit 28.1). A sample guide chart is shown in Exhibit 28.2. It covers scope of impact, one of the seven evaluative factors set forth in step 1.

Step 6. Correlate Total Points with Salary Data

Total point values for benchmark positions are correlated with their salaries. This is done to obtain an average or regression line. It is best to first conduct a salary survey, using the key positions, in order to obtain market data. It is possible that existing salaries may reflect distortions, errors, or rates otherwise at variance with markets. (The subject of conducting market surveys is discussed in the next chapter.) You may want to discard benchmark positions from the analysis when they greatly diverge from the average line. The data plot that results from this analysis also provides the basis for designing salary standardization (discussed in Chapter Twenty-Nine).

Step 7. Implement the Job Evaluation Plan

It is first necessary to develop manuals and training materials for position description writing and for allocation of positions to the job evaluation plan. If they are not already so, human resource management staff and supervisors must be trained in using the PDQ, writing position descriptions, and classifying positions, unless all or substantial parts of these responsibilities are to be retained by a central personnel agency. The preferred mode is to decentralize this responsibility to human resource personnel in various departments and agencies working closely with operating managers and supervisors.

Managers especially will consider trade-offs between higher- and lower-priced jobs within the total limitations of the personnel budget. For example, work might be redesigned to result in a decrease in the number of professional positions and an increase in technicians. Positions are allocated to the job evaluation plan as follows. For a given position description the appropriate subsystem

Exhibit 28.2. Sample Guide Chart.

Professional and Administrative Subsystem

Factor IV: Scope of Impact

Scope of impact covers relationships between the nature of the work and the effects of outputs within and outside the organization.

Degree	Point Value	Factor
1	15	The work involves the performance of specific, routine operations that include a few separate tasks or procedures. The work product or service is required to facilitate the work of others; however, it has little impact beyond the immediate organizational unit or beyond the timely provision of limited services to others.
2	30	The work involves the execution of specific rules, regulations, or procedures and typically comprises a complete segment of an assignment or project of broader scope. The work product or service affects the accuracy, reliability, or acceptability of further processes or services.
3	45	The work involves treating a variety of conventional problems, questions, or situations in conformance with established criteria. The work product or service affects the design or operation of systems, programs, or equipment; the adequacy of such activities as field investigations, testing operations, or research conclusions; or the social, psychological, and economic well-being of persons.
4	60	The work involves establishing criteria; formulating projects; assessing program effectiveness; or investigating or analyzing a variety of unusual conditions, problems, or questions. The work product or service affects a wide range of agency activities, major activities of industrial concerns, or the operation of other agencies.
5	75	The work involves isolating and defining unknown conditions, resolving critical problems, or developing new theories. The work product or service affects the work of other experts, the development of major aspects of administrative or scientific programs or missions, or the well-being of substantial numbers of people.
6	90	The work involves planning, developing, and carrying out vital administrative or scientific programs. The programs are essential to the missions of the agency or affect large numbers of people on a long-term or continuing basis.

is first determined. Then the type of work or occupational series is determined (for example, engineering or accounting). The manager next seeks benchmark position descriptions for this series. For example, if the position being classified is for a civil engineer and if there are civil engineering benchmark position descriptions, they should be compared with the description of the position to be allocated. If the latter corresponds to one of the benchmark descriptions, the manager awards the point values for the benchmark standard. If there is no related benchmark for type of work or there is considerable variance from a related standard, guide charts should be consulted. A combination of guide charts and benchmark descriptions may facilitate allocation through successive approximations of some factors.

CONCLUSION

This chapter should have familiarized the reader with job evaluation systems, including their evolution, importance, development, and uses. The reader should have gained sufficient understanding to be a critical consumer of such systems and should be able to judge organizational requirements for job evaluation. Sufficient information has been presented to lay the groundwork for development of a system.

The question remains: Is there a best job evaluation system? My bias is for use of broadbanding, under which maximum discretion and flexibility to manage are possible. An absence of resources and money may make broadbanding impractical for many organizations. However, the most fundamental requirement for this approach to work is an organizational human relations climate with a high degree of trust between management and the rest of the workforce. Highly adversarial labor-management relations create environments that are unlikely to support broadbanding, simplified job evaluation, and maximum management discretion.

Beyond the purely instrumental relationship between job evaluation and compensation, choice of a system might be governed by still other factors of organizational climate, especially these three important ones: the present and desired level of managers' authority to make human resource management decisions; the authority of employees, as individuals and in groups, to self-manage; and the degree of freedom permitted or restricted by the political leadership of the organization to take risks.

References

Americans with Disabilities Act of 1990. U.S. Code, vol. 42, sec. 12101 et seq.

Classification Act of 1923. U.S. Statutes at Large 42 (1923) 1488.

Hellriegel, D., and French, W. "A Critique of Jaques' Equitable Payment System." *Industrial Relations,* May 8, 1969, pp. 269–279.

Jaques, E. *Equitable Payment.* London: Heinemann, 1961.

Jaques, E. *Time-Span Handbook.* London: Heinemann, 1964.

Naval Ocean Systems Center, Naval Weapons Center, University of Southern California, School of Public Administration. "Adapting Private Sector Personnel Resource Management Methods for the More Effective Operation of Federal Government Organizations. Proposal for a Demonstration Project Authorized by Title VI of the Civil Service Reform Act of 1978." Unpublished proposal. Aug. 1979.

Paterson, T. T. *Job Evaluation.* London: Business Books, 1972.

Paterson, T. T., and Husband, T. M. "Decision-Making Responsibility: Yardstick for Job Evaluations." *Compensation Review,* 1970, *2,* 1–31.

Patten, T. H., Jr. *Fair Pay: The Managerial Challenge of Comparable Job Worth and Job Evaluation.* San Francisco: Jossey-Bass, 1988.

Richter, F. F. *A Summary of the Job Evaluation and Pay Review Task Force Report.* Washington, D.C.: Classification and Compensation Society, 1972.

Schay, B. W. *Broad-Banding in the Federal Government: Management Report.* Washington, D.C.: Personnel Systems Oversight Group, Office of Systems Innovation, U.S. Office of Personnel Management, 1993.

Schay, B. W. *Federal Demonstration Projects: Integrated Approaches to Pay, Performance Management and Position Classification.* Rand Forum on Public Sector Human Resource Management for the 8th Quadrennial Review of Military Compensation. Briefing Notes. Washington, D.C.: Rand, 1995.

"Study Identifies Two Broadbanding Approaches." *HR Focus,* Apr. 1995, p. 11.

U.S. Merit Systems Protection Board. *OPM's Classification and Qualification Systems: A Renewed Emphasis, a Changing Perspective.* Washington, D.C.: U.S. Government Printing Office, 1989.

CHAPTER TWENTY-NINE

Designing and Creating
an Effective Compensation Plan

Gilbert B. Siegel

Generally, the quality of a pay plan can be judged by criteria such as its internal equity, competitiveness with outside labor markets, usefulness to managers, political acceptability, and understandability. However, the emphasis on and importance of each of these criteria will vary with the objectives of a pay plan. Accordingly, this chapter begins with a consideration of compensation objectives.

Pay systems are also highly instrumental in personnel recruitment, retention, and motivation. Thus another important topic in this chapter is the relationship between compensation and performance, and several variations on individual and group merit pay systems are discussed. The latter part of this chapter is devoted to a step-by-step discussion of constructing and maintaining an effective salary structure, bringing together objectives, structural alternatives, and pay administration policies.

OBJECTIVES: WHAT DO WE PAY FOR?

Membership or Seniority

Traditional Civil Service Pay System. Objective setting is such a fundamental aspect of management that the need for it often goes without articulation. Sometimes the reason concern for objectives in compensation is obscured is that a system has been in use for so long that no one can imagine organizational life

608

without it. Such is the case for traditional civil service compensation systems, based as they have been on position classification, multiple-step or -rate salary ranges, and seniority pay progression. The objective in this type of system is pay for membership or seniority. The traditional model of civil service personnel administration has relied on merit competition to obtain qualified personnel. Once they are appointed, the idea is to make their employment so attractive that it is difficult for them to leave the service. This objective is supported by various forms of indirect compensation as well, such as generous retirement systems.

Realistically, however, not only have times changed but seniority-based systems can no longer be afforded by most governments. Neither the government revenue nor the political support for such largess is available. Yet costs continue to escalate as a result of the annual increases built into the public employee wage bill. Apart from growth in a public workforce for programmatic reasons, increases in costs can be attributed to the continuous pay increments required by seniority steps, cost-of-living increases and inflation adjustments, and adaptation to market rates. These upward adjustments result from inherent policies of the system and also from legislation, labor contracts, and the need to maintain competitive salaries.

Fringe Benefits. Like the objective of pay for membership, the objective of fringe benefits is to retain the workforce. Like the increases in pay for membership, increases in fringe benefits have driven up the cost of government labor. Public and private organizations are now attempting to retreat from generous fringe benefit entitlements. Nowhere is this better reflected than in health benefits, though retrenchment is also evident in such other entitlements as leave and pensions. Health insurance costs are being controlled through such varied containment strategies as enrolling employees in managed care, requiring employees to share or increase their share of premium costs, increasing deductibles or requiring them where they do not exist, requiring employees to share costs of treatment (coinsurance), and adding no new features to plans.

Costs of pension systems have been driven up by the demographic fact that people are living longer. Therefore the original actuarial assumptions of plans are often no longer valid. For the same reason, the past generosity of public employers toward retirees can no longer be tolerated. Thirty years ago, during the epoch of government union strength, political officials often agreed to sweetened pension benefits as a trade-off against higher salaries. Today's politicians are living with the consequences of these decisions. Accordingly, as a result of attempts to head off high future costs, it is not uncommon to see multitier systems with benefits based on date of hiring.

Another major adjustment governments are making is to switch pension funding from a defined-benefit to a defined-contribution approach. In government systems, the defined-benefit arrangement is normally financed by periodic monetary allocations from employers and employees, in amounts sufficient to provide determined monthly payouts upon retirement. The amount of these payments is based on a formula involving, for example, an individual's years of employment and the average of his or her three highest salaries. Assuming that contributions are made in a timely fashion, pension managers are able to meet liabilities of the system through fund investments and actuarial projections. Problems have arisen when public jurisdictions fall behind in meeting their contributory obligations. Sometimes the government is so in arrears that the system is transformed from an actuarial reserve to a pay-as-you-go basis of financing in order to meet current obligations to pensioners.

In contrast, the benefit system financed by defined contributions is more like a set of individual retirement accounts (IRAs). As with defined benefits, most governments contribute to employee accounts. The level of the contributions may or may not have been reduced during a transition between systems. For example, employees under more recent federal retirement plans receive even lower government allocations than employees covered by older entitlement systems. On the positive side, however, employees can increase personal funding with pretax dollars. Without this employee enhancement of funding, estimated retirement payouts are based on assumptions about length of work life, earnings, contributions, and compounded rates of investment return, including reinvestment of interest and other returns. These benefits are usually portable or at least the vested property of the employee. Portability of a pension account is important for the person who has earned minimal entitlements in more than one system but has not remained in one long enough to maximize retirement payouts.

Equity and Job Value

As discussed in the previous chapter, comparability of work and pay has been a sticking point with civil servants since the earliest civil service reforms in this country. In response the idea of internal organizational *equity* has been implemented as the basis for development of pay scales. Through job evaluation systems, positions are classified into jobs, jobs are given relative hierarchical value, or weighted, and this valuation is reflected in salary ranges to which similarly weighted jobs are allocated. The result is internal organizational equity. Although seemingly felicitous, this concept has some problems, as we will see.

Market Comparisons and Ability to Pay

Market Value. One problem with a pay system based on job evaluation is that it can be at variance with the market value of some jobs. For example, education and experience requirements for the job of social worker might lead to a range of pay that is higher than what the market will pay. Further, markets for some jobs vary on such dimensions as geography and proximity of work to residence. Labor-management negotiation of salaries, wages, and fringe benefits is a surrogate for the action of market forces. Presumably both sides are armed with market data preliminary to negotiations.

Comparable Worth. *Comparable worth* (sometimes called *gender equity*) refers to pay disparities between occupations, or job classifications, dominated by women and those dominated by men. The debate on this subject was settled by the U.S. Supreme Court in *County of Washington* v. *Gunther* (452 U.S. 161 [1981]). Advocates of comparable worth would like all jobs evaluated as having equal value to be compensated in the same range of pay. Furthermore, they would make job evaluation more uniformly inclusive, requiring a common set of factors and weights for all jobs in an organization, from janitor to highest executive, and would ignore differences in market rates of compensation for occupations otherwise seen as having equal value. However, the Court decided that unless comparable worth is legislated by a jurisdiction or agreed to under labor contract, market data can be considered in setting pay where job value is at variance with market value. This applies to jobs of equal weight that are not essentially the *same*. Under the Equal Pay Act of 1963, jobs that are basically the same must be compensated in the same pay range.

Ability to Pay. Governments sometimes find themselves in the position of being unable to compete for personnel. As a result, ability to pay becomes an unarticulated policy limitation on compensation. This limitation may apply only to certain occupations or be a problem in general. However, few governments have a formal ability-to-pay policy, such as to pay market or 10 percent below or above market. Such policies are more often seen in the private sector.

Knowledge or Skill

Knowledge or skill is a relatively new compensation objective (Lawler and Ledford, 1985; Gupta, Schweizer, and Jenkins, 1987; Gerson, 1987) that can be added either in job or in team contexts. Pay is for depth (more knowledge or skill in a specialized area), breadth (knowledge or skill that extends upstream, downstream, or parallel to original job), and height (expansion of management knowledge or skill). Further, pay is for performance capabilities, not necessarily for work performed. This pay objective may be important in situations requiring a cross-trained workforce or workforce flexibility and adaptability. It can be used with a broadband pay system. A given process performed by a team might be represented by a band, or alternatively, several bands could be segments of a still larger process. For positions each band might consist of several discrete skill or knowledge blocks that would be differentially compensated. If a job's compensation needed to be compared to market rates, the block with the highest aggregation of skill and knowledge would be compared to market. This compensation objective, with or without broadbanding, appears to be an alternative suitable for Total Quality Management/Continuous Quality Improvement (TQM/CQI) situations.

Performance, Achievement, or Merit

Performance, achievement, and *merit* are synonymous in compensation systems based on outputs or outcomes. Reward is for specified objectives achieved in quantitative or qualitative terms. Two types of such systems are distinct but share the reward-for-achievement attribute: individual performance and group performance systems.

Individual Merit Pay. The longest government experience with individual merit pay has been in the federal government, where this form of pay was first authorized under a demonstration project of the Civil Service Reform Act of 1978. The experiment, carried out in Navy research and development laboratories, was a success but occurred as part of a more comprehensive change in personnel management practices (Naval Ocean Systems Center, 1979). Initiation of the practice throughout the federal government has proved less of a success.

The following general introduction to merit pay will be helpful before we look at actual government experience in more detail. An objective of paying for individual merit is ideally suited for a broadbanding pay system because it is less restricted than other objectives by traditional pay range limitations and its emphasis on personal rank allows greater flexibility in personnel management. As noted in the previous chapter, broadbanding systems are not for all situations because they require fundamental change in the management culture, including empowerment of managers in areas of personnel management, performance measurement, and deviation from the ethos of equal pay for equal work as it has been generally interpreted.

Group Performance Systems. Although several group performance and reward systems are used in the private sector, this chapter primarily considers *gainsharing* and *goalsharing* (also called *winsharing*) (Bullock and Lawler, 1984; Schuster and Zingheim, 1992) because these are the most feasible for government organizations. These are group bonus plans in which monetary savings from improved performance are shared between the organization and employees of the better performing unit.

Under gainsharing, standard hours of direct labor in each unit of output are measured and compared with historically based long-term standard performance levels. Payouts are based on the value of productivity improvement. A variation is to use baseline work measurement standards based on current performance as performance criteria. The leading experience with gainsharing in government was the Air Force's Pacer Share Project, carried out by the Directorate of Distribution of the Sacramento Air Logistics Center at McClelland Air

Force Base in California (Siegel, 1994; Schay, 1993, 1995). Pacer Share was another demonstration project under the Civil Service Reform Act. A TQM/CQI intervention, it principally involved technical improvement of work processes, reductions in force, an extended period of negotiations with unions prior to project implementation, broad bands based on consolidation of pay grades, work allocated to six process categories based on contributions to common outputs, elimination of individual performance appraisal (the idea being that quality measurement for workgroups would substitute), pay levels adjusted automatically for federal government changed rates reflecting cost-of-living increases (comparability), and extensive TQM/CQI training. Productivity bonuses were distributed for beating baseline labor distributions relative to outputs—half to the federal government and half in equal shares to each worker.

In contrast is goalsharing, which is forward looking and bases payouts on group performance compared to predetermined goals, often with a quality modifier. Current productivity against previous standards may be measured as well. Payouts may be allocated as a percentage of base salary or as the same percentage of the market rate. This system might be combined with pay for membership or to compete with market rates, or it might be the sole basis for compensation. It requires a compensation infrastructure for determining goals and payouts and accounting systems that track contributions to organizational performance. A simpler version of a goalsharing system might be applied in the public service through management-determined or collectively negotiated goals.

MULTIPLE PAY SYSTEMS AND MULTIPLE OBJECTIVES

It is not likely that a public organization will have only one or few compensation objectives in the future. A current of environmental change is requiring governments to rethink traditional compensation systems that have rewarded mainly membership in multiple ways. Some of these important environmental changes are the reduction of government revenues; the introduction of reengineering and downsizing; and the flattening of organizations, accompanied by a recasting of vertically progressing careers to horizontally progressing careers requiring multiple roles, constant learning, and change.

This is not to argue that membership is to be avoided completely; it remains a factor in both workforce retention and the constant process of weeding out low performers. But in designing and creating a compensation plan, it is important to have in mind for what and how you are paying the workforce. Membership can be a reasonable objective because it promotes maintenance of the workforce, and perhaps fringe benefits are the best way to achieve this particular goal. Sensitivity to market changes in compensation is another way to prevent extensive turnover. What is important is not to emphasize or reward only membership.

However, if managers are to take compensation cost containment seriously, the annual-increase effects of multistep pay ranges need to be curtailed. Whether merit pay is to be applied or not, it is possible to use a system of flat rates or no more than two rates for each range (say, entry and fully competent levels); or the ranges themselves might be entry, journey, senior, and expert or supervisor. Salary adjustments other than for promotion would then be made based on performance or market rates, perhaps conditioned by the jurisdiction's ability to pay or by collective bargaining. A bonus system might be introduced for the part of compensation that is performance-based pay. Bonuses do not add to base salary and must be re-earned during each appraisal period.

In the previous sections, a series of objectives and systems have been described through which it is possible to produce and maintain a high-performing, flexible, and adaptive workforce. However, what may be a viable system for some employees may not be effective for all. Most of all, how systems are implemented is of critical importance. For these reasons, problems with performance-based systems are discussed in the next section.

PROBLEMS OF PERFORMANCE-BASED SYSTEMS

Individual Merit Pay

An important compound question is, Would/do government employees work harder/achieve more for higher compensation? The data are definitely mixed on these questions. The answers also evolve as contexts of government employment and economic and political environments change. On the one hand, data from the 1980s for some federal employees suggest that employees would not work harder for more money. What they feel to be important are coworkers, future pensions, and workplace comforts (Pearce and Perry, 1983). These may be the things that attracted them to federal employment in the first place. As recently as 1990, the Merit Systems Protection Board reported that 72 percent of federal supervisors felt that part of their pay should be based on performance, but only 42 percent would choose to be under a merit pay system. Only 38 percent of federal employees in general felt that pay is related to how well you perform (Schay, 1995). Rainey (1983) and Rainey, Traut, and Blunt (1986) came to the conclusion that state and local government employees have lower expectations for pay-for-performance links than do comparative private-sector groups. Rainey's study also revealed correlation of weak expectancies with the organizational constraints on pay-for-performance.

On the other hand, Navy and National Institute of Standards and Technology (NIST) experiments have shown positive attitudinal findings, such as employee perceptions that raises were linked to performance, that high performers stayed and low performers left the organization, and that individuals were satisfied with pay (Schay, 1995). Both of the experimental units involved are science and engineering organizations that were granted authority to significantly alter their personnel systems to support high-performance environments. Further, they did not commit many of the merit pay system implementation and administration errors that plagued first efforts at merit pay for GS 13 to 15 managers and supervisors and super-grade managers in the federal government: abrupt changes in agreed-upon levels of rewards (Silverman, 1982); lack of training in performance appraisal (U.S. General Accounting Office, 1984); lack of follow-through when planned performance objectives were no longer viable (Perry, Petrakis, and Miller, 1989); pursuit of planned objectives resulting in neglect of other duties (Pagano, 1985); use of a pay pool system of competing for rewards that did not work well (Pagano, 1985; U.S. General Accounting Office, 1983); insignificant amounts of money available for rewards (Harron, 1981; Pagano, 1985; Silverman, 1982); creation of individual performance contracts, resulting in divisiveness when coordination and interaction were required (Pagano, 1985); use of evaluation based on nonplanned objectives (U.S. General Accounting Office, 1984; Sauter, 1981); and general perception of favoritism in reward allocation (U.S. General Accounting Office, 1983).

In general, it can be concluded that individual merit pay can work well where certain conditions are met; conversely, their absence can result in failure. Desired achievements to be rewarded must be within the ability of the individual to carry out. Tasks or functions of positions so compensated should be ones for which the individual controls the pace of work and its achievement rather than being highly dependent upon others. Superiors and subordinates must be trained in the process of setting performance objectives (unless studied performance measurement systems already in place can be the basis of assessment). Performance objectives should be meaningful; they should be within the state of the art of the particular function involved. Undesired behaviors prompted by the setting and rewarding of specific objectives must be anticipated and circumscribed (for example, a concentration on rewarded objectives to the neglect of objectives that are not objects of special reward). The reward must be valued by the person who is to perform. The person must be able and willing to perform. Performance should be monitored and compared with plans; in other words, there must be feedback and evaluation. At this point questions may arise from the previous steps. Were any of the conditions changed in the process? Were either rewards or outcomes imprecisely or insufficiently identified? Finally, is the entire process worth it in cost-effectiveness or cost-benefit terms for the individual? for the organization? (Siegel, 1989). The requirements of individual merit pay are onerous if carried out continually by superiors and subordinates. As discussed, considerable investment in infrastructure such as training is needed, and a commitment to large amounts of time for goal setting, reviewing, evaluating, and rewarding is needed.

Skill-based pay is a special case of individual merit pay for which the research evidence is different. As of 1992, Schuster and Zingheim could find no evidence that organizations get direct financial gain from skill-based pay. However, other positive effects were discovered in a 1986 U.S. Department of Labor survey (pp. 143–144). Most organizations with skill-based pay improved workforce flexibility; improved employee satisfaction, commitment, and motivation; and increased output per hour worked. About half reduced labor costs and layoffs. Somewhat fewer reduced absenteeism and voluntary turnover. However, there were also disadvantages: costs increased as employees learned more skills, training and administrative costs increased, complex record keeping on individual certification and pay was required, and continual skill proficiency assessment presented problems.

Group Merit Pay

Growing numbers of private-sector organizations are embracing forms of team-based pay ("What's the Best Incentive for Employees?" 1992; "Companies Shift (Slowly) to Team-Based Pay," 1995). Bullock and Lawler (1984), in a study of thirty-three gainsharing programs, concluded that most resulted in improvements in such areas as productivity, quality, customer service, and reduced costs, accompanied by improvements in morale, attitudes, and quality of work life. However, they cautioned that relatively unchanging organizations are needed for such success, with no new technology introduced, flat learning curves (so managers can set standards from historical data), little capital investment planned, little use of overtime, high levels of trust, a largely nonunion workforce, a highly participative management style, and stable product lines.

Results from the Air Force's Pacer Share Project are mixed and raise more questions than they answer (Schay, 1993, 1995; Siegel, 1994). Although there were fewer grievances and the work climate improved, productivity did not increase relative to baseline data and in comparison with control groups. There was dissatisfaction with the connection between job performance and compensation and with opportunities for advancement. Quality measurement did not satisfactorily substitute for individual performance appraisal. Schay's interpretation (1993) was that "elimination of performance appraisal resulted in weakening of the pay-performance link" (p. 663), that line of sight that should exist between the individual's work, achievement, and ultimately, reward.

Some type of group bonus system is needed for TQM/CQI to work. It is possible to attain flexible, self-controlled workgroups where employees work harder and smarter. However, the organizational climate must support cooperation and employee empowerment. Workgroups do not function in highly competitive, individualistic cultures. As mentioned, a line-of-sight problem between work and reward may be unavoidable in any case. Some innovation, such as 360-degree performance evaluation (in which superiors, subordinates, and peers all evaluate each other), may alleviate this problem.

HOW TO CONSTRUCT AND MAINTAIN AN EFFECTIVE SALARY STRUCTURE

We now turn to a step-by-step approach to constructing and maintaining salary standardization, along with a discussion of design alternatives. The basic issues are (1) design structure and policies and (2) administration of pay. Both relate to the compensation objectives previously discussed.

Step 1. Design Pay Ranges

We learned in the previous chapter that point values for benchmark positions derived from job evaluation (as are found in a factor-point system) must be correlated with the pay rates for these positions. It is a good idea to go to the marketplace for these pay rates rather than to use internal organizational rates. In addition, the correlation should produce a tight cluster of values around the average line. Values that significantly vary should probably be removed from the analysis because they distort the average. (Market surveying of benchmarks is discussed later in this chapter.)

Figure 29.1 illustrates one model of pay range design. Focusing for the moment on the two diagonal lines, it can be seen that one represents averages derived from correlating pay medians with job evaluation point values for benchmark positions. The other represents the pay policy line, which in this case is below market. (Remember from the discussion on ability to pay earlier in this chapter that the organization may set a policy on what it will pay relative to market.)

Figure 29.1. Constructing Pay Ranges.

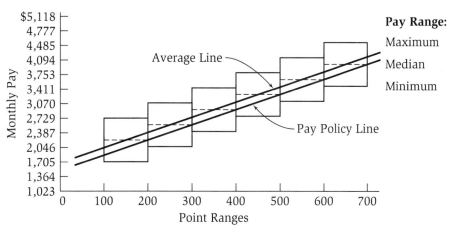

Pay range: Job A is worth 200 job evaluation points. It is allocated to range 2, which is 200 to 300 points. Range 2 is $2,046 to $3,070 per month.

Once the average line is available, a worksheet can be provided for trying out different pay range designs. Various point ranges on the x axis can be tested against ranges of pay on the y axis for pay periods of the jobs in the system. Most managerial, professional, clerical, and technical support jobs are compensated on a monthly basis (the pay period used in Figure 29.1), and blue-collar jobs are often paid hourly rates. It can be seen that the ranges in Figure 29.1 (indicated by the boxes) are linear. They also have a constant overlap of about one-third as they increase in points and dollars.

Once the pattern of ranges is designed, the pay ranges of the y axis are converted to tabular form, and the compensation levels available in each range are indicated based on the organization's policy on how employees will progress in the range: for example, step rates might be used (administration of pay within ranges is addressed further later). The point ranges on the x axis then become the guide for allocating positions (which have been previously job evaluated) to pay ranges, as the pay range example in Figure 29.1 illustrates.

Many pay range designs are possible, each with potential implications for pay policy or administration. For example, ranges may touch only at corner points as they ascend. This emphasizes a structure of flat rates without overlap in points or dollars. Overlap in pay ranges gives management the flexibility to reassign personnel to jobs allocated to neighboring ranges without having to increase or decrease pay. A corner point design might be the result of negotiated flat rates, particularly for craft jobs, where pay rates are considered to be separate for each craft.

Another design arrays the ranges on a positively inflected curve rather than a straight line. This, with no changes in the rest of the design features, means that higher compensated jobs begin at the point of upward inflection of the curve. The widths of the point ranges, however, remain constant, as do the widths of pay ranges. This outcome might occur when too broad a spectrum of jobs is encompassed by the job evaluation and pay plans, as when pay standardization covers all organizational jobs rather than separate subsystems.

Yet another design is positively curvilinear but with diminishing job evaluation points and higher levels of pay as the curve ascends. Here management wants to be less bound by job evaluation criteria and to be free to award increased pay for the higher-level jobs.

What would a broadband design look like? Assume that the graph is for jobs in a career progression, such as office clerical and technical personnel. Each box on the graph then represents career progression for a job, with possibility of movement to other boxes on the plot for designated jobs. However, pay range widths would be exaggerated, usually in excess of 100 percent (that is, maximum pay minus minimum pay, the result expressed as a percentage of the minimum). This design allows the personal rank concept to be applied to individual positions.

Step 2. Conduct a Pay Survey

Even though job evaluations represent the organization's value system for its jobs, the organization still must consider market rates in order to compete in recruiting, to adjust its pay policy relative to market rates, and to adjust its pay standardization to market averages. The latter purpose is also important for adjusting pay levels to reflect inflation in the general economy. Several U.S. Department of Labor indexes might be used to determine increases in cost of living, but they are based on selected purchases and subject to statistical artifacts, such as variations in the significance of the cost changes of the purchases and variations in the importance of the purchases as indicators. Better is to use average market rates for benchmark jobs, because these rates reflect both market adjustment to inflation and occupational supply and demand effects.

Survey data from other organizations might be relied upon solely or for comparative purposes. Various professional organizations do national surveys of their occupational specialties as do consulting companies, the U.S. Bureau of Labor Statistics, and several state agencies. Of course, comparability of benchmarks must be considered. Fundamental for an organization conducting its own survey are accurate job descriptions, particularly for benchmark jobs. As discussed under job evaluation, if the organization does not have a quantitatively based job evaluation system, it must develop one if it is to survey the market and design salary standardizations.

The geographic area to be surveyed will vary from job to job, depending upon the occupational specialty and the community of recruitment. For example, a small or medium-size city in a metropolitan area may survey only similar cities and local businesses for data on common clerical jobs. This is because many of these jobs are filled by secondary wage earners who prefer to work close to home. Many blue-collar jobs are filled locally as well. Even some professionals are attracted to a limited commuting distance and may be willing to trade off some salary for it. However, markets for most managers and professionals are at least regional, usually national, and even international in some cases. Because of the extensive spread and size of its workforce, the federal government has developed area rate adjustments for various metropolitan areas to supplement its General Schedule system. Whatever the geographic extent of the survey, mainly public and private employers from comparable size organizations should be surveyed. Other nonprofit organizations should be included where there are relevant specializations, such as social and health services jobs.

Optimally, data should be gathered by questionnaires that are followed up with visits or at least telephone conversations. For every job reported by an employer, the following minimum pay data should be gathered: the number of employees with the job title, their average rate of pay, and the number of hours in their work week. Compensation should be summarized by job surveyed to show the following (in separate lines for each employer and listed in columns): the date of the survey, number of employees in the class or job, number of hours in work weeks, and average pay of employees (converted to the same period for all employees). For each job or class, the surveyor should then compute the totals for employers, employees, and hours in the work week; the average work week per employer; and weighted average pay (employees × average pay/total number of employees).

Step 3. Gather Fringe Benefit Data

If possible, data on fringe benefits and perquisites should be gathered in the salary survey, and these rewards should be subtracted from salary and wage data. *Perquisites* differ from *fringes,* theoretically, in that they are allocated to particular jobs, services, or organizational levels as a requirement for proper functioning rather than as a form of compensation.

Because benefits often vary with the characteristics of employees (for instance, with age, salary, seniority, or marital status), it is important to be able to categorize data according to both the number of employees to whom the benefit applies and the differences in rates or amounts. Typical fringes and perquisites for which pay year costs should be gathered include

- Paid holidays (number)
- Severance pay per employee
- Paid vacation (number of days)
- Paid sick leave (number of days)
- Bonuses per employee
- Other leave (number of days)
- Profit sharing per employee
- Social Security benefits per employee
- Special allowances (food, clothing) per employee
- Pension cost per employee
- Life insurance per employee
- Health insurance per employee
- Automobile allowance or use of vehicles per employee
- Unemployment benefits per employee
- On-the-clock nonproductive time per employee (for example, transit time to and from the job)

It can be argued that this list of fringes is too detailed and perhaps not all items are worth the survey effort. Items that might be questioned are severance pay, bonuses, profit sharing, special allowances, and transit time. The answer to this argument is that it depends on how comparable a database is desired. These items are typical hidden forms of compensation, and *total compensation* implies all forms of monetary equivalents. The feasibility of surveying them must be decided by the comparing organization.

One approach to summarizing fringes is to develop a standardized cost under which costs for each benefit are computed, based on prototypical groups of the organization's employees. These groups are assembled to reflect combinations of variables, such as seniority and marital status, that represent the statistical variance in the employee population.

Finally, it is important for actors such as labor-management negotiators, compensation staff, and policymakers to be informed on total compensation—fringes plus direct pay—inasmuch as controversial public and private-sector comparisons are frequently made. Informed deliberation on pay policy should stem from total compensation data.

Step 4. Compute a Pay Line

Community job average rates must be regressed (points × dollars) to determine an average line of best fit. The shape of this line is usually curvilinear, rising more steeply at the upper end. Several regression formulas may have to be tried for best fit.

Given an existing pay plan, the current median of each range is adjusted for the new average line for all benchmarks. Thus the midpoint of each salary range will correspond to the intersection of median job evaluation points of the range and average data at that point from surveyed benchmarks. The new median ranges are then extrapolated to the extremes of each range. If there are steps or rates in the ranges, the structure of the standardization governs adjustments between bottom and top values of each range. The new medians of each range are, accordingly, the overall averages from the market survey. It is here that a policy to pay above or below the market may be applied. For example, if the policy is to pay 10 percent below market, the midpoint and extremes of each range are adjusted downward by 10 percent.

Step 5. Administrate Pay Within Ranges

This is the area where grade range design and compensation objectives come together. Exhibit 29.1 describes a few examples of ranges, which will be related to objectives.

Variables. Aside from the issues of the total size of the salary standardization and whether it is for subsystems or the entire organization, there are several variables that characterize salary schedule alternatives: the number of steps in ranges, the nature of difference between steps and between ranges (percentage

Exhibit 29.1. Examples of Salary Range Alternatives.

Example 1. Integrated Six-Step, Monthly Salaries

Grade	1	2	3	4	5	6
14	1915	2011	2112	2218	2329	2445
15	2011	2112	2218	2329	2445	2567
16	2112	2218	2329	2445	2567	2695

Example 2. Flat Rate, Nonintegrated Nine Steps, Monthly Salaries

Grade	1	2	3	4	5	6	7	8	9	Increment
14	1937	2029	2121	2213	2305	2397	2489	2581	2673	92
15	2050	2147	2244	2341	2438	2535	2632	2729	2826	97
16	2163	2266	2369	2472	2575	2678	2781	2884	2987	103

Example 3. Two-Step Flat Rate, Annual Salaries

Grade	Entrance Step	Competent Step
14	58140	61200
15	61560	64800
16	64980	68400

Example 4. Broadband, Annual Salaries

$26,000   career $60,000

Market = $32,000

$26,000 | $40,000 | ← broadband

| → Jones (assistant chemical engineer)

Example 5. Pay for Knowledge or Skill, Monthly Salaries

Entry Min K/S	25 percent of Team K/S	66 percent of Team K/S	100 percent of Team K/S
2000	2500	3320	4000

difference, constant percentage difference, constant dollar amount difference, whether ranges overlap or are flat rates, and width of ranges), and the compensation objective.

Some objectives work best with some designs and not well with others. For instance, examples 1 and 2 in Exhibit 29.1 are not good designs under a pay-for-individual-performance policy. Award of step increments could be made contingent upon performance, but how can individuals at the top step of the range be rewarded? More important, the performance obtained may not be worth the size of the step increment that would have to be awarded.

Traditional Pay System. Examples 1 and 2 of Exhibit 29.1 are the traditional systems that reward membership in the organization. The employee marches through the steps in each range, mainly based on time. Step 1 is usually the entry level, followed by a second step after the employee completes the probationary period. Other steps generally are time phased for different periods. If the standardization is not adjusted for changes in market and inflation, the individual does not achieve compensation above the extent of range values. Usually, without such adjustment, pay will be limited to the top step of the range unless the person is promoted or the job is reclassified.

Example 1 is known as an *integrated system* because of its constant percentage differences between maximum and minimum rates in ranges (width of near 28 percent), between steps in ranges (5 percent), and between ranges (about 5 percent). Thus, constant percentages provide the basis for integration as does a repetition of rates. Look diagonally up or down rates in ranges for repetition. Rate repetition provides an extension of the range overlap previously discussed. The design illustrated by example 1 has traditionally been used in small governments.

Example 2 has typically been used in large governments, where the great variety of occupations makes rate integration difficult. It is characterized by a flat rate system with constant dollar amounts (not percentages) between steps in a range and increasing dollar amounts between ranges. These types of systems sometimes use grade allocation criteria that are separate from those of the job evaluation plan for various levels of difficulty and responsibility.

Merit Pay. Example 3 eliminates multiple-step rates in ranges, except for a probationary step. Traditionally, this type of standardization has been associated with negotiated blue-collar rates. However, it can have great utility for compensating other employees in view of the trend toward government cost conservation. Its virtue is that it eliminates the annual-increase effects of multiple steps, exacerbated by cost-of-living and market adjustments.

Example 3 also provides the greatest potential for managerial flexibility with individual pay-for-performance. The ultimate in cost conservation and individual merit pay is this flat rate system, with rates increased only by market change and ability to pay and with performance rewarded through a bonus system. The jurisdiction that really wants to squeeze its workforce for performance might also make market change adjustments contingent upon performance. Because bonuses do not increase base salary and must be re-earned, bonus systems also make sense in pay-for-group-performance systems as well (such as goalsharing and gainsharing).

Sizing Merit Increments. A system of individual merit pay requires criteria for bridging performance appraisal to reward increments. The Navy demonstration project uses five performance appraisal thresholds for merit pay awards—two levels above and two below the level of *fully successful* (recall that the Navy and emerging federal government systems have collapsed multiple GS pay grade levels into pay bands). Fully successful performance is awarded *comparability.* Comparability is essentially the federal government's estimate of a national cost-of-living change, adjusted for political reality. Performance above fully successful is rewarded with comparability plus multiples of the salary increment for each pay level. One level below fully successful, comparability is halved, and two levels below it, zero is awarded.

Example 4, a broadbanding example, shows Jones, an assistant chemical engineer, placed at the market rate of $32,000, the center or median of a broad band. This band covers a career and spans a range of 131 percent. Private-sector applications use market rates as the basis for increasing or decreasing compensation for performance or competency growth (Hofrichter, 1993). This action suggests that pay for knowledge or skill, as well as for individual performance, can be accommodated with a broadbanding system. Market rate at the time the individual is appointed is the median of the band around which high and low percentiles are set. Pay is increased or decreased for performance or competency growth in percentile levels, just as the Navy system uses compressed GS grades. Individuals with exceptional qualifications might be initially appointed above the median.

Example 5 is a variation on broad bands in a pay for knowledge or skill system that rewards acquisition of team competencies.

CONCLUSION

From this chapter the reader should have learned that management needs to decide on compensation objectives and that objectives, in turn, can be translated to action through pay system structure and administration policies. Also, it should be clear that these various combinations have advantages and disadvantages. Further, the need for a job evaluation system and market survey data should be apparent. Finally, an understanding of the concept of total compensation (direct pay *and* fringe benefits) is fundamental. Although pay standardization and policies establish the direct pay, the fringe benefits must also be understood as important parts of any plan, albeit possibly for different objectives.

References

Bullock, R. J., and Lawler, E. E., III. "Gainsharing: A Few Questions and Fewer Answers." *Human Resource Management,* 1984, *5,* 197–212.

"Companies Shift (Slowly) to Team-Based Pay." *HR Focus,* July 1995, p. 11.

Equal Pay Act of 1963. U.S. Code, vol. 29, sec. 206 et seq.

Gerson, S. R. "Taking a Look at Pay-for-Knowledge." *Classifiers' Column,* Dec. 28, 1987, pp. 1–2.

Gupta, N., Schweizer, T. P., and Jenkins, G. D. "Pay-for-Knowledge Compensation Plans: Hypothesis and Survey Results." *Monthly Labor Review,* Oct. 1987, pp. 40–45.

Harron, M. "Another View of the Merit System." *Management,* Fall 1981, pp. 18–20.

Hofrichter, D. "Broadbanding: A 'Second Generation' Approach." *Compensation and Benefits Review,* Sept.–Oct. 1993, pp. 53–58.

Lawler, E. E., III, and Ledford, G. E., Jr. "Skill-Based Pay: A Concept That's Catching On." *Personnel,* Sept. 1985, pp. 30–37.

Naval Ocean Systems Center, Naval Weapons Center, University of Southern California, School of Public Administration. "Adapting Private Sector Personnel Resource Management Methods for the More Effective Operation of Federal Government Organizations. Proposal for a Demonstration Project Authorized by Title VI of the Civil Service Reform Act of 1978." Unpublished proposal. Aug. 1979.

Pagano, M. "Exploratory Evaluation of the Civil Service Reform Act's Merit Pay System for GS 13–15s: A Case Study of the U.S. Department of Health and Human Services." In D. H. Rosenbloom (ed.), *Public Personnel Policy: The Politics of the Civil Service.* Port Washington, N.Y.: Associated Faculty Press, 1985.

Pearce, J. L., and Perry, J. L. "Federal Merit Pay: A Longitudinal Analysis." *Public Administration Review,* 1983, *43,* 315–325.

Perry, J. L., Petrakis, B. A., and Miller, T. F. "Federal Merit Pay, Round II: An Analysis of the Performance Management and Recognition System." *Public Administration Review,* 1989, *49,* 29–37.

Rainey, H. G. "Public Agencies and Private Firms: Incentive Structures, Goals, and Individual Roles." *Administration and Society,* 1983, *15,* 207–242.

Rainey, H. G., Traut, C., and Blunt, B. "Reward Expectancies and Other Work-Related Attitudes in Public and Private Organizations: A Review and Extension." *Review of Public Personnel Administration,* 1986, *6*(2), 50–72.

Sauter, J. "Role of PRB in the Bonus Decision: Pitfalls to Avoid." *Public Personnel Management,* 1981, *10,* 296–298.

Schay, B. W. "In Search of the Holy Grail: Lessons in Performance Management." *Public Personnel Management,* 1993, *22,* 649–668.

Schay, B. W. *Federal Demonstration Projects: Integrated Approaches to Pay, Performance Management and Position Classification.* Rand Forum on Public Sector Human Resource Management for the 8th Quadrennial Review of Military Compensation. Briefing Notes. Washington, D.C.: Rand, Nov. 2, 1995.

Schuster, J. R., and Zingheim, P. K. *The New Pay: Linking Employee and Organizational Performance.* San Francisco: New Lexington Press, 1992.

Siegel, G. B. "Learning from Personnel Research, 1963–1988: Compensation, Benefits and Work Schedules." *Public Personnel Management,* 1989, *18,* 176–192.

Siegel, G. B. "Three Federal Demonstration Projects: Using Monetary Performance Rewards." *Public Personnel Management,* 1994, *23,* 153–164.

Silverman, B. R. "The Merit System." *Review of Public Personnel Administration,* 1982, *2*(2), 29–34.

U.S. Department of Labor, Bureau of Labor-Management Relations and Cooperative Programs. *Exploratory Investigations of Pay-for-Knowledge Systems.* Washington, D.C.: U.S. Government Printing Office, 1986.

U.S. General Accounting Office. *Analysis of OPM's Report on Pay for Performance in the Federal Government, 1980–1992.* Washington, D.C.: U.S. Government Printing Office, 1983.

U.S. General Accounting Office. *A Two-Year Appraisal of Merit Pay in Three Agencies.* Report to the Chairwoman, Subcommittee on Compensation and Employee Benefits, Committee on Post Office and Civil Service, House of Representatives of the United States. Washington, D.C.: U.S. Government Printing Office, 1984.

U.S. Merit Systems Protection Board. *Working for America.* Washington, D.C.: U.S. Government Printing Office, 1990.

"What's the Best Incentive for Employees? Study Says Small Group Incentive Plans Show Big Promise." *HR Focus,* May 1992, p. 22.

CHAPTER THIRTY

Merit Pay Mania

Transforming Polarized Support and Opposition into a Working Consensus

Gerald T. Gabris

The scene is familiar. A city manager who just a few years earlier fervently advocated and implemented a merit pay plan for his city, today just as ardently feels that merit pay does not work, and has abolished the plan he so earnestly implemented not that long ago. Attitudes surrounding merit pay can often be described as manic. Advocacy or rejection of merit pay can reflect enthusiasm or disenchantment that is extreme but also frequently transient. Generally, these extremes are grounded in assumptions that sound initially convincing and sensible but on deeper reflection are often found contradictory or inconsistent.

The purpose of this chapter is to explore the issue of merit pay, or incentive pay, as a practical tool for improving public agency performance. Building on the theme of merit pay mania, the chapter highlights reasons why some people like and some abhor merit pay as a personnel management tool. The topic of merit pay tends to evoke strong reactions among employees, especially in relation to how they perceive their self-interest affected by merit reward systems. Emotional battle lines are also drawn according to perceptions of equity, fairness, and the proper performance roles of employees in public organizations. Regarding merit pay, there are few easy or simple answers.

Fortunately, there exists an extensive literature on the topic of incentive pay for both the public and private sectors. Unfortunately, the more we research the topic, the less we seem to know about how to make it work consistently, especially in public-sector environments. If a pattern does exist, it implies that incentive pay has not worked effectively in the public sector, even after almost two decades of widespread application at all levels of government in just about all kinds of public organization situations (Heneman, 1992).

If merit pay has been no rose garden, and has not worked well in the public sector, then why study it further, why spend valuable space in a personnel management text reviewing a topic that has worn out its nascent welcome? My response is that merit pay will not go away solely because it has floundered in several settings. For managers seeking to influence employee behavior, it offers too potentially powerful a tool to be discarded. In the public sector especially, it is also intuitively extremely appealing as a vehicle for making public employees accountable for their performance. This is a political plus that professional public administrators cannot conveniently ignore.

Instead of witnessing the withering away of merit pay, we are more likely to see modifications, alterations, new experiments, and adaptations of the concept that have been customized and designed to much better fit specific situations, perhaps in limited and narrow applications. In short, merit pay is here to stay in some form. The real questions then become, What are the likely variants? And how might managers increase the odds for success?

The material is divided into several interconnected and intermingled discussions that should be conceived as phases rather than sequentially separate and distinct sections.

1. *Merit pay mania: basic working assumptions.* Why do employees hold extreme views toward merit pay, what do managers think merit pay should accomplish, and are these assumptions based more on emotions or facts? Answering these questions requires some understanding of the rich theoretical legacy of merit pay. How does theory say this process is supposed to work, according to psychological and economic models?

2. *Merit pay reality.* What do consulting observations and research show about what seems to work? Do merit pay theories pan out when subjected to field conditions?

3. *Strategies for mitigating merit pay mania.* What practical alternatives exist for practitioners and personnelists for making merit pay work better for improving work performance?

4. *Conclusion: why merit pay will not become extinct.* Merit pay will continue to be an important management tool into the twenty-first century, especially in the public sector. However, it will continue to experience a rocky road, full of pitfalls.

To summarize, the purpose or this chapter is to suggest ways of moving toward a more consensual, less bimodal debate on the practical utility of merit pay in the public sector. Although developing an effective merit pay plan is difficult, professional public managers need to search continually for incentive plans that on balance, are accepted by and motivate the most employees. Perhaps alternative kinds of incentive plans should be targeted toward different kinds of employees performing substantively different functions. But before we get too far ahead of the game, let us get back to the basics. Why does merit pay evoke extreme emotions, attitudes, and opinions?

MERIT PAY MANIA: BASIC WORKING ASSUMPTIONS

Prior to the passage of the 1978 Civil Service Reform Act, then president Jimmy Carter frequently spoke of the need to "remove the deadwood" from the bureaucracy (Ingraham and Ban, 1984). Back then, as today, many politicians and academic observers viewed public bureaucracy as stagnant and guided by the norm of mediocrity. Typical public employees were seen as comfortably stuck in a civil service system that barring egregious wrongdoing, protected them from aggressive external remediation. Within this context, public bureaucratic organizations and public employees were thought to perform poorly because they lacked adequate incentives and or competition. The now ubiquitous reinventing theme developed by Osborne and Gaebler (1992), makes noncompetitive government bureaucracy its central theme. Government organizations engage in rowing rather than steering because they operate in quasi-monopolistic systems and meaningful competitive pressures are absent. Mediocrity reigns supreme.

One solution has been to provide focused merit incentives that reward high performance and that at least indirectly, punish poor performers, the deadwood referred to by President Carter. Merit pay provides a seemingly quick and easy fix for increasing competition between employees by rewarding worker productivity.

The federal Civil Service Reform Act of 1978 mandated merit pay for higher-level supervisors in the federal workforce. Subsequent reformulations of this policy (Perry, 1991) remain today and encompass a much larger spectrum of federal workers. With the advent of merit pay at the federal level, most state and voluminous local governments followed suit by inaugurating their own brand of incentive pay plans, based on the premise that public bureaucracy and public employees need more than just a gentle kick in the buttocks (Golembiewski, 1986). Merit pay was viewed as a powerful tool available to policymakers and managers for making the public servant not only more productive, but also more accountable.

Yet, as merit plans were implemented during the 1970s and 1980s, strong opinions began to surface about their rationality, success rates, practicality, and fairness. Generally, merit pay has supporters or opponents—without much conceptually rich middle ground. Table 30.1 summarizes key assumptions and debates. These serve as a pathway for the discussion to follow.

Table 30.1. Merit Pay Mania: A Continuum of Support and Opposition.

Assumption Concept	Supporters Assume	Opponents Assume
Motivation	Incentives motivate by satisfying employee needs.	Incentives often demotivate or dissatisfy; they can lower self-esteem or they may not effect motivation at all.
Competition	Incentives create constructive competition between employees; lead to distributive justice.	Becomes destructive and win-lose. Reduces morale. Pits employee against employee. Is procedurally unfair.
Expectancy	Employees learn to expect that certain levels of behavior lead to certain levels of reward. This causes poorer performers to improve.	High performers may benefit but average to poor performers blame not themselves but biased managers for their lower performance. They feel the system is unfair. Poor performers do not change.
Supervisory leverage	Increases control of managers over workers. Makes workers more accountable.	Supervisors do not like to differentially reward employees; it creates friction and hurts teamwork.
Employee performance	Easily measurable via performance appraisal objectives, behavior, results, and traits. Performance is controlled by worker.	Very difficult to measure fairly. Rating errors lead to biased and unfair decisions systematically. Poor performance is really the fault of management and the system, not the worker.
Implementation	Easy; a technical-policy matter backed by strong managerial support. Generally, one size fits all. Incentives are contingent on funding. Is mandatory. Resonates with a bureaucratic control culture.	Highly complex. Often fails. More trouble than it is worth. No clear correlation between performance improvements and rewards. Erratic, insufficient funding. Technically flawed. Blames the wrong person. Reinforces a culture of fear and low trust.

Motivation

In its elemental form, supporters of incentive pay feel it serves as a superb *motivational* tool. Here, motivation is defined as the drive experienced by an employee to satisfy a need. For example, employees who want more pay (a need) work harder (experience a drive) to accomplish job-related tasks or goals. Incentives satisfy felt needs and thus motivate employees to work harder and more productively. This simple concept can be traced as far back as Frederick Winslow Taylor's differential piece rate plan, where plant workers producing more items per day were paid a higher rate (Schachter, 1989).

In contemporary theory, one of the stronger supporters of the idea that merit pay has powerful motivational properties is Edward Lawler (1971, 1981, 1990). With Victor Vroom (1964), Lawler (1973) is considered a codeveloper of the *expectancy theory* of motivation. This model suggests that a certain level of effort leads to a certain level of performance that is associated with a certain level of reward, with the *ability* of the worker serving as an intervening variable (Lawler, 1981).

For example, students learn quickly, we hope, that a certain amount of time spent studying (effort) leads to a desired level of performance (a score of 90 percent) that is rewarded with a letter grade (A). Probability also plays a role in determining reward success. Effort spent studying may not produce an anticipated score if ability is not also present or if the test is harder than expected. Probability may cause a student to study even harder and to exert greater effort if the reward, an A in the class, is highly valued.

To supporters of merit pay, this simple but elegant formulation explains how and why merit pay works. Management should create rewards employees value (usually money) and attach them to expected levels of performance. Presumably, this will motivate employees to work harder, so they can earn more money, especially when they know in advance the level of performance expected of them. Linking incentives to motivation sounds so intuitively and theoretically sensible, it is difficult for some supporters of merit pay to comprehend why employees do not like it or why it should not work. Merit pay seems mainly a policy and technical matter. Supply the valued incentives, design a performance measurement system, and presto—motivation to perform should logically follow.

Opponents point to several problems with this logic. First, not all agree that merit pay increases motivation to perform. Deci and Ryan (1985) argue that incentives may actually harm intrinsic motivation, insulting already high-performing employees by suggesting that their work needs to be rewarded. High performers perform high not for pay but because they are motivated by the sense of self-fulfillment that comes with high achievement.

Other theorists, such as Herzberg (1966, 1968), argue that factors that motivate are separate from those that demotivate. Generally, dissatisfaction with pay, which Herzberg classifies as a *hygiene factor*, leads to employee dissatisfaction. Giving employees an equitable pay raise does not necessarily motivate them; it just makes them less dissatisfied. Herzberg contends that what really motivates are incentives that appeal to an employee's higher psychological needs—such as greater responsibility, more involvement in decision making, and richer, more varied tasks. Hackman and Oldham (1980) make a somewhat similar argument about motivation in their description of work context.

In my consulting and research experience the enigma of linking pay incentives to motivation has often been borne out. Many employees, especially those in nonsupervisory, mid-skill positions, perceive merit pay as risky. When evaluated as only average or below average, they tend to blame management as biased rather than their own performance as inadequate when lower than expected merit increments are handed out. Moreover, very few commit to clear courses for improvement with the aim of securing higher merit pay raises in the future. Instead, average performers adhere to the self-justifying norm that no matter how well they perform, they will never be equitably trusted. Thus few experience motivation to improve.

Competition

Proponents argue merit pay generates healthy competition between employees, resulting in distributive justice. Aggressive, productive employees receive higher pay increments and average performers get what they deserve, which is something less. Two economic models, *implicit contract theory* (Gordon, 1974; Rosen, 1985) and *efficiency wage theory* (Salop, 1979; Stiglitz, 1987; Nalbandian, 1987) lend credence to this view. When incentives are linked to expected work output, employees feel they should provide an honest day's work for an honest day's pay. Those who do not, should receive less. Also, by paying higher producers premium wages, employers help ensure that the best workers remain with the organization.

According to *equity theory* (Adams, 1965; Jaques, 1961; Walster, Berscheid, and Walster, 1973; Lawler, 1981), employees frequently compare their job outputs and inputs (pay) to those of similar coworkers. If a productive worker is earning the same as a less productive employee in the same line of work, the former may eventually lower her productivity to a point where perceived equity is attained. Hence, rewarding those employees who compete and outproduce others has become a staple in the U.S. work ethic and can be observed in jobs ranging from players in professional sports to mechanics in a public works garage.

Winning is highly valued. Doing one's best and beating others at some game brings status, honor, and monetary reward. Opponents of merit pay point out, however, that this competitive philosophy exacts a price. Competition produces losers as well as winners. The merit raise of one employee is often financed by a reduced increment to a less fortunate coworker. Win-lose merit systems result, where the losers become angry, frustrated, or demotivated.

This is exactly what happened with initial merit pay efforts in the federal government, according to Frederick Thayer (1978). To Thayer, merit pay insults long-term employees who have mastered skills and who have attained high levels of proficiency in their jobs by forcing supervisors to artificially rank them. Arguably, senior administrators could find themselves in the bizarre situation of being evaluated as inadequate, and thus not deserving of a merit pay raise, while a peer receives a hefty monetary award. Thayer believes that merit pay creates unhealthy competition between employees, which in itself is bad enough but even worse from the standpoint that available empirical evidence does not support the assumption that competition increases overall performance (Perry, 1986). In a more recent reanalysis of his earlier position, Thayer feels that with merit pay, the "disaster continues" (1986).

Whether merit pay is perceived as creating unhealthy competition may have a lot to do with how successfully an employee has benefited from a specific system and the nature of the job. For example, in jobs requiring a high degree of teamwork, such as firefighting, employees may not want systems that differentiate between employees too much, for fear that this practice may actually weaken group camaraderie, which is crucial for success. I have found this same group norm operative in many blue-collar public-sector jobs. Blue-collar employees tend to prefer a high degree of internal equity between themselves, with relatively little pay differentiation based on merit. Alternatively, employees in supervisory and skilled white-collar positions are generally more predisposed toward a merit pay differentiator. Yet even here, well-conceived rules, evaluation instruments, and clear employee discretion over those areas being evaluated must be present. How difficult these factors are to achieve is illustrated in some early work by Peter Blau (1972).

In his study of a state employment office, Blau found that managerially induced competition between employees resulted in win-lose decisions that actually lowered the overall productivity of a work unit when compared to a work unit operating on a team-based, noncompetitive norm. In the former unit, employment officers actually hid job placement notices from each other to maximize their job placement success, even though such a practice clearly worked against the interests of their job-seeking clientele.

Expectancy

Research by Mitchell and me (Gabris and Mitchell, 1988) suggests the presence of a Matthew Effect in the distribution of merit pay incentives. This biblical aphorism prophesies that the rich shall get richer while the poor shall get poorer. High performers continually get rated high and continually reap the lion's share of merit payouts. Average to below average performers also get stereotyped and consistently receive lesser increments. To the high performer this reinforcement justifies his or her achievement, and he or she continues to produce well.

Expectancy theory, then, may describe what drives high but not low performers. Some research findings lend support to this view (Soden and Lovrich, 1988; Gabris, Giles, and Mitchell, 1988; Daley, 1988) by reporting that motivation strategies for high performers may not work equally well for average to below average producers. Employees not receiving merit pay disbursements perceive the system as biased, unfair, and as stacked against them. Thus they experience or feel little drive to improve, for what will they gain?

Supervisory Leverage

Another strong argument of merit pay supporters is that merit pay provides leverage to supervisors to reward those employees doing the best work. Immediate supervisors are most familiar with the work quantity and quality of their subordinates and thus are in the best strategic position to know who is performing. The capacity to award merit pay disbursements also gives supervisors a measure of control over their subordinates. Presumably, employees will be more motivated by and more receptive to a supervisor's suggestions for product quantity and quality improvement when they know that supervisor can reward their efforts. In short, merit pay should enhance supervisory credibility and thus enable supervisors to perform their roles better.

A problem with that view is that merit pay may give supervisors a responsibility they do not want. In an early assessment of performance appraisal, which is highly connected to merit pay disbursements, Douglas McGregor (1957) argues that supervisors dislike evaluating subordinates because it puts them in the position of playing God. They must differentiate and rank subordinates, some of whom they may consider friends. The obligation to provide subsequent feedback to employees is distasteful when the communication is negative and when the incentives backing up such an assessment are less than the employee expects he or she deserves. As a consequence, merit pay opponents feel that supervisors seek to avoid honest differentiation of ratees and instead prefer to rate them all above average and to give them all positive feedback and pay increments.

Some evidence exists for both points of view. On one hand, supervisors, as a group, clearly see more value in a merit pay system than do nonsupervisory employees (Gabris, 1986). Supervisors are more likely to believe a merit pay plan will work, that it will motivate, and that it serves a valuable purpose for the organization. To supervisors, merit pay represents a source of power. On the other hand, scattered evidence exists that supervisors refrain from rating their subordinates objectively. The widespread presence of rating errors, especially positive leniency, even when professionally developed performance appraisals are used, is one indicator of this (Latham and Wexley, 1981). When the federal government began implementing its merit pay plan, almost 90 percent of all ratees were found to exceed standards (Rappold, 1981). What was going on was that supervisors were rating all their employees high, thus forcing a relatively equal distribution of the merit pay pool. Supervisors simply did not want to hurt employees monetarily even though they had the power to finance larger incentives for the highest performers by giving less money to poorer producers.

To many supervisors the power to grant merit pay awards confronts them with a paradox. On the one hand, this capacity should increase managerial leverage over employees and enhance the credibility of a boss and thus the boss's ability to execute her or his priorities. On the other hand, differentially rewarding employees is likely to create perceptions of inequity and bias, which generate problems in morale and resistance. Having your cake and eating it too may be an impossible goal with merit pay. Another practice then is for supervisors to award merit pay raises and to claim they signify meaningful recognitions when in fact there is a relatively small range between the lowest and highest merit awards (Wallace and Fay, 1988). This way, supervisors give the impression that a specific employee is very important, yet by treating almost all employees the same way, they water down the symbolic value of such recognition.

Employee Performance

For merit pay to work, employee performance must be measurable. Supporters generally conceive the measurement issue as a technical problem solved through the implementation of a well-conceived performance appraisal instrument. Because Chapter Eighteen handles performance appraisal, not much must be said about it here, other than that the items normally measured include traits, behaviors, and results (Latham and Wexley, 1981; Bernardin and Beatty, 1984). Heneman (1992) defines merit pay as simply "individual pay increases based on the rated performance of individual employees in a previous time period" (p. 6).

Supporters feel that measuring individual performance makes an employee accountable for his or her productivity, or lack of it, and illustrates areas for improvement. On balance, most employees are evaluated about twice per year (Latham and Wexley, 1981; Heneman, 1992), and this affords an opportunity for the organization to correct defective behavior. It is assumed employees are responsible for improving themselves in those areas identified as weaknesses by management. Failure to improve can result in disciplinary action or even termination. Knowing that management has this much carrot-and-stick power over them, employees should perform better for fear of what may happen if they do not.

Opponents of merit pay find many problems in performance appraisal and measurement. The arguments here can be extensive, and because performance appraisals are covered elsewhere, I draw only a minimalist sketch of the debate. Essentially, some opponents argue that performance appraisal is a highly subjective enterprise under its guise of scientific methodology and that this subjectivity can lead to quite inaccurate and unfair rating decisions (Fox, 1991; Nalbandian, 1981; Lovrich, Shaffer, and Yale, 1980; Daley, 1988). Employees often come to fear performance appraisal and do not feel it accurately corresponds with their self-assessments of performance (Meyer, 1975).

Besides methodological problems in measurement that can lead to bias, W. Edwards Deming (1986) and Andrea Gabor (1990) find problems in the systems the ratees must work with. Gabor argues that most performance and quality problems (defects) can be traced to either common or special variation and that managers often blame employees for not performing well in situations where they are not to blame. They may have little control over the frequency of errors or defects because these are produced randomly by the system, not the employee, no matter how hard the employee strives to eliminate them. Deming argues it is the responsibility of management, not the employee, to making the system work. Continually improving systems would render voluminous performance appraisals (many of which are spurious anyway) unnecessary and thereby reduce a drain on management time that could be better spent elsewhere. Some have taken this view to heart and question the wisdom of widespread use of performance appraisal in government (Bowman, 1994).

Implementation

Finally, supporters feel that implementation of merit pay systems is primarily a mechanical, technical matter that must be backed up with strong managerial support. They may feel that implementation of such a plan is a matter of managerial will to make tough decisions regarding employee behavior and results. Supporters also feel that by following noncomplex, step-by-step, formulaic recipes for designing a measuring system and merit payout policy, any public organization can effectively implement a merit pay plan.

Such cookbook approaches are generally characterized by common attributes. First, most use a one-size-fits-all performance appraisal instrument for nonsupervisory employees, with usually only minor modifications allowed for assessing supervisors. Second, these plans rate employees once per annum with a rating instrument either totally or partially based on the personal traits of the ratee. This approach helps ensure maximum supervisory discretion, plus such instruments are very easy to develop. Many public organizations lack sophisticated in-house expertise for developing valid and reliable appraisal instruments, and even when they have this resource available, devising these documents usually takes so much time and costs so much money that few make the effort. Third, employees are given a global rating score with virtually no meaningful feedback about their performance or how performance scores will be translated into merit pay increments.

Management decisions on how to distribute merit pay payouts normally occur after evaluation, because only then does management possess sufficient information for predicting payout distributions contingent upon incentive money available. Usually, management refrains from saying in advance that a score of x will result in an incentive increment of y, because when too many employees earn the score of x, not all can receive increment y. Conventionally, merit pay payouts are awarded once per year, usually as a percentage of an employee's base pay, although more and more organizations are moving toward a fixed-dollar bonus that does not become part of the salary base (Heneman, 1992). Incentive pay supporters generally advocate a forced merit pay distribution based on employees' relative scoring patterns rather than a distribution that attaches specific increments to absolute score values. One method for doing the former is the despised (by employees) normal curve distribution. Here, only a small percentage of the employees can occupy the space on the curve indicating performance excellence, even when absolute scores suggest everyone is doing good work.

Botched implementation has been cited as one of the major reasons why merit pay does not work well in the public sector (Gabris and Giles, 1983b; Perry, 1986; Thayer, 1986; Lovrich, 1987; Daley, 1987). Problems with implementation segue into the topic of merit pay reality, for it is indeed in the details of implementation that most merit pay plans succeed—or more commonly fail. Consulting and research experience suggests that formulating merit pay theory and testing reward hypotheses in laboratory situations represents an easier and less complex endeavor than implementing merit pay in the field. Armchair philosophers aside, merit pay is probably one of the most difficult personnel management tools to implement successfully, among an almost endless panoply of personnel techniques. What follows reflects my personal experiences and observations more than detailed research findings and thus also reflects my own biases regarding merit pay implementation in the public sector. Nonetheless this discussion should offer clues for reformulating merit pay plans to lessen the hiatus between supporters and opponents.

OBSERVATIONS ABOUT MERIT PAY REALITY

Both supporters and opponents of merit pay express valid concerns, and both draw upon rich empirical and theoretical foundations to strengthen their arguments. Theories underlying merit pay practices—such as expectancy theory, need theory, goal theory (Locke and Latham, 1990), and economic theory—sound ostensibly convincing. One problem is that most of these theories have not been tested rigorously under field conditions, and if they have been subjected to empirical investigation at all, the medium has been the controlled laboratory—usually on a college campus (Locke and Latham, 1990). Transfer of laboratory findings to the field has been at best tenuous. Research findings from the field are often mixed because slight variations in conditions can lead to dramatically different results. Thus gaining a handle on exactly what works under general public-sector situations remains elusive.

This pattern, however, does not prohibit the following broad assertions about trends in public-sector merit pay that seem to influence implementation success. The reader should understand, though, that exceptions to these generalizations may exist.

1. Public organizations are notoriously inconsistent in funding merit pay pools at adequate levels. Available merit pay increments can change year to year from extremely generous amounts to nothing. This creates a roller-coaster effect that makes it difficult to link meaningful rewards to performance consistently.

The initial energy, enthusiasm, and financial support characterizing embryonic merit pay programs, frequently diminishes over time. This pattern precipitates a host of implementation dilemmas. First, higher levels of performance are not continually reinforced with commensurately equitable rewards. This inconsistency undermines the basic effort-performance-reward sequence vital to expectancy theory. Commonly, the amount of money public agencies make available for merit raise pools alternates dramatically—in a year when the pool is diminished the highest performer might conceivably earn an absolute increment that is smaller than the amount earned by an average performer during a year when the pool is flush.

As already indicated, even when merit money is available, the difference between the highest and lowest awards may be so nominal that to the high performer, merit pay signifies an insulting sham. Public organizations need to deal with the reality that their monetary reward systems are likely to wax and wane and therefore should not become the primary means for improving employee performance. Public organizations need to broaden their conception of acceptable incentives to include those more routinely available. This may require going beyond conventional financial incentives to more creative ways of rewarding productive employees. After all, an incentive is simply something that employees value, nothing else. How alternative incentives might be pursued by public organizations receives more attention shortly.

2. Merit payouts are not awarded frequently enough to reinforce preferred behaviors and/or results.

This problem is associated with the first but also reflects a substantively different issue. Reinforcement theory clearly suggests that rewards should recur frequently, although not predictably, if they are to have a positive reinforcing effect (Skinner, 1953; Burke, 1982).

Not only do most public agencies offer merit rewards that are too small and are inconsistent, they also do it too infrequently. The disbursement norm for most organizations is once per year, with a small number handing out the merit increment in two installments to spread out the effect. When a typical merit award is further marginalized via a monthly payout, the motivational effect is negligible; employees soon forget their merit award. Public organizations have countered this trend by giving two smaller rewards, juggling pay systems to reward employees at different times of the year, and more sensibly, by giving untaxed lump sum bonuses. Overall, however, a lag period between evaluation and merit payouts seems to diminish the motivational potential of merit pay.

3. Most merit pay plans are nested in bureaucratic structures that on balance, are merit pay unfriendly.

In a recent book on managing diversity, Robert T. Golembiewski (1995) makes the case for diversity friendly and unfriendly organizations. Much of his analysis applies to merit pay as well (Golembiewski, 1977, 1985, 1989). Golembiewski argues that typical public agencies are functionally structured bureaucracies that contain inherent weaknesses. Bureaucratic structure works when the environment remains stable, when tasks are routine, and when production technology is unsophisticated. Because these conditions rarely prevail in today's public arena, organizing strategies grounded in the bureaucratic model (Figure 30.1) are unable to effectively incorporate such modern management reforms as diversity management or merit pay other than in a superficial, cosmetic application (see also Gabris, 1995).

The organization depicted in Figure 30.1 exemplifies government agencies at all levels. The general manager (GM) is the only person who knows what transpires in the total system, with subunits (S units) specializing in functions that facilitate a sequential flow-of-work output process. This orthodox design, which remains so common, has many drawbacks. Others besides Golembiewski have critiqued the bureaucratic model and urged a postbureaucratic design (Osborne and Gaebler, 1992; Lawler, 1992; Denhardt, 1993; Hummel, 1987). Common bureaucratic dysfunctions, à la Golembiewski, can be summarized as follows.

First, bureaucratic structures encourage internal vertical and horizontal competitiveness, between employees for upward mobility and between S units. This

Figure 30.1. The Typical Bureaucratic Model.

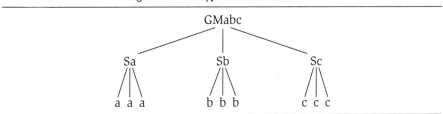

precipitates win-lose outcomes. Relationships between employees and between S units degenerate, exhibiting low trust, low openness (communication), high risk, and low owning (saying what one thinks). Under such conditions, energy for reform or innovation dwindles, employees and supervisors play their cards close to their vests, and do not rock the boat. A culture of defensive routines flourishes. Employees know the problems exist, but because the pain associated with dealing with them cuts deep (not to mention the risk), they become undiscussable (Argyris, 1985, 1991).

To further complicate things, bureaucratic organizations use command-and-control rule systems to obtain basic employee compliance, and employee commitment is generally treated as a rather hollow managerial ideal (Gabris, 1995). Personnel technology becomes a source of management's power to control the behavior of employees operating within narrow job descriptions. Now insert a merit pay plan into this degenerating, control-oriented culture, brimming with defensive routines, and guess what happens next?

The answer is obvious. Bureaucratic structure does not nurture the kind of trusting, open, risk-taking relationships between supervisors and subordinates crucial for making merit pay succeed. More likely, employees disgruntled the least bit with their reward increments will blame incompetent management rather than their own performance, reinforcing what is now known as the Dilbert principle (Adams, 1995). To employees in bureaucratic systems the annual performance evaluation leading to a merit award becomes a manipulative game. Consequently, learning how to *game,* or manipulate, the process to one's best advantage, even if such machinations are of dubious ethical bearing, becomes an accepted practice. That merit pay develops a negative stereotype under such conditions should not surprise. And the pattern of bureaucratic effects just described raises another important question. Can merit pay succeed as an isolated, discrete intervention, somehow remaining separate and untainted by potent organizational flaws? Or alternatively, can merit pay work only as part of an integrated set of multiple coordinated interventions that complement and add value to the larger system, as in a well-conducted culture change?

Golembiewski's (1995) and my observations suggest that merit pay cannot succeed as a lone ranger intervention; it cannot remain unaffected by the dysfunctions connected with typical bureaucratic structure. Other advocates of merit pay see merit pay more as working in concert with complementary change efforts, where the ultimate goal is substantive improvement in the overall culture of the work environment (Lawler, 1981, 1986, 1992). As Golembiewski (1995) convincingly argues, managers need to create organizational designs that are friendlier to complex managerial interventions. (What such postbureaucratic designs might look like and how reconceptualized merit pay plans can be made more congruent with larger system transitions will be addressed shortly.)

4. Typical merit pay plans focus solely on individual performance.
They exclude evaluation of team or group efforts and require the
use of sophisticated performance appraisals capable of measuring
specific individual contributions to tasks.

Noted organizational theorist Chester Barnard ([1938] 1968) has remarked
that the central reason organizations are created is to facilitate a system of coordinated and cooperative activity toward some purpose. The value of organizing stems from integrating the efforts of several individuals toward a common
goal. Success is not attained by just one person but grows out of the combined
effort of several persons working cooperatively. Most merit pay plans, however,
reward rated individual performance (Heneman, 1992) without considering that
individual performance may not be as salient as the performance of the whole
group or team. I have addressed this problem in earlier analyses (Gabris,
Mitchell, and McLemore, 1985), and it is related to a common merit pay assumption, namely:

5. Most merit pay systems assume performance
is controlled and determined by individual workers,
not by the systems and technology they use.

A common gripe heard from many employees derives from the fact that they
exercise nominal control over the tasks they are expected to perform and are
evaluated on. Moreover, the output of many other employees mainly involves
their contribution to a team or group effort, and attempts to extract minute individual contributions to that whole effort may be meaningless, misguided, or
highly inaccurate. For instance, the grant proposal one employee is responsible
for developing may require information developed by another employee, clerical
assistance from yet another, and computer software guidance from a staff person
being pulled in five directions at once. At any point in this flow-of-work process,
downtime by one contributor can easily stymie the speedy and efficient performance of the person ultimately responsible. By evaluating the last person on
the production chain as doing a good or bad job, managers are not taking into
account how that outcome would never have been possible without the cooperation and teamwork from other key contributors to the grant proposal. The
more meaningful measure is the quality of the grant proposal itself, rather than
the performance of a single contributor to the process.

There are many jobs where individual performance is measurable and meaningful and where the employee does enjoy a modicum of discretion. Here individual performance appraisals and merit rewards make sense. Equally, there are
many jobs, probably the great majority, that depend on teamwork and group
effort to create productive success (Hackman and Oldham, 1980; Lawler, 1992).

Conventional performance appraisal and concomitant merit pay plans typically ignore teamwork and do not reward group or team performance. This practice creates a gap between what is actually done and what is actually rewarded. By stressing individual contribution, merit pay plans encourage win-lose competition and emphasize for many public organizations the wrong level of performance.

By fixating on individual contributions, conventional merit pay plans also ignore management responsibility for system defects that reduce individual performance. The frustration felt by many employees involves their perception that they are blamed for performance glitches over which they have no control and that seem to emanate from managerial ineptness, ignorance, or avoidance. Compelling employees to improve in situations over which they have little influence results in several awkward, frustrating, and occasionally negative patterns.

As stress mounts, employees are likely to experience higher levels of job burnout (Golembiewski, Munzenrider, and Stevenson, 1986). As some employees burn out, they actually strive to work harder but only spin their wheels more. This exacerbates the situation and hastens their eventual running out of gas. This would not be a big deal if it were not for exceedingly strong evidence that high levels of job burnout exist in public organizations worldwide and that this occurrence is significantly related to most things we consider bad about organizations (Golembiewski, Boudreau, Sun, and Luo, 1996).

Additionally, employees become confused over what they can do to improve. When employee efforts do not normally result in predictable improvements, merit awards seem arbitrary and unfair. If an employee is lucky enough to work in an updated unit with good equipment and competent supervisors, that employee is more likely to be productive. Those less fortunate will seem less effective. Under such conditions, employees eventually develop a hard shell in order to survive and to work within what to them is an absurd expectation. They go along with the flow; they play the game, but they come to believe that merit pay is practiced more on paper than in reality.

6. Public employee unions have never met a merit pay plan they like.

7. Merit pay fixates on only one major variable for determining fairness in compensation, namely, individual equity. It generally ignores the salience of internal and external equity concerns.

These two assertions are fundamentally related to merit pay reality. The majority of employees I have dealt with, and especially those in blue-collar, low-skilled positions, are most concerned with pay stability, pay predictability, and internal equity (fairness in how the organization rewards employees performing roughly equivalent work).

As I have already discussed, merit pay tends to be erratic, unstable, and risky. Public organizations cannot clearly predict year to year how much money will be available in a merit pool. Relatedly, employees want to know how much money will be available to them in terms of an actual pay increment so they can plan accordingly. Merit pay emphasizes differences in individual performance and stresses the need to attach pay rewards to such differences. Equity theory would seem to warrant this kind of distribution (Adams, 1965). However, in the real world, employees are also very concerned with how their pay correlates with the external market (external equity), so they can determine whether their work organization is paying them appropriately. If a public agency awards decent merit increments, but employees perceive their base salaries as substantially below market, then the motivational impetus associated with the merit raise may be nil. Similarly, if an employee receives a merit raise but feels his or her base pay is substantially less than that of employees performing similar work, that employee's motivation to work hard may vaporize.

The point is this. A merit pay emphasis may focus too much attention on the wrong employee equity concern and do so in a way that does not enhance overall performance. Even though accountability, distributive justice, and retention of high performers may occur, these ideals may become hollow victories if the employees for whom they are targeted are more vitally concerned with elemental external and internal equity conditions.

Observations about merit pay reality, when complemented by the persuasive concerns of opponents, may give the rather dour impression that merit pay has become a dead issue in public administration. I do not think this is the case. On the contrary, merit pay is here to stay. Given what we know about what is wrong with current merit pay theory and applications, what reformulations of this technology might engender greater consensus and success? The following section now turns to this task.

STRATEGIES FOR MITIGATING MERIT PAY MANIA

Although no one best way for formulating and implementing merit pay probably exists, we should by now be better equipped for not shooting ourselves in the proverbial foot. We should be able to formulate more realistic, more consistent, and less controversial merit pay policies and techniques and intervene within our typical bureaucratic structures to make them more merit pay friendly. The suggestions just discussed may not resolve all the disagreements between merit pay supporters and opponents, and polarized positions are likely to persist. At the same time, these suggestions may help close the gap. So what might be done to make merit pay more user friendly, and thus enhance greater consensus between competing points of view?

1. Managers need to move away from using financial
or monetary incentives as the primary or sole incentive for
motivating employees via merit or incentive plans. They need to
creatively broaden what they consider valued incentives in order
to stabilize rewards and to make them consistently available.

This is not necessarily a new idea and I have addressed it on other occasions (Gabris and Giles, 1983a). The plain fact remains that most public organizations cannot offer large enough monetary incentives on a frequent enough basis for them to do much good. Politically, it is difficult to provide consistently high monetary incentives for public employees when, to many citizens and casual observers of government, government bureaucracy is the problem. Even when the political environment might support hefty merit pools, economic conditions may complicate and limit total monies available. Therefore public organizations have to have successful incentive programs and need to be more creative and innovative in devising rewards they can offer employees on a regular, consistent basis.

This translates into a greater organizational willingness to consider nonmonetary, nontraditional rewards that nonetheless satisfy employees' personal needs. A first step in such a program is to survey employees for the type of nonmonetary incentives they prefer and, second, to inventory what the public organization can make reasonably and consistently available. When this idea is presented to some public administrators, they allege it simply mimics and updates the old "atta boy," slap-on-the-back form of recognition practiced in the military. Or they worry that nonmonetary incentives will make employees perceive the organization as trying to get by on the cheap, which will be interpreted as a not-so-subtle slap in the face, leading to increased demotivation.

These dire predictions may prevail in crude heavy-handed and top-down development of an incentive program that tells employees what they will do. Here bureaucratic dysfunctions already highlighted will slip into gear, exacerbating already degenerating supervisor-subordinate relationships. Innovative, nonmonetary incentive reforms under such duress will certainly fail. On the other hand, managers now know that high-involvement cultures (Lawler, 1986, 1992) with credible leaders (Kouzes and Posner, 1987) using genuine recognition (Peters and Waterman, 1982) can be highly successful.

Leaders have to want to make a difference, have to take a new incentive reform seriously, and have to support it fully. Without intense leadership involvement not much positive will transpire. Leaders must step outside their comfortable bureaucratic niches and power structures. No empirical evidence suggests that employees will perceive nonmonetary rewards as too cheap. In fact, even if an agency can offer no monetary rewards, most employees would probably like having some alternative incentives and perquisites available. Some reward is better than none.

My nonscientific surveying of employees shows that what typical workers might consider a valued reward is quite broad and extensive. A partial list might include

- Extra time off, extra vacation, comp time
- Flexible work hours
- Better equipment, better working conditions
- More self-regulation and scheduling of work
- Perquisites such as better parking, travel, trips to conferences, small but meaningful monetary bonuses, formal recognition, extra fringe benefits, specialized training, job rotation, and employee discounts

All these incentives have costs, but normally, they are indirect and easier than merit pay for organizations to absorb over time. They should not totally replace monetary rewards but serve as stable supplements to monetary incentives that are less frequent and less hefty than desirable. Moreover, because an organization can generate a menu of nonmonetary incentives, employees could earn merit points and then spend those points on the incentives that satisfy their needs the best.

> **2. Merit pay cannot be implemented as an isolated, separate reform detached from the larger bureaucratic system. Instead, it should be implemented jointly with complementary interventions aimed at lessening the degenerative effects of bureaucratic structure.**

When merit pay becomes associated with a senior management change effort, rank-and-file employees often become skeptical and dubious about the staying power, seriousness, and fairness of what is being proposed. I have heard the following comment in various forms in more than one public agency: "We've learned more about our agency's merit pay program through the local newspaper than we have from our senior executives."

Senior executives feeling pressure from their political environments pursue the implementation of merit pay as essentially a technical problem. When sufficient in-house expertise is absent, which is often, a consulting firm is hired to develop the evaluation instrument and to recommend a merit pay policy. Experience suggests that consulting firms make the greatest profits after they have developed canned performance appraisal instruments that they can graft onto existing personnel systems. Some of these are well designed, and most consulting firms go through the motions of meeting with employees, presenting the instruments as the outcome of a highly scientific technical process.

The result is rather sterile, though outwardly spiffy, evaluation instruments that are plugged into a step-by-step cookbook formula for awarding merit raises. This incentive program is most often treated as an independent management reform that must stand or fall on its own merits (no pun intended). All management has to do is fund the program and allow it to manage itself, or put this task in the hands of the personnel department—which had to rely on external expertise to develop the system in the first place and now knows little about it.

Consultant-driven merit systems typically follow a four-stage cycle. Stage 1 can be described as guarded optimism among the target employees coupled with smug satisfaction among senior management that they have finessed a political need. They also feel they have accomplished a complex technical objective. Stage 2 involves mixed initial implementation reactions. Some employees get rewarded and are happy; many more receive less than expected and are upset. Supervisors calm employees by saying this was the typical first-year implementation snafu-a-rama and that subsequent iterations will be handled more fairly and equitably. Stage 3 usually follows one of two courses. In path A, merit pools remain flush. Here the Matthew Effect becomes more severe, with a growing gap between winners and losers. Employees not receiving what they consider fair awards become strong emotional critics and stalwart opponents of the system. In path B, merit pools dwindle (which is more common). Here, to avoid irking employees, supervisors rate everyone high, thus distributing what money is available equitably. Stage 4 soon follows and normally involves the elimination of or substantial reduction in the merit program, with a corresponding reemphasis on more stable, stepped pay increments. The cycle repeats itself when a new batch of politicians gets elected and they decide, often with the perception that they are the first to discover sliced bread, that merit pay can be used as a tool for generating greater employee accountability and performance.

Within this routine pattern, nothing much really changes the built-in bureaucratic unfriendliness toward merit pay because the culture of the organization remains intact. One discipline that strives to change the culture of the organization (Burke, 1982; Schein, 1985) and to improve organizational policies and structures (Golembiewski, 1989) to the benefit of both employees and management is *organizational development,* or OD.

Space does not permit a full review of this discipline, but OD provides a formidable array of diagnostic methodologies, intervention techniques, and normative values that have proven success in the field (Golembiewski, Proehl, and Sink, 1981; Burke, 1994; Porras, 1979). In fact, noted merit pay advocate Edward Lawler (1981) carefully tethers his conception of a successful merit pay program to OD. What OD does is to provide a rationale, a set of values, and a set of behavioral tools for moving typical public organizations into postbureaucratic settings (Golembiewski, 1995). OD makes public organizations more merit pay friendly by transforming the structures, infrastructures, and policies associated with bureaucratic ideation into systems grounded in regenerative interaction processes. This facilitates higher trust, higher openness, lower risk, and higher owning, all of which are fundamental if a merit pay plan is to be accepted by target employees as fair, meaningful, and motivational.

3. Merit pay should not target individuals as the sole recipients of merit awards. Public organizations need to reward and provide incentives to intact work teams and groups.

This is another issue I have addressed on previous occasions (for example, Gabris, Mitchell, and McLemore, 1985). Generally, merit pay rewards the rated past performance of individuals, not groups. Yet in reality, most work in public organizations is done by interactive work teams when outputs depend on overcoming problems connected with flow-of-work production processes. Therefore existing merit plans may be, first, rewarding output that is difficult to measure and, second, measuring the wrong level of output or, even worse, random variations in production (Deming, 1986). To address these deficiencies, merit pay plans in the future need to creatively broaden the kinds of performance that are both measured and rewarded.

The private sector has been evaluating and rewarding group productivity for a long time. An early model was the Scanlon plan, named after the union shop steward who conceptualized how blue-collar employees could save their companies money through more efficient work practices—especially when the employees could share in the savings (Frost, Wakely, and Ruh, 1974). More contemporaneously, this idea is referred to as *gainsharing* (Graham-Moore and Ross, 1990). The basic idea is that employees working on large group-based outputs are rewarded according to how well each group performs or saves money in the pursuit of some goal. Organizations have devised various formulas for distributing bonuses based on the level of performance or amount of money saved. More important, gainsharing has been found to work in a variety of government organization settings (Graham-Moore and Ross, 1990).

Another benefit of a team- or group-based incentive involves measurement itself. A group's output is typically larger than an individual's output. Focusing on the group output means that what is measured is usually clearer, easier to measure, and often comparable to past group outputs. Intact work units are also more likely than individuals to receive budget lines, and therefore it is easier to cost out a group-based product for the purpose of determining savings. Focusing on the group avoids the need for unwieldy and awkward individual performance measures and heeds Deming's caveat to avoid measuring the chance result of inherent system variation or a system defect when one means to measure the competency of an individual employee.

Team-based incentives reduce interpersonal win-lose competition by encouraging team cooperation rather than individual ways to win or beat the system. Performance appraisal can also be customized to measure each work unit's output, measuring what the unit does rather than some abstract individual trait. This should reduce subjectivity and rating errors by supervisors. By rewarding workgroups instead of individuals, public agencies will also reduce perceived internal inequities between employees, because employees will essentially share equally in bonus awards. Where individual-based performance appraisals and incentives are still necessary, they should be customized for each job so that activities or results measured are within the employee's discretion and are discrete units of output that can be reliably and consistently reassessed by the same measures.

In addition to all their benefits, however, team-based merit systems also have some drawbacks. One concern is that agency savings may be perceived by elected officials as simply excess fat that should not have been spent in the first place. Thus in subsequent budget years they may deduct any recent savings from the agency's base budget. This will serve as a disincentive for being efficient. There is some merit to this argument, especially as it reflects federal and some state and local government expenditure laws. Nonetheless, gainsharing also makes a lot of sense and can be used in a variety of government situations where money saved might be reallocated or saved for wiser purposes later (Osborne and Gaebler, 1992).

Another complaint is that slackers within teams will benefit from the productivity of the other team members and with no individual accountability will continue slacking off. Maybe so. However, this view ignores one of the most powerful forces in work organizations, namely, peer pressure to conform. It is doubtful that nonperformers on a team offered incentives for performance could easily escape the wrath of their coworkers if they persisted in nonperformance. Peer pressure may actually motivate nonperformers to improve in ways that negative supervisory feedback within traditional bureaucracies could never achieve.

Still another complaint is that not all jobs lend themselves to team or group work and that therefore this approach will work only under limited conditions. Maybe so. However, the opposite also applies. Not all jobs lend themselves to individual performance measurement and reward. Yet rewarding individuals has been the historical norm. Instead of taking an either-or approach, the sensible option may involve a synthesis or blended design that incorporates both individual- and team-based rewards where appropriate. This is not an insurmountable obstacle if managers tether such reforms to broader organizational change efforts, as suggested earlier, that make the work organization more merit pay friendly.

4. Compensation systems should reflect a balance among concerns for individual, internal, and external equity rather than fixate on only one type of emphasis.

Too frequently, merit plans stress the salience of individual equity to such a degree that somehow the motivational potential of competing equity strategies gets tossed out the window. In one in-depth treatment of this issue (Gabris, 1991), research findings from an actual public-sector merit plan application bore witness to this observation. When a municipal government received political pressure to implement a merit pay plan, the city manager and professional staff (mainly senior managers) contracted a consultant to develop a first-rate, by-the-book, technically sophisticated design. It involved reviewing existing job descriptions, job redesign, extensive and systematic rank-and-file employee participation throughout the process, reformulated performance appraisals, supervisory training in using the new system, plus multiple sources of merit raises and bonuses. This new system should have worked.

Originally, the total money available from the compensation pool was to be divided, with about 60 percent going for cost-of-living adjustments and automatic pay increases and 40 percent reserved for merit pay. When the elected officials heard this, they reversed the formula to 75 percent reserved for merit pay and 25 percent for cost-of-living increases. These political officials clearly wanted a strong merit message sent to employees.

The city's employees resisted such intense merit pay strategies, and the police department, to avoid the merit program, unionized that same year. After the efforts of cooler heads and the making of various compromises, the merit distribution went back more or less to the original sixty-forty split. Why was this so important to the rank-and-file employees? Why did they not want more resources put into the merit pool on the premise that if they performed well, they stood to receive considerable pay increases?

By and large, these employees, like others in the public sector, were more concerned with external and internal equity than with individual equity. One aspect of *external equity* exists when an employee perceives that his or her salary is relatively commensurate to market rates. This makes a great deal of sense. When an employee feels underpaid, he or she has a strong incentive to find a job that pays better. Merit raises, although helping, usually do not bring public agency base salaries up to market. What happens instead is that employees find their base salaries compressed in relation to what the market would currently pay someone with their level of skills and experience. This compression happens when people stay in the same jobs for long durations, receiving generally small base salary increases and only periodic merit raises. Ineluctably, these workers find new hires starting with base salaries not much below, and even in some cases above, their salaries.

Achieving external equity also requires keeping one's base salary high, because status and most fringe benefits, perks, and even merit raise awards are tethered to base salary. For example, if merit raises amount to a 5 percent increase in base salary, an employee earning $20,000 per year will receive $500 less in merit pay than someone earning $30,000. Getting base salary up, through periodic market surveys and salary realignments, will often increase an employee's long-term compensation and the value of a specific job much more than will periodic merit raises. Therefore, smart employees continually watch their base salaries vis-à-vis external market rates, and when they find the two out of sync, they become motivated to aggressively advocate realignment to usually new and higher salary levels.

Internal equity is another big issue and exists in several dimensions. First, many public employees, especially those performing blue-collar work, prefer pay systems that compensate people relatively equally rather than differentially. Blue-collar employees know they are never going to become rich through merit incentives and tend to prefer retention of workgroup camaraderie, even if this means receiving less compensation than they might earn via outcompeting their peers. The kind of pay format that best achieves internal equity is a *step plan*.

Step plans provide automatic, regular pay increments to base salary. A step plan represents to the employee a stable resource that can be depended upon, because once established, the plan conveys an aura of objectivity that cannot easily be tampered with by a devious management. Unions highly favor step plans for this reason. So do a majority of public employees who are not unionized.

Step plans are preferred over merit plans also because the they incur less risk. Employees know, generally, what they will get annually. This knowledge can be comforting when employees find themselves working in traditional bureaucratic structures conducive to degenerative interactions. Many employees simply do not trust their supervisors to reward them fairly and regularly under a merit system. For this reason most employees want the merit component of their compensation package minimized and the effects of internal and external equity maximized. Ideally, public organizations should strive to balance all three equity concerns, but the political attractiveness of incentive pay has made it the darling of politicians, often to the detriment of what, to the employee, represent more salient reward considerations.

So, what might be an alternative to this dilemma? What might reflect a higher level of consensus among employees, managers, and politicians? One option is to continue stressing external and internal equity concerns as the primary edifices of a public compensation system, with the proviso that some monies (usually a small percentage with which to form a pool) be set aside for merit pay bonuses. By *bonus*, I mean specifically an amount awarded in a lump sum on a semiannual basis. Like all bonuses these awards need to be re-earned time and time again and do not become part of base salary. Base salary in this option is kept at market levels and incremented regularly by a step plan that moves employees through a scheduled pay range. Even when employees are at the top of a scheduled pay range, they remain eligible for merit bonuses. When times are tight, public organizations can strive to protect base salaries by keeping up with the market and by providing small automatic pay increments. During austere times the amount of money allocated to merit bonus pools can be reduced, and because bonuses do not affect base salaries, most employees will not be too bothered by this.

By giving bonuses as lump sums, the public agency magnifies their motivational impact. With a $500 check an employee can go out and, if like me, purchase a new state-of-the-art fly rod. If the bonus is divided into twelve paychecks, or even twenty-four, then the bonus amount is minuscule each time and would hardly purchase a Zebco beginner's rod. Big deal. Lump sum merit bonuses afford much greater managerial leverage and can be customized to snugly fit already up and running compensation systems so that the positive effects of external and internal equity will not be lost. Furthermore, if merit bonuses are funded via a small percentage of the overall compensation pool, this amount can be stabilized so incentive pay does not evolve into a win-lose arrangement where a few high-performing employees are receiving increases by taking away compensation from those less fortunate.

The key is balance and movement toward a merit-friendly organizational structure. I agree that these suggestions may contradict various ongoing, traditional merit pay program practices and raise questions about their viability. Support for and opposition to merit pay will continue. At least now a sketch exists suggesting how managers might take these competing perspectives and transform them into a practical model. Finally, we need to recognize that merit pay will not simply vanish because we dislike it or because it has failed in various settings. The challenge is to make it work better.

CONCLUSION: MERIT PAY WILL NOT BECOME EXTINCT

Merit pay has exhibited a resilience and staying power unseen in some other management reforms, especially those in the public sector. Three interrelated reasons why this might be so have captured my perception.

Reason number one involves historical values and the general social culture of the United States. Unlike citizens in some countries, U.S. citizens have always placed value in individual achievement, pulling oneself up by one's bootstraps, and competition. They admire winners and deplore losers. The accomplishment of high-powered goals via aggressive, superior individual performance dovetails nicely with what nineteenth-century Americans equated with survival of the fittest, a kind of social Darwinism. The best win, and these winners should be justly rewarded, paralleling what takes place in nature. Although this interpretation of natural selection may both crudely and inaccurately apply to social situations, it describes how many people felt and still feel regarding the need for individual competition. Thus merit pay can be construed at least partially as a modern manifestation of the U.S. cultural heritage that celebrates individual achievement. Although challenged by other value systems, such as the Japanese, that downplay individual success, the focus on individuals seems ingrained in the U.S. general social culture.

Related to this historical cultural value is the strong political need to make public employees accountable. At the dawn of public service in the United States, appointees received their positions largely on the basis of family ties, education, land ownership, and aristocratic status. When Andrew Jackson was elected president in 1828, this tradition changed markedly. Jackson felt that just about anyone could serve effectively in public office and, more important, that by having newly elected officials appoint the people who would answer to them, employees would be more accountable.

In a democracy, elected officials want to feel that they can influence the behavior, direction, and performance of the employees they hire to do the job. Generally, most public employees are protected from direct political intervention or threats by long-established civil service laws. Most public employees are skilled professionals who take pride in their work and who make the best decisions possible for the people they serve. Nonetheless the perception held by many citizens and elected officials is that the public employee is not accountable and all too frequently is the maintainer of a system that is not working well.

Merit pay is seen as a vehicle for changing this, for allowing the elected official to influence the behavior and performance of public employees without dismantling the civil service infrastructure. Merit pay is actually embraced by many civil service systems as a valid and fair political intervention that is justified via rational, scientific, and theoretical models. Merit pay theory becomes useful in the actions of elected officials who want to influence a system where they ordinarily have little leverage. Because merit pay has received widespread and strong support by some scholars, researchers, and theorists, politicians can claim their interest in merit pay is based on genuine scientific as opposed to political considerations. Add to this the intuitive logic and sensibility of merit pay theory, and it is not difficult to fathom why merit pay is so appealing to politicians interested in making bureaucracy more accountable.

A third feature that drives merit pay is sociotechnical and stems from our continual and restless fascination with innovations, fads, gimmicks, technologies, and models that promise increases in performance and quality. Something may not initially work but that does not mean it will no longer be pursued. On the contrary, things that should work but do not often become intriguing puzzles that tease inquisitive minds to devise even better mousetraps. So it will likely be with merit pay. That merit pay has not worked well in the public sector may be the kind of kick in the rear compelling human resource managers and theorists to look more broadly into why it is not working and whether its success may be interconnected with broader organizational change efforts, culture, and structure.

New merit pay experiments will be devised. Bet on it. Merit pay development is iterative. Initially simple, noncomplex processes are generating unexpected problems and needs. Reformulated merit pay strategies may fix these unanticipated glitches for a short time, only to precipitate new glitches that require further treatment and further merit pay reformulations. What eventually transpires may be a merit program that looks, feels, and operates in a much different way than the one initially conceived. Through these iterations, managers and theorists learn a lot about what does and does not work. At times, they may even experience conceptual breakthroughs that enable them to take a management technique to a new level of sophistication and efficiency. U.S. managers like to tinker and, when risk is low, experiment with new ideas. Merit pay represents exactly the kind of management innovation that should work, that many scholars and leaders like to puzzle over and continually reformulate.

Thus for historical, political, and technical reasons, merit pay is likely to be around for some time as are continually revised ways of measuring performance through performance appraisal. Resistance to these developments will likely sustain the tension between the promise and the pitfalls associated with merit pay. A modicum of mania surrounding incentive plans will remain a reality, and perhaps this is how it should be for any management technique that fundamentally questions the basic worth, value, and contributions of typical employees. Within reasonable limits, merit pay mania reflects a robust and healthy tension between organizational skepticism and optimism (Gabris, Ihrke, and Maclin, forthcoming), which helps keep managers on their toes in an environment that is constantly changing. Complacency is the more dangerous condition, but with merit pay proposals always in the air the likelihood of complacency getting the upper hand remains doubtful. So ultimately, even though merit pay may not accomplish stated managerial purposes, it may inoculate public organizations against disease in indirect ways that neither supporters nor opponents have dreamed of.

References

Adams, L. S."Injustice in Social Exchange." In L. Berkowitz (ed.), *Advances in Experimental Social Psychology*. Orlando, Fla.: Academic Press, 1965.

Adams, S. *The Dilbert Principle*. New York: HarperCollins, 1995.

Argyris, C. *Strategy, Change, and Defensive Routines*. New York: HarperBusiness, 1985.

Argyris, C. *Overcoming Organizational Defenses*. Needham Heights, Mass.: Allyn & Bacon, 1991.

Barnard, C. I. *The Functions of the Executive*. Cambridge, Mass.: Harvard University Press, 1968. (Originally published 1938.)

Bernardin, H. J., and Beatty, R. W. *Performance Appraisal: Assessing Human Behavior at Work*. Boston: PWS-Kent, 1984.

Blau, P. *The Dynamics of Bureaucracy*. Chicago: University of Chicago Press, 1972.

Bowman, J. S. "At Last, an Alternative to Performance Appraisal: Total Quality Management." *Public Administration Review*, 1994, *54*, 129–136.

Burke, W. W. *Organization Development: Principles and Practices.* New York: Little, Brown, 1982.

Burke, W. W. *Organization Development: Process of Learning and Changing.* Reading, Mass.: Addison Wesley Longman, 1994.

Civil Service Reform Act of 1978. U.S. Code, vol. 5, sec. 1101 et seq.

Daley, D. "Merit Pay Enters with a Whimper: The Initial Federal Civil Service Reform Experience." *Review of Public Personnel Administration,* 1987, *7*(2), 72–79.

Daley, D. "Profile of the Uninvolved Worker: An Examination of Employee Attitudes Toward Management Practices." *International Journal of Public Administration,* 1988, *11,* 65–91.

Deci, E. L., and Ryan, R. M. *Intrinsic Motivation and Self Determination in Human Behavior.* New York: Plenum, 1985.

Deming, W. E. *Out of the Crisis.* Cambridge, Mass.: MIT Center for Advanced Engineering Study, 1986.

Denhardt, R. B. *The Pursuit of Significance: Strategies for Managerial Success in Public Organizations.* Belmont, Calif.: Wadsworth, 1993.

Fox, C. J. "Employee Performance Appraisal: The Keystone Made of Clay." In C. Ban and N. M. Riccucci (eds.), *Public Personnel Management: Current Concerns, Future Challenges.* (2nd ed.) New York: Longman, 1991.

Frost, C. F., Wakely, J. H., and Ruh, R. A. *The Scanlon Plan for Organizational Development: Identity Participation and Equity.* East Lansing: Michigan State University Press, 1974.

Gabor, A. *The Man Who Invented Quality.* New York: Penguin Books, 1990.

Gabris, G. T. "Can Merit Pay Systems Avoid Creating Discord Between Supervisors and Subordinates? Another Uneasy Look at Performance Appraisal." *Review of Public Personnel Administration,* 1986, *7*(1), 70–89.

Gabris, G. T. "Monetary Incentives and Performance: Is There an Administratively Meaningful Connection?" In M. Holzer (ed.), *Public Productivity Handbook.* New York: Dekker, 1991.

Gabris, G. T. "Benefits and Costs of Conventional Management Practices." In A. Halachmi and G. Bouckaert (eds.), *The Enduring Challenges in Public Management: Surviving and Excelling in Public Management.* San Francisco: Jossey-Bass, 1995.

Gabris, G. T., and Giles, W. A. "Improving Productivity and Performance Appraisal Through the Use of Non-Economic Incentives." *Public Productivity Review,* 1983a, *7,* 173–191.

Gabris, G. T., and Giles, W. A . "Level of Management, Performance Appraisal, and Productivity Reform in Complex Organizations." *Review of Public Personnel Administration,* 1983b, *3*(3), 45–63.

Gabris, G. T., Giles, W. A., and Mitchell, K. "Motivating the Uninvolved Worker: Some Conceptual and Empirical Observations." *International Journal of Public Administration,* 1988, *11,* 27–65.

Gabris, G. T., Ihrke, D., and Maclin, S. "The Leadership Enigma: Toward a Model of Organizational Optimism." *Journal of Management History,* forthcoming.

Gabris, G. T., and Mitchell, K. "The Impact of Merit Raise Scores on Employee Attitudes: The Matthew Effect of Performance Appraisal." *Public Personnel Management,* 1988, *17,* 369–387.

Gabris, G. T., Mitchell, K., and McLemore, R. "Rewarding Individual and Team Productivity: The Case of the Biloxi Merit Bonus Plan." *Public Productivity Review,* 1985, *14,* 231–245.

Golembiewski, R. T. *Public Administration as a Developing Discipline.* Vol. 1. New York: Dekker, 1977.

Golembiewski, R. T. *Humanizing Public Organizations.* Mt. Airy, Md.: Lomond Press, 1985.

Golembiewski, R. T. "OD Perspectives on High Performance: Some Good News About Merit Pay." *Review of Public Personnel Administration,* 1986, *7,* 9–27.

Golembiewski, R. T. *Organization Development: Ideas and Issues.* New Brunswick, N.J.: Transaction Press, 1989.

Golembiewski, R. T. *Managing Diversity in Organizations.* Tuscaloosa: University of Alabama Press, 1995.

Golembiewski, R. T., Boudreau, R., Sun, B. C., and Luo, H. "Burnout in Public Agencies Worldwide: How Many Employees Have Which Degrees of Burnout, and with What Consequences?" Paper presented at the National Conference of the American Society for Public Administration, Atlanta, Ga., 1996.

Golembiewski, R. T., Munzenrider, R., and Stevenson, J. *Stress in Organizations.* New York: Praeger, 1986.

Golembiewski, R. T., Proehl, C. W., and Sink, D. "Success of OD Applications in the Public Sector." *Public Administration Review,* 1981, *41,* 679–682.

Gordon, D. F. "A Neo-Classical Theory of Keynesian Unemployment." *Economic Inquiry,* 1974, *12,* 431–459.

Graham-Moore, B., and Ross, T. L. *Gainsharing.* Washington, D.C.: Bureau of National Affairs, 1990.

Hackman, J. R., and Oldham, G. R. *Work Redesign.* Reading, Mass.: Addison Wesley Longman, 1980.

Heneman, R. L. *Merit Pay.* Reading, Mass.: Addison Wesley Longman, 1992.

Herzberg, F. *Work and the Nature of Man.* Cleveland, Ohio: World Press, 1966.

Herzberg, F. "One More Time: How Do You Motivate Employees?" *Harvard Business Review,* Jan.-Feb. 1968, pp. 53–62.

Hummel, R. *The Bureaucratic Experience.* New York: St. Martin's Press, 1987.

Ingraham, P., and Ban, C. *Legislating Bureaucratic Change: The Civil Service Reform Act of 1978.* Albany: State University of New York Press, 1984.

Jaques, E. *Equitable Payment.* New York: Wiley, 1961.

Kouzes, J. M., and Posner, B. Z. *The Leadership Challenge: How to Get Extraordinary Things Done in Organizations.* San Francisco: Jossey-Bass, 1987.

Latham, G. P., and Wexley, K. *Increasing Productivity Through Performance Appraisal.* Reading, Mass.: Addison Wesley Longman, 1981.

Lawler, E. E., III. *Pay and Organizational Effectiveness.* New York: McGraw-Hill, 1971.

Lawler, E. E., III. *Motivation in Work Organizations.* Pacific Grove, Calif.: Brooks-Cole, 1973.

Lawler, E. E., III. *Pay and Organizational Development.* Reading, Mass.: Addison Wesley Longman, 1981.

Lawler, E. E., III. *High-Involvement Management: Participative Strategies for Improving Organizational Performance.* San Francisco: Jossey-Bass, 1986.

Lawler, E. E., III. *Strategic Pay: Aligning Organizational Strategies and Pay Systems.* San Francisco: Jossey-Bass, 1990.

Lawler, E. E., III. *The Ultimate Advantage: Creating the High-Involvement Organization.* San Francisco: Jossey-Bass, 1992.

Locke, E. A., and Latham, G. P. *Toward a Theory of Goal Setting and Task Performance.* Upper Saddle River, N.J.: Prentice Hall, 1990.

Lovrich, N. P. "Merit Pay and Motivation in the Public Workforce: Beyond Concerns of Technique to More Basic Considerations." *Review of Public Personnel Administration,* 1987, *7*(2), 54–72.

Lovrich, N. P., Shaffer, R. H., and Yale, D. "Public Employees and Performance Appraisal: Do Public Servants Welcome or Fear Merit Evaluation of Their Performance?" *Public Administration Review,* 1980, *40*, 214–222.

McGregor, D. "An Uneasy Look at Performance Appraisal." *Harvard Business Review,* May–June 1957, pp. 89–94.

Meyer, H. H. "The Pay for Performance Dilemma." *Organizational Dynamics* 1975, *3*, 39–50.

Nalbandian, H. R. "Incentive Compensation in Perspective." In H. R. Nalbandian (ed.), *Incentives. Cooperation, and Risk Sharing.* Lanham, Md.: Rowman & Littlefield, 1987.

Nalbandian, J. "Performance Appraisal: If Only People Were Not Involved." *Public Administration Review,* 1981, *41*, 392–396.

Osborne, D., and Gaebler, T. *Reinventing Government: How the Entrepreneurial Spirit Is Transforming the Public Sector.* Reading, Mass.: Addison Wesley Longman, 1992.

Perry, J. L. "Merit Pay in the Public Sector: The Case for a Failure of Theory." *Review of Public Personnel Administration,* 1986, *7*, 57–69.

Perry, J. L. "Linking Pay to Performance: The Controversy Continues." In C. Ban and N. M. Riccucci (eds.), *Public Personnel Management: Current Concerns, Future Challenges.* New York: Longman, 1991.

Peters, T. J., and Waterman, R. H., Jr. *In Search of Excellence.* New York: HarperCollins, 1982.

Porras, J. I. "The Comparative Impact of Different OD Techniques and Intervention Intensities." *Journal of Applied Behavioral Science,* 1979, *15,* 156–178.

Rappold, S. "The Merit Pay Payout: CAB's Experience the First Year." *Management,* 1981, *2,* 10–11.

Rosen, S. "Implicit Contracts: A Survey." *Journal of Economic Literature,* 1985, *23,* 1144–1175.

Salop, S. C. "A Model of the Natural Rate of Unemployment." *American Economic Review,* 1979, *69,* 117–125.

Schachter, H. L. *Frederick Taylor and the Public Administration Community.* Albany: State University of New York Press, 1989.

Schein, E. H. *Organizational Culture and Leadership.* San Francisco: Jossey-Bass, 1985.

Skinner, B. F. *Science and Human Behavior.* New York: Macmillan, 1953.

Soden, D. L., and Lovrich, N. P. "Motivating the Unmotivated State Employee Through Workplace Participation: Research Note from a Pre- and Post-Test Panel Study." *International Journal of Public Administration,* 1988, *11,* 91–117.

Stiglitz, J. E. "The Design of Labor Contracts: The Economics of Incentives and Risk Sharing." In H. R. Nalbandian (ed.), *Incentives, Cooperation, and Risk Sharing.* Lanham, Md.: Rowman & Littlefield, 1987.

Thayer, F. "The President's Management 'Reforms': Theory X Triumphant." *Public Administration Review,* 1978, *38,* 309–315.

Thayer, F. "Performance Appraisal and Merit Pay Systems: The Disasters Multiply." *Review of Public Personnel Administration,* 1986, *7*(2), 36–54.

Vroom, V. H. *Work and Motivation.* New York: Wiley, 1964.

Wallace, M. J., Jr., and Fay, C. H. *Compensation Theory and Practice.* (2nd ed.) Boston: PWS-Kent, 1988.

Walster, E., Berscheid, E., and Walster, W. "New Directions in Equity Research." *Journal of Personality and Social Psychology,* 1973, *25,* 151–176.

CHAPTER THIRTY-ONE

Employee Benefits

From Health Care to Pensions

N. Joseph Cayer

B enefits, as part of a total compensation package provided by employers, play an important role in attracting and retaining employees. Referred to as fringe benefits in the past, benefits now represent a central part of compensation systems. Especially as costs of all benefits continue to increase, employees consider the benefits package an important factor in deciding whether to accept a position or to remain in one. Employers constantly evaluate their benefits packages as well, recognizing the role they play in overall payroll costs. Although traditional benefits packages included pension plans and health care, contemporary approaches provide benefits that change with employees' life cycles and often are referred to as life cycle benefits (Adolf, 1993), addressing employees' differing needs as they move through educational opportunities, parenting, and retirement.

At the beginning of the twentieth century, virtually no employers offered any more than direct compensation. However, types and number of benefits have increased continually through the years since then (Hostetler and Pynes, 1995; Levine, 1993–1994; Wallace and Fay, 1988). In some ways, public employers have been leaders in providing innovative benefits; in others they follow the private sector. At the same time the number and types of benefits offered have grown, regulation of benefits has increased as well.

Public employers have traditionally offered more generous benefits across the board than private-sector employers, partly because government employees often receive lower direct pay than private-sector employees. Health care and retirement benefits in particular have been more generous. In the public sector the same level of benefits generally applies to all employees regardless of position level. In the private sector it is common to find different benefits packages for top-level executives and for rank-and-file employees. Such differentiation is difficult to justify in the political environment in which government organizations must operate. The electorate has little tolerance for treating some of its employees better than others, and this attitude has encouraged a leveling effect, although many elected officials (especially legislators) have been able to create especially generous plans for themselves (Zolkos and Philip, 1992). Government also typically covers more of the costs for public employees than private employers do, but the gap appears to be decreasing (Handel, 1992).

Generous public-sector plans have also resulted from another political reality. Because increased public-sector pay often results in negative reactions from the public, who see its potential immediate impact on taxes, elected political leaders try to avoid being too generous with pay hikes. However, benefits, especially retirement benefits, often have a delayed tax impact because they do not have to be funded until later. The costs can be put off until someone else is mayor, council member, or school board president, so elected officials have had less concern with negative political reaction.

However, changing demographics are affecting the types and costs of benefits. The current aging of the workforce is creating a need for different types of benefits. The greater diversity of the workforce is also suggesting the value of different types of benefits. Single parents, dual-career couples, unmarried partners, and people with disabilities need more diversity in benefits.

This chapter examines the structure of contemporary benefits plans. It describes the variety of mandated and discretionary benefits public agencies offer to their employees, compares public- and private-sector benefits, discusses how agencies are adapting to changing demographics and benefits needs, and suggests important challenges public employers must confront as they strive to maintain appropriate benefit plans for their employees in the present economic and political environment.

THE STRUCTURE OF BENEFITS PLANS

Although benefits packages in the public sector have been more generous than those in the private sector, the public sector has expanded its use of comparable pay, and as studies of pay levels in other jurisdictions and in the private sector come to form the major foundation for setting pay, the disparities between the public and private sectors are disappearing. Nevertheless, public employers still tend to cover more of the cost of benefits packages than is typical in the private sector. At the same time, however, funding levels are shrinking, making cost control an important element in benefits policy (Ellis, 1993).

Some benefits are mandated by national law or policy and others are voluntary (discretionary) on the part of the government unit (see Table 31.1 for a summary). Mandated benefits include Social Security, Unemployment Compensation, workers' compensation, and family medical leave. Discretionary benefits cover such things as health care, vacation leave, child care, elder care, employee assistance programs, and retirement pensions. In recent years the variety of benefits offered to employees by all employers has expanded greatly (Ellis, 1993; Levine, 1993–1994). For example, the newer discretionary benefits offered cover benefits for domestic partners, legal services protection, vision care, and dental plans. These benefits usually have been added to already existing plans. With the costs of many benefits escalating since the late 1980s, however, employers are trying to cap the funding to control costs. Between 1929 and 1989, the share of total payroll that supports benefits rose from 3 percent to 38.2 percent for U.S. employers (U.S. Chamber of Commerce, 1992, p. 6). The funding caps usually allow employees to choose those benefits most important to them within a specified monetary allowance.

Mandated Benefits

National government policy requires employers to provide some benefits to all of their employees. Often these benefits are referred to as *social insurance programs.* Many of them arose from the New Deal programs of the 1930s. As mentioned, they include Social Security, Unemployment Compensation, workers' compensation, and family and medical leave.

The *Social Security program* provides retirement income and also other types of social insurance that offer income security (disability benefits) to individuals who are unable to work because of injury or illness. Survivors of individuals who paid into Social Security also receive benefits. Medicare benefits are also part of the Social Security program. In 1983, the national government passed legislation requiring state and local government employers to participate in Social Security. (Prior to that time they could participate voluntarily.) Concern over the solvency of Social Security has led to discussion of limiting benefits and incorporating Social Security pensions into formulas for distribution of employer pensions. So far the ideas have not gone beyond such discussion for the most part, but political pressure for dealing with what some view as an impending Social Security crisis keeps the discussions going.

Unemployment Compensation, developed as part of the Social Security Act of 1935, provides temporary income to employees who have been laid off or have quit their jobs and are actively seeking employment. The program provides a fixed level of income for a specified number of weeks. Funding comes from a combination of employer contributions and federal monies. Employees unable to work because of work-related injuries are eligible for workers' compensation. These programs pay a part of an employee's wages and provide medical and

Table 31.1. Public Employee Benefits Summary.

Benefit Type	What It Provides	Funding Source
Mandatory		
Social Security	Retirement pension for employee and survivors.	Employer and employee contribution.
Unemployment compensation	Temporary income for employee who is laid off or quits and who actively seeks employment.	Employer contribution and federal funds.
Workers' compensation	Part payment of employee's wages or salary and medical and rehabilitation expenses.	Employer contribution.
Family and medical leave	Twelve weeks of unpaid leave during any twelve-month period for childbirth, adoption, and care of spouse, child, or parent as well as for employee's own serious illness.	Employer bears indirect cost of employee absence from work. Employee bears cost of no income.
Discretionary		
Vacation leave	Some specified number of days off with pay—typically one to four weeks depending on number of years worked.	Employer.
Sick leave	Some specified number of hours or days off with pay—typically a day per month for illness.	Employer.
Health care insurance	Medical and hospitalization coverage; often dental and mental health coverage. Preventive health measures: wellness, stress reduction, and exercise programs. Increasingly HMOs and PPOs.	Employer, traditionally. Increasingly, shared contribution between employer and employee.

Table 31.1. Public Employee Benefits Summary, cont'd.

Benefit Type	What It Provides	Funding Source
Disability	Long-term disability income.	Employee, at group rate.
Life insurance	Life insurance policy for a limited amount— employee may purchase more at group rate.	Employer often purchases limited-amount policy. Employee may purchase more at group rate.
Prepaid legal insurance	Policy to cover legal expenses.	Employee, at group rate.
Tuition reimbursement	Cost of work-related education and training paid.	Employer.
Employee assistance plans	Counseling and referral services for personal and family problems, including substance abuse, financial planning, and interpersonal problems.	Employer for a certain level of services. Referral to external services, at reduced rate.
Other work-related benefits	Travel support, employer vehicle, equipment (for example, computer). Suggestion awards— bonus in amount equal to some portion of cost savings from suggestion.	Employer.
Retirement pension	Income upon retirement from employment.	Employer, traditionally. Increasingly, employer and employee share contributions.

rehabilitation benefits as well. Employer contributions fund workers' compensation programs.

The newest mandated benefit, *family and medical leave,* results from the Family and Medical Leave Act of 1993. All employers with at least fifty employees must permit employees to take up to twelve weeks of unpaid family and medical leave during any twelve-month period for the birth of a child; adoption of a child or accepting a child for foster care; care of a spouse, child, or parent; or care of the employee's own serious health conditions. Experience with the new benefit suggests that it is working well although some private employers recommend modifying parts of it to fit requirements under other policies, such as the Americans with Disabilities Act, and to reduce the disruption of work flow (Buchanan, 1996).

Discretionary Benefits

Public employers offer many benefits at their own discretion. These optional benefits are intended to play important roles in attracting and retaining employees. Almost all public employers provide health care and retirement pension benefits as well as vacation and sick leave. Educational leave and reimbursement of tuition for job-related courses and training programs also are common. Increasingly, employers subsidize child-care and elder-care programs. The list of discretionary benefits continually expands (Boyd and Dickerson, 1990; Ellis, 1993; Levine, 1993–1994). To control costs, employers offer the options but cap the amount they will pay. Employees then choose the benefits most important to them within the amount of money the employer sets aside for benefits. These discretionary benefits can be categorized as leave, insurance, family care, personal and professional development, other work-related benefits, and retirement benefits.

Leave. Employers offer numerous types of leave to their employees, the most common being holiday, vacation, and sick leave. *Holiday leave* tends to follow the holiday policies of the national government, although there are variations from place to place. Most employees receive the national holidays, and some also receive other special days such as statehood day. Typically, these leave days add up to ten or twelve per year.

Vacation leave also is offered by most public employers. Typically, employees receive a week or two of annual paid vacation during the first two to five years of employment. Thereafter they may receive more on a gradual basis until they reach some fixed maximum, such as four weeks. Similarly, 95 percent of state and local employers offer *sick leave,* usually accrued according to time worked (U.S. Bureau of the Census, 1994, p. 321). Thus one day of sick leave a month, or the like, may be earned by the employee. The employee can use that sick day as necessary, although jurisdictions differ on whether illness must be verified through a doctor's note or other mechanism. Unused sick leave often is paid out in cash, but it also may be lost after a given period of time, such as a year. Many public employers offer maternity leave (59 percent) and paternity leave (44 percent) as well (U.S. Bureau of the Census, 1994). Some jurisdictions also offer *personal leave.* Personal leave usually is a day or two a year that an employee may take for any reason as long as it is planned in advance. Personal leave often is provided for an individual's birthday. Thus these days vary for each employee.

To streamline their leave policies many employers are experimenting with *comprehensive leave* policies. Agency members of the International Personnel Management Association reported in a recent survey that 43 percent of the members offer some form of comprehensive leave (Smith, 1996). Comprehensive leave combines vacation, sick, and personal leave into one block of time off permitted to each employee. As with each of the individual policies commonly used for vacation, sick, and personal leave, the employee may accrue time. Employers vary in whether or not they pay cash for unused leave time and whether they require that an employee must use at least a portion of it (such as forty hours continuous time off) before being eligible for payout on what is left over. Standardization of leave time under comprehensive leave helps alleviate some of the inequity arising from the differential use of sick leave and personal leave. Employees who do not use sick leave often are disadvantaged by sick leave policies. Some suggest, however, that eliminating sick leave per se may lead to people coming to work sick in order to save their comprehensive leave. Such a situation is not desirable either.

Insurance. Today employers offer insurance programs to protect against many eventualities. Health care insurance remains the most commonly offered insurance program. Long-term disability insurance, life insurance, and prepaid legal services insurance are other contemporary benefits offered by employers.

Typically, *health care benefits* cover many types of situations (Moore, 1991). Traditionally, the benefits covered medication and hospitalization to treat physical maladies and to maintain physical health. Gradually, mental and dental health care have been added to coverage. Ninety percent of state and local governments now offer medical insurance, 65 percent offer dental care coverage, and 89 percent provide mental health coverage (U.S. Bureau of the Census, 1994, p. 321). To help stem the tide of cost increases in health care, employers now also focus on preventive health measures, which include regular physical exams and wellness programs focusing on nutrition, healthy lifestyles, stress reduction, and regular exercise.

The various health care benefits are not only among the most commonly offered discretionary benefits but also among the most costly for employers. Health care costs in the United States have risen sharply in recent years, increasing 35 percent more than increases for all other goods and services. Health care expenditures in 1989 represented 11 percent ($600 billion) of the gross national product (GNP), and in 1992 it was estimated that they would reach 15 percent ($1.5 trillion) of GNP by the year 2000 (Brouder, 1992). The result has been rapidly increasing costs for health care benefits for all employers. In 1970, costs for medical coverage premiums were approximately $20 billion. By 1991, this figure had risen to $250 billion. These costs represented 3 percent of total payroll in 1970 and 7 percent of total payroll in 1991 (Beam and McFadden, 1994, p. 7).

Experiencing spiraling increases in health care costs, public employers, like their private-sector counterparts, have been searching for ways to contain costs. In addition to the preventive measures identified earlier, employers have turned to alternative ways of delivering services as a cost control measure (Cayer, 1995; Handel, 1992; Streib, 1996). The traditional indemnity plan offered employees free choice in the selection of services, and the plan paid the cost directly to the provider. Use of health maintenance organizations (HMOs) and preferred provider organizations (PPOs) instead cuts costs by reducing options for service. The employer contracts with an HMO or PPO to cover the health care costs of its employees, and each employee in the HMO program selects one of the group practices that has contracted with HMO to provide services and each employee in the PPO program chooses from a list of doctors who contract with the employer. The HMO or PPO agrees to deliver the service to employees on a fixed-cost basis. Employees may be required to pay some small fee for services. Even with these approaches to providing services, costs continue to increase. For traditional indemnity plans, average cost increases in recent years have been approximately 20 percent while costs for HMOs have increased an average of 8 to 12 percent. Increases for PPOs have ranged from 10 to 15 percent (Cayer, 1995, pp. 10–11; Brouder, 1992, pp. 27–28). These cost increases strain the budgets of government jurisdictions, as they tend to pay almost all the cost of health care coverage. For example, virtually all cities and counties provide health care coverage and rarely require employees to participate in the cost of it (Cayer, 1995). Twenty-six states pay the full cost of an employee's coverage; ten cover all the costs for family coverage as well. Of those that do not cover the full cost, most pay at least 80 percent of the employee premium, and half of these pay 80 percent of the family premium. Ten states also pay the full cost of retirees over age sixty-five (Handel, 1992, p. 11).

Rising health care costs stimulate public policy debate about employer responsibility for provision of coverage. Changes in the mid-1990s have, by law, extended the portability of health insurance and coverage of preexisting conditions. Insurance carriers will pass on the increased costs to premium payers including employers. Another controversial issue is universal coverage. If national policy should come to require universal coverage, employer provision of health care benefits likely would be affected.

Disability benefits beyond those mandated are another type of discretionary insurance (Finkle, 1997). Most public employees have short-term disability programs covered by their employer. Long-term disability usually is available, but the employee must pay for it. The insurance carrier for the employer makes the disability insurance available at a group rate, however, so the employee is able to access the coverage at a cost lower than if purchased individually. Similarly, many employers provide a life insurance policy for employees, often in the amount equivalent to a single year of salary. Employees then may purchase additional coverage at a group rate.

In recent years *legal insurance* has become available through employer benefits programs. Public-sector employees generally are indemnified for their activities as long as they act in good faith and within their authority; however, legal insurance allows additional coverage to be purchased for non-work-related legal services, and employees may opt for it as part of their benefits package. In some cases the coverage may be offered as part of a cafeteria plan; in most cases, however, it is offered as optional additional insurance that the employee pays for at a group rate.

Family Leave. The Family and Medical Leave Act of 1993, as mentioned, mandates leave to take care of ill family members, be home with a new child, or tend to employees' own serious health conditions. Employers often choose to offer other support for family responsibilities as well. Child-care subsidies are offered by 8 percent of state and local governments. On-premises child-care services sometimes are provided at a subsidized price. Otherwise, employees may receive a subsidy for off-premises child care. Even more state and local governments, 13 percent, offer elder-care programs, recognizing the responsibilities many employees have for elderly parents (U.S. Bureau of the Census, 1994, p. 321).

Personal and Professional Support and Development. In recognition of what Paul Sandwith (1993) calls "the triple threat of most organizations today . . . demands for improved quality, reduced costs, and constant innovation," employers encourage employees to participate in *human resource development activities* for professional growth. Thus most government employers reimburse tuition for employees taking job-related courses or degree programs. They also provide training and development programs. Many have their own internal human resource development programs and support employee attendance at external programs. In many cases, employees have a certain number of training and development dollars set aside that they may use for education and training programs. Increasingly, government jurisdictions require employees to participate in a minimum number of hours of training each year.

National government training and development programs serve as models for other levels of government. With the Government Employees Training Act of 1958 the national government recognized that employee skills quickly become obsolete, and the act created training and development programs for national government employees. The Intergovernmental Personnel Act (IPA) of 1970 supported training and development programs in state and local governments, providing funding to stimulate state and local governments to create programs specific to their needs. After IPA funding came to an end in the 1980s, state and local governments maintained their efforts on their own. With the increasingly rapid changes in U.S. society and in technology, continual learning is absolutely necessary (Van Wart, Cayer, and Cook, 1993). Human resource development programs allow employees to keep abreast of new developments and to maintain their ability to perform their jobs, thus benefitting employers and also the employees themselves.

The contemporary organization concerns itself with the personal needs of the employee to an extent never contemplated in the traditional organization. Recognizing that the performance of the employee is affected by many things in the employee's life, employers now attempt to deal with the whole person rather than just his or her organizational role. The stresses in the rest of an employee's life affect how well the employee can perform on the job. Starting with counseling for alcohol abuse, this employee focus has evolved into Employee Assistance Programs (EAPs) that help the employee deal with all kinds of personal problems that affect performance (Cayer and Perry, 1988; Johnson, 1985; Kemp, 1985). Employees are able to access assistance ranging from family counseling to counseling on legal and financial problems. Organizations sometimes have their own internal programs, but many contract with professional consultants for these services. The employee benefits by finding ways to resolve problems, and the employer benefits by having an employee who is able to focus on the work. Additionally, the employer is able to retain a valuable resource and does not have to bear the costs of replacing loyal employees and training new personnel.

A part of EAP services often focuses on stress management training. Stress and stress-related illnesses are the source of cost to employers. Training on how to avoid and manage stress helps in reducing those costs, especially in reducing absenteeism and reducing accidents and injury in the workplace.

Other Work-Related Support. Employees receive other work-related support from their employers that often is not considered a benefit but really is. For example, employees regularly receive travel support to attend conferences or for use of their own vehicles. Such support is appropriate in that it relates to the performance of the job. However, the employees also gain something from it, especially if the travel is to attend conferences. Many employees, especially high-level managers or public safety workers, are provided vehicles or other equipment, such as a home computer, to facilitate the performance of their duties. Although such equipment is not to be used for private purposes, it often is difficult to separate the job and private benefit.

Recent developments in work-related support include flexible work schedules and working by computer from home (Kemp, 1995). Flextime is particularly important to individuals who have family responsibilities that make it difficult for them to work a traditional schedule. This benefit also works to the advantage of the public employer and the general public because it permits offices to be open beyond the normal eight-to-five work shift. There is general public benefit to telecommuting as well in that cutting travel to and from work may reduce the emission of pollutants into the air. Allowing individuals to work at home when appropriate also fits well with contemporary approaches to holding employees accountable for what they accomplish rather than for the time they spend at work.

Most organizations also have suggestion award programs. Employees benefit by receiving some reward for suggestions that improve work. Commonly, an individual will receive 10 percent of the first-year savings brought about by the suggestion. Of course, the employing organization also benefits from the savings. Recognition programs are yet another benefit. They build morale within the organization and thus are likely to make employees more effective as well.

Retirement Pensions. Public *retirement pension programs,* with assets approximating $1 trillion, cover more than 33 million public employees (Beam and McFadden, 1994, p. 7). During the 1960s, public pension plans proliferated. In the public sector, *defined benefits plans* have dominated. Under these plans, an employee receives a guaranteed fixed benefit according to a formula using age and years of service (Pacelli, 1994; Zorn, 1994). Additionally, most public-sector plans have been pay-as-you-go, meaning that the government jurisdiction has to raise the money as employees retire and begin to take the benefit. Consequently, the generous retirement plans of the 1960s and 1970s resulted in great financial strain for governments, especially local governments, during the 1980s. These problems led to more experimentation with development of retirement funds and defined contribution plans. Most states now have a public pension fund that is invested and managed by trustees who are responsible for ensuring the financial solvency of the system. The national government still uses the pay-as-you-go system. At the local level, systems are mixed, with most governments using a forward-funding approach but some still using pay-as-you-go. Massachusetts, for example, established a statewide system to help bail out local systems that developed financial problems. Jurisdictions can now join the statewide system and pool resources and forward-fund their systems.

In the private sector, in contrast, *defined contribution plans* have been emphasized. These plans distribute benefits to a retired employee based on the amount of money invested in the retirement fund for that specific employee and on how well that investment performs. Typically, both the employer and the employee contribute to the fund. Many employers now allow employees to place their retirement funds in optional plans, using approved private financial planners to devise individual investment strategies.

Public pension funds have generated many controversies over the years. As noted, the costs, especially as they ballooned during the 1980s, created pressure for reform in the pay-as-you-go system. Even where forward funding has existed, however, the investment strategies of fund managers traditionally have been very conservative, dissatisfying many who thought that the funds could achieve higher yields resulting in higher benefits. During the 1980s, the conservative strategies of many pension funds gave way to what some considered reckless speculation. Additionally, pressures for social investing and investing in home state or local corporations resulted in some major financial losses for many pension systems (Mactas, 1992).

Many critics also raise concerns about employers' contributions to pension funds. Citing fiscal stress, many state governments turned to their public pension funds to deal with budget shortfalls. Many instances of "raiding" the funds to cover state operating costs posed problems for pension systems (Deutschman, 1992; Zolkos, 1992). States have also manipulated the actuarial standards used to determine how much money a fund needs to provide for the benefits it guarantees in defined benefits plans. By changing the actuarial figures, states can adjust how much they need to contribute in any given year. In lean years states are tempted to adjust the figures so that they can reduce their contributions; however, this also potentially puts the system's financial solvency in jeopardy.

The current aging of the workforce also presents challenges to retirement systems (Elliott, 1995). Concerns about the Social Security system arise from this fact that the population is aging and the corollary fact that the ratio of workers to retirees is declining. The same demographics affect employer-funded pension systems. In recent years, many employers have encouraged early retirement through buyouts or bonuses. However, early retirement exacerbates the financial solvency problem of pay-as-you-go pension plans. Longer life spans and early retirement also contribute to the financial pressures on health care programs because many jurisdictions, as noted earlier, pay for health care plans for retirees.

In addition to retirement pension plans, employers may offer employees *deferred compensation plans.* The Internal Revenue Code allows employees to set aside up to one-third of their pay or $7,500, whichever is lowest. The deferred compensation is excluded from federal income tax until it is actually paid out to the employee. An estimated 2 million state and local government employees participate in such programs, with total deferred compensation of approximately $28 billion (Harm, 1993).

ADAPTING TO CHANGING DEMOGRAPHICS AND NEEDS

Changing demographics require different employer approaches to the provision of benefits. The aging workforce already has been noted. It has implications for health and retirement benefits in particular but other implications as well. With the prohibition of mandatory retirement, employers find that many employees want to remain on the job well beyond the traditional retirement age of sixty-two or sixty-five. The benefits older employees use are often different from those needed by younger employees. Health care is usually much more of an issue for older workers, and costs of health care benefits may rise with the rise in worker age. At the same time, older workers diminish their dependence on other benefits, especially for education and child care.

The changing structure of families also has many benefits implications. The increase in the number of unmarried individuals living together is making domestic partnership benefits important. Unmarried couples increasingly demand the same benefits for partners as are offered to married couples. Controversy still surrounds domestic partnership benefits because many people equate them with support of homosexuality, still a hot-button issue in the current political environment. In reality, unmarried heterosexual couples far outnumber homosexual couples; thus they stand to gain most from domestic partnership benefits policies (Hostetler and Pynes, 1995).

Dual-career couples also have differing needs compared to other workers. When both members of the couple are employed and both have standard benefits packages, one package may be redundant. It makes more sense either to allow one person to opt out of some of the required benefits, assuming similar coverage can be acquired through the other person's employer, or to allow greater choice in the benefits taken.

Cafeteria benefits plans and *flexible spending accounts* represent strategies for accommodating benefits programs to changing demographics. Under these approaches, employees may choose the benefits that are most appropriate to them. In the cafeteria approach, the employer usually requires that the employee be covered under a health care plan and retirement system, either under that employer's plan or a spouse's employer's plan. Once that minimum is met, the employee may choose what is most appropriate for his or her needs from a range of benefit options. The flexible spending account is a variation of the cafeteria approach. It provides individual employees a fixed amount of money to spend on benefits, and they choose the specific benefits for which they want the money spent. For example, those who are trying to continue their education can choose to spend the money for coursework and training, and those who have elderly parents can choose to spend the money for elder care. Employees appreciate the opportunity to make their own choices. Currently, 5 percent of state and local government employers offer flexible benefits plans (U.S. Bureau of the Census, 1994, p. 321).

During this era of funding cutbacks and voter interest in smaller government, public employers face many challenges in paying for employee benefits within their budgets. The costs of benefits are increasing, like almost everything else. Health care cost increases, in particular, put pressure on the budget. To be able to continue to offer benefits to employees, public employers search for cost containment and cost-cutting alternatives. Flexible spending accounts are one option here, because as employees choose what they need, employers do not have to pay for benefits that are not likely to be used. Many alternatives for health care services are being explored. In particular, the health maintenance and preferred provider options mentioned earlier are being offered. Moreover, employees are increasingly asked to take some responsibility for their own needs. They are being encouraged to live healthier lives; thus wellness programs and employee assistance programs operate to prevent costly problems. And employers are asking employees to share in more of the cost of benefits as well. Public employers, who used to pay all the cost of most benefits, now are asking employees to pay part of the cost of their health care premiums, to pay copayment fees for their health care services, and to contribute to their pension funds. These practices help contain employers' costs.

Cooperative approaches to providing benefits present another way to contain costs. Alliances or consortia of governments have formed to contract with health care and other insurance providers. These consortia lead to larger numbers of employees to be covered, and thus they have more bargaining power to win lower per capita costs (Hackelman, 1994).

ASSESSING THE STATUS OF BENEFITS IN THE PUBLIC SECTOR

Public-sector benefits programs are reputed to be much better than plans in the private sector. The evidence suggests that in many respects the reputation reflects reality (Bergsman, 1995; Handel, 1992). Clearly, in the total picture, public-sector employees are covered under more types of plans and across job positions to a greater extent than are private-sector employees. Large private-sector employers come close to the public sector in coverage, but smaller private employers frequently have no discretionary benefits at all, and many have very limited programs. For example, 90 percent of public-sector employers make provision for medical care coverage while only 83 percent of large and medium-size private-sector employers and 71 percent of smaller private-sector employers do so. The differences are even more dramatic for retirement systems. Eighty-seven percent of state and local governments offer defined benefits pension plans while 59 percent of large and medium-size and 33 percent of small private employers do so (U.S. Bureau of the Census, 1994, pp. 321, 434). Being the most costly to employers, these two benefits represent very important parts of total compensation for government employees.

However, as the cost of providing benefits has continued to rise in both the public and private sectors, the public sector has been less successful in controlling costs than the private sector and has been less aggressive in requiring employees to share costs (Davis and Ward, 1995). Small private employers, in particular, often require larger employee contributions to the cost of plans. Thus, through their benefits, public employees continue to enjoy a substantial addition to direct compensation.

The aging workforce presents many challenges to employers, both public and private. As described earlier, not only is the number of retirees growing but life spans are increasing as well. The number of people sixty-five years old and older for every one hundred workers was twenty in 1985. By 2035, it is expected that there will be forty-one people sixty-five and over for every one hundred workers (Crampton, Hodge, and Mishra, 1996, p. 244). Thus over 40 percent of the population will be retirement age. The challenges are many as public employers attempt to remain competitive in the labor market.

CONCLUSION: BENEFITS CHALLENGES

Public-sector employers face many challenges in continuing to provide benefits to employees. Funding and controlling costs present the greatest challenges. The demand for benefits will continue to grow. Employers have to find ways to provide what is reasonable and prudent while working within financial constraints. Numerous strategies exist, although the public sector has been less aggressive than the private in adopting them.

Weaning employees from the *entitlement mentality* has been suggested as an overall strategy for controlling benefits costs (Haltom, 1995), especially in health care. Employers are encouraged to educate employees to accept responsibility for their own health. Thus wellness programs and healthier lifestyles constitute elements of many contemporary employer-sponsored programs. Employers are also shifting responsibility to employees for making choices about the benefits to be received. Similarly, employees are also being asked more frequently to cover part of the cost of premiums for various benefits. Although public employers have been reluctant to ask employees to pick up the current full cost of benefits, they increasingly require the employees to participate in funding any cost increases. With the rising costs of health care programs, it is especially likely in many public jurisdictions that employees are being asked to cover part of these premiums, to the point that their increased benefits costs often wipe out any increase they might receive in direct compensation.

Targeting the heavy users of health care services for education on health improvement and risk aversion has gained attention in recent years as a health care cost control strategy. Some evidence exists to suggest that a small portion of employees use a large part of health care services. One jurisdiction, for example, found that 1 to 2 percent of employees used 25 to 30 percent of the services and that about 80 percent of the services are used by about 20 percent of the employees (Hackelman, 1994). By changing the lifestyles and behavior of the employees who use the system heavily, employers may be able to make significant progress in controlling costs. Prevention and risk avoidance are more cost effective than treatment of health problems.

Cost containment also may be accomplished through the use of alliances or consortia for purchase of services (Cayer, 1995; Hackelman, 1994). Many communities across the country join consortia to purchase health care policies and participate in statewide pension programs to take advantage of the purchasing power of larger groups. The per unit cost usually is greatly reduced compared to the cost incurred by a lone employer. Small jurisdictions benefit most from such cooperative arrangements. Working with labor organizations also provides some employers with opportunities for cooperative plans and reduced costs (Brouder, 1992).

Employers are responding in some creative ways to the aging of the workforce. Typically, retirement meant ineligibility for many employee benefits, although the retirement pension and in some cases health care programs remained available. In recent years, especially with the prohibition of forced retirement, many employers have developed programs to retain older employees (West and Berman, 1996). Supportive workplace practices adapted to older workers' needs (for example, flexible working hours, part-time employment, and volunteer opportunities) and training designed for older employees are options that have been used. Elliott (1995) suggests such others as trial retirement, phased retirement, and return as part-time temporary employees, techniques that allow retirees to remain attached to the organization and to continue to contribute their expertise. These approaches can help lessen the strain on retirement pension systems and also keep retirees more healthy because they retain their sense of purpose.

A strategy often overlooked by employers is involving employees in the design of benefits programs (Davis and Ward, 1995). Employees know what is most important to them and are very creative in approaches if employers give them the opportunity. Employees who participate in the decisions about benefits plans are likely to have much higher satisfaction levels. Especially if employees are educated about the real costs of benefits plans, they can become advocates for the wise use of such plans and helpful in cost containment efforts.

Clearly, employee benefits programs cover the life span of employees. Employees have an interest in having as much variety as possible in the benefits available. As part of their contemporary management approaches, employers also want to have satisfied employees. At the same time, constraints on public-sector finances create pressures for limiting increases in costs. Adjusting benefits to the life cycle of employees makes much sense. The employer provides the most appropriate benefits to individual employees at any given time and keeps costs down by not paying for benefits that are not particularly relevant. Thus employers are likely to continue to refine the options available so that benefits truly range from the beginning of life (benefits addressing the birth of children) to the retirement and death of the employee (benefits offering pensions and life insurance) and cover all the needs in between as employees find their circumstances changing over their life spans.

References

Adolf, B. P. "Life Cycle Benefits." *Employee Benefits Journal,* Mar. 1993, pp. 13–20.

Americans with Disabilities Act of 1990. U.S. Code, vol. 42, sec. 12101 et seq.

Beam, B. T., and McFadden, J. J. *Employee Benefits.* (3rd rev. ed.) Chicago: Dearborn, 1994.

Bergsman, S. "How Shaky a Foundation?" *Pension Management,* 1995, *31*(7), 44–47.

Boyd, K. J., and Dickerson, S. D. *Local Government Personnel Compensation and Fringe Benefits.* Baseline Data Report, vol. 22, no. 3. Washington, D.C.: International City/County Management Association, 1990.

Brouder, J. "Labor-Management Cooperation Required to Address Health Care Costs." In M. J. Brzezinski (ed.), *Public Employee Benefit Plans.* Brookfield, Wis.: International Federation of Employee Benefit Plans, 1992.

Buchanan, C. N. "Oversight Hearing on the Family and Medical Leave Act." *IPMA News,* July 1996, pp. 7–8.

Cayer, N. J. "Local Government Health Care Benefits." In International City/County Management Association, *The Municipal Yearbook.* Washington, D.C.: International City/County Management Association, 1995.

Cayer, N. J., and Perry, R. W. "A Framework for Evaluating Employee Assistance Plans." *Employee Assistance Quarterly,* 1988, *3,* 151–168.

Crampton, S., Hodge, J., and Mishra, J. "Transition-Ready or Not: The Aging of America's Work Force." *Public Personnel Management,* 1996, *25,* 243–256.

Davis, E., and Ward, E. "Health Benefit Satisfaction in the Public and Private Sectors: The Role of Distributive and Procedural Justice." *Public Personnel Management,* 1995, *24,* 255–270.

Deutschman, A. "The Great Pension Robbery." *Forbes,* Jan. 13, 1992, pp. 76–78.

Elliott, R. H. "Human Resource Management's Role in the Future Aging of the Workforce." *Review of Public Personnel Administration,* 1995, *15*(2), 5–17.

Ellis, W. H. "Employee Benefits: Trends and Issues in the 1990s." *Compensation and Benefits Review,* Nov.-Dec. 1993, pp. 37–41.

Family and Medical Leave Act of 1993. U.S. Code, vol. 29, sec. 2601 et seq.

Finkle, A. L. "Designing a Safety Net for Employees." *Public Personnel Management,* 1997, *26,* 123–138.

Government Employees Training Act of 1958. U.S. Code, vol. 5, sec. 4101 et seq.

Hackelman, P. "Strategies in Controlling Health Care Costs for Public Employees." *Employee Benefits Journal,* Dec. 1994, pp. 8–12.

Haltom, C. "Shifting the Health Care Focus from Sickness to Wellness." *Compensation and Benefits Review,* Jan.-Feb. 1995, pp. 47–53.

Handel, B. "Financing Health Care Coverage in the Public Sector: Costs, Risks and Options." In M. J. Brzezinski (ed.), *Public Employee Benefit Plans.* Brookfield, Wis.: International Federation of Employee Benefit Plans, 1992.

Harm, K. J. *State and Local Government Deferred Compensation Programs.* Chicago: Government Finance Officers Association, 1993.

Hostetler, D., and Pynes, J. E. "Domestic Partnership Benefits: Dispelling the Myth." *Review of Public Personnel Administration,* 1995, *15,* 41–59.

Intergovernmental Personnel Act of 1970. U.S. Code, vol. 42, sec. 4701 et seq.

Johnson, A. "Municipal Employee Assistance Programs: Managing Troubled Employees." *Public Administration Review,* 1985, *45,* 383–390.

Kemp, D. "State Employee Assistance Programs: Organization and Services. *Public Administration Review,* 1985, *45,* 378–382.

Kemp, D. "Telecommuting in the Public Sector." *Review of Public Personnel Administration,* 1995, *15*(3), 5–16.

Levine, C. "Employee Benefits: Growing in Diversity and Cost." *Occupational Outlook Quarterly,* Winter 1993–1994, pp. 39–42.

Mactas, M. V. "Is Your State Underfunding Your Pension Plan?" In M. J. Brzezinski (ed.), *Public Employee Benefit Plans.* Brookfield, Wis.: International Federation of Employee Benefit Plans, 1992.

Moore, P. "Comparison of State and Local Employee Benefits and Private Employee Benefits." *Public Personnel Management,* 1991, *20,* 429–439.

Pacelli, J. D. *Benefit Design in Public Employee Retirement Systems.* Chicago: Government Finance Officers Association, 1994.

Sandwith, P. "A Hierarchy of Management Training Requirements: The Competence Domain Model." *Public Personnel Management,* 1993, *22,* 43–62.

Smith, K. D. "Comprehensive Leave: Pros and Cons." *IPMA News,* July 1996, pp. 20, 22–23.

Social Security Act of 1935. U.S. Code, vol. 42, sec. 301 et seq.

Streib, G. "Specialty Health Care Services in Municipal Government." *Review of Public Personnel Administration,* 1996, *16*(2), 57–72.

U.S. Bureau of the Census. *Statistical Abstract of the United States, 1994.* Washington, D.C.: U.S. Government Printing Office, 1994.

U.S. Chamber of Commerce. *Employee Benefits, 1992.* Washington, D.C.: U.S. Chamber of Commerce, 1992.

Van Wart, M., Cayer, N. J., and Cook, S. *Handbook of Training and Development for the Public Sector: A Comprehensive Resource.* San Francisco: Jossey-Bass, 1993.

Wallace, M. J., Jr., and Fay, C. H. *Compensation Theory and Practice.* (2nd ed.) Boston: PWS-Kent, 1988.

West, J. P., and Berman, E. M. "Managerial Responses to an Aging Municipal Workforce: A National Survey." *Review of Public Personnel Administration,* 1996, *16*(3), 38–58.

Zolkos, R. "Guvs Eye Pensions." *City and State,* June 1–14, 1992, pp. 1, 21.

Zolkos, R., and Philip, C. "Legislator's Pensions Soar." *City and State,* Aug. 10–23, 1992, pp. 1–2.

Zorn, P. *Survey of State and Local Government Employee Retirement Systems.* Chicago: Public Pension Coordinating Council, 1994.

Toward Effective
Human Resource Management

Stephen E. Condrey

The preceding thirty-one chapters, by thirty-eight authors, have brought together a wide-ranging compilation of insights into the study and practice of human resource management. The purpose of this concluding chapter is to highlight themes interwoven throughout this handbook and to suggest future avenues the HRM field should take.

THEMES AND DIRECTIONS

The *Handbook of Human Resource Management in Government* identifies ways in which human resource management must change to maintain its relevance to the academic community, elected officials, and most important, practicing managers.

The handbook contributors share four interrelated and overlapping themes:

- Human resource management should be strategically integrated into the functions and functioning of public organizations.

- Human resource managers should play an active role in developing and maintaining an organizational environment supportive of change and diversity.

- Effective human resource management requires a solid mix of technical and general management skills—human resource management should be viewed as an integral managerial tool.

- Public-sector human resource management is practiced in an increasingly complex environment.

The following pages discuss each of these insights in turn.

1. **Human resource management should be strategically integrated into the functions and functioning of public organizations.**

In a time of downsizing, rightsizing, decentralization, reinventing, and all-around general questioning of the roles and purposes of public organizations, human resource management and managers should seize the opportunity to become strategically integrated into the functioning of public organizations. David Carnevale (Chapter Twelve) urges human resource managers to assist in creating "high-performance work organizations." According to Carnevale, such organizations

- Push authority and responsibility for work processes down the line
- Strengthen the skills of employees through a strong commitment to human capital development and organizational learning programs
- Create less bureaucratic, more decentralized organizational arrangements to enable faster response times to client and customer demands
- Invest in technology to enhance information flow and to monitor organizational achievement
- Commit to quality as a premier measure of individual, group, and organizational performance

Carolyn Ban (Chapter One) urges human resource managers to break out of a myopic and rule-bound role to "new roles more aligned with management and more responsive to management's needs." Ban laments that too often personnel administration has focused on "enforcement of an increasingly convoluted set of laws, rules, and regulations" for governance of civil service systems. Ban also discusses three reform models—customer service, organizational development or consulting, and strategic human resource management. She proposes moving toward the strategic approach: "No longer should the focus be on carrying out the rules and regulations. [Human resource management's] new charge is to support the mission of the organization."

In a similar vein, Donald Klingner (Chapter Three) sees a change in the role of human resource managers: "The emergent paradigm has changed the role of the public personnel manager: from resolving conflict among competing values to implementing contract compliance and compliance with legislative limits. The role of public human resource managers is becoming more like the role of their private-sector counterparts, in that they are less responsible for resolving value conflicts than for increasing productivity."

2. Human resource managers should play an active role
   in developing and maintaining an organizational
   environment supportive of change and diversity.

At no other time in U.S. history have public organizations faced such rapid change—both technological and demographic. These dual challenges place the human resource manager in a pivotal position for helping create an organizational environment supportive of both. As James Danziger and Christopher Gianos explain in Chapter Twenty-Five: "An overall challenge for managers is to ensure that the fit among human resources, technology, and organizational needs is maximized." The impact of information technology (IT) on the workplace is considerable, and "managers must understand key technical issues associated with the efficient application of IT; grasp how IT can influence job domain, work routines, information flows, and worker morale; and be aware of the ways in which IT either supports or changes a manager's own responsibilities."

Danziger and Gianos challenge human resource managers to be anticipatory and proactive rather than reactive. Technological changes in the workplace will materially alter the nature and structure of public workforces. Human resource managers should strive to maintain an anticipatory stance to facilitate the training and retraining of skilled personnel. Additionally, they should become skilled at adapting communication systems, reporting processes, and human resource reward structures to coincide with the new organizational landscape.

Technological change notwithstanding, changes in the demographic makeup of public organizations will visibly alter the nature and character of public organizations in the decades to come. Mary Guy and Meredith Newman (Chapter Four) and Jonathan West (Chapter Five) demonstrate that the racial, age, and gender composition of U.S. workforces will change significantly over the coming years. Guy and Newman stress that human resource managers should value the prospect of a diverse workplace: "Diversity promotes equity in the workplace just as democracy promotes equity in the community. Human resource managers who skillfully choreograph changes in the workforce with every new hire, promotion, and training opportunity take advantage of the best that the American labor force has to offer."

Demographic changes in the workforce will not be restricted to racial and gender composition. Continuing the pattern of diversity in the workplace, workers with disabilities will also increasingly take a prominent role in staffing and managing public organizations (thanks in part to the Americans with Disabilities Act, discussed by David Pfeiffer in Chapter Ten). Thus the role of the human resource manager is not only to ameliorate the effects of past and current discrimination but to help create an organizational milieu receptive of diversity, broadly defined.

3. Effective human resource management requires a solid mix
of technical and general management skills—human resource
management should be viewed as an integral managerial tool.

A primary focus of the *Handbook of Human Resource Management in Government* is to broaden the expectations and vision of human resource managers so that they can become more fully integrated into the overall management of public agencies. The fourth section of the handbook is devoted to the theme that human resource management is an integral management function, crucial to the effective operation of government organizations. Adding key skills in benchmarking organizational productivity (Chapter Nineteen, by David Ammons), developing strategic plans (Chapter Twenty, by Mary Maureen Brown and Roger Brown), designing and conducting employee attitude surveys (Chapter Twenty-One, by Gary Roberts), implementing Total Quality Management programs (Chapter Twenty-Two, by Robert Durant), developing budgets (Chapter Twenty-Six, by Charles Coe and Catherine Reese), using volunteers (Chapter Twenty-Four, by Jeffrey Brudney), and effectively employing consultants (Chapter Twenty-Three, by Glenn Rainey) not only will make the human resource manager more effective in accomplishing traditional personnel functions but also will broaden the managerial perspective and impact of human resource professionals.

Of course traditional personnel functions such as compensation, recruitment, and selection are of continuing importance to human resource managers. Increased professionalization of these functions will continue to enhance the role and function of human resource professionals in public organizations. Although not every manager will be expected to construct a classification and pay plan or devise an entire set of assessment center exercises, practical examples of the effective application of these techniques (see Parts Three and Five) assist the manager in becoming an effective judge of the efficacy of the current and future use of these techniques in his or her organization.

4. Public-sector human resource management is practiced
in an increasingly complex environment.

Much of this handbook emphasizes the complex environment in which public human resource management is practiced. As Donald Klingner stresses (Chapter Three), public-sector human resource management is value infused. As keepers of the public trust, human resource managers serve as gatekeepers and arbiters of an important resource—public jobs. The human resource manager must serve as referee of the often competing values of efficiency, social equity, responsiveness, and employee rights. Klingner points out that value conflicts will surely become more prevalent as the emerging values of personal accountability, limited government, and community responsibility continue to influence the field through catalysts such as the National Performance Review and the reinventing government movement.

The environment in which human resource management is practiced is increasingly concerned with legal issues. Gerald Hartman, Gregory Homer, and John Menditto (Chapter Seven) document the recent and dramatic rise in employment discrimination suits—increasing over 50 percent in the three-year period between 1991 and 1994. Additionally, legislative mandates such as the Americans with Disabilities Act of 1990 add complication to an already complex human resource legal environment (see Chapter Ten). And as Michele Hoyman and Lana Stein demonstrate (Chapter Nine), charges of sexual harassment are still not rare in public-sector workplaces.

Any discussion of the environment of public-sector human resource management would not be complete without mentioning the influence of employee groups and unions. Unions are often the source of much distrust and antagonism in public organizations. Robert Tobias (Chapter Thirteen) states that as the relationship between public personnel administrators and employee unions matures, "there is a growing awareness that unions and managers must create a more cooperative, less adversarial relationship in order to maximize productivity, efficiency, and employee satisfaction."

The 1990s have produced a convergence of social, political, and legal forces that have taken direct aim at the structure and practice of public-sector human resource management. Even though these forces add to the complexity of the environment surrounding human resource management, they also enliven the field, making the public sector one of the most challenging and rewarding arenas in which to practice human resource management.

JOINING THEORY AND PRACTICE

The *Handbook of Human Resource Management in Government* has brought together an extensive compilation of scholarly knowledge, practical advice, and examples of specific applications in public-sector human resource management. The primary aim of the handbook has been to forge an alliance between effective human resource management theory and practice; that is, to develop a relationship in which theory informs practice and practice informs theory. This handbook should serve as a valuable resource for practicing managers and scholars as they guide the human resource management field into the next century.

NAME INDEX

SUBJECT INDEX